1908

Where the Fleet Begins

Where the Fleet Begins

A History of the
David Taylor Research Center

1898–1998

Rodney P. Carlisle

Naval Historical Center
Department of the Navy
Washington
1998

Library of Congress Cataloging-in-Publication Data

Carlisle, Rodney P.
    Where the fleet begins : a history of the David Taylor Research
Center, 1898–1998 / Rodney P. Carlisle.
       p   cm.
    Includes bibliographical references and index.
    1. David Taylor Research Center—History.   I. Title.
VM623.A9C37 1998
 359'.07'0973—DC21   98–24955

For sale by the U.S. Government Printing Office
Superintendent of Documents, Mail Stop: SSOP, Washington, DC 20402-9328
ISBN 0-16-049442-7

Contents

Appendices

Bibliographical Notes   603

Bibliography   606

Index   627

Tables

Illustrations

Foreword

Yesterday, Today, and Tomorrow

A S THE CARDEROCK DIVISION OF THE Naval Surface Warfare Center celebrates one hundred years of service to the Nation, the Navy, Marine Corps, and Coast Guard as well as this country's maritime activities, it is fitting that we look back over our history as we look forward to the twenty-first century. For this reason, we have commissioned the completion of this historical study to capture our heritage.

The long view which comes from reading and thinking about our history helps to bring together yesterday, today, and tomorrow. Looking back through our yesterdays, this book shows us how we are connected to a distinguished past, a past that flows directly from our founders David W. Taylor and George W. Melville. They took a strong leadership role in developing the methods and tools of science and engineering and applying them to the task of designing better ships for the U.S. Navy. The institutions they founded have evolved, have been relocated, and have moved again and again within the Navy's command structure and on its organizational charts. Through all of those changes, however, the fundamental principles to which Taylor, Melville, and their colleagues were dedicated continue to guide us.

Today, the Carderock Division provides the Navy's technical leadership for both surface ship and submarine systems. As such, it provides two fundamental and over-arching roles critical to the present and future Navy.

> It expands the breadth and depth of all technologies vital to ensuring mission effectiveness of Navy surface and subsurface systems over their entire life cycle. It links science and engineering in design, acquisition, and operational support to meet the needs of the fleet. The Division is "keel to masthead and cradle to grave" in scope and capability.

> It provides long-term stewardship of the knowledge base and specific national assets to ensure that critical technologies are available to maintain naval superiority for the United States, despite changing economic conditions. It works closely in partnership with industry but is distinct from industry in that it must preserve many critical technologies and capabilities that, over the long haul, do not offer the basis for a profit-making enterprise in the private sector.

With these two primary roles of linking science and engineering and serving as a steward of accumulated knowledge and Navy-critical technology, the Division is crucial both to the present and to the future Navy.

For the present Navy, it assists in the procurement of systems, provides working solutions to difficult fleet problems, and enhances the performance of older fleet assets.

For the future Navy, the Division provides the innovation and vision for new and sometimes revolutionary warfare capabilities, applies science and technology to develop and engineer future systems and develop and maintain technical capabilities essential to support future acquisitions.

Out of the heritage that goes back to Taylor and Melville, the Division plays many roles that span both the present and the future:

Naval Scientist and Engineer
Architect and Custodian of the Corporate Knowledge Base
Catalyst for Innovation
Systems Integrator
Educator and Trainer
Advisor to the Navy as a Smart Buyer
Facilitator in Navy/Industrial Relationships
Life Cycle Manager
Facility Developer and Operator

We must develop and sustain the critical technologies and capabilities that underwrite U.S. naval superiority and, at the same time, contribute to the technological superiority of U.S. industry.

We have been entrusted as the steward of these capabilities and we must ensure that there is no compromise of them for perceived short term gain. We are confident that despite the uncertainties of the current environment, with emphasis on downsizing and outsourcing, our roles will continue to be necessary even though the details and perhaps the magnitude of execution will change.

Like our predecessors, we will "steer by the stars and not by our wake," remaining focused on our mission and vision, and partnering with industry and academia in the most effective way to develop the technologies, facilities, and systems which will continue to ensure that the U.S. Navy is the best in the world.

We believe that this historical study will play an important part in helping us maintain a consciousness of our heritage and in keeping these roles and values active into the next century.

Richard E. Metrey
Director, Carderock Division, NSWC
Spring 1998

Acknowledgments

THE RESEARCH AND WRITING OF THIS WORK was supported under a contract from the Director of Navy Laboratories, which funded research expenses of the author, research assistants, and support staff at History Associates, Incorporated, located in Rockville, Maryland. The author is indebted to several of his associates at HAI for their contributions, including Philip Cantelon, Richard Hewlett, Ruth Dudgeon, Dian Belanger, Margaret Rung, Anne Davidson, Gail Mathews, Carol Spielman, DyAnn Gates, Kim Kilpatrick, and Margaret Belke.

At the David Taylor Research Center, a number of individuals gave their time and the benefit of their experience in interviews, as listed in Appendix H. Several of those interviewees read portions of the manuscript and offered supplementary suggestions that proved most helpful, including Ernest Rogers, William M. Ellsworth, G. Richard Garritson, and Richard E. Metrey. The center also provided an advisory board, made up of staff and outside volunteers, which reviewed every chapter, advised as to style and content, and graciously left interpretive questions to the author's judgment. Serving on the advisory board were Dean Allard (former Director of Naval History), Sylvia Fries (Historian at NASA), David Allison, Paul Shatzberg, Seth Hawkins, and Joseph Marchese. Allison and Marchese also served as Contracting Officer's Technical Representatives on the contract as civilian historians employed by the Navy on the work completed in the 1980s.

Other employees of the center, especially James M. Scott in the Public Affairs Office, Joanne Lappin in the Technical Information Center, and Carol Nowicke, archivist in the Historian's Office, all provided directions to sources. As in any work of this scale, informal critiques, suggestions, and information from personal contacts proved valuable, and thanks go to Norman Friedman, Gary Weir, William (Trey) Addington, Theresa Francheschini, and Lew Graham. Particular archivists went out of their way to help, including Richard von Doenhoff at the National Archives and Dean Allard at the Naval Historical Center.

In 1996 and 1997, the manuscript was revised and prepared for publication based on suggestions provided by the newly constituted Editorial Advisory Board (EAB). Material to bring the book from 1987 to 1997 was also provided through the EAB. Comments by the board on the earlier portions of the manuscript proved invaluable in revision, and as a source for contemporary information. Various documentation supplied by the EAB is contained in the Advisory Board Information File (ABIF) in the library of the Carderock Division, Naval Surface Warfare Center and is cited in the chapter endnotes. The 1996–1997 Editorial Advisory Board, ably headed by Dennis Clark and William Ellsworth, included Larry Argiro, Brian Bowers, Harvey Chaplin, Gene Gleissner, Dick Messalle, Peter Montana, William Morgan, Justin McCarthy, William Murray, Harold Nutt, Peter Palermo, Maurice Sevik, Charles Schoman, Joe Sheehan, and George Wacker. Through the board, input from a variety of other information sources was provided, including Mary Charlotte Crook, Martin Krenzke, Howard Law, Mike Marshall, Gloria Patterson, Geraldine Yarnall, Walt Dumbeck, and Edward Wenk. The knowledgeable support of Mike Marshall, Dennis Clark, William Ellsworth, and Howard Law in handling many administrative matters made working on the revision a truly collegial experience in the best sense of the word.

The final manuscript was ably steered towards publication with excellent editorial assistance from Lynn Gemmell and staff at the Naval Historical Center, including its Director, William F. Dudley (who also serves as Director of Naval History), and Sandra Doyle. The final work would not have been possible without Ms. Doyle's patient attention to matters of style and her help in coordination. The excellent support and cooperation given by John Grier of the Government Printing Office in preparing the book for final publication is also gratefully acknowledged.

The author, of course, takes responsibility for any inaccuracy or error in the final work.

Rodney P. Carlisle
History Associates, Incorporated
1998

Institutional Names

T HE INSTITUTION WHOSE HISTORY IS detailed here underwent several reorganizations and renamings. In the text, the contemporary name was utilized. The following list will assist the reader through the changes of nomenclature:

1898–1940 Experimental Model Basin, Washington Navy Yard (EMB)
1940–1967 David Taylor Model Basin, Carderock (DTMB)
1907–1963 Engineering Experiment Station, Annapolis (EES)
1963–1967 Marine Engineering Laboratory, Annapolis (MEL)

Following the merger of Carderock and Annapolis facilities in 1967:

1967–1973 Naval Ship Research and Development Center (NSRDC)
1974–1987 David Taylor Naval Ship R&D Center (DTNSRDC)
1987–1992 David Taylor Research Center (DTRC)
1992–   Carderock Division, Naval Surface Warfare Center (CDNSWC)

Where the Fleet Begins

CHAPTER 1

Introduction

I N 1907 PRESIDENT THEODORE ROOSEVELT sent the Great White Fleet
on a tour of the world. The pride of the Navy, the heavily armored
fleet, with its straight, wave-cutting bows, with its belching smokestacks and coal-fired boilers, proudly and successfully showed the
American flag. Today, with considerably less fanfare and far more might,
the U.S. Navy cruises the oceans of the world, still embodying the nation's influence, power, and technology. Today's fleet is propelled by nuclear power, armed with missiles, and cuts through the water with bulbous bows. Each individual part of the ship, from bow to propeller, from
armor plate to frame, from waterline to clustered radar and radio antennae, is the result of decades of incremental innovation.

Such innovation came out of patient, structured research, conducted for the most part in laboratories and research and development
centers owned and operated by the Navy itself. The modern fleet begins,
not in the shipyard, but in the laboratory. Tomorrow's ships are on the
drawing boards and in the computers of today's scientists, engineers,
and technicians.

Two of the laboratories that housed the Navy's ship research were located near the nation's capital. These two facilities, which after 1967 were
merged under the same administration, bore the unwieldy name, the
David Taylor Naval Ship Research and Development Center, through the
early 1980s. DTNSRDC, carrying the longest acronym among the laboratories housing the Navy's research, is the first of such centers established
to consolidate previous naval technical facilities into more effective instruments for invention and development. In 1987, Captain Clark (Corky)
Graham was successful in getting the name changed to the David Taylor
Research Center. Unfortunately, this name change was to be short lived.

David Taylor's Annapolis detachment sits on the scenic and rustic northeast shore of the Severn River, directly across from the U.S. Naval Academy. Opened in 1908 by the Navy's Bureau of Engineering, the Annapolis branch, originally named the Engineering Experiment Station, rises on a carefully tended 65-acre plot, with its own docks, office buildings, laboratory structures, and a small harbor sheltering vessels from the Severn's occasionally choppy waters, commanding a beautiful view across the river to the Academy. The facility was founded in 1905 by Chief of the Bureau of Steam Engineering George W. Melville, who had passionately championed the professionalization of naval engineering before Congress and within the Navy for more than a decade. In the mid-1990s, the Annapolis detachment was scheduled for closure.

The newer facility, opened in 1940 as the David Taylor Model Basin, nestles in a wooded setting near the Washington beltway on the Potomac River, at Carderock, Maryland. As on a university campus, its striking white facades emerge from a 186-acre carefully tended greensward. The most impressive structure is a single white concrete building, nearly a mile long, housing one of the largest towing tanks or model basins in the world. Inside, scientists and engineers test hull designs and parts on a model scale, prior to incorporation into new naval ships.

Carderock is the successor to an earlier, less precisely constructed model basin, founded in 1898 by David Watson Taylor at the Washington Navy Yard on the Anacostia River. Captain Taylor, who directed the navy yard Experimental Model Basin for the Bureau of Construction and Repair, exemplified the late nineteenth- and early twentieth-century officer-scientist. Like several contemporaries, he brought the best qualities from both the scientific and naval professions to his work, rising in international scientific repute as a leading naval architect and eventually an admiral. As the facility nears its centennial, ten decades after he established the navy yard basin, it is appropriate that the modern successor model basin continues to bear his name.

The laboratory at Carderock is the largest and most comprehensive ship research facility in the Western world. It has a dual mission. On the one hand it serves as the principal U.S. Navy research, development, test, and evaluation (RDT&E) center for naval vehicles, experimental aerodynamics, and naval logistics. Its other mission, receiving more attention as the nation converts military capabilities to peaceful requirements, is to provide RDT&E support to the nation's commercial maritime industry. Within the Navy, the principal sponsor of the work of the center has been the Naval Sea Systems Command (NAVSEA), and its predecessor organization, the Bureau of Ships (BUSHIPS).

This book tells the story of the two consolidated laboratories that comprise the David Taylor Research Center. A laboratory history, like the story of Mount Vernon or of the Capitol building, cannot be told solely by reviewing the physical structure and its furnishings or its organizational evolution. A study of the people reveals the complexity of modern research and innovation: how a massive laboratory is organized; how policy stimulated or retarded progress; and how personal careers intersected with institutional life. At one level, there were the administrators and decision makers who set the funding, chose the projects, and organized the work. At another level were researchers, pursuing individual professional careers while seeking to apply their technical and scientific training to the changing needs in naval ships and weapons.

Early in the century, men like David Taylor at the navy yard model basin, or his counterpart, Walter F. Worthington, at the Engineering Experiment Station, combined in their own persons a variety of skills. Taylor and Worthington filled several roles at once: advisors to the bureau chiefs who set priorities, facility administrators, researchers, contract monitors, and, if needed, repair technicians.

In the period when the Navy built and opened the two laboratories, groups of scientists, engineers, and naval officers were engaged in converting their specialized skills and backgrounds into professions. Like men and women in other American occupations at the time, they sought to define standards, develop definitions of merit and accomplishment, and form organizations to embody those aspirations. Each of the emerging professions at the laboratories contributed ideas about naval ships and ship research. Although scientists, engineers, and naval officers shared certain ideals, they sometimes parted ways. Running through the laboratories' histories were constant tension and often outright disagreement over which profession could best define the Navy's technical needs.

In a period of rapid technological advance and scientific discovery, researchers became more specialized, concentrating on narrower fields in greater depth. Whole new disciplines evolved in airplane design, electronics, structural mechanics, material sciences, and in particular, engineering areas such as diesel engine, propeller, and electric motor design. Each decade required different educational backgrounds, new skills, and fresh personalities. All such human factors produced constant cycles of change.

But those changes occurred within the tradition-bound structure of the Navy. As the laboratories grew, they only gradually altered their original internal organizational units. As new specializations were added, new departments or divisions grew around them to survive for decades. Although the bureaus that established the laboratories faced several reorganizations over the years, they too maintained their internal, technical groups.

As technology became more intricate and the number of electrical and mechanical devices aboard ships increased, those bureau offices responsible for designing and purchasing the Navy fleet constantly turned to these two laboratories for innovative work and ideas. Even ten years after the laboratories opened, a comprehensive description of the work and the mission was difficult to articulate.

Despite the mixed array of projects and the many separate episodes of innovation, a careful retrospective view can uncover themes and recurrent problems. Similar questions arose in each decade: Who influenced and changed the laboratories' definitions of their own missions? How did officers, scientists, and engineers come to accommodations among themselves in selecting ship designs? How did particular designs developed at the laboratories find their way into the fleet? This book has been written to address these questions.

In the vast document collections housed by the National Archives and Records Administration, boxes containing yellowing correspondence, draft reports, weekly and monthly progress statements, memoranda between researchers, and meeting agendas can sometimes reveal tantalizing hints about the scientific research process itself. The history of technology is often told as pure advancement and accomplishment, led by brilliant men forging ahead against ignorance and obstructionism. That view is essentially a fantasy. Progress and invention included experiments that failed. Daily frustrations arose from equipment breakdown, personnel change, or lack of funds. Where documentation is adequate, those difficulties are sketched in so that the reader may recognize that progress was neither automatic nor falsely heroic.

A rich record of the work can be found in the reports published by the researchers themselves. From the beginning, Taylor announced his results at conferences of naval architects, and the published papers of those conferences detail equipment, method, and results. In later years, others followed in his footsteps, presenting their results in a growing array of reports, articles, and conference papers, most of which are indexed and available at the Carderock facility's own research library. Although the engineers at Annapolis attended fewer conferences in the early years, their carefully detailed and illustrated reports, often published in only four copies, explicitly spelled out the specific problem and its particular solution. Both scientists and engineers were careful to detail their false starts as well as their successes, leaving a record for contemporaries and later generations.

The record, however, does not always reveal the crucial actors at the policy level. Naval officers traditionally wrote in the passive voice, a style designed to conceal personal identity. Rather than giving a direct order, an officer might state that "it has been decided" to proceed. That style, in itself, confounds the historian who seeks to assign credit or responsibility for the policy choices in the inventive process. But the history of technical advance and scientific research is more than a catalog of individuals and their choices. The policy was frequently shaped, not so much by individuals, but by larger forces, including technical progress from outside the laboratory, the needs of the Navy, and the evolution of various disciplines involved.

Research, invention, and development are national concerns and the subject of many studies, both within and outside the defense establishment. Such investigations bring to bear theoretical frameworks regarding management, psychology, organizational concepts, or the philosophy of science. To set the David Taylor laboratory in its context, management and administrative history, the history of technology, and naval weapons history have proven very useful. Within the confines of the laboratories, such larger considerations find constant reflection.

Born out of late nineteenth-century naval policies, the two laboratories evolved against a background of war and peace, congressional constraints on funding, and a world arms race. Naval officers sought particular paths of inquiry to support defined naval missions. Those missions grew out of the officers' perceptions of past, present, and future wars. Although the Navy wanted to present a united front when dealing with Congress, internal naval disagreements frequently surfaced over such problems as ship design, the role of submarines and aircraft, and the proper defense against new weapons.

The laboratories were the creatures of the naval bureaucracy from their origins, subject to control by the Navy's bureaus. In the late nineteenth century, the bureaus produced, and the Navy line consumed, the weapons, equipment, ships, and facilities. Although ships of war were manufactured by private firms under contract, several bureaus controlled the selection of particular designs. The Annapolis branch, established by the Bureau of Engineering, originally focused on propulsion equipment, particularly the reciprocating steam engine, and the steam turbine introduced to the Navy about the time the laboratory opened. The Bureau of Construction and Repair had oversight of hull design, and Taylor founded the Experimental Model Basin to bring more scientific procedures to hull choices, concentrating at first on destroyers and capital ships. Even though the power exercised by the bureaus and their successor commands was never absolute, headquarters control of budget was essential to the story. Records of the bureaus and of the naval commands that succeeded them reflect some of the decisions over budget, technology, organization structure, and even day-to-day management concerns.

Science and technology also came from outside the fences that surrounded the facilities. Despite careful and legitimate efforts to guard all secret development, progress and change naturally derived from the flow and transfer of ideas and information across national boundaries, from conference to journal, between laboratory and shop, and back and forth between private firms and government-owned facilities.

International competition in ship, aircraft, and weapons technology drove the laboratories' growth. Early in the century, as the United States sought to match the navies of Britain and Germany, the first concern was to build effective capital ships and destroyers. World War I saw the introduction of radio, submarines, and aircraft. The first passive sonars, large underwater microphones, added a new means of sensing the presence of an enemy. A realization of the new dimension of air warfare and its implications led to the construction of aircraft carriers and a host of seaplanes through the interwar years.

Ship propulsion moved from the inefficient reciprocating steam engines of the turn of the century through rapid modernization. Steam turbines and reduction gears powered many of the ships of World War I, while the smaller vessels were driven by internal combustion gasoline and diesel engines. Larger and larger diesels, combined with electric motor drives, powered some ships between the wars. Germany, despite its defeat in World War I, proceeded with engine design, and the U.S. Navy sought to match German progress in reducing the power-to-weight ratio of diesel engines to make them more practical for submarines and small craft.

World War II brought a burst of engineering and scientific advances to naval warfare in a surprisingly short period. German progress in jet aircraft, submarines, and missiles required American responses. American science produced microwave radar and the nuclear weapon. Improved mines, torpedoes, the proximity fuse, and sonar all brought new specialists and techniques to the laboratories. Although Taylor had a predisposition to research, his laboratory and that at Annapolis had focused on engineering and design rather than on research. The advances by both Germany and the United States during World War II changed the Navy's emphasis. Funds for research no longer had to be covered as overhead expenses of engineering and design facilities, but could be openly carried on the books. The Navy built expensive, large-scale equipment suitable for fundamental studies on the interaction of ships and aircraft with their fluid media. But the Navy still kept the focus on application, not theory. Both laboratories continued to generate innovative designs and devices, as well as the less dramatic incremental improvements.

In the period following World War II, science and weaponry advanced hand in hand. Missiles, nuclear weapons, radar, and computers altered the shape and mission of the Navy's ships. Nuclear propulsion changed the nature of the submarine from a submersible surface ship to a true submarine, capable of long-range underwater cruises, and gave surface vessels new tactical advantages. When wedded to nuclear-tipped guided missiles, the nuclear-powered submarine became part of the nation's strategic defense. To protect this fundamental element of retaliatory power from surprise attack and destruction, a whole science of underwater acoustics evolved, and the laboratory responded with new facilities and specialists. At both Carderock and Annapolis, researchers worked on a wide variety of means of quieting engines, auxiliary equipment, drive gear, and propellers to prevent their detection by emitted sound. The jet aircraft demanded larger aircraft carriers, and the structural and propulsion problems generated by such craft impinged on the laboratory's work. The laboratory appended specialties in fire control, nuclear blast protection, catapult design, weapons handling, and aircraft and missile interaction. Hovercraft, hydrofoils, and helicopters with special naval missions brought new challenges, and specialists at the center would establish national and international reputations for their inventions in these areas. Gas turbine engines opened new possibilities in the propulsion of ships.

Within the limits of time and resources dedicated to this work, we have sought to show how the Navy built, operated, expanded, and utilized the dual laboratories. This book proceeds chronologically, tracing the origins and founding, the expansion, and the widely varied accomplishments. More than half the chapters deal with the period since the World War II, an era that saw the greatest application of science and technology to the arts of war. Separate chapters focus on organizational reform and facility construction to provide background for the specific technical work.

The story of technical progress waxed and waned. War or peace changed the tempo. Policy and funding could advance or retard the pace of progress. An encouraging tale emerges from behind the uneven growth and change. By the late 1980s the Navy justly took pride in its "Center of Excellence" and its record of achievement. Through reorganization in the 1990s, the facility remained the place "where the fleet begins."

Two New Facilities for the New Navy

B OTH THE EXPERIMENTAL MODEL BASIN at the Washington Navy Yard and the Engineering Experiment Station at Annapolis grew out of efforts during the late nineteenth century to integrate advances of technology into the Navy and thereby create a more effective instrument of foreign policy. Individual officers and civilian inventors had pioneered in bringing steam and the screw propeller to the Navy before the Civil War. But by the 1880s, naval innovators and reformers were pushing for a wide array of improvements that soon came to be called the "New Navy" movement. While various historians have analyzed particular elements of the New Navy, that movement is best understood not as a conscious and concerted single reform, but rather as a group of related advocates and achievements in maritime technology, naval strategic thinking, professionalization of the officer corps, and the modernization of shore facilities. The ancestry and birth of both the model basin and the experiment station are found in the cluster of reforms and innovations that historians have labeled "navalism."

Technology and the New Navy

Particular technological advances and choices of all kinds, whether in the military or civilian sphere, can be viewed as incremental results of the "push" of technical development, which creates possible alternatives, and the "pull" of economic, marketing, or policy requirements, which lead to advances down a particular path. The push of naval technology in the mid-nineteenth century could have led to any of several paths of development, dependent upon the pull of naval policy requirements.

Several European naval engagements between 1849 and 1856 proved the efficacy of the exploding shell against unarmored or lightly armored wooden ships. Rethinking the strategic and tactical implications of both weapons and defense systems, European naval planners responded with new doctrine that required further innovation from shipyards, gun factories, and the metal industries. A cycle of improved designs, technical advances that created new alternatives, and renewed requirements based on the developments of potential adversaries, soon led in the 1860s to the first modern technological naval arms race, as Great Britain and France attempted to match each other's progress.

That arms race culminated in the emergence of the modern capital ship. The 9,300-ton British *Devastation*, launched in 1868, provided the prototype for future European development. Designed by Edward James Reed, the steam-driven, sailless, oceangoing ship included many components of subsequent battleships, with iron armor up to 14 inches thick over wood and two revolving turrets, each mounting two 12-inch guns.[1]

The various thrusts of the New Navy movement in the 1880s and 1890s in the United States had the purpose of bringing the Navy to rank with the navies of Europe. Although American industrial and naval capacity made it theoretically feasible to match European naval developments a decade earlier, that choice was not immediately taken. Instead, in the years following the Civil War, U.S. naval planners at first engaged in a postwar process of analysis that required, in the words of naval historian Bernard Brodie, "years of hard thinking and debate and the most exhaustive examination of accumulated evidence."[2]

In the United States, Civil War naval battles had utilized and demonstrated only some of the potentials of the developing technology. As a consequence, the European doctrinal requirement that armored and turreted ships also be capable of high-seas steaming was largely overlooked. One major reason for the American delay, until the mid- and late 1880s, of the development of ships to rank with the 1868 *Devastation* can be found in the striking impression made by the battle of *Monitor* and *Virginia*, the former *Merrimack*.

On 8 and 9 March 1862, the 1,200-ton Union *Monitor* successfully turned back the 3,500-ton Confederate *Virginia* at their classic engagement at Hampton Roads. With some irony, the victory of *Monitor* (which closer examination proved to have been more of a draw) contributed to a kind of technical immobility in post-Civil War ship development.

The battle of *Monitor* and *Virginia*, while the first engagement of two ironclads, lived on in American legend as the event that introduced ironclads—a legend patently untrue. Although bureau chiefs in the Navy recommended a deep-water modernized fleet in 1865, that choice of requirements had little appeal.[3]

In the years between 1865 and 1885, *Monitor* dominated American naval thought, imposing an almost hypnotic fixation on that one type of design (especially in the popular press). The "*Monitor* craze" retarded American ship development, claimed the critics, while European nations proceeded with oceangoing capital ships designed along the lines of *Devastation*, with higher freeboard, multiple turrets, higher speed, and longer range. As a consequence, by the early 1880s the United States had a twenty-one-ship fleet comprised of relatively new, but, by European standards already outmoded, coastal defense monitors and a few cruisers powered by sail with auxiliary steam plants. Advocates of modernization judged the 1880 Navy, not as second-rate, but as twelfth-rate, no match even for the navies of Chile, China, Spain, or Italy. It should be remembered, however, that for the limited policy of coastal defense, the fleet was, in 1880, probably quite sufficient.[4]

Ships of the New Navy

In 1881, President James A. Garfield's Secretary of the Navy William H. Hunt appointed a Naval Advisory Board headed by Rear Admiral John Rodgers to make recommendations for modernization of the fleet. The Rodgers board proposed an ambitious plan to build sixty-eight new ships, entirely of steel. After the death of Garfield, President Chester A. Arthur's Secretary of the Navy, William Chandler, appointed a second advisory board, headed by Commodore Robert Shufeldt, recently returned from a world cruise on board the cruiser *Ticonderoga*. Shufeldt's board produced a more politically realistic and conservative plan for five ships. Congress approved four of these ships in 1883 with an appropriation of $1,300,000. Arthur signed into law the bill authorizing the construction of three oceangoing steel cruisers, *Atlanta*, *Boston*, and *Chicago*, and a dispatch vessel, *Dolphin*—the so-called "ABCD ships."

Despite many shortcomings, ABCD ships, used for tactical and operational training, became the "Squadron of Evolution." Rapidly rendered obsolete, the first four vessels of the American steel navy nevertheless served for decades—the last to leave service was *Boston*, in 1946. Over the ten years following the construction of ABCD ships, the Navy expanded rapidly with new cruisers, battleships, gunboats, torpedo boats, and torpedo-boat destroyers, the forerunners of destroyers.

In stepping up ship construction from 1885 through the 1890s, Congress and the Navy sorted through a variety of budgetary and technical questions, none of which had simple answers. Members of Congress of both parties hoped to achieve improvements at the lowest possible cost, and evaluated each technical change against its impact upon federal expenditure. To what extent should armor be sacrificed for speed, especially in cruisers? How many engines and screws should be used to propel the most powerful, heaviest ships? Should double- or triple-expansion engines be used? How should propellers be modified to improve their efficiency? In such debates, the Navy's four technical bureaus—Ordnance, Construction and Repair, Equipment and Recruiting, and Steam Engineering—each provided expert advice.

Two Navy bureaus, Construction and Repair, and Steam Engineering, quietly worked to bring science into ship construction and engine design. In a very real sense, the Experimental Model Basin was born as an integral part of the New Navy, in the mid-1880s. The Naval Advisory Board recommended in 1884 the building of an experimental model basin to allow the Bureau of Construction and Repair to test scientifically ship hull forms prior to construction, but Congress did not implement this recommendation for another twelve years. And on the engineering side, the Bureau of Steam Engineering sought a facility for testing the plethora of machines and materials turned out by industry for the New Navy as the demands for continuous, accurate evaluation of newly procured items increased in the 1890s.

By the time both the model basin and engineering station were completed and put into service, the New Navy fleet was well under way. In 1893 the fast cruiser *Columbia* broke speed records at 22 knots; *Minneapolis* made over 23 knots the next year. By 1898, a year before the model basin opened, the fleet consisted of four first-class seagoing battleships, two second-class battleships, two armored cruisers, ten partially armored or "protected" fast cruisers, and a large number of new gunboats, monitors, and torpedo boats. When the station opened in 1908, the U.S. Navy at last competed with Germany for second place after the British navy. It was, indeed, a New Navy.[6]

Navalism and the New Navy

One force behind the "naval renaissance" was the desire of naval officers to re-equip themselves with ships on which to serve. Officers had become a powerful political force in themselves, creating institutions to develop, express, and fight for their objectives, such as the Naval Institute (1873), the Office of Naval Intelligence (1882), the Naval War College (1884), and the Navy League (1903). Officers needed ships to command—a phenomenon that one historian has cynically labeled as career anxiety. There was a real basis for such anxiety in the fact that in 1883, before the ABCD ships, the Navy had a total of only thirty-one ships, yet there were 1,817 active naval officers.[7]

Another factor in the birth and rapid growth of the New Navy fleet was the early emergence of cooperative interaction between steelmakers, shipbuilders, and naval procurement boards, in which both industry and the Navy put pressure upon Congress. Some observers have found in this development the birth of what a later generation has described as the military-industrial complex. The spirit of cooperation between suppliers and the Navy was tempered by naval suspicion of the profit-driven private sector. The relationship between the Navy and its suppliers reflected a larger ambivalence characteristic of the late nineteenth-century and early twentieth-century relationship between the government and private enterprise in the United States. On the one hand, a mercantilist tradition of government aid and support continued to flourish; on the other hand, suspicion of private greed required government vigilance. The Navy established increasingly strict standards to ensure value, quality, and meeting of design specifications.[8]

Some of the political navalists argued that even the traditional role of the Navy could no longer be performed without improving its equipment. The old Navy had been built to implement a dual strategy: coastal defense and overseas protection of American commerce, missionary activity, and political influence through occasional "gunboat" diplomacy missions in the underdeveloped areas of Asia, Africa, and Latin America. While monitors might serve as coastal defense long enough to allow for mobilization and shipbuilding in case of a major invasion threat, the older cruisers were no longer adequate even to "show the flag" in the face of navies equipped with steel hulls and armor, powerful steam engines, and rifled guns.[9]

Other advocates of a stronger navy were even more ambitious, and visualized a greater role for the fleet than coastal defense and traditional overseas commerce protection. Through the 1880s, congressmen, journalists, and some naval officers who fought for a strengthened navy reflected a new spirit of nationalism and a new world role for the United States that we associate with the writings of Alfred Thayer Mahan in the 1890s and 1900s.

Historian Robert Seager has detailed the basis of the political navalism which characterized this "Mahanism before Mahan." The movement reflected a desire for overseas markets, the growing acceptance of a Social Darwinist belief in strength, and a new realization that the oceans were highways of travel, not protective moats. Bringing all these views together was an advocacy of sea power as early as 1880, fully a decade before Mahan's views were in print.[10]

In 1890, Mahan published *The Influence of Sea Power Upon History, 1660–1783,* the first of ten works that documented, codified, and popularized the viewpoints already expressed by navalists since 1880. Although he authored an analysis of European affairs, Mahan explicitly proposed "to draw from the lessons of history inferences applicable to one's own country and service." Mahan's biographer, William Puleston, believed that Mahan told his story "so simply and convincingly that the world accepted his theory in his lifetime and transmitted it as axiomatic." Reduced to its most fundamental level, Mahan's theory is straightforward: history has demonstrated that a nation's greatness would flow from a strong maritime commerce and a strong navy to protect that commerce.[11]

The ideology of sea power had found its most articulate spokesman. The logic and ideas of navalism, as codified by Mahan, became the basis of courses at Annapolis and the Naval War College and the bedside reading of Kaiser Wilhelm, Theodore Roosevelt, and a generation of naval modernization advocates in Europe as well as the United States.

In a narrow sense Mahan's writings simply stressed protection of overseas commerce that had been one side of the American traditional dual strategy of defense of coasts and commerce. Yet Mahan's writings reflected more than a shift of emphasis: if the Navy heeded the lessons he drew from European history, the United States would go beyond limited gunboat diplomacy to become a major sea-trading and naval power.

Offsetting the navalist arguments for shipbuilding expenditures, Congress placed severe limits on its support through an equally pervasive concern for strict control on the federal budget. Congress carefully eyed ship construction for evidence of waste or favoritism. Some congressmen suspected that contracts were let to friends of their political opponents and that "jingoism" and the naval arms race were simply schemes to get rich at public expense. Democrats, for example, gleefully noted that the builder of *Dolphin* was a personal friend of Republican Secretary Chandler when the ship's poor performance in sea trials became apparent. Ship construction decisions taken by Congress resulted only after agonizing examination of alternatives, both technical and financial, down to the design and cost details of individual ships. As a consequence, the New Navy was built at a surprisingly low price, with total naval budgets averaging under $20 million a year through the 1880s and 1890s, only slightly above the average budgets for the Navy in the 1870s, before the massive buildup began.[12]

As built, the New Navy soon made possible a more active pursuit of the nation's new role, providing the instrument of policy to project American interests and influence abroad. Along with older vessels and commercial steamers, the new ships soon proved their value. From 1891 to 1893, cruisers and gunboats of the New Navy showed the flag, landed troops, or blockaded ports in actions in Chile, Hawaii, Brazil, and Nicaragua, dealing with local political crises and protecting American commercial interests.

The second-class battleship *Maine* steamed to Havana to show the flag during an uprising of Cubans against Spanish rule. When an apparently internal explosion sank her, 15 February 1898, with the loss of 266 lives, the assumption she had been sabotaged precipitated the war with Spain that began 21 April 1898. At the outbreak of that war, the U.S. Navy had fifty-three new warships. By contrast, the Spanish navy possessed only thirteen modern vessels.[13]

The six-month Spanish American War was America's first blue-water war; unlike all previous major American wars, it was fought entirely off the North American continent. During that war, the protected cruiser *Charleston* won Guam, since that time an American possession, without firing a shot. In battles at Manila Bay and in waters off Cuba the New Navy demonstrated that the United States had become a world power. The war established major territorial commitments in the Caribbean and Pacific, and Mahan's vision seemed on the way to fruition.

As a nation, the United States by 1900 had adopted a policy that recognized the nature of world military power and that viewed the navies of Europe, South America, and Asia as potentially threatening to American interests and ideals. Anti-imperialists and pacifists argued that a naval arms race itself ran counter to American ideals and that an empire of colonies was incompatible with a democratic system. But by the era of Theodore Roosevelt and William Howard Taft, "Mahanism" was in its ascendancy and Congress annually supported an appropriation for the "Increase of the Navy."

Professional and Institutional Reform

The New Navy movement produced not only warships to meet the needs of an expansionist ideology, but new kinds of naval officers as well—technical professionals. Members of this class of officers would be instrumental in the establishment of the laboratories at the Washington Navy Yard and Annapolis.

The naval profession followed the same pattern as other professions in the late nineteenth century, with raised educational standards and limits on admission to its own ranks. The Naval Academy at Annapolis, founded as an officer cadet school in 1845, had evolved in the period before the Civil War toward the direction of improved standards of admission, conduct, scholarship, and training. A series of reforms after the Civil War, under Admiral David D. Porter as superintendent and Lieutenant Commander Stephen B. Luce as commandant of midshipmen, converted the Academy into a training ground for a truly well-educated officer elite.[14]

The role of engineers in the Navy and in naval education had been fraught with controversy since the introduction of steam before the Civil War. Engineers were at first drawn from civilian educational backgrounds and vied with Annapolis-trained line officers for rank and standing. At the Naval Academy steam engineering was introduced to the curriculum in 1861; in 1863 the Academy initiated a program to train "cadet engineers" as well as "cadet midshipmen." The cadet engineer program had very limited success until the 1870s, then was dropped entirely in 1882. After 1882 Academy cadets could elect special training in engineering at the Department of Steam Engineering but few availed themselves of the option. Postgraduate training in steam engineering could not be found in American colleges—an occasional engineer would be funded for a year's study in Britain; the New York Navy Yard provided some research and study facilities for engineers in the 1890s. Appointments to engineer rank continued to be made from outside the Academy-trained officers.[15]

As staff officers (along with medical officers, pursers, and chaplains), engineers faced a series of career discriminations in regard to promotion, quarters, pay, and status that often deterred ambitious Academy graduates from pursuing staff careers. The issue was resolved in 1899 by an act that merged line and staff officers and eliminated the distinction. In order to ensure that engineering officers received an education that would meet the increasingly technical requirements of the New Navy, naval engineers advocated that the specialized course at Annapolis be extended, that an experiment station serve as a training ground for cadets, and that a postgraduate department or school be created. [16]

The "Construction Corps" of naval architects was a far smaller group than the "Engineer Corps" that manned the ships. While every steam-driven ship would have an Engineering officer, only a limited number of Construction and Repair officers, serving as inspectors at navy yards and private shipbuilding yards and in the Navy's design office, were needed. To fill its few slots, the Bureau of Construction and Repair drew upon Academy graduates, usually encouraging the two or three highest ranking students from each class to pursue graduate training in naval architecture. Beginning in 1884, the Navy sent two Annapolis graduates each year as "assistant constructors" to study at the British Royal Naval College, providing a small but steady flow of young men for the elite corps. In 1899 the Navy worked with the Massachusetts Institute of Technology to shift its postgraduate naval architecture education to that institution; each year thereafter one or two Academy graduates engaged in a two-year graduate course at MIT under internationally famed naval architect William Hovgaard.[17]

The career of Francis T. Bowles, secretary to the second Naval Advisory Board and author of the first formal recommendation for an experimental model tank, reflects the Construction and Repair career path in the period. After Bowles graduated from Annapolis, the Navy sent him to the British Royal Naval College at Greenwich for postgraduate training in shipbuilding. By 1884 he had earned the position of assistant constructor. Later, Secretary of the Navy John D. Long would appoint Bowles Chief Constructor and Chief of the Bureau of Construction and Repair, in 1901.[18]

The younger, Annapolis-trained officers drawn to the Construction Corps included Virginia-born David Watson Taylor, later to found and direct the model basin. Taylor was probably the most brilliant of the officers of his generation, finishing first in his class at the Academy in 1885, with the highest grade point average of any graduate up to his time. Like Bowles, after graduation, he studied in Britain at the Royal Naval College, completing the three-year course in 1888, first in his class there as well. Taylor's potential, his training, and his career path allowed his scientific and mathematical talents to flourish. In 1893 he published *Resistance of Ships and Screw Propulsion*. By 1896, when he was barely thirty, Taylor was a naval constructor.[19]

In the early days of the New Navy, some of the best engineering officers rose to positions of authority, although they had never attended the Naval Academy. George W. Melville, a naval engineer who had studied steam engine operation at Brooklyn Polytechnic Institute prior to his naval service, won national recognition for heroic emergency repair work and rescue efforts on the De Long Arctic Expedition of 1878–1879. Melville rose to Engineer in Chief and Chief of the Bureau of Steam Engineering by 1887. A large, impressive, full-bearded naval man of the old school, Melville brought practical engineering genius and striking leadership to the bureau. Like many fellow engineers, he faced discrimination in advancement and worked to raise the status of engineering officers by eliminating the distinction in rank between en-

Admiral David W. Taylor.   A talented naval architect and forceful officer, Taylor established the first Experimental Model Basin at the Washington Navy Yard.

Admiral George W. Melville. Former Arctic explorer and Chief of the Bureau of Steam Engineering, Melville advocated the establishment of an engineering experiment station at Annapolis and a fuel oil testing plant in Philadelphia to meet the needs of the New Navy.

gineering and line officers. Under his direction, the bureau planned the Engineering Experiment Station. Specializing in propulsion, he later perfected, with Joseph MacAlpine, a type of marine reduction gear, after his retirement from the Navy in mid-1903.[20]

Other men of technical ability and ambition chose line, that is, ship-command, careers, rather than bureau staff careers. Naval Academy graduate Bradley Fiske, a prolific inventor, with patents for an electric ammunition hoist, a range finder, a telescopic sight, and an engine room telegraph, later developed the release devices needed for torpedo bombing from aircraft, all while serving as a line officer. When the Engineer Corps won legislation in 1899 that gave engineers the same promotion potential as line officers, some ambitious young naval careerists were encouraged to pursue advancement through the technical bureaus, rather than following Fiske's example of officer-inventor in line service. Thus, after 1900, the bureaus could continue to attract energetic and talented professionals and could reward them with promotions and rank equivalent to officers of the line. But the line career continued to attract energetic reformers and inventive minds long after the merger of staff and line.[21]

The New Navy and its new corps of professionals not only sought ships to rank with those of Europe, but created institutions and shore facilities modeled on those of the most modern forces of the world. Congress funded a $10 million construction program for the Naval Academy that got under way in 1900. Educational reforms included improved Academy training in steam engineering, the MIT courses in naval architecture from 1899, and the Engineering Postgraduate Department at the Academy after 1909.

The moves to build new testing facilities for Construction and Repair and for Steam Engineering were parts of a wider Navy effort to improve shore facilities. The Bureau of Ordnance established the Naval Gun Factory at the Washington Navy Yard in 1886. The Bureau of Construction and Repair refurbished and reopened facilities at Portsmouth, Boston, League Island, and Pensacola in 1899, and opened new navy yards at Charleston and Puget Sound. Between 1897 and 1905 the number of employees at navy yards and naval stations increased from under 7,000 to over 24,000.[22]

The professionalism of both the Engineer Corps and the Construction Corps and the growth of the Navy's shore establishment that characterized the New Navy can be viewed as part of the wider movement in American society to develop specialized technical skills and bureaucratic structures. Reforms of the Progressive era and earlier movements in civil service reform, municipal reform, and the professionalization of various occupations all sprang from similar concerns to place society on a more rational basis. The New Navy, in its organizational, educational, and scientific aspects, reflected that same late nineteenth-century attempt to rationalize and systematize traditional institutions.

Viewed as a whole, this cluster of New Navy reforms and ideas went well beyond the creation of a steel navy, although the fleet itself was the most visible and central aspect of the movement. The professional officer corps in naval architecture and in engineering developed an esprit matching that in the best European navies. The Navy of ships and men had evolved rapidly from twelfth place to second place through the modernization of educational facilities, ship-procurement methods, repair facilities, and the Navy's increasing scientific and technical capability.

The Model Basin and the New Navy

A close examination of the origins of the Experimental Model Basin and the Engineering Experiment Station shows how intimately those two facilities grew out of the New Navy. As the Navy modernized its ships, specifications and requirements became increasingly demanding. The two technical bureaus, staffed by professionals like Bowles, Taylor, and Melville, needed adequate equipment to accomplish their missions of design and test of new ships and engines. The scale of naval expenditures, particularly after 1898, made the requests for the essentially inexpensive shore facilities required by the two bureaus seem reasonable and prudent, despite congressional scrutiny.

In the first recommendation for a towing tank from the Naval Advisory Board in 1884, Assistant Constructor and Board Secretary Bowles pointed out that the most "important question in naval architecture" was the "relation of resistance, speed and engine power of ships." The Navy determined that relationship by measured mile trials with completed ships. Bowles, just returned from his British postgraduate training, prepared a paper explaining the economic advantages and the principles of determining resistance by the towing of models and showed that Scot shipbuilder William Denny of Dumbarton had used a privately owned tank and models to predetermine the speed and power relationships prior to ship construction.[23]

The intellectual and policy roots of the Experimental Model Basin go back to advances made first in Britain in understanding ship design problems and in the rapid emulation of British advances by the other major naval powers. In the 1870s, the English civil engineer William Froude had carried out experiments for the British Admiralty to calculate the total resistance of a full-sized ship, to determine the power lost

in the propeller and machinery, and to work out the relationship between full-sized ships and scale models. Using scaling laws developed by
French mathematician Joseph Bertrand and French naval architect
Frederic Reech, Froude proposed to solve the problem of ship resistance by the use of models rather than by test of full-scale ships. Froude
suggested that the wavemaking resistance, or residual resistance, of a
ship could be calculated from a tested model, if a scale of frictional resistance could be determined. Allowing for this frictional resistance,
and applying the scaling laws to the residual resistance of the model, he
believed he could calculate the basic wave-making resistance of various
ship forms.[24]

The Admiralty funded Froude's project and a model tank at his home
in Torquay, England. Froude first established the scale of frictional resistance by testing the resistance of simple planks. Once the frictional resistances at various speeds were known, Froude subtracted that factor from
the total resistance of models. Then applying the scaling law developed by
Bertrand and Reech, Froude calculated the resistance of a full-scale ship
from the model. The scaling law worked on the principle that if the speeds
of model and ship were held in proportion to the square root of the ratio
of model length and ship length, then the resistance of the model and ship
would vary by the cube of the same ratio of model and ship length. Using
that principle, with a known projected ship length, a known model length,
a known model speed, and a measured and therefore known model resistance, it would be a simple matter to calculate the resistance of the full-
scale ship of a particular hull design at a particular speed, as long as he
made allowance for the frictional resistance of the ship.[25]

Once Froude had established his frictional resistance tables from
his tests with planks, he tested and demonstrated his model method. In
1874 Froude published results of a towing test of both the model and
the full-scale HMS *Greyhound*. Although the test proved his predictions
not precisely accurate, he did establish the principle that experiments
with models could allow one to predict, more or less accurately, the top
speed of a full-scale ship with a given hull and power plant. Out of
Froude's formula and his first experiments, the science of ship hydrodynamics was born.[26]

In 1876 Britain pretested the design for HMS *Inflexible*, which was
the first ship to be built from a hydrodynamic model. In the same year,
Froude, working from his own experiments and from data collected by
Denny, published papers on the relationship of indicated to effective
horsepower and on the comparative resistance of various designs of
"long ships." He presented his basic conclusions and formulas in "The

Fundamental Principles of the Resistance of Ships" in the *Proceedings of the Royal Institution of Naval Architects.*[27]

The linkage between British naval science, the arms race, and the stimulus to create an American model basin was very clear, as the recommendations of the 1880s demonstrate. From his own studies in Britain between 1881 and 1883, Bowles was familiar with Froude's pioneering work in hydrodynamics and his proof of the usefulness of model work to predict resistance. Bowles explicitly tied the U.S. Navy towing tank proposal to the scientifically demonstrated advantages of model testing and other work already accomplished by Froude and Denny. If the U.S. Navy was ever to compete in the European naval arms race, he argued, it would have to have the capacity to pretest designs in a towing tank. In 1884 the Naval Advisory Board that had planned the first ABCD ships forwarded Bowles's recommendations and reports on British work to Secretary of the Navy Chandler, strongly recommending the construction of an American towing tank at an estimated construction cost of $50,000.[28]

Each year, from 1891 through 1895, the Secretaries of the Navy forwarded to Congress the recommendation of the Chief Constructor for the establishment of a "model tank." The arguments for these recommendations were technical, military, and fiscal and repeatedly echoed national and congressional concerns regarding the strength of the U.S. Navy in comparison to the fleets of potential adversaries. The work of Froude and Denny had shown that a tank was needed to check discrepancies in trials and more generally in the preparation of naval designs. Rear Admiral Philip Hichborn, Chief Constructor, pointed with alarm to the growing European naval arms race, as he gave details of the British tanks at Torquay and Haslar, of the Italian tank at Spezzia, and the Russian tank at St. Petersburg that allowed those nations' navies to use modern science to achieve efficiency and speed. By 1894 Britain was constructing all of her warships from pretested models.[29]

Hichborn noted the inaccuracy of information from foreign speed trials, and complained that "all the principal foreign countries have model tanks, and hence to that extent have an advantage over us." Hichborn pointed out that especially for planned fast torpedo-boat destroyers, the small ship that evolved into the modern destroyer, a model tank was "almost a necessity." Without a model tank, Hichborn implied, the United States would only fall farther behind in the naval arms race. The constant pressure from the Bureau of Construction demonstrated that in the 1890s American naval officers were articulate advocates of the view that adequate scientific test equipment, under naval control, was essential to the defense of the nation. But the advocates advanced further arguments.[30]

The Chief Constructor also appealed to congressional concerns for thrift, explaining that up to 1 January 1896, the builders of thirteen ships of the New Navy had received speed premiums, that is, bonuses, for exceeding speed requirements, with the average speed exceeding predictions by 1.5 knots. The total premiums paid to date had been about $2 million. If the government had a tank to pretest models, he estimated that it would have been unlikely for finished ships to exceed predictions by more than three-quarters of a knot, resulting in a saving of about $1 million. Since speed premiums had just been abolished, he anticipated no such direct saving in the future. Yet penalties remained for falling below predicted speed. Since bidders factored into their estimates extra power to avoid penalty, the unpredictability of resistance still cost the government money. With more accurate predictions based on model tests, low bids would not include the insurance factor built in under the current system.[31]

Hichborn pointed to the precedent for such a facility in the construction of a large plant for the testing of iron and steel at the Watertown Arsenal, Watertown, New York, administered by the Army's Bureau of Ordnance. Congress had directed that the test facilities at Watertown be used, at cost, by private persons. The value, not only to the Army, but to the country at large, was well known. Hichborn, finally, stressed the fact that the tank, like the Watertown facility, would be too costly for private venture capital. He fully endorsed the idea of private use of the tank at cost, as an encouragement to the development of shipbuilding.[32]

Republican Congressman Samuel G. Hilborn of Oakland, California, introduced a bill (H.R. 4045) "providing for a model tank for the United States Navy" on 15 January 1896. The bill directed the Secretary of the Navy to "establish a model tank, with all proper appliances, for the purpose of investigating and determining the most suitable and desirable shapes and forms to be adopted for U.S. naval vessels." Total cost was to be $100,000.[33]

Congressman Hilborn included a provision that private shipbuilders be authorized to have experiments conducted there for actual cost of materials and labor, and then, within a few days, wrote to shipbuilders around the country asking what they thought of the idea. He received more than a dozen prompt, enthusiastic replies "heartily endorsing" the "inestimable value" of the proposed tank for helping to make shipbuilding an "exact science."[34]

The congressman also sent a copy of his bill to Secretary of the Navy Hilary Herbert on 10 February. Herbert responded with favorable comment and a copy of Hichborn's memorandum of endorsement and justification. The Secretary noted only that "for want of room" at the Washington Navy Yard, the site specified in the original bill, the old observatory grounds in Washington might be a more "suitable" location for the model tank.[35]

Model tank legislation wound a tortuous path through Congress. Hilborn's bill never emerged from committee, but the naval appropriations bill (H.R. 7542) of 27 March 1896 contained a brief paragraph allowing $7,500 to be spent for "preliminary work toward the construction of a model tank." The bill passed the House but the Senate struck the model tank provision with neither explanation nor comment, in a group of amendments proposed by the Appropriations Committee to reallocate spending priorities. Despite the fact that the naval appropriation as a whole supported naval expansion, no one present in the committee brought up the relationship of the model tank to New Navy objectives at first, and an apparent lack of understanding of the proposal contributed to its near elimination. An opponent, Senator Wilkinson Call, a Democrat from Florida, complained that "I do not know where this idea comes from, or why it is necessary to build a tank to exhibit a little model of a ship." His fellow Floridian, Senator Samuel Pasco, also a Democrat, then helped resurrect the tank by reading into the record lengthy and cogent scientific and strategic arguments of Chief Constructor Hichborn. Hichborn's report once again tied the proposal to the range of New Navy issues as he reminded Congress of the competition of European navies and their use of model tanks, the economies of model versus full-scale testing, and the proposed services to private industry. He noted that the Bureau of Construction and Repair had already received "several communications from private shipbuilders throughout the country expressing gratification at the prospect that the United States was at last in a fair way to be on a par with foreign nations in this important respect."[36]

In the end, the Senate approved the legislation, with only minor modifications. Despite Herbert's concern for lack of space at the navy yard, the Senate specified that the basin be located there rather than at the observatory, the Secretary's preferred location. The comprehensive Naval Appropriations Bill, including $7,500 for the towing tank, passed both houses after several conferences; President Grover Cleveland signed it into law on 10 June 1896. Congress approved the $92,500 balance of the original model basin cost proposal the following year without difficulty, again including the funding as a minor aspect of the total naval budget.[37]

Construction of the Model Basin

With passage of the authorizing appropriation, the Bureau of Construction and Repair drew up plans and began initial work on the construction of the model basin. Naval Constructor Taylor, in charge of the project, worked from exact specifications. Plans called for a basin that would be 14 feet 8 inches deep, 42 feet wide at the surface, sloping inward at 35 degrees to a 3-foot-wide shelf at a depth of 4 feet, then dropping the remaining 10 feet vertically to an 8-foot width at the bottom. Its length was to be 470 feet. The tank would hold a million gallons of water, taken from Washington city water mains, to be treated with alum to coagulate and precipitate out mud and then passed through an animal bone filter. A brick structure would house the basin, to be situated in the navy yard immediately to the west of the existing ship house and railway within a few feet of the Anacostia River. The 500-foot-long basin building would have no windows, but a skylight would stretch the length of the roof.[38]

Naval Imaging Command

Experimental Model Basin Under Construction.   At the start of construction in February 1897 a first step was driving foundation piles.

From the beginning, Taylor fought against problems arising from the tank's location; the foundation rested on a sandstone base, 8 or 9 feet below the mean tide level of the nearby Anacostia River, which could undermine dangerously the foundation and the tank itself. In order to provide stability and a watertight tank, Taylor accepted strengthening modifications to the original specifications. Under the tank, a layer of broken stone would be covered with a thin layer of concrete, a half-inch of asphalt, and 9 inches of concrete in 16-foot lengths. The joints of the concrete and the whole inside were then coated with a different grade of asphalt. The side walls would rest on a double row of pilings, and sheet pilings with a retaining function would extend around the deeper section.[39] The Navy itself would drive the pilings necessary for supporting the foundation walls and the sheet pilings. A contractor would handle excavation and building.[40]

While planning proceeded, the bureau used some of its initial appropriation to fund work by the Bureau of Yards and Docks to shift railroad tracks and to begin initial piling work. The Navy workers encountered several difficulties in driving the pilings, as they found an old wharf below the surface. Hichborn requested that Yards and Docks put men on 12-hour shifts to complete the work, as allowed by tides, prior to turning the site over to the contractor.[41]

The bureau solicited bids for construction 3 May 1897, and opened the bids 7 June. The bureau awarded the contract for the main construction to the lowest bidder, Penn Bridge Company of Beaver Falls, Pennsylvania, for $50,000; Penn Bridge subcontracted the concrete work to Cranford Paving Company of Washington, D.C.[42]

Under Taylor's direction, the bureau developed designs and plans for the towing carriage and recording equipment while construction proceeded on the basin and building. Taylor kept meticulous records of all design decisions. The towing carriage for models would rest on two pairs of steel rails that paralleled the basin. Power was to be provided by a reciprocating steam engine in a nearby building, which would drive three electric dynamos. That power would in turn drive four 50-horsepower motors that drove the carriage. The electric drive of the carriage allowed for a speed range from 0.5 to 18 knots, at increments between 0.1 and 0.3 knots. Only one generator and one motor would be used at the slowest carriage speeds and lowest acceleration rates. For the maximum speed and fast acceleration, all three generators and all four motors would be put in service. The generators and motors were provided under contract by General Electric, and William Sellers Company of Washington built the carriage. Braking the 40-ton carriage would be accomplished by reversing the motors' direct current, converting them to generators. As a further backup, a pair of friction brakes and an emergency underwater hydraulic brake would be installed.[43]

Taylor took particular care with the scientific apparatus at the basin. The dynamometer for measuring model resistance would consist of a horizontal coiled spring about 15 inches long and 3 inches in diameter. A recording drum and pen would record seconds of time and the position of both ends of the spring, as well as changes of level of the bow and stern of the model. The spring was set in line with the fore-aft axis of the model; its stretch would measure the model's resistance. Technicians calibrated the spring by placing known weights on a scale pan and observing and recording on the drum the amount of stretch necessary to balance the weights. Displaying his characteristic foresight and concern for precision, Taylor fought to keep the device as simple as possible in order to avoid errors that might come in from friction in more complex linkages. Another pen marking half-second intervals on a drum driven by the carriage wheels recorded carriage speed. Saegmuller of Washington City, a firm specializing in instruments for the Navy, built the dynamometer and recording devices.[44]

Two pumps would provide for drainage of the basin. The larger 12-inch electrical centrifugal pump could empty the million-gallon tank in about four hours. A smaller, 4-inch centrifugal pump would drain the remaining shallow water from the basin and was also to be used to pump tidal seepage from the underlying rock foundation when the tank was empty. Without such a pump, pressure from the external tidal water could crack the tank walls when the tank water pressure was removed during emptying and cleaning. Engineers later learned the severity of the threat as the Anacostia tides generally rose to a level within 6 feet of the surface of the tank water.[45]

Taylor calmly adjusted to several delays during construction. Tidal seepage during excavation continued to set back the schedule several months through 1897, and the bureau granted contract modifications to Penn Bridge to allow for that and other added costs. Through 1897 Taylor recommended and Hichborn approved several contract changes and cost increases submitted by Penn Bridge for strengthening and protecting the basin in its precarious location: plans for improved roof trusses, improved skylight design, improved external drainage, additional concrete for strengthening the basin itself, an improved formula for the concrete mix, changed details of asphalt application, and an increased use of interlaced barbed wire, iron rails, and pipe within the concrete lining as reinforcement. Springs and quicksand uncovered in excavation required more extensive digging and concrete filling.[46]

Experimental Model Basin, 1898–1940.   This building housed the lead
U.S. facility for hydrodynamic model testing of proposed naval and commercial
ships for four decades.

Despite the changes and delays, the basin itself was completed in
1898. Contractors for the electrical and towing equipment fell behind in
performance in mid-1898, due, Taylor conceded, to pressure of other
government work during the Spanish American War. The electrical generators were delivered late in 1898.[47]

The original total appropriation of $100,000 proved insufficient to
pay for additional equipment, the modifications, and the cost of delays.
Government budget for piling, excavation, and sheet piling together
with changes for the towing carriage with its driving equipment, pumps,
and later additions, including a wavemaking apparatus, a shallow-water
platform, and tools for construction of models, raised the eventual total
cost of the equipped basin, by Taylor's own calculation, to $143,874.96.[48]

By mid-1899 the tank was in working order; the towing and register-
ing equipment had been installed, inspected, and tested. Despite the numerous applications both from private firms and from other bureaus of

the Navy for testing time, Taylor planned to use the first months of the
basin operation for standardizing the equipment.[49]

Two years after the Penn Bridge contract was awarded, a justly
proud Taylor announced the completion of the new basin in a press release dated 4 July 1899. Despite setbacks in schedule brought on by tidal
seepage and by the Spanish American War in 1898, and despite some degree of cost overrun, the basin met exacting specifications. Reflecting
the New Navy awareness of European competition and of the need to
professionalize and make more scientific the process of ship design, the
press release listed specifics that alluded to those concerns. The 470-foot
by 42-foot basin was the largest in the world, exceeding the dimensions
of the large 400-foot by 20-foot British tank at Haslar and the 500-foot by
22-foot Italian tank at La Spezia. Basin equipment was brand new and
in good working order; its testing and recording devices, designed by
the bureau and constructed with precision, would allow for extremely
accurate measurement. A backlog of work had accumulated, and Taylor
was eager to begin. Planned new destroyers and cruisers could be

EMB Towing Tank.   Construction engineers survey the completed tank and
building in 1898.

Office Staff, 1898.   Admiral D. W. Taylor, Naval Constructor for the Bureau of Construction and Repair, stands with the bureau's Navy Yard Department staff. Several in the back row, including Lyman Hewins (left rear), stayed with the towing tank for decades.

pretested, promising economies for the government. Private ship-builders had built up a demand and waited in line for available time. Even another naval bureau, Steam Engineering, sought its turn to test propellers. Research work on the fundamentals of ship resistance, begun by Froude, could be scheduled. The new century would begin with a hectic schedule that held great promise for the advancement of naval technology.

Creation of the Engineering Experiment Station

The Engineering Experiment Station at Annapolis grew out of the same New Navy concerns to match European advances, to improve the scientific capability of the Navy, to provide facilities for the increasing numbers of professional officers, to improve the quality of education in the Navy, and to recognize the growth of the engineering profession it-

self. Over the years of advocacy and building of the model basin, the
Bureau of Steam Engineering worked to establish its own facility for testing and evaluating new equipment. Public discussion of such a facility
can be traced to 1895, when former Assistant Engineer F. C. Bieg published an article in the *Journal of the American Society of Naval Engineers.*[50]
Bieg's proposal incorporated the solution of two separate problems in a
single plan. First, he wanted a well-equipped station to conduct experiments and research on engines and materials. Second, he addressed the
need for postgraduate training of engineers in the Navy. At the time,
commissioned engineering officers from the Naval Academy had studied
only one elementary engineering course. Bieg visualized a kind of engineering institute with graduate students pursuing a course of study, retired officers giving guest lectures, and researchers drawn from the engineer ranks proposing and conducting their own projects at the facilities,
under the direction of senior engineers.

Bieg suggested that the proposed school and station should be near
"still and deep water," and that it also be near engineering and manufacturing centers. However, he believed it should not be located either at a
navy yard or at the Naval Academy. Routine work at a navy yard would
interfere with research duties. Commissioned officers, studying at the
postgraduate level, should not be subjected to the discipline of cadets at
the Academy. He outlined some of the categories of work that might be
taken on as part of the experimental program at such a station: practical
engineering, chemistry, metallurgy, propeller studies, lubrication work,
and research into boiler deterioration. He anticipated that ideas for research in all of these areas would be suggested by naval engineers. They
would submit a plan of research—a proposal—which, if approved by the
director, himself a senior engineer, would result in the detailing of the
officer making the proposal to the station for a tour of duty to conduct
his experiment using his own methods. This system, Bieg believed,
would preserve and enhance the engineer's esprit de corps.[51]

The *Journal of the American Society of Naval Engineers* published comments on Bieg's proposal from twenty-one prominent naval and civilian
engineers. The commentators disagreed over details of location, exact
orientation and organization, and the methods of ensuring continuity of
work, but most agreed that a facility for research and training along the
lines suggested by Bieg was a necessity. Several alluded to the growth of
engineering as a profession and drew parallels to the Navy's other new
facilities, including the War College, the Torpedo Station, and the Naval
Gun Factory. The group agreed that current training, with the short
course at the Academy and hit-or-miss postgraduate training either at
the New York Navy Yard or in foreign schools, was entirely inadequate.[52]

The discussion stimulated by Bieg's paper continued outside the forum of the American Society of Naval Engineers. Both Chief of the Bureau of Steam Engineering George Melville and William S. Aldrich, an Academy graduate and professor of engineering at West Virginia University, considered the issue of engineering research and education at the 1895 annual meeting of the Society of Naval Architects and Marine Engineers (SNAME). Aldrich recommended that federally funded engineering laboratories be established at the Academy and at every land grant college following the example of government supported agricultural stations at the land grant schools. Melville generally supported the ideas put forward by Aldrich, but in the case of the Navy, he expressed doubts as to whether such a station should be associated with the Academy. "Systematic efforts are required," he argued, "to achieve quality experimental work for the Navy and for the mercantile interests." Such efforts, he believed, "can be exerted and lasting results obtained only in a special place." Agreeing with the point made earlier by Bieg, Melville said, "I do not think that the Naval Academy or any of our constructing or repair navy yards would be suitable for a Naval Experimental Station. A station should not be subordinated to the multifarious duties of a navy yard or the routine of the Naval Academy."[53]

During this period Melville saw the need for an experiment station as a higher priority than the problem of engineering education, and he worked to establish the station as a testing facility rather than as a training school. In 1900 he advocated an experiment station and reported on the expansion of testing work by the Bureau of Steam Engineering. Like his counterpart in Construction and Repair when arguing for the model basin, he noted with concern the competitive example of European experiment stations, particularly the German facilities. In a clear departure from the approach of Construction and Repair, however, Melville argued that full-scale tests were necessary for evaluation of such items as propellers, shafts, and engines. "Experiments with models," he pointed out, "can do no more than indicate in a doubtful degree changes desirable [*sic*], owing to the reduction in size and the increased difficulty in observing delicate differences." Melville agreed that the variety of research carried on by the bureau in scattered locations created a pressing need for a separate testing station.[54]

Despite his initial objection to tying the station to the Naval Academy, Melville decided by 1901, apparently out of a pragmatic concern, that the station should be built to link the establishment of the station to Academy expansion. His original ambivalence on this question colored the whole question of location of the station, its eventual creation with an administrative and educational relationship with the

Academy, and its evolution in the direction of an establishment independent of the Academy over its first decades. However, the massive appropriations for Academy expansion approved in 1899 and expanded in 1900 provided a convenient shelter for Melville's relatively modest request for funds. In 1901 and again in 1902 Melville explicitly tied the idea of the station to the authorization for expenditure of $10 million in improvements of buildings at the Academy. For want of an independent establishment, Melville argued, Annapolis presented some advantages. He proposed to cooperate in the administration of the station with the Bureau of Navigation, which operated the Academy. In defense of Senate bill S. 2471 in the 57th Congress, introduced early in 1902, Melville proposed a building at the Academy to cost $250,000, with a budget of $150,000 for equipment. Unlike the legislation to establish the model basin, station authorization encountered no recorded debate; it was smoothly eliminated as a separate bill and then incorporated in the yearly general naval appropriations bill, passing almost unnoticed in the generally pro-Navy political atmosphere of the first Theodore Roosevelt administration, and in the wake of the successes of the Navy in the Spanish American War of 1898.[55]

In arguing for the appropriation Melville pointed out that the station would conduct work to benefit the Navy and the engineering profession at large. It would be used to test "patent appliances" that inventors offered to the government. He listed a range of possible problems to be considered at the station: the form, size, and location of propellers; the character and area of propeller blades; systematic tests of the endurance of electrical systems; corrosion of boilers and condenser tubes; form and type of watertube boilers; compressed air systems; balancing of marine engines; storage battery improvement; efficiency of gas engines; and perfection of joints and connections for hydraulic, steam, and pneumatic systems.[56]

A regular force of engineers working at a specified location would have several advantages over the ad hoc arrangements for testing which the bureau had used to date. Tests could be carried on continuously and efficiently. Independent inventors, unable to finance their own experiments, would be stimulated to submit ideas for consideration by the Navy. Naval officers with inventive ideas—here he was thinking of men like Bradley Fiske—could continue to invent appliances and improvements that could be tested and put in service. Unlike Bieg, however, Melville did not propose that the inventive officers run their experiments on short assignments at the station.[57]

The new station would serve the larger goals of the New Navy. Melville pointed quite explicitly to European competition. He noted that Germany, with its engineering station connected with a technical school at Charlottenburg in the Berlin suburbs, had made great strides in engineering over the previous decade. Melville saw an irony in the fact that the Navy did not even have a laboratory for engineering work which could compete with civilian undergraduate academic institutions in the United States. "I am simply requesting," he said, "that the Academy be placed upon an equality with several universities whose colleges of mechanic arts and science equipment far surpass the engineering outfit of the Academy plant."[58]

In 1902 the budget legislation was approved, with the amounts requested by Melville authorized for expenditure in 1903. Melville secured the approval of the Bureau of Navigation for location of the facility at the Academy. Some of the initial appropriation was used to establish a small testing facility with a Parsons turbine engine under the jurisdiction of the Steam Engineering Department at the Academy. The Parsons engine, invented and manufactured by C. J. Parsons in Britain, was the first practical marine steam turbine; its use as a propulsion plant on board ships had been demonstrated in the experimental British vessel, *Turbina*, launched in 1893. In 1903 the U.S. Navy considered the acquisition of turbine plants for warships; the first in U.S. naval vessels were a Parsons engine in the cruiser *Chester* (1908) and a Curtis turbine in the cruiser *Salem* (1908). The acquisition of the pathbreaking Parsons engine, later to revolutionize ship propulsion because of its high efficiency for small size, reflected Melville's concern that the Navy keep up with the state of the art.[59]

Melville's firm endorsement of the need for a station and his specific proposals carried great weight. He was probably the most influential naval engineer in the United States. Appointed Chief of the Bureau of Steam Engineering in 1887, Melville was a colorful and well-known national figure; Congress had recognized his heroic performance on the Arctic exploration in 1878–1879 by advancing him fifteen places in the naval promotional system. Even so, his direct influence in the particulars of planning of the experiment station was hardly as pronounced as Taylor's personal direction of the construction of the model basin, because Melville retired from the service in 1903, the first year that congressionally approved funds for the project became available.[60]

In one of his last official communications as a naval officer, in June 1903, Melville wrote to Superintendent Willard H. Brownson of the Academy, arguing once again for locating the station off the Academy grounds. "The place selected . . . is cramped; it gives no opportunity for expansion." Furthermore, he noted that tests with steam generators, with steam and coal smoke pouring forth "night and day," would be "a nuisance inside the Academy grounds." The head of the Academy's Steam Engineering Department, Edgar T. Warburton, concurred that a location off the grounds should be secured. Melville had requested that architect Ernest Flagg, who had been engaged to design new Academy buildings, draw up preliminary plans, but Melville noted that the exact spot must be fixed upon before laying out the buildings in detail. In general, however, Melville envisioned a single-story, firm, light building with arched roof with light-colored brick to suit the color and general appearance of the Academy buildings. Although Melville advocated that the new station be located off the grounds, he was not suggesting a complete detachment from the Academy; he visualized a station organization still tied to the Academy.[61]

In 1903 a site selection board, headed by Rear Admiral W. C. Field, approved a location across the Severn River, a half-mile across from the wharf where the Academy moored its prison-ship, the hulk *Santee*. An advantage of the site was that the river was already dredged to a 30-foot depth, about 200 yards from the shore. The board noted that, with very little further dredging, a channel could allow for a battleship to approach within 50 feet of the structure.[62]

View Across Severn River.   From the site of the Engineering Experiment Station, the U.S. Naval Academy could be seen directly across the river.

Captain Walter F. Worthington.
Director of the Engineering Experiment Station, 1904–1910, posed here in his full dress uniform.

C. W. Rae, Melville's successor at the bureau, reported other advantages. He noted that when ships visited the Academy, they could be moored at the station and "new machines could be tested at the new facility." By proceeding in this manner, there would ultimately be accumulated a mass of reliable data concerning the working of every type of machine used in the naval service. Centralized evaluations would be more useful than tests at the builders' works. A further advantage of the location would be the supply of water for use in propeller-testing tanks; ships bringing heavy machinery, coal, and other supplies could discharge their cargoes directly to the station. On the hill rising 60 feet behind the proposed location a water reservoir could be constructed; wells had tapped good fresh water at 15 to 30 feet. On the hills farther behind the station, excellent locations could be had for the construction of dwellings for future officers and employees.[63]

Execution of the plan and oversight of construction fell to Commander Walter F. Worthington, a practical and hard-headed engineer with a good command of day-to-day detail, who fumed over the contractor's excuses for delay and requests for rescheduling. Like Taylor, Worthington faced numerous requests for contract modification and extension, but unlike Taylor, Worthington had little patience for excuses and no patience whatsoever with private concerns seeking profit from Navy work. The contract for foundation work was signed 12 January 1906, but was not received by the contractor, Latta and Terry Company of Philadelphia, who bid $68,990, until two weeks later, 26 January 1906. The contractor requested an extension of three weeks to make up for this initial delay. Other delays derived from time taken in inspection of piling timbers at Jacksonville, Florida, inclement winter weather, delayed delivery of the pile driver and the piles themselves by schooner, attempting to drive piles during unexpectedly adverse weather in June and July 1906, redesigning of the building, and conflicts of timing in getting local oystermen to haul gravel and sand in their boats during their own heavy work season. Altogether, the contractor requested allowance for seventeen weeks of delay. Worthington, always concerned that naval funds be wisely spent, denied most of the contractor's claims, and explicitly recommended approval of only five of the requested weeks.[64]

Worthington grew increasingly angered by the performance of the architect. As an engineer, Worthington carefully checked Flagg's drawings and calculations, finding them full of inaccuracies and errors. The architect's commission was to be calculated as 5 percent of construction costs. When Flagg billed for a commission on foundation as well as building costs, Worthington put his foot down. He dashed off a strongly worded case for denial of the commission. Flagg's foundation sketches had been in error; his negligence with correspondence led to contractor delays; he had not bothered to check core samples; his estimates of bearings on pilings had been dangerously low; his plans had to be entirely reworked by Worthington himself. Worthington found Flagg's delays "inexcusable, his figures incorrect," and his demand for funds without the "slightest title." The bureau offered a reduction to a one percent commission, about $600, for Flagg's work on the foundation but the dispute dragged on.[65]

Construction on the foundation for the main building was finally completed 17 January 1907. Bids on construction of the building were opened 15 October 1906, the originally proposed date for completion of the foundation work. Noel Construction Company, after revising its bid downward to $157,000, won the contract for the building 1 February 1907. Construction work began in the spring of 1907, with planned completion scheduled for 1 March 1908.[66]

The main building was 316 feet long, 66 feet 8 inches wide, and 29 feet to the eaves. The lower half was brick, steel, and concrete, with steel

Engineering Experiment Station. Fronting on the Severn River, the Station provided easy off-loading for coal, heaped at quay-side on the right.

sash on the upper half. It was laid out northeast by southwest. Worthington and Flagg squared off in an acrimonious debate over the color of the brick to be used for the building's exterior. While Flagg insisted on "blue-gray" to match the Academy buildings across the river, Worthington believed such a concern to be frivolous, considering the distance to the other buildings and the utilitarian function of the station. Worthington said Flagg's ideas were "based on a misconception of the kind of work to be done. . . . The place will be an industrial establishment pure and simple." Flagg argued for clean aesthetics with great fervor, sorely stretching Worthington's patience. On this score, however, the naval engineer yielded to the architect, because Flagg finally recommended brick that was no more expensive than alternative materials.[67]

Through 1907–1908 Worthington sent out requisitions for equipment to be brought to the site for assembly and installation. A 15-ton electric crane ran the full width of the main building on overhead tracks, and could travel the full length of the building. The building was divided in half: the northern end contained offices, laboratories, storeroom, and tool room, with testing machines in the central space. The southern half contained a machinery laboratory and a machine shop to be equipped with lathes, planer, shaper, milling machine, drill press, and pipe-cutting and threading equipment. A well-equipped woodworking shop was also planned. Worthington ordered steam condensers, an experimental boiler and a second boiler to be used both for tests and for heating and lighting the building, a carbon dioxide recording instrument that could be used to test the efficiency of fire-stoking crews, and a coal-testing calorimeter.[68]

Worthington successfully got the building itself completed on schedule and ordered staff to move in over the period 17 March–6 April 1908. He oversaw the installation of the electric traveling crane, a Curtis turbo-generator, an auxiliary condenser, and freshwater and saltwater pumps. The $150,000 fund for new equipment proved more than adequate, allowing for continued judicious acquisition of new machinery during the first months of the station's operation. Through 1908 the station acquired the original Parsons marine turbine used previously at the Academy, two types of surface condensers, and fireroom blower engines. Private firms supplied sheet packing for steam and water joints and a collection of boiler water gauges to be tested. Worthington planned to acquire a standard naval distilling plant, a safety-valve testing apparatus, and more equipment.[69]

The two major ship procurement bureaus of the Navy—Construction and Repair, and Steam Engineering—had successfully opened two major facilities. Both the model basin on the Anacostia and the engineering station on the Severn were concerned with aspects of ship research and design. Each was adequately funded and equipped; each was competitive in equipment and design with parallel institutions in the service of first-ranking European naval powers. The technical staff at each facility looked forward eagerly to a range of challenging work that would apply the most modern methods, the newest equipment, and the talents of trained naval and civilian personnel to the design of ships and engines.

Endnotes

1. William Hovgaard, *Modern History of Warships* (London: E. & F. N. Spon, 1920), 7; Edgar C. Smith, *A Short History of Naval and Marine Engineering* (Cambridge, Eng.: The University Press, 1938), 153.
2. Bernard Brodie, *Sea Power and the Machine Age* (Princeton: Princeton University Press, 1941), 19. See also I. B. Holley, *Ideas and Weapons* (1953; reprint, Hamden, CT: Archon Books, 1971, copyright 1953), vii–xiii.
3. Hovgaard, *Warships*, 22; James Phinney Baxter III, *The Introduction of the Ironclad Warship* (Hamden, CT: Archon Books, 1968), 302–303.
4. Hovgaard, *Warships*, 66; Augusta C. Buell, *The Memoirs of Charles H. Cramp* (Philadelphia and London: Lippincott, 1906), 79; John D. Alden, *The American Steel Navy* (Annapolis: Naval Institute Press, 1972), 4.
5. Alden, *American Steel Navy*, 13–16.
6. Donald J. Sexton, "Forging the Sword: Congress and the American Naval Renaissance, 1880–1890," Ph.D. diss., University of Tennessee, 1976, 291; E. B. Potter, *Sea Power: A Naval History*, 2d ed. (Annapolis: Naval Institute Press, 1981), 160, 194.
7. Sexton, "Forging the Sword," 291; Charles Oscar Paullin, *Paullin's History of Naval Administration, 1775–1911* (1912; Annapolis: Naval Institute Press, 1968), 418. Depending upon exactly what classes of ships are counted, the U.S. fleet was in the range of 21 to 31 ships in 1880.
8. B. Franklin Cooling, "The Formative Years of Naval Industrial Complex: The Meaning of Studies of Institutions Today," *Naval War College Review* 27 (Mar–Apr 1975): 53–61.
9. Kenneth J. Hagan, *American Gunboat Diplomacy and the Old Navy, 1877–1889*, Contributions in Military History 4 (Westport, CT: Greenwood Press, 1973), 4–10.
10. Robert Seager II, "Ten Years Before Mahan: The Unofficial Case for the New Navy", 1880–1890, *Mississippi Valley Historical Review* 40 (Dec 1953): 491–512.
11. William Dilworth Puleston, *Mahan: The Life and Work of Captain Alfred Thayer Mahan, USN* (New Haven, CT: Yale University Press, 1939), 94, 104.
12. George T. Davis, *A Navy Second to None: The Development of Modern American Naval Policy* (New York: Harcourt, 1940), 40–45.
13. Donald W. Mitchell, *History of the Modern American Navy from 1883 through Pearl Harbor* (New York: Knopf, 1946), 35–54.
14. Ronald Spector, *Professors of War: The Naval War College and the Development of the Naval Profession* (Newport: Naval War College Press, 1977).
15. Monte A. Calvert, *The Mechanical Engineer in America, 1830–1910: Professional Cultures in Conflict* (Baltimore: Johns Hopkins Press, 1967), 255.
16. Paullin, *History of Naval Administration, 1775–1911*, 460–463.
17. Rear Admiral Julius Augustus Furer, *Administration of the Navy Department in World War II* (Washington: GPO, 1959), 234–235.
18. Obituary, *New York Times*, 4 Aug 1927, 21; *Who Was Who in America*, vol. 1, *1897–1942* (Chicago: Marquis, 1943); U.S. Naval Academy Alumni Association, *Register of Alumni, 1945–1985*, #01440.

19. William Hovgaard, "Biographical Memoirs of David Watson Taylor, 1864–1940," *Biographical Memoirs of the National Academy of Sciences*, vol. 22 (Washington: National Academy of Sciences, 1941). No full-length biography of David W. Taylor exists. Taylor biographical materials for this and the following chapter are drawn from various standard references and primary sources.

20. William Ledyard Cathcart, "George Wallace Melville," *Journal of the American Society of Naval Engineers* (hereafter *JASNE*) 24 (1912): 477–511; *Who Was Who* 1:329.

21. Clark G. Reynolds, *Famous American Admirals* (New York: Van Nostrand Reinhold, 1978), 117–119. For a full biography, see Paolo Coletta, *Admiral Bradley A. Fiske and the American Navy* (Lawrence, KS: Regents Press, 1979), or Fiske's autobiography, *From Midshipman to Rear Admiral* (New York: The Century Co., 1919).

22. Paullin, *History of Naval Administration*, 478–479.

23. Rear Admiral E. Simpson to W. E. Chandler, Secretary of the Navy, 17 Apr 1884, DTNSRDC RC 7-1, box 2, Naval Advisory Board President Simpson transmitted Bowles memorandum recommending a towing tank.

24. Charles Singer, E. J. Holmyard, A. R. Hall, and Trevor I. Williams, *A History of Technology*, vol. 5 (Oxford: Clarendon Press, 1958), 386–390; Frederick H. Todd, "The Fundamentals of Ship Model Testing," *Transactions of the Society of Naval Architects and Marine Engineers* (hereafter *TSNAME*) (1951): 850–862.

25. Ibid.

26. Ibid., 852.

27. William Froude, "On the Ratio of Indicated to Effective Horse-power as Elucidated by Mr. Dennys M.M. Trials at Varied Speeds," "On the Comparative Resistances of Long Ships of Several Types," and "The Fundamental Principles of the Resistance of Ships," collected in *The Papers of William Froude, 1810–1879*, Wescott Abell, ed. (London: Royal Institution of Naval Architects, 1955).

28. Simpson to Chandler, 17 Apr 1984, supra 23.

29. *Annual Reports of the Navy Department for the Year 1894, Annual Report of the Secretary of the Navy*, 436–437; ibid., 1895, 338–40 (hereafter *SECNAV Annual Report*).

30. Philip Hichborn, Chief Constructor, USN, Second Endorsement of H.R. 4045 "Providing for a Model Tank for the United States Navy, Bureau of Construction and Repair," 1896–1911, National Archives and Records Administration (hereafter NARA), RG 19, entry 88, box 107, file 372/A.

31. Ibid.

32. Ibid.

33. H.R. 4045, 54th Cong., 1st sess., 1896.

34. NARA, RG 80, box 175, file 5457.

35. H. H. Herbert to S. G. Hilborn, 18 Feb 1896, NARA, RG 19, entry 88, Bureau of Contstruction and Repair 1896–1911, box 107, file 372/A.

36. H.R. 7542, 54th Cong., 1st sess., 1896; U.S. Congress, Senate, 54th Cong., 1st sess., 2 May 1896; *Congressional Record* 28:4736; *SECNAV Annual Report, 1896*, 374.

37. *Congressional Record* 28:4735–37, 5916, 6022, 6326, 6357, 6365, 6441; *SECNAV Annual Report, 1897*, 351; H.R. 10336, 54th Cong., 2d sess., 1897. The Appropriations Act passed 3 March 1897.

38. Hichborn to Herbert, on model basin specifications, 29 Mar 1897, NARA, RG 19, entry 88, box 107, file 372/A; Taylor, *The Experimental Model Basin*, EMB Report #54, Jul 1922, DTNSRDC RC 7-1, box 3.

39. Text of press announcement on EMB to be released 4 Jun 1899, NARA, RG 19, entry 88, Bureau of Construction and Repair 1896–1911, box 107.

40. Hichborn to Herbert, 29 Mar 1897, supra 38.

41. Hichborn to Chief, Bureau of Yards and Docks, 17 Sep 1896; and Hichborn to Commandant, Navy Yard, 5 May 1897, NARA, RG 19, entry 88, Bureau of Construction and Repair, 1896–1911, box 107.

42. *SECNAV Annual Report, 1897,* 351; Theodore Roosevelt to Chief, Bureau of Construction and Repair, 15 Jun 1897, NARA, RG 19, entry 88, Bureau of Construction and Repair 1896–1911, box 107.

43. EMB Press Release, 4 Jul 1899; EMB Report 54.

44. Ibid.

45. EMB Press Release, 4 Jul 1899.

46. Contract and Changes, NARA, RG 19, entry 88, Bureau of Construction and Repair 1896–1911, box 107, doc 372/A220.

47. *SECNAV Annual Report, 1898,* 522.

48. D. W. Taylor to D. W. Dickie, 17 May 1918, Bureau of Construction and Repair 1912–1925, NARA, RG 19, entry 88, box 20.

49. *SECNAV Annual Report, 1899,* 563; Hichborn to John H. Dialogue, 23 Jun 1899, Bureau of Construction and Repair, 1896–1911, NARA, RG 19, entry 88, box, 408, file 4113/A3.

50. F. C. Bieg, "On the Necessity and Value of Scientific Research in Naval Engineering Matters as Related to the U.S. Navy and the Necessity of an Engineer Training for the Younger Members of the Engineer Corps of the U.S. Navy," *JASNE* (7 Aug 1895): 449–453.

51. Ibid., 451–452.

52. Ibid., 454–483.

53. William S. Aldrich, "Engineering Research in the Navy," *TSNAME* 3 (1895): 185–193; Melville's discussion, 192.

54. *SECNAV Annual Report, 1900,* 842–843.

55. *SECNAV Annual Report, 1902,* 715–721; S. 2471, 57th Cong., 1st sess. 1902; U.S. Congress, Senate, "Naval Engineering Experiment Station at Annapolis, Maryland," S.Doc. 93, 57th Cong., 1st sess., 1902, 2.

56. S.Doc. 93, 1902, 2–4.

57. Ibid., 4–5.

58. Ibid., 5; *SECNAV Annual Report, 1902,* 715–717.

59. *SECNAV Annual Report, 1904,* 894. This report did not specify the Parsons engine, but later correspondence and reports detail experiments with the Parsons engine; see chapter 3. Emil E. Keller and Francis Hodgkinson, "The Steam Turbine in the United States; I-Developments by the Westinghouse Machine Company," *Mechanical Engineering* (Nov 1936): 683–696. Westinghouse, by licensing agreement reached in 1895, acquired exclusive rights to the manufacture and sale of Parsons steam turbines in the United States, except for those used in marine propulsion.

60. *Who Was Who in America* 1:829. See also, Cathcart, *George Wallace Melville,* 477–511.

61. George Melville to Captain Willard H. Brownson, Superintendent, U.S. Naval Academy, 24 Jun 1903, Washington National Record Center (hereafter WNRC) RG 181, acc. 2794, EES General Correspondence 1905–1941, box 1 (General Correspondence 1905–06–07); Comment from Joe Sheehan, David Taylor Research Center, Advisory Board Information File (hereafter ABIF).

62. Rear Admiral W. C. Field, et al., "Site Recommended for Steam Engineering Experiment Station," 19 Nov 1903, WNRC, RG 181, acc. 2794, box 1.

63. *SECNAV Annual Report, 1904,* 893–894. C. W. Rae, Chief of the Bureau of Steam Engineering, based his arguments for the location on a letter from Lieutenant Commander Walter F. Worthington, 2 Sep 1904, WNRC, RG 181, acc. 2794, box 1.

64. Contract, Charles Bonaparte, Secretary of the Navy, with Latta and Terry Construction Company, 12 Jan 1906, WNRC, RG 181, acc. 2794, box 1.

65. Worthington, letter draft, 20 Aug 1906, General Records of the Secretary of the Navy, 1897–1915, NARA, RG 80, box 550, file 1224-22, 1224-35; Worthington to C. W. Rae, Chief, Bureau of Steam Engineering, 4 Aug 1906; and Worthington to Superintendent, Naval Academy, 2 Mar 1908, WNRC, RG 181, acc. 2794, box 1.

66. Worthington to Superintendent, Naval Academy, 5 Oct 1907, WNRC, RG 181, acc. 2794, box 1. Bid offer of 15 Oct 1906, folder B165.1, same location, provided a flexible price based upon optional features.

67. Correspondence between Worthington and Ernest Flagg, 20 Nov 1905, 23 Nov 1905, 23 Nov 1905, 20 Nov 1905, 8 Dec 1905 (quoted), 11 Dec 1905, 27 Jan 1906, 29 Jan 1906, WNRC, RG 181, acc. 2794, box 2. Correspondence on the topic continued well into 1908.

68. Worthington reported in great detail on the building and equipment in a variety of correspondence, WNRC, RG 181, acc. 2794, box 1.

69. Worthington to C. W. Rae, 16 Jan 1908, DTNSRDC RC 7-2, box 1.

CHAPTER 3

Finding Roles

I N THE FIRST TWO DECADES OF THE TWENTIETH century, the model basin and the experiment station faced similar difficulties in growth, setting routines, acquiring and installing equipment, and recruiting staff. But by 1920, the well-established institutional personalities of the facilities revealed pronounced differences between the two. The experiment station became the Navy's center for testing products and devices for use on board naval ships and had issued reports on over 1,000 items. The model basin, too, had made solid contributions, with tests on over 2,000 models. But in addition, the basin had produced a body of more basic research work, attracting national and international recognition for fundamental advances in the science of hydrodynamics and, to a lesser extent, in aerodynamics, through wind tunnel studies of airfoils and wind speed indicators.

Each facility was highly professional and productive. Engineers at the station, like naval architects at the basin, attended conferences and published in journals. Both used innovative methods and accurate measuring procedures. Officers and civilian staff worked closely with innovators in the private sector.

The original missions of the two laboratories were quite different, leading to two kinds of investigation. The fundamental research at the basin came as a natural corollary to design testing and data gathering, much of it useful in refining various aspects of hydrodynamic theory. By contrast, only rarely could the testing of completed products or equipment as conducted at the station lead to such fundamental research. Despite their more limited opportunity for making original contributions, the engineers at the station justly took pride in several major innovations, as well as in their more routine evaluative work.

The theoretical work at the basin grew out of the opportunity presented both by the unique equipment and by the heavy load of naval and commercial design testing. Since the time of William Froude, a range of experiments had filled in and amplified scientific understanding and mathematical expression of the interaction of solid shapes and fluids, and had raised a range of unsolved problems whose solutions required experimental observation. In essence, hydrodynamics as a science had always required a relatively heavy investment base. Even Froude's earliest work had been government-sponsored. Yet government and shipbuilder-owned basins in Europe had full schedules of hull testing growing out of the intense naval arms race of the 1890s and 1900s, and time and energy for research of a more basic nature were always difficult to find.

David Taylor's contribution grew from his ability and concern to create procedural efficiencies for naval work that themselves led to several developments in hydrodynamics. With the hardware, a mathematical approach to the problems, insights into the best methods to be employed, and the drive to find underlying principles, the frontiers could be pushed forward. Taylor recognized that the applied discipline and the theoretical discipline required the same methods, equipment, and training. And even practical design results and systematic observations could be derived from the very same test runs if properly organized and managed.

The work at the experiment station cut across many of the subdisciplines of mechanics, chemistry, thermodynamics, and the physics of materials. While sometimes requiring adaptation to a particular test, the equipment of the experiment station was largely purchased off the shelf. Sometimes, in fact, it was acquired at no cost, as the station's directors begged equipment that had fallen into disuse, found salvage from sunken or scrapped vessels, and scrounged surplus gear from academic institutions and private companies. From time to time these common pieces of testing equipment could be turned to developing systematic observations that could add to the body of technological knowledge.

David W. Taylor, 1899–1914

The achievement of bringing model basin equipment and personnel to bear on fundamental research as well as on naval applications can rightfully be attributed to the interest, drive, and ability of Taylor. Because he built and managed the basin and served as the only scientific officer in its first years, a review of the work of the basin will necessarily seem like a chapter of a biography of one man. He designed the experiments, did calculations, wrote reports, delivered conference papers, and established routines that could be carried out by a small staff of assistants. His interests and research concerns ranged widely; much of the future schedule of the basin would reflect institutional survivals of some of those interests.

As a young officer, Taylor had shown great promise with his excellent record at the Naval Academy, at the Royal Naval College, and as a naval architect in the decade following his 1885 graduation. Upon his return from the Royal Naval College, he went to Charles Cramp's shipyard in Philadelphia as assistant naval constructor. In 1889, he served on a board of experts considering defects in the battleship *Texas,* under construction at Norfolk. In 1891 he was promoted to naval constructor, and he served from 1892 to 1894 as the construction officer at the navy yard at Mare Island, California. In 1894 he transferred to Washington as the principal assistant to Chief Constructor Philip Hichborn, and it was in that duty that he took personal charge of the model basin construction, 1896–1899. On its completion 4 July 1899, four months to the day after his thirty-fifth birthday, he was at an age when he could bring both the vigor of youth and the maturity of experience to bear on the job ahead.[1]

Taylor directly managed the model basin from its opening in 1899 through 1914. In that year, he was promoted to chief constructor and bureau chief with the rank rear admiral and served in that post through 1922, retiring in January 1923 after forty-one years of naval service. At the basin, he was succeeded by Naval Constructor William McEntee (Naval Academy, 1900), who directed the facility until 1920.

Even before Taylor could fully test and standardize the equipment at the basin, he plunged into a hectic schedule of model testing for newly authorized battleships of the *Idaho* class. As a result, he admitted, "the work of the basin has not been carried on during its first year in an ideal manner." He still planned, "as time permits," experiments to establish constants for frictional resistance that would apply to his tank, rather than continuing to rely on possibly inapplicable figures from foreign basins, derived under slightly different conditions of temperature and details of equipment.[2]

All of Taylor's routine work was characterized by a willingness to depart from the precedents established by European predecessors. The length of the basin allowed models to be constructed in 20-foot lengths, rather than at the 12- to 14-foot standards customary in the European tanks. Taylor noted several advantages of the larger models, deriving from the scaling law itself. For a 240-foot ship, a 20-foot model represented 1/1,728 the displacement of the ship; for a 480-foot ship, a 20-

foot model would represent 1/13,824. Using the traditional 12-foot models, the figures would be 1/8,000 and 1/64,000, respectively. The 20-foot models allowed for more accurate prediction of ship performance, because instrument error would not be multiplied by the larger scale factors present with the smaller size European models.[3]

The hot Washington summers precluded the use of paraffin models common in the basins in Europe. Again, Taylor's departure from standard practice brought some advantages, particularly since wood held its shape and the wooden models were far stronger than paraffin ones, offsetting the disadvantage of added expense, and allowing the longer model size. The wooden models were built up using glued blocks of white pine, shaped to conform to the ship plan. The resulting surface, unlike the paraffin model surfaces, needed to be coated with a special varnish to ensure a uniform smooth finish. Once the varnish was applied and dried, the model's frictional resistance would be consistent.[4]

Within the first year Taylor established a routine for testing naval ship models, whose carefully structured procedures demonstrated the experimental technique that he brought to practical problems. He would run five tests of a model: one with displacement as planned for the ship, with no trim. Against this baseline, he would run a second test with trim at the head changed 4 inches and a third test with trim changed 4 inches at the stern. He would then run two tests with no trim, but at 10 percent heavier and 10 percent lighter displacement. The basic five-part test, with its baseline and variation runs, was a general approach rather than a single-condition approach. Tests with variations in displacement or trim might lead to a recommendation for hull redesign; the mass of comparable results could build data useful to an understanding of the resistance forces at work in a more general fashion.[5]

In 1900 Taylor attempted to draw systematic conclusions from the very first tests, hoping to make a "contribution to the solution of the general problem of resistance." From a group of tests with beam and draft variations of the gunboat *Yorktown* design, Taylor concluded "that given the length and displacement of vessels of usual forms, the resistance is not materially changed by practicable changes in shape, beam, draught, etc."[6]

Within two years Taylor recognized that his 1900 statement was in error, and he noted that "experience at the model basin has materially modified my former ideas." After experimentation, he found that resistance was indeed very much influenced by "comparatively slight variations of form" and that many factors besides displacement and length were crucial. In the pattern of his very early routine experiments, he developed the approach that in a few years would lead him to a number of major contributions to the "general problem of resistance." First, he had the desire to use model testing, even in routine design problems, to accumulate data toward the more general problem. Second, he already worked with variations of a single design, to determine in a controlled way how each variation would affect results. Later he would perfect that approach and produce major papers and a full-length monograph that lasted as solid contributions in the field of hydrodynamics.[7]

When Professor William Hovgaard of the Massachusetts Institute of Technology, his friend and professional colleague, sent Taylor a tentative manuscript in 1903 on the forms of ships and their impact on the issue of resistance, Taylor was well aware that he needed to gather more information to fully work out the effects of form on resistance. "You cannot do much better in the present state of our knowledge," he told Hovgaard in reference to the manuscript. Taylor supplied some tentative conclusions drawn from his comparative trim runs regarding the impact on resistance of changes in a fore and aft direction of the center of buoyancy. Beyond those ideas, he hoped to develop a more systematic and comprehensive approach, if he had the time. "If I stay here three or four years longer," he told Hovgaard, "I think I could give you definite facts."[8] He stayed another ten years, and he did indeed develop the "definite facts." But in the first years concern for the daily mundane tasks of model construction, purchasing, keeping up correspondence, dealing with private parties seeking tests, and following the rapid advances in marine engineering all prevented an exclusive focus on such fundamental research.

Taylor's precision of approach was evident in the care he took, even on the smallest issues, to proceed with scientific method. When an employee of the Ordnance Department urged adoption of his own glue for the models, Taylor conducted a controlled experiment comparing this "Wachter's Army and Navy Glue" with "Cooper's White Glue" currently used in building up the pine blocks for turning into models. Six pairs of glued blocks, three with each product, were prepared according to the maker's specifications, and immersed in the model tank for seventeen days. Those blocks glued with Mr. Wachter's formula came apart at various times—all carefully noted and recorded while the Cooper-glued blocks held admirably and could not even be split apart with wedges at the glued seam. Accordingly, the basin continued to use the Cooper glue, which, Taylor told Bureau Chief Francis T. Bowles with dryly ironic satisfaction, was ten cents a gallon less expensive than the inferior product.[9]

Taylor constantly sought shortcuts and efficient methods. He took considerable pride in what he called "machine-made model forms." The

EMB Model Shop.   Craftsmen constructed the body of ship models using innovative methods developed by Taylor, transferring the design from paper to wooden templates to model, itself shaped by machine. Only the bow and stern would be finished by hand.

drafting shop produced large-scale drawings from the original ship plans. Using a pantograph or eidograph, the lines of cross section were then transferred at model size to paper, then to wooden templates that in turn served as guides for machining down the raw glued-up white pine block to the planned hull form. Only the bow and stern would be shaped or "faired" by hand, using a small electric disc sander. Such machine-made hull forms could be produced much faster than entirely hand-built models, and made it easier to slightly vary alternative models of a basic ship design.[10]

During the Progressive era, the federal government sought to assist industry through impartial services, insisting that costs be paid by the user, not the general taxpayer. As planned in the original enabling legislation, the basin was to work out a method and a set of charges for private use of the equipment. For a deposit of $300, a model could be constructed and tested, with the unused balance, usually about $50, returned to the shipbuilder. By 1902 the rate of private model testing had reached five to ten per year. Increasingly over the decade 1900–1910, private shipbuilders would come to rely on Navy pretesting; however, American commercial ships did not compete with British or German vessels in sophistication of design, speed, or equipment.

Taylor worked out an efficient schedule for such private model testing at the basin. In the model shop an outside order would be given priority over "standing work" of alternative model forms and naval designs. In all, from the time the ship "lines" were received in blueprint form, until the final report was issued, would take three weeks, of which one week was devoted to painting, varnishing, and drying the model. Taylor estimated that by using quick-drying paint and imposing a requirement that ship designs be submitted in a standard form, one could cut the turnaround time from three weeks to six days, if one cared to operate a basin on a strictly commercial basis. As it was, the shipbuilder could expect results, once the model was put in the water, in about two days of testing, measuring, and reporting.[11]

The report took the form of simple curves plotted on charts, without analysis, as the Navy's position was that private naval architects would not appreciate the Navy's providing such professional consultation at no charge in competition with them. The report would include three resistance curves at different displacements, and two at the designed displacement with the trim off at the bow and stern, just as reported on the naval ship models. Thus, even in private testing, Taylor could assemble data on fundamental questions, building a consistent and structured collection of information, as well as producing the practical, needed test results.[12]

Taylor's Range of Contributions

In addition to conducting naval and private model testing and overseeing details of management, Taylor kept in touch with crucial developments in related fields such as shiphandling safety, propeller and engine design, turbine and reduction gear machinery, gyroscope applications, and aeronautics. As the manager of the basin, Taylor was under no orders to pursue these lines of research; rather, they grew out of his personal interest as a professional naval architect. Many of Taylor's own technical sidelines would become permanent research interests for the model basin.

He frequently strayed into fields that fell in the purview of the Bureau of Steam Engineering, rather than his own Bureau of Construction and Repair. Corresponding with F. W. Brady of the Holland Torpedo Boat Company regarding submarine engines, and

EMB Towing Carriage Under Way. Using scaling laws developed by William Froude in Britain in 1874, the resistance of a ship at sea is predicted by measuring the resistance of its model towed on a carriage through the basin.

with C. G. Curtis, the inventor of the Curtis turbine, Taylor supplied detailed recommendations as to speed trial methods to determine propeller horsepower outputs from comparison of speed with engine revolution. Similarly, he continued to advise engineers at Cramp Ship Yard, propeller designers at General Electric Company, Admiralty naval constructors in Great Britain, naval architecture Professors Cecil H. Peabody and William Hovgaard at MIT, and other marine engineers and naval architects regarding specifics of propeller and turbine design. In the area of turbines, General Electric and Westinghouse competed commercially and followed different fundamental designs. General Electric adopted the Curtis turbine, while Westinghouse held a license to market the British Parsons design. Perhaps reflecting an early rivalry, Taylor worked with Curtis and General Electric, while Melville in the Bureau of Steam Engineering worked closely with Westinghouse.

Although Taylor was not a leader in the application of the turbine engine to marine use, he took a close interest in this fast-moving technology. In Britain, A. F. Yarrow was working on the problem of reducing turbine output at high speed to the necessary slower speed and higher torque of propellers. Similar to Cramp in the United States, Yarrow was a leading shipbuilder and key innovator in ship design. He had formed a shipbuilding firm in 1866 and had to his credit innovations in the use of high-tensile steel and aluminum and a patented system to reduce ship vibration. In 1905 Taylor wrote to Yarrow, encouraging him to investigate the use of a chain drive to reduce high-speed turbine output to the propeller shaft speed needed. Taylor indicated that Americans were experimenting with chain transmissions for DeLaval turbines, and that the idea held great promise for Curtis and Rateau turbines as well. While helical-cut reduction gears developed by Melville and Joseph MacAlpine and marketed by Westinghouse soon solved the turbine transmission problem by an entirely different method, Taylor's concern and interest in the issue in 1905 demonstrated his professional involvement in a wide range of current marine technological issues.[14]

Yarrow's patented system for the balancing of reciprocating steam engines was licensed in the United States through the firm of Manning, Maxwell and Moore of New York, and that company contacted Taylor to serve as a consultant "to give assistance where necessary in technical matters as regards calculations." He was to be paid out of the licensing fee for advice and details supplied to American firms. Taylor's appointment as a technical consultant to the firm apparently grew out of his presentation, in 1901, of a mathematical analysis of the Yarrow system. His article received a $100 SNAME prize. In the same year, Melville submitted an article on engine balancing for the same prize, losing to the younger officer. The Bureau of Steam Engineering had not adopted the Yarrow system, despite its wide acceptance abroad, because Melville believed it was ineffective in eliminating high-order vibrations, and he believed that Taylor's mathematical analysis of the system also failed to properly account for higher order vibrations. Taylor's prize essay in Melville's own field, and one that took a position so directly opposed to his own and his bureau's position, clearly angered him; the two officers exchanged a rash of heated letters in the pages of the *Transactions of SNAME* over a period of two years in which each more or less politely accused the other of ignoring crucial elements of the problem.[15]

In a rapid piece of research completed in 1903, Taylor produced a report that had a lasting impact on a minor but crucial industry. Until he published his findings, there was no fundamental understanding of the physics of ventilation. In two articles, one published in the *American Machinist* and the other in the *Transactions of SNAME*, Taylor presented, for the first time, a mathematical analysis of the design of vent pipes, elbows, joints, and ventilating fans themselves and developed methods for measuring "head" or ventilating air pressure.[16]

In 1904–1906 Taylor conducted experiments with ship propellers, establishing through a range of runs at different angles and speeds, with series of identical or slightly varied propellers, which factors influenced efficiency. He admitted by 1906 that his test series were only a beginning on the complexities of propeller design, but he had determined several principles. He found that a "rake" or tilt of the propeller on the shaft fore or aft had little effect on efficiency. He also studied the effect of blade thickness, blade form or section, and blade shape. His tentative conclusions pointed to changes in blade section as having a major impact on propeller efficiency. He also attempted to answer the basic question of whether propellers followed the law of comparison—would model propellers yield results that could be scaled up to full-sized propellers? A meticulous comparison of 24-inch- and 8-inch-diameter propellers designed and made with the shape as identical as possible led Taylor to conclude that the scaling law did not apply with exactness, but that "We can rely with a good deal of confidence upon model propeller results extended by the law of comparison." Here, too, his rivalry with Melville surfaced. Earlier, Melville had forcefully argued that propeller model work was of "doubtful reliability" and that full-scale work was the only appropriate research technique in this field.[17]

In the same period in which he conducted the theoretical work on propeller fundamentals, Taylor designed and patented a set of propellers with a "hollow" on the back of the blades near the tips, and worked with Curtis, who arranged for their manufacture in a shop in Philadelphia, to conduct speed trials and tests of the propellers. Taylor worked with representatives in Britain to obtain patent rights there to the same propeller. Taylor also provided Curtis with his opinions on the efficiency of twin screws compared to triple screws as a propulsive system.[18]

Taylor's interests included the question of "suction" or reduced pressure that occurs between two ships, traveling in the same direction, when one overtakes and passes the other too closely. He saw the problem as a demonstration of the principle of streamline flow, in which he had been interested since the 1890s. As early as 1902 Taylor explained the principles based on streamline theory over and over in his correspondence. In 1909 he published a paper resulting from model basin experiments, demonstrating how reduced pressure between closely passing ships tended to force them closer together with danger of collision. In late 1911 Taylor traveled to Britain to testify at an admiralty law case as an expert witness. *Olympia* and *Hawke* had collided in a narrow waterway; the issue of fault hinged on whether the ships could have avoided collision or had been forced together by the action of the water. Taylor's explanation of suction was accepted, but he noted with his usual dry humor that the British judge took the attitude "that suction might appear in American or German waters, but that it had never been heard of in England, and hence should be regarded with the greatest of suspicion." The judge did accept the principle of suction as a cause, but preferred to regard the proper term as "forces set up in the water" which carried *Hawke* "towards *Olympia* in a swerve which was beyond her control."[19]

Taylor became an enthusiastic supporter of the work of Elmer Sperry, a prolific inventor with background in electric motors, streetcar propulsion, the electric car, and the battery. Sperry sought to design a gyroscope to enhance ship stability, beginning in the winter of 1907–1908. Improving upon a German invention of 1904, he filed a patent application for an active ship-stabilizing gyroscope in May 1908. Sperry's device would be able to head off a ship roll by beginning its counteracting force before the full rolling effect of a wave was felt, through an electrical linkage that actuated the gyroscope at the first tilting effect of a wave. In early 1908 Sperry discussed his ideas with Taylor, beginning a long and crucial association between Sperry and the Navy. Taylor agreed to test a model of Sperry's stabilizer at the basin, and in July 1910 he drafted a forty-page report explaining in mathematical terms the stabilizing effect of Sperry's machinery.[20]

Taylor feared that his own report and Sperry's innovative gyroscopic stabilizer would "land permanently in the pigeonholes of the Dept.," and he offered to rewrite the report for the Naval Institute *Proceedings*,[21] but Sperry himself spread the word through a 1910 article in the *Transactions of SNAME*.[22] In the same year Sperry developed his first plans for a gyrocompass, following a suggestion from Taylor that the Navy was seeking an American-manufactured compass superior to a German-designed one already on the market. Sperry proceeded with both the stabilizer and the compass; over the decade following 1915, both came increasingly into naval service. Through the 1910 testing of the stabilizer at the basin, Taylor provided Sperry not only with valuable test facilities and encouragement, but also with a range of specific technical suggestions for improvement. Sperry's biographer has found in this cooperation between Taylor and Sperry a major foreshadowing of "a new era in the history of research and development," much more characteristic of mid and late twentieth-century patterns than of the 1910 period.[23] In the context of Taylor's own interests, his support for Sperry followed the pattern of cooperation with private manufacturers like Yarrow, Curtis, and Cramp, as well as academics like Peabody and Hovgaard.

The Speed and Power of Ships

Taylor's wide-ranging interests did not distract him from his intention to use the data collected from routine model testing to make a contribution to the fundamental understanding of the problems of ship resistance. Through his work in pretesting ship hull forms for the *Idaho* class, Taylor developed a practical shortcut to finding the best hull form—that is, the development of a series of like forms, each slightly varied from the next. Minute variations in bow angle, bow shape, water line, and section and stern configuration produced variations in resistance requiring a complete revision of his 1900 remarks that suggested that such factors played no appreciable part in residual resistance. Rather than regarding the variations as too complex to analyze, he sought to isolate the factors affecting resistance and to develop curves of predicted effects known from experiment. "Very early in the operation of the experimental model basin," he noted with reference to the *Idaho* class work, "it became evident that there was need for some method of deriving quickly the lines of a model possessing certain desired characteristics, and even more need for practicable and easy methods of systematically varying characteristics of models in order to enable a number to be made and the most desirable one to be selected."[24]

The idea for a "standard series" appears to have its origin in this search for practical shortcuts to useful designs. It was well known that longer ships with displacement and tonnage equal to shorter ships encountered less resistance. Taylor conducted a set of experiments to determine why lengthening ships—increasing the "parallel middle body"—allowed for increased capacity with only minimal increased resistance. In 1907 Taylor ran a series of tests with forty models to determine the effect of midship section upon resistance of ships. Naval architects had various opinions on the best shape of hull in midships. Taylor's conclusion was that as long as the area of midship section was held constant, the variations of usual hull forms through midships had little bearing on resistance.

In these same years he developed a method for making water streamlines around hulls visible. The technique would allow for very simple, yet fundamental, observations of flow. The model hull would be coated with an iron compound set in glue. During model runs, small amounts of diluted pyrogallic acid would be injected through minute holes from inside the model, to flow out into the passing water. The acid would stain the hull, leaving a streak aft a distance of two to four feet from the hole. After a short run, the model would be removed, and a new hole drilled to continue the streamline. The laborious process required half a day of testing to determine six lines of flow on a standard twenty-foot model. This simple demonstration, however, allowed Taylor to come to a major conclusion. Water was not "parted" at the bow to flow out to the sides, as most mariners assumed, but rather flowed down and under the vessel. When combined with later observations, this point would allow Taylor to suggest major modification in the bows of high-speed ships.[25]

In the space of a few years the Experimental Model Basin and Taylor produced several articles explaining these techniques and gradually emerging theories, and continued to collect a large mass of data on the effects upon resistance of variation of hull, bow, length, and configuration on hypothetical ship forms which had never been submitted as actual plans for specific vessels. By 1908 Taylor worked from "parent forms" in which certain factors would be held constant and others varied. In reference to a test run of that year, he noted, "All the models tested had the same midships section and ratio of beam to draught, variations being in longitudinal coefficient, in size and in shape of curves of sectional area."[26] Using parent forms, he tested three series of models, with each series containing twenty models. Each series consisted of four different-sized models, each size with five different models with different curves of sectional area. Each of the three series of twenty models held to a single longitudinal coefficient. The experiments yielded optimum percentages of parallel middle body for each of the three longitudinal coefficients.

In 1911 Taylor published *The Speed and Power of Ships,* putting together his calculations on series, which provided a guide to hull design. The standard series detailed in that work eventually became known as the "Taylor Series," which for the next twenty-five years generated the designs for U.S. Navy ships and served as a guide for other navies as well. The series data continue to be used by naval architects throughout the world today.

The conclusion that "bulbous bows" rather than sharp bows can be better suited to high-speed ships emerged as the most widely recognized and revolutionary conclusion of Taylor's series work. Taylor's reconsideration of bow form was part of a larger effort to bring the hull testing capability of the model basin to bear on battleship design. Charged with developing a design that would increase speed, the Bureau of Construction and Repair experimented with a variety of changes. Taylor's conclusion that a rounded bow would be more efficient than a sharp bow seemed contrary to common sense, and his careful experiments to demonstrate the point attracted the attention of fellow naval architects throughout the world.[27]

In a summary paper given in 1911 at the SNAME conference, Taylor explained the principles that he used to determine the best hull forms at bow and stern, by series, for different sizes and predicted speeds. He used two series of sixteen models—resulting from the use of four sectional area curves with four different model lines. The models were constructed so that each bow type could be combined with each stern type. If all combinations of the two series had been tried, he would have had to run 256 configurations in each. However, he did not use all possible combinations, only practicable ones. Careful comparison led him to conclude that entirely different bow designs were suitable for most efficiency at low speed and for high speed, recommending the U-shaped or bulbous bow.

He explained his conclusions in commonsense terms, as well as mathematically, making clear the simple principle behind the efficiency of the bulbous bow, derived from the insights of the streamline flow demonstrations and from tests of alternative bow shapes:

> At the high speeds . . . the whole forebody has to do with the creation of the waves, and we decrease resistance by making the waterline as fine as possible and putting as much as possible of the displacement well below water where the pressures due to its thrusting itself into undisturbed water will be as much as possible absorbed in doing the necessary pumping aft of the water and not in raising the surface into waves.[28]

Taylor's work, with its "standard series" and his analysis of the bulbous bow, changed the look of naval ships drastically and fundamentally over the next decades. Perhaps the easiest way to visualize that difference is to glance at two pictures: one that is "pre-Taylor," the cruiser *Olympia* with its forward-cutting sharp bow; the other "after Taylor," the *Iowa*-class battleship *New Jersey* (BB 62), with its swept-back, curved bow and a forward-jutting bulb under the water line. The characteristic bows of later high-speed ships reflect the Taylor lines so widely that, without too much exaggeration, one could regard modern naval fleets themselves as floating monuments to his achievement.

By the end of the first decade of operation, Taylor had established the model basin not only as a facility for testing proposed naval and commercial ship designs, but as an important contributor to scientific knowledge and as a source of information and support to innovative private manufacturers. The regular publication of articles in the *Transactions of SNAME,* followed by the publication of *The Speed and Power*

***Olympia* and *New Jersey*.** The two photographs illustrate the hull forms of cruiser *Olympia*, laid down in 1891, and battleship *New Jersey*, laid down in 1941 and designed according to scientific principles and techniques developed by David Taylor.

of Ships, had demonstrated that the U.S. Navy was in the forefront of the field of hydrodynamics.

Engineering Experiment Station—Emergence of an Agenda

In the first twelve years of operation of the Engineering Experiment Station, Officers in Charge Walter Worthington (through 1910) and Thomas W. Kinkaid (through 1920) would shape the role and establish the agenda for that facility. Just as Taylor and his successor, William McEntee, would leave the imprint of their personalities and their disciplinary orientations on the model basin, so Worthington and Kinkaid would leave a lasting heritage at the station.

Although Melville had envisioned an experimental engineering facility devoted to innovation in ship engine development and had expected the new facility to meet at least some of F. C. Bieg's expectations for academic training of naval engineers, the station's character soon developed along slightly different lines, partly because of the simultaneous opening of the Postgraduate School at the Academy. Under Worthington, whose background was as a fleet engineer and whose interests tended in the direction of inspection and testing, the facility soon took on an emphasis on specification development and evaluation of equipment, materials, and lubricants, rather than engine development or education.

The emergence of testing to specification in American industry had taken place during the New Navy period and the new field had been partly shaped by the burst of naval development. The hallmarks of American industry in the mid-nineteenth century had been the development of careful measurement, machine tools, and standardization and interchangeability of parts in what contemporary observers and later historians have called the "American System of Manufactures."[29]

After the Civil War, strength-testing machinery and regularized specifications for material strength that could be physically tested had spread rapidly through American industry. In 1877 the Bureau of Steam Engineering required that all wrought-iron boiler plate be subjected to standard strength tests by a specified testing machine, produced by the Riehle brothers in Philadelphia, a firm that had taken a lead in platform scales and then had branched into the production of material testing machines in the post-Civil War decade. The Pennsylvania Railroad had established one of the first large-scale testing laboratories in its shops in Altoona, Pennsylvania, in the early 1880s, using the Navy-approved Riehle machines for the purpose of checking purchased materials against specifications. Other companies, hearing rumors of the savings generated at Altoona, soon emulated the railroad, until, by the 1890s, there were dozens of such laboratories. The fields of specification, standards, and testing, like other emerging fields in the last decades of the century, became professionalized; the American Society of Testing and Materials was founded in 1898. Although Worthington never specifically stated the establishment of such a testing facility as his objective, his background, personality, and proclivities led him to develop the station along the lines of the industrial testing precedent rather than as an engineering research laboratory.[30]

The types of equipment purchased would play an important role in determining the types of research that would be performed. On the other hand, certain experiments ordered by the bureau required that specific equipment be obtained or constructed. Did the equipment determine the selection of experiment or did the experiment determine the equipment acquired? As we search for the answer to this chicken-or-egg causation question, we find that the process usually worked as follows: a mandated experiment, especially in the very early days, would require the addition of new equipment and sometimes the recruitment of staff with a particular skill or background. In turn, that equipment would provide the capability of doing further work along the same lines, and a single line of testing ordered on one occasion could thus become a regular part of the station's capability, setting up an institutional momentum. However, from time to time Worthington would obtain some equipment, either as surplus or as a loan from another Navy organization, and its opportune addition to the station would help establish future sorts of work.

Even before the station formally opened, the acquisition of equipment and the emergence of a pattern of research were intimately intertwined. During the long period of four years from his appointment until the final opening of the station, Worthington attempted to build up a collection of machines and begin a modest testing program at the Department of Steam Engineering at the Academy. Following up on Melville's interest in current engine design, Worthington used the Parsons steam turbine as a centerpiece, proposing several tests with it. In this case, at least, the machine led to the proposed work. Worthington wanted to see if dividing the condenser tubes would increase efficiency, as claimed in a patented "Contraflo" condenser. He also proposed to determine the ideal vacuum that could be applied to the turbine—a question that remained unresolved for all turbines at the time. After review, Bureau Chief C. W. Rae, Melville's successor, authorized Worthington to proceed with these experiments.[31]

Yet the emergence of a schedule of research was not always a passive response to orders or to the potential of equipment. Worthington, Kinkaid, bureau officers, and staff at the station all spoke cogently about the function of the facility, and there is ample evidence regarding plans in their words as well as in their work.

Worthington's philosophy as officer in charge of the station was thoroughly rooted in his background as fleet engineer. He had served in the Squadron of Evolution, on board *Atlanta* and *Chicago,* both of which had been plagued by design and construction defects, as well as on other ships in the 1880s and 1890s. He was instructor in steam engineering at the Academy 1893–1895; after his tour at the station, he went on to serve as chief inspector of materials for Steam Engineering at the Navy's Munhall, Pennsylvania, facility and, later, at the Brooklyn Navy Yard. He recognized that there was a fundamental difference in method between private purchasers of manufactured items and the government as purchaser. In the case of private purchasers, when they received inferior merchandise, "it is within their power to discontinue dealings . . . and this possibility is in the nature of a penalty continually operating." "Not so with the Navy," he complained. The Navy had to treat all bidders as equal, even if some were known to have produced inferior products in the past. Yet good products for the Navy were life-and-death matters and could determine the course of a naval battle: "If a single tube gives out, the boiler is out of service . . . and one boiler cut out means the ship cannot maneuver at full power. . . . " For this reason, inspection and testing to determine conformity with clear specifications were essential.[32]

Worthington had little patience with a bidder who could not produce promised items, or with a salesman who, from eagerness to sell or ignorance of engineering principles and his company's capabilities, would sign a contract that could not be met. He was particularly incensed at contracting firms that he believed intentionally misread specifications in order to find loopholes that would allow for inferior or cheaper materials.[33]

In his day-to-day management Worthington constantly suspected contractors of fraud, abuse, or incompetence. Before the station opened, he continued to struggle with architect Ernest Flagg, carrying on the dispute for at least a year after the opening. He complained, "When I came to Annapolis, the Architect seemed to be 'running amuck.' It struck me that there must be some law to govern him as well as other people and after some delay I have found there is and it is doubtful if he is entitled to any compensation whatsoever."[34]

Worthington had similar difficulties with the Racine Boat Company of Muskegon, Michigan, the firm that supplied a launch for ferry duty across the Severn to and from the Academy bringing staff, many of whom used the boat to commute from their homes in Annapolis. After delivery with a bent shaft and other defects, eventually repaired by company representatives, the launch could not be brought up to the specified 8 knots. After months of further repairs, using station staff and Academy tools, and increasingly testy correspondence between Worthington and the company, the launch achieved 7.5 knots. Worthington rejected it, complaining that if the company had pretested their boats, as promised in their literature, they would have known the vessel was a half-knot defective. He recommended that Racine "be allowed no further compensation and that a boat be procured from some reliable manufacturer."[35]

The contrast between the styles of Taylor and Worthington when dealing with building contractors and other suppliers reflected their different backgrounds as well as their different personalities. As a naval architect, Taylor worked with the Penn Bridge Company to redesign the model basin building to meet the conditions of the site; the cost overrun did not distress Taylor unduly, nor did the delays imposed by factors outside his control, such as the Spanish American War or the tides on the Anacostia River. When confronted with competing products, Taylor would run a scientific test to determine the better product, finding the decision a simple matter of test results, not ethics. Worthington, on the other hand, found Flagg's behavior reprehensible, and he engaged in running debates with several contractors that lasted for years. Worthington, as a fleet engineer imbued with the values of a bureau inspector, drew from a different background and experience, in which a failure to meet a specification in armor plate, boiler plate, or propeller shaft could spell the death of comrades. His moral tone in ensuring that the Navy got its money's worth derived from such perceptions and experience. Worthington's exacting care with the details of contractor responsibility paid off; by contrast to the 44 percent cost overrun incurred by Taylor on the model basin, the experiment station building was constructed within budget.

In their two approaches Taylor and Worthington reflected two sides of the progressive relationship with the private sector. Taylor supervised the conduct of service tests for industry at cost, and cooperated with Curtis and Sperry to encourage and promote their inventions. Reflecting the "mercantilist" side of progressivism, Taylor believed good engineering and scientific practice in the private sector should be promoted by the government through aid and encouragement. Worthington, with his opposition to what he saw as contractor chicanery and his scrupulous adherence to testing standards, reflected the regulatory side of the Progressive era government-industry relationship, which would ensure that good engineering standards be achieved through inspection, specification, and control of industry. If left to its own devices, Worthington believed, private industry would tend to be slipshod, prone to errors like Flagg, or false in its advertised claims as the Racine Boat Company.

For Worthington, the function of testing was to ensure that the Navy purchased satisfactory products. Yet such a hard-headed orientation could also contribute to technical progress. By establishing high standards, by publicizing and enforcing them, Worthington made sure the tests and experiments at the station would advance the state of the art. Other naval officers at the station besides Worthington saw and understood this relationship of testing to progress. Lieutenant Commander Ernest J. King, who was later to reach the rank of Fleet Admiral and serve as Commander in Chief and Chief of Naval Operations during World War II, had a brief tour of duty at the station, 1912–1914. While there, he considered the relationship of the station's work to more fundamental technical development, summing up some of his ideas in a journal article:

> Though attention has been called to the fact that the Experiment Station has so far had little time for original research, mention should be made of the general practice obtaining wherein all "tests" are investigations into the merits of the subject of test [and] recommendations are worked out with a view to the probable improvement of the subject of test. . . . There will always be progress; and it is the work of the Experiment Station to assist in determining what is progress and what is not.[36]

Along the same lines, Worthington viewed technical investigation and innovation—the process a later generation would call "research and development"—as an incidental, if refreshingly stimulating, by-product of the main testing task of the facility. "In many instances during the progress of the work," he noted, "rather interesting questions have arisen and it would have been very profitable to pursue the investigations far beyond the point originally intended. In some instances, also it became evident that a slight change in the design or construction of the apparatus would probably result in improving its operation. In such cases, no change was made at the station, but if thought important, the inventor or manufacturer was notified and his cooperation sought."[37]

Despite his rejection of direct research as an appropriate major role for the station, Worthington took some pride in several such recommended improvements, noting their serendipitous quality: "Interesting and useful information is sometimes unexpectedly obtained." He drew attention of the bureau to several small recommended improvements in gauge glasses, by coating the inside with mica to prevent opaque and corrosive buildup of silicious deposit, in piping, and in a water tap system for saltwater evaporators.[38]

However, under Worthington's direction, the staff spent far more time and energy on their first priorities, evaluating the conformity of materials and devices to specifications and the framing of specifications themselves, than they did on recommendations for design changes. For a surprisingly wide variety of procured items, the Navy by 1908 had either no specifications at all or only the most vague and ill-defined or unenforceable specifications. The experiment station moved rapidly to fill that gap by regularizing and modernizing purchasing and holding manufacturers to accountable systems of performance. In response to an early request that the station produce specifications for asbestos sheet packing, Worthington explained his views regarding specifications: "As a general rule it is bad policy to limit the manufacturer to any one process. He should be told definitely and clearly what tests his products will have to stand and then allowed pretty free scope as to his method of getting the results. Also there is another important principle often overlooked in specifications; and that is, do not specify anything that the inspector cannot enforce."[39]

Here Worthington stated a key to his approach: enforceable specifications had to be developed where none existed, and then they had to be enforced. Without such a system, the Navy would be a constant victim of contractors run "amuck"; with controls, purchasing could be put on a rational and efficient basis.

In the case of asbestos packing, Worthington noted that although there had been industrial improvements in the product, manufacturers continued to send materials meeting outdated, but not officially altered, Navy specifications. With his usual ill-concealed contempt, he noted, "Some manufacture their material to satisfy the [obsolete] specifications regardless of whether or not the goods will or will not be serviceable."[40]

In 1908–1909 Worthington conducted a major series of evaluation tests on two different products to determine their quality and to set specifications: safety valves and gauges for the Isthmian Canal Commission and asbestos sheet packing in response to Bureau of Steam Engineering requests. He also initiated work in March 1909 to set up apparatus to test the effect of various commercially produced soda compounds on boilers, gauges, and boiler tubes, to prevent corrosion. In addition to such specification work, he continued the engine work: running 926 hours of testing on a 26-inch Sirocco blower, driven by a small, Swedish-designed DeLaval 20-horsepower steam turbine. He ordered from the leading testing machine company, Riehle Brothers, a 20,000-pound oil testing machine. On delivery, he found the Riehle machine defective and, after some delays, had company representatives repair it. He planned that the machine would be used to test "samples of every lot of lubricating oil furnished to the Navy."[41]

Worthington's caution about suppliers soon caused a major problem. The Sundry Civil Appropriation Act of 1909 required that funds appropriated in earlier years be expended in the current year. Since the original appropriation for the station and its equipment had been passed in 1903, and two years had been taken up in delays over clearing title to the land, Worthington found it difficult to accept that the reversion of funding would apply to his operation. Nevertheless, he lost over $45,000 in equipment funds through failure to commit the expenditure before the deadline of July 1909.[42]

The Kinkaid Years

Commander Thomas W. Kinkaid replaced Worthington at the station on 26 September 1910. Kinkaid, like Worthington, had served at sea, with duty during the Spanish American War and as fleet engineer for the Pacific Squadron; he had also worked as an inspector at the Norfolk Navy Yard, as inspector of engineering material at Chester, Pennsylvania, and had been on duty at the station as Worthington's assistant since 16 December 1909.

On the day he took over, Kinkaid issued a set of directions to researchers, which he labeled very clearly "ROUTINE," spelling out the most minute details of procedure, style, maintenance of a log, necessity of quadruplicate filing of reports, and the routing of all outside communications through his office. No commas were to be used in Arabic numerals, and "ten thousand" was to be represented as "10000." The reports on tests soon became so thorough and detailed that his superiors in the Bureau of Steam Engineering insisted on simplification. They requested that repeated statement of routine methods be eliminated, and the history of a material or machine being tested be included.[43]

Kinkaid did not bring quite the same moral fervor to his specification and testing work as did Worthington. Instead, Kinkaid appeared to be a quantifier, looking for concrete measures of accomplishment. He continually compiled lists of tests and pointed with pride to the increased workload of the station under his administration.

In that spirit, Kinkaid reported in his first year the increase in serial number of tests from 81 to 163 and, in his second year, the increase to 267. By 1919 the station had conducted over 1,300 tests. His pride in quantity of output was infectious; reports by others in the laboratory during this period abound with enumerations, listings, and statistical calculations of hours expended. Such measurement did in fact help convey the variety and range of work. One running tally of station tests of products and materials produced in 1917 showed that the station had approved for naval use the following products, listed in the report, each by brand name:

2 boiler compounds	4 metal alloys	84 oils	16 gauge glasses
5 evaporators	5 fuels	26 packing materials	12 gaskets
9 fan blowers	7 steam traps	14 pumps	53 miscellaneous categories[44]
2 feed water heaters	2 governors	21 valves	

Like Worthington, Kinkaid took pride in the occasional research product of the station, although he struggled to convey to bureau officials the more routine and massive regular specification testing. He noted that confidential bulletins on packing issued by the station had eliminated some inferior manufacturers and that, overall, the price of packing had been reduced as a result of the station specification work. In 1908 the Navy paid $1.28 a pound for sheet asbestos; by 1912, as a result of station standards, the Navy paid $0.35 a pound. He also claimed credit for the fact that sheet rubber came down from $0.51 a pound to $0.30 a pound in the same period.[45]

Once the apparatus for testing soda compounds was set up, Commander Frank Lyon conducted experiments that led, in uncharacteristic research and development style, to the establishment of a new product, a standard Navy boiler compound to inhibit corrosion. It was well known that a bright piece of metal immersed in a solution of sodium carbonate would not rust. After experimenting with various dilutions of sodium carbonate, Lyon determined that a "three-percent solution," or 4.29 pounds of NA_2CO_3 dissolved in 1,000 pounds of distilled water, was ideal. Sodium carbonate, or soda ash, was the cheapest of several alkali materials that could form the basic ingredient of the compound. In order to reduce priming (adherence of grease particles and other precipitates to the exposed metal surfaces), trisodium phosphate (TSP) was added; tannic acid would be included to hold precipitates in suspension and prevent adhesion of scale-forming salts. Lyon's eventual specifications for an ideal boiler compound gave specific percentages for soda ash, TSP, glucose, and tannic acid.

This specific formula was adopted in 1911 and became known as "Standard Navy Boiler Compound." The chief of the bureau credited this station-developed compound with prolonging navy boiler life by three times; the cost of the compound, once standardized, fell in less than three years from $0.22 a pound to $0.03 a pound. With the increasing use of turbine engines, the development of feed water or boiler water compound was essential; the compound contributed in a major way to the rapid shift from reciprocating engines to turbines over the following decade.[46]

Since many of the results of tests were issued in confidential bulletins for use by naval engineers or in reports directly to the manufacturer, members of the station staff often felt that their work received little public attention or even recognition within the relatively narrow world of engineering and naval circles. While statistical counts of tests run and products approved could serve in internal reports to demonstrate the workload, such lists had little glamor and could not be readily used to publicize station accomplishments. Thus, the uncharacteristic research and development work, which had a bit more public appeal, received a disproportionate share of attention. Lyon's work on boiler compounds in 1911 was mentioned over and over as a demonstration of the work of the station. Similarly, the early recommendation to add mica to gauge glasses to reduce fractures and buildup of deposition on the glass, a minor by-product of a 1909 study, was mentioned repeatedly as a significant advance in both contemporary reports and in later memoirs and historical pieces about the early days at the station.

William N. Berkely, station chemist, argued for systematizing test procedures in 1911, when all oil testing was consolidated at the station from the navy yards. He pointed out that the variety of testing methods at different yards created "discreditable" conditions. "There can never be any proper enforcement of specifications for naval suppliers," Berkely complained, "unless the methods used to determine the properties prescribed by the specifications are absolutely uniform."[47]

A short flyer set forth rules stating that prior to acceptance by the Navy, a material had to be tested at the station and subjected to a service test aboard a naval vessel; tests would be taken only on written application to the bureau by the "exhibitor" or manufacturer; the exhibitor would bear the cost of the test; the test results could not be used in advertisement. In addition, the flyer gave exact specifications and methods of testing for a particular commodity or material such as oil or gaskets.[48]

In 1912 Kinkaid obtained photomicrographic and test equipment that allowed the testing of the strength and composition of metals. In 1913 a portable micrographic outfit was added that allowed for inspection by station staff at the navy yards. The new equipment could be used to investigate failed materials from ships, determining flaws in design and in metal working that could be changed in future construction. The station studied and published work on broken shafts from *Connecticut, Vermont, New Jersey, Tacoma,* and *Kentucky.* Defective boiler plates and tubes from *Aylwin, Lamson, Blair, New Mexico,* and *Georgia* were tested, as well as a variety of other defective or ruptured parts from at least seven other naval ships over the period 1914–1918.[49]

Testing at the station soon proliferated into a variety of areas, and even the staff members admitted that it was difficult to see a pattern in the work. By 1913, five years after the station opened, King could already categorize the majority of work into ten broad areas, exclusive of a range of odd and miscellaneous tests:

- Machinery tests
- Heat transmission apparatus
- Boiler fittings and accessories
- Pump and engine fittings
- Valves and pipe fittings
- Coal studies
- Lubricants
- Packings and gasket materials
- Metals
- Chemical analysis[50]

While some other experiments did not fit these categories, the pattern of these ten areas, set by 1913, and the equipment acquired to operate the tests shaped the agenda for the next decades.

Looking at the tests in terms of function, rather than subject or material, several different types could be categorized, each providing a slightly different benefit to the Navy. Staff members Harold Bowen and Leo Loeb concluded after the first five years that the benefits included ten categories of practical reductions in cost and eliminations of waste for the Navy.[51]

World War I appeared to have little direct impact on the research schedules of the station, although it did present Kinkaid with several administrative problems. He found his staff of officers reduced as lieutenants were assigned to sea duty. The sudden national shortage of trained manpower affected the civilian staff, which had grown under Kinkaid's administration to 112 by 1917. He hired several women to fill vacant posts, particularly as "laboratorians" or laboratory assistants, and even applied for permission to put a female chauffeur on staff. The Navy drew the line there, however, and permission was denied. Despite shortages, Kinkaid brought new personnel in, bringing the 1918 complement to 168. The war had another impact on the station in that it

Laboratorians at the Engineering Experiment Station. *Top row, left to right:* Sue Gantt, Officer in Charge Captain Thomas Kinkaid, Helen Vincent, and Gladys Hook. *Bottom row, left to right:* Emma Engle, Bessie London, and Ruth Dumbroko.

Aircraft Testing, c. 1910.   The Navy's first "aviation camp" was established on the Severn River, next to EES.

allowed him to find more surplus equipment: engines from Ford-produced Eagle boats, airplane engines, diesel engines, and auxiliary and surplus equipment of all types were begged and borrowed during the 1917–1918 period. [52]

During Kinkaid's administration several new research lines for the station were temporarily opened up, only to be reassigned elsewhere as the technology became more advanced and the Navy developed other organizations and facilities to house the new work. In 1910–1911 launches assigned to the station experimented with "radiotelegraphy," determining ranges of equipment under operating conditions. After the war, radio work eventually was concentrated at the new Naval Research Laboratory in Washington. In 1910–1913 the Navy's first "aviation camp" was established on the Severn River next to the station; in the spring and summer months, aviators from the camp used station equipment for repairs and modifications. It was on one of this first generation of Navy airplanes that King took his first flight, in 1912. However, the Navy's aviation specialist, Washington Irving Chambers, opposed making the camp permanent, and in 1913 the camp was transferred to Pensacola, Florida. Work on aileron strengths in 1912 and on aircraft engines in 1916–1917 later became consolidated under the direction of the Navy's new Bureau of Aeronautics, formally set up in 1921. In 1919 Harvey Hayes transferred from New London, bringing with him major accomplishments in underwater depth finding and hydrophone detection of ships. This early acoustics work, like the radio research, was transferred in 1923 to the newly opened Naval Research Laboratory. The station's contributions in each of these areas—radio, aeronautics, and sonar—which would later play vital roles in naval technology, took the form of providing temporary housing for a research effort later taken up on a larger scale elsewhere; such work did not set precedents for major new departures or permanent additions to the station's capacities.[53]

Similarly, during 1912–1917 the idea of using the station facilities more directly in education was temporarily revived. King took charge of the program to instruct several student officers from the Postgraduate School at the Academy. Not an engineer himself, King, like Bradley Fiske, was a line officer with an interest in technical matters and an ambitious drive to make a good record on each of his career assignments. He worked closely with the chairman of the Postgraduate School, J. P. Merten, and arranged for an initial group of nine students to study at the station over the winter 1912–1913.

King worked out a detailed schedule in which the students rotated as laboratory assistants in the chemistry laboratory working on oils, through mechanical laboratories working on packing, valves, and a variety of steam machinery, to the photomicrographic section. King himself supervised student work in the testing of boiler water. After King's departure in 1914, the

Naval Academy Students at EES. The Engineering Experiment Station provided hands-on experience for naval cadets, under close supervision of instructor-officers.

program continued through early 1917, to be discontinued because of the war, when the whole postgraduate course of study at the Academy was suspended.[54]

The mission of the station had evolved in the decade after 1910 in specific directions never predicted by F. C. Bieg in 1895 or by Melville in 1903. By 1920 the station had taken on work in at least ten separate engineering areas; fundamental research was an admittedly rare event; training of students from the Academy became a minor adjunct to the Academy's new postgraduate program. The development of specifications and testing of materials and products to those established standards by a large staff with varied backgrounds gave the station a unique character. The very diversity of work at the station contrasted sharply with the single-discipline pattern at the model basin. Despite Taylor's wide-ranging personal interests in engines, propellers, gyroscopic balancing, ventilation, turbines, and maritime safety, the basin, after all, had concentrated on model testing of ship forms and the concurrent development of general hydrodynamic principles that could be tested by the same methods as the day-to-day experimentation on particular designs. However, Taylor and his successor, William McEntee, would make a major effort over the same decade, 1910–1920, to expand the role of the basin into a new, but related, discipline.

Aeronautic Work at the Model Basin

At the Experimental Model Basin, McEntee would strive to continue Taylor's programs, just as Kinkaid had kept in place the initiatives set up by Worthington. Besides the well-established reputation for scientific work on hydrodynamics, McEntee inherited from Taylor another major undertaking, a plan to build up aeronautical research as a permanent part of the basin's mission. When Taylor moved up from the basin to serve as bureau chief and chief constructor, he continued his interest in, and support for, aeronautical work. Together, Taylor and McIntee had far more success than Kinkaid in keeping aircraft research as part of their facility's mission.

Aeronautic research work at the basin evolved against a background of interagency disputes over the proper location for all aircraft-related research in the government. Taylor took a personal interest in the dispute, advocating a major role for the Navy and for the Bureau of Construction and Repair over the period 1911–1915. Taylor was particularly concerned that plans to create an aeronautical research laboratory under either Smithsonian administration or in the Bureau of Standards, or as a wholly independent laboratory, not preempt a naval role in this new field.

In 1911 a group of aeronautics enthusiasts, organized in a national aeronautical society, advocated a Smithsonian-directed laboratory. Rear Admiral R. M. Watt, Chief of the Bureau of Construction and Repair, protested to the Secretary of the Navy that such a plan would duplicate and ignore work at the model basin and at the experiment station at Annapolis. The Navy's objections prevented President William Howard Taft's endorsement of the plan. Through 1911 and 1912 Taylor remained active in opposing a similar plan that would concentrate government aeronautic work under the administration of the Smithsonian Institution, which was advocated by Chambers, special advisor to the Secretary of the Navy on aeronautic affairs. The Woodward Commission, a group set up by Taft to recommend a course of organization for air research, also endorsed a centralization of aeronautic research under civilian control. The organizational dispute continued until, by 1915, Congress approved a clumsy compromise in which a formal advisory committee would be established. The National Advisory Committee for Aeronautics (NACA), modeled on a British advisory committee, in turn created an array of subcommittees to issue reports on specific aeronautic research topics and to arrange a few preliminary research contracts. Taylor was an advocate of NACA and was appointed to the committee in 1917 as a replacement for charter member Holden C. Richardson.[55]

Through this same period of interagency rivalry, Taylor and his assistant, McEntee, worked to establish a major role for the model basin in the new field. There are a number of striking parallels between the construction of the model basin in 1896–1899 and the building of the first Navy wind tunnel, set up

Wind Tunnel Work at EMB. David Taylor took the logical step from hydrodynamics to aerodynamics with construction of a small wind tunnel at the Navy Yard in 1914. Here a biplane is subjected to oscillation tests to measure effects of turbulent loads.

by Taylor at the navy yard under model basin jurisdiction, in 1912–1914. Both facilities would make possible a program of Navy directed research in a new and opening discipline. The Navy's model basin itself was the first such basin in the United States and provided the basic tool for significant new work in its first decade. The wind tunnel built at the Washington Navy Yard was only the third one put in operation in the United States, but the two earlier ones were already out of use. The first, built by Professor Albert F. Zahm of Catholic University in 1901, had operated through 1908; another, on a small scale, built by Orville and Wilbur Wright in Dayton, Ohio, had been used to pretest their first experimental craft. Therefore, the Navy's wind tunnel, like the basin, was to be a state of the art facility; for some years it was one of only a very few of its type in the world. The parallel was made explicit: the new facility was called the Experimental Wind Tunnel; the towing tank had been called the Experimental Model Basin.

The Navy's wind tunnel was similar to the basin in its basic scientific principles as well. It was a structure in which the resistance of shapes in a flow of fluids could be tested. Instead of moving a model through a fluid, as in the basin, the wind tunnel would move the fluid, in this case air, past a fixed model. Speed would be carefully controlled and measured; a delicate tension-recording device would measure the forces on the model; scaling laws would be applied to translate the experimental results into practical design principles.

The first working wind tunnel for testing aircraft shapes had been built at exactly the same time Froude constructed his first model tank at Torquay. In 1871 Francis H. Wenham in Greenwich, England conducted tests in his steam-powered tunnel, which was 18 inches square in cross-section and capable of air speeds up to 40 miles per hour. In the United States Samuel Langley of the Smithsonian Institution began systematic investigation of aerodynamics in 1888, using a different principle—a whirling arm that would move the model through the air at speeds up to 70 miles per hour. By 1903 thirteen wind tunnels had been built throughout the world, including the Wrights' in Dayton and Zahm's in Washington. In France, Gustave Eiffel, the wealthy inventor and engineer, built a tunnel first at the foot of his tower in Paris and then at Autiel, France. He conducted studies comparing the two techniques, movement of models through air (which he conducted by tethered drop tests from the tower), with wind tunnel tests. In 1911 Eiffel published his results in *La Résistance de l'air et l'aviation,* showing that both techniques achieved similar results.[56]

In 1910 Congressman Butler Ames, a West Point graduate with an engineering degree from MIT and experience in textile and automotive parts manufacturing, requested permission to use the towing carriage at the model basin to test a model of a flying machine of his own design. Ames had attempted, unsuccessfully, to conduct the test on an automobile, but complained he could not locate a road sufficiently smooth or wide enough to allow equestrian traffic to pass in the opposite direction; a further problem was finding a road that would head into the wind. The idea of using the towing carriage was a viable one, but Taylor encouraged Ames to apply through channels to test the machine on board a vessel. On 22 July 1910, a team from the experiment station, headed by Frank Lyon, tested the Ames' machine on board the torpedo boat *Bagley.* Lift was provided by a rotating drum equipped with vanes that Ames hoped would lift a flying machine even when the engines failed. The machine was quite unworkable, although Lyon reported graciously on the congressman's good ideas; Lyon conservatively reported that the equipment was itself too heavy to overcome the lift forces generated. Perhaps wisely, Taylor had passed up this early opportunity to establish a foothold in aeronautical research.[57]

In early March 1912 Taylor began planning construction of the wind tunnel at the navy yard. The proposal to construct the wind tunnel received quiet approval in the Bureau of Construction and Repair; neither Taylor nor Bureau Chief Watt sought special congressional endorsement or funding, which might have proven difficult in the face of the ongoing national debate over the proper location for aeronautic work. Taylor wrote to the American Blower Company describing tentative plans for a "testing duct for aeroplane investigations." After several inquiries to industrial firms supplying fans and blowers, Taylor drew up specifications and secured a low-keyed and rapid go-ahead from Watt; on 21 February 1913, Taylor awarded a contract to General Electric for a 500-horsepower motor to drive the fan. Through 1913, Taylor proceeded with construction of the foundation and the tunnel walls, and worked on details of the measuring devices, securing the aid of the Office of Naval Intelligence to inquire into purchase of plans for a British torsion balance. By July 1914 Taylor had completed calibration and regulation work, and began to look for a "man to keep on aeronautic work only." He wrote to Jerome Hunsaker, a young officer interested in aeronautics, while he was still in his naval architecture course at MIT. Hunsaker was later to work for Taylor in the field of aeronautics, and became famous as a pioneer in naval aeronautics. In later life, Hunsaker would chair the National Advisory Committee for Aeronautics from 1941 to 1956. Taylor departed for his position as chief of the bureau before finding someone to put in charge of the wind tunnel.[58]

Like the model basin, when the tunnel was completed it was the largest in the world, and it incorporated several departures from earlier precedents. One revolutionary feature was the fact that the tunnel was designed as a closed circuit, so that exhaust air would return to the intake. The tunnel was 8 feet square at the model testing point. The direct-current, 500-horsepower engine drove an overshot Sirocco blower fan capable of achieving air speeds up to 75 miles per hour. In order to reduce eddies and ensure a smooth flow of air past the model, sixty-four 1-foot-square, 8-foot-long tubes served as baffles, keeping the airflow uniform with a less than 2 percent variation. The tunnel walls were constructed of two layers of tongue-and-groove sheathing. The overall length of the tunnel, including the curved return section, was about 86 feet; the testing wind chamber itself was 33 feet long.[59]

The air speed was checked with an array of twelve Pitot tubes, which had been calibrated both at MIT and at Britain's National Physical Laboratory. The model, which could be up to 36 inches in wingspan, would be mounted on a steel spindle connected through the top of the tunnel to a weighing scale, or torsion balance, which could record deflection in three axes. This arrangement, based on a design originated by Eiffel, allowed for measurement of shifts in horizontal and vertical directions, and could indicate the line of application of the force to the model, which could be varied by altering the angle of the model on the spindle. The scale was accurate to about .002 pound. Control of speed and measurement were conducted from a platform over the tunnel.[60]

Upon Taylor's promotion to chief of the bureau on 16 December 1914, McEntee took over management of the model basin and the new wind tunnel. While McEntee continued an interest in hydrodynamics, both he and some of his staff members came to be known as naval aviation pioneers largely because of their work with the tunnel. McEntee had already suggested a scientific rationale for conducting aerodynamic work at the basin, and he had thus established himself as one of a limited number of naval officers taking an interest in the new field. In 1911 McEntee read a paper at the annual meeting of the Society of Naval Architects and Marine Engineers, showing several parallels between the principles of naval architecture and aeronautics and particularly discussing transverse and longitudinal stability and proportion of frictional resistance to total resistance. "As in naval architecture," he pointed out, "the practical elements dealt with in aeronautics are weight or displacement, buoyancy, stability, resistance, propulsion, and speed. For higher theoretical investigations, the mathematics of streamlines or fluid motion are equally applicable to each." He concentrated on heavier-than-air craft and on the issues of stability and propulsion.[61]

Over the period 1912–1916 Holden C. Richardson, also later honored as a naval aviation pioneer, worked with Taylor and McEntee at the model basin. A 1901 Annapolis graduate, he studied naval architecture at MIT following the Construction Corps education and career path. In 1912, as naval constructor, he translated Eiffel's work on the resistance of air; that translation was useful in the design and construction of the wind tunnel. In 1913 Richardson conducted a thorough series of tests of seaplane float forms in the model basin. In 1915 Richardson learned to fly, becoming "Naval Aviator #13," and he worked on airplane design, including the first Navy two-engine aircraft, 82-A, first flown in 1916. A model of the 82-A was reputed to be the first complete airplane model tested in the tunnel. Throughout the period, Richardson worked on a wide range of aeronautic experiments; although no evidence has come to light to show that he was in charge of the wind tunnel at this time, he certainly worked closely with McEntee and Taylor and was one of a limited number of aircraft designers with access to the tunnel.[62]

Albert F. Zahm

McEntee's greatest coup in recruitment was Albert F. Zahm. Zahm had a long record in aeronautic research. He had earned a master of science degree at Notre Dame in 1890, a master of engineering at Cornell in 1892, and the Ph.D. at Johns Hopkins in 1898 with a dissertation on aerodynamics. As early as 1889 at Notre Dame, he had worked with airplane models. He was already credited with many "firsts," including the invention in 1893 of the airplane control "stick," and construction of the first wind tunnel in the United States, which he had planned and built in 1901. In a report on that work, Zahm coined the term "wind tunnel." He had developed measuring instruments for wind tunnel work and had published widely on the topic before 1910. He was a cofounder of the Aero Club in Washington, and an active advocate of a Smithsonian-operated laboratory. He also became involved in a long-running patent dispute between Glenn H. Curtiss and the Wright brothers, defending Curtiss's position that prior work by Langley had placed fundamental airplane design in the public domain before the Wrights' invention. In 1914–1916 he organized Curtiss's aeronautical laboratories, and was one of the first members of NACA.[63]

Within a year after recruiting Zahm to operate the tunnel built earlier by Taylor, McEntee secured approval for Zahm to design a smaller, supplementary tunnel to take on the extra work beginning to accumulate. He directly supervised wind tunnel work as expert aeronautical aide to Bureau Chief Taylor. Through the war years, Zahm recruited assis-

Chain of Command, c. 1915. Left to right, a vigorous Franklin D. Roosevelt (Assistant Secretary of the Navy), Admiral David W. Taylor (Chief, Bureau of Construction and Repair), Josephus Daniels (Secretary of the Navy), Brigadier General C. H. Laucheimer (Inspector General of the U.S. Marine Corps), Admiral William F. Benson (Chief of Naval Operations).

tants, including Louis H. Crook and S. S. Rathbun. Zahm served at the model basin in charge of aeronautic research from 1917 through 1929.[64]

By the time Zahm came to the navy yard, Secretary of the Navy Josephus Daniels organized the service's rapidly growing air research, dividing functions between the various bureaus. Construction and Repair, under Taylor, was charged with preparing and preserving aircraft plans; planning, preparing, and conducting model experiments; and issuing instructions for manufacture and repair of aircraft. Steam Engineering was to be in charge of power plants; Navigation was to be in charge of instruments and to handle recruitment of air officers; Ordnance would prepare aircraft weaponry.[65]

On his arrival, Zahm encountered a well-equipped and going operation. The large wind tunnel was housed in a three-story brick building, 40 by 100 feet. The first floor contained the large tunnel; the second floor had the observation room for the tunnel and space for the smaller tunnel to be designed by Zahm, an instrument shop, and rooms for models and testing apparatus. Zahm's smaller tunnel, built in 1918, was 4 feet in section and 20 feet in length, designed with a return loop as in the larger tunnel. A 25-horsepower motor produced winds up to 50 or 60 miles per hour.[66]

In a phenomenal burst of creative research over the period from the United States entry into World War I in April 1917 through June 1919, Zahm and his staff produced over two hundred reports. The variety and range of work at the wind tunnel bore a striking parallel to the varied and practical engineering work of the experiment station in the same period. The aeronautical work of Zahm and his staff, partly due to the pressures of wartime demand, tended to focus on problems of application, rather than on the type of theoretical issues with which Taylor had dealt in his first years at the basin. Large groups of tests were conducted on complete airplane models, on airplane wing sections, on airship models, on airplane engine radiators, and on speed meters. Smaller numbers of tests were conducted on airplane bodies, struts, propellers, inclinometers, and wind-driven gasoline pumps.[67]

The tunnel allowed for testing airplane designs for stability, often resulting in redesign and retesting to ensure the change was useful. Dozens of tests on airplanes and components resulted in immediately ordered changes in design. The major innovation supplied by Zahm's group during the war was a "waterproof speed nozzle" to measure air speed. Once the design had been worked out, both the Army and Navy cooperated in ordering 40,000 of the speed indicators; 12,000 were manufactured and delivered before the end of the war.[68]

Zahm redesigned the torsion balance for both wind tunnels. The original balance could measure forces in three directions, based on Eiffel's design. Zahm's rebuilt torsion device measured drag, side force, and lift as well as the roll, pitch, and yaw moments measured by the Eiffel balance. It appears that this invention followed a design Zahm had developed while working for Curtiss.[69]

Zahm continued to produce papers, designs, reports, and patents at a prolific rate. His work touched a wide number of aspects of aeronautics, including instrument design, propeller design, model designing and construction tools, automatic speed control for the tunnels, slide rules and protractors for calculating air force from measurements, shock recorders, airship design, and helicopter planning and design.[70]

One of the better-known contributions of the aeronautics group at the Bureau of Construction and Repair during the period was the design and testing of the "NC" aircraft. Recommended by Taylor during the

Naval Historical Center

Flying Boat NC-4. The NC-4, fourth of a seaplane class originally recommended by Taylor, made a historic flight across the Atlantic well before the solo flight of Charles Lindbergh.

war, these "flying boats" or seaplanes were designed by Richardson and Hunsaker, along with others, to be flown across the Atlantic for delivery in Britain in case submarine attacks by the Germans interdicted surface transport. Although the war ended before the planes were completed, three were manufactured and flown, one by Captain Richardson. While he and another pilot had to bring their craft down in seas too rough for takeoff, a third, the NC-4, made it to the Azores and Great Britain in the historic first flight across the Atlantic, May 1919, eight years before Charles Lindbergh's solo, nonstop flight in the *Spirit of St. Louis*.[71]

By the end of the war, Taylor advocated a combination of naval aeronautic research and procurement in a new bureau. His plan would be implemented in 1921; however, the model basin retained the wind tunnel, Zahm and his staff, and the assignment of work that grew out of the equipment and the talents of the men. Zahm stayed on until 1929 and his assistant, Crook, continued through the period, although not as a permanent basin employee. Taylor and McEntee, despite the stormy winds of aeronautic politics, succeeded in making one branch of research in aeronautics, aerodynamics, a long-lasting part of the work of the model basin.

While McEntee supervised the research of Richardson and Zahm, he continued to participate directly in model basin work, as Taylor had done. McEntee carried forward several smaller projects in the basin initiated by Taylor. One study reported on the effect of external lubrication on frictional resistance of ship hulls, including oil, graphite, and Ivory Soap. McEntee conducted a series of tests on the frictional resistance of the surfaces of propellers; he reported on the effect of air resistance on ships. His major contribution in the area of hydrodynamics could be found in an extension of the standard series concept to nonnaval ships. In 1917 he released data on a series of designs for barges, colliers, freighters, and broad-beamed cargo ships. He also published work on the propulsive efficiency of single-screw cargo ships in 1918, reporting on the first use of self-propelled models in tests.[72]

Personality, Institution, and Style

Taylor, McEntee, Worthington, and Kinkaid had shaped the destiny of the New Navy's two facilities within two decades of opening. A source of the distinctions in style of operations of the model basin and the experiment station could be found in the differences between naval architects in the Bureau of Construction and Repair and the engineers in the Bureau of Steam Engineering. Taylor's training and experience made the search for fundamental knowledge a natural use of the facility. Worthington's background with its emphasis on "inspection" led him to compare products and to seek the most economical and efficient one that met a specified naval purpose with the least risk to officers and men on board ships.

Kinkaid built on the base set by Worthington, carrying forward testing work in a growing range of areas in which Navy purchasing had previously been chaotic, unspecified, and uneconomical. New work and research were eagerly welcomed. Yet the massive task of putting equipment and material purchasing on a scientific basis was so overwhelming that original research could only be peripheral to the central mission; the rare research and development work focused on the creation of specifications where none had existed before or on recommending modifications to existing machinery.

At the model basin, Taylor and McEntee successfully added a second scientific area and brought in a leading pioneer in the field to take charge of it. However, under the pressure of war, Zahm's aeronautical work, like that of the engineers at Annapolis, was strictly in the realm of applied rather than fundamental science.

In the decades to follow, both facilities would slowly evolve in new directions; yet the imprint of their New Navy origins and their first years would remain. The brief 19-month participation of the United States in

World War I would lead the Navy to reassess the strategic and tactical uses of its ships and aircraft, to revise doctrine, and to examine closely the functioning of the bureau system. As naval policymakers evaluated the "lessons of the war," the effort to harness science and technology would suggest changes of style, organization, and method at both facilities. Nevertheless, the early emphases brought by Taylor and McEntee to the basin and by Worthington and Kinkaid to the station would continue with the force of naval tradition long after those founding administrators had passed from the scene.

Endnotes

1. Hovgaard, "Biographical Memoir of David Watson Taylor, 1864–1940," *Biographical Memoirs of the National Academy of Sciences*, vol. 22.
2. David W. Taylor, "The United States Experimental Model Basin," *TSNAME* 8 (1900): 37.
3. Ibid., 42.
4. Ibid., 41–42.
5. Ibid., 42–43.
6. Ibid., 44.
7. Taylor, "On Ships' Forms Derived by Formulae," *TSNAME* 11 (1903): 243.
8. Taylor to William Hovgaard, 15 Apr 1903, DWT LB-1.
9. Taylor to Francis Bowles, 22 Apr 1902, DWT Reports, 1901–1906.
10. Taylor, "On Ships' Forms Derived by Formulae," 245.
11. Taylor to R. W. Dana, 18 Mar 1902, DWT LB-1.
12. Ibid.
13. Taylor to F. W. Brady, 1 Feb 1902; Taylor to C. G. Curtis, 28 Feb 1902; and Taylor to N. Towne, 14 Dec 1904, DWT LB-1; Taylor to C. H. Peabody, 14 Feb 1912, DWT LB-5; Taylor to J. W. Kellogg of General Electric, 11 Feb 1909, DWT LB-3; see also Ben Keppel, *Taylor Correspondence Data Base* (DTNSRDC, 1984), for range of other correspondence.
14. Taylor to A. F. Yarrow, 12 Jan 1905, DWT LB-1; George Westinghouse to G. L. Von Meyer, Secretary of the Navy, 5 Oct 1909, and 8 Oct 1909, NARA, RG 80, 1897–1915, box 1435, file 27308.
15. Taylor to Harlan & Hollingsworth Corporation, 15 Aug 1912, DWT LB- 5; D. K. Allison to B. F. Tibbitts, 3 May 1984, citing correspondence in *TSNAME* (1901 and 1902), memo entitled "Battle of the Titans."
16. Taylor, "A Dynamometer and Revolution Counter for Fan Testing," *American Machinist*, 11 Jun 1903, 833–836; Office of Naval Intelligence, *The United States Navy as an Industrial Asset—What the Navy Has Done for Commerce and Industry*, ONI-1922 (Washington: Government Printing Office, 1923), 100–102.
17. Taylor, "Some Recent Experiments at the Model Basin," *TSNAME* 12 (1904): 107; A. V. Curtis and L. F. Hewing, "Some Results of Tests of Model Propellers," *TSNAME* 13 (1905): 87; Taylor, "Model Basin Gleanings," *TSNAME* 14 (1906): 65, quotation 78; *SECNAV Annual Report, 1990*, 842–843.
18. Taylor to C. G. Curtis, 16 Jan 1902, 28 Feb 1902, 10 Mar 1903, and 11 Jan 1904; and Taylor to W. H. White, 26 Aug 1910, DWT LB-4.
19. Taylor, "Some Model Experiments on Suction of Vessels," *TSNAME* 17 (1909); Taylor to W. H. Faust, 29 Nov 1902, DWT LB-1; Taylor to Harvey Goulder, 23 Jan 1912, DWT LB-5.
20. Thomas Hughes, *Elmer Sperry: Inventor and Engineer* (Baltimore: Johns Hopkins, 1971), 112, 120–124; Taylor to Elmer Sperry, 28 Dec 1910, DWT LB-1.
21. Taylor to D. R. Alger, 16 Aug 1910, DWT LB-4.
22. Elmer Sperry, "The Gyroscope for Marine Purposes," *TSNAME* 18 (1910): 144.
23. Hughes, *Sperry*, 103.

24. Taylor, "On Ships' Forms Derived by Formulae," 243.

25. Taylor, "An Experimental Investigation of Stream Lines Around Ships' Models," *TSNAME* 15 (1907): 1. Note that Taylor and his contemporaries referred to streamlines as "stream lines."

26. Taylor, "The Effect of Parallel Middle Body Upon Resistance,"*TSNAME* 17 (1909): 171.

27. John C. Reilly and Robert L. Scheina, *American Battleships, 1886–1923* (Annapolis: Naval Institute Press, 1980), 142, 163, 191, 197.

28. Taylor, "Some Model Basin Investigations of the Influence of Form of Ships Upon the Resistance," *TSNAME* 19 (Nov 1911): 59–66, quotation 64.

29. Merritt Roe Smith, *Harpers Ferry Armory and the New Technology: The Challenge of Change* (Ithaca: Cornell University Press, 1980); David A. Hounshell, *From the American System to Mass Production, 1800–1932: The Development of Manufacturing Technology in the United States* (Baltimore: Johns Hopkins Press, 1984).

30. Riehle Brothers, *Evolution of the Testing Machine*, privately published, 1927; "Testing—Riehle" file, Division of Mechanical and Civil Engineering, National Museum of American History, Smithsonian Institution.

31. Walter F. Worthington to C. W. Rae, 16 Jan 1908; and Rae to Worthington, 20 Jan 1908, DTNSRDC RC 7-2, box 1, folder 3; Worthington to Rae, 19 Oct 1908, WNRC, RG 181, acc. 2794, box 2; and Worthington to G. W. Melville, 27 Oct 1909, RG 181, acc 2794, box 1.

32. Worthington, "Government Testing and Inspection for the Naval Service," *JASNE* 24 (1912): 931–947.

33. Ibid.

34. Worthington to R. S. Griffin, Assistant Chief, Bureau of Steam Engineering, 18 Nov 1908, WNRC, RG 181, acc. 2794, box 2.

35. Worthington to Superintendent, Naval Academy, 16 Sep 1907, WNRC, RG 181, acc. 2794, box 2.

36. Ernest J. King, "The U.S. Naval Engineering Experiment Station, Annapolis, Md." *JASNE* 25 (Aug 1913): 445–446.

37. EES Annual Report, 2 Jun 1910, DTNSRDC RC 7-2, box 1, folder 3.

38. Ibid. For gauge glasses, see also Bowen & Loeb, "EES, Some Results," *JASNE* 26 (1914): 707.

39. Worthington to John K. Robinson, 22 Oct 1909, WNRC, RG 181, acc. 2794, box 2.

40. EES Annual Report, 2 Jul 1910, DTNSRDC RC 7-2, box 1, folder 3.

41. EES Annual Report, 6 Jul 1909, DTNSRDC RC 7-2, box 1, folder 3; Worthington to Riehle Brothers, 3 May 1910, WNRC, RG 181, acc. 2794, box 2.

42. Worthington to J. K. Robinson, 14 Jun 1909, WNRC, RG 181, acc. 2794, box 2.

43. T. W. Kinkaid, "Routine," 26 Sep 1910, and H. I. Cone to Kinkaid, 30 Jul 1912, box 2; and R. S. Griffin to Kinkaid, 28 Mar 1916, WNRC, RG 181, acc. 2794, box 6.

44. "List of Material and Appliances Recommended for Naval Use up to 1 Dec 1917," WNRC, RG 181, acc. 2794, box 10.

45. H. G. Bowen and Leo Loeb, "The Engineering Experiment Station; Some Results," *JASNE* 26 (1914): 706–723.

46. Ibid.; H. S. Cone to Superintendent, Naval Academy, 6 Jan 1911, WNRC, RG 181, acc. 2794, box 2. Bowen and Loeb reported different percentages for the compound, but those shown are given in the official specification issued 10 May 1911 (box 2).

47. W. N. Berkeley to Kinkaid, 18 May 1911, WNRC, RG 181, acc. 2794, box 2.

48. "Information Concerning Tests of Lubricating Oil at the Engineering Experiment Station," 7 Feb 1916, WNRC, RG 181, acc. 2794, box 6.

49. "Report on Tests," for the month ending 31 Oct 1918, WNRC, RG 181, Acc. 2794, box 14.

50. King, "U.S. Naval Engineering Experiment Station," 440–442.

51. Bowen and Loeb, "The EES, Some Results," *JASNE* (1914).

52. EES Annual Reports, 1916, 1917, 1918, DTNSRDC RC 7-2, box 1, folder 3; Kinkaid to Superintendent, Naval Academy, on chauffeur, 28 May 1918, and Superintendent to Kinkaid, 6 Jul 1918, WNRC, RG 181, acc. 2794, box 12, "Employees" file.

53. EES Annual Reports, 1912–1919, DTNSRDC RC 7-1, box 1, folder 3, for Chambers' position on the aviation camp, see W. I. Chambers to Division of Material, 1 Dec 1913, WNRC, RG 181, acc. 2794, box 3.

54. Ernest King to Head, Naval Engineering Experiment Station, 3 Feb 1913, DTNSRDC RC 7-2, box 1, folder 3; EES Annual Report, 1 Jul 1918, DTNSRDC RC 7-2, box 1, folder 3.

55. For a full treatment of the relationship between Zahm, Taylor, and Captain Washington Irving Chambers, the special advisor to the Secretary of the Navy on aviation matters, see Alex Roland, *Model Research: The National Advisory Committee for Aeronautics, 1915–1958*, vol. 1 (Washington: NASA, 1985), 4–25.; R. M. Watt to Secretary of the Navy, 24 Apr 1911, NARA, RG 80, 1897–1915, box 1688, file 28229-2; Third Annual Report of the National Advisory Committee on Aeronautics, 13 Dec 1917 (Washington: GPO, 1918).

56. N. H. Randers-Pehrson, "Pioneer Wind Tunnels," *Smithsonian Miscellaneous Collections* 93, no. 4 (19 Jan 1935); Gustave Eiffel, *La Résistance de l'air et l'aviation: experiences effectuees au laboratoire du Champs-de-Mars* (Paris: H. Dunot et E. Pinat, 1911).

57. Frank Lyon to J. A. Bowyer, 15 Aug 1910, NARA, RG 80, 1897–1915, box 1384, file 26983-45 (also listed as 2689345); *Biographical Directory of the American Congress, 1774–1961*, 476; Taylor to Butler Ames, 20 Jun 1910, DWT LB-4.

58. Taylor to R. B. Bedford, American Blower Company, 20 Mar 1912 and 16 Jul 1912; Taylor to Maxwell Day, General Electric, 12 Apr 1912; and Taylor to J. C. Hunsaker, 29 May 1912, DWT LB-5; Taylor to Director, Office of Naval Intelligence, 27 Aug 1915; and R. T. Glazebrook to Naval Attache, 20 Sep 1915, NARA, RG 19, 1897–1915, box 173, file 1356 A50.

59. William McEntee, "United States Experimental Wind Tunnel," Navy Department, Bureau of Construction and Repair Bulletin #70, 15 Mar 1916, DTNSRDC RC 7-1, box 2.

60. Ibid.

61. William McEntee, "Some Applications of the Principles of Naval Architecture to Aeronautics," *TSNAME* 19 (1911): 287–295, quotation 287. McEntee is listed in the *Register of Commissioned and Warrant Officers of the United States Navy and Marine Corps, 1941* as fluent in both French and German; it is possible that he had read both the work of Eiffel and that of German pioneer Ludwig Prandtl in the original at this date. English versions of their works were not available. Prandtl had published a basic work on aerodynamics based on research on water flow in 1905 in the *Proceedings of the Third International Mathematical Congress, Heidelberg, 1904*.

62. H. C. Richardson, "Hydromechanic Experiments with Flying Boat Hulls," *Smithsonian Miscellaneous Collections* 62, no. 2 (1923); J. C. Hunsaker, "Forty Years of Aeronautical Research," *Annual Report of Board of Regents of the Smithsonian Institution, 1955* (Washington: Government Printing Office, 1956), 241–271. Taylor himself was not appointed to NACA until 1917. The lacuna in records of the first two and a half years of the wind tunnel is due, according to J. Norman Fresh, to a fire in 1918 that destroyed early log books and other information. J. Norman Fresh, *The Aerodynamics Laboratory—The First 50 Years*, DTNSRDC RC 7-1, box 14.

63. Library of Congress, Aeronautics Division, "Biographical Sketch of A. F. Zahm—in Aeronautics," DTNSRDC RC 7-1, box 1.
64. Ibid.
65. Josephus Daniels to Bureau of Construction and Repair, et al., NARA, RG 45, box 780, subject file ZGU.
66. Lieutenant Mary Ford, "The Role of Wind Tunnels in Aerodynamic Research for the United States Navy" (Aviation History Unit, 1945), DTNSRDC RC 7-1, box 2.
67. "War Work of the Aerodynamical Laboratory," NARA, RG 45, 1911–1927, box 838.
68. Ibid.
69. McEntee to Commandant, Washington Navy Yard, 19 Dec 1917, NARA, RG 19, 1912–1925, box 173, file 1356 A50; Ford, "Role of Wind Tunnels," 1945, DTNSRDC RC 7-1, box 2.
70. Ibid.; see also Library of Congress, "Biographical Sketch of A. F. Zahm."
71. Westervelt, George Conrad, Commander Holder Chester Richardson, and Lieutenant Commander Albert Cushing Read, *The Triumph of the NCs* (Garden City, NY: Doubleday and Page, 1920).
72. *TSNAME* publications by McEntee include "Variation of Frictional Resistance of Ships with Condition of Wetted Surface" (1915); "Notes from the Model Basin" (1916); "Cargo Ship Lines of Simple Form" (1917); "Variations of Shaft Horsepower, Propeller Revolutions, and Propulsive Coefficient with Longitudinal Position of Parallel Middle Body in a Single Screw Cargo Ship" (1918); "The Propulsive Efficiency of Single Screw Cargo Ships" (1919).

CHAPTER **4**

Between the Wars

THE PERIOD BETWEEN THE TWO WORLD WARS was one of an ambivalent policy toward armaments, naval armaments in particular. On the one hand, national public sentiment and national policy entered a period of intense isolationism and rejection of military preparedness, especially during the 1920s. On the other hand, naval planners and elements of the political structure advocated a strong and modernized defense, particularly against a possible threat from Japan. In a period of uncertain support for military research, the expansion of research work at the two laboratories reflected the shifts in policy.[1]

A great many outside factors influenced the nature of the overall research problems sent to the two facilities by their respective bureaus and submitted by private firms during the interwar decades. In the 1920s evaluations by the General Board and by the bureaus of the events of World War I led to new technical problems of concern to the Navy. Those General Board policies were themselves set against the background of national politics and international diplomacy.

National revulsion with war focused on naval armaments; with some justification, American isolationists believed that the naval arms race that had preceded the Great War had been a contributing cause of the war itself. The naval "parades" and exhibitions, such as those typified by the visit in 1907–1909 around the world by President Theodore Roosevelt's Great White Fleet, had brought international naval competition into the public eye. The U.S. entry into the war had been caused by naval events; it was Germany's announced unrestricted submarine attacks upon Allied and neutral shipping, February–April 1917, that forced President Woodrow Wilson to ask Congress for a Declaration of War. The disillusionment with war prevalent in both Europe and

America after the Armistice contributed to the Washington Naval Conference in 1921–1922 and to a system of naval arms limitations set up then and modified in subsequent conferences in London in 1930 and 1936.[2]

Those treaties limited the number and tonnage of capital ships that the United States could produce; they allowed the construction of cruiser-sized aircraft carriers; they limited the weight of destroyers; they allowed the expansion of submarine fleets. The particular sizes and specifications of U.S. Navy ships were thus structured by a set of international agreements. In general, to meet the limits imposed on tonnage, and to achieve maximum firepower and speed within those weight limits, American naval ships needed to be of lighter construction. The weight reduction consideration would guide much of American interwar ship design, affect the design of many auxiliary machines and main propulsion plants, and change the details of ship fabrication itself. Many of the specific studies at both the Engineering Experiment Station (EES) and the Experimental Model Basin (EMB) in the interwar period were driven by the effort to cut weight.[3]

Naval planners recognized that submarines and aircraft had the potential for completely revolutionizing warfare at sea. While the General Board and others in the Navy and Congress struggled with the doctrinal and administrative issues surrounding these new craft and their management, staff members at both EES and EMB dealt with hundreds of major and minor technical aspects, from improving engines and propulsion, through design of hull and construction methods. These advances by themselves would have made the decades between World War I and II exciting and creative; as international tensions increased in the 1930s, work at both facilities took on added urgency. Any future war would be won or lost with the naval craft they designed; whatever the mood of the country, naval engineers and architects believed that the fate of the nation rested with them. Events would prove that belief well founded.

The use of the submarine in World War I conveyed particular lessons. The adoption of the convoy shipping plan, in which a large group of merchant ships traveling together would be protected by flanking warships, proved a somewhat successful strategy for defense against the submarine after American entry in the war. The destroyer, originally an unarmored, fast, seagoing gunship designed to overpower small torpedo boats, emerged during World War I as the major convoy escort defense against submarines, when equipped with depth charges and subtracking hydrophones. Improvement in speed, maneuverability, and range of the destroyer, and improvement of its sound-detection capability to counter the threat of the submarine, would become major naval technological priorities in the interwar period.[4]

The submarine itself would be thoroughly redesigned, leading to research problems in strengthening the hull and structure against depth charges, to redesign of hull and conning tower, improvement of rescue equipment, and concern for more powerful and lighter power plants. Through the interwar period, the development of a "fleet submarine" capable of long range and relatively high speed became a naval objective due to the long cruising radius required by a Pacific Ocean-oriented strategy. Both facilities during the period contributed to these developments.[5]

The proper use and effect of aircraft in naval warfare generated a decade of debate about the exact lessons of World War I in this new dimension. Lighter-than-air ships held the potential for the transport of troops and supplies over long distances, possibly serving as bombers above the ceiling altitude of fighter aircraft. Small planes launched from ships could serve as scouts and spotters; one or two catapult-released seaplanes could be placed aboard capital ships. Larger groups of fighters could be based on specially designed aircraft carriers.[6]

Bomb and torpedo attacks from such aircraft might require a re-thinking of the role and vulnerability of major capital ships. General Billy Mitchell attracted both public and official attention by the demonstration bombing in 1921 of former German warships used as targets, stirring a controversy regarding questions of air doctrine that overflowed the usual confines of Navy General Board and Army staff discussion. Navy decisions to concentrate aircraft work in the new Bureau of Aeronautics, to push piston-driven aircraft engines to the limits of their potential for speed and power and to construct a limited number of aircraft carriers, would all have direct impact at both the EES and EMB. The Bureau of Aeronautics, while coordinating aircraft work after 1922, placed specific projects, with supporting funding, at both facilities. Through the late 1930s, both Construction and Repair and Engineering concentrated on the basic question of the strengthening of ship structures against explosive shock, bringing new classes of research into the laboratories.[7]

Japan's acquisition of German territories in the South Pacific after World War I immediately renewed naval concerns about Japan as a possible enemy. As a consequence, considerable naval war planning in the 1920s and 1930s focused on the Pacific as a possible theater of operations, leading to the concern that new naval craft be designed to handle immense distances. Aircraft would require carriers because the United States had few bases. Destroyers would need extraordinary steaming radii; submarines would have to be built to handle high-seas maneuvers. Such considerations also drove technology.[8]

The push of outside technological development in several non-weapons areas affected the research at the two laboratories. German advances in diesel engine design made clear that American technology had to concentrate on this area in order to stay current. In regard to steam turbine engines, advocates of longer range major ships believed that technical advances in shore-based electrical power-generating turbines pointed the way to superior designs for marine applications. Harold Bowen, Chief of the Bureau of Engineering, 1933–1939, who had served briefly at EES under Kinkaid before World War I, complained that American marine engine builders were too dependent on British designs, in particular on the Parsons turbine, and he fought to build up an American marine turbine industry that would incorporate the advances of the American electrical industry.[9]

German progress in diesels and power station progress in steam turbines made American ship propulsion technology appear retarded or even theoretically obsolete by comparison. Bowen pressured American firms to improve both turbine and diesel design, especially to meet the doctrinal requirements of a potential war in the Pacific, and to keep up with German progress. As American manufacturers attempted to meet the challenge of more efficient diesels and turbines, as specified by Bureau of Engineering designs, the volume of machinery, parts, and materials to be tested at EES for conformity to those designs climbed dramatically.[10]

The mood of the nation and Congress in the 1920s had been so opposed to armaments that funding could not be obtained to build ships even up to the levels allowed under the Washington treaty. Despite the lessons of the war regarding destroyers, no new ships of this class were built between 1920 and 1932. In 1929–1933, naval expenditures under President Herbert Hoover increased, and under President Franklin Roosevelt, a much larger naval expansion budget came through, at first partially justified as economic relief in the National Industrial Recovery Act (NIRA) of 1933. NIRA funding of $238 million allowed for new design work and new generations of ships, incorporating literally hundreds of major and minor improvements. The resultant burst of work through the mid-1930s created severe strains at both EES and EMB, and management at both laboratories attempted to meet the challenge and to keep up with the increased demand for output of design and materials analyses. By the late 1930s, defense and shipbuilding funding picked up and both facilities could then use naval appropriations to expand to an even larger scale of operation.[11]

Officers in charge faced several dilemmas typical of such institutions. When pressure for results and immediate production was highest, as in World War I, it was difficult to find staff, equipment, or the time for planned growth. When the hectic work pace slackened, and administrative attention could be turned to organizational growth, budget would be scarce, as in the mid-1920s. When the pace picked up again, under New Deal funding, heightened technical demand, and rearmament in the 1930s, EMB faced the embarrassment of having seriously outdated and inadequate equipment, difficulties in retaining experienced staff, and a resultant tendency to fall behind scheduled delivery dates. The Bureau of Construction and Repair under Bureau Chiefs J. D. Beuret, George Rock, and Emory Land and the Bureau of Engineering under Harold Bowen took several steps to increase central supervision and monitoring of performance, reducing the independence of both facilities.

Administrators of both laboratories, driven by the imperatives of their own careers and those working under them, sought opportunities to expand their institutions and to provide some degree of upward mobility for their talented staff members. Increased projects and departments would provide one source of positions; yet such additions of new scientific disciplines and new responsibilities were relatively rare events. One danger was that a few individuals might move up by moving out of the institution entirely; management struggled to promote and retain good men, usually with success.

For such reasons, EES laboratory heads often displayed extensive longevity, a pattern established by the 1920s. At the same time, day-to-day research and its direction began to shift away from military men to the civilian department heads. After the first two military directors, never again would military officers command for such long periods. Walter F. Worthington and Thomas W. Kinkaid managed EES for a total of sixteen years. Thereafter, military management came and went in a more or less steady succession of 3- or (rarely) 6-year tours of duty. As longevity of office shifted to the civilian department heads, so did responsibility and daily direction, producing a degree of internal independence despite concerted bureau effort to exercise control and to monitor the agenda. Through the 1930s officers in charge at EES worked to retain internal military control by spreading their few staff officers over the expanding departments. But civilian growth rapidly outstripped military.

The station succeeded in recruiting and keeping, for various periods, several civilian "stars" during the period, such as metallurgist Dunlap J. McAdam and chemist James G. O'Neill. As the naval officers in charge of EES began to serve shorter terms, the number, quality, and

1. CARTER
2. O'NEILL
3. WEBERT
4. HECKLER
5. McADAM

6. COLE
7. DE BAUFRE
8. KINKAID
9. STUART
10. BERKELEY

Engineering Experiment Station Staff, c. 1915. Captain Thomas W. Kinkaid, in the front row, had firm ideas about keeping up appearances. High button shoes were the order of the day.

seniority of some of the civilian engineering personnel contributed to the growth of the departments as independent and powerful substructures. By the 1930s EES had acquired a largely civilian character, and through an incremental process it had come to implement the concept of a permanent laboratory, funded and managed by the Navy but almost entirely staffed by civilian employees. Naval supervision and control kept the facility purely Navy in its objectives while it was almost purely civilian in its manpower.

Progress toward a civilian-staffed naval facility at EMB was somewhat slower. By contrast to conditions at EES, naval officers continued to manage and serve on the staff of the basin through the interwar years, as naval architects from the Construction Corps stayed on and conducted research, wrote technical reports, published articles, and to some extent followed the research career exemplified by Taylor. Captain Ernest Eggert served as officer in charge at EMB for fourteen years; William McEntee served a return term of three years in the 1920s. Harold E. Saunders served as Eggert's second in command from 1930, with a short hiatus for sea duty in the mid-1930s. McEntee, Eggert, and Saunders all actively engaged in basin research, in addition to their administrative duties.

Even at the basin, however, an increasing number of civilian scientists came in; after the resignation of Albert F. Zahm in 1930, Eggert worked diligently to provide sufficiently attractive conditions and to allow for some independent research, hoping to recruit and hold good specialists from the civilian sector. The work pace, the relative obscurity of the research, and the aging condition of the large model basin made staff recruitment difficult. However, by the end of the decade, the prospect of working at the new basin to be constructed at Carderock, the slightly increased prestige attached to civil service work as a result of the great expansion of government employment during the New Deal, and the increased concern with defense in the light of world tensions all became added inducements in civilian staff recruitment.

As the demand for output increased, both laboratories flourished. Despite the national isolationism and the opposition to naval rearmament, the interwar period was one in which both laboratories grew and matured. Their identities as major facilities became even more firmly established in these two decades. Ship, propeller, and naval aircraft designs would be tested at the basin, and theoretical scientific work would be kept up; specifications for metals, gaskets, valves, gauges, packing, engine parts, and oils would be set at the station and products would be evaluated against the specifications. Although most of the categories of work at the two laboratories in 1939 bore a striking resemblance to those in the period 1910–1915, the value, the mission, and the significance of the two laboratories had all changed drastically. By the end of the interwar period, each had established that it was crucial to the modernization of the Navy. American ships, aircraft, and submarines of World War II would go into battle carrying the ideas, the ingenuity, and the hard work of basin and station staff.

Expansion at the Engineering Experiment Station

The civilian employee force at EES fluctuated through the first post-World War I decade, climbing from 148 in 1918 to a high of 169 in late 1919, and dropping to a low of 121 at the end of 1923. By 1928 the force had climbed back to its 1918 level, partly through the temporary addition of a team to replace a boiler that had exploded in August 1926. Appropriations for the station fell from $225,000 in 1920 and 1921, to $200,000 in 1922, and to $175,000 each year for the period 1923–1929.[12]

Through the late 1920s the commanding officers of the station argued with some vigor for increase in appropriations back to the 1921 level, pointing to increased workload, increased salary levels that required reduction in staff totals while consuming the same dollar amount, and stressing the cost effectiveness of the station. Captain Henry C. Dinger carefully and fully documented his arguments for growth in personnel, higher civil service ratings, and increases in numbers of laboratories.

Dinger complained in 1929 that every effort had been made to increase allotments from other bureaus of the Navy to cover work done for those bureaus, but without success. "It is considered highly desirable," he noted, "to concentrate all testing work in the particular fields now developed here to this Station; but, to do this successfully, some additional funds are required." Efficiency in research approach would suggest that the Navy should do all of its metals, machinery, and chemical testing at the station.[13]

Looking ahead, he expected naval growth to lead to expansion: "In view of the increase in volume of work for other government activities and the expected increase in connection with inspection service due to the new [ship] building program," he requested an increase from $175,000 per annum to $200,000. That increase was not forthcoming. Dinger pointed out that curtailing the budget of the station was in "no way a saving." If the work in areas of specialization of the station, conducted in "a more or less desultory fashion" at the various navy yards, were all stopped at those yards and concentrated at the station, the bureau would save more than the cost of the additional personnel needed at the station. Dinger claimed that $50,000 in additional funding would increase the "useful output" of the station by 50 percent.[14]

Dinger's argument for concentration of work at the station was part of a larger concern of his, that all naval research be better defined, coordinated, and planned. In a lengthy draft essay he prepared in 1928 for submission to the *Journal of the American Society of Naval Engineers*, Dinger proposed the creation of the "Coordinating Board for Naval Testing and Experimental Work," which would coordinate research schedules and work to avoid duplication. Dinger's critique of the Navy's existing scattered research system as managed through the material bureaus called for reforms that would not be implemented for another fifteen to twenty years. In correspondence to Bureau Chief H. E. Yarnell, Dinger complained, "At present, the only way that I can find out at all what any other Laboratory is doing is to pay a visit."[15]

Through the 1920s the station had based work on traditional and established areas of expertise. Even though budget and staffing fell, the three officers in charge during the 1920s, Captains John Halligan Jr. through 1923, Paul Dungan through 1926, and Henry Dinger through

1930, all worked to secure promotions, upgrading job definitions such as raising the designation for a position from junior engineer to assistant engineer, and arguing for individual wage increases within the civil service framework. Halligan and Dungan did not, however, attempt to argue for new categories of work or for added divisions or laboratories, concentrating on playing from strength, as Dinger did in his 1929 budget request for fiscal year 1930.

By 1930 EES was organized into three laboratories. The Metals Laboratory was headed by Dunlap J. McAdam, metallurgist, who had a staff consisting of two associate metallurgists, an assistant chemist, an assistant metallurgist, a junior metallurgist, and six to seven "laboratorians" or laboratory assistants. The Mechanical Laboratory was directed by Joseph B. Lincoln, mechanical engineer, with a staff of an associate mechanical engineer, a junior mechanical engineer, a mechanical drafts-

Engineering Experiment Station, c. 1923. Across the Severn River from the Engineering Experiment Station, the U.S. Naval Academy included the old Steam Building, with smokestacks on the right. The Steam Building had housed EES 1904–1908, while the new station was under construction.

man, and five laboratorians. James G. O'Neill, with a B.S. in chemistry from Cornell, headed the Chemical Laboratory; he had a staff of four. A clerical force of eleven handled administrative duties, including accounting, requisitions, payroll, equipment reports, invoices, shipping records, personnel paperwork, correspondence, and manuscript writing. Another 119 civilian mechanics, helpers, and laborers provided the maintenance and shop force.[16]

By contrast to this civilian staff of 157, Dinger had the assistance of four naval personnel: two lieutenant commanders (one of whom was on temporary assignment) and two lieutenants. While one naval officer was listed in staff reports as "in charge of tests," it was clear that both management of research and most of the research itself were conducted by the civilian staff.

Dinger issued an order in 1929 spelling out the duties of the most junior of the lieutenants assigned to the station as assistant test officer. Among other tasks, Dinger expected this officer to "specially familiarize" himself with the work of the Metals Laboratory, leaving the higher ranking test officer "to look out more particularly for the scheduling of test work and the work involved in the Chemical and Mechanical Laboratories." In 1929–1930, the civilian heads of the laboratories were not separately supervised by specific naval officers—that pattern would not emerge until 1931, when both the civilian and military staff grew; but it was clear that as early as 1929, Dinger hoped to move in the direction of assigning specific naval officers to take on supervisory tasks over each of the three internal laboratories. In 1929, however, Dinger was careful to reassure his civilian engineers that "the presence of the Assistant Test Officer does not change the status of the responsibility of the heads of the laboratories from that hitherto exercised."[17]

Each of the three laboratories continued to work in the areas as set out by Worthington and Kinkaid. The Metals Laboratory tested failed materials, and studied stress, breaking, and endurance of new alloys. The Mechanical Laboratory tested engine parts and electrical devices and did some minor redesign of components. The Chemical Laboratory tested lubricants, packing materials, gauge glasses, and insulation.

Early forced-feed lubrication systems on steam turbines encountered difficulties as the oils would clog lines, a problem often blamed on the practice of mixing two or more different oils. O'Neill developed an oil testing machine to determine whether mixing of different brands of oil of the same grade caused the difficulty, and determined that the mixing practice was not at fault. An expanded use of this machine illustrates the principle of how the availability of equipment and skills led to new areas of research within the broadly defined parameters of work, without any concerted management decision to expand.[18]

The testing machine worked by injecting a film of oil under pressure into a bearing surface between a steel journal and a bearing made of a babbitt metal. A 3-horsepower electric motor would revolve the journal under a constant pressure maintained by springs. A counter would record the revolutions of the journal, and a gauge would monitor the foot-pounds lost to friction at various speeds. After a set number of hours, either 100 or 150, the foot-pound loss would be recomputed. The machine could thus allow a reading of the loss of lubricating ability of the oil after a standardized period of running, by comparing the foot-pound loss at the beginning of the run with the loss at the end of the run. O'Neill began to develop this principle into a standardized measure of the durability of oils, publishing a journal article on the subject in 1921.[19]

His comparative study of a paraffin-based oil, a naphtha-based oil, and sperm whale oil showed the utility of the test as a means of comparing different lubricants. By 1923 O'Neill produced a standardized rating of oils, based on 100-hour runs on two machines; by running two nearly identical machine tests, instrument error and variation could be reduced by cross-checking results. Through the 1920s O'Neill's test began to attract attention in naval circles; the Bureau of Aeronautics' Naval Aircraft Factory in Philadelphia requested reprints, in 1925, of all of O'Neill's lubricant tests over the period 1923–1924. By 1928 twenty other government bureaus and agencies requested their own studies of lubricants, using what O'Neill was now calling the "Navy Standard Work Factor Test." The agencies ranged from the Marine Corps and Coast Guard through the Customs Service, the Department of Agriculture, and the Indian Service. In 1928 Dinger requested $6,000 extra allotment to cover the cost of such service work to outside agencies, again without success.[20]

Dinger noted that, by 1928, the oil testing work had doubled over the rate in the early 1920s, creating pressure not only on staff but on the testing machines themselves. He requested funds to build two additional endurance machines, one of which would then be devoted entirely to aircraft work for the Bureau of Aeronautics. The "large volume of aviation oils now being tested," Dinger noted, made such additional equipment essential. The funding was not provided.[21]

By 1932 Dinger's successor, Captain Halford R. Greenlee, noted that the work factor test, although resisted by some oil manufacturers, had become recognized as a major contribution in the area of standardized testing. A subcommittee of the American Society of Mechanical

Engineers had ranked the Navy's work factor test as the only test in the United States that classified oil in the order of service performance quality, and in this area, the Navy had established a lead in the industrial standards movement.[22]

Greenlee believed that the test had greatly improved the quality of lubricants purchased by the Navy over the late 1920s; indeed, using the standardized tests, the average "score" of performance of the oils had in fact gradually, but visibly, risen over the decade. Greenlee claimed, with apparent logic, that the improved quality of the Navy's oil, resulting from the work factor test, had reduced wear and tear on Navy machinery, and thereby reduced maintenance costs, far beyond the cost of the testing, the personnel, and the equipment itself. Greenlee did not point out, however, that it was impossible to calculate such a cost-benefit analysis with any precision. Like his predecessor, he used such arguments to ask for an increase in funding, or permission to raise the charge to manufacturers for the test, which ran at $50 per test run through the 1920s.[23]

Another traditional area which saw continued work and incremental change was the question of boiler compound. The 1911 specifications for the compound developed by Frank Lyon were originally used for boiler feed water in both reciprocating and turbine steam engines. With a gradual increase in the use of turbines, and increases in their speed, temperature, and operating pressure, any slight impurities or scaling in boiler feed water took on added importance. At the high speed and close tolerance of balance in turbines, impurities could lead to turbine failure. Boiler tube buildup of scale remained dangerous. Through the late 1920s, treatment of boiler water with the standard compound in order to remove scale deposits had not always proven successful; salt impurities or the use of hard water from shore facilities, rather than distilled seawater, in boilers had produced a variety of difficult scaling problems.[24]

For such reasons, a review of the quality of the specifications for boiler compound was needed by the late 1920s. On a special project through 1931–1932, Lieutenant Commander Thorvald Solberg and civilian chemist A. Robert Adams worked on revision of the compound specification to meet the increased demand for pure steam. The bureau issued in 1933 its new "Standard Navy Boiler Compound Specifications."[25]

Solberg served on temporary assignment for the project; Adams worked on special contract for this project alone, together with a laboratory assistant. On completion of the project, Adams moved to a regular staff position in O'Neill's Chemical Laboratory. Solberg continued his career, rising after World War II to rear admiral and chief of the Office of Naval Research (ONR), a post created in 1946, in which he implemented some of Dinger's proposed reforms.[26]

Another group of major advances within the range of the traditional work came with McAdam's studies of metal fatigue. His World War I studies of propeller shaft failures convinced him that metal parts subjected to cyclic or repeated stress showed weakening or fatigue much more rapidly when subjected to the corrosive action of water. Through the early and mid-twenties, he published several papers and a number of internal reports, developing this concept of corrosion fatigue, and applying it to nonferrous as well as ferrous alloys. In 1927 he was awarded the first annual Dudley medal of the American Society for Testing Materials for his 1926 paper on the topic before the society. He received a job offer in 1930 for a post with another government laboratory; despite efforts by Dinger to offer inducement, McAdam moved on to the new job. At the station, his work was taken up by a bright young internal replacement, W. C. Stewart, whom Dinger promptly put up for promotion in pay, civil service status, and responsibility.[27]

In later summaries and command histories, these developments—the work factor test for oil, the new boiler compound, and the metal fatigue studies—were treated, fairly enough, as major milestones of accomplishment. Just as in the first decade of the station, it would be the unusual project that made for good publicity, rather than the workaday issuance of confidential test reports on metals, gaskets, insulation, and engine parts. The rate of production of such reports had climbed, despite the relatively stable staffing level, from some 100–200 per year in the Kinkaid years to an average of about 300 per year through the mid-1920s, to over 700 a year by the period of Dinger's administration.[28]

In 1928 the test report production schedule became the station's official and formalized measure of productivity, and monthly statements of inspection test report progress submitted to bureau headquarters provided a clearly quantifiable measure of output over the next decade. In fact, such statistics, coupled with growth of staff, reflect in a very tangible fashion the relatively surprising growth of the station in the interwar years.[29]

In 1929 Dinger began to collect information regarding two new areas of work that would lead within a few years to expansion of the station's mission and growth of the organization through new personnel: the fields of welding and diesel engine design. Navy yards had developed skills and interest in new welding techniques during World War I when the yards were called upon to repair sabotage-damaged ships of the Central Powers that had been interned in American waters. Because the German and Austrian crews broke up equipment with sledge hammers in hopes of immobilizing the vessels in a few hours prior to their own removal from the ships, ingenious repair work had to be done on the auxiliary engines, piping, and shafts. Since manufactured replacement parts for these foreign-built ships could not be obtained, shattered parts needed to be repaired and patched if the confiscated vessels were to serve the Allied cause. In many cases, welding provided the answer.[30]

During the 1920s, advances in the art of welding in the private sector had led to strengthening of welds to the point at which they were as strong or stronger than the surrounding metal: gas shielding of electric welding to protect the weld against oxidation while hot; development of new alloys for welding rods; improvement in the craft skills of applying clean beads of welding. Such developments all helped provide outside technological push to the internal naval work.[31]

Requirements for lighter ships induced interest in welding through doctrinal "pull." A welded ship hull would be considerably lighter than a riveted hull, not only through saving the weight of the rivets themselves, but because a welded joint would not require that the adjoined metal plates overlap, but instead butt up against each other. If welding could replace riveting on a wide scale, then similar weight reductions could be achieved through the welding of internal structural members and auxiliary machinery casings.

In December 1928 Dinger submitted to bureau headquarters a very carefully written argument for the creation of a staff position for a welding expert, "so as to furnish expert consultant and testing service on welding and apparatus on the basis of acceptable lists and work factor value." Dinger enclosed with his brief for welding his draft essay on naval research reorganization, thus placing his own request in the broader context of general improvement and rationalization.[32]

While his recommendation for the addition of welding research wound its way through bureau approvals, he continued to lobby for welding in the Navy. In 1929 Dinger publicized the fact that pipe and pipe flanges welded at the Norfolk Navy Yard and tested at the station resisted a bursting pressure of 7,800 pounds; steel plates and rods welded together showed tensile strength up to 60,000 pounds. Dinger advised naval engineers through the *Bulletin of Engineering Information* to train personnel for welding whenever possible; welding, he said, "is really an art in itself and requires much previous practice and study to perform satisfactory work."[33]

At the same time, Dinger received a copy of a report from the Office of Naval Intelligence's attaché in Berlin describing diesel engine design progress there. In particular, German engine companies had begun to develop engines with drastically reduced weight-to-horsepower ratios, which would make them suitable for high-speed long-range sub-marines, as well as for a variety of other small naval vessel applications. Without appropriations or new personnel lines, Dinger got started in this area in 1929, acquiring diesel engines from the Naval Postgraduate School and from the Smithsonian, where captured German World War I submarine engines were stored.[34]

EES Growth in the 1930s

Dinger's cogent advocacy of both diesel and welding work through channels, his logical arguments, and his careful laying of groundwork for expansion into both fields paid off over the next years, after his depar-ture from the station, as did his effort to assign junior officers a direct role in supervision of departments. In a relatively short period, Dinger's successors implemented his hoped-for organizational reforms and new lines of research. In 1931 an additional lieutenant was assigned, allowing Greenlee to develop some administrative specialization and to appoint a separate lieutenant as the supervisor of each of the three laboratories.[35]

In addition, Greenlee obtained new funding for the recruitment of a senior engineer, Bela Ronay, to set up a Welding Laboratory, adminis-tratively under the Metals Laboratory. In 1933 specialists in diesel engine work were concentrated in a new, deceptively acronymed, Internal Combustion Engine (ICE) Laboratory, originally staffed by a mechanical engineer, Nicholas Setchkin, assisted by an associate and an assistant en-gineer. Within two years Setchkin was replaced by William Joachim, hired as a senior mechanical engineer. Joachim would head the labora-tory for the next two decades. Greenlee's successor, Captain Ormond Cox, obtained appointment for another lieutenant so that each of the four laboratories could be supervised by a naval officer as well as a civil-ian engineer, with the exception of Ronay's Welding Laboratory, which continued under the supervision of the same officer supervising the Metals Lab.[36]

The balance of technical management at the station shifted in the direction of civilians through the 1930s. Lincoln in the Mechanical Laboratory, Stewart in Metals, O'Neill in Chemistry, Ronay in Welding, and Joachim in Diesels were senior engineers whose research direction of their laboratories was clear-cut; the assigned naval officer, usually a lieutenant who was almost always younger than the civilian engineer, assisted in naval liaison matters, reported to the officer in charge re-garding priorities, and helped publicize the findings and results of their departments to the engineers with the fleet. The supervising naval officers served short tours of duty, usually two or three years; as they moved on to fleet engineer or navy yard posts, their stay at the station served in their careers as a kind of advanced learning experience. Even though the officers had the title of "Superintendent" and outranked the civilian "Head of Laboratory," the length of civilian tenure and the depth of the civilians' experience gave them a degree of informal clout. The high positions eventually obtained by men like King, Bowen, and Solberg reflected the fact that a tour of duty at the station could be a valuable stepping-stone in the naval engineer's career path. By contrast, the civilian engineers usually made all or most of their careers at the station, heading their departments for periods of a decade or two; the departure of Department Head McAdam was the exception rather than the rule.[37]

Cox sought to increase the responsibility of the naval officers, converting their work from a consulting role to more direct supervision. In 1935 he argued for making the seven-man officer complement permanent, noting, "The personnel organization of the Station parallels somewhat that of a capital ship in that the laboratory superintendents act as heads of departments." In this context, Cox referred to the naval lieutenants and lieutenant commanders when he wrote of "laboratory superintendents." By contrast to their "test officer" role under Dinger, Cox claimed, "At present the laboratory superintendents are held responsible for progress of test work, for the methods of testing and for preparing the test and inspection reports." Cox asserted that military control led to an increase in test and inspection reports issued between 1933, when the station completed 1,004 reports, and 1935, when the output had nearly doubled to 1,938 reports. Despite his claims, a host of other factors besides Cox's command style helped account for the increase.[38]

Early in Cox's tour of duty, several long-term changes had already become well established. Both welding and diesel engine work had been added. Furthermore, between 1929 and 1933, the number of civilian employees had grown from 140 to 232, partly due to the staffing of the new laboratories and to an increase in shop personnel. The striking improvement, however, came from the growth of the "classified force" representing clerical, laboratory, and engineering staff from a range of 35 to 40, which had remained quite constant from 1923 to 1930, to the range of 60 to 70 by January 1934. No doubt, the approximate doubling of the classified force would help account for the increase in report production, rather than the slight reorganization of officer control.[39]

The sheer size of the various laboratories in personnel was striking by contrast with the pattern under Dinger, with the most notable numerical growth in the Chemical Laboratory as shown in table 4–1.

Table 4–1
Laboratory Personnel

January 1930	January 1934
Metals 13	Metals 16
Mechanical 9	Mechanical 15
Chemical 5	Chemical 18
	Welding 1
	Internal Combustion 3
Clerical force 11	Clerical force 15

Dinger, Greenlee, and Cox had converted the pressure for work in both welding and diesel engines into permanent new staff, new equipment, new organization, and new budget. Under the Franklin Roosevelt administration, appropriations soon climbed to $230,000, finally meeting Dinger's earlier requested level, while additional special funds allowed for the purchase of new equipment. Steadily increased work on new lubricants and fuels for aircraft and lubricants for diesel engines, and continued work in traditional areas including feed water, coatings for fuel tanks, asbestos, and packing materials, required and justified spectacular growth in the staff of the Chemical Laboratory.[40]

Internal Combustion Engine Laboratory.   In the ICE Lab, EES carried out extensive studies on a variety of diesel engines of a range of sizes, as well as their fuels and lubricants.

The Internal Combustion Engine Laboratory conducted studies of submarine and small boat diesel engines submitted by manufacturers through 1934 and 1935. At the urging of Bureau Chief Bowen, Charles (Ket) Kettering, director of research at General Motors, purchased a small diesel engine manufacturing company, Winton Engines, and the ICE Laboratory tested engines produced by GM-Winton, Fairbanks-Morse, Hoovens-Owens-Rentschler, Sun Oil & Shipbuilding, and Stearns Engine Company. Cummins and Treiber engines tested were not ready for Navy use. In addition, the laboratory tested diesels for small boats manufactured by Buda, Hercules, and Hill companies.[41]

Working at first in isolated test spaces for three or four engines, the ICE Laboratory continued to seek increase in space, acquiring two buildings and stands for testing seventeen to twenty engines by 1941. Reports and work covered a range of diesel engine questions, from design of fuel injectors, engine blocks and heads, and pistons and rings, through cold-starting tests under refrigerated conditions. In the years 1937–1939 the laboratory took up a host of weight-reduction attempts through the use of aluminum engine parts, submitted by private companies in response to carefully written detailed specifications. A major goal was to reduce the weight-to-horsepower ratio of diesel engines, and dozens of separate experiments reflected that effort. One outcome of the engine work was the approval of the General Motors Series 71 diesel engine, approved in 1939 at EES. This engine became the workhorse auxiliary and small power boat engine of World War II, powering all except the largest landing craft.[42]

While the writing of specifications conformed to the practices established under Worthington and Kinkaid, by the late 1930s the setting of detailed specifications for engine parts was no longer simply a kind of responsive testing of private sector designs. Through the process of establishing by experiment more and more strenuous requirements and receiving submissions from manufacturers, the station had moved closer to the model of a laboratory that conducted research. In effect, private firms were building bureau-designed engines. The nature of the work had moved, gradually and unobtrusively, away from passive testing to active design development.[43]

By 1936 the ICE Laboratory moved increasingly into the area of testing of various diesel fuels. Joachim arranged his laboratory into three subdepartments, one devoted to large engines, one to small engines, and a third to fuels, lubricants, and auxiliaries. The fuels section was operated in 1938 by Harold V. (Hi) Nutt, recruited as a graduate student from MIT. After a one-year contract, he was brought on board as a civil servant and remained a station employee for more than four decades. Nutt worked on lubricating oil specifications and fuel specifications, developing a specialized engine for testing the ignitability of diesel oil. By 1939 each of the ICE Laboratory subdepartments maintained a staff and output as large as that of a whole department a decade earlier.[44]

In the Welding Laboratory, Ronay continued to work alone and later with two assistants through the 1930s, producing exactly the kinds of specifications and tests that Dinger had anticipated. In particular, he tested new welding rod alloys, worked with methods of welding higher tensile steels, and examined a variety of welding apparatus. By 1939 Ronay worked with techniques of welding carbon-molybdenum and chromium-copper steel alloys, studied the performance of welding electrodes in light of their chemical composition, studied silver brazing techniques to be used with bonding together plastic composition fittings and copper tubing, examined methods for the repair of propellers, evaluated new techniques of oxyacetylene gas welding, and conducted qualification tests of various brands of electrodes. Ronay provided a course in welding to students of the Naval Postgraduate School that consisted of twelve hours of lecture and thirty hours of demonstrations; the text he prepared was adopted for training of welding supervisors in navy yards. Ronay cooperated with the metals department in testing welded assemblies submitted by contractors for approval.[45]

By 1939 the EES organization chart was quite complex, reflecting the military supervision of departments, the addition of the new areas of work, and the internal divisions within the laboratories. Dinger's 1929 goals for both expansion and military supervision had become fully implemented by the end of Cox's tour of duty.

Over the 1930s, work in the new areas had flowed forth in a steady stream; together with ongoing production in established areas, the report level climbed. Under Dinger, about 700 test reports a year had been produced; in Greenlee's three-year administration the report production climbed to about 1,000 per year; under Cox, production soared to about 2,000 per year by the mid-1930s, and even higher by the end of the decade. Dinger's estimate in 1929 that a $50,000 increase in budget would increase productivity by fifty percent proved modest.[46]

During the two decades between the wars, EES had responded to the challenges of technology by adaptation and growth. By 1939, civilian staff, now 400 strong, working under the small seven-man naval complement, had firmly established the primacy of the station in five areas: steam mechanics, diesel design, materials testing, welding, and petroleum product testing. Reliable, lightweight diesel engines had moved into the fleet; class by class, naval ships had exchanged structural weight for fighting power; the Navy demanded and received higher quality lubricants and fuels for its new ships and aircraft.

The Model Basin—The Navy Redesigned

In 1939 Construction and Repair Bureau Chief William DuBose had his staff prepare a massive, detailed memorandum for the Assistant Secretary of the Navy spelling out with pride the basic changes in ship design and construction carried out by the bureau over the interwar years. In this rare retrospective document, too detailed for full reproduction here, the bureau recapitulated all the major changes in the interwar years, class by class, in both major ships and auxiliaries. Every accomplishment of the Bureau of Construction and Repair that DuBose listed derived from design or engineering. The achievements were indeed striking.

DuBose noted that over the previous two decades, the Navy had worked to increase fighting power per ton, the strengthening of ships against underwater explosions, the development of the fleet submarine and the aircraft carrier, and improvements in destroyer performance. Use of welding and the construction of all-welded auxiliary vessels, reboilering and reengining of battleships, addition of deck protection and underwater blisters, and elevation of gun turrets had all gone on in the 1920s.[47]

In the early 1930s the Navy improved the habitability of submarines and other ships, used new steel alloys, employed more welding, replaced transverse framing members with longitudinal members, increased the use of aluminum, introduced new cruiser and destroyer designs, and developed submarine rescue devices. DuBose noted that each hull form improvement had required model basin testing.[48]

Such engineering changes, often incremental in nature, collectively modernized the fighting fleet despite the dribble of appropriations for shipbuilding during the two decades. Although much of the engineering work went on at EES, the basin was called upon throughout the period to test every new ship design. The planned hull form of each lead ship of each class, down to details of keel, rudder, and stern-shape, was submitted to the basin for modeling to determine powering requirements and resistance.

Ship design projects, reflecting the emphasis of the 1939 DuBose retrospective analysis, were the mainstay of the model basin work in terms of manpower, hours, budget, and quantity of projects. A selection of such projects at the basin is shown in table 4–2.

Table 4–2
Design Projects, Model Basin, 1928–1939[49]
Listed as "On Hand," 19 June—:

Project	Year	'28	'29	'30	'31	'32	'33	'34	'35	'36	'37	'38	'39
China River Gunboats		▓											
Coast Guard Cutters 52,55		▓	▓		▓			▓	▓	▓	▓	▓	▓
Battleship designs			▓										
Light Cruisers 32–41				▓									
Light Cruisers 40–43								▓					
Light Cruisers 55–56													▓
Destroyers					▓	▓	▓						
356–363								▓					
364–379								▓					
409–420											▓	▓	
Ranger (CV 4)				▓									
Wasp (CV 7)									▓				
Submarines 176–181													
Submarines 182–187													
Farragut (DD 348)					▓	▓							▓

The Navy's ships that fought in the initial battles of World War II included many that had been through Lyman Hewins's drafting room during the 1930s, and whose models had been tested in the basin at the navy yard. Using radar-assisted fire control, light cruiser *Cleveland* (CL 55) was credited with the sinking of the Japanese cruiser *Sendai* and assisted in the American invasion of the Philippines. *Farragut* (DD 348) survived the attack on Pearl Harbor by rapidly steaming out to sea. *Farragut* saw action at Coral Sea and in the Solomons, guarding convoys and, later, aircraft carriers. *Ranger* (CV 4) served in the Atlantic to provide air cover off North Africa and Norway. *Yorktown* (CV 5), tested in the basin in 1932 and launched in 1934, was famous for actions at Coral Sea and Midway. After playing a crucial role in the defense of Midway, she was hit by bombs and was lost despite valiant salvage efforts. Each of the other ships and classes that passed through the basin testing stage in the 1930s would have similarly dramatic careers in the period 1941–1945.[50]

Model Storage at EMB.   Every planned hull form for the lead ship of each class of naval vessels was tested and the models stored, creating a kind of three-dimensional database. Keel shapes with projecting rudders and propeller housings can be seen on the storage racks.

The basin made essential contributions to the rebuilt American Navy and proved responsive to the bureau's constant requests for detailed and informed testing and consultation on literally hundreds of design questions affecting the whole surface and subsurface fleet. Each design innovation affecting hull or structure in the period involved the Basin. *Farragut*, launched in 1934, was the first destroyer commissioned by the Navy in fourteen years; as such, she served as a testing, development, and training ship in the late 1930s. Improvements worked out by basin staff on *Farragut* became incorporated in the later groups of destroyers.

Old Methods and Equipment

Every week through the interwar decades, the design section at the Bureau of Construction and Repair would request detailed tests, constantly asking for evaluation of sometimes very minor modifications.

Hewins operated the drafting room at the basin in a style little changed from the tried and true methods developed in the first decade of the century. His drafting assistants perched on Dickensian stools before large tables, tracing drawings for polygraph transfer to templates. Later, pine-block models would be constructed in the shop, using gluing and shaping methods worked out by Hewins and Taylor thirty years before. Then the models would be tested in the tank, again using equipment designed and built in 1900 and in service constantly ever since.

Eggert served as officer in charge at the model basin, 1920–1924 and 1928–1938. During the period 1924–1927, McEntee returned for a three-year tour, and Captain Everett Gayhart briefly filled in before the return of Eggert. Since Eggert managed the basin for fourteen years in the interwar period, he was the dominant management personality in the two decades. His long term of office at the basin contrasted rather sharply with the more typical naval turnover of command at the station.

Through his administration, Eggert faced severe difficulties in meeting the demanding schedule. By the mid-1930s the basin was forty years old and, in some respects, quite decrepit. Periodic river flooding, fire damage to the building, settlement of the foundation into the soft soil on the bank of the Anacostia, and recurrent repairs and cleaning of the aging equipment all took a toll of workdays. While detailed records are not available for every year, data in table 4–3 suggest the constant nature of the problem.

Table 4–3
Time Lost During Repairs of Model Basin

Fiscal Year	Time Lost	% Time*
1929	23 basin days	8.0
1932	100 hours	3.6
1936	146 hours	7.2
1937	71 hours	3.5
1938	75 hours	3.7

* The percentages, as given in the internal annual reports are based on different-length work-years, dependent on the number of shifts. Information compiled from internal reports.

Good personnel were difficult to attract and hold. Eggert faced a chronic shortage of both naval officers and civilian engineers sufficiently well trained and enthusiastic enough to work at the basin under the trying conditions. Despite problems in recruitment and retention, total staff rose during the interwar years from a complement of two officers and seventeen civilians in the mid-1920s to five officers and thirty to forty civilians by the late 1930s. Eggert blamed part of the difficulty in re-cruitment on the lack of publicity of the basin's work; even when salaried vacancies opened up, Eggert could not find a sufficient candidate list from which to select anyone of high quality, he noted in 1930.[51]

Other factors contributed to limitations on productivity. Shallow-water tests on towboats, barges, and ferries required that, to simulate shallow conditions, a platform be lowered into the basin; its assembly and disassembly each took a day. Thus, shallow-water projects would be held off and accumulated; when the platform was in place, regular work would be backlogged. The opening of a smaller 30-foot basin that could be used for shallow-water testing in 1924 alleviated the problem without offending the "inland waterway interests" by closing the operation entirely.[52]

Although the original, large model basin was plagued with problems due to age, Eggert also managed several relatively new facilities. The facilities and activities under Eggert's jurisdiction by the late thirties are listed in table 4–4.

Table 4–4

EMB Facilities & Activities

Unit	First Year of Operation
Large model basin	1899
Small model basin (30-foot)	1924
8-foot by 8-foot wind tunnel	1914
6-foot-4-inch wind tunnel	1932
12-inch var.-press. water tunnel	1929
Structural research laboratory	1932
Experimental diving unit*	1927
Bio-chemical laboratory	c. 1932
Arc welding research	c. 1934

* The experimental diving unit had been set up in the wake of naval submarine losses by accident during the 1920s. This unit conducted experiments on diving equipment, salvage gear, and underwater cutting and welding techniques and, by the mid-1930s, had developed a group investigating the human biology of diving.

The smaller, 30-foot basin built in 1924 had been intended for testing of river craft and other shallow-water vessels. By the early 1930s it provided space for working on what Eggert called "radical ideas," by which he meant theoretical and scientific research. Thirty-inch models tested bulbous bow principles. Staff experimented with planes towed in fresh water and then in a solution of glycerine to compare the effects of a fluid's viscosity on friction. Eggert was generous in allowing staff mem-

bers time and access to the facility to run their own, independent projects, and in this quiet and unobtrusive way, Eggert structured the work
so that the Bureau of Construction and Repair through the model basin
served as a kind of patron for fundamental research.[53]

The variable-pressure water tunnel, which would operate like a
wind tunnel by forcing the fluid past the model, had been designed to
develop comparability between water tunnel tests and open water
model basin tests. The tunnel held out promise for evaluating propeller
designs and for investigation into problems of cavitation, although difficulties in developing a means of measuring true water speed in the tunnel prevented full exploitation of the equipment for experimental
work. Fluid interactions between propeller blades, as one blade caused
change of the flow around the next, was studied through an analogous
experiment testing a cascade of airfoils, placed parallel to each other,
in the wind tunnel.[54]

The wind tunnels continued to be used to test seaplane, flying boat,
and airplane models and full-scale parts under request and funding
from the Bureau of Aeronautics, producing a steady flow of some twenty
reports a year. The bulk of basin tests for the Bureau of Aeronautics consisted of testing seaplane float forms in water.

Through 1930 Zahm had run the wind tunnel as a separate operation "under the cognizance" of the Bureau of Aeronautics; his successor, James A. McCrary, assisted by two staff members, continued the
round of testing for the Bureau of Aeronautics. Operating somewhat independently of the rest of the basin, the wind tunnel staff concentrated
on improved airfoils, body shapes, cockpit, and windshield design.
Every naval aircraft in the period was pretested in the wind tunnel, including not only fighter craft and seaplanes, but blimps, rigid airships,
and kite balloons. All main parts of aircraft, including nacelles, controls, struts, and stays, were tested; the steady stream of reports followed
the pattern set by Zahm: scale drawings, scale models, wind velocity and
dynamometer readings, pressure tables, and concise, mathematically
documented brief reports.[55]

In 1917 NACA had constructed a laboratory at Langley Field near
Washington and, by 1920, made the facility permanent. Wind tunnels
there and the 1931 construction of a 2,000-foot towing tank for testing
of seaplane hulls and floats turned Langley into a primary center for
aeronautical research. NACA's experiments with cowlings for engines,
monoplane design, and wing-mounted engines faired into the wing, all
changed the basic look of airplanes. By the early 1930s, NACA research
had produced an aerodynamic form for aircraft that was already suffi-

cient to offer minimal air resistance at speeds higher than those that could be obtained at the time by piston-driven aircraft engines.[56]

With the center of advanced aeronautical research under direct NACA control, the wind tunnel under Eggert's command concentrated on specific design studies for the Navy's own Bureau of Aeronautics, with little excursion into independent research projects along the lines of Zahm's earliest work. Engineering research took place at the Bureau of Aeronautics, in the hands of an elite Aeronautic Construction Corps made up of Academy-trained officers with postgraduate training at MIT. Increasingly in the 1930s, the aeronautical designers at the bureau turned for routine tests to a variety of facilities, including NACA's Langley facility, Wright Field, and private laboratories, as the volume of design tests outgrew the Navy's capacity at the navy yard. Such pressures for continued output kept the wind tunnel role similar to that originally legislated for the Experimental Model Basin, to test specific plans supplied by the design division of the bureau.[57]

A Crisis in Ship-Powering Predictions

At the model basin, it was not simply aging equipment that caused difficulties. From the perspective of many scientifically trained naval architects it was clear that theoretical hydrodynamic research should precede model testing of designs. The problem was even more fundamental. The quality of the equipment and a variety of unresolved basic issues in hydrodynamics led many in the profession by the late 1920s to seriously question the reliability of ship-powering predictions based on model tests at the basin. In some cases it was difficult to find two runs of the same model that yielded identical results; discarding of anomalous data sometimes made true testing of hypotheses difficult.

Doubts about model testing as practiced at the basin were widely shared. N. W. Akimoff, a successful designer and owner of a propeller manufacturing firm in Philadelphia, with several SNAME publications to his credit, wrote to George Rock, Assistant Chief of the Bureau of Construction and Repair, listing his critiques in 1925. Among other points, Akimoff suggested that "The question of resistance proper should be revised from head to foot." He doubted the reliability of self-propelled testing, suggesting that the theory was "based on ridiculous assumptions" that could discredit the whole bureau. "The fact," he noted, "that in isolated cases it was possible to force some of the model basin findings into apparent coincidence with the results of [full-scale ship] trials, in itself, of course, does not mean anything, if the solid foundation is lacking. There should be less Taylorism (referring to Frederick

Winslow Taylor) and more sincerity, less doctrine and more Physics, less tolerance and more desire to check things up, less tendency to follow the other tanks and more inclination to firmly stand on one's own feet." Rock's reply suggested he thought Akimoff a disgruntled inventor; Akimoff pointed out that model basin tests, unreliable as they were, had won him Navy contracts, and if he simply followed his economic interests, he would not bring his complaints to the attention of the bureau.[58]

Eggert, as a Construction Corps-trained naval architect, shared some of Akimoff's doubts about the usefulness of model testing, but phrased his objections in less heated terms. Nevertheless, Eggert constantly reminded his superior officers of the unreliability of model prediction. He believed that extrapolation of model testing results contained so many approximations as to appropriate adjustments to make for frictional resistance, wind resistance, wave action, and actual shaft horsepower as to be almost useless for many designs, especially new designs that did not emerge from a standardized, fully tested series.[59]

Commenting through internal bureau correspondence on a SNAME conference paper, Eggert noted of frictional coefficients, "The natural conclusion of one studying these data, without complete information, is that model basin testing is a very uncertain process, and that the results are not to be relied on. This is not wholly without foundation."[60]

Eggert noted that models could yield only an approximation to the resistance of a ship, accurate only within 10 percent. "This," he said, "is a rather discouraging state of affairs, when we remember how the opinion has been fostered, and is gaining ground, that model basin results are precise and definite. Especially has the opinion prevailed that for comparisons with different though related forms model results are particularly useful, even though precise absolute results were unattainable. Yet it is in exactly this field that model results are most uncertain. Individual models do not always give consistent results. The comparison between two models can then give decidedly erroneous results."[61]

"One must regret," he wrote, "in view of the universal faith in model results, to report a disturbing truth, that the cases of models with erratic results are becoming rather frequent. In such cases, the obvious course is taken, the model is rerun, but this means delay frequently annoying and the new results are then by no means beyond suspicion." By implication, Eggert saw uncritical belief in model work as a kind of ritual or magic, rather than as true science. A proper use of the basin, he believed, would be to proceed with correcting the theoretical side of the discipline through rigorous and long-term experiments; he was deeply troubled by the constant pressure for results from those with a blind faith in model testing under the conditions imposed by both inadequate equipment and incomplete theory.[62]

Despite such disclaimers, the quiet work of some of the civilian staff members on their own research projects vindicated the intellectual commitment of Eggert and Saunders to the value of scientific inquiry as opposed to everyday, practical design work. The most notable success was that of Karl Schoenherr, whose 1932 work on the frictional resistance of flat plates provided a crucial advance in the extrapolation of model resistance data to full scale. Plotted on a graph, his "Schoenherr Line" served as the standard for scaling frictional resistance from model to full scale, and was adopted in 1946 by the American Towing Tank Conference. It served as the baseline for the "Correlation Line" adopted in 1957 by the International Towing Tank Conference.

Schoenherr's personal career was hardly typical of scientists, and the story of his ambition and ultimate success has elements of the romanticized Horatio Alger stories of earlier decades. After his graduation from a German gymnasium in 1909, he went to sea, shipping on board sailing vessels and steamers in the German merchant marine in the South American trade. He fought in the German army in World War I. In 1914, after a dramatic escape from a French prisoner of war camp, he moved to the United States, took out American citizenship, and then signed on board American vessels, including molasses and oil tankers and private yachts. At the end of World War I, he decided to pursue his education and applied to MIT for admission on the basis of qualifying examinations. His German secondary education had prepared him well for most of the tests, and he was admitted in 1918.[63]

Schoenherr enrolled in the curriculum set up by William Hovgaard, the naval architects program, usually filled by the top graduates of the Naval Academy, as preparation for careers in the Construction Corps. Schoenherr completed the curriculum in 1922; he then found himself not only distrusted as a German immigrant, but thrown into the labor market in the midst of the maritime recession of the early 1920s. He took a temporary position as a shipfitter's helper and reassessed his career. As an MIT student, he had tested a yacht design at the model basin in Washington, where he had met some of the staff.

Among his contacts there was the chief of the design section, Lyman Hewins, who needed an assistant draftsman and had casually mentioned the opening. Since private shipbuilding appeared to be in a slump, Schoenherr followed Hewins's suggestion and went to work as an assistant, on a part-time basis, in 1922. His naval architecture training, the equal of those of the top officers of the bureau, certainly over-qualified him for an apprentice-like status at the bottom of the basin hierarchy, tracing design changes. Schoenherr's natural ambition could only have been fueled by the ignominy of his position.

Seeking further education, Schoenherr enrolled in a masters of arts program at George Washington University in physics, and suggested as a thesis subject the question of the relationship of frictional resistance to the viscosity of the fluid; by varying temperature, he could experimentally determine the pattern. Soon, under Eggert's encouragement, he used the small model basin, running experiments under cold conditions and then heating the water to create a range of data. Through the period, Eggert listed the work as a model basin research project: "General Study of Laminar Flow."

Upon his completion of the master's degree thesis, Schoenherr enrolled at Johns Hopkins for doctoral degree work. Although he would have preferred to take a doctorate in physics, in the early 1930s at Hopkins the field was dominated by interest in nuclear science. Because he was a "hydrodynamicist," the only appropriate higher degree at Hopkins would be in engineering. His professors there encouraged him to continue his work on the question of laminar flow, or the layers of fluid that were crucial to the questions of frictional resistance. At the model basin, Eggert continued to provide time and space at the small basin for the doctoral project.

For the dissertation research, Schoenherr correlated data from a wide variety of sources and attempted to develop a unified approach. The Reynolds number, which is the ratio of inertial to viscous forces in a fluid flow, differed by two to three orders of magnitude in going from model to full-scale ships. By comparing data from the library study of reports from other basins, reviewing detailed data from the model basin, and filling in the gaps with experiments and with results from recorded full-scale ship trials, he manipulated various formulas using the Reynolds number until he established a single formula that explained the apparent variation of resistance at low and high speeds.

Schoenherr knew that several other researchers were studying approaches to the same set of problems, and he worked intensively through 1931 and 1932, recording data on massive sheets of graph paper after hours on the high tables in the drafting room at the basin. He explained his intensive drive to his professors at Hopkins, "Whoever comes out first with an answer that seems to be internationally acceptable, has something that builds a reputation."

With the completion of his dissertation in 1932, Schoenherr achieved both his doctorate and the international reputation he so conscientiously sought. On a local level, his work demonstrated the value of a science-before-design emphasis and a desire for more fundamental research, and at the same time addressed some of the disturbing problems with extrapolation of model basin data. The larger crisis in applying model studies to ship design that had troubled specialists from Akimoff to Eggert, and the practical difficulties resulting from the stalemate in theory, had led to one breakthrough.[64]

Schoenherr's accomplishment served as an inspiring example to some of the younger researchers Eggert succeeded in bringing in through the mid-1930s. As Louis Landweber, who arrived in 1932, would note later, most of the staff members in the basin's model drafting room had bachelor's degrees; some held technical diplomas from institutions such as Webb Institute of Naval Architecture. But Schoenherr's ambition and dedication impressed Landweber; the support of Eggert and Saunders was powerful. Landweber enrolled in a night program at George Washington University to begin work on an M.A. Like Schoenherr, he would utilize the basin "patronage" for graduate research. Landweber's first ambition was to revise Schoenherr's own work; fifteen years later, he did in fact publish a refinement of the Schoenherr Line.[65]

Both Schoenherr and Landweber later credited Eggert and Saunders for their foresight in sponsoring research at the basin; Landweber was encouraged by the fact that Eggert began to allow the authorship of model basin reports to be included on the reports' title pages. He believed that the training inherent in meeting the report standard set by the officers at the basin was his first step in advancing to outside publication in journals. While pursuit of graduate degrees among civil servants was rare in the decade, Saunders and Eggert actively encouraged graduate work. Although the Navy would not fund attendance of the civilian staff at universities or even conferences, except in extraordinary circumstances, a few ambitious young researchers would expend their own time and money. Research, while not among the Navy's highest priorities, was at least tolerated; at the basin it received quiet encouragement.

The need for fundamental research before proceeding with innovative development and design work would become, in a later age, a standard way of looking at the relationship between science and engineering. In the early and mid-1930s, however, the science-first and development-second orientation was shared in the Navy by only a few science-trained officers like Saunders and Eggert and by civilian scientists like Schoenherr, whose training, like that of the Construction Corps officers, had been in naval architecture. Such men viewed themselves as a small, brave band committed to bringing the scientific perspective to the Navy.

Europeans, particularly Germans, structured their approach to research in a hierarchical fashion, giving prestige and fame to scientists and less prestige to engineers. The social structure of German research reflected a view of the primacy of science: University professors did pure research; they also trained Ph.D.s and Doctors of Engineering. The best and brightest would go on in research and eventually replace their mentors in the professorial chairs. The lower ranking Doctors of Philosophy and Engineering would work for industry and teach in the hundreds of technical high schools, to produce a large and excellent corps of technicians. Unlike the American self-taught mechanic, the German technician was also an academic product, albeit from the lowest rung in an intellectual hierarchy. In such a culture, with its Platonic assumptions, it was easy and natural to view engineering and design as "applied" thought.

In the United States, by contrast, academic research was rarely credited with the great advances. The prestige and the financial rewards derived from innovation rarely went to academics. At least according to legend, men like Thomas Edison and Orville and Wilbur Wright were the heroes of invention—practical men with grease under their fingernails. Their cut-and-try methods, so it was believed, reflected the shop and craft heritage—good old American know-how. The facts, closely examined, would not have entirely supported that view. Edison organized his research in a methodical fashion; the Wright brothers had conducted aeronautical research in a wind tunnel and had produced an innovative development, the aircraft, only after the pursuit of research.

But in the 1930s the legend of practical hard work and shop know-how as the path to innovation was dominant. Academically trained scientists were often viewed as dreamers—men who loved to speculate about unsolvable problems but whose usefulness to innovation remained problematic. In such an atmosphere, men like Saunders, Eggert, Schoenherr, and their younger scientifically trained colleagues, had justifiable cause to feel themselves isolated.

The Navy, however, as a sophisticated institution for the recruitment and utilization of talent, was not so simplistic in its view of science as Eggert feared. Science was respected, with caution. A few of the graduates of the Naval Academy went through the MIT program and served in the Construction Corps, and some officers in the Bureau of Construction and Repair Design Group fully understood the value of scientific procedure and theoretical work. The Navy's commitment to hydrodynamic science was not new but had a tradition going back to the early days of Francis Bowles and David Taylor in the previous century. Indeed, the Navy had sponsored scientific work in other fields well before the Civil War. But unlike Taylor, Eggert did not have a strong personal publication record. However, as a quiet patron of scientific work at the basin, he did his best to keep alive the Taylor tradition.[66]

In light of the continued day-to-day production of routine evaluation work at the model basin and its real importance, the extensive hand-wringing of the scientists there over the need for more fundamental work took on a quality of exaggerated rhetoric. Eggert, Saunders, and Schoenherr believed they had to defend an unpopular position. Eggert's complaints about facilities and about the need for time to conduct research would seem to the bureau chiefs self-serving: a request for more funds and more time and a reduction in demand for tangible product construed as a plea for more research freedom. During the period, the tension between the scientists who wanted more research time and the bureau that pushed for more design production generated a running struggle over management.

Management of Design Work

Writing in the characteristic Navy style that conveyed every personal opinion as an abstract state of mind, Eggert noted, "It is felt that [the basin's] primary function, that of experiment and research, is one that should constantly be borne in mind in any consideration of its status, its program and its work." Since he regarded "experimental development and research work" as the central mission of the basin, the constant pressure for specific tests of alternative rudders, keels, propeller shaft supports, stern forms, and other practical applied designs for the Navy and of hull designs for tugboats, barges, freighters, tankers, and even yachts for private parties could only be regarded as interference with the mission as he wished it viewed. It is indicative of the change in the standing of fundamental research between the 1930s and the 1980s that Eggert, even when advocating more emphasis on research, spoke of "developmental and research work"; in the post–World War II era, the primacy of science in government weapons development became established, and the phrase would become "research and development." But in the 1930s even the advocates of research recognized, in their language, the order of official priorities.[67]

In a cogent summary of his argument for emphasis on research over testing, Eggert noted: "The model basin should concentrate its time and activities more on research work than on routine testing. More time should be spent upon each research model and each research project than is now the case. As an example may be mentioned the matter of frictional resistance of ship models, which is not yet established upon a firm basis after more than fifty years of work."[68]

Eggert particularly complained of the constant influx of private work as a distraction, both financially and intellectually, from research projects. By 1936 Eggert greeted with relief the reduction in the percentage of private work to eleven percent, partly through the falling off of the shipbuilding business due to the Great Depression.[69]

But as the percentage of private shipbuilding design work declined, the model basin turned to a variety of new projects in naval ship design. In 1932 the basin tested a series of submarine diving planes and rudders, designed at the Portsmouth Navy Yard. Basin staff worked on destroyer stern shapes for the class DD 348–352, using a nine-model series with two different designs. Self-propelled model tests revealed that mounting propeller shafts in bossings, or enclosed shapes, produced less resistance than mounting the shafts by struts. Characteristically cautious, Eggert concluded that the bossings were preferable, "assuming the model predictions to be fulfilled on the ship." Despite his hesitations, the routine work proceeded, with the naval side picking up gradually as the private work declined.[70]

Eggert sought to gain more control over decisions regarding whether or not to test a particular naval design problem through the use of a model, preferring to have his staff serve in a consulting capacity from their background of data and knowledge, rather than simply testing every suggested design submitted by the bureau or private parties. He worked to avoid what he saw as time-wasting projects, to increase the proportion of naval over private projects, to select a mix of fast-turnaround problems of some immediate value to design of new ships, and to take on groups of longer range problems of more general research value.[71]

The pressure to solve specific issues and design problems increased greatly through the 1930s. Design of destroyers, development of rudder designs for fast-turning vessels, choices between strut and bossing mounts for propeller shafts, propeller design, hull and keel form for new classes of submarines, destroyers, cruisers, aircraft carriers, and battleships—all these needed predictive decisions, whether or not the basin was troubled by issues of scheduling, manpower, inadequate equipment, or Eggert's doubts about the accuracy of predicting full-scale power requirements.

In the late 1930s bureau efforts to increase hull and structural resistance to shock from shells, bombs, torpedoes, and in the case of submarines, depth charges all required new studies of the structural mechanics of ships. For example, experiments with rearrangement of the internal structural members from tightly spaced cross members to tightly spaced longitudinal members to increase structural integrity without increase in weight required new means of testing structural strength. Through the mid-1930s this work became more formally organized and new equipment for testing of strain, vibration, and plate strength was added. In 1938 the research group working on such problems was headed by Dwight F. Windenberg, an administrator deeply concerned with staffing levels and the interests of his staff. The group greatly expanded in mission, and was renamed the Applied Mechanics Laboratory.

In 1930 Bureau Chief George Rock blamed Eggert for poor management, if not incompetence, and he initiated a series of controls, including tightening the monthly reporting system. Rock extended his efforts to control the basin after review of Eggert's 1 February 1930, monthly report, complaining that the work was "in arrears." Eggert replied, defending the present program of work and stating flatly that the bureau was "incorrect" in its assessment. "The items now on hand," he said, "represent only two or three months' work and to keep the force efficiently employed work must always be kept on schedule for at least such a period."[72]

A review of the 1 February report in detail makes clear the source of Rock's dismay. There were forty projects "on hand," nowhere near a two-months' output of results. Only two of the projects were listed as "completed." The status of all the others was explained in terms that implied delay: twelve were shown as "not started," "not ready," "no progress," "scheduled," or "postponed." Another thirteen were shown as in one or another state of progress: seven were "ready for test," five were "in shop," and one project was listed as worked on "when opportunity permits." From the point of view of those concerned with production of design results, such descriptions of status of projects "in hand" rather than tallies of projects finished seemed to be excuses.

From the perspective of later systems approaches to scientific research, the problem lay not with a dilatory approach of the laboratory, but with the reporting language and structure itself. Incoming design projects went through several stages, including preparation of drawings, preparation of model in the shop, conduct of model tests, analysis of data, and preparation of report. A modern, project-tracing report would spell out each step and its percentage of completion, allowing for justifiable slippage and rescheduling with unexpected problems.

While it is anachronistic to suggest that Eggert should have used methods not developed for another twenty-five years, management tools available at the time could have been useful. Many industrial practices of the period derived from the efficiency-enhancing methods of Frederick Winslow Taylor, the very "Taylorism" objected to by Akimoff in 1925. Ford Motor Company used operation sheets that divided an overall task into separate operations, a system which would have sufficed to show progress by stages and output of product. Although research and testing always involves unpredictable outcomes and hence is never readily subjected to rigorous scheduling, the simple problem of reporting on progress and its impediments presented Eggert with a continuing difficulty. His reports did not convey project progress, but simply appeared to be a tally of reasons why the final report had not been completed.[73]

Eggert, however, took the attitude of a research scientist, not an administrator. He pointed out that scientific work is difficult to subject to a clear-cut management logic. "It will be appreciated that, by the very nature of experimental work, the facilities needed, the methods to be adopted, and the procedure to be followed cannot always be worked out beforehand, hence an estimate of the date of completion is more difficult than if the work were entirely known beforehand and carried through on a production basis." Exactly those difficulties of subjecting the research process to management have continued to haunt laboratories ever since.[74]

In the case of the 1930s work of the basin in preparation of designs, however, the projects had clearly predictable requirements for time and were hardly similar to the unpredictable nature of more theoretical work. Despite Eggert's view, much of the basin work was indeed more like industrial production than "pure" research. The bureau chief could not be blamed for demanding a tighter, more clear-cut schedule of design work. The tension between the bureau and Eggert revealed the difficulty in converting work perceived as independent research into structured output of an organization. Eggert simply did not possess or care to use the management language, even as developed by contemporary private sector industry, that would have allowed for a convincing presentation of the basin's activities to his command.[75]

All the players in the 1930s viewed the management issue differently. Eggert saw the scheduling problem as intrinsic to scientific work itself, exacerbated by an excess of day-to-day projects, submitted because of a misguided blind faith in model testing, which interfered in the further development of hydrodynamic theory. He never attempted the marriage of applied and fundamental work that David Taylor achieved. Rock perceived the slow progress as the result of a lack of firm command on the part of Eggert. Later, a more sympathetic bureau chief, Emory Land, would blame the decrepit equipment and he worked to get the entire basin rebuilt.

Through 1932, Commander L. A. Kniskern from the bureau's design staff visited Eggert regularly, conducting and reporting on detailed discussions of project after project. But when Kniskern wanted to talk about management, Eggert would talk about hydrodynamic theory. Eggert explained his guesses and estimates on such matters as the resistance of forward-facing butt edges of hull plating, torpedo bulkhead installation, difficulties encountered on rolling tests, his own theory regarding heel during turns, the value of various keel forms, theories of cavitation, and specific tests on destroyers, cruisers, and carriers. Kniskern reported on the discussions, clearly from closely kept notes, with Eggert's citations to journal literature in both English and German, and with fully explained formulae for resistance theories. Eggert was quite frank with Kniskern in explaining that much prediction from the basin was guesswork—informed guesswork, but nevertheless not always a matter of scientifically accurate prediction.

When Kniskern relayed bureau concerns, Eggert continued to resist control. For example, in one report of a visit, Kniskern noted, "I handed Captain Eggert a brief memorandum . . . showing the Model Basin tests outstanding on the *Farragut* class destroyers and indicating the relative priority of those tests." Eggert replied rather coldly; as Kniskern noted, "Captain Eggert said he had no comment to make on the memorandum." Eggert, however, continued a strenuous program of turning tests on the *Farragut* models, rigging lights on masts to photograph angles of heel.[76]

In July 1932 Kniskern noted a query on his copy of Eggert's monthly report regarding the Spindle of Revolution, already carried for years as a model basin research project to be worked on "as opportunity permitted," Kniskern guessed the topic to be bulbous bow studies, but for months, nothing had been done. On his next visit, Kniskern asked Eggert to explain. The problem had nothing to do with the classic question of bulbous bow resistance, but rather referred to the testing of an ideal shape of a submarine hull; unlike surface ships, a submarine's model had to be fully immersed for resistance testing. In order to be supported underwater, some towing arm would need to be connected, offering resistance itself. The problem was a classic case of the Heisenberg "uncertainty principle," in which the tools of the experiment would alter the results. Kniskern was left somewhat puzzled, for it appeared that the problem, although carried on the books for years, might never be solved. It was a measure of Eggert's foresight to work on the problem; an ideal-shaped submarine would not be developed until after World War II, when revolutionary propulsion systems made concern with high speed under water a practical consideration. The project was dropped after 1936.[77]

The Engineering Decades

In the 1920s and 1930s science was the poor stepchild of design and technology, funded almost as an afterthought. The Bureau of Construction and Repair needed warships, the Bureau of Aeronautics needed aircraft, and private firms and the federal Maritime Commission needed new classes of freighters and tankers. Those entities would provide the bread-and-butter work; whatever research could be squeezed in was tolerated with a rare expression of minor curiosity by officials of the administering bureau. Eggert's claim that research should be done before tests were conducted usually fell on deaf ears; the research accomplishment of Schoenherr is a testament to his own dedication and to the personal commitment of Eggert and Saunders in quietly endorsing projects outside of any formal naval approval or funding.

At the Engineering Experiment Station, the Navy's concentration on technology rather than science produced no distress. Engineers thrived in that environment, and the station force more than doubled while its output soared by a factor of over 700 percent. The challenges of redesigned naval ships created hundreds of specific technical problems for both station and basin. While both facilities met those challenges, the contrast remained—engineers at the station rightfully prided themselves on being on the cutting edge of their profession; a handful of scientists at the basin did the work but constantly searched for the opportunity to get back to research.

In retrospect, Schoenherr and Landweber would look back on Saunders and Eggert as men who had the foresight to fight for a research organization and for good equipment. Yet, at the time, only the argument that the equipment needed to be rebuilt impressed bureau leadership. The scientific issues partially addressed by Schoenherr's research were regarded by Kniskern, Rock, Beuret, and others at the bureau level as interesting, but primarily the concerns of eccentric scientists. The Navy wanted ships designed and, as of 1938–1939, no one at the basin could command the national and international research reputation necessary to convince the bureau of the need for work on fundamentals first.

By the last years of the 1930s, a group working under Saunders devoted more and more time to planning and supervising the details of the new model basin to be constructed at Carderock, Maryland. Other changes were in the wind. Ever since the beginnings of the New Navy in the 1880s, many thoughtful critics of Navy policy had argued that the two major ship procurement bureaus—Engineering and Construction and Repair—should not be separate. The reorganization of these two bureaus into a new Bureau of Ships came just as staff began to shift to the new facility. The story of these two basic reforms, one in physical plant, the other in command, is the subject of the next chapter.

Endnotes

1. Stephen Roskill, *Naval Policy Between the Wars* (London: Collins, 1968).
2. Ibid.
3. Peter Hodges and Norman Friedman, *Destroyer Weapons of World War II* (Annapolis: Naval Institute Press, 1979). DuBose, Chief, Bureau of Construction and Repair, to Assistant Secretary of the Navy, 13 Feb 1939, NARA, RG 19, General Correspondence 1925–1942, entry 115 , 51- 1(1), vol. 2.
4. Hodges and Friedman, *Destroyer Weapons of World War II*, 109–115. The development of the convoy is the subject of various works; an early treatment reflecting contemporary thought on the subject is in C. Ernest Fayle, *The War and the Shipping Industry* (London: Oxford, 1927).
5. John Alden, *The Fleet Submarine in the U.S. Navy, A Design and Construction History* (Annapolis: Naval Institute Press, 1979).
6. There is a rich literature on naval air development between the wars. See especially, Norman Friedman, *U.S. Aircraft Carriers* (Annapolis: Naval Institute Press, 1983) and I. B. Holley, *Ideas and Weapons* (New Haven: Yale University Press, 1953). Brodie identifies air, submarine, and radio as the three most important developments in naval warfare in the early 20th century. Bernard Brodie, *A Guide to Naval History* (Princeton: Princeton University Press, 1955).
7. Archibald D. Turnbull and Clifford Lee Lord, *History of United States Naval Aviation* (New Haven: Yale University Press, 1949).
8. The Japanese islands as a strategic Achilles' heel are discussed in Harold and Margaret Sprout, *Towards a New Order of Sea Power: American Naval Policy and the World Scene, 1918–1922* (Princeton: Princeton University Press, 1940, 1943).
9. Harold G. Bowen, *Ships, Machinery and Mossbacks: An Autobiography of a Naval Engineer* (Princeton: Princeton University Press, 1954), 56–59.
10. Ibid., 127–136.
11. Historical Section, Bureau of Ships, "An Administrative History of the Bureau of Ships During World War II" (MS on deposit at Navy Department Library, Washington Navy Yard), 8.
12. H. C. Dinger to Bureau of Engineering, 4 Feb 1929; and "Appropriation," EES: EES Letter, WNRC, RG 181, acc. 2794, box 55, NP116/L10-5.
13. Dinger to Bureau of Engineering, 4 Feb 1929.
14. Ibid.
15. H. C. Dinger to Rear Admiral H. E. Yarnell, 15 Dec 1928, DTNSRDC RC 7-2, acc. 83-4, box 1.
16. "EES Reports of Personnel," 1928–1939, WNRC, RG 19, entry 993, P/NP16. (Entry 993 of the Bureau of Ships records at the WNRC is an extremely rich source; note that the entry is mislabeled "933.")
17. "EES order #5-29," 20 Nov 1929, WNRC, RG 181, acc. 2794, box 55; also, 13 Aug 1931, WNRC, RG 19, entry 993, P/NP16.
18. Richard L. Mohon, "Command History," DTNSRDC RC 7-2, acc. 83-4, box 2.
19. J. G. O'Neill, "Examination of Oils from the Atlantic Fleet Before and After Use," *JASNE* 29 (1917): 325–341; "Endurance Test of Force Feed Oils," *JASNE* 33 (1921):

248–260.

20. Manager, Naval Aircraft Factory, to Chief of the Bureau of Engineering, 16 Jun 1925, WNRC, RG 19, entry 993, L5/NP16; request for funding, same location, 24 Dec 1928.

21. H. C. Dinger to Bureau of Engineering, 3 Jul 1928, WNRC, RG 19, entry 993, NP16/N8.

22. Lecture, H. R. Greenlee, "The U.S. Naval Engineering Experiment Station," DTNSRDC RC 7-2, acc. 83-4, box 1. For oil companies, the work factor test presented a problem; if they claimed that used oil was as good as new oil, they would be arguing against the practice of disposing used oil. If that practice declined, consumption of the product would decline. If companies accepted the test and its results, they would have to spend money to marginally improve the product. In fact, the loss of lubricating ability, as long as the oil remained clean, was very slight.

23. Greenlee Lecture, 1932, DTNSRDC RC 7-3, acc. 83-4, box 1; charges are covered in 25 Oct 1926, WNRC, RG 19, entry 993, L5/NP16.

24. H. C. Dinger, "Scale Removal by Use of Navy Boiler Compound," *Bulletin of Engineering Information* 38 (1 Mar 1929).

25. Wilson D. Leggett, "The U.S. Engineering Experiment Station," U.S. Naval Institute *Proceedings* 77 (May 1951): 517–536.

26. Ibid.

27. D. J. McAdam, "Stress-strain cycle relationship and corrosion-fatigue of metals," ASTM paper, 1926; mentioned in *SECNAV Annual Report, 1927*, 39.

28. Such comments are typical of internal histories; see for example, Leggett, "The U.S. Engineering Experiment Station.".

29. EES Reports of Personnel, 1928–1939.

30. References to the stimulus to welding provided by the repair of sabotaged ships were common in the interwar period. See for example, DuBose, Chief, Bureau of Construction and Repair, to Assistant Secretary of the Navy, 13 Feb 1939, NARA, RG 19, entry 115, General Correspondence 1925–1942, S1-1(1), vol. 2. This document is a valuable summary of interwar ship design and technology issues from a 1939 perspective.

31. Ibid.

32. Dinger, "Memorandum for Engineer in Chief," 15 Dec 1928, WNRC, RG 19, entry 993, NP16/L5-2; see also DTNSRDC RC 7-2, acc. 83-4, box 1, folder 3.

33. "Notes from the Engineering Station," *Bulletin of Engineering Information* (1 Jul 1929).

34. Johnson, Director of Naval Intelligence, to Dinger, 6 Apr 1929, WNRC, RG 181, acc. 2794, box 55; Bennet to Dinger, 4 May 1929, NARA, RG 19, entry 993, NP16/N8.

35. The assignment of various numbers of naval officers on temporary or permanent duty and their task assignments have been traced through monthly EES Reports of Personnel, WNRC, RG 19, entry 993, NP16/LL.

36. EES Reports of Personnel, 1928–1939, WNRC, RG 19, entry 993, NP16/LL.

37. Longevity of term has been summarized from a review of the monthly EES Reports of Personnel.

38. Cox to Bureau of Navigation, 4 Sep 1935, WNRC, RG 19, entry 993, NP16/N8.

39. EES Reports of Personnel, 1928–1939, WNRC, RG 19, entry 993, NP16/LL.

40. S. M. Robinson, Chief of Engineering, to Director, EES, 13 Jun 1933, NARA, RG 19, General Correspondence 1925–1940, box 3293, NP16(8).

41. "DEMA-ICE Laboratory Talk," W. F. Joachim, 22 Oct 1953, DTNSRDC RC 7-2, acc. 83-2, box 2; Stuart Leslie, *Boss Kettering* (New York: Columbia University Press, 1983), 229–275, on diesels; Bowen, *Ships, Machinery, and Mossbacks*, 127–136. Source for Cummins and Treiber engines: James Blose comments, ABIF.

42. Bowen, *Ships, Machinery, and Mossbacks*, 135; see also, John O. Hughes to Capt. Johnson, 18 Mar 1929, WNRC, RG 181, acc. 2794, box 55. Series 71: James Blose comments, ABIF.

43. "Bureau-designed" engines as a policy had been announced earlier. See *Annual Report of the Chief of the Bureau of Engineering, Fiscal Year 1923*, 5. Testing of Bureau designs and components continued through the early 1930s, and by 1936 the ICE Lab was the specialized center for diesels.

44. H. V. Nutt comments, ABIF; *Annual Report of Laboratory Activities: Five Laboratories of the Engineering Experiment Station*, 31 Dec 1939, NARA, RG 19, entry 115, NP16/1.

45. Ibid.

46. The sheer volume of such work as a measure of productivity is impressive; however, it renders difficult any depiction of the type of work through review of the reports. Bureau management recognized that difficulty and sought narrative and summary reports on the station's research work as a whole that would yield a more comprehensive view of the facility's growth and changing character. Much of the general observation of trend and work summarized above derives from the 50-page 1939 report cited above, as well as from a review of technical reports and report titles.

47. DuBose, Chief, Bureau of Construction and Repair, to Assistant Secretary of the Navy, 13 Feb 1939, NARA, RG 19, entry 115, General Correspondence 1925–1942, 51-1(1), vol. 2.

48. Ibid.

49. EMB Monthly Reports are in NARA, RG 19, entry 115, NY5/S1-2, vols. 1–3. "NY5" was the *Navy Filing Manual Code for the Washington Navy Yard*; "51-2" referred to ship design. This table is derived from monthly "on-hand" status reports of the basin's work, reflecting only that work on hand as of June in the years shown. Thus, the table does not include many other design projects which came and went in the rest of the year, and serves only as an indication of the variety and range of ship design work, rather than a complete presentation.

50. Action information on vessels drawn from *Dictionary of American Naval Fighting Ships* published by the Naval Historical Center.

51. Eggert to Rock, Apr 1930, NARA, RG 19, entry 115, NY5/S1-2, vol. 1.

52. H. A. Schade, Report of Visit to Model Basin, 10 Nov 1933, NARA, RG 19, entry 115, NY5/S1-2, vol. 2.

53. *Annual Report of Model Basin Activities*, 5 Aug 1932, NARA, RG 19, entry 115, NY5/S1-2, vol. 1.

54. Ibid.

55. Library of Congress, Aeronautical Section, "Biographical Sketch of A. F. Zahm, DTNSRDC RC 7-1, box 1; Mary Ford, "The Role of Wind Tunnels in Aerodynamic Research for the United States Navy," (MS), Aviation History Unit, 1945, in DTNSRDC RC 7-1, box 2.

56. Edward Constant, *The Origins of the Turbojet Revolution* (Baltimore: Johns Hopkins University Press, 1980), 152–160; Jerome Hunsaker, "Forty Years of Aeronautical Research," *Annual Report of the Smithsonian Institution* (1955).

57. Frank H. Featherstone, "A.E.D.O.: A History and Heritage," U.S. Naval Institute *Proceedings* 94 (Feb 1968): 33–45.

58. Akimoff to Rock, 4 Nov 1925; Rock to Akimoff, 16 Nov 1925; Akimoff to Rock, 27 Nov 1925, NARA, RG 19, entry 115, NY5/S1-2, vol. 1.

59. Eggert's correspondence and the visit reports by Design officers contain many indications of Eggert's uncertainty about the theoretical base of hydrodynamics. For example: Kniskern report dated 21 May 1932 discusses Eggert's doubts about the

basin's method of computing frictional resistance; the day before, 20 May 1932, Eggert wrote to the Chief Constructor regarding guessing resistance: "This whole subject is in such a vague condition that out and out dicta of authorities must be looked at with suspicion. NARA, RG 19, entry 115, General Correspondence 1926–1942, 51-2(1), vol. 8. While contemporary hydrodynamicists would have viewed his doubts as the mark of a good scientist, his naval superiors evinced some degree of impatience with his hesitancy.

60. Eggert to Chief Constructor, 7 Nov 1929, NARA, RG 19, entry 115, NY5/S1-2, vol. 1. The paper was by basin staff member Roop.

61. Ibid.

62. Ibid.

63. Karl Schoenherr, interview by David K. Allison, 15 Apr 1985, DTNSRDC RC

64. Thomas Kuhn, *The Structure of Scientific Revolutions,* 2d edition (Chicago: University of Chicago Press, 1970), 52–65. Kuhn would view the debates over frictional resistance as evidence of a "crisis" in theory.

65. Dr. Lou Landweber, interview by Seth Hawkins, 28 Oct 1983, DTNSRDC RC The relationship of science and technology in the pre- and post-World War II periods is nicely spelled out in George Wise, "Science and Technology," *OSIRIS,* vol. 1, 2d series (Philadelphia: Univ. of Pennsylvania, 1985), 229–246. The professionalization of technological work is addressed in Louis Galambos, "Technology, Political Economy and Professionalization: Central Themes of the Organizational Synthesis," *Business History Review* 57 (Winter 1983): 471–493.

66. A. Hunter Dupree, *Science in the Federal Government* (1957; reprint Baltimore, MD: Johns Hopkins University Press, 1986).

67. Eggert to Chief of Bureau of Construction and Repair, 9 Apr 1930, 14–15, NARA, RG 18, entry 115, NY5/S1-2, vol. 1. Eggert's defense against charges of delay was extensive, painfully documenting all of his concerns about personnel, equipment, theory, workload, and intrusion of irrelevant work.

68. Ibid.

69. *Summary of Work U.S. Experimental Model Basin and Related Activities for the Year Ending 30 Jun 1936,* NARA, RG 19, entry 115, NY5/S1-2, vol. 3.

70. *Annual Report of Model Basin Activities,* 5 Aug 1932, NARA, RG 19, entry 115, NY5/S1-2, vol. 1.

71. Eggert to Rock, 29 Mar 1930, NARA, RG 19, entry 115, NY5/S1-2, vol. 1.

72. Eggert to Chief of Bureau of Construction and Repair, 30 Apr 1930, NARA, RG 19, entry 115, NY5/S1-2, vol. 1.

73. David Hounshell, "Ford Eagle Boats and Mass Production during World War I," in Merritt Roe Smith, ed., *Military Enterprise and Technological Change: Perspectives on the American Experience* (Cambridge: MIT Press, 1985).

74. Eggert to Chief, Bureau of Construction and Repair, 30 Apr 1930, NARA, RG 19, entry 115, NY5/S1-2, vol. 1.

75. 1 Mar report, 3 Mar 1930, NARA, RG 19, entry 115, NY5/S1-2, vol. 1.

76. L. A. Kniskern Reports of Visits, 15 and 29 Jul 1932, NARA, RG 19, entry 115, NY5/S1-2, vol. 1.

77. Kniskern Visit Report, 29 Jul 1932, NARA, RG 19, entry 115, NY5/S1- 2, vol. 1.

CHAPTER 5

New Quarters, New Command

P ART OF THE MODERNIZATION OF THE NAVY in the 1930s extended to review and restructuring of the Navy's bureau organization itself. The bureau reforms would affect both EES and EMB, bringing the two laboratories into the same administrative unit for the first time in their history. In addition, the Navy merged the officer corps of naval engineers and naval architects. Physical shore facilities were also modernized and improved. The building of a new basin to replace the one designed and constructed under David Taylor's leadership in 1896–1899 brought sudden and dramatic physical modernization in equipment, architectural setting, capacity, and potential for technical accuracy. Both transitions, organizational and physical, grew out of intense political conflicts.

New Quarters—The Fight for a New Basin

The pressures for a new basin had been mounting for about a decade before legislation finally authorized funding. The original model basin had been built in a low-lying section of the Washington Navy Yard, and Taylor had expended considerable time and incurred a cost overrun in attempting to strengthen the foundations of the basin with pilings and massive, extra concrete work. Despite careful preparation of the site, the basin, undermined by springs and resting on an unsteady foundation, presented problems of physical deterioration.

In the 1920s and 1930s Ernest Eggert found himself struggling with physical problems that hampered the time available for either design or research experimentation, ranging from minor breakdowns in the carriage or motors, to major crises like the 1933 flooding of the basin and its electrical equipment. But in addition to such difficulties intrinsic to an aging facility built in an inappropriate location, the basin had become technically inadequate to meet the demands of both commercial users and the rapidly modernizing Navy. It was not simply that the basin was getting old and decrepit; for economic, technological, and military reasons it had become outmoded.

Among the difficulties faced by basin managers had been the problems surrounding shallow-water tests. Since private shipping interests concerned with river and canal vessels were widely distributed throughout the country, and hence had dispersed geographic representation both in organizations and in Congress, the pressure from such interests for improvement in the basin could be readily converted into organizational support for expenditure. On the other hand, if nothing were done to satisfy the inland waterway people, their displeasure and complaint could lead to public criticism of naval policy. The political use of pressure was a delicate task.

As early as 1931, Eggert supplied Bureau Chief George Rock with details of the shallow-water problems. In order to mount such tests, a platform would be lowered into the basin. Eggert pointed out that from 1925 to 1928, the platform, which would prevent deep-water model tests, was in the basin for commercial shallow-water tests about one-fourth of the time. Even so, Eggert had been unable to meet all the requests of commercial interests for model work. In the period 1929–1931 the "work had to be curtailed and the basin closed to such work on account of the rush of deep sea work." Despite the increase in towboat and barge construction, Eggert noted, such shipbuilding was "being done with very little help from scientific research. This constitutes a neglect that is certain to be costly to the country." Eggert indicated that about one-third of the basin time "ought normally" to be devoted to shallow-water testing.[1]

Eggert carefully documented his comments with a complete recapitulation of all the shallow-water work at the model basin between 1903 and 1928, showing that 371 basin days had been devoted to these tests. Over the twenty-five year period the total basin-days had amounted to more than 5,000. Therefore, shallow-water work had occupied, in terms of number of days, less than 8 percent of the time. It would appear that Eggert's suggestion that 33 percent would be "normal" was based on his sense of an economic ideal and recent trends in ship construction, rather than upon historical experience.[2]

In 1933 Lieutenant H. A. Schade reviewed Eggert's 1931 information about shallow-water testing for possible political use, noting that the construction of a new basin would be of "direct interest to all those concerned with inland waterway commerce, and it should be possible to obtain the backing of these interests for this project."[3]

Small, 15-inch models could be tested in the new 30-foot basin; however, such tests, because of the small scale of both model and basin, greatly magnified error and were not satisfactory. Eggert preferred to set aside the small basin for independent research projects like those of Karl Schoenherr and Louis Landweber.[4]

Rock, in arguing for construction of a new model basin in 1931, made note of the limitation on shallow-water work, and included it as an important item among other, more technically based fundamental problems with the existing basin. Other difficulties he identified were:

- Inadequate length with no possibility of extension
- Unstable foundations
- Insufficiently level tracks
- Depth and form of cross section unfavorable
- Limited width prevented turning tests beyond one-quarter of a full circle
- Carriage speed limit of fifteen knots prevented tests of high-speed vessels such as seaplanes
- Limited length prevented accurate calculation of frictional resistance of longer models
- Propeller testing required larger models than could be run[5]

Rock particularly emphasized the problem of the basin's overall length and lack of solid foundations. Neither of these flaws could be addressed through reconstruction or remodeling of the basin in its navy yard location. He did not raise such issues simply because they supported claims for a new construction budget; the technical limitations were real, and becoming more and more crucial as the tempo of work picked up. The basin suffered from more than wear and tear or depreciation; its built-in design could not be adapted to naval problems of high-speed testing, turning tests, and testing of self-propelled models with large-scale propellers.[6]

Rock, like his predecessors in the 1890s, noted the world naval competition, particularly emphasizing work in Germany, France, Italy, Holland, Norway, Russia, and Japan with new and remodeled basins either completed or under way. He warned that if a new American basin was not soon built, "ship design in this country will lag hopelessly behind." Again, this was no mere hyperbole, but a real assessment of the situation.[7]

Among the problems noted by Rock, the difficulty of adequately conducting model turning tests became a severe one during the expanded destroyer construction of the 1930s. *Farragut* tests in 1932 were limited by the fact that the 10- and 12-foot models used could be turned

90 degrees, but would then strike the side of the basin after a very short observed turning run. Rock, with a rare pun, admitted that the testing inadequacy left the bureau "more or less at sea as to what the turning circle will actually be." Schade noted that "in view of the somewhat doubtful validity of model basin turning tests," the Navy should plan careful full-scale ship trials with the finished *Farragut*, rather than relying on the doubtful predictability of the basin.[8]

As the bureau worked on higher speed destroyer designs and strove for better maneuverability and turning at those high speeds not possible in 1900, the basin's very shape became archaic. Accurate turning tests for contemporary ships just could not be conducted with any accuracy. Even if the basin had been built on solid ground and its rails been kept perfectly level, its sheer dimensions would no longer be adequate. The Navy now needed a long, level, high-speed tank with facilities for adequate tests of turning radii; both the Navy and commercial interests needed another facility for shallow-water testing; propeller design and self-propelled models required a new facility as well.

As the pressure arising from new naval ship design questions mounted through the 1930s, the inadequacy of the basin became a more and more serious problem. Eggert and his team could not conduct sufficiently accurate and consistent tests; the variation between separate runs of the same model led to constant guesswork, reflected in Eggert's frequent discussions with A. H. Van Keuren, Schade, and L. A. Kniskern. While Eggert was right to insist that model tests could not be used to answer many of the questions raised in the design branch of the bureau, the alternative of trying out various new ideas in full-scale trials of the completed ship was not only expensive but politically dangerous.

The practical consequences of inaccuracy in prediction of ship performance became severe when the true dimensions of problems showed up only in full-scale trials, rather than at the model stage. By the late 1930s, several design flaws would become newsworthy in themselves, causing troublesome inquiries. Essentially minor problems requiring redesign on lead ships of a class would appear to the public as built-in errors; elements of the press could sensationalize the sea-trial difficulties as evidence of naval incompetence. Several such front-page news stories brought public attention to the question of naval research administrative organization.

Although Eggert constantly argued that basic hydrodynamic theory needed more work, Bureau Chiefs Rock and Emory Land concentrated their efforts on the problem of the facility and sought a solution through building new equipment. In a very explicit fashion, the engineering viewpoint and the scientific viewpoint led to two slightly different emphases on how to solve the problem. For the scientists, theory needed to be improved, and such improvements, when applied, would lead to breakthroughs in design. Inadequate equipment was an annoyance that sometimes stood in the way of developing better theory. For those with an engineering viewpoint, improvement in equipment would allow for the needed accuracy of testing. The advantage of the latter viewpoint was that it led to practical and achievable bureaucratic solutions. Money could produce new equipment on a schedule. However, getting the money would require political know-how and connections. The promotion of Land to bureau chief in 1933 had come at an opportune time for the new basin fight.

Land Takes Charge

Admiral Land, a 1903 Naval Academy graduate, was hardly typical of the intellectually elite Construction Corps. A colorful figure who was both the delight and despair of journalists, Land had been a football hero at the Academy. He was constantly in the news throughout his career. President Theodore Roosevelt had personally delivered Land's Academy commission on graduation to his hospital bedside as he recov-

Admiral Emory S. Land.   In this 1936 photo, Land wore the full dress uniform of Rear Admiral, while serving as Chief of the Bureau of Construction and Repair.

Naval Historical Center

ered from a football injury. A cousin of Charles Lindbergh, Land acted as family representative in aspects of the famous kidnapping case. In the 1930s Land astounded the press by walking, rather than riding, to and from work daily, a round trip of perhaps six miles. Usually smoking a pipe, he was a photogenic officer, with bright, alert eyes, clenched chin, sharp features, and steely-gray hair. His salty vocabulary often made his off-hand remarks about organized labor or advocates of disarmament unprintable by 1930s standards. Journalists even found Land's after-dinner speeches at staid organizations such as engineering societies and shipowners associations worthy of national coverage for his outspoken opinions and sometimes controversial positions.[9]

In 1933 Land mounted an intensive lobbying campaign through his wide contacts in private scientific, engineering, and commercial sectors, urging Secretary of the Interior Harold Ickes to place a model basin construction project on the public works budget. R. L. Hague, at Land's urging, secured time on the agenda of the 1933 American Steamship Owners Association to obtain an endorsement of the project and then used the resolution of the association to pressure Ickes. H. G. Smith, president of the National Council of the American Shipbuilders Association, attempted to visit Ickes, but had to settle for relaying his opinions by mail via Ickes's secretary, Fred Marx. SNAME adopted a resolution favoring a new basin at its November 1931 meeting, and Land revived that resolution in 1933 to get leverage with various members, urging them, in turn, to contact Ickes. Other individuals tapped by Land for support included John Warner, general manager of the Society of Automotive Engineers, H. I. Cone of the advisory committee to the U.S. Shipping Board, H. Gerrish Smith, secretary-treasurer of SNAME, and Jerome Hunsaker, former basin staff member under Taylor and later serving as president of the Institute of Aeronautical Sciences.[10]

Land anticipated difficulties with Ickes, because he sensed a general "feeling that the Navy has had perhaps an undue share of public works appropriation," through NIRA funding of shipbuilding. He suggested to his correspondents that they "stress the national character" of the new basin and its value to private shipping interests more than its military necessity. Some of those Land approached were lukewarm in support, and a few institutions and agencies refused his entreaties. Nevertheless, the organized letter campaign through the fall of 1933 did include some impressive figures in shipping and related industries.

As part of his effort to stress the practical, private side of the new basin, Land argued that the basin was not intended for pure research. He pointed out that the recently completed 2,000-foot basin at Langley Field was designed and operated particularly for research, but he commented that the function of the Navy's new basin would be "one of experimentation and development in contradistinction to research." Land was politically astute enough to recognize that the Public Works Administration would not have supported the expenditure of several million dollars for a research facility, especially if there was the slightest possibility that the expenditure represented a duplication of effort. When construed as an effort to assist private shipping, however, "experimentation and development" might win support.[11]

Despite his intensive efforts and the support of key groups like SNAME, Land did not succeed in convincing Ickes of the propriety of including the basin in the NIRA public works projects. Land may have been correct in his assumption that because NIRA funding of naval shipbuilding had already drawn unfavorable comments, the timing was poor for another naval expenditure from the civilian employment program no matter how carefully phrased as an effort to stimulate private experimentation. Ickes, with President Franklin Roosevelt's agreement, refused the model basin project.

In a more fundamental sense, the 1933 campaign for a new model basin was doomed by the political atmosphere. Despite hints of international difficulties, such as the recent Japanese takeover of Manchuria, isolationist and antiarmaments feelings ran strong. Congressional investigations would soon begin looking into the cause of American entry in World War I. A special congressional committee under Senator Gerald Nye held hearings beginning in 1934 that resulted in new neutrality legislation and attested to the widespread nature of such sentiments. "Munitions makers" and shipping interests in the private sector had been singled out as a crucial influence in preventing true neutrality during 1914–1916 by the Nye investigation; a model basin supported by major shipbuilders could hardly bring wide popular support in such an antibusiness and antipreparedness political atmosphere. Within a few years, however, events in the Far East and in Europe would bring a slight but significant shift in popular and congressional attitudes.

Land turned to Congress, mounting a new campaign. As a part of his effort to secure political support for the new basin, Land hit on the idea of naming the basin after David Taylor, who had been partially paralyzed by a stroke in 1931. Taylor's name was well known to the younger generation of naval architects and engineers who had gone to work during the 1920s and 1930s, not only because of his naval work, but because of the wide circulation of his 1910 work presenting the standard series of ship forms, used by ship designers all over the world as a database. The "Taylor Series" information served as handbook data and Taylor had been recognized as a founding father of hydrodynamics in the United States. In 1931 Taylor was awarded the John Fritz Medal by four major engineering societies, placing him in the distinguished company of former medalists including Lord Kelvin, Thomas Edison, Orville Wright, and Herbert Hoover.[12]

By construing the new model basin as a monument to Taylor, Land could appeal to ship designers both inside and outside the Navy to lend their support to a special congressional appropriation. The idea caught on, and in letters of support written through 1936, a wide range of advocates of the new basin referred to it as the "David Taylor Model Basin" prior to any official decision so designating it. On 13 April 1936, Land secured President Roosevelt's endorsement of the name, and the title became official with an announcement by Secretary of the Navy Claude Swanson on 13 May 1937, and formally implemented 5 October 1937, with a naval Executive Order.

As he worked for passage of a special appropriation to fund the basin, Land once again called on a range of engineering, shipping, and pro-Navy supporters to bring pressure on Congress. Land claimed that the basin proposal "had about the best backing of any project ever presented to Congress," including "every branch of the Government in any way concerned with ships or aircraft, practically all technical societies in the United States interested in ships or shipping, the Public Parks Commission and the Fine Arts Commission." Coupling arguments from science, technology, and national pride with the emotional appeal of honoring Taylor, Land had worked strenuously to win the necessary funds.[13]

In his memoirs, Land noted his personal satisfaction that he had won the fight before retiring from the bureau post to take up membership on the newly formed Maritime Commission. On his file copy of the press release announcing the approved name and its rationale, Land noted with evident pride, "My final act as Chief Constructor."[14]

But it was the changing climate of opinion, as much as Land's lobbying tactics, that accounts for the success of the effort in 1936. Advocates of a stronger Navy had succeeded in launching a shipbuilding effort, and a variety of recent world events made early 1936 a more auspicious time for a degree of preparedness than 1933. In 1934 Japan renounced the terms of the 1922 Washington Naval Treaty, and when the United States refused to grant warship parity at a London conference on the topic, Japan withdrew from the conference on 15 January 1936. The agreement, signed in March by Britain, France, and the United States, while continuing the principle of limitation of warship construction, provided "escape clauses" that in effect brought the effort at naval limitation to an end. In October 1935, Italian forces invaded Ethiopia, and on 7 March 1936, Germany reoccupied the Rhineland, a demilitarized zone since the Versailles treaty.

While all such events were distant, they nevertheless made headlines in the United States. Advocates of a stronger Navy, like Representative Carl Vinson of Georgia, succeeded in obtaining authorization for an expanded fleet in 1934, although appropriation of major funds did not come through until 1938. Despite such setbacks for those who argued for a stronger defense, Congress considered and passed a variety of bills in 1936 with preparedness aspects, including legislation providing for nationalization of the National Guard in an emergency, and a Merchant Marine bill that provided subsidies for shipbuilders who would design freighters to meet military specifications.

In early 1936, at Land's urging, and with the endorsement of the Secretary of the Navy, Vinson introduced a separate bill (H.R. 10135) authorizing $3 million for "the construction of a model basin on 55 acres of land, more or less, in the vicinity of Cabin John, Maryland." The House Committee on Naval Affairs altered the bill, allowing more flexibility in the selection of a site—"at a cost not to exceed $100,000 in the vicinity of Washington, D.C." [15]

The bill passed the House without debate. Senate approval took longer, with Senators Millard Tydings of Maryland and Thomas J. Walsh of Montana arguing strongly in its favor. They pointed to the decrepit condition of the old basin, to European advances in model basin work, to the cost advantages of model testing in general, and to the need for "scientific construction" in both commercial and naval shipbuilding. Following the principles from EMB, Public Law No. 568 noted that "experiments may be made at this establishment for private parties, who shall defray the cost thereof." The appropriation of $3 million was approved 27 April 1937, supplemented the next year by an additional appropriation of $500,000. In an apparent concession to army and NACA concerns about the Navy's deep involvement in aerodynamic research, both appropriations specifically prohibited expenditures for research except in surface and subsurface vessels, thereby excluding wind tunnel work from the new construction. However, aerodynamic research remained on the agenda of the laboratory, and wind tunnels were added under later appropriations. [16]

Construction Planning

During the period that Rock and Land had worked on the political effort to secure funding, both through Ickes's office and later through

Congress, planning of the specific details of a new basin went forward in Eggert's staff in a group under the direction of Harold E. Saunders.

Harold Saunders graduated from the Naval Academy in 1912, after an outstanding academic performance there in which he earned the highest scholastic record since that of David Taylor. Perhaps in tribute, he earned from his classmates the nickname "Savvy." In 1914, he took postgraduate training in naval architecture at the Academy and at MIT, earning the master of science degree in 1917. During the 1920s, he served with the Bureau of Construction and Repair as head of the submarine design and construction section. In 1929, he transferred to the Washington Navy Yard, as assistant to Eggert at EMB. It was on this tour of duty that Saunders first developed the preliminary plans and detailed specifications for the proposed new basin. By the fall of 1933, Saunders supplied Eggert with detailed plans for carriages and tracks of the new basin, and the plans were ready to turn over to navy yard or private contractors to convert into working plans, should the funding come through Ickes's office. After sea duty as Force Constructor with the Battle Force, U.S. Fleet, Saunders served as liaison officer between the Bureau of Construction and Repair and the model basin. In 1939, he was promoted to the rank of captain, at that time, the youngest captain in the Navy. He remained in the liaison post overseeing construction and design through the completion of the model basin.

Many of the details of Saunders's original 1929–1933 plans were kept and used later. The new carriages were to be triangular in shape when viewed from above, with the base of the triangle on one track and the apex on the other. The carriages were to be driven by four driving wheels on the base side, propelled by hydraulic gear. An alternating current motor would run the hydraulic pressure pump. This arrangement would allow for smooth propulsion without the necessity of a direct current motor and its required electric substation.[17]

Saunders later specifically credited Eggert with insisting that the planning for the new basin be based on a thorough understanding of the difficulties inherent in the older basin. As a consequence, the early plans reflected what Saunders called fundamental requirements:

- Firm and unyielding foundation, preferably bedrock
- Several basins, each with separate function
- Basins long enough to allow eight-second constant velocity runs
- Space for 100 percent expansion in fifty years
- Adequate freshwater supply
- Easy access from Navy offices in Washington[18]

Another retained feature of the 1933 plan was a system for very precisely calculated leveling of the tracks, accounting even for the slight

Captain Harold E. Saunders. Saunders set demanding standards for the planned new model basin to replace EMB at the Washington Navy Yard.

Carderock Site of New Model Basin.   The setting for the new model basin met stringent requirements for close proximity to Washington, D.C., with good water supply and level ground both visible from this aerial photo of the open meadow that was chosen.

curvature of the earth over the length of the basin, and the consequent minute curvature of the water surface. To achieve the desired precision, Eggert estimated in 1931 that laying and adjusting the tracks would require about one year. This particular feature, and the nearly absolute precision it implied, became one that Saunders carefully documented and one that would fascinate and attract journalists and public relations officers in future decades. The precision of the track laying would nicely symbolize the contrast between the older navy yard basin and the accuracy and scale of the new one. But the significance of the precision was not simply symbolic; the care given to the precision of the new equipment directly addressed the central problem of the predictive work of model testing. As men with a scientific orientation designed their own equipment, they pushed accuracy to the limits that were possible at the time; their foresight would help determine the type of research conducted at the new basin for decades to come.[19]

In the Bureau of Yards and Docks, specific architectural plans were put together under the leadership of Commander Ben Moreell. His design called for a long rectangular basin building running east and west, covered by a barrel arch roof with a 110-foot span. The arches would be hinged at the base of each arch to allow for expansion and contraction. The windowless basin area could lead to better climate control.[20]

The large structure would house four basins. The high-speed basin was originally planned to be 1,600 feet long, 21 feet wide, and 10 feet deep. Later limitations of funding required the length to be cut to 1,168 feet. A deep-water basin would be 693 feet long, 51 feet wide, and 22 feet deep, capable of handling large models with minimal wall and tank-bottom effect. During the final stages of planning, this basin was lengthened to 963 feet. A 303-foot-long shallow-water turning basin at the west end would allow for maneuvering tests impossible at the old basin. In addition, the shallow-water basin, with a 10-foot depth that could be drained for specific lower depth runs, would meet the need for commercial and naval river and canal vessel testing.[21]

Carderock Model Basin Construction. One of the reasons Harold Saunders chose the Carderock site in 1937 for the new model basin was the firm bedrock strata immediately below the ground surface.

Moreell also designed a three-story combination office-laboratory-shop building to be built next to, and connecting with, the basin structure. In planning the facade and other details of this facility, Moreell conformed to what a later generation has designated the art moderne variant of art deco, often associated with the 1939 World's Fair structures and other massive public work projects in Europe and the United States in the period. His designs won him an Association of Federal Architects' award, and the final structure has remained a classic example of the style.[22]

After congressional passage of the funding authorization, a site selection committee headed by Saunders looked into more than twenty sites and settled on a flat meadowland of about 107 acres in Carderock, Maryland. The location met the requirements for firm bedrock, a relatively level terrain, nearby water supply, and accessibility from downtown Washington. The site had further advantages: it was more than twenty feet above the flood stage of the Potomac, it was secluded from industrial development which might cause vibration or smoke and noise, yet the area was convenient to residential areas northwest of Washington in Bethesda, Chevy Chase, and Glen Echo. Furthermore, Saunders noted, there was plenty of room for future expansion. The years of cramped quarters at the navy yard had given Eggert and Saunders an unusual degree of foresight regarding the restrictions imposed by limited space.[23]

Groundbreaking took place 8 September 1937, and Saunders continued to head the team from the navy yard model basin to represent the Bureau of Construction and Repair during the construction. Saunders was well aware of the parallels between his own role in planning and direction of the work and that of Taylor in constructing the original model basin at the navy yard. During construction, Saunders reminded members of SNAME that "about four years elapsed from the time that the first appropriation was made for the present Washington Tank until the first model was towed. While it is now possible to accomplish many building operations more expeditiously than was formerly the case, the increasingly severe modern specification requirements more than compensate for this feature."[24]

Despite such disclaimers, the work moved along at a steady clip, partly because in the case of the new basin, detailed advance planning had taken place before the first appropriation, whereas Taylor had started detailed plans only after congressional approval. The construction of the basins, the arched building covering the basins, and the connecting office-shop-laboratory building was completed less than two years after groundbreaking, by June 1939. The track-laying and leveling procedure began in March 1939 and continued for fifteen months

Photo by Captain Harold Saunders

Carderock Model Basin Walls. June 1938, contractors Potts and Callahan use rock from the site excavation to fill the walls of the new basin ahead of the arched frame for the basin roof.

through the late summer of 1940, while testing machines and other equipment were installed in the laboratory building.

A formal dedication was held during these stages of final construction, 4 November 1939, after completion of landscaping. The occasion served as a kind of reunion of Navy Department employees who had worked with Taylor, as well as the current staff of EMB. Taylor himself attended, confined to a wheelchair; within a year he would be dead.

While 4 November 1939 is usually taken as the date of formal opening of the David Taylor Model Basin (DTMB), the actual transition of equipment, personnel, and projects from EMB to the new site was a more drawn-out process lasting from early 1939 through 1941. Wind tunnel work continued at the navy yard until 1943, when equipment and staff were transferred to the new facility.

During the period from early 1939 through late 1940, Saunders and his group worked constantly at Carderock to ensure accurate construction to specifications. The original 1930 specifications had called for tolerances of 0.005 inch in the track leveling and alignment; during

Ceremony When Laying First Rail, 1939. Saunders insisted on a high
degree of precision in laying the rails which would carry the model basin carriage.

installation, Saunders upgraded the allowable tolerance to 0.002 inch.
He and his group devised a number of methods to attain that accuracy
over the long stretches of rail, and developed for each alignment
method several alternative checks and verifications.[25]

One of the means of checking the level of the tracks was to float a
"leveling bridge" in the basin, with a micrometer set to first level the
chair or metal base, then to level the final track. Every effort was made
to prevent waves in the basin that would disturb the floating bridge,
through closing off outside ventilation, limiting nearby construction traffic, and even prohibiting walking on portions of the basin wall. These
measures reduced wave motion in the basins to 0.001 inch while leveling
was in progress.[26]

The towing equipment incorporated other innovations in technology. The carriages, with 4-inch-diameter tubular frames, reflected a
novel method of joining tube members, with 10-inch spherical joints taking up to ten different angled tubes. The advantage of this method was
that it allowed right-angle cuts on tube ends and thus reduced the

David Taylor Model Basin Completion, 1939. With the model basin complete, and connected laboratory-office structure to the right, the extensive grounds had not yet been landscaped.

amount of precision cutting and welding on the connected tubular structural members.[27]

To check that the weight of the carriages was distributed evenly, short sections of each track were designed as weighing scales. The towing carriage and dynamometer allowed for towage in either direction with only minor adjustments. As in the original basin, the linkage and recording device for the dynamometer were kept clean and simple to reduce error.

The hydraulic motors allowed for stopping the carriage by "regenerative braking." When the controls were moved to a lower speed indicator, the hydraulic motors would act as pumps, the hydraulic pumps would act as motors, the electric motors would act as generators, and electric power would be "pumped" back into the line. Two mechanical back-up braking systems served in case of electrical or hydraulic failure.[28]

New and relocated equipment came from several sources. The model-making methods used at the old basin were continued, with a new press for clamping the glued blocks of wood together. Pieces of

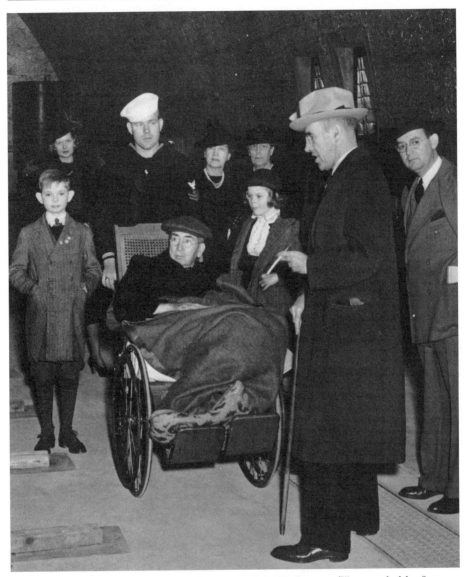

Dedication, 4 November 1939. David W. Taylor, age 75, attended by family members at the dedication of new basin, named in his honor as the David Taylor Model Basin.

equipment from EMB moved to the new facility included the 12-inch variable-pressure water tunnel and a 600,000-pound universal testing machine. A new 27-inch variable-pressure water tunnel built at EES for propeller testing was also transferred to the new facility (later modified to 24-inch).[29]

Facade of the DTMB Main Building.   Facing a broad open greensward, here dusted with snow, the striking art moderne design by naval engineer Ben Moreell won a Federal Architects' Award.

Towing Basin Carriage.   The DTMB towing carriages were constructed of 4-inch tubular sections, connected by 10-inch hollow spherical joints making an extremely rigid structure.

To an unusual extent, various parts of the new basin were built and tested first on a model or sample scale. A 1:4 scale model of the concrete arch basin roof was tested at the navy yard in 1934. Pilot testing of chairs and rails was done in the new laboratory building at Carderock. A balsa wood and airplane-glue model of a towing carriage was constructed at 1:48 scale, to assist in estimating the rigidity of the complex three-dimensional shape.[30]

The precision of test-equipment construction struck members of the naval architect profession as unusual, but fascinating for the opportunities it opened and the questions it raised. Simply put, ship hydrodynamics had been haunted by a recurrent problem: were inconsistencies in data attributable to hydrodynamic sources or to mechanical sources? As in many physical sciences, instrumentation was crucial, but in hydrodynamic experimentation with models, the problem was especially severe. On some experiments, very small mechanical irregularities could multiply into large errors when taken to full scale. By reducing the variations in mechanical forces to a known and defined minimum, the possibility for isolating hydrodynamic causes for variation was heightened. The new basin squarely faced these difficulties and offered the promise of a new level of predictive accuracy.[31]

Saunders described the problem at the old basin when working with two nearly identical models or with successive changes on a single model. "In many cases we were forced literally to throw up our hands on particular problems, not knowing whether the changes were due to changes in the model or were the result of vagaries of the track or the carriage or the dynamometer."

Nevertheless, Saunders claimed, he looked at the old basin equipment "quite reverently." In 1940 he pointed out, "Very few instruments of precision are still in use which were designed and placed in operation as far as four decades back." Saunders' work had a similar longevity. His own equipment, first planned in 1929 and then installed in 1939, remained in operation well over four decades later. Although the architectural design of the outside structure would convey to a later eye many subtle echoes of the 1930s, the basic equipment of the basin would meet the "high-tech" standard of the late twentieth century.[32]

Eggert and Saunders had established that the details of the instrumentation of the new facility would be designed by the naval architects themselves. In the Navy system that practice was itself very rare—ships were used by line officers and sailors but designed and supplied by the procurement bureaus; shore facilities used by those bureaus were built by Yards and Docks. The Navy's organizational division into "providers" and "consumers" had operated as a kind of miniature check-and-balance system. David Taylor had participated in the design of the navy yard basin, but in site choice and construction, he had yielded to Congress and to Yards and Docks. Worthington had fought architect Ernest Flagg and the contractors every step of the way in the completion of EES in 1904–1908. But in the case of the new model basin, the ultimate users had wrested control of location, design of equipment, and confirmation of accuracy into their own hands. Saunders and Eggert took full advantage of that circumstance to create the ideal model basin at the very limits of achievable accuracy.

Saunders was appointed the first technical director of the DTMB in 1940 and served in that capacity through World War II. In 1946, he was appointed director of the model basin, retiring in 1949. Like Taylor, Saunders was a naval officer who combined administrative and technical excellence. He wrote some forty papers and reports in the field of naval architecture, and the first two volumes of his work, *The Hydrodynamics of Ship Design,* were published by the Society of Naval Architects and Marine Engineers. Like Taylor, he remained active in retirement, serving in the American Towing Tank Conference and the International Towing Tank Conference. He was the American representative to the standing committee of the International Towing Tank Conference, 1954–1960. Saunders's influence at the new model basin would be as profound as that of Taylor at the old EMB. Over the decade 1929–1939, Saunders played the key role in planning, design, and construction, and in the years 1939–1947 as technical director and then director, he, like Taylor before him, was an inspiring leader whose personal achievements in the discipline won him respect from his staff and colleagues as well as from the wider profession.

New Command—The Creation of the Bureau of Ships

Simultaneously with the final construction of the new basin, Congress considered proposals from the Secretary of the Navy to reorganize naval administration. The bureau system, created in 1842, had become severely dated by the twentieth century. The Bureau of Construction and Repair had been created by the original act in 1842; the Bureau of Steam Engineering had been added in 1862, and renamed the Bureau of Engineering in 1920. As ships incorporated industrial technology through the period of New Navy expansion, the Bureau of Construction and Repair concentrated more and more on overall hull and ship design, while other procurement or "provider" bureaus concentrated on other elements. Engineering provided propulsion units, drive and propeller systems, and auxiliary machinery while Ordnance concentrated on armor and weapons.

The need to coordinate such diverse functions had been apparent with the birth of the New Navy. Secretary of the Navy William Chandler recommended in 1883 uniting the two bureaus into a "single Bureau of Naval Construction." Similar recommendations were made in 1886 by Admiral of the Navy David Porter, in 1899 by Secretary of the Navy John D. Long, and in 1909 by Secretary of the Navy Truman Newberry. Newberry effected a practical and working unification of the two bureaus by appointing Washington L. Capps to head both, but Newberry was overruled by Congress.[33]

Each bureau continued to develop its own budget; the Secretary of the Navy's annual report to Congress represented a compilation of bureau chief reports; and each bureau chief held his appointment from Congress. Under such conditions, the bureaus acted as separate, nearly independent, entities. Bureau chiefs, expert in their own areas and supported by a large group of technical staff members, were responsible only to the civilian Secretary of the Navy, who rarely had the knowledge or willingness to challenge their power.

With the creation of the Bureau of Aeronautics, the Navy had moved to a new approach more adapted to the increasing technical complexity of modern weaponry, which pointed up the continuing diverse, complex, and outmoded nature of the administrative arrangement in ship procurement. With the creation of a separate Bureau of Aeronautics, research and perfection of various elements continued to be handled at facilities managed by existing bureaus, but Aeronautics provided funding and coordination. Thus, through the 1920s and 1930s, EES continued to work on aircraft engine components, and EMB tested seaplane floats in the basins and wing and body shapes in the wind tunnels. In effect, both laboratories worked "on contract" for the Bureau of Aeronautics. Nevertheless, Aeronautics set a precedent for a logical, coordinated approach to the procurement of craft. Although Aeronautics had shown one way to modernized procurement, the design of warships continued another seventeen years under the divided system that had survived all critics since the 1880s.

Rear Admiral Harold Bowen, head of the Bureau of Engineering, agreed that reform was needed. As an advocate of increasing the operating pressure and temperature of steam turbines during the 1930s, Bowen believed that the bureau arrangement as constituted gave too much power to those who wished to prevent change. "Naturally," he said, "there were a lot of people out looking for my scalp." The system itself allowed "mossbacks" to dominate, in his view. In particular, Bowen found his objectives opposed by William DuBose, Chief of the Bureau of Construction and Repair, and some of Bowen's own officers, such as Ormond Cox at the Engineering Station. The General Board as well as an interbureau Board of Inspection and Survey also worked against Bowen's ideas in new technology. Support for his own positions came from Assistant Secretary of the Navy Charles Edison and some of the junior officers in Engineering, together with a few fleet engineers and commanding officers who served aboard some of the more efficient, but still experimental, high-pressure turbine-driven vessels. Bowen believed that the bureau system allowed for the perpetuation of old systems; he hoped that unification of the two bureaus would consolidate power over shipbuilding and ship design into one forward-looking organization. He hoped to head that organization himself.[34]

Even before any formally structured internal merger of the two ship bureaus, Engineering and Construction and Repair cooperated on a wide variety of minor questions, sending each other reports and setting up systems of automatic exchange of project lists between the laboratories. After 1928 EES sent detailed monthly reports to Construction and Repair; similarly, EMB sent its reports of work on hand to Engineering. Other forms of low-level coordination and cooperation were common: EMB tested propellers for Engineering throughout the 1930s, and EES supplied Construction and Repair with copies of its technical reports on a regular basis.[35]

Yet, on many crucial issues, specialists in the two bureaus would disagree. In 1934, for example, Bureau of Engineering designers attributed vibration on *Farragut* to the propeller and insisted on substitution of a new design. Eggert, at Construction and Repair's model basin, suggested to Schade of Engineering's design division that the vibration probably derived from the shaft itself. The two bureaus often disagreed on smaller problems such as stern design and rudder strength.[36]

Reasonable disagreements arose out of the overlapping responsibility for ship design. But when engineering and design issues were expressed and held by strong personalities, each advocating what he viewed as the best interests of the Navy and the nation, public controversy became almost inevitable. A series of problems with some of the new ships built in the 1930s brought public attention to the need for even closer cooperation between the two bureaus. In fact, many of the problems with the ships had more to do with other causes, such as the inadequacy of model testing, experimentation with new designs, increased use of auxiliary equipment and heavier ordnance, and the inexperience of shipyard workers with warship construction, brought on by the long hiatus in naval construction during the 1920s. Yet press and public seized on ship defects through the late 1930s as proof of scandalously poor naval administration.

In 1938 the General Board reviewed several matters of controversy, including not only Bowen's concern with the rate at which the Navy converted to high-temperature, high-pressure steam turbines, but more specialized problems with cracked sternposts and excessive rolling of heavy cruisers, defective ground tackle on the *Brooklyn* (CL 40) class of light cruisers, and a variety of engine problems in diesel submarines and steam-driven turbines. The twenty-eight ships in the *Mahan* (DD 364) class of destroyers seemed particularly plagued with difficulties, including cracked deck plating, structural weakness, and leaking "cone-shaped" joints in high-pressure steam lines. Bowen later recalled in his memoirs that the criticism focused on "gadgets" used on the *Mahan* class. Bowen believed that the great variety of problems partly derived from the haste with which the ships were constructed in order to demonstrate increased employment during the depth of the Depression. Even the normally reserved *New York Times*, however, simply treated such difficulties as hints of defective naval administration and "red tape."[37]

The situation that drew the most public and congressional unfavorable attention to the two bureaus also surfaced in 1938. The so-called top-heavy destroyers presented a set of problems that could be rather readily solved; yet the press seized on the fact that two bureaus had failed to coordinate—one building the hull, and a second building the equipment leading to ships that were unstable. This illustrated, in the eyes of the press and Congress, a simple administrative problem, with an apparently simple solution. Rather than completely reviewing and reanalyzing the whole complex structure of naval administration, Congress could order the two bureaus merged, leaving further naval organizational reforms to a later period.

The thirty-five vessels in the *Anderson* (DD 411) class of destroyers incorporated a design flaw, which could be corrected only by more heavily weighting the keel, thus reducing operating speed. Because of equipment, the ships of the *Anderson* class were top heavy—that is, their metacentric heights and their centers of gravity were too close. Although the ships were not, as the public came to believe, on the verge of capsizing, their stability was reduced when they ran low on fuel oil or on ammunition and other stores.

Through 1938 and 1939 the press converted the engineering problem into a search for responsibility. Gibbs and Cox, the design firm responsible for *Anderson*, had warned as early as 1934 that the ships would lack stability unless modified. Construction and Repair, which held responsibility for coordinating structure and content of the ships, had de-

cided against modification. As a consequence of the publicity surrounding earlier delays in construction, Secretary of the Navy Claude Swanson
ordered Assistant Secretary Charles Edison to serve as "coordinator of
shipbuilding" on 31 March 1938; in this new position, Edison had to
take personal charge of the problem of the top-heavy or overweight destroyers by early 1939.

Edison took several steps. The first was to transfer DuBose from his
position as Chief of the Bureau of Construction and Repair. Then, in
August 1939, he ordered the consolidation of the design divisions of
Engineering and Construction and Repair. On the death of Secretary
Swanson, Edison assumed the duties of Secretary, and appointed Rear
Admiral Samuel M. Robinson as both Chief of the Bureau of
Engineering and to take over Edison's own newly assigned task as coor-
dinator of shipbuilding. As part of that responsibility, Edison also asked
Robinson to head a committee to study the merger of the two design di-
visions. That special board, with Edison's blessing, went beyond its origi-
nal mandate to review the merger of the design divisions and recommended a full merger of the two bureaus. The recommendation from
the board had the support of both bureau chiefs, Robinson in
Engineering and Van Keuren in Construction and Repair.

Edison then authorized Van Keuren and Robinson to work closely
together, merging planning groups and units over the period between
September 1939 and mid-1940. The new conciliatory relationship between the two bureaus could be attributed to the fact that Edison had
handpicked the two bureau chiefs with the idea of cooperation and consolidation in mind. Furthermore, the outbreak of World War II in
Europe, 1 September 1939, added a degree of urgency to all preparedness work in the United States; in itself, the war crisis could provide a rationale for improved efficiency and the sacrifice of tradition.

Robinson, Van Keuren, and Edison testified before Congress several times in late 1939 and early 1940 in favor of fully merging the two
bureaus. Although Edison argued that the top-heavy destroyer issue
raised in committee was a false one, he accepted the congressional endorsement of reorganization as something that was very practical and
that could readily be done in the direction of administrative reform.

One issue that concerned Congress and the naval officers involved
was exactly how to merge the two different naval professions of naval architect and naval engineer. The Construction Corps, with its architects,
was a small, elite force, drawn from the top two or three Academy graduates each year. Corps officers received graduate scientific training, either
in Europe or at the naval architecture program started by William
Hovgaard at MIT. Always designated "CC" after their rank, such officers

were excluded from sea duty. By contrast, naval engineers had been merged with line officers in 1900, in pay, in promotion opportunity, and in obligation to perform sea duty. With the creation of Engineering Duty Only (EDO) status in 1916, they were excluded from ship command positions, but, nevertheless, all served tours at sea.

Some engineers, like Bowen, were concerned that their group included many officers with only marginal engineering training; however, the highest ranking engineers had often served not only on board ships and in navy yard and private shipyard inspection duties but also at EES, which had provided a great many of those who rose to the top with an informal stage of postgraduate research education. Exactly how to ensure that the office of chief of the new bureau would rotate between the two types of professions, and how to merge them comfortably in the new bureau, absorbed many hours of congressional hearing and much soul searching. The eventual outcome exposed naval architects to the requirement of sea duty. The separate elite Construction Corps was abolished in the new arrangement.

By June 1940 Congress approved the creation of the new bureau. Edison appointed Robinson Chief of the Bureau of Ships, with Van Keuren as assistant chief. Bowen received appointment as director of the Naval Research Laboratory, which was separated entirely from its former connection with the Bureau of Engineering. Bowen believed that Edison's dismissal of DuBose had been an appropriate step, and a proper reprimand to the "mossbacks." He remained bitter because, as a leading proponent of reorganization, he believed he should head up the new bureau. Of course, the creation of the Bureau of Ships was also supported by a wide variety of naval officers, many of whom did not share his contentious style. Those who had worked most diplomatically through 1939 and 1940 to effect the merger, Robinson and Van Keuren, were appropriately enough chosen to administer the new bureau.

Modernized Equipment, Merged Bureaus

New schedules of work at EES and at DTMB through 1939 and 1940 reflected the joint administration, even before the Bureau of Ships was officially in place. The combined design divisions began to set priorities, in effect coordinating the research at the two laboratories as early as the summer of 1939.

How would the merger of the small group of science-oriented naval architects into the larger community of naval engineers affect the almost clandestine efforts of some of those officers to bring theoretical research into the business of ship design? Could men like Saunders, outnumbered even in the Bureau of Construction and Repair, realistically expect to preserve a scientific emphasis in the new Bureau of Ships? The warship design priorities of 1939 left little room for the behind-the-scenes scientific research characteristic of the early 1930s.

The full consequences of the dramatic changes of 1939–1940 would not be felt for years. Over the months, while staff moved into the new facility at Carderock and designers in the two bureaus sat down together, the "Phony War" in Europe gave way to the Battle of Britain as Adolf Hitler planned Operation Sea Lion. The Navy faced the coming war years with a thoroughly modernized model basin, a large, well-staffed Engineering Experiment Station, a reshuffled administrative structure, and a fleet of relatively untried, but recently designed and engineered, ships. The demands of World War II would put to the test the ships, the facilities, and the approaches to research inherited from the interwar years.

Endnotes

1. Eggert to Chief Constructor, USN, 31 Jan 1931, NARA, RG 19, Bureau of Construction and Repair, General Correspondence 1925–1940, box 3293, NP21-(l), vol. 1.
2. Ibid.
3. H. A. Schade, Visits to Model Basin, 10 Nov 1933, NARA, RG 19, General Correspondence 1926–1942, entry 115, 51-2(1), vol. 2.
4. Schoenherr, interview by David K. Allison, 15 Apr 1985, DTNSRDC RC 6-5, acc. 84-13; Dr. Lou Landweber, interview by Seth Hawkins, 28 Oct 1983, DTNSRDC RC 6-5, acc. 84-21.
5. George Rock to Dean Cooley, 24 Jan 1931, NARA, RG 19, Bureau of Construction and Repair, General Correspondence 1925–1940, box 3293, NP21-(1), vol. 1.
6. Ibid.
7. Ibid.
8. A. H. VanKueren, Memo for Design, 18 Aug 1932; and H. A. Schade, Memo for File, 7 May 1934, NARA, RG 19, entry 115, DD348-355/S1-2.
9. Emory S. Land, *Winning the War with Ships* (New York: R. M. McBride, 1958).
10. R. L. Hague to R. J. Baker, 24 Oct 1933; H. G. Smith to T. L. Marx, 27 Oct 1933; E. Land to H. G. Smith, 16 Sep 1933; and Claude Swanson to Harold Ickes, 17 Nov 1933, NARA, RG 19, Bureau of Construction and Repair, General Correspondence 1925–1940, box 3293, NP21-(1), vol. 1.
11. E. Land to Secretary of the Navy, 4 Mar 1937, NARA, RG 19, Bureau of Construction and Repair, General Correspondence 1925–1940, box 3294, NP21-(1), vol. 2. For discussion of Langley towing tank, see Chapter 4, page113.
12. *TSNAME Special Supplement*, 1931, DTNSRDC RC 5, box 6.
13. Land had used the term "D. W. Taylor Model Basin" as early as 1933, about three years before the term was officially approved. Land to Dickinson, 25 Jul 1933; Land to Wilson Brown, 17 Mar 1936; and Land, Memo for File, 15 Mar 1937, NARA, RG 19, Bureau of Construction and Repair, General Correspondence 1925–1940, box 3294, NP21-(1), vol. 2.
14. Land, *Winning the War with Ships*; Land, Memo for File, 15 Mar 1937.
15. House Committee on Naval Affairs, *Construction of the Model Basin Establishment*: Report to Accompany H.R. 10135, 74th Cong., 2d sess., 1936, H.Rept. 2022.
16. [U.S. Congress, Senate, *Congressional Record*, 74th Cong., 2d sess., 6038–39.
17. H. A. Schade, Visit Report, 14 Oct 1933, NARA, RG 19, entry 115, General Correspondence 1926–1942, 51-2 (1), vol. 2.
18. H. E. Saunders, "The David W. Taylor Model Basin," *TSNAME* 46, pt. 1 (1939).
19. Eggert to Chief Constructor, 15 Jan 1931, NARA, RG 19, Bureau of Construction and Repair, General Correspondence 1925–1940, box 3293; Saunders, "The David W. Taylor Model Basin," *TSNAME* 46, pt. 1 (1939).
20. Saunders, "The David W. Taylor Model Basin," 315.
21. Ibid., 312–315.
22. Ibid., 311.
23. Ibid., 309.

24. Ibid., 318.
25. H. E. Saunders, "The David W. Taylor Model Basin," *TSNAME* 48, pt. 2 (1939): 48, 178.
26. Ibid.
27. Ibid., 184.
28. Ibid., 184–185.
29. Ibid., 187.
30. Ibid., 187–191.
31. Ibid.; Comments by Professor Kenneth S. M. Davidson, Commander Hugo Fischer, 206–208.
32. Comments by Saunders, 208–209; comments by Davidson and Fischer.
33. Historical Section, Bureau of Ships, *An Administrative History of the Bureau of Ships During World War II* (MS), 17–21.
34. H. G. Bowen, *Ships, Machinery, and Mossbacks* (Princeton, NJ: Princeton University Press, 1954), 120.
35. EMB Monthly Reports are in NARA, RG 19, entry 115, NY5 51-2, vols. 1–3; EES Monthly Reports are in WNRC, RG 19, entry 993, NP16/L5.
36. Schade, Visits to Model Basin, 10 Nov 1933, NARA, RG 19, entry 115, General Correspondence 1926–1942, 51-2(1), vol. 2.
37. Bowen, *Ships, Machinery, and Mossbacks*, 63; *New York Times*, 4 Nov 1930, A1.

CHAPTER 6

R&D in War and Peace

ALTHOUGH WORLD WAR II SERVED AS A turning point in the development of U.S. technology and science, concentration on the transformations that occurred should not obscure the continuities from the late 1930s through the late 1940s. Many things stayed the same at both the Engineering Experiment Station and the David Taylor Model Basin. Most of the prewar types of work and the internal departmental divisions remained in place, with some significant additions, between 1939 and 1949. Individual personnel continued—much of the senior staff in 1939 was still on board in 1949. Bela Ronay continued to head the welding group at EES. Karl Schoenherr and Louis Landweber were still at the model basin, and Dwight Windenberg remained in charge of Structural Mechanics.

The growth and striking changes of the war and postwar years can be held in better perspective if viewed against that context of persistent institutional settings and continuing personal careers. The most outwardly obvious change was a spectacular growth of facilities and staff at the model basin. Harold Saunders and a succession of commanding officers secured funding for over $13 million in additional construction. Unlike much of the rapid construction of buildings elsewhere during the war—a period noted for temporary housing developments, hastily constructed industrial plants and shipyards that would become decaying and rusting relics within two decades—some of the new facilities at the model basin met the same exacting standards of quality and permanence as the first basin building there. Many of the war-built facilities at DTMB continued to provide good service for decades.

With the new structures and equipment came a vastly increased civilian staff that soon crowded even the offices and laboratories to capacity. The number of civilian personnel grew from 200 in 1940 to 870 by the end of the war, 1,050 by 1946, and about 1,200 by 1949. Facilities drew staff; together they drew new types of work; added categories of research, in turn, justified more staff. That circular explanation of growth, however, gives little clue to the fundamental changes in the nature of the research or the continued success of the model basin.[1]

By 1949 the model basin had become one of the new "Big Science" institutions, alongside the laboratories of the Atomic Energy Commission, the burgeoning university laboratories, and the massive research centers of private industry. Together with such institutions, the Navy's own research laboratories had become a part of the war's legacy to the postwar generation. The growth of civilian staff was not simply quantitative—DTMB had taken on a new character, at once less military and more dedicated to the dictates of the disciplines of its civilian staff. By the end of the decade, members of DTMB staff took up a surprisingly wide range of fundamental research questions. No longer a job shop for the design division of the Bureau of Ships, DTMB became a research institution, taking on projects that frequently went well beyond questions of immediate naval application.

This transformation of mission became quite explicit. More important, from the perspective of later years, was the Navy's own postwar recognition of the basin's role as a research and development institution. The underlying causes of the changeover lay in the new national regard for scientific research between 1940 and 1946. The basin's conversion to a research laboratory can be seen as a case study of the impact of underlying national change; it demonstrated exactly how that broader development, noted by historians on a level of national policy, worked itself out in a local setting in the lives and careers of individuals.

The national emphasis on scientific research and the view that the advances of science had to precede the advances of technology—reflected in the emergence of the phrase "research and development" with the explicit primacy placed upon research, tended to reduce engineering and technology to a second place after science. Earlier, before the war, the Navy and the nation as a whole had anticipated that American engineering would lead to victory if the nation entered the war. Industrial production of warships, engines, aircraft, munitions, transport equipment—all would overwhelm the enemy. But by 1946 it was easy to argue that science had also played a crucial role—radar-directed fire control, the proximity fuse, and advances in acoustic detection revolutionized sea warfare, while the use of the atomic bomb at Hiroshima and Nagasaki made it possible to believe that science had won the war. Even though such technical advances in the arts of war had derived from technological and engineering work, it was science that received much of the credit.

Many of the new ships and weapons of World War II were the result of the application of standard technological and engineering principles and the step-by-step improvement in existing equipment rather than the consequence of more purely scientific breakthroughs. Yet by war's end, the employment of scientists in the United States, Britain, and Germany in the development of new weapons had been demonstrably effective. In the United States, the marshaling of scientific talent through university contracts and through direct employment grew overnight into a large-scale enterprise, coordinated through new agencies. The scientists who headed those agencies became articulate postwar spokespersons for continued national expenditure on weapons-related scientific research. Whatever the real balance between the contributions of science and engineering may have been, during and after the war, spokespersons for science succeeded in convincing policymakers in government, the press, and the public at large that organized scientific research was essential to the national safety. National security, they argued, would require continued massive funding and support. At a national level, the case for heavy funding of science was made by men such as Vannevar Bush, James Conant, and Harold Bowen. Bush was chairman of the National Defense Research Council (NDRC) from its formation in 1940, and later headed the Office of Scientific Research and Development (OSRD). Conant was Bush's successor on NDRC. In the Navy, Bowen, who had been Chief of the Bureau of Engineering, ran the Navy's new Office of Naval Research in 1946. Even though Bowen was himself an "alumnus" of EES and had a lifetime career as a naval engineer, and although he and Bush developed a series of bitter interagency disagreements, nevertheless, Bowen, like the more prominent Bush and Conant, became a powerful and effective advocate of a concerted postwar scientific research effort. During the immediate postwar years, the leading source of federal funding for basic research was ONR.[2]

The lesson pointed out by Bush, Conant, and Bowen was clear: without vigilant mobilization of scientific talent, the United States could readily be overwhelmed by potential enemies. Bush argued that science presented an "endless frontier" to be vigorously promoted for future health, welfare, and especially the military security of the United States. The wartime matching of weapons with counterweapons, the German advances, and the nuclear weapon itself, all became pieces of evidence in their arguments for a science-based permanent arms race. As a consequence of such thinking, no longer did military policymakers believe they could achieve modernization primarily through testing commercially produced items to meet military specifications. The early mission of the Engineering Experiment Station, based on such testing, no longer held even the limited glamor that it had in 1939. The decline of EES from its prominence as the Bureau of Engineering's most important laboratory sprang not so much from the merger of the Bureau of Engineering with Construction and Repair in 1940, but rather from the decline of product testing and the rise of government-directed research and development in the military and national priorities that began in the mid-1940s.

Within a few years, the warnings of leaders like Bush, Conant, and Bowen would prove prophetic: the Soviet explosion of a nuclear device in 1949 and the launching of Sputnik in 1957 would send shock waves through the American political and public opinion structures. By the early 1960s, with the John F. Kennedy administration, the nation and its defense establishment would accept the concept of a permanent scientific arms race as essential to the survival of the nation. Militarily directed research and development had become a regular part of the national budget; the private and governmental laboratories that developed the innovations grew to gigantic proportions when compared to their pre-World War II counterparts and predecessors. Navy laboratories would not be merely little-known sites of the Navy's shore establishment. By the 1960s they would become command posts for the Navy's silent war of science and technology. With the perspective derived from such later developments, questions about the events at the two facilities in the 1940s take on heightened importance.

Some of the immediate effects of the war hardly seemed conducive to long-term research or scientific advance. Particular necessities of wartime management would adversely affect the freedoms of scientists and engineers at both facilities. The imposition of security classification would limit communication of scientists with their intellectual peers in academia and abroad, and the communication of engineers with their professional colleagues in industry. The demand for strategic materials required a structured priority system that posed problems for researchers working at the unpredictable frontiers of their disciplines. The military draft system cut into the ranks of talented civilians. The Navy reaction of enlisting many of the younger staff members and assigning them to their former civilian jobs led such scientists and technicians to temporarily take on the uniform and some of the behavior of military discipline, with all its frustrations and its unfamiliar rigidities of command structure and military courtesy. Furthermore, the war work itself tended to take both facilities away from research and toward testing: the war produced a flood of new products to be tested at EES; the shipbuild-

Operating the Towing Carriage.   *Left to right:* Grace Ann Sipes, Mildred Smith, Mary Cavanaugh, Ann Cavanaugh, Helen Burnison, and Arvella Brake. During World War II, women became an integral part of the technical work force.

ing and weapons program pushed the new facilities of DTMB to capacity—but the capacity was used primarily for design testing.

Advocates of increased federal support for science feared that the research momentum of the war years might not survive demobilization, as the nation returned to peace. Civilian scientists and engineers would be drawn to private employment. Congress might no longer approve the needed massive funding. At the two laboratories, such national debates had another side. Even if research and development were to be funded, could the recently expanded testing roles of both EES and DTMB provide a basis for sharing in new avenues of research?

In 1946 men like Saunders pointed to the hiatus in development of naval technology in the decade following World War I as an illustration of earlier short sightedness. The danger was that the nation would once again allow its naval shipbuilding and its weapons research to go underfunded until international threats once again forced it to rebuild, redesign, and attempt to catch up. The next attempt might be less successful than the crash program of the late 1930s. While Bush, Conant, and

Bowen carried those arguments to a national and congressional audience, Saunders and his colleagues kept the issue alive in naval circles and in the Bureau of Ships.[3]

Yet the argument had to proceed on two levels. First, science advocates had to secure national commitment to continued research funding. Second and more vitally for the staffs at EES and DTMB, that commitment would have to work itself out in a successful local changeover to the new priority, getting both laboratories to convert from hectic applied studies to a research and development orientation.

The conversion to a wartime mission, the reconversion to peace, and the changing national perspectives on science were no distant abstractions for the staff members at EES and DTMB. War and peace brought changes to their daily lives, to their projects and studies, and to personal long-range careers.

EES and the War

Several factors kept the staff at EES from fully adapting to the new emphasis on research and development. The station had always been oriented toward testing and toward engineering solutions of programmed design problems. Even though the engineering problems there were crucial ones, and their solutions would represent technical breakthroughs, the established procedure was not for EES staff to proceed towards developmental solutions but rather to test alternative devices or products submitted by private manufacturers who were seeking to solve a particular problem. Engineering progress came out of the intimate relationship with industry, in which Navy-established specifications or desired improvements would be announced after consultations with EES staff, products submitted would be measured for conformity to standard, and EES would endorse a product for Navy use only. Approval for use would be the reward to the developing firm, by establishing the Navy as a customer for the product.

EES tradition and staff were strongly rooted in the Navy's Bureau of Engineering, with its heritage from the days of Admiral George Melville. Practical men sought practical solutions; the shop and craft traditions, despite the professionalization of engineering, were strong. EES internal laboratories followed a successful pattern of evaluating manufacturers' claims; prolific, yet careful, engineering test reports were their tangible product.

That pattern and practice continued and greatly expanded under the pressure of wartime. The sheer volume of the problems dealt with and the mechanics of expanding the various EES laboratories' ability to handle the flood of design innovations, the issuance of literally thousands of brief reports detailing the test results, and the task of management of the increased staff, which grew from 400 to 1,200 during the war, reduced the likelihood that EES would take on a number of larger innovation and development tasks for itself.[4]

In light of the state of engine and auxiliary design in 1939–1940, the EES focus was not only understandable but precisely what was needed. After prodding from the Navy, several firms had developed lighter diesel engines for marine use, including General Motors through its purchase of the Winton Company, which it later renamed and reorganized as the Cleveland Motors Division. Other entrants to the marine diesel field included Buda Motor Works, Fairbanks-Morse, Cummins, and several lesser firms. In addition, many smaller firms concentrated on parts manufacture for the new engines. Despite weight-to-horsepower reductions, the marine diesel was plagued by several performance problems: cylinder heads overheated, pistons scuffed the cast-iron cylinder liners causing excessive wear and loss of compression, main bearings and piston bearings gave out, diesels tended to balk in cold weather and overheat in hot weather, defective and worn piston rings led to gas blow-by and resultant crankcase explosions. Each of these problems was approached by a "cut and try" method as a variety of engine-parts manufacturers came out with new alloys for bearings, cylinder liners, piston rings, cooling systems, and engine fuel injection systems. Similarly, petroleum refiners marketed fuel additives, new lubricants, and better diesel fuels.[5]

The new products held promise, yet the manufacturers' explicit interest in their own contributions would make their claims of performance less than objective. EES was in an ideal position to test the products: as the major purchaser of marine diesels, the Navy's choice would influence which development was pursued; EES, with its careful methods, would make technically accurate but financially "disinterested" decisions. Since the improved fuels, lubricants, cylinder liners, piston rings, bearings, and so forth, would interact in an engine, a controlled experimental approach by an objective outside interest was obviously necessary if progress was to come out of the flurry of invention, claim, and counter claim.

In the late 1930s and early 1940s, the relationship of the Navy to technical progress in industry varied, depending on the state of the art and the scale of the Navy purchases in the particular technology. In some fields, the Navy was only one of many purchasers, and its decisions, while important to a particular supplier, would not so clearly shape the wider course of innovation. But in the area of the application of the diesel engine to heavy-duty maritime use, the Navy's decisions, formulated at EES, were critical. In this particular area, the process of testing evolved into development coordination; that evolution did not go quite so far in other areas of technology in which the Navy's influence as major purchaser was less powerful.

For such reasons in 1939–1941, the EES role in testing was crucial to the defense of the nation. Item by item, in a flood of reports, EES helped find a way through multiple design alternatives. The Internal Combustion Engine Laboratory engineers studied all the alternative solutions that could lead to technological advance in their field; their reports would lead to Navy orders that could make the fortune of a manufacturer, and which would produce better marine diesel engines. ICE staff had every reason to see their own work as interesting, challenging, and on the forefront of progress.

The work of the other departments at EES reflected a similar pattern of reports that focused on alternative industrial solutions to contemporary technical problems of naval interest. In the Metals Laboratory, test machinery determined the effect of welded seams on the endurance properties of thin wall steel tubing, and other tests determined the fatigue-resistance of copper- and brass-covered steel rods. Gear teeth and roller bearings under compressive loading led to problems of jamming of heavy gun turrets; various new manufacturer-provided alloys could be tested in search of a solution. Diesel engine problems of the smoothness of bearings, journals, cylinder liners, and other parts also crowded the Metals schedule. The routine work of studying up to two hundred metal specimens per 8-hour shift under metallurgical microscopes allowed for the laboratory to pass on the actual forgings used on board ship, rather than simply testing random manufacturers' samples.[6]

Through the war years, the Welding Laboratory continued to develop suitability tests for commercially supplied welding materials and apparatus, and to develop process approval tests and operator's qualification tests. Much of the lab's time was consumed in suitability tests; just as in the ICE Laboratory, the conflicting or overlapping claims for improvement among welding rod alloy manufacturer, flux manufacturer, transformer, coil and generator manufacturers, all had to be sorted out. In welding, however, the Navy was only one of many major purchasers of equipment and materials. Ronay's group, as a consequence, exercised less power in shaping the overall trend of welding development than William Joachim's ICE group in marine diesels.[7]

The Chemical Laboratory conducted analytic work for the ICE, Metals, and Welding Labs, and routine tests of petroleum and thousands of tests of metals for the inspectors of naval material in shipyards consumed the bulk of the staff time. Similarly, the Mechanical Laboratory tested auxiliary machinery and steam propulsion equipment. Special equipment to test blowers and steam condensers allowed for competitive testing of the claims of the manufacturers of such special pieces of marine equipment.[8]

The procedures adopted at EES under the pressure of rapid wartime industrial innovation incorporated methods that allowed for the simultaneous evaluation of several variables with the same equipment. In the ICE Laboratory, a 12-cylinder Winton diesel test engine would be run with a single oil, a single brand oil filter, but with a wide variety of parts in each cylinder. Each would have a different combination of head, liner, piston ring assembly, piston pin bearing, and crank-pin bearing. After some 300 hours of running, the wear on parts would be measured and rings, liners, bearings, and heads could be evaluated for quality. By 1943 the laboratory had over sixty engines, with nine devoted to multiple component testing. Others were dedicated to evaluating filters, fuels, lubricants, or simply the overall life of a particular engine.[9]

Getting multiple uses out of the same machine became something of a challenge at the station during the war. Metals, Welding, Mechanical, and Chemistry Labs also reported on ingenious methods of using equipment for widely different purposes. For example, a Metals Laboratory machine for measuring the frictional resistance of pipe to saltwater at various velocities could be adapted to experiments on protective coatings such as synthetic rubber and resinous coatings and paints, either under water or under spray conditions.[10]

The rich variety of projects in the ICE Lab continued through the war. By 1943 that laboratory alone had a staff that exceeded the size of the whole EES of fifteen years earlier, with 22 Naval Reserve officers, 29 professionals and subprofessionals, and 135 unclassified workers. Work covered piston rods, toxicity of diesel exhaust from fuel to which an amyl nitrate dope had been added, new lubricants for diesel and aircraft engines, bimetallic piston rings, and continuing evaluation of lubricants, fuels, bearings, rings, liners, heads, filters, and cooling systems, as well as whole engines.[11]

By setting requirements for manufacturers, testing, and selecting the best of several experimental solutions to design problems, the station had taken a more active role in development over the 1930s. During the war years that same interaction with industry in the development process continued. However, by no means did the increased pressure for new products convert the station over to a laboratory that conducted in-house research and development.

The crush of war work on the Bureau of Ships laboratories led to massive problems of coordination. By early 1944 the bureau attempted to sort out the complexities with some internal controls. As laboratories at navy yards took on new projects, some of them, the bureau noted with disapproval, began "branching out into development work." In an effort to prevent duplication, the chief of the bureau prohibited developmental studies by such laboratories without first clearing the details with the bureau.[12] The bureau requested the commandants of all the navy yards and the directors of EES, DTMB, and NRL to follow a single format in monthly reporting of all tests involving "Research, Development, Suitability for Naval Use, or Specifications."[13]

When Thorvald Solberg attempted to provide further coordination, the system he established gave a clear picture of how bureau headquarters regarded the mission of EES during the war. He directed that each Bureau of Ships' laboratory send copies of its monthly reports to selected other laboratories, so that separate staffs working on similar problems would keep abreast of each others' work. The details of the report exchange system he developed put EES in the same category with the navy yards, rather than with NRL and DTMB. From Solberg's point of view at the Bureau of Ships, the bulk of regular work done at EES held primary interest only for the navy yard testing laboratories and he apparently assumed that the greatest likelihood of duplication of EES work could be found among the testing labs rather than the more research-oriented labs. Implicitly, Solberg ranked EES as a test shop.[14]

Shortly after Pearl Harbor, the Bureau of Ships relaxed its inspection requirements and permitted the acceptance of material that did not meet contract and specification requirements, in order to speed up ship and equipment deliveries. By June 1944, however, because of failure of materials and equipment that required repair and special-order manufacture of replacement parts, which in itself slowed down regular industrial production, Bureau Chief E. L. Cochrane reinstituted higher standards. At the same time, he ordered naval inspectors to cooperate with manufacturers closely to upgrade their own inspection operations and to maintain both high quality and rapid delivery. Despite the temporary relaxation of inspection, EES continued to receive literally thousands of samples of material, fuels, lubricants, and equipment for testing.[15]

However perceived by headquarters, the testing by EES was not simply a passive response to industrial suppliers. The ICE Laboratory used inspection testing of lubricants and engine parts to develop detailed maintenance schedules for main propulsion submarine diesel engines, spelling out oil change, filter check, test run, and inspection breakdown schedules to be conducted while afloat by engineers on the boats. In effect, EES developed a manual for the fleet that in its particulars was more sensitive to the actual performance of the engines and to its collection of parts manufactured by diverse firms than the schedules of maintenance proposed by the manufacturers.[16]

The independence and leadership position taken by EES in development was even more subtle and complex. While the laboratory rarely directly engaged in developmental work, its ability to sort through literally hundreds of simultaneously developing private solutions to find the most useful one, to direct the assembly of components through setting of standards, and the selection of particular products as suitable for naval use meant that despite the bureau's conception that the laboratory was not devoted to development, it did in fact define, direct, and coordinate industrial development in several areas of technology.

The Engineering Experiment Station could accelerate and determine technological development, especially when numerous small firms competed for the Navy market. In case after case, corporate officials appealed for EES approval or reconsideration of disapproval. The Eisemann Magneto Company submitted a lightweight diesel fuel injection system for test, but the station rejected it until the company could work out its adaptation to an engine already in naval use. After two years of company developmental work and repeated requests from the company, EES accepted the system for testing.[17] In another case, the Savage Muffler Company appealed a negative EES ruling, requesting that the Norfolk Navy Yard be allowed to test their muffler on a gasoline engine "before we are excluded from Navy business." [18]

In other cases, the support of EES for well-designed or innovative equipment was so enthusiastic that the Navy ran the risk of openly endorsing the product. Vanderhorst cylinder liners represented such a great advance that EES recommended them by name to a wide distribution list of naval personnel, but the staff were careful to prohibit the use of Navy test results by Vanderhorst in commercial advertising.[19] The prohibition against the use of EES test results in manufacturers' advertising was enforced throughout the period.[20]

In some cases, as in work on the successful bimetallic piston ring, EES managers debated whether to hire the inventor directly or to place a major contract with the firm in order to ensure that the development work not become a "lost art." The Navy opted for an order of 2,000 rings, and put the company on the road to success.[21]

The power of Navy purchasing was such that even the largest companies responded to EES suggestions. When an EES report indicated that a General Motors 6-71 diesel engine was unsuitable because of cracked cylinder liners, carbonization and sticking of piston rings, and accumulation of carbon deposits inside the spray tips of the fuel injectors, the company responded with design changes in piston clearance, altered rings, and a changed retention system for the piston pin, all carefully explained in detail by the chief engineer of GM's Small Diesel Engine Plant. EES then gave approval for naval use. Similarly, the Buda Company responded to EES reports promptly by redesign of bearings.[22]

A recommendation against naval use was so extreme a sanction for some companies that, in cases of minor defects, station engineers and officers reserved the right to make confidential, informal adverse comments for internal naval use, even while recommending formal acceptance of the product. At least one naval officer at EES suspected that engineers would carefully phrase their reports so "as not to offend the manufacturer," and he recommended that the informal, more frank confidential report be institutionalized formally in the interests of "added information" to the bureau and for the sake of staff morale.[23]

EES was less successful in influencing development directly through contract work than indirectly through the acceptance versus rejection process. Directly contracted development work faced the difficulty that under the press of the war, companies often could not perform contracted development work on time. Priorities for machine tools, high-temperature resistant alloys, and staff time all delayed performance on experimental development work by several companies involved in gas turbine designs.[24]

Several companies worked on Navy contracts administered through EES, from 1940 through the war to develop a 3,500-horsepower drive gas turbine. Allis Chalmers, DeLaval, General Electric, Westinghouse, and Elliott all proposed alternative designs and worked under separate contracts.[25] J. T. Rettaliata, working for Allis Chalmers, was a recognized expert in the field with several publications on the problems and prospects of gas turbines. Rettaliata headed the project at Allis Chalmers and kept EES posted with detailed monthly reports. In 1942 he noted that the priority set for the gas turbine did not allow Allis Chalmers to devote shop time, personnel, or materials to the project in the face of higher priority war work.[26] Delivery dates were set back from November 1941 to August 1942 to March 1943. Finally, in 1944 EES began testing the Allis Chalmers model, after several delays of its own in acquiring testing equipment, but by that time it became clear that gas turbine applications would not be completed in time for the current war.[27]

By the end of the war the station had made many contributions to the technology of naval warfare, through the indirect method of selecting products for naval use. Yet, like most of the earlier specification work of the station, the results were not widely identified as EES achievements. Rather, the small and large firms that developed the final pieces of equipment received the credit. The station's limited-circulation reports on products and equipment also did very little to enhance the reputation of the station, even in naval circles. The internally produced command histories, or the occasional public relations piece detailing the background of the station, could not adequately capture the magnitude of the dispersed and varied EES contributions to the development of diesels, welding, metals, and petroleum chemistry. Even today, with access to previously classified documents, a fully detailed account of their coordination role in development would require a lengthy monographic treatment in itself. During the war years, Bureau of Ships policy, the reliance on manufacturers for innovation, the difficulty of directing long-term development projects under contract through industry, together with the long-established testing emphasis, all mitigated against a transformation of the station into a different kind of laboratory more clearly fitting the postwar fashion of in-house research and development.

3500-HP Allis Chalmers Gas Turbine.   Tested during World War II at the Engineering Experiment Station, this gas turbine was not ready for application until after the war.

Goddard and Rocket Work at EES

One of the efforts of in-house development at EES during the war years reflected many of the Navy's difficulties in managing innovation. Throughout his professional career, Robert H. Goddard (1882–1945) had attempted to convince the U.S. military of the potentials of his rocket research. His relationship with the Navy further demonstrates the same pre-World War II lack of enthusiasm for scientific research that Schoenherr and his colleagues encountered. As early as 1916 he wrote to the Smithsonian claiming that his "devices" would be capable of "propelling masses, such as explosives, for very great distances, and hence would be very likely useful in warfare." Although he realized the civilian applications of his work, as in meteorology, he continued to appeal for military support.[28]

In order to fund his work, Goddard relied upon a variety of grants. Soon after he finished his dissertation at Clark University, Princeton awarded him a research fellowship to work on rocket motion, but a diagnosis of tuberculosis in 1913 ended that project. The Smithsonian gave him $11,000 in the period 1917–1929 to continue his work on liquid propulsion of vertical thrust rockets. During these years he worked on an innovative oxygen-gasoline fuel, an injection system, and a gyroscopic stabilizer. Goddard launched the first liquid-propelled rocket on 15 March 1926, in Worcester, Massachusetts.

When Charles Lindbergh arranged for a two-year Guggenheim grant of $100,000 to Goddard, he began to pursue his research full-time. Complaints from Worcester residents and city officials concerning the noise and danger from his experiments prompted him to look for a new research site. Taking into consideration his poor health and the need for an isolated area in which to conduct flight tests, he settled on the dry climate and wide-open space of Roswell, New Mexico. After buying the Mescalero Ranch, he set up shop with his dedicated wife, Esther, and four assistants. Although the grants were not luxurious by the standards of a later generation, they provided Goddard with considerable latitude in arranging his own work, conducting rocket and instrumentation development at his own pace, and devoting care to safety considerations and careful record keeping of test results.[29]

The military establishment was not as willing as the Guggenheim Foundation to take a chance with Goddard. After suggesting in 1939 and 1940 that the Navy cosponsor with the Foundation work on the "exploration of new chambers for accelerating bombs," Goddard and Guggenheim representatives visited Washington to make a personal plea for funds. Frustrated with the skepticism he encountered, Goddard

JATO Test Stand.   Under urging from Robert H. Goddard, the Navy experimented with jet-assisted take-off, testing the rockets in stationary stands here in December 1943.

returned to Roswell and continued to urge that his work "be turned to national defense lines, on as powerful a footing as possible." [30]

The Army Air Corps through the National Research Council did begin funding a jet propulsion project, but the funds went to Theodore von Karman and his team at the California Institute of Technology's Guggenheim Aeronautical Laboratory. Learning of this, Goddard wrote to a friend, "From remarks that were dropped I imagine they are starting work with liners in chambers, which I did 26 years ago." Although the Cal Tech people discussed the possibility of Goddard collaborating with them, von Karman and others believed that Goddard did not want to turn over to others what "he had learned through years of work and sacrifice." Goddard, for his part, correctly assumed that without his consultation, time and money would be wasted repeating his research.[31]

In 1941 Goddard suggested research begin on antiaircraft projectiles, long-range and high-speed artillery, assisted take-off devices for airplanes, and special jet motors. He predicted that "jet propulsion making use of liquid oxygen and a fuel pump system will provide rocket projectiles of the greatest speed and range, and jet propulsion for airplanes of the greatest power for a given weight." As war raged in Europe, he warned that "interruption or abandonment of such fundamental research as this would seem unwise under the present conditions."[32]

By September 1941 Goddard finally negotiated a contract with the Navy's Bureau of Aeronautics to work on one of his suggestions, jet-assisted take-off (JATO) units. Jointly funded by the Army Air Corps, the contract stipulated that Goddard begin work in November. However, ignoring the formal contract terms, he eagerly began work in September, making rapid progress by December. Although enthusiastic about the Navy project, he soon encountered difficulties.[33]

Goddard complained of the obstacles to independent research that arose under contract work. "The contract fits the corporation supplying commodities to the Government for profit. I, on the other hand, am attempting to solve a research problem without profit." He pointed out that "the spirit of the contract as originally agreed upon was more in the nature of a research grant, for which I agreed to obtain certain results in a definite time, rather than contract for supplying commodities." Details of contract administration soon interrupted research time: "I would certainly welcome the opportunity of doing my worrying on the jet-propulsion unit exclusively, rather than dividing it with financial matters."[34]

During the spring of 1942, the Navy sought to monitor Goddard's work even more closely and requested that he move to the Engineering Experiment Station at Annapolis over the summer. A Navy team headed by Lieutenant Robert C. Truax was already in place at EES working on a similar JATO project but was plagued by problems with the propellant. An engine had exploded after the propellants were allowed to sit too long in the combustion chamber before igniting. Goddard, too, encountered problems with his liquid oxygen-gasoline mix, forcing him to try different combinations. The Truax team finally settled on a mixture of nitric acid and aniline and began to work on solid propellants. Goddard, with his more deliberate and cautious style developed over years of independent, grant-funded research, found some of Truax's procedures questionable. An acid explosion in January 1943 prompted Goddard to write a memo stating his objections and refusing to assume responsibility for accidents with nitric acid. He suggested equipping acid motors with the same safety devices he had recommended for use on liquid oxygen motors.[35]

The relationship between the Goddard and Truax teams at EES reflected the tension that arose from the divergent approaches to development taken by scientists and engineers in the era. Lieutenant Harold Nutt of the fuels division and later the technical director of EES, claimed that Truax "displayed some disdain for the older, theoretical physicist who was not a 'real' engineer." For his part, Goddard simply "put up" with the Navy personnel, as he believed they were toying with theories and ideas he had already developed, sometimes following procedures he had established as dangerous or unproductive. From his perspective, the engineers would use cut-and-try methods without regard for already established basic principles. His sometimes arrogant manner did not help matters, despite a general respect for his intellect.[36]

Meanwhile, Lieutenant Charles F. Fischer of the Bureau of Aeronautics, with whom Goddard worked closely in arranging the contract, pressured Goddard to test a JATO-equipped PBY plane. Fischer even insisted that he fly the test craft himself. Goddard, always concerned with safety, cautioned against too many successive tests of the still developmental JATO. He finally agreed to a 23 September 1942 test flight. The first six take-offs succeeded, but during the seventh test a long flame appeared, indicating an excess of oxygen. With a sudden rise in pressure, resultant shock, and a break in the liquid oxygen line, a small fire broke out, and Fischer crash-landed the plane in the Severn. Neither Fischer nor his co-pilot were hurt, but Goddard, chafing under Navy-imposed expectations of scheduled results, promptly wrote a memo formally advocating necessary safety precautions.[37]

After the accident, the Navy decided to halt EES work on JATO while continuing work on jets and rockets at Cal Tech and successor laboratories in California. Goddard's assignments at EES then concentrated on component-part development, rather than development of a whole propulsion system. He began work on the improvement of rotating chambers, the perfection of a variable-thrust motor, and the development of pumps and igniters. He remained frustrated and disappointed that the Navy would not fund his vertical, liquid-propelled rocket research. When his health began to deteriorate in 1943, however, he had to accept the fact that he would have to leave rocket development to others.[38]

Meanwhile, the Navy grew increasingly interested in captured German technology. Parts of a V-2 rocket were sent to EES for examination in the spring of 1945, and Goddard excitedly noted the striking similarities between the German rockets and his own. Indeed, the V-2 design was practically identical to the pump-operated rockets he had developed in New Mexico. Although Goddard believed that the Germans had read his theories and searched out his patents, Peenemunde scientists later claimed that they reached their parallel conclusions quite independently. Similarities between the world-famous

V-2 and Goddard's earlier, more obscure work drew attention to his pioneering research.[39]

Goddard died of cancer in a Maryland hospital on 10 August 1945, before the American rocket program started in earnest. He received posthumous recognition by the National Aeronautics and Space Administration in the naming of the Goddard Space Flight Center north of Washington, D.C., and in Roswell, New Mexico, with the construction of a beautifully maintained small museum. Such belated honors tend to cast Goddard in the classic role of "a man ahead of his time." The story was neither so simple nor quite so tragic. The Navy, constantly flooded by thousands of crank inventors' often half-baked ideas, was understandably cautious about Goddard's visionary suggestions; it is to the credit of Fischer and others in the Bureau of Aeronautics that they even attempted to harness his genius. Used to working as a loner, Goddard may have found the more structured environment at EES uncomfortable. Despite a degree of hesitant, yet intelligent, receptivity to new ideas, the Navy and EES did not quite know how best to utilize the skills of a man like Goddard in the prewar and early war years.

The Postwar Mission of EES

The persistence of the station's testing mission through the war into the postwar years was made explicit as the bureau continued its efforts to coordinate and spell out the overlapping responsibilities of the bureau labs. In 1945 EES retained exclusive responsibility for naval inspection testing of aviation gasoline, grease, bearings, pressure gauges, gasoline meters, thermometers, carbon-molybdenum steel, nonferrous metals, underwater cutting tools, welding materials, packing materials, boiler compounds and boiler water, and metal polishes. By 1948, EES retained exclusive testing jurisdiction for those same categories, while for a few other classes of materials, EES was one of several laboratories assigned, on a regional basis, for inspection testing. The traditional testing role remained the mainstay.[40]

By the end of the 1940s the Bureau of Ships officially endorsed an expanded mission for EES in research and development in a general mission statement for the facility issued in 1949. In broad terms, EES was to "conduct research and development, investigations and tests on engineering equipment, materials, fuels and lubricants" in the fields of chemistry, metallurgy, welding, internal combustion engine mechanics and acoustics, vibration, and shock. But when the statement spelled out details at length, the traditional mission appeared to persist more strongly than the new mission statement suggested: to examine the causes of service failures of materials, develop specifications, test items for compliance with those specifications, and investigate causes of machine failure.[41] Walter Worthington would have recognized that list. The official statement, while giving lip-service to research and development, did not recognize the quietly expanded and intricate relationship between the Navy and private industry in which testing and product selection had, for a few years, guided development.

War Work at DTMB

It is a contemporary cliché that war provides a stimulus to science. But the immediate effect of World War II on the schedule of work at the model basin was at first quite the opposite. The new basin at Carderock had been open slightly over a year by December 1941. On the eve of Pearl Harbor, the basin had already begun model testing of warship designs. American entry into the war only increased the pressure to complete the work and to move ahead with new ships. As the tempo quick-

Army Encampment, WWII.   With its 107 acres, the DTMB grounds provided space for tents and barracks to house U.S. Army troops on duty in the Washington Metropolitan area.

ened, staff members had little time or opportunity for fundamental or theoretical research as distinct from practical work on ship and weapon design problems.[42] In 1941 the Navy continued to view theoretical research as a luxury; whereas Ernest Eggert had permitted Schoenherr to conduct his dissertation study as model basin research in the early thirties, no such generous scheduling could be arranged under wartime priorities. At the model basin, the wartime workload had a complex effect, producing growth and expansion of staff and facilities with the potential for research. Furthermore, DTMB did considerable new developmental work.

Research had a solid, if minor, place on the schedule in the last two years before the war. The official annual report for 1939–1940 estimated that the model basin devoted about 8.3 percent of its time to research projects.[43] Staff used the more accurate Carderock basin to do design work on battleships 57–64, carriers 6–9, cruisers, submarines and a variety of destroyers, torpedo boats, and other small vessels. In 1940, research included several long-standing projects. Studies of wakes and eddies, series of propellers, and series of tests on middle body shapes were all in the "research" category. One project involved tests of *San Francisco,* a German merchant ship; various basins in the United States cooperated on tests of identical models of this vessel to compare results and to produce some standardization of calculation from one basin to another. However, the war interrupted progress on this cooperative project and on most of the other long-range research interests.[44]

Within two months after the attack on Pearl Harbor, the model towing schedule had been converted over to two full shifts at DTMB and a full shift at the older basin at the Washington Navy Yard. Although the Bureau of Ships had planned to transfer all the activities from the navy yard and to provide the model basin storage space and other facilities there to the Naval Gun Factory, the press of work required keeping both the old and new towing tanks operating simultaneously.[45]

"The chief function of this organization in war time," wrote DTMB Director Captain H. S. Howard, in 1943, "is to give as nearly as possible immediate solutions or answers to problems submitted to it to meet special situations brought forth by the war." Enumerating the most notable contributions in the first twenty months of the war, Howard listed the developmental and design problems that had consumed basin time on a large scale. Each project had indeed been in response to an immediate need:

- Development work for Bureau of Ordnance on new torpedoes
- New gear for minesweeping
- Propeller and ship noise reduction

- Vibration observation on battleships and cruisers
- Work on Carriers 41–44 resulting in new lines
- Speed and powering of landing craft
- Design data work on DD 692 class
- Turning tests to provide tactical data
- Depth charge firing tests [46]

Howard's view of the relationship between research and the immediate developmental projects was explicit; in 1943 he conceived of research as having provided a base of knowledge from which to work. "Research which has been and is being continuously carried on at this establishment gives the background of knowledge which makes it possible to undertake and furnish the solution to these urgent problems." [47] Howard made a clear-headed connection between research and problem solving, a position that reflected the orientation of an engineer rather than a research scientist. As he saw it, knowledge was crucial for the use to which it could be put in the solution of problems. In the midst of the war, Howard, like many of his contemporaries, did not choose to characterize research as a pursuit valuable for the goal of clarifying the fundamentals of knowledge.

Schoenherr, under Lieutenant Commander E. Alvey Wright, worked on the development of the design for an air-dropped acoustic homing torpedo. Even though Schoenherr had already built a reputation as a theoretical hydrodynamicist, his approach to the torpedo problem reflected that of an engineer. Rejecting a number of ideas he regarded as "futuristic," Schoenherr asked a set of practical engineering questions: How big was the airplane bombing bay that would carry the torpedo? How large did the explosive charge have to be? What minimal speed would be acceptable? How sturdy did the drive and propeller system have to be to withstand the shock of the drop to the water? Within the straightforward design parameters provided by the answers to such questions, Schoenherr worked with draftsmen, metalworkers, and mechanics to construct a durable model of the torpedo, incorporating a simple propeller of his own design. Other laboratories designed the battery drive and acoustic homing components. When asked to perfect the streamlining to reduce resistance and increase speed further, Schoenherr rejected the approach of a mathematically formulated curve for the nose shape, insisting that an elementary traced curve would be perfectly adequate for the proposed speeds. He later remarked, "That is the difference between the pure mathematician and the mathematician with his feet on the ground." Put in the language of a later generation, Schoenherr's wartime research on the air-dropped torpedo was strictly requirements driven. [48]

Men like Schoenherr and Landweber turned their skills to other immediate and practical problems under the pressure of wartime needs. Basin staff later remembered as personal contributions to the war effort their developmental work on new instruments to measure explosive shock, research with towed minesweeping and target gear, and rapid designs for landing craft. Landweber worked on predictive formulas for the resistance of towed gear and on a difficult problem of developing a set of towed cylinders that would emit an underwater sound whose characteristics would detonate acoustic mines. Even though the resistance of the cables on such gear raised interesting theoretical issues, Landweber postponed investigation and reporting on the hydrodynamics of cables until after the war.[49]

Although a number of challenging and unique developmental projects engaged the scientists at the basin during the war, the bulk of double-shift basin time was spent on ship model tests. The shipbuilding effort in the United States during the war is legendary—in the one-year period March 1944 to March 1945 alone, the Navy acquired over 43,000 vessels, including landing craft and auxiliaries. Research on materials, structures, and machines led to a continual introduction of new weapons, devices, and tactics as a result of war experience. Major and minor modifications were constantly brought into the fleet. The Bureau of Ships claimed in early 1945 that, in order to keep up with demand of continual modification, "The Taylor Model Basin is operating at nearly its peak load on ship model tests."[50]

While full-time ship model testing proceeded for battleships, carriers, cruisers, frigates, destroyers, destroyer escorts, submarines, landing craft, torpedo boats, and auxiliaries, the basin continued to take on a variety of special projects of high priority. Special tests of launchings in restricted waterways were held for models of *Alabama* (BB 60), *Kentucky* (BB 66), and *New Jersey* (BB 62).[51] The staff mounted vibration generators on board battleships *North Carolina* (BB 55), *Washington* (BB 56), and *South Dakota* (BB 57) and recorded the natural frequencies of the fire control instruments and the director towers.[52] As in the prewar days, teams continued to participate in full-scale trials, but the Penobscot Bay area off Maine no longer provided quite the picnic spot it once had for the visiting group from the model basin, as it was regarded as in the "theater of operations of enemy submarines."[53]

Other one-time tests included experiments with periscopes to identify wake configurations at the Experimental Model Basin in Washington,[54] a test to see if an aircraft carrier could transit the Panama Canal, and construction of a miniature beach in the small model basin to test landing craft models. Other special projects included cavitation

Panama Canal Simulation.   An early test in the model basin replicated part of the Panama Canal to determine if WWII-era aircraft carriers could transit locks and turns in the canal.

tests for the propellers of *North Carolina* and *Washington,* leading to re-design of those propellers to suppress their excessive vibration, and special studies of ammunition handling and landing-craft loading practices.[55] The British sought information on some of the basin's unique projects, including studies of torpedo net resistance, acceleration measurements on torpedo boats, resistance of towing cables, and determination of ship's speeds from photographs of wakes.[56]

By mid-1945 the pressures increased to a point at which Schoenherr, heading the hydromechanics section, complained that he had enough. It was time that professionals no longer be required to do the day-to-day carriage work of instrument reading. "The practice of using professional employees as substitutes for sub-professionals," he complained in an angry memorandum to Saunders, "delays the calculation and report work and also has a bad influence on the morale of the lower grade professional employees." Although war work was beginning to decline, work for private shipbuilders had increased. Schoenherr recommended a group of personnel shifts to alleviate the problem, mostly consisting of the transfer of subprofessional employees to his own group. However, two days after his memo, *Enola Gay* bombed Hiroshima, and V-J day came eight days later. The war was over, and the intense workload declined.[57]

Science Delayed

The effect of the war upon the DTMB agenda ran deeper than simple increased volume and heightened demand for practical results. The war affected the choice of work by interrupting the international dialogue among hydrodynamicists over several problems of theory that had arisen during the interwar decades and that underlay the problem of measurement and prediction which had earlier plagued observers like Akimoff and Eggert.

In 1940 model basin hydrodynamicists anticipated using the new equipment to address such issues. The precisely laid track, sturdy carriage, and excellent climate control at the new Carderock basin would reduce equipment error in the prediction of ship performance. The older navy yard basin had been so prone to error that experimenters had been unable to determine whether prediction discrepancies should be traced to weaknesses in theory, human error, variation in equipment performance, or some set of controllable variables such as temperature. With the new basin, continued variation between ship performance predictions based on models and performance of the full-scale ship could now be studied closely, in isolation from the effects of inconsistent machine and instrument operation. The new equipment could allow development and accurate testing of more sophisticated theories. But, even in 1940, warship design priorities pushed the study of fundamentals to the back burner. Science had to wait.

Many issues of hydrodynamic theory remained unresolved. William Froude's original method of calculation of frictional resistance was based on limited empirical data for smooth plates. An empirical factor had to be applied to correct for the difference between predictions based on smooth-hulled models and the results from rough-hulled ships; Schoenherr called the correction the "roughness factor." Later investigations determined that several considerations besides the roughness of ships contributed to the discrepancies. In the late 1930s different basins in Europe and Japan had adopted various standards for applying Froude's frictional resistance calculations; in 1933 and 1937, towing tank superintendents in Europe met to work toward a standard on questions such as correction factors for temperature and methods of calculating frictional resistance.[58]

Americans had not participated as official delegates at either conference but had organized their own group of model basin directors. The American Towing Tank Conference (ATTC) had met twice before sessions were postponed due to the war. The war also interrupted the ATTC program of research and standard setting, as it had those of the European conferences. Between 1939 and 1945, most cooperative efforts between Britain, Germany, Italy, the Netherlands, and other nations were impossible, and American communication with European basins virtually stopped. When the war ended, the issues discussed at the towing tank conferences prior to 1939 could be revived, and the cooperative effort could begin anew.

The war not only interrupted work on outstanding theoretical problems but postponed investigation into newly raised theoretical issues growing out of wartime weapon development. As Schoenherr, Landweber, and other scientists at the basin turned their efforts to problems of torpedoes and towlines, they had to avoid some of the interesting larger questions suggested by the experiments if they sought rapid innovation. Saunders summarized some of the postponed issues in an informal presentation at SNAME in 1946. "Time was when all we had to worry about was heeling and rolling and turning," he said, but the advent of the torpedo, guided missiles, and improved mines required ship designers "to think very definitely in the same sort of terms that have been necessary for the airplane people." High-speed submarines, together with the other developments, meant that the basic question of maneuverability of forms under the surface, as well as on the surface, now required study and a new nomenclature to make the study possible. Hydrodynamicists would have to think in three dimensions.[59]

Thus, by the end of the war, hydrodynamicists hoped to take up two classes of pent-up scientific research issues if provided with the time and budget: long-standing problems with the fundamental theory on which progress had been interrupted by the war, and new issues raised by wartime development but postponed in the interests of immediate practical results.

Two months after the Japanese surrender, Howard detailed current and planned research. He tended to stress the postponed war-related problems more than the long-standing theoretical issues: "During World War II, the facilities of the DTMB have naturally been devoted primarily to specific projects of immediate military urgency. With the cessation of hostilities, this laboratory must assume a greatly enlarged scope of fundamental research, particularly in the fields in which actual war service experience and possible fantastic weapons of the future indicate that basin investigations must be undertaken if our national safety is to be insured."[60]

A specific set of fundamental research priorities, with just such an "enlarged scope" came from Landweber in the form of a list of twenty-one theoretical problems for the future agenda. The problems of interest to Landweber included very few with a direct relationship to recent or future weapons. He divided the theoretical issues into five categories:

- Determination of velocity and pressure fields about bodies immersed in a stream
- Non-uniform motions of a body through a fluid
- Vortex formation and interactions
- Turbulence studies
- Studies of phenomena at the interface between different fluids[61]

About three-quarters of the particular problems suggested by Landweber under these headings dealt with the interrupted theoretical pursuits, on some of which the beginnings of an international dialogue can be found in the late 1930s, including studies of boundary layers, wave effects, determination of "roughness" allowances, shallow-water and channel effects, and cavitation and vortex studies. A few of the topics he saw as interesting did grow out of the war, and represented an effort to establish theoretical explanations for the noted effects of fast cut-and-try projects. Such projects included theoretical studies related to launching of ships, the interaction of periscopes and cables with their shed vortices, the study of "air-water entry," and a closer study along the lines suggested by Saunders of the motion of submerged bodies, that is to say, torpedoes and submarines.[62]

Although the war had interrupted scientific research of a fundamental kind in favor of applied work, that did not mean that the war in a larger sense prevented or delayed progress. From the scientists' viewpoint, wartime haste to innovation raised tantalizing new avenues to explore on a theoretical level. The war also helped provide the tools that would make such exploration possible.

New Facilities at DTMB

The growth of facilities at the Carderock location over the decade following the opening in 1940 was extraordinary. Considering the original delays and difficulties in getting funding in the 1930s for the new plant, and considering the pressures during the war years for funding and for manpower, the basin's success in growth and the quality of the additions require explanation. It is not sufficient to say that the Navy added the new facilities because they were needed; in the competitive and hectic war years, new facilities on a massive scale both in America and abroad had good claim to resources. All the standard arguments against growth or expenditure in any particular location could now be strengthened by the fact that other efforts had high priority.

Saunders and Howard used some prosaic arguments to win funding for new equipment. The model basin site at Carderock had been an excellent choice, and the factors that made it excellent in 1938 became good arguments for locating further buildings and facilities there. The land was close to Washington; it was already quite level; there was a good deal of acreage in the original compound and more was readily added; the granite that served as perfect foundation for the basin itself was appropriate for other installations and additions.

Saunders and Howard marshaled several more subtle arguments, requiring more justification. Some of the facilities requested were unique, and the existing investment in the model basin and the presence of staff trained in its use made the addition of unique structures there logical. When other laboratories claimed that their own facilities should be the location for a particular improvement, model basin advocates lined up internal naval support in the competition. Particularly helpful "lobbying" came from the Bureau of Ordnance in the effort to extend the basin itself in order to test torpedoes; Aeronautics helped argue that wind tunnels at the navy yard should be established at Carderock, a move once opposed by NACA.

Of all the new facilities added, the most striking was the extension of the overall length of the basin to 2,968 feet and the building housing it to 3,145 feet. The original basin had been cut back for economy reasons in the 1938–1939 construction to 963 feet. The extension was requested in 1941, and approval for $8 million required for the work came in July 1944. Paralleling the deep-water basin, a single high-speed basin of a total length of 2,968 feet allowed long runs at high speed. Howard successfully argued that high-speed work on torpedoes required the longer tank, and naval ordnance agreed. Construction began in 1944 and the basin was open for its first work in August 1946, twelve months after the end of the war, although regular testing could not get under way until 1948.[63]

While interior work continued on the basin extension through 1947, the range of facilities and equipment at Carderock and improvements on existing facilities brought during the war and early postwar years added up to considerable growth of capacity. During construction of the basin extension, technicians checked the tracks on the high-speed basin. Because of aging of concrete and shifts in the earth's crust, some

Model Basin Extension, 1944–1946.   Captain H. S. Howard fought for the extension of the towing basin to a length of 2,968 feet despite competing claims to resources in the peak WWII years. In the distance, the connected office-lab building can be seen to the left of the original basin.

of the original precision of the tracks had eroded, leading to deviations "several times greater than allowable tolerances." Staff shimmed and re-aligned the chairs and tracks in the 1944–1945 construction, with mini-mal interruption of the work schedule.[64]

Two water tunnels, one with a 12-inch-diameter test section brought from the older model basin at the navy yard in the original Carderock construction, and a second tunnel with a 24-inch diameter, opened in 1941, both operated like wind tunnels by forcing water past a model. The "closed" feature of the water tunnels allowed for variation in pres-sure necessary to simulate operating conditions of propellers, and the tunnels could be used to predict propeller cavitation at various speeds and depths.[65]

A circulating water channel, opened in 1944, allowed for a variety of other tests. The walls and bottom of the channel were fitted with large viewing windows, allowing observation of flow around ship models, periscope vibration tests, observation of underwater exhaust systems,

DDG 51 Model in Circulating Water Channel. Opened in 1944, the water channel allowed for stationary models to be tested and the water flow lines to be captured in photographs. Here small tuffs and dye reveal the flow lines around the bulbous bow.

Pentagonal Explosives Test Pond. Constructed in 1943, the test pond was lined with Gunite and the bottom roughened to avoid reflections of pressure waves. A worker in the center provides a sense of scale.

and observation of positions of mines in currents and tideways. Researchers could measure the deployment angles and drag of underwater towed devices like paravanes used to cut mine moorings and could observe flow around underwater appendages such as struts, rudders, and diving planes. While some of these tests could be carried on in an open basin, the circulating water channel simplified photography and observation procedures, since in this facility, as in the water tunnels and wind tunnels, the model remained stationary while the fluid moved past it.[66]

For tests of explosives, a pentagonal test pond was constructed in 1943, in which small charges of TNT could simulate the effects of full-scale underwater blasts.[67] For the testing of structures, three massive machines for measuring either tension or compression on metal samples were rated at 30,000 pounds, 150,000 pounds, and 600,000 pounds. In 1947 a fourth testing machine rated at 250,000 pounds was under construction, designed to allow for reversing the load from compression to tension.[68]

Altogether, four wind tunnels were in operation, two at the old navy yard facility, and two at Carderock, which opened for tests in 1944. The older tunnels at the navy yard were not decommissioned until 1952. James A. McCrary, Albert Zahm's successor at the wind tunnel operation at the navy yard, planned and set the specifications for the two Carderock wind tunnels constructed during the war and carefully arranged that shops and offices would be adequate and convenient to the operation. McCrary, whose training was in mechanical engineering, and who had served with the basin since 1920 as an electrical and mechanical specialist, perceived the facility as a design-test, rather than a research, operation. In planning the tunnels, he remained committed to what he viewed as a practical, rather than a research, approach.[69] "Extreme accuracy in experimental work," wrote McCrary, in an obvious critique of the time-consuming leveling of basin tracks, "is scarcely ever necessary, for it is relative and not absolute quantities that are generally sought and used."[70]

Despite McCrary's disclaimer, the wind tunnel equipment, including both air deflectors and the measuring dynamometers, achieved a high degree of accuracy. McCrary's approach was to use equipment that could be constantly adjusted for accuracy, rather than building in from the beginning an attempt at perfect accuracy. Correction, he believed, was cheaper and more practical than pursuit of permanent precision. In connection with the difference of philosophy between McCrary and Saunders, it may be pertinent to note that before the tunnels were to open, Saunders ordered McCrary to a purely consulting and writing task, in January 1944, removing him entirely from adminis-

DTMB Wind Tunnel Construction, 1942.   James A. McCrary designed the wind tunnels at Carderock with less accuracy than the basins, criticizing the precise design style of Harold Saunders.

tration of the new tunnels whose construction he had planned and overseen to that point.[71]

When Saunders sought to calibrate the new tunnels more accurately early in 1944, the Bureau of Aeronautics complained. "The paramount purpose in creating these facilities was to provide wind tunnels suitable to conduct tests of a purely engineering nature as required in connection with the development and operation of naval aircraft and to relieve NACA of much of this work, thereby freeing their facilities for basic research." The Bureau of Aeronautics repeated previously supplied allowable tolerances, already present in the tunnels, and urged Saunders to put the tunnels to work without further delay. "The wind tunnels in their present basic form will meet all the Bureau's needs that can be foreseen at this time," the bureau noted. Saunders was forced to comply, however reluctantly, and within two months, both new tunnels were open for Bureau of Aeronautics-funded tests.[72]

For staff members, Carderock continued to be cramped after the war, with office and laboratory space at a premium. Temporary remodeling into office space of the lobby and museum area in the main office building, with its attractive mosaic illustrations of historic American ships, promised in 1947 to become a permanent alteration. Not until the 1980s would the space be restored to its originally planned use as a display and reception area.

The original 107 acres at Carderock were extended during the war with the addition of 47 acres, finalized in 1943, and another 55 acres in 1945. The domain grew further in 1946, with the addition of a field station for testing of underwater acoustic effects in Lake Pend Oreille, an exceptionally deep and clear lake in Idaho.

During the rapid expansion over the period 1943–1947, Howard, Saunders, and other staff members engaged in the planning gave considerable attention to such features as appearance, future expansion, and possible growth and extension of the nearby George Washington Parkway, as well as to convenience, utility, and accuracy of the facilities.[73] In 1945 Howard described the general future growth of the buildings, suggesting that the meadow area in front of the office-laboratory should be kept clear of construction. "Having in mind the architecture of the main building, I visualize something in the nature of a college campus or graduate school grown up around and in front of the main building. A row of buildings might well grow to the east and to the west of the main building toward the south but the central area should be kept free of building so that eventually a U-shaped group is formed with the open end toward the Highway."[74] Howard's foresight, based on pride in the striking design of the original buildings, led, in fact, to just the effect he desired. The U-shaped space, flanked by eastern and western extensions, is still apparent fifty years later with a clear view from the parkway across a wide lawn to the front of architect Ben Moreell's classic facade. The explosives test pond and its access road represented the beginning of what Howard visualized as the eastern branch of the "U-shape," while the wind tunnel and aeronautics laboratory represented the beginning of the western side of the U, supplemented in the 1990s with the transfer of the Ship Materials efforts from Annapolis to a striking new building along that same side. From the parkway entrance, the vista remains.

Postwar Research at DTMB

In 1946 the American public, Congress, and the military establishment became convinced that massive expenditures for research and development were essential to a strong defense. The dramatic product of the Manhattan Engineer District was the most obvious and most often cited factor in bringing about new support for science and technology.

Lake Pend Oreille.   The DTMB facility at Bayview, Idaho, provided still, clear, and quiet waters for the measurement of acoustics characteristics of submarine models.

David Taylor Model Basin, c. 1946.   Despite wartime expansion, the park-like expanse between the Moreell-designed facade and the Potomac River was largely preserved.

More subtle, but perhaps as essential in this conversion process, was the growing recognition of the sophisticated use of science by the German war machine.

Project Paperclip brought captured German equipment, laboratories, and personnel to the United States, a striking case of what a later generation would call technology transfer from one system to another. The project was established to enrich the scientific strength of a wide variety of U.S. research institutions. Included in this group were three men who were to have a profound influence on the future work and attitudes at DTMB: Georg Weinblum, a ship hydrodynamicist and specialist in wave theory; Herman Lerbs, a world authority on design of propellers; and Alfred Keil, an underwater explosions expert. Keil came to DTMB later than the other two, after a period at the Norfolk Navy Yard. Weinblum returned to Germany during the early 1950s to become director of Institut fur Schiffbau at Hamburg University. Lerbs also returned later to become director of the Hamburg Ship Model Basin. After serving first at the Underwater Explosions Research Detachment (UERD), Keil moved on to DTMB to become the head of the Structures Department and, later, the first civilian technical director of DTMB, serving from 1963 to 1967. Through such individuals Paperclip strengthened one laboratory after another. But it had an even broader importance in its contribution to the American recognition of the defense value of basic research.

As U.S. Army and Navy officers toured German laboratories and interviewed German scientists and engineers to gain data and to select Paperclip recruits, they expressed admiration and a degree of shock. A few months before the defeat of Germany, the Wehrmacht had a host of weapons that had passed from research through development to prototype or early production stages. Jet aircraft, revolutionary submarines, V-2s—all were either in production and use, or within a few more months could have been thrown effectively into the war effort. Project Alsos, an investigation of German nuclear development, uncovered the fact that German progress in this area had been retarded by policy decisions, not by scientific capability. Members of the Naval Technical Mission in Europe were duly impressed by what they found, and at times they appeared to exaggerate the quality of German work they found. They used the materials they found to offer a warning similar to that laid out by Vannevar Bush. The implication of their message, often explicitly stated, was that German science came close to dramatically affecting the outcome of the war.

The evidence that the officers on the Paperclip, Alsos, and Naval Technical Missions accumulated was stated in sobering language. In report after report, they reiterated the assertion that German research—had it been better organized, marshaled, properly funded—had come close to winning the war for Adolf Hitler. The very policy errors on the part of Germany that had delayed development were frighteningly ordinary—similar policies could easily have prevented American science from making its contributions. Young German scientists and engineers had been drafted for military service; scientific advice was not always heeded by policymakers; bureaucracy and materials priorities impeded the scientists in their work. It sounded all too familiar. The lesson was not only that science was essential but that it had to be protected, funded, and given a free hand, or its full effect might be too late.[75]

American science had also organized for the war, and now the story could be told. In articles, books, and memoirs, participants and observers publicized the impressive details. The works of James Conant, Bush, and commentators like James Phinney Baxter III, as well as official and journalistic accounts of the Manhattan Engineer District and of other previously secret research by new and old laboratories for the Army and Navy, helped build almost overnight a widespread recognition of the relationship between research and weaponry.[76]

For those working inside the Navy's laboratories, the new willingness and even eagerness on the part of the bureaus to fund basic research had sweeping effects, varying from laboratory to laboratory. At the Naval Research Laboratory, scientists quickly argued that testing responsibilities there should be shifted elsewhere and that basic research should expand. At EES the growth of small development responsibility during the war eroded as the pace of Navy procurement tapered off. The end of massive purchasing closed that opportunity to direct development. Within a few years, EES went back to the traditional task of testing regularly supplied and already standardized petroleum products, boiler compounds, alloys, and machine and engine parts.[77]

At DTMB as well, the vision of the basin as a research facility could have remained simply an unfulfilled hope. At the postwar forking of the path, the model basin could easily return to a design-testing role, leaving research into the newly raised and continuing theoretical issues as the province of academia or industry. During the war, under the pressure of ship, torpedo, and minesweeping work, fundamental problems of hydrodynamics were postponed or interrupted; at least twenty-five such problems were placed out on contract at university towing tanks, particularly at MIT, Stevens Institute of Technology, Caltech, the University of California, and the University of Minnesota. At some colleges, swimming pools were commandeered and converted into temporary model basins.

For such reasons, over the war years, the programs and policies did not necessarily augur well for a conversion to more research.[78]

The conversion of Navy leaders to a commitment to research sprang from the broad causes suggested here. At an institutional and organizational level, signs of that change were manifest as early as the spring of 1944, when a large group of Army and Navy officers met with Vannevar Bush from the Office of Scientific Research and Development under the leadership of Rear Admiral J. A. Furer, serving as the Navy's coordinator of research and development, to discuss the role of scientific research in postwar planning. Among the thirty-eight officers participating in the meeting and discussion was Rear Admiral H. S. Howard, in his role as director of DTMB. Several alumni and friends of both EES and the older EMB also attended, including Thorvald Solberg from the Bureau of Ships and Jerome Hunsaker, as well as A. H. Van Keuren, formerly with the Construction Corps Design Office, who had worked with Eggert and now served as director of NRL. Supported by such colleagues, Howard had every reason to understand well before the war was over that the marshaling of scientific talent and facilities would become a major postwar priority in the military.[79]

Even with Howard's early participation in such discussions, however, the change in emphasis from testing to research and development on the part of the Navy could have bypassed DTMB had not Howard and his staff consciously sensed the importance of the change and adapted to it promptly. Within two months after V-J Day, Assistant Secretary of the Navy H. Struve Hensel queried bureau chiefs and through them laboratories, regarding the Navy's research capacity. His inquiry itself reflected some ambivalence as to whether the model basin would be destined for a research role: "Neither personnel qualification nor facilities with Bureau of Ships' laboratories generally require fundamental research such as is conducted by the Naval Research Laboratory," asserted Hensel. Yet in a slight opening, seized on eagerly by Howard and his staff, Hensel referred to "research projects" performed at not only NRL but also at "TMB" (Taylor Model Basin) and those contracted out through the National Defense Research Council. That research, Hensel noted, required explanation.[80]

In response to this crucial inquiry, Howard signed off on a lengthy rationale for research work at the model basin prepared by Alvey Wright, who had consulted with Schoenherr and Landweber about prospects, facilities, and opportunities. Setting some distance between DTMB and the laboratories in the Bureau of Ships that had less potential for research, Howard's statement explicitly laid claim to a large and growing research role: "Unlike most of the laboratories under the

Bureau of Ships which serve primarily for quality control of materials, the David Taylor Model Basin is responsible for fundamental research and specific development projects in the fields of structural mechanics, hydromechanics and aeromechanics." Although Howard and Wright could not stress personnel strength in 1945 as proof of capacity, they gave full details of recently completed facilities and those under construction as explicit arguments for an enhanced research role.[81]

In the weeks following, Wright feared that the commitment of highly placed friends of DTMB, like Bureau Chief Cochrane and Solberg as coordinator for naval research, might be lost if any one of them were detached for other service. In November 1945 Wright warned that if that happened, "We would have to start our campaign all over again . . . some quite senior officer in the Bureau must find the time to pick up and carry our torches." He sought a commitment in writing from Cochrane affirming the basin's research role. Saunders, Howard, and Wright all perceived DTMB's adjustment to R&D as a "campaign" requiring bureau-level support. That basin campaign did in fact succeed.[82]

The commitment and drive for research materialized in the form of training, equipment, projects, and published reports. The cadre of scientists at the basin with higher degrees had increased somewhat during the war, but of the higher ranking civilian personnel, only Windenberg in Structures and Schoenherr in Hydromechanics had doctorates. Wright had taken graduate training in naval architecture at MIT, and he and Saunders went through the older Construction Corps elite scientific education. Landweber, who had followed in Schoenherr's footsteps to work on a master of arts degree in his own time in the late 1930s, had not pursued his studies further during the war. In later years, Landweber and Schoenherr, despite their differences and disagreements, both remembered the 1930s and early 1940s as a period of "little academic strength"—that is, few research-oriented staff members, only occasional sympathy for the scientific point of view on the part of naval officers, no interest in graduate training on the part of most of the other civilians, and not much sense of belonging to a national or international community of scholars. However, both of them also remembered the period from 1946 to 1950 as one of drastic change, personally and for the basin staff as a whole.[83]

In the immediate postwar period, the Navy encouraged graduate study for its civilian staff, gradually increasing the support and ease of graduate work from verbal encouragement through providing time off for class attendance, and arranging that University of Maryland courses be taught at the basin. Later the Navy provided tuition support and eventually even full fellowships for full time Ph.D. study by selected staff. Landweber himself took up the challenge, earning his doctorate in 1950.[84]

Although Schoenherr held a Johns Hopkins doctorate since the mid-1930s, he had exercised little personal leadership in his group. He was something of a loner, and others found his personality abrasive. Landweber, who during the war headed the hydrodynamics group, however, encouraged his younger staff members in the postwar period to emulate his own pursuit of education; individuals studied particular courses in mathematics or physics or took up work toward degrees. Landweber himself headed the professional development committee that arranged courses and related administrative details.[85]

Through the late 1940s DTMB purchased and developed a range of new instruments and equipment to further enhance the capacity for research. Landweber requested improved instruments for study of flow phenomena, including an electronic recorder to measure, record, and analyze the roughness of surfaces. Such equipment would allow a correlation of physical evidence with the empirically derived "roughness" factor calculated at 0.0004 on the average.[86] Analysis of the roughness issue remained a major research issue through 1947–1949.[87] Some of the new scientific equipment was designed and constructed at the basin: a group of Pitot tubes and manometers for measuring underwater pressure around models, which could help in determining the boundary layer transition between laminar flow and turbulent flow in model testing, were fully reviewed by one of the older, less scientifically trained staff members, C. E. Janes, in this postwar burst of work.[88]

At the same time, the nature of research changed rapidly. Postponed and interrupted projects at the forefront of the field in hydrodynamics soon replaced the wartime ship design problems. The new training and the new equipment meshed. In the early 1950s, naval architect F. H. Todd, who had moved to the basin from Britain, both shocked and impressed his former colleagues with a report on a recent U.S. Navy Bureau of Ships research program. Instead of testing particular destroyer or PT boat designs, Todd reported, the basin investigated fundamental problems such as the determination of the ingredients in the roughness factor used to adjust the Schoenherr Friction Line to full-scale ship performance, the effect of seaway and waves on resistance, and the effect of ship motion and seaworthiness on ships. Several new parent series lines were under way by the end of the 1940s, and university contracts on cavitation problems as well as planned in-house cavitation work all attested to the successful conversion to an emphasis on basics.[89]

A personal triumph for Schoenherr and incidentally a tribute to the basin's earlier pioneering work in fundamental problems in the 1930s came with the 1947 adoption by the American Towing Tank Conference of the Schoenherr Friction Line as a standard for member tanks in the United States and Canada when calculating frictional resistance.[90] Schoenherr himself defended his research in correspondence, modestly disclaiming he had any "axe to grind." His work, he claimed, needed refinement, but he also believed it "stood on its own feet." With a touch of bravado, he asserted, "If some of my statements made 15 years ago are disproved by more recent work, I shall be the first to welcome it." The challenge to "disprove" his work was not met and the ATTC adopted the Line.[91]

Other projects of a fundamental nature in the 1947–1950 period included the study of thermal currents in basins, the development and testing of a "hot wire anemometer" for measuring turbulence and boundary layer transition on models, and Morton Gertler's reanalysis of the Taylor Standard Series using the Schoenherr Line. A cooperative project with other basins involved the revival of the *San Francisco* model series tests and another cooperative series on Liberty ship models. Cooperating with the tank at Princeton University, the basin ran a set of systematic towing tests on a variety of geometric forms.[92] Test series with propellers reflected the application of the parent and series methods to propellers, an extension and continuation of a research item from the 1930s. William Morgan gave the series approach a new twist with propeller studies using a system of variable pitch and different numbers of blades that could be mounted on a single hub.[93]

Projects with more immediate application to naval use were not entirely crowded off the schedule, however. Such work included rudder design data, tests of reaction of floating drydocks to wind and current, and the effect of beam winds and lateral drift on stability.[94] The Structural Mechanics Laboratory tested flight deck strength on aircraft carriers in 1947.[95] Bureau of Ships orders continued to come in, reflecting current concerns. Hydrophone arrays needed to be properly housed and towed, and a test of special hydrophone towing struts for resistance and noise generation in 1948 was one such project.[96]

Over the period 1947–1950 new data for ships from series designated Series 56 through Series 61 covered several issues with clear contemporary and future practical application, yet reflected the traditional parent and series approach that had yielded systematic data. Each of the studies constituted an extension of the hull form parameters originally studied by David Taylor in the first decade of the twentieth century. Series 56 and Series 61 investigated the effects of size and length-to-beam ratio on planing boat resistance, with application to PT boats. Series 57 and Series 60 investigated the effects of block coefficient and longitudinal center of buoyancy on merchant ship powering performance. Series 59 dealt with the effects of bow and stern shape on aircraft carrier resistance. Series 58 led to a revolutionary tear drop hull design for submarines, first evaluated at full-scale on *Albacore* (AGSS 569), perhaps the best-known and historically important DTMB project with a specific naval application in this period. Work on the Walters engine and speculation regarding other self-contained propulsion systems, including engines driven by an aluminum oxide or magnesium oxide combustion process, as well as the impending completion of a nuclear power plant with submarine application, had stimulated the search for the ideal shape of a low- drag submarine. Later, *Skipjack* (SSN 585) combined a near optimum hull form with nuclear power. Series 58 and these two revolutionary vessels formed the basis for all future U.S. nuclear submarines.[97]

Researchers pursued other projects suggesting that the emphasis on fundamental research would have practical, but highly futuristic, weapons applications. In 1947 such work already included studies of seaworthiness at high speeds, propeller quieting, magnetic minesweeping gear, and acoustic countermeasures, against both homing torpedoes and shipborne sonar, as well as extensive DTMB participation in the Navy's nuclear test series at Bikini Atoll, code-named Operation Crossroads.[98]

By 1950 the Chief of the Bureau of Ships officially endorsed the basin's fundamental research thrust. W. S. Estabrook asked that the Hydromechanics Laboratory conduct research in six areas, all of which were already under study:

1. Mechanics of boundary layer transition in fluid flow
2. Effect of transverse curvature on frictional resistance (a question already under investigation by Phillip Eisenberg and Landweber)
3. Mechanism of resistance due to surface roughness (as already noted, basin investigators had been working on this problem since 1947)
4. Mechanism of turbulence and turbulence stimulation in relation to frictional resistance (the hot wire projects)
5. Resistance on flat plate surfaces due to paint roughness
6. Empirical studies of turbulence stimulation on specific types of ship models[99]

The prolific production of research over the brief period from 1947 through 1949 had won official approval and even a Bureau of Ships "request" for some of the very work of a fundamental nature that the model basin staff already had taken up. Eggert had been able to propose and pay for a handful of basin research projects in the mid-1930s. L. B.

McBride had reported in 1940 that about 8 percent of the basin time reflected basin-initiated research. But by the end of the 1940s the bureau responded as Wright had hoped it would at the end of the war, with official recognition that fundamental research was appropriate at DTMB and that the basin should proceed. Bureau of Ships projects now included science projects, not simply ship projects. The campaign to achieve that goal and to link it to facilities and staff expansion had succeeded with the beginning of a steady flow of reports and work.

The Laboratories and the New World of Research

Although the basin had entered the postwar era with a strong job-shop orientation made even more pronounced by the war work and its pressures, two crucial factors account for the successful transformation of the basin into a research institution in response to the national shift in priorities. One of those factors was the assortment of particular individuals and their leadership and professional qualities. At the local administrative level, Howard, Saunders, and Wright advocated more science. Not only were they personally committed to the growth and survival of the basin, they were believers, with their scientific orientation typical of the old Construction Corps, in the concept that fundamental research was a necessary prerequisite to technological innovation. Like their counterparts in academia and like their fellow scientifically committed officers in other bureaus of the Navy and in the Army, they welcomed the R&D world.

At first very few DTMB key civilians held graduate degrees in the sciences or mathematics; Schoenherr, who had attained international recognition, had his doctorate in engineering. Nevertheless, the basin had assembled a young and eager generation of science and engineering graduates willing to move into further study. The influx of German scientists, some with very impressive academic and publication credentials, included Georg Weinblum, Herman Lerbs, and Alfred Keil. Such men soon provided another level of example and leadership.

The second factor crucial to the adjustment was the fact that the staff had designed and built a truly first-class set of facilities. The sheer weight of the investment cried out for proper use, a point not lost on Navy bureau chiefs and assistant secretaries. Staff members soon added to the facilities a range of smaller scale equipment necessary for research. When they used the new facilities and equipment to respond eagerly to the new national priority, within a very few years the transition took hold.

On the other hand, the beginnings of an evolution of the Engineering Experiment Station into a more development-oriented laboratory tapered off after the war. One by one, the more advanced development projects were terminated, transferred, or wound up, without being replaced. Without the clout of massive procurement, EES could not shape any major technology. After his death in 1945, Goddard's work on rockets moved to California, to be merged with university contract work there and to form the core of what became the Naval Weapons Center at China Lake in later years. However, the postwar era would bring new challenges to EES.

Endnotes

1. *David Taylor Model Basin History, October 5, 1937, to December 31, 1958,* copy in Naval Historical Center (NHC), Navy Laborary/Center Coordinating Group (NLCCG) Archives, RC 1/2, box 2, folder 10.
2. Harvey M. Sapolsky, "Academic Science and the Military: The Years Since the Second World War," *The Sciences in the American Context: New Perspectives,* Nathan Reingold, ed. (Washington: Smithsonian Press, 1979), 381–384; James Phinney Baxter III, *Scientists Against Time* (Boston: Little, Brown, 1946); Vannevar Bush, *Modern Arms and Free Men* (New York: Simon and Schuster, 1949). Bush's most impassioned plea for research was in *Science: The Endless Frontier: A Report to the President* (Washington: GPO, 1945), a work reprinted several times in later years.
3. H. E. Saunders to Captain G. C. Weaver, USN, 30 Sep 1946, WNRC, acc. 4818, box 25, SS/Misc.; H. F. D. Davis, "Building Major Combatant Ships in World War II," U.S. Naval Institute *Proceedings* 73 (May 1947): 579.
4. EES personnel figure derived from EES Annual Reports in WNRC, RG 19, entry 1267, box 11.
5. E. C. Magdenburger, "Diesel Engine in the United States Navy," *JASNE* 61 (1949): 66; Carl Hoegh, *The Cylinder Wear in Diesel Engines* (New York: Chemical Publishing Co., 1945); D.S.D. Williams, *The Modern Diesel* (London: Newnes-Butterworths, 1972); John F. Nichols, "The Development of Marine Engineering," *Historical Transactions, 1893–1943* (1945); E. C. Forsyth to Director, EES, 16 Sep 1940, WNRC, RG 19, entry 1266, Bureau of Ships General Correspondence 1940–1945, box 414, 541-1, vol. 5; E. C. Forsyth to Director, EES, 16 May 1940; and E. C. Forsyth to Director, EES, 29 Apr 1940, WNRC, RG 19, entry 1266, box 413, 541-3, vol. 1; Hamilton to Director, EES, 24 Oct 1940; and A. T. Church to Bureau of Ships, 15 Aug 1940, WNRC, RG 19, entry 1266, box 415, 541-3, vol. 9; A. T. Church to Bureau of Ships, 14 Jan 1941, WNRC, RG 19, entry 1266, box 401, 541-1, vol. 2; M. M. Dana, Memo to Head of Design Division, 4 Feb 1941, WNRC, RG 19, entry 1266, box 416, 541-3, vol. 11.
6. *Annual Report of Laboratory Activities at the EES for Year Ending December 31, 1943,* WNRC, RG 19, entry 1267, EES Reports, box 11.
7. Ibid., 49–56.
8. Ibid., 64–67.
9. A. T. Church to Bureau of Ships, 30 Jan 1942, WNRC, RG 19, entry 1266, box 411, 541-2, vol. 1.
10. *Annual Report of Laboratory Activities at the EES for Year Ending December 31, 1943,* WNRC, RG 19, entry 1267, box 11.
11. H. A. Ingram to Director, DTMB, 5 Jul 1941, WNRC, acc. 4818, box 10, L5-2/N32-3-(3D); A. T. Church to Bureau of Ships, 16 Mar 1942, WNRC, RG 19, entry 1266, box 420, 541-3, vol. 22; C. C. Ross to Bureau of Ships, 21 Jul 1941, RG 19, entry 1266, box 416, 541-3, vol. 14; A. T. Church to Bureau of Ships, 29 May 1941, WNRC, RG 19, entry 1266, box 416, 541-3, vol. 12; A. F. Pola, J. C. Broach, and Bela Ronay to Office of the Judge Advocate General, 13 Oct 1941, WNRC, RG 19, entry 1266, box 418, 541-3, vol. 17.

12. C. D. Wheelock to Commandants, All Navy Yards, 8 Jan 1944, WNRC, RG 19, entry 1266, box 140, L5-3, vol. 2.

13. W. C. Latrobe to Commandants and Directors, 5 Jan 1944, WNRC, RG 19, entry 1266, box 140, L5-2, vol. 2.

14. Solberg to Director, EES, 5 May 1944, WNRC, RG 19, entry 1266, box 141, L5-2, vol. 3.

15. E. L. Cochrane to All Supervisors of Shipbuilding, Inspectors of Naval Material, and Inspectors of Machinery, 15 Jun 1944, WNRC, RG 19, entry 1266, box 135, L5-1, vol. 3.

16. A. T. Church to Bureau of Ships, 26 May 1941, WNRC, RG 19, entry 1266, box 416, 541-3, vol. 12.

17. A. R. Joyce to Bureau of Ships, Jun 28, 1940, WNRC, RG 19, cntry 1266, box 414, 541-3, vol. 4.

18. S. Parker to Bureau of Ships, 20 May 1941, WNRC, RG 19, entry 1266, box 417, 541-3, vol. 13.

19. John O. Huse to Commandants, 17 Jan 1942, WNRC, RG 19, entry 1266, box 419, 541-3, vol. 20; E. F. Keyes to Chrysler Marine Engines Sales and Service, 20 Feb 1942, WNRC, RG 19, entry 1266, box 420, 541-3, vol. 22; A. T. Church to Bureau of Ships, 13 Apr 1942, WNRC, RG 19, entry 1266, box 420, 541-3, vol. 24.

20. W. C. Latrobe to Eisemann Magneto Corp., 30 Jul 1940, WNRC, RG 19, entry 1266, box 414, 541-3, vol. 4; "Rules Governing the Restricted Status of Test Data Pertaining to a Manufacturer's Product When Such Test Data are Obtained at a Naval Laboratory," WNRC, RG 19, entry 1266, box 135, L5-1, vol. 3.

21. L. T. Barnes to Bureau of Ships, 5 Jan 1942; M. M. Dana to Code 502, 7 Jan 1942; and W. C. Latrobe to Director, EES, 26 Feb 1942, WNRC, RG 19, entry 1266, box 411, 541-2, vol. 1.

22. A. T. Church to Bureau of Ships, 4 Mar 1942, WNRC, RG 19, entry 1266, box 420, 541-3, vol. 22; C. C. Ross to Bureau of Ships, 25 Apr 1941, WNRC, RG 19, entry 1266, box 416, 541-3, vol. 11.

23. P. 5. Johnson to Code 335, 22 Jan 1945, WNRC, RG 19, entry 1266, box 135. L5-1, vol. 3.

24. Most of the EES correspondence and memoranda relating to delay problems with gas turbine work are located in WNRC, RG 19, entry 1266, boxes 402 and 403, 541-1, vols. 1–8.

25. G. W. Nelson to Chief, Bureau of Ships, 12 Jan 1942, WNRC, RG 19, entry 1266, box 402, 541-1, vol. 5; Robert V. Kleinschmidt to Contractors on Gas Turbines, 30 Sep 1942, WNRC, RG 19, entry 1266, box 403, 541-1, vol. 8.

26. J. T. Rettaliata to R. N. Landreth, 10 Mar 1942, WNRC, RG 19, entry 1266, box 402, 541-1, vol. 6.

27. A. T. Scott to Code 330A, 27 Oct 1944, WNRC, RG 19, entry 1266, box 410, CS41-1, vol. 3; Note Solberg recommendation that DTMB take over in November 1945; DTMB looks into adding German personnel to do the work.

28. R. Goddard to President, Smithsonian Institution, 27 Sep 1916, Robert H. Goddard/Smithsonian Institution Correspondence, 7 Sep 1916–30 Apr 1918, Rare Book Room, National Air and Space Museum (NASM).

29. Robert Goddard's early work is nicely summarized in two unpublished manuscripts written by Robert Goddard and McFall Kerbey circa 1940. Both manuscripts are located in the Research Branch, National Geographic Society, Washington, DC.

30. Albert B. Christman, *Sailors, Scientists, and Rockets: Origins of the Navy Rocket Program and of the Naval Ordnance Test Station, Inyokern*, vol. 1 (Washington: Naval History Division, 1971), 98.

31. Ibid., 97–99.
32. Christman, *Sailors, Scientists, and Rockets*, 102; R. Goddard to T. Taylor, 7 Jun 1941, Biographical File on Robert Goddard, NASA History Office Archives.
33. The contract he signed also stipulated that he move his work to the EES upon request. Merely one week after the contract with the Navy officially began (November 1941), Goddard had an experimental model ready for a static test. On 3 December he ran the first test of the motor in the horizontal position. Progress Report to Asst. Chief, Material Division, Army Air Forces, 24 Dec 1941, in Esther C. Goddard and G. Edward Pendray, eds., *Papers of Robert H. Goddard*, vol. 3, *1938–1945* (New York: McGraw Hill, 1970), 1444–1451.
34. R. Goddard to Lt. C. F. Fischer, 1 Dec 1941, in ibid., 1439–1440.
35. "Goddard's Years at the Engineering Experiment Station," *Centerline*, 19 Jul 1981, 4; Goddard and Pendray, eds., *Papers of Robert H. Goddard* 3:1488.
36. "Goddard's Years at the Experiment Station," 4; Elizabeth F. Edmondo (Goddard's secretary at the EES), "Goddard's Years," 4.
37. Goddard and Pendray, eds., *Papers of Robert H. Goddard* 3:1479–1481.
38. Christman, *Soldiers, Sailors, and Rockets*, 113.
39. Jul–Aug 1944 Diary entries, Goddard and Pendray, eds., *Papers of Robert H. Goddard* 3:1537–1540; Ernst Steinhoff on Robert H. Goddard, Frank H. Winter, Memo for File (undated), Goddard Biographical File, NASM Library.
40. W. R. Hibbard to Laboratory Committee, 31 Oct 1945, WNRC, RG 19, entry 1266, box 11, L5-2, vol. 5; W. R. Millis to Commanders and Directors, 19 Apr 1948, WNRC, RG 19, acc. 5300, box 163, L5-2.
41. E. E. Sprung to Directors, EES and DTMB, 13 Jul 1949, WNRC, acc. 11414, box 160-1, A3-1.
42. *David Taylor Model Basin Command History, 5 October 1937–31 December 1958.*
43. *Annual Report of the Bureau of Ships for the Fiscal Year Ending Jun 30, 1940.*
44. Saunders to Chief, Bureau of Ships, 4 Oct 1940, WNRC, RG 19, entry 1266, box 141, L5-2.
45. L. B. McBride to Chief, Bureau of Ships, 31 Jan 1942, WNRC, acc. 4818, box 16, NY5/A3-(1).
46. Description of the David Taylor Model Basin for Commander in Chief's Annual Report, 23 Oct 1943, WNRC, acc. 4818, box 15, NP 21, 1943–1945; C. Lester Walker, "We Model Our Fighting Ships" (Reprinted from *Harper's Magazine*, Nov 1943), DTNSRDC RC 7-1, box 3.
47. Ibid.
48. Karl Schoenherr, interview by David K. Allison, 15 Apr 1985, transcript in DTNSRDC RC
49. Dr. Louis Landweber, interview by Seth Hawkins, 28 Oct 1983; Dr. Louis Landweber, interview by David K. Allison, 20 Jan 1986, transcripts in DTNSRDC RC
50. C. L. Brand to Director of Naval Intelligence, 5 Mar 1945, WNRC, RG 19, Entry 1266, box 71, A9-1.
51. Baker to David Taylor Model Basin, 2 Mar 1942; L. B. McBride to Commandant, Norfolk Navy Yard, 20 Mar 1942; and H. E. Saunders to E. H. Rigg, 29 Mar 1943, WNRC, acc. 4818, box 4, BB61-66/S6, vol. 1.
52. Vibration Tests on USS. *South Dakota* (BB 57), 9 Apr 1942, acc. 4818, BB/S1-2-(3), vol. 2.
53. E. A. Wright to Commander C. D. Wheelock, USN, Jul 23, 1942, WNRC, acc. 4818, box 20, 58-8, vol. 3.
54. H. N. Wallin to Director, EMB, 24 Jan 1941, WNRC, acc. 4818, box 25, SS/S1-2-(6) also discussed in EMB Report 152 of May 1943.

55. C. Lester Walker, "We Model Our Fighting Ships" (reprint from *Harper's Magazine*, Nov 1943), DTNSRDC RC 7-1, box 3.
56. Commander, U.S. Naval Forces in Europe, to Director, David Taylor Model Basin, 3 May 1945, WNRC, RG 19, entry 1266, box 634, NP21/A1.
57. K. E. Schoenherr to Director, DTMB, 4 Aug 1945, WNRC, acc. 5144, box 1, NP21/A3-1.
58. E. A. Wright, *Reports on Visits to European Model Basins, Jul–Aug 1939*, WNRC, acc. 4818, box 12, N8-5/EF.
59. H. E. Saunders, "Brief Statement of Recommendations made to Council of ," Appendix II, 13 Nov 1946, WNRC, acc. 12608, box 8, N8-5/A19.
60. H. S. Howard, Memorandum, 17 Oct 1945, WNRC, acc. 4818, box 15, NP21 1943–1945.
61. Landweber to Commander Wright, 22 Mar 1946, WNRC, acc. 7681, box 4, NN/A3-1.
62. Ibid.
63. C. O. Kell to Chief, Bureau of Ships, Code 740, 26 Jul 1949, WNRC, acc. 11414, box 160-1, A3-1.
64. W. Roop to Test Facilities, 13 May 1944, WNRC, acc. 4818, box 15, NP21/P.
65. H. E. Saunders, "The David Taylor Model Basin: A Manual for Visitors to the DTMB," Apr 1947, DTMB Report 569, 39–41.
66. C. U. Hubbard to H. E. Saunders, 21 May 1942, WNRC, acc. 4818, box 13, N8-5-(1a)/NP21.
67. H. E. Saunders, "The David Taylor Model Basin: A Manual for Visitors to the DTMB," Apr 1947, DTMB Report 569, 31–32.
68. Ibid.
69. J. A. McCrary, "The Development of Naval Sea and Aircraft and Experimental Model Basins and Wind Tunnels, 1898–1945: Historical Observations," DTNSRDC RC 7-1, box 13, 29-D.
70. Ibid., 34-D.
71. H. E. Saunders to J. A. McCrary, 27 Dec 1943, WNRC, acc. 5144, box 1, NP21/A-31.
72. L. B. Richardson to Director, DTMB, 23 May 1944, WNRC, acc. 4818, box 6, F1-2/EN11.
73. H. S. Howard to Chief, Bureau of Ships, Jul 29, 1944, WNRC, acc. 4818, box 15, NP21/'43-'45.
74. H. E. Saunders, Memorandum, 2 Apr 1945, WNRC, acc. 4818, box 15, NP21/1943–45.
75. Clarence G. Lasby, *Project Paperclip: German Scientists and the Cold War* (New York: Atheneum, 1971); U.S. Technical Mission in Europe, "Comments on the German Aeronautical Research Program," Sep 1945, Technical Report No. 501-45, OA, box 43; and U.S. Technical Mission in Europe, "The Organization of Research in Germany," Oct 1945, Technical Report No. 472-45, OA, box 42.
76. Julius A. Furer, "Naval Research and Development in World War II," *JASNE* 62 (Feb 1950); Baxter, *Scientists Against Time*.
77. David K. Allison, *New Eye for the Navy: The Origins of Radar at the Naval Research Laboratory* (Washington: Naval Research Laboratory, 1981), 185.
78. *David Taylor Model Basin History, October 5, 1937, to December 31, 1958.*
79. *Minutes of Conference to Consider Needs for Post War Research and Development for the Army and Navy*, 26 Apr 1944, WNRC, RG 19, entry 1266, box 21, A3-1, vol. 2.
80. H. Struve Hensel to Chiefs of Bureaus, 8 Oct 1945, WNRC, RG 19, acc. 4818, box 15, NP21/1943–45.
81. H. S. Howard, Memorandum, 17 Oct 1945, WNRC, RG 19, acc. 4818, box 15, NP21/1943–45.

82. E. A. Wright, Memorandum for the Director, WNRC, RG 19, acc. 4818, box 15, NP21/1943–45.

83. Schoenherr interview, 15 Apr 1985; Landweber interview by Hawkins, 28 Oct 1983; and Landweber interview by Allison, 20 Jan 1986, transcripts in DTNSRDC RC; *David Taylor Model Basin History, October 5, 1937, to December 31, 1958*; Administrative Memo, M-3/50, 6 Jan 1950, DTMB Records Management Office, Administrative Memos, 1950.

84. Ibid.

85. Landweber, interviews with Hawkins, 28 Oct 1983, and 20 Jan 1986, DTNSRDC RC.

86. L. Landweber to Hydromechanics Officer, 20 Dec 1949, WNRC, acc. 12608, box 4 All/Cavitation, vol. 1.

87. H. E. Saunders, ed., *Sixth International Conference of Ship Tank Superintendents: International Committee Reports, Introductory Remarks, Discussions, and Conclusions*, 10–15 Sep 1951 (New York: 1953); *Progress Report on Research in Frictional Resistance*, Sep 1950, DTMB Report No. 726; G. Hughes, ed., *Fifth Conference of Ship Tank Superintendents: Papers and Discussions*, 14–17 Sep 1948 (London: His Majesty's Stationery Office, 1949); Louis Landweber, "Skin Friction: A Contribution to the Discussion of Subject 2," *The Sixth International Conference of Ship Tank Superintendents: Discussions, Conclusions and Comments*, Sep 1951 (Washington: 1951); Morton Gertler, *A Reanalysis of the Original Test Data for the Taylor Standard Series*, Mar 1954, DTMB Report No. 806.

88. C. E. Janes, *Instruments and Methods for Measuring the Flow of Water around Ships and Sea Models*, Mar 1948, DTMB Report No. 487.

89. F. H. Todd, "Hydrodynamics Research Programme of the Bureau of Ships, U.S. Navy," *Transactions of the Institution of Naval Architects* 96 (1954).

90. J. Comstock to Landweber, Davidson, and Rouse, 2 Dec 1946, WNRC, acc. 12608, box 8, N8-5/A19; Gertler, *A Reanalysis of the Original Test Data for the Taylor Standard Series*, Mar 1954, DTMB Report No. 806.

91. J. D. Comstock to Landweber, Davidson, and Rouse, 2 Dec 1946, acc. 12608, Box 8, N8-5/A19.

92. "Progress Report on Hydrodynamic Research at the David Taylor Model Basin," Prepared for presentation at the American Towing Tank Conference, Oct 1948, TMB Contribution File, No. 134.

93. William B. Morgan, *Open Water Test Series of a Controllable Pitch Propeller with Varying Number of Blades*, Nov 1954, DTMB Report No. 932.

94. *Current Hydrodynamic Research at the David Taylor Model Basin*, Oct 1947, WNRC, acc. 8883, box 6, P8-2/NAME-(3).

95. R. A. Hinners to Chief, Bureau of Ships, 15 Dec 1947, WNRC, acc. 8883, box 3, F1-2/EN 28.

96. Joseph E. Joers and Leo F. Fehlner, *Development of a Hydrophone Towing System for Investigation of Ship Noise*, Dec 1948, DTMB Report No. C-154.

97. J. M. Farrin, "Model Series at the U.S. Experimental Model Basin, 1900–1940: Addendum 1941–1956," Jan 1957 Addendum to DTMB Report No. 475; K. H. Wilcoxon, Memorandum, 25 Oct 1949, WNRC, acc. 12608, box 14, SS/S1-2-(5); supplemented by information provided by Justin McCarthy, ABIF.

98. W. C. Mehaffey, Administrative Memorandum, 5 Sep 1947, DTMB Records Management Office, Administrative Memos 1947.

99. W. S. Estabrook to Commanding Officer and Director, DTMB, 30 Jun 1950, WNRC, acc. 12608, box 4, All/Resistance.

CHAPTER 7

Research Directions

IN THE DECADE AND A HALF FOLLOWING 1950, both the David Taylor Model Basin and the Engineering Experiment Station worked to achieve standing as major research and development institutions. Progress toward this goal at the two facilities proceeded differently. At DTMB, with its stronger research tradition, the process would be viewed in retrospect as "coming to maturity." At EES, the increased Navy emphasis on research and development also brought change, later viewed by leaders there as "a period of transition," capped in 1963 with the renaming of the facility as the Marine Engineering Laboratory. This chapter outlines research directions at both institutions during the period; the following two chapters explore major contributions in the areas of submarines and surface ships.[1]

During the war and immediate postwar years (1941–1947), Captain Harold E. Saunders had served as director at DTMB. When he retired in 1947, Rear Admiral Claude O. Kell became director of the model basin. Until 1948, the commanding officer also formally held the post of director. Through the administrations of George A. Holderness, Albert G. Mumma, William H. Leahy, E. Alvey Wright, and Jack A. Obermeyer, actual technical direction was handled at the department or laboratory level, where technical leadership sometimes rotated among department heads. Under Kell, the four major departments—Structural Mechanics, Hydromechanics, Aerodynamics, and Applied Physics—were each renamed laboratories with representatives from each serving on a planning council which reported directly to the commanding officer. Each laboratory sought its own budget from codes in the Bureau of Ships. Coordination and direction varied with the laboratory heads, but the commanding officers through the decade had a diminished role to play in leading or directing the relatively autonomous laboratories.

While a tradition of research was well established at the model basin by 1950, the "maturation" of DTMB into a research facility was hardly painless. The design-test tradition ran deep. Aeronautics and Structures both had evolved as departments dedicated to testing; Hydromechanics, although including in its staff some scientists eager to work on theoretical problems, also was strongly rooted in a tradition of testing ship designs.

The development and availability of early computers and the recognition of their potential impact on research and development led the Bureau of Ships and DTMB to establish a computer laboratory, first with a UNIVAC-A in 1953, followed by two more UNIVACs, expanded in 1960 with a Livermore Atomic Research Computer (LARC). Established as the Applied Mathematics Laboratory in 1952 even before the machinery went into operation, the new specialists hoped to conduct their own research into computer engineering and into basic mathematics and programming logic. However, the major objective of the laboratory was *applied* mathematics, that is, the application of mathematics and

LARC at Carderock.   The Livermore Atomic Research Computer was among the first computers at Carderock to add new methods of modelling and analysis to the Navy's research capability.

computing to the solution of real problems in science, engineering, management, and operations. Still another laboratory came out of work that had been conducted in Applied Physics and Hydromechanics. Concern with silencing ships led to the formation, in 1963, of the Acoustics and Vibration Laboratory, drawing people and projects from the others.

While Navy policymakers believed that the future of America's ability to wage war at sea depended on "research," the practical meaning of that term and the mechanics of research management had to be defined. Through the 1950s and into the early 1960s, the organization of research in the Navy underwent a series of restructurings designed to address the issues of how best to fund and manage research. For the man or woman at the bench, such changes and discussions usually seemed remote. At best, position papers and plans, alternating every three or four years between centralization and decentralization, could sometimes be utilized to urge a greater effort or to explain a shift in personnel.

The rate of progress toward a greater emphasis on research and development at DTMB depended on unpredictable factors such as leadership, funding opportunities, the impact of new equipment, the growth of teams with good internal mutual respect, and the emergence of individual talent, rather than on more intentional factors such as management plans and mission statements. The evolution of management theory or naval reorganization at first had little direct impact on either the quality or the nature of the scientific and technical work at the basin, yet even so, as the staff and agenda grew more diverse, the need for centralized planning and direction seemed ever more crucial.

Of all the changes in the naval research organization during the period, probably the most important to the laboratories was the decision by the Bureau of Ships, in the late 1950s, to appoint civilian technical directors to such laboratories, while retaining a naval commanding officer. Harold V. Nutt, an engineer with twenty-five years of service, beginning in the Internal Combustion Engine Laboratory under William Joachim in 1937, became the first EES civilian technical director in 1958. At the model basin, Alfred Keil, a Paperclip German scientist with prior experience at the Underwater Explosions Research Division (UERD) of the Norfolk Navy Yard and as the head of the Structural Mechanics Laboratory from 1959, became civilian technical director of DTMB in 1963. Both men, eager to produce results, diplomatic in interpersonal skills, and intensely interested in good management, brought years of background as civilians in research work for the Navy to their posts. Each sought to harness the skills and energies of their staffs and to move the labs forward in the transition to research and development. When they took over research direction of the laboratories, Nutt and Keil inherited a number of unresolved problems; they also inherited strong and well-equipped institutions with long-standing records of accomplishment.

Some of the changes naturally brought personality conflicts to the surface. Perhaps the most notable arose when Keil, after service at the basin only since 1959 as head of the Structural Mechanics Laboratory, was selected to be technical director. "Under those conditions, I resign," Karl Schoenherr said, according to the later memory of Keil. However, Schoenherr had been with the organization since 1922, and his compulsory retirement at age seventy was due in any case. Keil was relieved—for he anticipated that Schoenherr would have been the most difficult individual to work with as he took over the top supervisory position. However, he did not believe that his own German origin or his previous status as a Paperclip scientist led to enmity among others. Quite the contrary, he found American hospitality, acceptance, and recognition of his talents both natural and pleasant.[2]

Keil was remembered by his colleagues as a natural leader, an engaging personality, and a man who quickly adapted to American manners and to the American sense of humor. In 1949, during a test sinking of an old German U-boat *(U 1105)* off Piney Point, Maryland, Keil was along as an observer from UERD. A young engineer, Hubert Cosner, had taken motion pictures documenting the event, which would demonstrate some blast effects, with whipping of rigid flagpoles mounted on the sub. On the way back to their lab in Norfolk, Keil casually asked Cosner if he had remembered to take the lens cap off the camera. Cosner insisted that the car be stopped so he could check his camera; he remained nervous until the film was developed. The story became legend. For years, people would automatically ask Cosner if he had the lens cap off.[3]

By the early 1960s, the need to coordinate projects at DTMB that had ramifications in more than one laboratory, and to conduct systematic research into completely new types of ships with innovative hull forms, including air cushion vehicles and hydrofoils, led to the beginning of advanced ship design groups, drawing staff and skills from the other laboratories. The language of systems management, developed at Rand Corporation, carried forward in the Navy in the Polaris project, and implemented from the top down throughout the Department of Defense during the John F. Kennedy administration, would provide tools for such coordination and management. But success depended not on paper plans but on the men and women engaged in the work.

Growing Pains and the Research Emphasis

At both EES and DTMB, the conversion to a research emphasis over the 1950s and early 1960s meant that each group of staff members faced different kinds of career developments. At EES the overall size of the staff declined from around 1,200 to about 1,000 in the 1950s. Through reductions-in-force in 1948, retirement, and easing-out of some individuals, the proportion of support technicians and shopworkers was cut in favor of higher ranking engineers. Department managers, operating on department budgets that they had obtained separately from bureau codes, found that the need to carry excess numbers of shopworkers raised the cost of each project; the financial incentive to reduce the burden of unneeded technicians led to resentment at the assignment of excess staff members to their own projects. "Thank God for the Civil Service rules," remarked Harold Nutt later, in reference to opportunities for early retirement, for promotion, and for reductions-in-force—all of which made the manager's task somewhat easier. Some department heads actively assisted in the search for alternative career opportunities for those they needed to drop, sweetening the bitter pill as much as possible.[4]

The avenue of upgrading was open to many. In the mid-1950s EES technicians and engineers were encouraged to take courses—to earn bachelor's degrees, or if holding a bachelor's, to pursue graduate work. Classes beginning at 1600 hours at the University of Maryland proved convenient, as did a similar program at George Washington University. The station released those attending classes at 1500 hours, providing them with an hour's paid commuting time. The class and return home would be done on the staff member's own time, but the early release hour at least gave some assistance. In Annapolis, as at Carderock, a few courses would be taught on location.[5]

Hiring to fill vacancies took on a new style, as the station placed advertisements not only through bulletin board announcements but through Baltimore and Washington newspapers, and as far afield as the *Wall Street Journal* and national association newsletters. Networks of college faculty were tapped for promising graduates. Recruitment became a strenuous talent search rather than a simple hiring process.[6]

A similar shift in emphasis, under way earlier, continued at the model basin. Keil eagerly sought the graduates of MIT, Stevens Institute of Technology, University of Minnesota, and Stanford. At both DTMB and EES, measurement of career achievement took on a more professional cast: participation in conferences, publication in the open literature, and achievement of higher degrees all began to supplement time-in-service and limited circulation report production as a significant part of the standard for promotion. For each individual, the changes in emphasis would have a different effect. For some, it was a time of personal opportunity leading to more responsibility and more reward. For others, especially the shop staff and technicians, the handwriting was on the wall: retirement or a job in the private sector provided a ticket out of Navy employment. On the other hand, new opportunities for technicians arose in the many positions created to deal with the operation and maintenance of the new computer facilities.

In group after group, new appointees from outside often received higher-ranking posts, leaving old-timers often feeling bypassed. The results were mixed. Sometimes, as with Keil, a combination of diplomacy, hard work, and mutual recognition of achievement could smooth over the rough spots. In other cases, minor reorganizations of groups and creation of special task groups, cosmetically presented as growing out of the nature of the project, could separate two incompatible individuals or provide an avenue for advancement for a promising, but junior scientist. Department heads consumed weeks in patient negotiation, peacekeeping, and smoothing of ruffled feathers.

Yet good will and diplomacy, reshuffling, and careful management could achieve only so much. By 1960 it was apparent to basin staff and to the Bureau of Ships that the sometimes haphazard effort to improve skill levels and infuse new talent had both positive and negative effects. In that year the bureau ordered a review and evaluation of the model basin, appointing a team composed of civilian scientists from Naval Research Laboratory and from nominees suggested by the National Academy of Sciences. After a series of visits, interviews, and meetings, the evaluation team produced a full report, together with twenty-eight recommendations for improvement.

The recommendations ranged from major reorganization measures to minor details of supply management and budgeting. Most crucial and important was the proposal to appoint a technical director for the laboratory as a whole. In addition, the evaluation team suggested that the formation of "splinter groups" cease; that unrelated functions be moved out of Carderock; that local management keep the bureau informed whenever "law or regulation promotes mediocrity or hinders operations;" that the basin review the use of underused facilities and reduce supervision and administrative "overload"; and that another twenty or so minor reforms of group and shop management be instituted. Within a year, Commanding Officer Obermeyer could report internal progress on most of the reforms, while still awaiting bureau action on the appointment of a technical director.[7]

The report itself was hard-hitting, pointing to a "downhill tendency" in performance, attributed by staff to a wide range of conditions but especially to a lack of leadership from the top. Of course, under the diffused management of the 1950s, such complaints were well justified. In particular, the evaluation report singled out for attention the financial problems and lack of direction of the new Applied Mathematics Laboratory. The report also noted poor morale in several areas, particularly the Aerodynamics Laboratory, which seemed to have been "orphaned" by its separate funding and by its status as the only laboratory without a civilian director.

Since the 1930s, at both institutions the relationship of civilians and naval officers had been at best an uneasy alliance, and at worst a source of friction. Although most of the management crises and morale difficulties at both facilities could be traced to the transition from testing facility to research and development laboratories, with the attendant crosscurrents of career shifts, the delicate question of naval supervision of civilian employees haunted many of the contemporary analyses of difficulties and the retrospective comments of those who survived the period. Nutt noted that the relationship was more complex than simply between officers and civilians. Indeed, he felt that several factors underlay the relationship: as a reservist who had gone on active duty during the war, he noted from experience that when civilians became officers they changed their style of behavior. Officers were themselves divided between those with Engineering Duty Only background, whose attitudes and training made them sympathetic to the work of engineers and scientists, and line officers, who typically viewed EDO officers as well as civilian engineers as "technicians." Despite all such sources of potential division or tension, Nutt and many other civilians recognized and appreciated the talents of most of the naval officers assigned to EES. Incidents of friction often came down to simple personality clashes between individuals, rather than any deep-seated cultural conflict. Yet some broader patterns could be discerned.[8]

Long-range changes in naval structure had affected the relationship of officers and civilians, particularly at the model basin. With the 1940 merger of officers in the Construction Corps with the engineering officers, the numbers of Construction Corps-trained officers, in the tradition of David Taylor, Ernest Eggert, Saunders, and Wright, soon declined. Officers in the Construction Corps, always a small cadre, either qualified personally as first-rate naval architects or at least were highly sympathetic to the concerns of scientists and engineers. As the last of the Construction Corps generation of the late 1930s reached retirement age in the 1950s and the 1960s, the military-civilian gulf at the model basin began to widen.

Other long-range developments also contributed to the difficulties faced by naval officers managing civilian staffs. Both EES and DTMB had become very large institutions—each employing over 1,000 civilians, with a small officer complement in charge. At both facilities the emergence of civilian department heads with decades of service and experience, when combined with the Navy policy of rotating officers in three- or four-year billets, created an imbalance of local experience and seniority weighted heavily in favor of the civilians. Officers, no matter how diplomatic and understanding of the needs of researchers, would naturally find it hard to "handle" civilians who expected the Navy men to run interference with the bureau "downtown" and to keep the lawns mowed, but to stay clear of research matters. With such attitudes, even the most well-meaning and sensitive officer might find the deck stacked against him. Some would win support through sheer intellect and personal charm. Keil had "extremely fond" memories of Captain Dennett K. Ela, commanding officer of the basin, 1964–1967, admiring both his quality of mind and personality. However, Keil remembered that Obermeyer, commanding officer and director, 1960–1963, while a brilliant officer, had attempted to do too much in handling both tasks. Many of the scientists saw the appointment of a civilian technical director as one of the signs of maturation of the laboratory, and a welcome change that would resolve some of the difficulties of military-led local management.[9]

To review the sometimes painful aspects of the transition and maturation of the two facilities could create an incorrect impression of conflict. The reality was hardly so unpleasant. Managers might concentrate their energies and, later, focus their memories on the growing pains. However, for the individual researcher and engineer, the personal achievement of career goals and the output of good work remained primary concerns. Particular achievements in research earned both local enthusiasm and wider recognition. Reform could possibly make both laboratories more efficient and more responsive to Navy needs; better budgeting and direction would make them better places to work. But in the end what counted was not management style but achievement of research and development results. Regardless of management problems and attempts to solve them, the output of work during the period attested to the growing skills and the quality of equipment at both laboratories. At the station, the transition from testing to development slowly took hold, while at the basin, the quality and significance of research increased.[10]

EES—Transition to Development, 1950–1965

Two of the most promising research areas at EES in the postwar period were designed to free submarines of the necessity of surface operation to recharge batteries: the "snorkel" that would permit regular diesels to run submerged, and the closed-cycle hydrogen peroxide engine based on the Walters design. By 1946, EES had succeeded in running American two-cycle diesel engines with a modified snorkel, and in 1948, the station could proclaim the first successful operation in the United States of the closed-cycle system. Paperclip German engineers, including Wolfgang Lang, assisted with the submarine closed cycle and diesel engine systems. Yet, as Nutt was to remark later, the advent of the nuclear submarine meant that the "whole house of cards flopped." However, he and others believed that the work on such projects was not entirely in vain. Should such studies ever be needed in the future, the work was completed and the reports were "on the shelf."[11]

The area in which EES could effectively work at first seemed to be narrowed from both ends. Not only were promising in-house development projects terminated, but even the former mainstay of station work, specification testing, dropped off severely in the 1950s. Under the Dwight D. Eisenhower administration, the Navy cooperated with the Army and the Air Force in establishing a set of guidelines for manufacturers so that they could conduct testing of fuels and lubricants. In area after area, new technology development and testing of products to standards was turned over to private industry, leaving the station, in effect, on the sidelines. For those trained in the EES tradition of product evaluation and working with manufacturers to ensure that changes in design and manufacture led to improvement, the change in emphasis was unsettling. At the practical level of day-to-day management, the change meant that shop staff, formerly used to set up tests and to read instruments, was now redundant.[12]

Despite the narrowing of the field of activity, during the 1950s and early 1960s, the station continued to work in two directions. One entailed some limited in-house development on less dramatic and far-reaching projects than closed-cycle engines or jet-assisted take-off. The second path included projects in which the older method of industrial liaison and specification-guided development could be effective. The two different methods or styles of development continued side-by-side through the period.

The coming of nuclear submarines, while bringing an end to other underwater propulsion alternatives, generated new technical problems, some of them addressed at EES through in-house development. The

new work included, in 1949, development of a water-lubricated submarine shaft bearing, ready for installation in 1952. Another EES project involved development of a hull-noise damping system using a chromate-
felt treatment, installed in nuclear submarines after 1957. By 1960 EES
could claim that its own development work had contributed twenty-one
separate improved component parts or systems for use in nuclear submarines, including newly designed shaft bearings, auxiliary diesel power
engines, reactor piping, and fire-resistant hydraulic fluids.[13]

Other in-house developments could be found in less dramatic but
also crucial, areas. Through the decade, EES staff worked on low-fre-
quency shock-noise isolation mounts constructed of rubber or synthetic
materials for shipboard machinery. By 1958 the staff set up a complete
set of mounts, accepting loads ranging from 50 pounds to 2,000 pounds.
The relatively unspectacular mounts not only reduced noise and vibration but represented a successful venture of the station in the research,
evaluation, redesign, and development of an innovation for naval use.[14]

A bearings project begun in 1946 led to several products and applications through the 1950s, including a method of measuring bearing
temperature as a warning system. Nutt later recalled that Watt Smith of
the bearings group "did more than any other human being in the area
of naval bearings." Smith personally worked on saltwater lubricated bearings, developed bearings made of composite materials to replace
wooden ones used in supporting propeller shafts, and redesigned main
thrust bearings for large ships. Smith perfected a design for very large
thrust bearings, which took tremendous pressure as they transmitted the
propulsive force from the shaft to the ship itself, so that they could contain and self-circulate lubricants. He not only personally designed such
high-load thrust bearings but also set up procedures and methods for
packaging tiny, delicate ball bearings so as to prevent corrosion from
minute atmospheric contaminants.[15]

In 1953 two explosions of hydraulic catapults aboard aircraft carriers led to a thorough investigation. Small amounts of air had mixed with
hydraulic fluid in lines, allowing the fluid to explode from the heat of
compression—essentially, to "diesel." The explosions had been disas-
trous, leading to loss of life and extensive fires. EES conducted the investigation and recommended the development of a nonflammable, substitute hydraulic fluid. Through the late 1950s the station developed a
fluid and adapted it for use in other hydraulic applications.[16]

Although the Navy chose to order no more diesel-electric submarines after 1954, hundreds of other fleet uses of diesel engines remained. The Internal Combustion Engine Laboratory evaluated the performance and recommended a series of design changes on an

all-aluminum Packard diesel engine in 1955. The engine, after incorporating the changes, found over 500 applications in the fleet. Among the suggestions of the ICE Lab on this engine were corrections for excessive wear of main bearings and turbocharger bearings, solution of combustion gas leakage past cylinder head gaskets, and strengthened valve tappets to prevent breakage. [17]

Among the in-house development contributions of EES during the 1950s were a variety of shock, vibration, and noise-reduction methods, redesigned gauges, an ocean-water salinity testing device, improvements in instrument light systems, and high-efficiency flame and spark arrestors for small engines. As in the past, the station's contributions ranged over a wide area; what was new was that in case after case through the 1950s, development work began to replace testing of products. These innovations, undramatic as they might be, were coming full-blown from the station rather than from manufacturers. In the 1950s, EES contributed more purely in-house development of devices, instruments, materials, and systems than it had in all its previous four decades of work put together.

USS *Turbot* (SS 427).   In 1950 the Navy provided *Turbot* to the Engineering Experiment Station for use as a floating laboratory to begin a program of submarine noise reduction.

In 1950 the station acquired *Turbot* (SS 427), a World War II submarine, to use as a floating laboratory for noise-reduction research. Station personnel acted as consultants in a program to reduce noise output from machinery on board *Grouper* (SS 214) during its modification into a killer submarine at Mare Island Naval Shipyard. As a result, *Grouper* became the quietest submarine in the fleet to date. Out of the study group working on *Grouper,* and using *Turbot* as a test facility, the Station established a program on machinery noise reduction.[18]

A variety of projects came out of the noise-reduction work, including development of specifications for special quiet ball bearings in 1952 and development of design criteria for the manufacture of gears. Investigations proved that the main reduction gears were the primary source of noise generation on board ships. In 1952 a large-scale evaluation stand was built in an acoustically and structurally isolated building. Further research on reduction gears revealed that the most important factors in noise generation were tooth-mesh frequency and tooth design. Technicians improved the test stand to take greater loads and speeds of revolution up to 10,000 rpm. This facility became the Navy's central test facility for new gears.[19]

Nutt later noted that some of the work with gear design perfectly illustrated the need for the Navy to continue to be a "knowledgeable buyer." When a set of gears built from a new alloy failed, the propulsion plant on a destroyer had to be redesigned to accommodate an older set of gears constructed from more conventional steel. After studying the problem, Nutt believed that the Navy had erred in setting a specification that could not be reached. "We had not done our homework," he remembered. When asked by the bureau officer in charge of the project why Westinghouse could not be forced to produce the new gears to contract specifications or to pay for the expense of the problem, Nutt pointed out that the courts could not be expected to force the company to pick up the cost of redesign of the propulsion plant to adjust for Navy error in setting technically unachievable parameters. In short, the case illustrated the need for the Navy to continue to thoroughly review designs and specifications prior to procurement and, in areas of newly developing techniques, to work closely with the manufacturer in management, adjustment, and redesign. "You've got to know that you can get what you want," said Nutt, sounding very much like Walter Worthington forty years earlier. Clearly, Nutt understood the importance of the EES method of guiding development through purchase that had brought diesel progress; even in the 1950s and 1960s, opportunities to use such a method came along from time to time, despite expectations on the part of some Bureau of Ships officers that manufacturers would manage and direct their own development projects.[20]

Some aircraft on board Mediterranean Fleet carriers were immobilized during the Suez Crisis of 1956 because of the inability of the carriers to refuel aircraft with clean fuel. Heavy emulsions of dirt, rust, and water contaminated jet fuel. The station successfully undertook the job of setting specifications and working through manufacturers to improve jet fuel filters. In this case, the method of guiding development through specifications and through close liaison with manufacturers recommended by Nutt, and so well demonstrated in earlier years, continued to survive as the development- management procedure.[21]

At the station, silencing work expanded in 1953 with the acquisition of an acoustic range for measuring noise signatures of ships. Work on *Turbot* led to the perfection of the chromate-felt treatment for hull-noise damping, which was installed on nuclear submarines constructed after 1956. In 1959 the station engaged in a program to test the first of each class of nuclear submarines to ensure that machinery vibration and machinery noise generation was held to a minimum. Thus, between isolation mountings, the hull-damping work, and improvements in machinery installation and full-scale vessel testing, EES contributed greatly over the period 1950–1960 to submarine silencing work. Submarine stealth remained the primary responsibility of the Acoustics Department (Code 19) at Carderock; the isolation-mounting and hull-damping studies were collaborative efforts between Code 19 and Annapolis.[22]

In 1959 the station set up a facility to evaluate the generation of magnetic fields from electrical equipment on board minesweepers. This "Stray Magnetic Field Facility" tested motor generator sets and other electrical equipment to determine how they might be improved to make magnetic minesweeping more effective.[23]

When Nutt took over as EES technical director in late 1958, he continued to advocate specification work and cooperation with manufacturers as well as in-house development work as the proper provinces for the station, and to upgrade the staff through retraining, promotion, and identification of promising and talented younger workers. Despite the constriction on the station's opportunities, he kept searching for new development areas. As in the past, some of the more exciting projects that had started at the station would be transferred away. The station briefly housed a study of fuel cells, a system of chemically regenerated batteries, with the idea of providing a power source for Navy-operated space satellites. The fuel cell work was discontinued, to be carried forward by National Aeronautics and Space Administration.[24]

By the early 1960s the station's areas of expertise earned some recognition: machinery silencing and vibration damping, gear and bearing innovations, development of specialized machinery and electrical items for naval use, and study of nonflammable hydraulic fluids. Guided external development continued in a few areas, as in the work on the Packard diesel, the development of jet fuel filters, and the testing of magnetic equipment and reduction gears. When the Bureau of Ships clearly demonstrated excessive reliance on outside manufacturers, neglecting the Navy's need to be a "knowledgeable buyer," Nutt and his colleagues reasserted the value of the specification tradition, quietly affirming that the station could play a role in development, even in the age of massive research and development contracts to giant corporations. Under Nutt, the transition from a testing facility to a development facility quietly became more explicit.

In 1963 Nutt conducted a "contest" to produce a new name for the facility that would reflect the emerging new identity. After considering several suggestions, many of which sought to memorialize Admiral George Melville through naming the facility the "Melville Engineering Center," perhaps echoing the naming of the Carderock facility after Melville's one-time rival, David Taylor, the selection committee settled on "MEL"—the U.S. Navy Marine Engineering Laboratory—finally abandoning the turn-of-the-century "Experiment Station" concept in favor of a more contemporary "Laboratory" designation. The Navy formally changed the name on 1 July 1963.[25]

As Nutt led the transition from experiment station to laboratory, the nature of the work continued to reflect engineering and development, not fundamental research. Development work, whether in-house or through manufacturers, continued to lead to step-by-step improvements rather than spectacular breakthroughs. The nature of the projects, including the most notable such as noise damping and a nonflammable hydraulic fluid, fell in the tradition of incremental engineering advances or applications of existing technology to special problems.

Although for decades station managers and bureau officers had placed highly promising projects at the facility, the most advanced and innovative projects had, over time, been transferred away or had been bypassed by other technologies. In retrospect, the station had played a role, often for only a few years, in some of the most exciting naval developments of the twentieth century: aircraft testing, 1911–1913, before transfer to San Diego; sonar work under Harvey Hayes, 1919–1923, before transfer to NRL; JATO work under Robert Goddard, 1941–1942, before the concentration of Navy rocket work at China Lake; snorkel and Walters engine work before the advent of the nuclear submarine,

1916–1948; and fuel cell development. While the station had temporarily pursued work on each of those revolutionary developments, none of them led to lasting institutional or research follow-through at EES.

Although the reasons these projects were briefly situated at the station differed and the reasons for their transfer to other facilities or their termination varied, some common threads in the pattern would be obvious as EES converted to MEL in the 1960s. As a testing station with well-equipped shops and a deep-water location close to Washington, the station had been an ideal spot to house a self-contained innovative project with engineering aspects. However, the engineering and testing orientation of staff and facilities was best suited to the incremental development of technology, especially in machinery and engines, and was so viewed both by local administrators and by bureau decision makers. The station could assist in evaluating prototype devices, such as aircraft or sonar, but for continued development of the new technology, the Navy would turn elsewhere. For control of sonar self-noise for submarines and surface ships, Carderock's Code 19 took the lead. With the advent of the research and development conception during and after World War II, the station could undergo a transition to a development facility but only in those areas of its central strength, narrowly defined.

Maturation of Research at Carderock, 1950–1965

The adjustment to the Navy's emphasis on research and development at DTMB required less dislocation than at EES. The basin's work under the leadership of Saunders and Wright in the immediate postwar period had already built a reputation, a capability, and a self-image of scientific work, especially in fundamental hydrodynamic issues and in follow-through on research questions raised during the war years. Several new specialties and new research directions opened up for the model basin in the 1950s and the 1960s.

With the advent of large computers, one of the more important major additions to the basin's capabilities came with the creation of the Applied Mathematics Laboratory (AML) in 1952. When the building housing the UNIVAC-A opened in 1953, it was the first new structure at Carderock to house research work since the completion of war period-initiated construction in 1949. The new staff of thirty, headed by Harry Polachek, visualized several functions for the new facility. Polachek established three divisions: Theory and Analysis, Planning and Programming, and Engineering and Development. In 1955 the divisions were reorganized, reflecting the evolving workload. The Theory group did research in methods of calculation, Mathematical Computations found solutions to specific engineering research problems, and Management Data Analysis focused on management and logistics and served clients throughout the Navy and in other branches of government. Engineering and Development handled operation, maintenance, and design improvements on the computer. In 1961 Polachek received the Department of Defense's Distinguished Civilian Scientist Award for his work in establishing this new capability.

The types of work handled in the Applied Mathematics Laboratory included a wide range of problems, some having impact far beyond DTMB. The sheer ability of the UNIVAC to process massive amounts of data proved useful. For example, it was used to produce a set of tables with over 400,000 entries for Congress to include in the Uniformed Services Survivors' Benefit Program in 1954.[26]

More directly related to Navy use, but still reflecting a departure from the model basin's traditional areas of concern, the laboratory produced calculations on the lifetime of submarine nuclear reactors that were used by Rear Admiral Hyman Rickover's Nuclear Reactors Directorate within the Bureau of Ships. The work for this project produced the first practically applicable mathematical models and computer programs for describing reactor core behavior. The programs computed the diffusion of neutrons through the core, taking into account the core geometry and composition, then simulated the depletion of the fuel and the buildup of fission by-products, and calculated the "criticality factor"—that is, the power-producing capability of the overall reactor design.[27]

For planning purposes, perhaps the most important product of the program were predictions of core life, allowing accurate refueling projections. Reactors used on submarines of the *Skate* (SSN 578) and *Skipjack* (SSN 585) classes as well as the aircraft carrier *Enterprise* (CVAN 65) were all designed using these projections, as were the replacement cores for *Nautilus* (SSN 571) and *Seawolf* (SSN 575). Elizabeth Cuthill and Joanna Schot, two of the first members of the AML staff, developed these computer programs. Cuthill and Schot turned the methods and algorithms over to Westinghouse and General Electric for use in design of reactors for electric utility purposes. With later modification, the Cuthill-Schot programs continued to provide calculations for alternative designs and proved essential in the manufacture of most reactors produced in the United States over the following two and a half decades.[28]

By the late 1950s, computer methods had entered the full range of work at DTMB, from on-line collection, sorting and analysis of experimental data to numerical solution of some of the never-before-attempted, most complex problems of computational fluid and structural

Elizabeth Cuthill and Joanna Schot.   In the early 1960s, Cuthill and Schot developed computer programs to predict nuclear reactor core behavior, essential in the design of propulsion and power reactors over the next decade.

mechanics for the researchers in the departments of Hydromechanics and Structural Mechanics. Computers added an all-important tool to those employed for analytic and experimental work by ship researchers and naval architects in all of the departments at DTMB. Significant progress was made on some 118 computational problems. In Hydromechanics alone, problems included potential flows around two- and three-dimensional forms, spectrum analysis of ocean wave records, pressure fields around shiplike bodies, calculations on submarine hull form Series 58 (the *Albacore* project), and analysis of irregular waves. Problems that focused on management data analysis and logistics included material requirements for shipbuilding programs, an inventory system for a ship parts control center, a demonstration payroll, and a study of electronic equipment failure rates.[29]

The range of analysis included effective horsepower calculations, shaft horsepower calculations, evaluations of "transient excitation" or blast effects on ship hulls, calculations of probabilities in minesweeping operations, statistical analysis of the properties of new alloys, studies of blast transmission, and determination of the natural frequencies and normal modes of vibration of various structures. Studies of propellers, speedboat resistance, and acoustic problems crowded the schedule by the end of the decade.[30]

In 1957 Alvey Wright, addressing a group of naval engineers, recognized the fundamental impact that the computer would have on the work of the basin and of all engaged in naval engineering work. "Across the face of our profession, rooted in mathematics and embracing every physical science, is quietly bursting a tremendous new versatility and power that will surely carry naval engineering far beyond present design frontiers. It is the rapid automation of ship calculations. . . . This young dimension might be called naval mathematics."[31]

By the time the UNIVAC-A was "retired" in 1962, it had been in operation about 45,000 hours. In addition to the areas already mentioned, among its major projects had been calculations to obtain general instability collapse pressures of submarine hulls; calculations of fallout patterns from nuclear explosions under various scenarios of nuclear attack on the United States, prepared for the Naval Radiological Defense Laboratory; and calculation of gamma- and neutron-shielding properties of materials. Not all the computer laboratory work had such direct application to strictly naval and defense problems. Indeed, among mathematicians, the laboratory received worldwide recognition when John Wrench and Dan Shanks, eminent mathematicians, announced their computation of pi to 100,000 places on the IBM 7090, an outstanding feat for its time. This accomplishment continued to be noted for decades in mathematical histories.

As hydrodynamicists turned their attention from conditions in still water, typical of model basins but rare in actual fleet operations, to problems of ships in sea waves, the computer would prove crucial. The extremely rich numerical representation of water motion would be handled by computer; "hand" calculation simply did not have the power to slog through all the thousands of calculations necessary to analyze the effects of waves. Problems studied would include lateral motions of ships in oblique waves and a variety of water motion analyses.

As in other areas, the UNIVAC represented a technological revolution in tools and instruments that would bring advances in science. Engineers sometimes rebut the scientist's assertion that engineering is "only" applied science by demonstrating that science itself is often "applied technology." A case in point for the impact of tools on scientific theory came with the revolution in seakeeping hydrodynamics, made possible by the application of the computer. The new computer proved essential when, in the mid-1950s, a group of hydrodynamicists, including

Manley St. Denis at the basin, Willard Pierson at New York University, and other scientists at Stevens Institute of Technology, MIT, University of Michigan, and Stanford, developed a realistic statistical model for the motions of a ship in a "seaway"—that is, for the actual conditions of waves on the high seas.[33]

The St. Denis work on modeling ship motions in a realistic seaway served as a source of local pride. Like the contributions of David Taylor and Karl Schoenherr, the work of St. Denis illustrated that the U.S. Navy could conduct and coordinate fundamental hydromechanics theoretical research, and that the model basin stood in the forefront in this science. St. Denis and the others used the computer to study records of actual ocean wave spectra and to test their statistical models against those records. Spectrum analysis of detailed wave records confirmed that heights of natural waves in a fully developed sea—that is, a sea over which wind speed and direction had been constant for some time—followed a Gaussian distribution. This meant that a knowledge of the average wave height for a given sea condition could be used to predict how often a wave of specified very large height was likely to be encountered.

Ground Breaking for the Maneuvering and Seakeeping (MASK) Facility.   In Navy Seabee style, on 1 August 1956, Captain E. A.Wright conducts ground breaking by bulldozer for the new MASK facility, completed in 1962.

Construction of the MASK Facility.   Heavy concrete piers supported a vast vaulted roof to cover the rotating arm basin, a section of the MASK facility. The central pillar to support the rotating arm is being worked on.

Eventually the theoretical understanding, together with the power of the computer, would allow for study of many effects of the interaction of ships and waves previously beyond the reach of hydrodynamicists, including wave-induced loads, slamming, shipping of green water, added hull resistance due to waves, and ship-roll prediction.

In 1962 Carderock added a new facility, the Maneuvering and Seakeeping Basin (MASK). This addition permitted performance of seakeeping experiments with large ship models in oblique, regular, and random waves, allowing for model testing of the calculated predictions based on the computer work. The two new tools or instruments—the dedicated computer and the MASK—brought a full-scale maturation of a whole scientific discipline. Two decades earlier, such problems, while interesting, were regarded as almost hopelessly complex.[34]

MASK consisted of two separate basins housed in the same building: a rotating arm basin for testing maneuvering during turns, and a rectangular basin with a complex wavemaking capacity for conducting tests of ships' seakeeping ability under ocean conditions. A circular

MASK Rotating Arm. When filled, this basin could accommodate surface models up to 30 feet in length, and by rotating the model around the circular tank, could achieve speeds up to 50 knots.

basin of reinforced concrete, 266 feet in diameter and 21 feet deep, provided the tank for the rotating arm facility. In order to test the forces that induce and maintain a turn, models needed a longer run than possible in the J-basin constructed on the west end of the towing tank in 1940. The large dimensions of the circular basin could accommodate submarine models up to 20 feet in length and surface models up to 30 feet in length. By running in a circle, higher speeds could be attained. At a radius of 120 feet, speeds up to 30 knots could be reached in one half revolution, and up to 50 knots in just over one full revolution.

Motor-driven wheels mounted on a track around the periphery of the tank drove the rotating arm, which pivoted on a tower in the middle of the tank. The track alignment itself incorporated a precision approaching the original Carderock basin, with accuracy to within a factor of plus or minus 0.006 inch, measured from the water surface. Experimenters could position models under the arm at a range of angles, governing roll, pitch, and yaw.

The MASK allowed for the study of irregular wave conditions and their impact on ships. Although earlier model basins had sometimes contained wavemakers, those waves were usually regular, long-crested waves, a type that only rarely occurred under actual ocean conditions. When at sea, ships encountered trains of waves of different lengths and heights that simultaneously interfered with each other, establishing complex patterns such as those studied and predicted by St. Denis. In attempting to simulate actual conditions, planners designed the basin so that irregular wave patterns could be created by several separate wavemaker units.

The wavemakers operated along two adjacent sides of the 360-foot by 240-foot basin, and they could be programmed to make long- and short-crested, as well as regular and irregular, waves, simulating seas up to gale force conditions. Concrete bar grids opposite the wavemaking sides acted like beaches, absorbing and breaking up the wave pattern rather than bouncing it back to create unwanted sloshing that would interfere with the generated waves. The wave absorbers consisted of 2-inch concrete bars

MASK Basin. This 360-by-240-foot seakeeping basin can be programmed to make both regular and irregular waves. The sloping "beach" and grids to absorb wave action can be seen at the basin's edge.

arranged in a sloped grid with an overall thickness of about 3 feet and nearly 36 feet long, suspended at an angle into the basin.

The pneumatic wavemakers departed from the design of earlier mechanical-flapper wavemakers. Two generators supplied power to twenty-one separate motor-driven blowers that, in turn, were each dynamically valved to control the air pressure in a dome acting on the water surface at the edge of the tank. In order to provide control to achieve maximum flexibility, each of the eight pneumatic wavemakers on one side of the basin could be individually controlled. A magnetic tape would be programmed for a particular wave pattern and the planned sea conditions would be played out automatically.

After initial calibration testing and correlation of test results, the basin began testing bulk carriers under heavy sea conditions and a model of the aircraft carrier *Forrestal.* Early tests also included a group of experiments on slamming conditions. Within its first year of operation, the basin was also used to test smaller auxiliary ships such as supply vessels and fire control ships under ocean wave conditions.[35]

By the 1970s seakeeping research moved from the theoretical phase to itself becoming applied in ship design: seakeeping hydrodynamics began to influence early hull designs for destroyers and design and performance assessment of roll stabilizer systems. Seakeeping hydrodynamics would provide the beginnings of the ability to predict weapon, sensor, and aircraft operational capabilities in true sea environments, and would open a range of other possibilities. Smaller, more economical ships might be able to perform missions previously reserved for larger ships under rough sea conditions. Ships of every class, designed with the new principles, might have the capacity to operate in higher sea states than previously acceptable for the class.

Hull series work continued through 1963 with Series 60 for merchant ships, Series 61 and 62 for planing hulls, and Series 64 for high-speed displacement hulls. The work, under the direction of Frederick Todd, followed in the footsteps of the earlier series work undertaken by David Taylor in the first decades of the century. As with the original Taylor Series, the new series data allowed ship designers to assess powering requirements during preliminary design and to plan trade-offs of hull form changes affecting resistance. The series for high-speed displacement forms, Series 64, was used in design calculations for *Ashville* (PG 84)-class gunboats, while the work on Series 62 was used in design work for the "Coastal Patrol Interdiction Craft," as well as for other small Navy boats.[36]

Between 1945 and 1970, DTMB conducted model powering experiments for more than 150 merchant ship designs under contract to the

Athena Research Ships.   A result of high speed tests of DTMB Series 64, these former *Ashville*-class gunboats were designed in the early 1960s and saw action in Vietnam. These are two of three provided to the center that were converted to *Athena* research ships.

Maritime Administration and many of America's leading shipbuilders, shipowners, and design offices. Over the 25-year period, this work averaged out to about six evaluations per year, down from about twice that number tested at EMB each year in the five years preceding World War II. Tests were conducted on cargo and passenger ships, ore and bulk carriers, roll-on-roll-off and container ships, tugs and barges, ferries, towboats, yachts, and ocean platforms. Researchers investigated the application of contrarotating propellers to tankers in 1964 and to containerships in 1972; the first highly skewed propeller for a merchant ship was designed and evaluated at full scale in 1973. By 1970, shipbuilding had declined in the United States, with the majority of U.S.-owned merchant ship construction and associated model testing being conducted in Europe and Japan.[37]

The 1950s and 1960s are spoken of as the "Golden Age of Hydrodynamics Research" at DTMB. The establishment in 1952 of the Bureau of Ships Fundamental Hydromechanics Research (FHR)

Model Shop. The DTMB model shop in full swing. The wide variety of naval and commercial hulls under construction in the 1950s included (front to back) an LCVP (a 36-foot high speed landing craft), a U.S. Coast Guard icebreaker with ducted propellers, a frigate (DL), a guided missile cruiser (nuclear powered), a Navy refrigeration stores ship, and a plastic model of the experimental submarine *Albacore.*

Program, administered by DTMB, provided a funding stimulus that, coupled with the computational and model-testing tools, produced lasting contributions to the technology base. By 1967, the program supported an average of about eighty work years of research each year, with about 75 percent of it done at DTMB and the remainder at universities. The impact and success of the program can be judged from the first six issues of SNAME's *Journal of Ship Research,* where nearly two-thirds of the papers were written by current or former DTMB employees or by academics supported by the FHR Program. Research support at DTMB was further strengthened in 1963 with the introduction of the Independent Research and Independent Exploratory Development (IR/IED) Program originating with the Office of Naval Research, which provided discretionary funding for naval laboratories to bolster R&D efforts. At its high point in 1967, the IR/IED Program supported about one hundred person years of effort.[38]

A few leading examples of the seminal research contributions of DTMB hydrodynamicists during the period 1952–1968 demonstrate the richness of the work.

- 1952 Herman W. Lerbs: *Theory of moderately loaded propellers with arbitrary circulation distribution*
- 1953 Manley St. Denis and Willard J. Pierson (New York University): *Theory of ship motions in confused seas*
- 1955 Marshall Tulin: *Linearized theory of supercavitating foils*
- 1956 Leonard Pode: *Theory of cable-towed systems*
- 1957 William E. Cummins: *Theory of time-dependent forces and moments on moving bodies*
- 1961 Pao C. Pien: *Evaluation of propeller lifting surface theory*
- 1962 Morton Gertler and Alex Goodman: *Patenting of planar motion mechanism for vehicle dynamics*
- 1964 J. Nicholas Newman and Ernest O. Tuck: *Slender-body theory of ship motions*
- 1968 Paul S. Granville: *Velocity similarity laws for drag-reducing polymer solutions*

Tools and Research

The cross-fertilization or application between the two fields of engineering on the one hand and science on the other reflected a deep-seated aspect of the maturation of DTMB in the 1950s. Scientists, using the new instrument technology, could leap forward with theoretical advances. Engineers and designers could then apply those advances in ship technology. Housing science and applied engineering in the same facility, DTMB began to demonstrate a healthy interaction of the two ways of thinking in a burst of research and development that could meet both practical naval needs and attract the attention of the international community of science. In an earlier era, David Taylor designed the tools, evaluated designs, used the data to generate design criteria that could then be applied to the design of ships. But now, on a large institutional basis, the stimulating interaction between science and technology proceeded from group to group, from specialist to specialist. In its maturity, the model basin began to fulfill the promise of its youth.

At both EES and DTMB, new opportunities produced responsive work. The basin's capabilities expanded, with the addition of the computer facility, with the MASK, and with the pressure tanks. The fundamental progress in areas outside the basin—in steel alloys from the metals industry and in the development of nuclear propulsion—presented new challenges and opportunities. The decade and a half had opened new directions at both facilities. At the station, development work increased. Studies of machine silencing and a group of in-house development projects in hydraulics, electronics, welding, and engine mounts solidified the station's reputation in those areas. New instruments such as the gear test stand, submarine shaft seal and thrust bearing set-ups, and the stray magnetic field facility made new research possible.

At the basin, the new capacity for computational work produced many solutions in the decade of the 1950s. Metallurgical research with the new steels, work on hull structures, and the extension of hydrodynamics into the area of actual sea conditions all showed promise for the future, while series work showed new ways of building on the tried-and-true methods established by Taylor fifty years before. In area after area, research moved more quickly with new tools; increasingly, the scientific work could lead to new weapons, systems, and ships. During the decade and a half from 1950 through the mid-1960s, the facilities would be central to the introduction of a new generation of submarines, surface ships, and aircraft to the fleet. One of the most dramatic of these new naval systems was the nuclear-powered submarine, the subject of the next chapter.

Endnotes

1. Alfred Keil, interview by David K. Allison, 2 Nov 1984, Harold V. Nutt, interview by David K. Allison, 22 Oct 1982, DTNSRDC RC 6-5, box 1.
2. Keil interview, 2 Nov 1984.
3. William Murray, ABIF, 29 Feb 1996
4. Nutt interview, 22 Oct 1982; *Our Diligent Neighbor* [no author], DTNSRDC RC 7-2, box 2.
5. Nutt interview, 22 Oct 1982.
6. Ibid.
7. *Summary of Status of DTMB Survey Recommendations*, Nov–Dec 1961, 1–4, DTNSRDC RC 7-1, box 14.
8. Nutt interview, 22 Oct 1982.
9. Keil interview, 2 Nov 1984.
10. T. K. Fordyce, "Officer-Civilian Relationships in Semi-Military Technical Organizations," *JASNE* 65 (Feb 1953): 9–22; Nutt interview, 22 Oct 1982.
11. Nutt interview, 22 Oct 1982.
12. Ibid.
13. *U.S. Naval Engineering Experiment Station Progress Report* [no author], Jan 1961, DTNSRDC RC 7-2, box 2.
14. Ibid.
15. Nutt interview, 22 Oct 1982.
16. *U.S. Naval Engineering Experiment Station Progress Report*, 153.
17. Ibid., 146–147.
18. Ibid., 150.
19. Ibid., 151.
20. Nutt interview, 22 Oct 1982.
21. *U.S. Naval Engineering Experiment Station Progress Report*, 156.
22. Ibid., 157.
23. Nutt interview, 22 Oct 1982.
24. Ibid.
25. Ibid.
26. "Fact Sheet on David Taylor Model Basin LARC," DTNSRDC RC 7-1, box 10.
27. "Nuclear Reactor Design Methods of Ships and Submarines," DTNSRDC Major Accomplishments, No. 18, DTNSRDC RC 3-2, box 3; Richard G. Hewlett and Francis Duncan, *Nuclear Navy, 1946–1962* (Chicago: University of Chicago Press, 1974).
28. "Nuclear Reactor Design Methods for Ships and Submarines," DTNSRDC Major Accomplishments, No. 18, DTNSRDC RC 3-2, box 3 Joanna W. Schot, "Nuclear Reactor Design Calculations," May 1961, DTNSRDC Report No. 1519, 224–255; Elizabeth H. Cuthill, "FLAME, A Three-Dimensional Burn-up Code for LARC," *Codes for Reactor Computations* (Vienna: International Atomic Energy Agency, 1961); Cuthill, "Digital Computers in Nuclear Reactor Design," *Advances in Computers* (New York: Academic Press, 1964), 289–347; Cuthill and Schot document the FLAME Code Program in 1965 DTNSRDC Reports: *Specifications*, No. 1477; *User's Manual*, No. 1937; *Reference Manual*, No. 1939; *Operations Manual*, No. 1938; *Master Control System*, No. 1863.

29. Smith and L. Acton, *Problems Solved on High-Speed Computing Equipment of the Applied Mathematics Laboratory*, Jan 1959, DTMB Report No. 1295.

30. Ibid.

31. E. A. Wright, *Naval Mathematics at the David Taylor Model Basin*, Jul 1957, DTMB Report No. 1144; also see *JASNE* 29, no. 2 (May 1957). (A copy of this article is in DTNSRDC RC 7-1, box 10.)

32. D. Shanks and J. W. Wrench Jr.,"Calculation of Pi to 100,000 Decimals," *Mathematics of Computation*, 16 (1962): 76–99.

33. "Surface Ship Seakeeping Research and Development," DTNSRDC Major Accomplishments, No. 7, DTNSRDC RC 3-2, box 3; Manley St. Denis and Willard J. Pierson, "On the Motions of Ships in Confused Seas," *T* 61 (1963): 280–357.

34. Ibid.

35. W. F. Brownell, *Two New Hydromechanics Research Facilities at DTMB*, 13–26; Brownell, *A Rotating Arm and Maneuvering Basin*, Jul 1956, DTMB Report No. 1053; Brownell, interview by Rodney Carlisle, 27 Apr 1986.

36. "Development of Surface Ship Hull Forms," DTNSRDC Major Accomplishments, No. 5, DTNSRDC RC 3-2, box 3; M. Gertler, *A Reanalysis of the Original Test Data for the Taylor Standard Series*, Mar 1954, DTMB Report No. 806; F. Todd, *Series 60, Methodical Experiments with Models of Single-Screw Merchant Ships*, Jul 1963, DTMB Report No. 1712; H. Y. H. Yeh, "Series 64, Resistance Experiments on High-Speed Displacement Forms," *Maritime Technology* (2 Jul 1953); Lasky, *Performance of High-Speed Naval Ships, Part II, Results of Resistance Tests in Smooth Water on Nine Hull Forms (LCB/LCF Effect)* (U), Nov 1970, NSRDC Report No. C-3311.

37. Justin H. McCarthy, "David Taylor Research Center," in H. Benford and W. A. Fox, eds., *A Half Century of Marine Technology, 1943–1993* (Jersey City: SNAME, 1993), 26–41.

38. Ibid.

CHAPTER 8

From Submersible to Submarine

E VER SINCE JOHN P. HOLLAND DESIGNED and built the boat purchased by the U.S. Navy and commissioned in 1900 as *Holland*, the English-speaking world had referred to such vessels as "submarines." Yet, strictly speaking, the submarines of World Wars I and II were more literally submersible craft, capable of cruising on the surface, then submerging for a limited amount of time and conducting undersea operations at a reduced speed. By the late 1930s, the major navies of the world had settled on diesel-electric propulsion, in which diesel engines would propel the boat on the surface, simultaneously charging a bank of batteries, which in turn would supply power to electric motors for undersea maneuvers. One virtue of the electric system underwater was that it did not consume oxygen. However, all subsurface cruising was limited, usually to a few hours' time, by the storage capacity of the batteries. Batteries themselves were heavy; as electric capacity increased, so did the weight carried.[1]

The naval doctrine that evolved for the submarine reflected the fact that it was not truly a submarine cruising vessel but a submersible surface craft. During World War II, German U-boats motored on the surface at night, submerging during the day to avoid detection by Allied aircraft. The U-boats established extended picket lines to intercept convoys of shipping. When a submarine detected a convoy, the commander would radio Berlin in code with the location, so that a group of subs might converge on the rich target. Then, to attack, the vessel submerged, advanced at periscope depth, launched a salvo of torpedoes, dived to avoid retaliatory depth charge strikes by destroyer escorts, and eventually, if surviving, surfaced and cruised off again under diesel power to arrange another kill, rendezvous with comrades, or return to base.[2]

Antisubmarine doctrine, too, recognized the potentials and limitations of the boats. Allied attacks against German submarines increased in effectiveness during the war because of several innovations, some technical, some tactical. As German submarine commanders radioed their coded messages to headquarters to assemble groups of U-boats, Allied radio interception provided both decrypted messages, through cracking of the German code system (the Ultra source), and radio location through a High Frequency Direction Finding device (HF-DF or Huff-Duff). Allied destroyers, working in pairs as hunter-killer groups, would utilize sonar to zero in on the exact location of submarines. U-boats could sometimes evade sonar detection when immediately beneath the attacking vessel, but the tactic of paired attack would allow one vessel to utilize sonar and to relay location information to the other, which would then position itself and drop depth charges.[3]

Very rarely would one submarine be used to track or attack an enemy sub during World War II. However, the few incidents of such attacks fascinated naval analysts after the war. In only one case, the attack by *Gudgeon* (SS 211) on Japanese *I-173*, 27 January 1942, did one submarine sink another while both were submerged. Yet the concept of submarine dogfights like those of aircraft held out the possibility of using the submarine itself as part of an antisubmarine strategy. If detection and maneuverability could be vastly improved, the mission of the submarine might be redefined to include a hunter-killer role of its own.[4]

By 1943 Allied airborne radar assisted the code breakers in location of surfaced submarines. In response to this aerial threat, the German navy developed between April and September 1943 the schnorchel, a 20- to 30-foot breathing tube that allowed extended subsurface running on diesel power. The tube, with a simple float valve at the top, allowed intake of air, while exhaust could be bubbled out below the surface. If a wave overran the top of the intake tube, the valve temporarily closed to prevent seawater from flooding the engine. The Allied microwave radar, which the Germans never detected, became so highly advanced that it could locate even the small protruding tip of the schnorchel pipes. Surface and air hunter-killer groups could then converge, seek out, and destroy the submarine.[5]

In response, German designers and operating crews agreed that "the submarine of today must be able to operate submerged continuously in order to exist as a useful type." The next step in the technological arms race in submarine development during the war took the U-boat one step closer to the truly submarine vessel and away from its submersible surface ship heritage.[6]

A possible approach came from an innovative idea developed a decade earlier in Germany, but applied late in the war to submarine technology. By 1930 Herman Walters had developed the concept of an engine which ran on decomposed hydrogen peroxide (H_2O_2). The oxygen released from the hydrogen peroxide had obvious applications to the problem of sustained underwater diesel operation of submarines. If perfected, the Walters engine would allow extended underwater operation completely closed off from the outside atmosphere, in a closed cycle.[7]

The closed-cycle engine offered the possibility of extended submerged running, which, as German designers were quick to realize, meant that the submarine hull no longer needed to be designed for surface cruising. While a submersible surface craft, cruising on the surface, needed a bow suitable for surface maneuvering and handling, a true submarine would benefit from a blunter, more bulbous bow and no deck equipment. Using these principles, German designers produced Type XXI, capable of submerged speeds of about eighteen knots, nearly double the operating speed of the earlier designs.[8]

By the last days of war in Europe, German advances in submarine design set the stage for many of the postwar developments in submarines. But the German advances did not simply foreshadow future developments. The victorious Allies, borrowed, improved, and incorporated major German advances. Technology transfer from Germany to the Soviet Union, Great Britain, and the United States did not happen by accident. Instead, scientists and engineers, including those at DTMB and EES, made a conscious, calculated, and decade-long effort to apply what the Germans had learned.[9]

At the end of the war in Europe Germans sought to scuttle and destroy their advanced models. Nevertheless, schnorchel-building plants, several samples of Type XVIII through Type XXI boats, and some of the H_2O_2 plants and engines were all eagerly captured and studied by Soviet, British, and American teams. Engineers and technicians from DTMB and EES served on the Naval Technical Mission in Europe that examined the confiscated German equipment. As they studied the captured booty, the American teams reported that the Walters engine and the high-speed underwater U-boats of the last classes could have prolonged the war. Almost by chance, bombing raids and German army use of H_2O_2 for V-1 and V-2 weapons had kept most of the new advanced undersea craft from deployment.[10]

Technical Mission staff noted that Germany sought "a new concept of submarine warfare" in which submarines "must remain submerged indefinitely, attain speeds heretofore considered impossible, operate at great depths, and must be highly maneuverable." The American technical observers identified the core of the concept. The search for a means of indefinite submergence became an immediate postwar research and development objective.[11]

American submarine development in the postwar decade, while limited by a peacetime budget and by a general tendency to demobilize the whole fleet, showed direct continuity from the German advances, as American naval designers hoped to counter real and projected Soviet submarine threats. American designers adopted all the goals that the wartime German designers had pursued: extended underwater operation, evasion of detection, greater depth, higher submerged speeds. At first, both DTMB and EES specialists followed the German technical solutions: the schnorchel, the closed-cycle engine not dependent on outside oxygen, and the improved hull form.

The "snorkel" (as the Americans began to spell the German invention) had not been perfected but rather suffered frequent problems in regular operation. Typically, the snorkel tube itself created resistance, limiting the submerged speed of boats so equipped to eight or ten knots. When the snorkel valve closed to cut off seawater, the engines would draw air from the interior of the vessel, creating a momentary ear-popping vacuum. In 1946 an EES team worked on adapting the snorkel to the American two-cycle diesel engine. Two-cycle engines drew air at a much faster rate than the German four-cycle engines, resulting in even more severe pressure drops. With remodeling of both snorkel and engine, *Irex* (SS 482) demonstrated a preliminary model of a telescoping snorkel tube at work with an American diesel in 1946.[12]

The possibility that nuclear power could be harnessed to a propulsion plant had interested the Navy and, in particular, Chief of Naval Research Rear Admiral Harold Bowen from the early days of the Manhattan Project. Like the H_2O_2 engine, nuclear propulsion offered the possibility of extended subsurface operation; the nuclear power plant, if workable, would be capable of more extended use than the H_2O_2 cycle engine that had offered six hours of high-speed performance underwater. But in 1946 both types of engine seemed in the realm of science fiction; the next decade would determine if either of the ideas could be turned into a working reality for the American fleet.[13]

At the Bureau of Ships, a special group designated Code 390 and headed by Captain (later, Rear Admiral) Hyman Rickover worked with industry to perfect a working model of a nuclear reactor and steam tur-

Hyman Rickover Visit to Carderock. Retired Admiral Hyman Rickover, center, meets with Technical Director Alan Powell and Commanding Officer Captain Barrick F. Tibbitts, after his retirement from the Navy.

bine suitable for submarine propulsion. At EES, several experiments with the Walters closed-cycle engine went forward in the period 1946–1954. While not perceived as a "race" between the two technologies, both the nuclear project and the peroxide project proceeded toward the same goal—the development of an engine that would make possible a true submarine.[14]

In the late 1940s planners could not predict if the new propulsion systems would ever be economically feasible, fully workable, safe, or capable of being produced in numbers. Other ideas were clearly practicable and could be used immediately while research and development on the nuclear and H_2O_2 engines went forward. The snorkel, despite its obvious drawbacks, had proven itself. The huge fleet of American submarines could be selectively outfitted with snorkels, if the telescoping snorkel adaptation on *Irex* (SS 482) could be perfected for American engines.

With hull modifications similar to those used by the Germans in Type XXI, submerged speed on electric power could be increased. The Guppy program, an acronym derived from "Greater Underwater

Propulsive Power," led to refitting over fifty submarines to achieve much higher speeds, approaching the 18- to 20-knot level of the most advanced German models. Guppy conversions required stripping away wooden decks, streamlining conning towers, removing deck guns, reducing and lightening the battery package, equipping vessels with collapsible snorkels, and in some cases, stripping out one diesel engine from boats with two.[15]

DTMB and EES both contributed essential designs and evaluations to the Guppy conversions. EES obtained U.S. shipyard blueprints of snorkel exhaust piping and modifications of planned installations. Using such information, and designing new test apparatus, EES engineers supplied the Chief of Naval Research with details regarding the composition of snorkel exhaust gases, and the kinds of pressures at inlet and exhaust valves generated in snorkeling modes. Numerous EES test reports focused on design details associated with operating diesels under the strenuous conditions imposed by snorkel arrangements, leading to improved performance.[16]

The Guppy class was a very diverse school of fish. To begin with, there were several generations of Guppy modifications. Furthermore, different navy yards developed their own particular styles of conversion. Even more fundamental to the problem of diversity was the fact that each submarine modified, while originally a World War II fleet type, was already slightly different in design and power because of pre-Guppy repairs and refittings. The Guppy class consisted of a wide variety of reconstructed fleet submarines; it was a class in which each boat performed and handled uniquely. When instructors at the New London Submarine School sought help from DTMB in determining the predicted angle of dive for the Guppy class at different speeds with bow and stern planes set at specified angles, the reply could not simply consist of a model-based dive-entry chart.

Regarding the diving predictions, Morton Gertler in Hydrodynamics explained that a difference of three or four degrees and four or five seconds of response time would be observed on every individual boat. A standard handbook, based on DTMB information for a class of boats, simply could not be issued for the Guppies.[17]

The design of improved ship control features was necessary to safely and effectively exploit the new speed capability of the Guppies. Ship control and maneuvering predictions needed to design and safely operate these submarines challenged the technical community. Adequate prediction capability for the dynamic features of high-speed submarines required extension of test devices, analysis techniques, and predictive equations to enable non-linear analysis and simulation, whereas linear techniques had sufficed for slower speed, less maneuverable submarines. DTMB pioneered new towing tank apparatus, analysis techniques, simulation capabilities, and full-scale trial methods to support development of needed prediction tools.

The Subsea Arms Race

In the postwar decade and a half, the Soviets engaged in a research and construction program in submarines, which, like the American program, started from where the Germans had left off. In one sense, the intense submarine arms race of World War II, with advances in offense and defense, concealment and detection, speed and sustained submergence, continued unabated in the peacetime arms race between Soviet and American technical experts. American sources estimated that between 1945 and 1960, the Soviets constructed over 300 new submarines; in the same period, the United States built only about thirty-five new vessels, in addition to the conversions of existing fleet types to improved Guppy status. Both sides, however, experimented with new types and designs.[18]

Before American nuclear submarines went into production in the mid-1950s, it was clear that the Soviets had a marked lead in the field of underwater warfare, both in numbers and in some aspects of technology. Much of the Soviet technology had been acquired from the Germans, but that thought offered little consolation to American planners in the period before 1953, because the American improvements like the snorkel and the Guppy conversions also represented "borrowed" German ideas. The Soviets succeeded in acquiring and adapting closed-cycle plants and faster hull designs and in launching a large fleet using the adaptations.

While there were certain similarities between the approaches of the Soviet and American navies, certain Soviet developments worried American Navy planners. The massive Soviet production of the high-speed W type, equivalent to the German Type XXI, provided a submarine that was fast, elusive, and possibly beyond the American ability to catch and destroy with existing equipment and tactics.[19]

In January 1949, the Chief of Naval Operations directed each fleet to set aside a submarine group devoted to developing tactics and techniques "to detect and destroy submarines having characteristics of Guppy conversion." The Guppy conversions, in 1949, were as close as the Americans could come to the suspected capacity of the Soviet W class. Methods developed to track and attack the Guppy conversions might approach those required for the W.[20]

In May 1949 the Atlantic Fleet established its submarine research team at New London, Connecticut, Submarine Development Group 2, called in naval acronymic terminology, "SUBDEVGRU-2." This organization brought together scientists, engineers, submarine officers, and enlisted men in an effort to evaluate a wide variety of ideas on tactics, equipment, and procedure. Line officers instructed subordinates, down through the naval chain of command, to cooperate with civilians in the research effort. James Fife, commander of the Atlantic Fleet Submarine Force, discontinued a system of classified "Guppy diaries," which had been maintained by submarine commanders, and set up a less rigid system in which commanding officers of Guppies and snorkel submarines were to "consider the developmental nature of their special installation and arrangements" and to communicate anything of interest to design authorities by letter report. Fife forwarded such letters, noting anomalies and problems, to the appropriate research groups.[21]

While the fleet engaged in supplying reports on performance and problems, SUBDEVGRU-2 headed up the primary investigation. Among the first group of scientists attached for temporary duty to the New London SUBDEVGRU was DTMB physicist Marvin Lasky. Lasky had worked in a section of the Hydromechanics Laboratory devoted to "hydrodynamic noise" since 1948, and his new work concentrated in the growing areas of sound detection and sound analysis.[22]

While at New London on his six-month tour, Lasky learned of severe noise problems with Guppy conversions. The intermittently roaring diesels, the clanking valve on the snorkel pipe, and the wake of the pipe itself appeared to emit so much noise as to render the submarine's own sonars ineffective. Even worse, on the relatively quiet electric motors, running at fifteen knots, propeller cavitation, flow-generated noise, and transient noise from operation of rudders and planes would reveal the sub's location to any enemy. Although the Guppy boats were capable of high speed and could probably evade many surface destroyers sent to catch them, they simply could not sneak up on any vessel equipped with listening gear. The emitted sound problem suggested that a Guppy could not catch a Guppy. If the Soviet W class met or exceeded Guppy characteristics, which was the CNO's working assumption, the Guppy could not qualify as a killer submarine directed at Soviet W's unless it could be quieted down.[23]

The U.S. Navy Underwater Sound Laboratory and EES contributed to the sound studies of Guppy, along with DTMB. By the end of 1949, W. L. Pryor at the Underwater Sound Laboratory closely reviewed an EES report on the sound emitted by *Dogfish* (SS 350), a Guppy conversion. After reconciling measurement methods between EES and the

Evolution of Submersible Surface Ship to Submarine.   The Fleet type was made less resistant in the Guppy class by bow modification, conversion of the conning tower, and removing deck equipment. *Albacore* (AGSS 569) foreshadowed the nuclear classes to follow, with a hull designed as a true submersible with high underwater speed.

Sound Laboratory, Pryor concluded that the snorkel itself did not contribute significantly to the problem of Guppy submarines being located by other ships. Although "qualitative evidence" (that is, a gut feeling) prior to the tests had led to predictions of severe snorkel noise, the test results indicated that the device produced levels only about three decibels above noise contributions from other onboard sources, an amount that could not be "distinguished from the experimental uncertainty." He found that, with the state of equipment in 1949 and the interference of many other noises from the submarine, he could not isolate snorkel noise.[24]

Pryor concluded that one could not identify the snorkel as the major culprit in the noisy Guppies. Nevertheless, it remained clear that Guppy submarines, even when operating on battery power underwater, could not evade detection. The search for a proper hunter-killer design would have to go beyond Guppy.[25]

Beyond Guppy to *Albacore*

Within the Office of Naval Research, the Committee on Undersea Warfare, aware of SUBDEVGRU findings, recommended the construction of a high-speed research submarine. The goals of the design would include minimum drag and optimal shape. A feature of the design that would be crucial in light of the Guppy findings would be the reduction of self-emitted noise. Working toward the goal of a fast submarine could help in the search for a quiet submarine. An ideal shape, low-drag features, and optimized flow of water into the propellers would reduce the onset of propeller cavitation, cutting down on one major noise source during electric propulsion underwater. The optimum design concept recalled the problem that Ernest Eggert had toyed with in the 1930s—the perfect "spindle of revolution" and studies of ideal airship shapes over many years. Body of revolution hull test Series 58, evaluated at model scale in 1950, yielded low-drag shapes for the hull. Rear Admiral Albert Mumma, serving as commanding officer and director at DTMB,

***Albacore* Launching.**   In 1953, the diesel-powered *Albacore* hull design came out of research at the David Taylor Model Basin on Hull Series 58, carried out in 1950 in search of an optimum shape for submerged cruising.

1951–1954, insisted on seeing the vessel through to completion. The result was the diesel-driven *Albacore* launched in 1953. In its revolutionary body-of-revolution shape, *Albacore* would change the future of submarines; its shape was a model basin achievement and would rank with nuclear propulsion itself as a major American step toward the true submarine. Indeed, for many at the Carderock facility, the *Albacore* design would be considered as the single greatest contribution of the institution over its century of innovation and invention.[26]

DTMB civilian personnel, many of whom had spent a tour at SUB-DEVGRU-2, began acoustic trials on *Albacore* in 1953. The acoustic testing continued intermittently for the next fifteen years. While the hydrodynamic shape of the Guppy class and of the later *Tang* (SS 563) class, a close emulation of the German Type XXI, had resulted in improved speeds, *Albacore* represented a beneficial departure in the direction of both hydrodynamic and acoustic ideals, suitable to concealed as well as fast underwater maneuvering.[27]

The Navy designated both *Albacore* and *Dolphin* with AG series numbers, respectively AGSS 569 and AGSS 555, indicating both as experimental or research submarines. *Albacore* was to test the best hydrodynamic and acoustic shape, and *Dolphin* to test deep-diving possibilities and later, experimental sonars. Both boats hosted a variety of research projects of interest to Navy researchers from different laboratories and facilities around the nation. The commanding officer of the model basin held overall responsibility for research schedules and priorities for both boats.[28]

Through the 1950s and 1960s DTMB oversaw dozens of sound tests, tests of hydrophone arrays, boundary layer investigations, propeller torque and thrust measurements, and methods of reducing noise on board *Albacore*. Specialized test runs included study of the vibration and sound emitted by nearly every conceivable part of the boat, including ballast tanks and superstructure vents. Researchers traced flow noise around the anchor and anchor chain, hatches and escape trunks, towing padeyes, stern light and cleats, handrails, whip antennae, stern planes and dorsal rudder, periscope housing, and sonar domes.[29]

While DTMB staff conducted some of these tests, the Underwater Sound Laboratory, specialists from other labs, and the boat's own crew also did some measurement work. DTMB staff coordinated closely with the shipyard staff to arrange installation of test gear, removal or modification of equipment that generated noise, and modification of controls so as to allow "flying by feel" as with an airplane.[30]

The major change on *Albacore* was a redesign and rebuilding of the stern shape to increase hydrodynamic stability. Through 1956 DTMB staff followed the sea trials closely to measure the effect of these particular changes. This information along with constant advances in dynamic prediction capabilities initiated for the Guppies, enabled the design of a greatly improved stern control surface arrangement. *Albacore* served as a true test boat for improvement in speed, handling, and quiet operation. Over and over, lessons of the *Albacore* tests would be incorporated in later nuclear submarine classes.

Sometimes to make improvements suggested by engineers would require that carefully constructed and extensive dependable databases be abandoned as no longer applicable, as well as interfering with satisfactory existing conditions, developments not easily accepted by the more scientifically inclined researchers. In 1958 Karl Schoenherr reacted unfavorably to a suggestion that the bow of *Albacore* be modified to house a new sonar transducer (transmitting-receiving unit). The change would require a new plastic sonar dome to replace one earlier designed and manufactured at DTMB. Schoenherr, serving as civilian head of the Hydrodynamics Laboratory at the time, believed that "as a result of considerable quieting effort" the boat had become "an effective sonar platform whose acoustic characteristics are well established over her entire range of speeds and submergence." Rather than changing the hull form and ruining the data continuity through addition of a new sonar dome, which would increase power requirements and reduce speed, he suggested that the sonar active unit be installed in the sail of the submarine and that a listening or passive sonar be set up in the existing bow dome.[31]

Propulsion Plant Experiments at EES

Before *Albacore* had been launched, the intense race to modernize the submarine fleet and to match possible Soviet advances also filled the work schedule of EES with a host of submarine-related studies. For nearly a decade the hunt for a means to propel the submarine at high speed underwater, through the use of a modified hydrogen peroxide engine or some other closed-cycle alternative, absorbed several groups at the station.

At EES, study of the H_2O_2 alternative went forward as Project Hill— so named because the facilities to store the relatively dangerous hydrogen peroxide were located on a hill at some distance from the main EES buildings. Development contracts with commercial manufacturers, together with in-house research on pumps, valves, and catalysts for the peroxide engine, testified to the magnitude of the research effort in this area between 1946 and 1954. EES staff knew that if nuclear propulsion proved successful, the Navy would call off further work on hydrogen peroxide options for the main propulsion unit of full-scale submarines. Nevertheless, they kept up hope for other Walters cycle roles—as a midget submarine drive plant or as a motor for a long-range, high-speed torpedo. Project Hill staff also followed with interest the British experiments with a kerosene-compressed air closed-cycle engine, the "B-cycle," which held promise for torpedo propulsion.[32]

Work on the H_2O_2 engines posed a range of technical and procurement problems. German Ingolene, or hydrogen peroxide, had been manufactured to a high degree of purity. Like other German wartime products, such as synthetic diesel fuel derived from coal, cost had been no object. Maintaining supply, whatever the price, had been a major German problem because of issues of priority, as well as bombing attacks on plants and transport. A shortage of hydrogen peroxide continued to plague Project Hill, even in the peacetime setting of 1947. EES staff arranged shipment of confiscated German supplies to the United States, studied the German plants for production and engineering shortcuts, and arranged for the shipment to the United States of complete hydrogen peroxide plants as "reparations."[33]

Project Hill researchers sought to keep track of the few existing Walters engines and to prevent their destruction as scrap metal. In the period 1946–1947 naval officers in Europe, acting on requests from EES, scrambled to identify and seize the test plants and submarine engines that had escaped bombing or scuttling.[34]

Details of the Soviet capture of Walters experimental and production facilities at Blankenburg and intelligence regarding Soviet study and use of both German equipment and technicians increased the sense of urgency for Project Hill staff. Since the Germans had not settled on a particular final design, it was not clear which path the Soviets would choose nor which was most practicable for wartime use. Each of several possible ideas needed to be explored.[35]

In the H_2O_2 propulsion studies the Navy worked with two contractors, each to design a separate approach, just as they had earlier with gas turbine development and as they would with the more well-known nuclear project. The two contractors, Allis Chalmers and Westinghouse, worked toward slightly different objectives in peroxide engines, starting from the same basic idea. Both the Allis Chalmers Alton and the Westinghouse Wolverine used a diesel-driven gas turbine.[36]

In the Alton system, surface and snorkel propulsion used a conventional diesel-electric system. Double armature electric motors took power from the diesel generating plant, and the boat's speed was electrically controlled. The hydrogen peroxide plant itself was reserved for underwater high-speed forward cruising in which the gas turbine was driven by diesel fuel, with hydrogen peroxide providing the oxidant for combustion. Slower, quiet, forward underwater propulsion, as well as astern operation underwater, would rely on battery-electric propulsion. The Alton design configuration would allow a return to base under conventional power if the experimental peroxide system broke down.[37]

The Wolverine plant also had alternate propulsion modes, with two different sets of alternatives considered. In one pattern, both forward and astern submerged propulsion were electric drive from batteries that were charged by the Wolverine Walters plant; in the other, all submerged propulsion relied on the peroxide-diesel turbine.[38]

Another method of providing subsurface oxygen was the Kreislauf cycle, which depended on stored oxygen either in compressed form or as liquid oxygen. This system, code-named Ellis, also had several alternate approaches for propulsion arrangements.[39]

EES engineers conducted an in-house study of the Ellis, Alton, and Wolverine alternatives, considering several options within each. All the systems required solutions to a range of novel engineering challenges, including chemical storage and corrosion, gas discharge systems, and clutching arrangements. None of the engineering problems was insuperable, but as in all ship design, trade-offs between options and approaches had to be considered carefully.[40]

In both the Alton and Wolverine engines, a discouraging consideration was the cost of H_2O_2 itself. One calculation, assuming a price of $0.35 per pound of hydrogen peroxide, resulted in a predicted cost of $147,000 for a single 10-hour run. To provide perspective, an aircraft carrier burned only $16,000 worth of fuel in a 10-hour period.[41]

Difficult technical problems abounded. Both Walters designs required a special valve that would control the flow of H_2O_2, water, and diesel fuel; perfection of this three-way proportioning valve required major expenditures of funds in the 1947–1949 period. Under a development contract with Buffalo Electro-Chemical Company, a valve, code-named Bessie, began to prove operable in 1949. Both Alton and Wolverine required similar special design and fabrication of pumps, compressor coolers, turbines, combustion chambers, piping systems, control panels, and clutches. Only rarely could the overall design accommodate a ready-made, off-the-shelf part. As a consequence, the scheduling of completion of the complex assemblies presented intricate management tasks to the Project Hill staff. By 1950 weekly "newsletters" kept the Bureau of Ships officers, researchers, and contractors informed as to schedule slippage and expected completion dates of components.[42]

Sea Trial of X-1. This small experimental submarine was powered by a diesel engine with oxygen supplied from hydrogen-peroxide, a follow-on from German designs at the end of WWII. Nuclear power overshadowed this technological pathway, and *X-1* was soon retired.

X-1, a midget submarine design, utilized a converted Hercules piston diesel engine, supplied with oxygen from decomposed H_2O_2. Combustion products were compressed and disposed overboard. Although Italy and Japan had designed numerous midget submarines for clandestine attacks on enemy harbors, the United States had never developed the type. *X-1*, if successful in a technical sense, would require new doctrinal thinking. A fully working model of this boat was completed, but an explosion of the stowed hydrogen peroxide interrupted the tests, culminating a series of engineering and design problems. After discontinuation, the stripped-out *X-1* hull was placed on display for over two decades near the entrance gate to the Annapolis facility and later moved to the grounds of the Naval Academy.[43]

Among the closed-cycle alternatives considered at EES during this period were some brief conceptual studies of the possibility of using aluminum oxide or magnesium oxide as a fuel source. These compounds, supplying their own oxygen, would burn at extremely high temperatures, creating further design problems. Unlike the Walters alternatives, these exotic engine concepts did not even make it to the drawing board.[44]

In January 1954 the Chief of Naval Operations shut down research on all nonnuclear closed-cycle engines for submarine use; the order signaled the victory of nuclear technology over the other alternatives. Since nuclear propulsion came to dominate American submarine development in the next decade, the story of the nuclear submarine is well known. In effect, the "Atomic Sub" consigned the Walters engine to the dustbin of technological history.[45]

Like the Stanley Steamer, the Zeppelin, and Howard Hughes's "Spruce Goose," the Walters engine represented a technology bypassed and outmoded while still in the developmental stage. Like those other technologies, sometimes remembered as "follies" because of notorious failures or spectacular accidents, commentators associated the Walters system's dangers and liabilities with the demise of the technology, as if the unresolved risks caused the ultimate decision to abandon development. The Walters engine, however, represented a bypassed technology, which, in the words of Hi Nutt at EES, went "on the shelf" for future reference. Like a few other projects at both facilities, the Walters and related closed-cycle work represented a path not taken. Such projects, often little-noticed in historical treatments that focused solely on success stories, would loom large in the memories of the researchers, and are an essential part of the story of technology.[46]

Project Hill groups at EES had always known that the nuclear plant, if perfected, would put them out of business. But with the closing of Alton, Wolverine, and Ellis research, and with the decision to construct only nuclear-propelled submarines, a whole era at EES came to an end. The station no longer worked on the main engine of the submarine. Henceforth, EES could help with auxiliary equipment and solve crucial electrical, mechanical, and materials problems, some of them essential to safe or effective cruising. But the glory days for submarine internal combustion engines were gone.

Nuclear Classes

Nuclear submarine development over the decade from the mid-1950s through the mid-1960s continued apace. The hull shapes of the first six nuclear-powered submarines followed several patterns similar to the *Tang* class of diesel-powered submarines, a modification of German Type XXI. The body-of-revolution design of *Albacore*, suitable both for high speed and designed to reduce flow-generated noise and propeller cavitation noise, "married" the nuclear propulsion plant in the *Skipjack* class and later classes.[47]

The nuclear submarine, embodying the objectives of undetectable, long-range subsurface cruising, would generate new strategy and doctrine. After a period of experimentation in which nuclear submarines explored under the North Pole, circumnavigated the globe submerged, and broke a variety of endurance records, the Navy searched for a suitable new mission. One idea explored and then abandoned came with plans for *Triton* (SSRN 586) to serve as a radar picket station for control of guided missiles. The Navy canceled that mission even before the boat was launched. The older role of torpedo attack on merchant and naval ships could be replaced by a true hunter-killer function, presaged by the *Gudgeon* attack during World War II and by the diesel-powered SSK class of the 1950s. Furthermore, if the new submarine could evade acoustic detection and take full advantage of the concealing depths, it would also provide an ideal missile launching platform.[48]

In the politics of defense funding, a submarine that could launch long-range missiles became an intriguing possibility. Although some observers believed that the nuclear bomb had made the surface Navy obsolete, if a submarine could be developed that would carry an effective and accurate long-range missile, then the Navy could join the Air Force in claiming funds for a "strategic deterrent," that is, a system capable of delivery of nuclear weapons in a major war and hence serving to deter or diminish the likelihood of such a war.[49]

The first ballistic missile submarines of the *George Washington* (SSBN 598) class were built on a crash program. The management and accelerated production of this Polaris missile program under Rear Admiral William (Red) Raborn vindicated a group of new research and development management methods that would later be implemented throughout the military's research establishment. The crash program added several new challenging kinds of work at DTMB and EES.[50]

Both Carderock and Annapolis laboratories found critical niches in the rapid expansion and redesign effort for the nuclear submarine fleet. As already mentioned, DTMB computational work was essential to nuclear reactor design. At EES, decades of experience with auxiliary machinery and materials design provided a pool of information crucial in the construction of quieter and deeper diving boats. At DTMB, continuing work on acoustics and the testing program on *Albacore* assured a vital role in the new developments, since it was essential that a missile-launching submarine, like a hunter-killer, be both fast and capable of evading detection.

Electric Boat Corporation

George Washington **(SSBN 598).** The rapidly developed Polaris missile program led to this first ballistic missile submarine and a host of new projects for the Model Basin and the Engineering Experiment Station.

Deeper diving submarines with longer undersea endurance, designed to run as silently as possible, led to a wide range of tasks suited to the diverse backgrounds and technical capacities of the Annapolis facility. Harold Singerman, a chemist at EES, traced toxic materials in submarine atmospheres that, on long undersea runs with no fresh air, could represent health hazards to the crew. He traced one elusive compound to a slowly evaporating solvent in the adhesive used to hold down floor tiles. Using his work, the laboratory developed a new adhesive and the flooring was replaced.[51]

Other aspects of the new classes of submarines developed through the 1950s generated many projects at EES, as engineers there resolved numerous crucial technical details:

- Deep-diving propeller shaft seals
- Deep submergence valves
- New shaft bearings
- Auxiliary diesel engine design
- Turbine steam line isolation joints

- Machinery lubricants
- Reactor piping
- Main circulating pump design
- Control panel lighting
- Radar mast seals
- Underwater speed log
- Submarine atmospheric control program
- New welding techniques for high-strength steel alloys[52]

Descriptions of all of these contributions would take a volume in itself. A few examples will suffice to show the range of contributions of the wide variety of engineering groups at EES. The new submarines could cruise for almost unlimited periods underwater, as the engines, unlike the diesel-electric systems, did not require oxygen. However, the crew did. One of the major efforts in the period 1954–1960 regarding the nuclear submarine fleet was the definition of the oxygen required and the amount of carbon dioxide generated by a crew of about one hundred in a closed system for sixty days and the development, testing, and evaluation of reliable continuous chemical engineering processes to achieve and maintain the desired levels. High-pressure electrolysis of water was chosen to provide the oxygen, while carbon dioxide was removed by concurrent "scrubbing" with a solution of monoethanolamine (MEA). Working with the Bureau of Ships and manufacturers, most of these systems were evaluated and upgraded at Annapolis, and then evaluated on board submarines. Later research, in the period 1960–1970, was directed toward increasing the reliability of the oxygen generator and improving the carbon dioxide removal process. Researchers at Annapolis were able to modify the MEA system to lower the carbon dioxide level from 1.0 percent to 0.2 percent. The atmospheric problem in *Snook* (SSN 592) in mid-1961 was so severe that the ship could not be delivered unless the problem was corrected. Annapolis staff traced the problem to the oil heaters that preceded the centrifugal separators. Air in the heaters insulated the heaters from the oil, and resulted in charring, yielding chemicals that vented to the atmosphere and caused severe eye irritation to the crew. A simple design change, later incorporated in every nuclear submarine, was made, once the problem was tracked to its source. Other studies revealed that ordinary solvents, such as methyl chloroform, used to clean up the adhesives that secured tiles to the decks of the submarines, generated problems with the catalyst in the oxidizer equipment. New rules eliminating the use of this solvent and other paint solvents for a week before getting under way and while under way controlled the problem. These findings led to a program that continued from the mid-1960s to the early 1990s to analyze all the nonmetallic materials that go into the submarine and to determine if they would have a negative effect on the environment. A data sheet was generated, a forerunner of a Material Safety Data Sheet later required by law.[53]

Manufactured by Treadwell Company, the electrolytic oxygen generators (EOGs) had to be made larger as bigger nuclear submarines were designed and built. The larger EOGs required higher amperage, eventually reaching 1,000 amps in the mid-1970s. The high amperage generated excessive heat, causing failure of an asbestos cloth separator used to wrap the cathode in the system. One solution was to surround the EOG cells with a cooling jacket, but the lower temperature reduced the current and reduced the oxygen production rate. Attempted fixes with epoxy used to partially fill the cooling jackets caused an alarming failure rate. The problem was turned over to Annapolis in 1975, which led to a redesign of the EOG that could then run at 2,500 amperes. The 2,500-amp oxygen generating cells became standard on all U.S. nuclear submarines equipped with the Treadwell EOG.[54]

The new submarines generated a host of specific problems that established groups at both the laboratories could address. Improved panel lighting was handled by a small group established at EES in 1949 with the transfer of several technicians and engineers from NRL to form the Interior Communications and Fire Control (ICFC) Section attached to the Welding and Electrical Laboratory. ICFC tested a wide range of equipment such as salinity indicators, wind indicators, bearing temperature monitors, engine order telegraphs, compass repeaters, and a variety of bells, buzzers and sirens. In the early 1950s ICFC conducted tests on a University of Cincinnati-designed electromagnetic log for determining ship speed through water. At the model basin, a towed "knotmeter" was developed that could be used as a calibration or reference instrument to check the accuracy of the electromagnetic log; the log had to be calibrated for each ship. In 1963, ICFC developed a flowmeter fo[r controlling discharge of ballast on board *George Washington*-class missile submarines. When a missile was fired, a precise amount of ballast had to be discharged in order to compensate for the added weight of water flooding into the empty missile tube. The ICFC-designed flowmeter used the same principle as the electromagnetic log, incorporating all solid-state electronics, that were newly available. Tests on the flowmeter were successful, and EES managed a contract to build and install the flowmeters on board the rest of the class of submarines.[55]

Silencing Work—Annapolis and Carderock

In May 1953, even before the launching of *Nautilus*, the Bureau of Ships established a program of submarine noise reduction that set up a schedule of acoustic surveys. In 1959 and 1964 commanders of the Pacific and Atlantic Fleets modified the survey schedules, and in 1966 the bureau reviewed all existing acoustic survey procedures. The bureau attempted to coordinate and delineate responsibility for different types of acoustic surveys that had grown up over the years since the 1953 directive.[56]

Through the 1950s Marvin Lasky from Carderock and Larry Argiro from Annapolis closely followed acoustic developments, and each helped establish continuing roles for both laboratories in the intricate ever-expanding requirement of conducting acoustic surveys and preparing trial reports. In 1956 testing of sound from *Seawolf* led to a conference hosted by the Underwater Sound Laboratory in New London. At that conference, Argiro and Lasky participated in parceling out acoustic responsibilities. Measurement of sound during builders' trials, acoustic testing in the Bahamas, and continuous self-noise measurements all seemed appropriate to the skills at the laboratories. Lasky's group acquired responsibility for the overall testing program and the final report of tests during such experiments; EES was to focus on the structure-borne, airborne, and overside tests, particularly gathering data from machinery and machinery foundations. Even under nuclear power, the modern submarine held many sound-emitting conventional machines; EES would concentrate on detection and reduction of sound from air conditioners, boiler feed pumps and water pumps, oil pumps, and hydraulic plants.[57]

The original division of work in acoustics survived organizational changes through both the naval chain of command and within the laboratory organization. Groups at both laboratories continued the mission along the lines set up in the 1950s. In 1963, the Acoustics and Vibrations Divisions in the Hydrodynamics and Structures Laboratories merged in an Acoustics and Vibrations Laboratory (AVL), bringing to five the number of major laboratories at the model basin. (The prior four laboratories were Hydromechanics, Aerodynamics, Structural Mechanics, and Applied Mathematics.) Argiro and his EES group retained responsibility for testing and analyzing machinery noise; AVL at Carderock concentrated on hydrodynamically generated noise, sonar self-noise, and radiated noise during underway operation. Carderock staff ran sound tests in the Bahamas, while the remote station at Lake Pend Oreille, Idaho provided a location for towed array, acoustic and radar countermeasures, and small buoyant body testing.

With increasing design and operational requirements in terms of size, speed, and powering, AVL greatly expanded efforts to measure and understand noise-producing mechanisms aboard the vessel itself to improve acoustic stealth. When the Bureau of Ships received notice of a noise problem associated with a particular ship, AVL would be tasked to localize the source, determine its root cause, and recommend a fix. Often, AVL personnel installed special sensors and rode on board the ship to listen to the noise, acquire data, and attempt localization using sonar and installed sensors. They would examine regions of the hull or outboard equipment at points from which the noise appeared to emanate. They would perform theoretical calculations that provided insight into the noise-producing mechanism to lead to a silencing solution. Many early noise problems were associated with flow disturbances such as cavitation occurring on propellers and at hull surface discontinuities, various cavity resonances, flow oscillations induced by improperly shaped struts and ladder rungs, and singing propeller blades. The laboratory's multitiered approach to solving fleet noise problems became more extensive and organized over time as more and more stringent requirements were set for acoustic stealth. The approach required joint and coordinated efforts between AVL, Hydrodynamics, and Structural Mechanics personnel as silencing solutions to fleet noise problems became more difficult to achieve because the solutions impacted basic submarine and surface ship design.[58]

Structural Mechanics and Submarines

The loss of the submarine *Thresher* (SSN 593) in 1963 led to increased naval interest in deep submergence vessels for exploration, observation, and possible search and rescue application. The basin became a leader in the development of safe and lighter pressure hulls and buoyancy systems for deep submergence vessels, with applications to 20,000 feet. Results of this pioneering work found application in several submersibles for the Navy and for private industry. Work on titanium hulls and new foam buoyancy materials provided the base for modifications of the deep submersible *Sea Cliff* to extend its operating depth from 6,500 feet to 20,000 feet.[59]

As the Navy sought to design submarines and deep submergence rescue vessels with ever-greater depth capability, designers confronted the issue of testing new shapes against the effects of pressure or "external hydrostatic loading." Early pressure tanks at the basin included a 37-inch-diameter tank constructed before 1951, which had a limited capacity and could not be used to test welding or structural details. By 1954 the basin built an 8-foot-diameter tank with an internal "deflectometer" to measure variation from true roundness in models before and during pressure testing. This tank used oil as a pressure medium, both for ease of handling and to prevent corrosion of electrical connections. Constructed from available materials at a cost of only $15,000, the 8-foot tank's load of 900 psi proved insufficient for model testing of the new generation of deep-diving vessels planned in the 1960s and 1970s.[60]

From 1961 through 1976 the Structural Mechanics Laboratory developed a series of highly capable tanks for testing research and design-confirmation models and full-scale hulls of deep submersibles. Stemming from deep-dive tests of *Thresher*, which revealed that the test results showed little agreement with classical theory, a group including Martin Krenzke, Thomas Kiernan, Kane Nishida, and others began investigating the causes for the disparity. Through tests of small carefully machined scaled models the problem was traced to local flat spots on the surface of the sphere that had escaped the rather coarse original measurements of sphericity. By following up these tests with a series of realistic, fabricated models, a new design procedure was developed that accounted for the weakening effects of local flat spots, as well as the effects of local thin spots developed during the fabrication process. This

DTMB Structural Mechanics Laboratory Construction. With new emphasis on deep submergence, DTMB constructed a new structures test facility with three pressure tanks.

Structural Mechanics Laboratory. As the new tanks were added in building 19, the open greensward in front of the Main Building was preserved.

improved design procedure found widespread use both in the United States and abroad in the design of submarine and small submersible pressure hulls. The structures staff under Edward Wenk Jr. also investigated a variety of potential hull configurations and materials for submersibles including nested spheres, sandwich shells, higher strength steel alloys, aluminum, titanium, fiber-reinforced plastics, and even "massive glass" and ceramics. Eventually Structural Mechanics researchers Rich L. Waterman, David T. McDevitt, and Peter M. Palermo conducted over 40 deep submergence trials of new submarines during the period from 1951 to 1983. Some of these submarines were tested two to four additional times. The additional tests resulted from studies stimulated by the loss of *Thresher* and from the special problem of developing a suitable junction at the intersection of the missile tubes and the pressure hull on the deeper diving 608-class ballistic missile submarines.[61]

With the creation of the Navy's Deep Submergence Systems Office, which had the explicit objective of developing small submersibles for search, rescue, and recovery, researchers turned to specific applications,

Jacques Cousteau. On a visit to Carderock, Jacques Cousteau listens attentively while Martin Krenzke demonstrates the mounting of a plexiglass view port in a deep submergence rescue vehicle.

concentrating on development of candidate pressure hull designs for a deep submergence rescue vehicle (DSRV) and a deep submergence search vehicle (DSSV) for operations to 20,000-foot depths. Using new alloys of steel, with high-yield strengths of 100,000 and 130,000 psi (HY-100 and HY-130) and titanium alloy ($Ti_6Al_2Cb_1Ta_{0.8}Mo$), the basin became directly involved in the structural design, construction, and validation testing of spherical pressure hulls for *Alvin, Turtle, Sea Cliff,* and DSRV. The use of the new steels for deep submergence vehicles represented a practical test of metal working methods and capabilities of such high-strength materials for possible use in regular attack and missile submarines. Krenzke and Kiernan conducted research and developed procedures for the design of doubly curved shells for submarine end closures and for the hulls of the DSRVs. Similarly, work on fiberglass and massive glass had possible applications in full-size submarines, as well as in instrument casings and floats used at various depths in the ocean. At its peak in the mid-1960s, the work on deep submergence hulls and materials was funded at about $2 million a year, from a variety of sources.[62]

Improvements to DSRV-1.   The Deep Submergence Rescue Vehicle served as a test bed for dozens of innovative concepts developed by different groups at the center, including new high-strength steel alloys.

The significance and usefulness of the work on deep submergence vessels was demonstrated in January 1966, when *Alvin* participated in the recovery of the "broken arrow" nuclear weapon lost off Palomares, Spain. The unarmed thermonuclear weapon was recovered from 2,850 feet of water, in an effort which took three months, dozens of ships and aircraft, thousands of people, and millions of dollars. The highly publicized event reemphasized the national importance of an expanded capability for search and recovery systems in the deep ocean. The Navy introduced a new program to develop deep-ocean technology, with a priority program implemented in fiscal year 1968, running through 1988.

The Deep Ocean Technology Program generated a library of engineering data and numerous prototype hardware contributions. Eight handbooks were authored at the Annapolis laboratory, providing engineering data over the period 1968–1980. The handbooks covered the design of various systems for use in deep-ocean environments, including electric cables, shaft seals, lubricants, electric and electronic circuit breakers, imaging systems, insulation materials, electric drives, and hydraulic systems.[63]

Hardware contributions to the deep-diving effort abounded at the Annapolis lab. In 1973 a variable seawater ballast system was developed for the Woods Hole Oceanographic Institution's submersible *Alvin.* In the same year a prototype electric-drive pontoon emplacement vehicle system was developed for the salvage of large objects. A prototype hydraulic power supply for the 20,000-foot manipulative work system package was developed in 1977. Research and development deliverables for the conversion of *Sea Cliff* to a 20,000-foot-depth capability included program coordination, titanium hull and air flask materials selection, the variable ballast system, and electric motors and electrical switching devices. For the 20,000-foot advanced tethered vehicle, a team developed a prototype high-voltage and power control system in 1987.[64]

A program deriving from the deep submergence effort was a plan to develop a 60 kw, 1,000 kwhr fuel-cell system for operation at 20,000-foot depths. The reactants in this fuel cell, hydrogen and oxygen,

Submersible *Orion* Entering Pressure Tank.   When the two sections of this large pressure tank at EES closed, it could test full-scale submersibles and large-scale models, simulating depths to 20,000 feet.

needed to be stored at high pressures: the hydrogen at 7,500 psi and the oxygen at 4,500 psi. Annapolis staff determined the effect of hydrogen on the fracture toughness of high-strength containment materials, finally selecting HY-100 steel alloy as the optimum material. A 30 kw, 700 kwhr fuel cell power system was installed on *Deep Quest* for at-sea tests. Although the fuel cell proved itself as an advanced and efficient underwater power source, it was never used on a DSRV because of the improvement of more conventional silver-zinc batteries. However, this background work on fuel cells held promise for future applications.

In order to ensure a high degree of confidence in the structural reliability and safety of the submarine fleet, the Structures Department worked with the Bureau of Ships in developing a rigorous process for determining hull scantlings and construction tolerances, and for confirming design adequacy. In the lab, this work was initiated by engineers who had survived a drastic cutback in the Structures Department in 1949–1950 when the staff was reduced from sixty to eighteen. Of those, six more left because they were demoralized. By 1951, when the nation was engaged in the Korean War and personnel ceilings were lifted, recruitment efforts pushed by Edward Wenk succeeded in attracting the necessary talent in analytic and experimental structural mechanics to build a solid foundation for submarine structural design.[65]

In the late 1940s, as designers anticipated that submarines should be made capable of much greater depth. The Bureau of Ships anticipated that the maximum operating depth would be increased significantly to enlarge the safe operating envelope for much faster submarines and to gain other operational advantages. Increases in operating depth and propulsion weight placed a much greater emphasis on structural weight reduction and resulted in the use of new structural configurations such as doubly curved end closures, much greater structural optimization, and higher strength steel hulls.

As a consequence of such planning, the bureau approved a research program to develop a submarine hull steel that was much stronger than the current yield strength of 44,000 psi to 47,000 psi. Nine different steels were investigated, but they offered minimal improvements at best. Special treatment steel (STS), developed by Krupp in Germany in the 1890s, had been used for armor plating by the U.S. Navy as early as 1912. Modified low-carbon special treatment steel (LC-STS) was developed by industry, incorporating a modification of the amounts of nickel and carbon in the alloy, and the addition of a small quantity of molybdenum. The bureau specified this alloy as the hull material for *Albacore,* for the magazine protection system for the aircraft carrier *Forrestal* (CVA 59), and for the missile hangars on *Growler* (SS 215). The bureau redesignated LC-STS as "HY-80," for high-yield strength, 80,000 psi special treatment steel. In 1956, the bureau specified HY-80 for the hull and stiffening system for *Skipjack* and for most follow-on submarines.

However, shipyards continued to use older systems and procedures for welding the new alloy. By 1957, excessive cracking of weldments in highly restrained or stressed structural members occurred on board the new submarines, leading to an expensive and time-consuming repair process of literally hundreds of feet of HY-80 welds. The nuclear submarine program suffered a major crisis: the question remained—would the repaired welds crack again in a few years?

Cracking occurred not only at one shipyard or at one company. Electric Boat's *George Washington* as well as *Patrick Henry* (SSBN 599), *Scorpion* (SSN 589), *Tullibee* (SSN 597), and *Ethan Allen* (SSBN 608) all showed welding cracks. Similar cracks occurred on welds on *Theodore Roosevelt* (SSBN 600) under construction at the Mare Island Naval Shipyard and on *Abraham Lincoln* (SSBN 602), at the Portsmouth Navy Yard. Construction under way at other shipyards, including Newport News, Ingalls, and New York Shipbuilding revealed similar problems with welding HY-80 steel.[66]

It was obvious that the fabrication experience developed with *Albacore, Forrestal,* and *Growler* was insufficient and that something more had to be done to explain the cracking and to alleviate the problem. Capable personnel from industry, academia, Navy laboratories, ship operators, and the Bureau of Ships sought to define and bound the problem and develop an approach to its solution. In the end, a series of related actions and requirements addressed the issue. On the one hand, industry and EES personnel developed new welding procedures and welding materials. On the other hand, researchers studied the cause and effects of the cracks.

At the basin, Ralph Allnutt of the Structures Lab, working with Paul Day of the Industrial Department, developed and patented a unique scheme for conducting cyclic fatigue tests of submarine scale models without subjecting the test tank to fatigue loadings. The method involved holding the test tank pressure at the maximum test pressure and varying the pressure on the inside of the models from zero to the maximum test pressure. In that way, the model saw the equivalent of a varying external pressure. This scheme was then utilized at other test facilities and at private laboratories for conducting cyclic tests of submarine models. pressurizing the inside of the model. Then Palermo and McDevitt developed procedures for cyclic loading fatigue tests and prediction methods of HY-80 submarine models, while others developed shipyard welding procedures and controls. The teams recommended softer or "more forgiving" welding materials and new alloy compounding methods, with reduced sulfur, phosphorus, and hydrogen content that would reduce weld repairs. The development of new welding materials, procedures, and supervision concepts reduced repair, fabrication, and maintenance costs.

In this effort, staff from both the Structures Laboratory at the basin and the Welding Laboratory at the Marine Engineering Laboratory—formerly Bela Ronay's group at EES—cooperated in research and publication of results. Reports from the studies were published as DTMB reports, MEL reports, and Naval Research Laboratory reports. The crash program to resolve shipyard problems was completed by 1960; the more comprehensive study characterizing dynamic, metallurgical, and static HY-80 weld properties continued through 1966. [67]

Nuclear submarines in general and the later generation of Polaris class missile submarines in particular presented a variety of problems to the Structures Department that had not been faced earlier in conventional submarine design. For example, the size and layout of the nuclear power plant required a large increase in submarine pressure hull diameter. This led the designers to replace the traditional double-hull construction with single hull construction for the reactor compartment, and eventually to adopt predominantly single hull construction with ballast tanks located only at the bow and stern. Stiffeners were moved to the inside of the pressure hull to achieve an acceptable hydrodynamic outer surface. The high horsepower developed by the nuclear power plant led to the requirement for long machinery compartments, with large deep frames used to provide the structural support normally provided by relatively closely spaced bulkheads. Steep conical shells were introduced to transition more rapidly from the large diameter to smaller diameter, externally stiffened cylindrical hull sections.

A new structural design was introduced to eliminate the cone-cylinder juncture ring, and a new design of the transition ring reduced measured stresses by over 30 percent. In order to achieve ballistic missile launch capability, two rows of relatively large diameter tubes, which housed Polaris missiles, were placed vertically in the missile compartment, with the tubes penetrating the hull at the crown. The submarine structural design process that evolved consisted of four essential steps. First, failure modes were identified for each hull configuration, material, and fabrication process through a combination of analytical and experimental investigations. Then methods for predicting each of the failure modes were developed and verified through carefully controlled experiments. The second step was to use these validated prediction

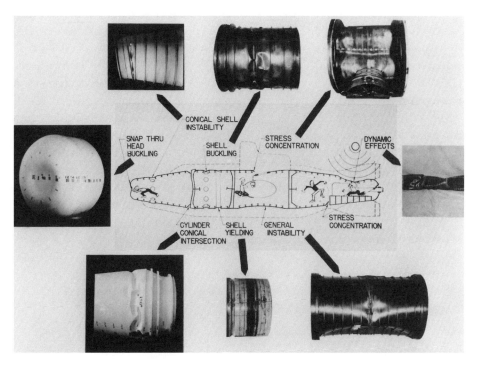

Pressure Hull Studies.   Researchers investigated different possible modes of collapse of pressure hull models.

methods to develop user-oriented design procedures that were compiled in a Navy Submarine Structures Design Manual. This design manual, in which 80 percent to 90 percent of the references were from DTMB, would be invoked in the contract for each new submarine. Next, when a new submarine design was developed, the drawings were reviewed to identify any significant departure from previous hull designs. If any such features were found, a confirmation model of typically 1/6 to 1/3 scale was fabricated and tested in a DTMB pressure tank to demonstrate structural behavior and collapse strength. The final step was to conduct a manned deep dive, during which strain measurements were taken.

In designing the first ballistic submarine, *George Washington*, Structures Department personnel worked feverishly with the Bureau of Ships in conducting model tests and deep dives, back fits and more model tests and deep dives, until a satisfactory, semi-empirically based design with adequate collapse strength as well as fatigue life was finally achieved.[68]

By the mid-1960s the Navy had replaced the submersible with a true submarine. When the nuclear submarine moved into the fleet, it reflected and embodied work of every department at both DTMB and EES. The resources of DTMB, particularly in its long-established hydrodynamics and structures groups, proved essential. The *Albacore* design itself, a product of the DTMB Series 58, introduced a faster and quieter shape to the U.S. nuclear submarine fleet. The nuclear boats ran safer, faster, and deeper, because of the work of the laboratories. Recovery of submarine personnel and nuclear weapons from the ocean depths stimulated a variety of programs to design vehicles that could dive to extreme depths and face the harsh environments found there. And a new science of underwater acoustics, discussed in the following chapter, would help the new submarines run more quietly and detect more effectively the presence of potential adversaries while submerged. Like the development of applications of nuclear fission and jet propulsion during World War II, advances in underwater acoustics would bring new responsibilities and new talents to the two laboratories.

Endnotes

1. John B. Alden, *The Fleet Submarine in the U.S. Navy: A Design and Construction History* (Annapolis: Naval Institute Press, 1979), 42–44.
2. Erminio Bagnasco, *Submarines of World War Two* (Annapolis: Naval Institute Press, 1977), 54.
3. Ibid., 33, 56.
4. Naval History Division, *The Submarine in the United States Navy*, 3d ed., selected chronology (Washington: Government Printing Office, 1969); Bagnasco, *Submarines of World War Two*, 33–36.
5. Bagnasco, *Submarines of World War Two*, 33–34, 57.
6. Ibid., 57; U.S. Naval Technical Mission in Europe, *The German Schnorchel*, Technical Report No. 517-45, Oct 1945, OA, box 44.
7. U.S. Technical Mission in Europe, "Advance Report on Walter Werk Keil," Letter Report No. 52-45, 16 May 1945, OA, box 9, Letter Reports; U.S. Naval Technical Mission in Europe, *Thermodynamics and Tests of the Walter Propulsion System*, Technical Report No. 188-45, Aug 1945, OA, box 24.
8. Bagnasco, *Submarines of World War Two*, 34, 56–57, 76; U.S. Naval Mission in Europe, *The German Schnorchel*, Technical Report No. 517- 45; U.S. Naval Technical Mission in Europe, *German Submarine Design, 1935–1945*, Technical Report No. 312-45, OA, box 32.
9. Clarence Lasby, *Project Paperclip: German Scientists and the Cold War* (New York: Atheneum, 1971).
10. U.S. Naval Technical Mission in Europe, *The German Schnorchel*, Technical Report No. 517-45; U.S. Technical Mission in Europe, *German Submarine Design, 1935–1945*, Technical Report No. 312-45.
11. U.S. Naval Technical Mission in Europe, *German Submarine Design, 1935–1945*, Technical Report No. 312-45.
12. U.S. Technical Mission in Europe, *The German Schnorchel*, Technical Report No. 517-45; Naval History Division, *The Submarine in the United States Navy*, 3d ed. (Washington: GPO, 1969) selected chronology.
13. Norman Polmar, *The American Submarine* (Annapolis: Nautical & Aviation Publishing Company of America, 1983), 109.
14. Richard G. Hewlett and Francis Duncan, *Nuclear Navy 1946–1962* (Chicago: University of Chicago Press, 1974), 76; J. H. Reinerston, L. E. Alsager, and Morley, "The Submarine Propulsion Plant—Development and Prospects," *Naval Engineers Journal* 75 (May 1963): 357–360.
15. Polmar, *The American Submarine*, 79–83.
16. Ibid., 75–97; J. J. Scheilbeier to Director, EES, 12 Jan 1949; and F. W. Walton and G. C. Humphreys to Chief of Naval Research, 21 Sep 1951, WNRC, RG 181, acc. 73A2733, box 13, 030058-2.
17. M. Gertler to Officer in Charge, USN Submarine School, 17 Feb 1956, WNRC, RG 181, acc. 63A2152, box 8.
18. Marvin Lasky, "Historical Review of Undersea Warfare Planning and Organization 1945–1960, with Emphasis on the Role of the Office of Naval Research," *Journal of Underwater Acoustics* 26 (1976): 327–357.

19. Ibid., 330–341. The U.S. policy was based on a close awareness of Soviet capture of German submarine types, as discussed at the Low, Hartwell, and Nobska Conferences. For a detailed review of submarine policy as deriving from these conferences, see Gary Weir, *Forged in War* (Washington: Naval Historical Center, 1993), 133–147.
20. Lasky, "A Historical Review," 345–346.
21. *Ibid.*, 346; J. Fife to Commander Submarine Force, U.S. Atlantic Fleet, et al., 17 Feb 1949, WNRC, RG 181, acc. 12608, box 14, SS/S1-2-5 Subs, vol. 1.
22. Lasky, "A Historical Review," 345–346.
23. Ibid.
24. W. L. Pryor, Jr., to Director, EES, 7 Dec 1949, WNRC, RG 181, acc. 73A2733, box 7, 3364.
25. Ibid.
26. Lasky, "A Historical Review," 346–347.
27. Ibid.
28. H. C. Mason to Commanding Officer and Director, DTMB, 29 Oct 1965, WNRC, RG 181, acc. 69A5171, box A52-3, 540: 1965.
29. L. A. Rupp to K. Taylor, 11 Jan 1956, WNRC, RG 181, acc. 63A2152, box 5, S8/USS *Albacore*. Auxiliaries, General Sub 1956.
30. L. A. Rupp to K. Taylor, Jan 11, 1956; J. R. Baylis to Commanding Officer and Director, DTMB, May 14, 1956, WNRC, RG 181, acc. 63A2152, box 5, S8/USS *Albacore* Auxiliaries, General.
31. K. E. Schoenherr to Chief, Bureau of Ships, 14 Jul 1958, WNRC, RG 181, acc. 65A4256, box 4, S8/USS *Albacore*.
32. J. H. Reinerston, et al., "The Submarine Propulsion Plant-Development and Prospects," 349–364; H. E. Strange, *Supplementary Report on Walter Submarine Propulsion Unit Combustion Chamber*, 3 Aug 1948, EES Report No. C-2533-A(5), WNRC, RG 181, acc. 73A2733, box 10; F. W. Heep to Chief, Bureau of Ships, 13 Nov 1951, WNRC, RG 181, acc. 73A2733, box 12; Harold V. Nutt, interview by David K. Allison, 22 Oct 1982, DTNSRDC RC 6-5, box 1.
33. Director, EES, to Chief, Bureau of Ships, 4 Oct 1946; J. S. Crenshaw to Chief of Naval Operations, 23 Jul 1947; and J. S. Crenshaw to Chief of Naval Operations, 19 Sep 1947, WNRC, RG 181, acc. 73A2733, box 16, 030077; J. 5. Crenshaw to Chief of Naval Operations, 7 May 1947, WNRC, RG 181, acc. 73A2733, box 16, 30077-2.
34. L. B. Slater to Assistant Chief of Staff, British Naval Forces, Germany, 13 Aug 1947; and J. S. Crenshaw to Chief of Naval Operations, 23 Jul 1947, WNRC, RG 181, acc. 73A2733, box 16, 030077.
35. J. S. Crenshaw to Chief of Naval Operations, May 19, 1947, WNRC, RG 181, acc. 73A2733, box 16, 030077.
36. John J. Dinan, *Shore Test of Project Alton Submarine*, 19 Nov 1954, EES Evaluation Report 030077, WNRC, RG 181, acc. 73A2733, box 14; R. C. Davis, *Final Test Report of Wolverine Gas Turbine Plant*, 14 Aug 1956, EES Research and Development Report 030076, WNRC, RG 181, acc. 73A2733, box 13.
37. Dinan, *Shore Test of Project Alton Submarine Plant*, EES Evaluation Report 030077.
38. Davis, *Final Test Report of Wolverine Gas Turbine Plant*, EES Research and Development Report 030076.
39. Reinerston, et al., *The Submarine Propulsion Plant-Development and Prospects*, 357–360.
40. Ibid.
41. Ibid.

42. D. J. Nairn to Code 432, W. C. Karl, 22 Sep 1950, WNRC, RG 181, acc. 73A2733, box 12, 030077-6; F. W. Haus to Chief, Bureau of Ships, 21 May 1947, WNRC, RG 181, acc. 73A2733, box 12, 030077-2; C. L. Sayre to EES, 23 Aug 1949, WNRC, RG 181, acc. 73A2733, box 12, 030077.

43. Reinerston, et al., *The Submarine Propulsion Plant—Developments and Prospects*, 347–350.

44. K. H. Wilcoxon, Memorandum, 25 Oct 1949, WNRC, RG 181, acc. 12608, box 14, SS/S1-2-(5), Subs Vol. 1, 1950.

45. R. C. Davis, *Final Test Report of Wolverine Gas Turbine Plant*, EES Research and Development Report 030076.

46. Nutt interview, 22 Oct 1982.

47. Polmar, *The American Submarine*, 93–97, 119.

48. Ibid., 119.

49. Ibid., 123.

50. Harvey Sapolsky, *The Polaris System Development: Bureaucratic and Programmatic Success in Government* (Cambridge, MA: Harvard University Press, 1972).

51. Harold Singerman, interview by Rodney Carlisle, 7 Jul 1986.

52. [No author], "U.S. Naval Engineering Experiment Station Progress Report," Jan 1961, DTNSRDC RC 7-2, box 2.

53. Harold Singerman, 24 Jul 1996, "A Brief Unclassified History of the Submarine Atmospheric Control Program at the Annapolis Laboratory," ABIF.

54. R. E. Smith, "Submarine Electrolytic Oxygen Generator," ABIF.

55. Tom Mansfield, ABIF communication, 7 May 1996.

56. L. H. Beck to DTMB, et al., May 9, 1966, WNRC, RG 181, acc. 70A5757, box A52-1, 3900/Noise.

57. R. W. Vollenweider to Supervisor of Shipbuilding, et al., 27 Jun 1956, WNRC, RG 181, acc. 63A2152, box 6, S8/*Seawolf*, WNRC.

58. Brian Bowers, ABIF communication, 8 Oct 1996.

59. "Deep Submersible Hulls," DTNSRDC Major Accomplishments, No. 17, DTNSRDC RC 3-2, box 3.

60. E. E. Johnson, *Pressure Tank and Instrumentation Facilities for Studying the Strength of Vessels Subjected to External Loading*. Apr 1956, DTMB Report No. 979.

61. "Deep Submersible Hulls," DTNSRDC Major Accomplishments, No. 17; communication from Marty Krenzke; from Peter Palermo; from William Morgan, ABIF; Wenk interview, 17 Apr 1987.

62. "Deep Submersible Hulls," DTNSRDC Major Accomplishments, No. 17.

63. The eight handbooks were among a series of eleven, available through the Defense Technical Information Center. Topics and publication numbers were Electric Cables: AD 877-774; Shaft-seals: AD899-330(L); Fluids and Lubricants: AD 869-350L; Depth-compensating fluid systems: AD 894-795; Circuit-interrupting Devices: AD889-829; Underwater imaging: AD 904-472 (L); Electrical Insulation: B012737(L); Electric Drive: B022859(L); Hydraulic Systems: ADB062769.

64. R. Chomo: "Deep Ocean Technology," ABIF.

65. Edward Wenk Jr., *Making Waves: Engineering, Politics, and the Social Management of Technology* (Urbana: University of Illinois Press, 1995), 30, 34.

66. "Development of Welding Materials and Welding Procedures for HY-80 Steel," DTNSRDC Major Accomplishments, No. 25, DTNSRDC RC 3-2, box 3; ABIF material from Peter Palermo.

67. "Development of Welding," DTNSRDC Major Accomplishments, No. 25; Peter Palermo, et al., *Cyclic Loading Tests of Scaled Submarine Models*, Jun 1961, DTMB

Report No. C-1282; Abner R. Wilner and Marcel E. Salive, *Effects of Austenitizing and Tempering on Mechanical Properties of Fully Quenched HY-80 Steels*, Nov 1961, DTMB Report No. 1523; William G. Schreitz, *Restrained Cracking Technique for Use in Simulated Weld Thermal Cycling Studies*, Jun 1964, MEL Report No. 90/64; William S. Pellini, et al., *Review of Concepts and Status of Procedures for Fracture-Safe Design of Complex Welded Structures Involving Low to Ultra-High Strength Levels*, Jun 1965, NRL Report No. 6300; Irving L. Stern and Abraham Pollack, "Semi-Automatic Inert Gas Metal Arc (MIG) Welding of HY-80-LINDE 103 Filler Wire," Dec 1963, NASL L.P. No. 9300-1 TM#5.

68. Martin Krenzke, ABIF communication, May 12, 1996.

CHAPTER 9

Ship Silencing and Ship Protection

I N THE WANING DAYS OF THE THIRD REICH, late in 1944, a Messerschmitt
Me 262 screamed out of nowhere to attack Allied bombers. The first
jet fighter plane, the Me 262 could fly 540 miles per hour at 20,000
feet, climb at over 3,900 feet per minute, and reach a maximum ceiling
over 37,000 feet. Germany produced 1,400 Me 262s, but only 200
reached squadron service.[1] Seven months later, over a desert in southern
New Mexico, the scientists and engineers of the Manhattan Engineer
District set off Trinity, the first nuclear explosion. The "gadget," an im-
ploded sphere of plutonium, yielded the equivalent of some 13,000 tons
of TNT. A simpler, uranium-fueled weapon devastated Hiroshima 6
August 1945, and three days later a Trinity-type weapon destroyed a portion of Nagasaki.

The jet and the atomic bomb revolutionized the future of warfare. In the postwar period all military planners confronted a new age
of weaponry. For the Carderock and Annapolis laboratories, the jet
and the nuclear weapon shaped dozens of projects in the 1950s and
1960s. Admirals asked if the surface Navy would have a role in the face
of the devastating force of the atomic bomb; nuclear weapons added
airblast and vastly greater underwater shock effects to the threats already faced by a surface ship from torpedoes, high-explosive bombs,
shells, and mines.

Other wartime weapons work also required follow-up at the labs, including innovations in acoustic detection of ships and several promising
innovations in ship propeller design through the 1950s and 1960s. The
lessons and innovations of World War II in the areas of surface ship pro-

tection against shock and silencing of ships and submarines to evade acoustic detection would establish much of the exciting research agenda of these decades.

With closer coordination, the introduction of flexible and powerful computer hardware and software, a better-trained professional staff, and improved physical plant, the two labs responded more efficiently to naval needs than had been the case when two separate, competing, and often feuding bureaus controlled the laboratories. No longer faced with the wartime pressures, the two laboratories embarked on parallel paths that often brought them into cooperation and a coordinated partnership on particular projects, new weapons, and new defensive systems. A variety of research and development projects growing out of the new technologies often cut across the remaining organizational barriers between the Carderock and Annapolis laboratories. After the consolidation of the two laboratories in 1967, discussed in the following chapter, cooperation and joint projects in the new areas could move ahead even more efficiently.

Underwater Acoustics—A New Science

During and immediately after World War II, the Navy asked General Electric (GE) to develop acoustic homing torpedoes, incorporating an active sonar system. Earlier antisubmarine torpedoes had operated on a simpler, sound-homing principle that utilized a passive rather than active sonar, and basically aimed at a noise source. Submariners could evade the approaching torpedo by slowly circling, by emitting a train of bubbles, or by using a simple sound-emitting decoy. But the planned Mark 32 torpedo developed by a small team at GE's Schenectady plant used an echo-ranging system that would be much harder to evade. In February 1944 GE reported its first successful test. At the end of the war, work on the active sonar torpedo ended, just as the weapon entered production. A year later the Navy issued another contract to GE to improve the Mark 32 and to build its compact sonar system into even more effective "fish."[2]

Improved passive listening devices as well as the development of more compact active sonars as in the Mark 32 meant that defense against detecting and targeting by sound would become a major research priority in the postwar period. Both submarines and surface vessels would have to carry sonars, run quietly, and develop an effective set of countermeasures to combat new detection methods. At the model basin, Rear Admiral H. S. Howard was quick to note opportunities. Even before the war ended, he told Harold Saunders that Rear Admiral J. A.

Furer, research coordinator, had tipped him that the Office of Scientific Research and Development was closing up their own work on using models in sound detection work. Furer and Howard had agreed that such work "could come here better than anywhere else." Furer and Saunders planned to increase the basin's schedule of acoustic work.[3]

The new Bureau of Ships (BUSHIPS), managing both laboratories, made it possible to bring together individuals formerly isolated by separate control of the two laboratories. Wesley Curtis had started his career in 1939 at EES. The bureau shifted him to Carderock, along with the partially assembled twelve-inch water tunnel for propeller testing. In 1948 Curtis worked in the Vibration and Acoustics Branch in the Applied Physics Laboratory until the absorption of its programs into the Hydromechanics Laboratory in 1950; he then headed the Underwater Acoustics Branch of the Hydromechanics Laboratory set up in 1954. After the establishment, in 1963, of the Acoustics and Vibrations Laboratory, Curtis continued to run the Facilities Branch within the laboratory and to serve in other administrative posts in the lab. Through the war years, Murray Strasberg, supported by others, conducted measurements of propeller noise on submarines of the SS 212 class. The results of this effort and the measurements he obtained in the 24-inch variable-pressure water tunnel led to an improved understanding of propeller-generated sound and methods of suppressing propeller cavitation. Strasberg continued to work on hydrodynamic sources of sound through the 1950s. Other staff members with early experience stayed on in a similar fashion, allowing the model basin to build staff strength in acoustics on internal experience and continuity of personnel. The variety of seemingly random projects in acoustics and vibration eventually solidified, by the mid-1950s, into a set of regular commitments and programs.[4]

The work required a new set of procedures to protect security and classification. In October 1945 Commander J. O. Baker worked out a procedure for storing acoustics documents, including working notebooks as well as draft reports, in the main vault. Although vault storage led to the inconvenience of checking out pertinent documents each day, the system offered far tighter security for the classified material than storage in locked file cabinets. Baker noted that the internal procedure was even more secure than that required by Navy regulations.[5]

Anticipating a "probable expansion" in the underwater sound mission, Rear Admiral Claude Kell established a course, equivalent to a three-credit-hour university course, for training in the fundamentals of sound and sonar. Complete with prerequisites in calculus and college physics, a syllabus, examinations, and a strenuous set of projects and readings, the course would lead to qualification to work in the growing section of Applied Physics Laboratory devoted to acoustics. Topics included acoustic instrumentation, sound phenomena, sound fields, sound generation, and physics of sea and underwater sound measurements. The development of such a course demonstrated how the basin recognized the growing emphasis on education when no regular university courses could be taken because the field was so new and so militarily sensitive.[6] A few months later, Kell announced a course presented by two naval officers who were themselves "undergoing indoctrination," set up through the Bureau of Ships. Kell did not, in this case, offer the suggestion that taking the course might open opportunities for transfer to the acoustics group. Rather, the lecture series from the Bureau of Ships office was perceived more as an orientation rather than a true, rigorous, university-level course.[7]

Opportunities to do acoustics work arose when model basin staff found that they could offer equipment or expert knowledge that filled a need not met elsewhere in the Navy. In January 1949, Strasberg reported a rumor that the Underwater Sound Laboratory had indicated it would have to postpone measurements of propeller noise. Strasberg urged the model basin to step into the breach, using a towed hydrophone system that had already been the subject of a basin report. The towed hydrophones, streamlined to reduce self-noise, would be towed alongside a destroyer by a cable array from a strut on the side of the destroyer. Experimental propellers drove the ship, while staff observed through special ports cut in the stern and compared visual observations of cavitation with measurements of cavitation sound inception points made through the hydrophone array.[8]

At times the basin had to defend, as well as to promote, its growing collection of equipment in the acoustics area. When the head of the Bureau of Ships section on noise, shock and vibration questioned the authority of the basin to design and build a stethoscope for measuring full-scale ships' noise, Rear Admiral Kell shot back with extensive arguments. This "invaluable instrument" would define and clear up objectionable noise sources of full-scale ships, and it might make unnecessary the construction of a variable pressure facility at much greater expense. The stethoscope would only cost $2,000, and Kell asked for speedy approval of the expense in order to get ready for upcoming full-scale trials.[9]

Through 1949 Baker, the physicist in charge of the Applied Physics Laboratory over the small acoustics group, arranged transfer of 1950 allocated funds to the model basin for acoustics activities. New budget lines would be approved for full-scale ship tests on a 60-inch sonar dome and for construction of a strut system for the mounting of towed hydrophone arrays.[10] Kell arranged for internal transfers of funds from various other projects at the basin to continue the work in acoustics.[11]

As SUBDEVGRU-2 conducted investigations in New London in early 1950, model basin staff continued to develop proposals for further work. Louis Landweber proposed a study by a model basin staff member to be performed on a visit to the New London group, recommending to the commander of SUBDEVGRU-2 a series of investigations into the background noise picked up on a JT sonar system being tested. Landweber proposed a careful analysis to determine whether the background noise came from self-generated noise, bubbles, turbulence, vortices, cavitation, or vibration of metal.[12]

The pattern of specialization in various aspects of acoustics at both EES and DTMB was shaped by early choices of projects. In this way the accidents of capability of staff and equipment in the immediate postwar years determined the work of a later decade. Strasberg, Curtis, Lasky, and others at the basin built up reputations in specialized problems associated with flow-generated and cavitation-generated noise of propellers and of sonar devices themselves. As concern with the generation of noise aboard ship grew, both DTMB and EES staff continued to stake out a new set of specialties. In 1953 Mark Harrison at the basin studied the problem of sound isolation mountings of sonar equipment. Although a system of sound-isolating mountings with a fluid cushion had worked quite well when tested in air, the system did not prevent the transmission of noise when tested at sea. Harrison reviewed the mathematics of vibration and vibration damping and suggested a design in which several smaller mountings would substitute for one larger one.[13]

At the same time, at the Engineering Experiment Station in Annapolis, researchers worked on reduction of noise from gears and pinions. Both empirical and fundamental research approaches yielded basic information about how various factors such as material, geometry, finish, and hardness of the component metal affected the noise emitted. A machine powered by a 300-kilowatt motor driving a gear box, itself acoustically isolated from the motor and from torque testing devices, allowed for running and testing of gears and pinions under varying speeds and loads. Staff ran accurate tests of both structure-borne and airborne noise by mounting the gears in an anechoic room isolated acoustically from the motor. As in earlier EES tests of diesel engines through interchange of alternative parts, the research revealed which variable—lubrication, tooth geometry, finish, or material—contributed to particular noises.[14]

By the mid-1950s the naval engineering community began to discuss the fact that sound propagation was a crucial issue in the design of surface ships as well as submarines. Avoidance of acoustic torpedoes and evasion of submarines equipped with listening devices required quieter ships, designed from the drawing board to be quiet rather than simply being quieted down after construction. At the bureau a special office devoted to underwater sound provided funding and encouragement for specialized studies by 1954.

On the eve of the launching and sea trials of *Albacore* in 1955, Admiral Frederick Furth commented on the fact that for a decade the Navy had held annual symposia on underwater sound. These meetings had drawn specialists in a wide range of disciplines to exchange ideas and findings, including "applied physicists," biologists, chemists, oceanographers, and a variety of specialists in the study of materials. Unlike other areas, the field of underwater sound was of interest only to the Navy, and specialists could not count on broad-based industrial support or shared investment from other branches of the military or the civilian government departments.[15] Navy support for work in the area had begun to create a unique Navy-funded technical-scientific discipline drawing from a variety of long-established sciences. The Navy had, in effect, created a new Navy-controlled and highly classified interdisciplinary area of scientific research and development. Naval recognition of the new field grew more and more explicit.[16]

Robert Taggart, in charge of the noise section of the Applied Science Division of the Bureau of Ships, asserted that the scientific acoustic work showed the need for new engineering, not only on submarines but on aircraft carriers. He called for examination of engine room design, to silence all equipment. The goal would be to prevent noise from revealing a ship's position and to eliminate interference in a ship's own listening devices. Naval engineers, he argued, had to become familiar with the basics revealed by the scientists at the symposia, and he sought to explain the unclassified fundamentals through a widely distributed open publication.[17]

Taggart himself published a study of noise reduction goals for minesweepers engaged in clearing the seas of acoustic mines. Such ships would either have to be run intentionally on a noisy basis to set off mines or would have to be so silent as to work through minefields, towing a sound-emitting device. Taggart worked through the mathematics of both approaches, exploring possible measures and countermeasures.[18]

The official recognition of the major role of acoustics at the Bureau of Ships level and in the naval research establishment more generally, led to a variety of studies, cooperative projects between laboratories, and increases in equipment resources over the decade from the mid-1950s through the mid-1960s. The model basin offered to share its facility at

Lake Pend Oreille, which it had acquired in 1946, with other laboratories, particularly the Naval Research Laboratory. In turn, basin staff hoped to be able to share with NRL the use of a reservoir thirty miles north of Washington, D.C., in sound work.[19]

By 1958 Marvin Lasky, who had contributed to submarine silencing work and represented the basin at SUBDEVGRU-2 meetings, had moved on to work at NRL, but he continued to cooperate with his former colleagues at the basin. Together, Lasky and E. Alvey Wright, commanding officer of the basin, worked out a proposal for the two laboratories to study jointly the fundamental characteristics of hydrophone towing cables.[20]

In addition to such cooperative efforts, the basin worked with outside contractors, including Arthur D. Little and Westinghouse to study various acoustic effects. One such operation entailed not only those two firms but also cooperation with the Naval Electronics Laboratory, the Engineering Experiment Station, and several navy yards to study the mechanical principles of sound. In the same period, the model basin also independently studied resilient mountings of nonrigid machinery to nonrigid foundations.[21]

The postwar emphasis on submarine stealth, the complex nature of a ship's contribution to acoustical signatures and efficient silencing, and the increased numbers of deployed Navy ships contributed to the increased importance of ship acoustical work in the early 1960s. In recognition of the growing significance of such work, DTMB Technical Director Alfred Keil formed the Acoustics and Vibration Laboratory in 1963. He first temporarily formed the Office of Underwater Acoustics in 1962 from personnel in the Hydromechanics Laboratory, with this office reporting directly to him. When he created the AVL, he added personnel from the vibration division of the Structural Mechanics Laboratory to the Office of Underwater Acoustics. Until Captain Pat Leehey was appointed head of the AVL in late 1963, Wesley Curtis and Henry Gilbert intermittently acted as head of the new laboratory. Leehey was the principal advocate of submarine silencing at the Naval Sea Systems Command (NAVSEA), and he had served on the President's Scientific Advisory Committee. Alan Powell took over as head of AVL in early 1965. Leehey's interests in ship silencing and Powell's earlier work in aerodynamics, boundary-layer pressures, general turbulence effects, vortex sounds, and jet and rocket engine noises provided a broad base of technical understanding and support in investigating the many sources of ship-related machinery-and flow-induced noise.

Over the 1960s, AVL was involved in several important Navy ship acoustical programs, to reduce noise from ships to reduce interference with on board passive sonar, to reduce emitted noise that might give away the ship's position, and to reduce the ship's reflection of enemy active sonars. Significantly reduced radiated noise allowed a submarine under power to blend closely into the natural acoustic background of the sea and remain undetected at certain distances. Reduced self-noise surrounding passive sonars would allow a submarine to listen at significantly greater distances for potential adversaries. The establishment of an organized acoustical trial program with dedicated branches of technical personnel supporting both ship-radiated noise and sonar self-noise measurements at either Carr Inlet Acoustic Range in the Pacific or *Monob* in the Atlantic provided intensive, rapid identification and fixes of existing noise deficiencies. AVL branches worked with Hydromechanics and Structures and with the Machinery and Structureborne-Noise Branch at Annapolis in a coordinated manner to understand and provide silencing solutions for increasingly complex

***Monob* Acoustic Research Barge.**   With heightened awareness of the importance of ship and submarine silencing, testing aboard *Monob* allowed rapid identification and fixes of noise deficiencies.

shipboard noise sources and associated noise propagation paths through the ship structure.

As the specialties of the two laboratories developed, cooperation and lines of delineation between the work of various naval facilities in the acoustics field became easier. By the end of the 1960s the model basin had established a reputation for work on the electronics of full-scale ship trials that evaluated both emitted noise and sonar effectiveness, in the testing of transducers and transducer towing equipment, and for handling questions of research into exactly how various shapes emitted sound as they passed through water. EES had developed specialized competence in the silencing of machinery and in developing and testing flexible mountings for machinery.

Although much of the work in underwater sound remained classified, specialists followed professional careers in this new interdisciplinary field much as they would in more open or widely supported scientific and engineering areas. Similar to some other scientific and technical disciplines essential to defense, such as nuclear science and cryptographic theory, the Navy's own "secret science," underwater acoustics, involved an apparent conflict between the need for security and the free exchange of ideas and conclusions among specialists essential for progress.

As in all scientific and technical fields, individual reputations could only be built on the production of published reports and studies that established the author's recognition among his peers. The affiliation of a productive and innovative investigator with a particular institution enhanced the standing of that institution. In this field, as in the other new secret sciences of the postwar era, much of the advanced work remained too sensitive for wide distribution, and a solution to this conflict between the need for recognition by professionals and the need to closely guard release of information in the interest of security came through the issuance of classified reports with limited circulation and the publication of a small group of classified journals and periodicals whose subscribers held clearances and a need to know the material.

Of course, a "publication" that was not publicly distributed could seem to an outsider a contradiction in terms. Nevertheless, such classified publishing spread knowledge of the work of specialists and enhanced the reputation of their institutions among a cadre of colleagues and research administrators at other naval facilities. Through such means, the secret science could be both professional and secure. When the Carderock and Annapolis laboratories merged in 1967, each had earned a well-deserved reputation within the naval research establish-

ment for competence and excellence in specific areas within the new secret science of acoustics.

Ship Protection

The nuclear weapons exploded at the end of World War II
promised to revolutionize naval warfare. But the exact doctrinal implications of atomic bombs were not clear. As naval planners debated exactly
how to plan for the future, several scientific and technical questions fell
to the model basin and the experiment station. As in acoustics, personnel strengths and equipment built up during the war and postwar years
determined the role of the facilities and set a pattern for new long-term
research areas.

Ship designers and builders, together with the research specialists
who provided them with basic data, recognized that public attention and
therefore congressional and governmental attention were captivated by
the A-bombs and jets. At the 1946 meeting of SNAME, Wright urged the
naval architectural profession not to despair at the nonnaval character
of the new "atomic and supersonic furor." [22]

Responding to that emphasis, the Navy planned an extensive but
hurriedly organized series of experiments to evaluate the effect of both
air and subsurface nuclear blasts on ships. Operation Crossroads, held at
Bikini Atoll in the Pacific in April 1946, provided the Navy with a chance
to prove that surface ships and submarines could survive a nuclear war.
That purpose, critics charged, reflected the long-standing and newly intensified interservice rivalry of the postwar period. Researchers sought a
more scientific and less political orientation, to evaluate carefully
weapons effects in order to develop appropriate countermeasures. [23]

Carderock was already in a good position to study the correlation
between the effects of small charges of high explosive with nuclear blasts
measured in kilotons of TNT. An explosives test pond built during the
war to evaluate the effects of depth charges and other underwater explosions through the use of small charges had served as a precursor to the
nuclear work. A series of high-explosive charges, set off with small models, helped establish the correlations by comparing the results of small
model tests with the final Crossroads results. Experiments at a separate,
specially constructed temporary test pond could be publicized, utilizing
the Bikini events as a "news hook." Basin press releases touted the
"Miniature Atomic Bomb Tests." [24]

Even within the naval bureaucracy, nuclear fever ran. In later
brochures, memorandums, and public documents, this relatively inciden-

Test in Explosives Test Pond. This July 1962 test reflected increased concern with underwater shock loading on ships from both nuclear and conventional weapons.

tal program received repeated coverage. The very "atomic furor" to which Wright referred made the experiment one of great public interest.[25]

When, in the late 1950s, the design of the next generation of naval ships allowed for the introduction of protection against the effects of nuclear weapons, the data from Crossroads were carefully reviewed to provide a scientific basis for design choices, rather than simply to prove that

the Navy would still float after nuclear airblast. One problem with nuclear testing, from the point of view of many of the scientists engaged in
it, was that the weapons required such expensive and massive test organizations that it was difficult to arrange new "experiments." For that reason, the documentation from Crossroads had to be treated as a set of
historical documents from which new conclusions could be derived.

But for basin staff and other researchers, the massive archival and
documentary products of a complex nuclear test operation represented
a paperwork nightmare. As scientists who were trained and who preferred to verify data for themselves by running their own experiments, a
review of the work of others in the past in order to massage out new data
seemed an awkward and, at times, nearly impossible task. As early as
1949 Captain Francis X. Forest, serving in the Hydromechanics
Laboratory, sought photographs of the target ship *Prinz Eugen* showing
her state immediately prior to departure for Bikini. Hoping to track the
photos and a letter report he had written at the time to files at San
Pedro, California, Forest plaintively remarked, less than thirty-six
months after Bikini, that the pictures "apparently have been lost
through the years."[26]

Forest was diligent and lucky, however. He was able to supply the
hydrodynamicists at the basin with a copy of his own inspection memorandum from 1946 and a set of photographs and blueprints which he finally traced to the files of the Long Beach Naval Shipyard.[27] As years
passed, however, the primary documents and data records became difficult, if not impossible, to locate.

Because the raw data from the 1946 test were dispersed among the
files of various participating laboratories, researchers confronted an apparently overwhelming set of archival and jurisdictional hurdles if they
sought to reexamine the evidence. The dispersal of raw data sheets soon
forced scientists to rely on the slightly more available collections of limited-circulation classified reports as sources. Such derivative material
would be less than ideal, from the perspective of both historians and
physicists, but it was sometimes the best or only information available. In
1957, eleven years after Bikini, some scientists conducted research by
using some of the classic methods of the historian.[28]

A group of structural engineers at the Massachusetts Institute of
Technology proposed to use Crossroads information to develop a preliminary design of a blast-resistant stack for a destroyer. This particular
proposal meshed with the model basin's commitment "to coordinate the
whole Bureau of Ships research program leading to improved ship designs better fitted to withstand nuclear explosions."[29]

In April 1957 the model basin started to stake out one particular aspect of the nuclear effects question. While other laboratories would concentrate on issues of the radiological effects, ballistic protection, and underwater explosions, the model basin managed contracts and conducted in-house research on the issue of strengthening ship structures to withstand airblast effects of a nuclear explosion. The basin hosted an airblast conference, which served to inform the naval research community of its interest in the area. Through 1957 basin management secured both budget and formal Bureau of Ships assignment of responsibility for the airblast structures work.[30]

The airblast research generated improved design features that gradually would be worked into new ships. In 1957 DTMB provided recommendations for a destroyer deckhouse design, based on the preliminary findings of the airblast studies, in a criticism of working plans held by the designers, Gibbs & Cox. Pointing out the apparent defects in the preliminary designs, basin staff suggested an informal proposal to develop a more resistant design. After a few weeks' internal review, Gibbs and Cox responded with a specific research proposal that addressed the issues at a very modest cost.[31]

Nuclear weapons detonated under water, however, transmitted destructive force by shock. Earlier work on elastic mountings to reduce the effect of shell impacts both on equipment and personnel and to provide for reduced acoustic transmission of vibration from equipment to hull seemed to be a useful approach to the problem of protection against some of the problems of explosive shock loading. In 1962 George Chertock of the model basin presented a paper at a symposium in which he analyzed motions induced in structures by the sudden shock front of an underwater explosion.[32]

The shift of interest on the part of the U.S. Navy after the war, toward assessing and improving the survivability of ships in the vicinity of nuclear bursts brought out the relative vulnerability of shipboard equipments (compared to the structural hull) much more starkly. In the case of underwater nuclear bursts, in particular, the loading affected the entire ship, not just a portion. Nuclear bursts tended to make lots of equipment fail, not just the relatively small number caused by high explosive bursts. The Umbrella and Wahoo shots of Operation Hardtack in 1957 demonstrated the point with the three destroyers involved. The combat capability of U.S. warships of World War II vintage could be destroyed by weapons that missed their ship targets at ranges considerably in excess of those which would have resulted in ship sinkings. Some of this work was carried on at the Underwater Explosions Research Detachment Norfolk, before that unit came under the model basin and Keil moved

"Sailor Hat" Test. After the 1963 atmospheric nuclear test ban, the center participated in several large-scale high explosive tests, like this 1965 shot to evaluate blast effects on destroyers.

to Carderock. Work at UERD led by Keil had clearly pointed to the great influence of the pulsating gas bubble and the associated whipping of the ship. Chertock, at DTMB, developed for his doctoral dissertation an idealized theoretical treatment of this situation, limited to ship structural stresses in the elastic range and to high explosive (HE) explosions. Bill Sette, at Carderock, developed a computational scheme for estimating shock-wave produced pressures at the surface of a fixed rigid cylinder. William Murray, at UERD, developed for his doctoral dissertation a theory for finding the body velocity of a rigid but moveable cylinder impacted by a spherical shock wave of both the HE and the nuclear type. In 1960, Keil issued a paper, "Shock Vulnerability of Present U.S. Navy Ships," which was widely distributed within the Bureau of Ships and made available to the Bureau of Naval Weapons and the fleet. This document helped in winning acceptance by the fleet of shock-testing operational ships and contributed to the success of the entire shock protection program. Criteria for protecting equipment were developed, and a variety of protection methods were tested and adopted after comparison tests on ships.[32]

Building on the earlier work on vibrations and explosions, the basin established by the mid-1960s a clear reputation for work in the strengthening of ships against both conventional and nuclear weapons. In building a new generation of ships in the 1960s, the Navy adopted a program of "shock hardening," that is, the protection of ships, auxiliary equipment, electronics, and weapons themselves against the impact of a shock wave from a nuclear or conventional explosion. The basin was in a position to take the lead. The shock-hardening of ordnance fell under the jurisdiction of the Bureau of Naval Weapons (BUWEPS), but by special arrangement, they and the Bureau of Ships agreed that the work, even when under their technical direction and control, would be conducted at the basin. Technical information, as distinct from administrative communication, flowed directly from the basin to BUWEPS under the arrangement.[33]

Specifically, the Bureau of Ships assigned to the model basin, in January 1965, the responsibility to serve as technical director of a Bureau of Weapons research program to ensure that new weapons "will be capable of surviving an airblast or a near-miss underwater explosion."

Shock Trial of CVN 71. In 1963, the Bureau of Ships assigned to the David Taylor Model Basin the task of evaluating the capability of ships to survive the underwater shock wave of a near-miss nuclear explosion.

But basin management complained that the time-consuming work for BUWEPS could set back work on other high-priority projects by structures researchers, including bottom protection, tests on full-scale targets, and even work for the Defense Atomic Support Agency (DASA) on the combined effects of nuclear weapons.[34]

DTMB personnel and personnel at UERD who later transferred to DTMB participated in most of the Pacific tests of nuclear weapons, and in several of the tests at the Nevada Test Site. As already mentioned, researchers at DTMB used a temporary small test pond and small HE charges with models to develop a damage scale that was used at Crossroads in 1946. A few DTMB staff members attended the test to help measure phenomena. Under the lead of the Office of Naval Research, personnel working at UERD, helped design three 4/5-scale submarine targets, called Squaws. Beginning in 1952, systems for predicting underwater blast effects were developed under Keil's leadership. This information was applied in the deep-water atomic blast test code-named Wigwam, in 1955 under the task force commander Rear Admiral Charles B. (Swede) Momsen, the inventor of the Momsen Lung. A DTMB team headed by Harry Rich instrumented the Squaws and analyzed the data, despite the loss of the two which had been submerged. A small nuclear device (Small Boy) in the Dominic series at the Nevada test site was used to test a scaled model deckhouse, a modeled smokestack, and several modeled antennae. DTMB personnel provided instrumentation for these targets and analyzed the results. William Murray was appointed scientific director for the Swordfish test, 11 May 1962, of a destroyer-delivered, underwater atomic weapon, one of the last tests before the test-ban treaty with the Soviet Union precluded further such explosions. One crucial question was the safe range at which the destroyer could deliver the weapon. Murray wrote the scientific director's report on this test, and was awarded the Navy's Distinguished Civilian Service Award in 1963 for the work. In all these tests, DTMB and UERD personnel cooperated with personnel from the Naval Research Laboratory, the Naval Ordnance Laboratory, and the Navy Radiological Defense Laboratory, as well as Bureau of Ships personnel.[35] Earlier work at EES in the development of resilient, sound-absorbing mountings provided a base for that laboratory to assist in the weapons-hardening project. In 1965, now organized as the Marine Engineering Lab, the Annapolis facility cooperated with Carderock to study the shock-isolating and shock-mitigating properties of resilient mountings. MEL also worked on the development of new shock testing machines and the publication of the *Structural Dynamic Analysis Handbook* to train technicians working on shock studies. Other MEL projects included response studies of decks and upper structures to underwater shocks, the analysis and calibration of an underwater explosion test platform, and plans to participate in full-scale shock test trials of *Atlanta* (former CL 104).[36]

MEL staff reported to the commander of DTMB on the weapons hardening work, but its particular aspect of work fell within the old EES tradition of specification setting. MEL gathered all the information on specifications and performance ratings on both BUSHIPS and BUWEPS equipment and worked to develop a single sheet to "display principal mount parameters." Despite the modern tone, the work was a continuation of the strong tradition of gathering, coordinating, and publishing technical specifications.[37]

Implementing shock-hardening findings on *John F. Kennedy* (CVA 67), under construction at the time, presented headaches to BUWEPS. It had responsibility for the catapult to launch aircraft, the arresting gear, and visual aids equipment, and strove to incorporate shock-hardening concepts immediately. To make the new equipment meet the "high-shock requirements" and still meet building deadlines required a tight schedule of redesign and close cooperation between the bureaus.[38]

In 1965, however, much of the work connected with the study of the effect of airblast and shock on equipment had become routine testing, and Captain Dennett K. (Deke) Ela, serving as commanding officer and technical director in that year, sought relief. In order to concentrate on scientific work which fell within the basin's traditional areas, the routine work would have to taper off. Ela pointed out that no matter what the bureau decided as a policy matter, the basin would simply have to refuse requests for routine testing of equipment on floating shock platforms.[39]

By the end of the decade, DTMB still played a role in experimental rather than routine work in the area of shock. The Dial Pack test, which involved the explosion of 500 tons of high explosives conducted in Canada, entailed a study for the Navy by Carderock personnel of the effects of airblast on topside equipment and ship superstructures. Since above-ground nuclear testing had been terminated under international agreement by 1963, such a test of high explosives with a blast yield in the range of a small nuclear weapon in the open air was anything but routine. Just as at the nuclear test series, in this situation, Carderock cooperated with many groups of experimenters from a variety of facilities. At the basin, researchers continued to investigate in a theoretical fashion the fundamental questions of physics involved in transmission of shock through structures, studying both abstract conical and cylindrical shapes and small models of the *Kennedy* in several series through 1969.[40]

Jets and Super Carriers

As they pioneered new research avenues in acoustics and strengthening ships against airblast and shock, the model basin and the station also took on the scientific challenges associated with jet aircraft. Carderock's aeronautic work and wind-tunnel capabilities, which had developed during the 1930s and 1940s, and the station's strong background in fuels and lubricants meshed following the war.

The technologies of the jet engine and the jet airframe evolved over the postwar decade. For the Navy, progress in both fields went forward at corporate, rather than government, facilities. General Electric, Pratt and Whitney, and Westinghouse took the lead in engines, while McDonnell, Chance-Vought, Douglas, and other firms competed for Navy contracts for new classes of fighters and bombers suitable for aircraft carrier launching and landing. For the Carderock people, their participation was limited to the airframe itself and its ability to deliver weapons.[41]

The higher speeds and specialized designs of the new aircraft required testing of overall aerodynamic properties, improved materials to resist heat generated at high speed, and redesigned control surfaces (flaps and rudders). Various new methods of attaching and releasing "stores," such as bombs, rockets, and disposable fuel tanks, were investigated. The projects led the wind tunnel staff at Carderock into research work and away from the more routine testing characteristic of the war years.

McDonnell built the Phantom, the first jet airplane of that company to enter production and the first Navy operational jet in 1946. A later version of the Phantom remained the standard U.S. Navy fighter, as the F-4, well into the 1970s. New aircraft by McDonnell and by Northrup, North American, Chance-Vought, and Douglas rapidly followed as the Bureau of Aeronautics tested both aircraft designs and air-war doctrine in a rapid evolution through the 1950s and 1960s. Night-fighters, fighter-bombers, and high-performance experimental craft kept the testing and evaluation schedule at the wind tunnels crowded with work through the two postwar decades. Innovations in radar and missiles and constantly improving speed, endurance, range, and handling characteristics led to several "design contests" between firms, continuing the Navy's procurement tradition of sponsoring competing private research paths on the same weapons development.[42]

By 1963 six main areas of aircraft technology research defined the Aerodynamics Department at Carderock. Four of the areas directly reflected the impact of the turbojet revolution. In the field of "Carrier

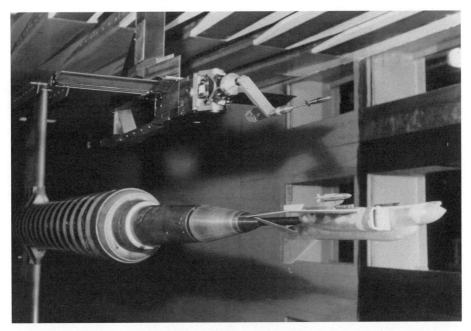

Aircraft Stores Separation.   In the mid-1960s, transonic wind tunnel studies focused on the separation of "stores," such as weapons or external gas tanks, from high speed jet aircraft, with this F-4 model mounted bottom up.

Approach-Path Flow Fields," researchers investigated the characteristics of the air wake of the carrier itself and its interference with jet landing and take-off. "Captive Flight/Launch Aerodynamics of Aircraft Stores" included a range of problems associated with the buffeting and flight path of weapons launched from moving aircraft at jet speeds. "Dynamic Stability" studies involved more theoretical work to perfect the state of the art so that designers could better predict performance. For example, generalized theoretical models allowed researchers to study the effects of wing sweep and wing-tail interference at speeds up to Mach 4 on proposed variable-sweep designs. "Super/Hypersonic Aerodynamics" involved the more conventional testing of models of proposed jet craft. In addition, other research areas included work on innovations such as vertical short take-off and landing (V/STOL) craft and those depending on "interface aerodynamics," such as the hovercraft that utilized ground effect.[43]

Specific research projects included a close study of the trade-offs in hypersonic aircraft. Aerodynamic heating, researchers discovered, required redesign of leading edges of the aircraft. Teams worked on the drag of various cones and spiked noses, modifications of the wind tunnel equipment itself, and a range of studies on proposed experimental craft.

Bell Aerospace

***Osprey* V-22 V/STOL**.   After decades of experimenting with vertical short take-off and landing concepts, the V-22 was introduced to the fleet. The center focused on reducing aircraft drag and tail buffeting.

Carrying weapons under jet wings at high speeds imposed drag, leading to a series of studies through the mid-1960s focused on that particular problem.[44]

At EES, materials problems and specialized questions regarding the composition, transportation, storage, and handling of jet fuel gave new dimension to the work of the existing fuels and lubrication group at the station. Jet fuel, a type of kerosene, resembled diesel and bunker fuel in composition, opening possibilities for cross-fueling of ships and aircraft. In 1955 EES tested the high-flash-point "Aircraft Turbine and Jet Engine Fuel," designated JP-5, as an emergency fuel for diesel engines. Routine tests at EES of the flash point and explosivity of JP-5, and of JP-5 blended with standard kerosene and diesel fuels, provided the Bureau of Ships with data that soon allowed mixing of ship bunker fuel and aircraft fuel. This practice significantly increased the effective range of the new jet plane-carrier weapon system by extending the period a carrier could support its aircraft before resupply.[45]

In standard Navy practice aboard carriers, as JP-5 was used it would be replaced with seawater in order to ballast the tanks and provide proper trim for the ship. The interior of the tank would readily corrode under alternate exposure to the fuel and saltwater, eventually contaminating the fuel with bits of the tank lining material. Through the mid-1950s EES researchers studied a variety of filters, additives, coatings, and alternative metals for such tanks, leading to reduced problems with corrosion.[46]

While contractors provided the Navy with jet aircraft, the Navy took a far more active role in the research, design, construction, and modification program for the new flattops to carry the jets. Consequently, both Carderock and Annapolis participated in the creation of the Navy's super carrier fleet.

The new aircraft produced a new carrier design. Jets had higher fuel consumption, higher stall speed, and shorter flight time per mission than piston aircraft. With more limited sortie time, a carrier simply had to be larger to accommodate more planes. Furthermore, jet aircraft characteristics began to control flight deck lengths and overall size of the carrier. Higher launching speeds demanded more powerful catapults, while higher landing speeds required greater deck length and stronger arresting gear. Jet aircraft weighed more than propeller aircraft; the elevators to lift the planes from the hangars to the flight deck had to be increased in capacity. To conserve deck space, the elevators would be mounted on the ships' sides. In a word, the price for jet speed was larger carrier size.[47]

The carrier innovations of the 1950s—the angled deck, the steam catapult, and the "super carrier" size—reflected the new requirements of jet planes. The angled deck allowed for greater flexibility in landing, refueling, and simultaneously handling more flights for an overall higher rate than possible on a straight deck. A more powerful catapult helped launch jets, least efficient at slow take-off speeds.

Since jets consumed greater quantities of both fuel and ordnance, handling and storage of both became more dangerous. The masses of fuel alone had increased by an order of magnitude over the fuel loads of World War II carriers. *Essex* (CV 9) carried 209,000 gallons of aircraft gasoline in 1940. Twenty years later, *Forrestal* carried 750,000 gallons. Once JP-5 fuel could be interchanged with ship bunker fuel, capacities rose to over 2,000,000 gallons. Ordnance, too, reached unprecedented levels. *John F. Kennedy*, commissioned in 1968, carried some 2,000 tons of aircraft bombs and missiles, compared to only 458 tons on board the whole carrier task force that raided Tokyo in February 1945.[48]

The attack carriers (CVAs) of the 1950s and 1960s, exceeding 55,000 tons displacement, all qualified as super carriers. Each year

Notional Aircraft Carrier Model. Later aircraft carriers would extend ideas developed in this 1951 concept design: angled decks and vast size.

through these decades, one or more was under construction. Design, testing, adjustment, and adaptation employed thousands of men through the two decades at shipyards and laboratories, as well as at the factories of industrial contractors.

The super carriers presented a number of unique challenges to other laboratories and to private industry, and for some of the issues basin staff could serve as consultants. Shock studies conducted by Harry Rich on submarines drew the interest of engineers at Westinghouse Bettis Atomic Power Division, as they adapted nuclear engines for carrier propulsion. As Westinghouse geared up to construct twelve power plants for *Enterprise*, Rich worked closely with the firm's Plant Apparatus Department.[49] Again, the basic computational work on nuclear reactor design continued to assist in building the power plants. As the Bureau of Aeronautics designed missiles for safe stowage aboard the new carriers, they sought DTMB estimates of aircraft carrier shock spectra.[50]

The more massive research demanded by the new ships spilled over to the laboratory's traditional work. Model basin staff, operating under BUSHIPS orders, installed instruments on board *Ranger* to study her structural and hydrodynamic seaworthiness during a cruise around Cape Horn in 1958. The scientists measured a wide variety of effects during the rough voyage, including studies of the intensity and characteristics of hull stress and motions caused by slamming and whipping. Other instruments recorded dynamic water pressures acting on the bow and on the port flight deck sponson and measured the hull stress and motions during all sorts of sea states, speeds, and courses in order to predict stress over the life of the ship. Well within the traditional sea-trial role of the basin, the work on new types of installations included the magnitude and character of vibration affecting radar installations, and the stresses around the side openings in the shell necessary for the huge elevators used to raise aircraft to the flight deck. In addition to the electronic data gathering, researchers set up an extensive system of photo recording of plate cracking and other damage. Simultaneous photo recording of the sea state allowed vivid comparison of damage with weather conditions. Even the super carrier faced the old challenges of ships in heavy seas.[51]

With the massive quantities of fuel and ordnance required on board super carriers, the questions of fire-hazard and fire-fighting capacity became even more crucial. An accidental fire on board *Enterprise* in 1969, which killed twenty-seven men, intensified the concern. Annapolis staff under the leadership of A. Waldron cooperated with the Aberdeen Proving Grounds, the Naval Applied Science Laboratory at Brooklyn, and staff at China Lake, California, to test high-powered fire-fighting pump rigs. Waldron attached heat-measuring instruments to bombs and missiles and exposed them at various distances from 2 feet to 9 feet from open JP-5 fuel fires to record temperatures and cooling rates.[52]

Behind the innovative work, both Carderock and Annapolis routinely performed much of the basic design and testing work for super carriers. In 1957, for example, on completion of *Saratoga* (CVA 60), basin staff conducted trials on the ship off Guantanamo Bay, Cuba. Acoustic work included study of machinery and propeller noise. A test of the characteristic noise of the ship, its acoustic signature, was recorded. Airborne noise surveys checked the ventilation and air conditioning system. Hull and vibration trials, tests of fuel economy, radio interference, ventilation efficiency, and ship handling under tactical maneuvers extended over a five-week spring cruise. Such routine trials, typical of all new ships, did not produce spectacular research findings or startling design departures. Nevertheless, such constant participation in the traditional manner going back to the 1930s was an essential part of the construction of each modern carrier. From such trials, the ship's defects could be corrected and her actual performance could be determined for the men who would trust their lives to her.[53]

Eyes on the Future

As product testing shifted from EES to suppliers through the 1950s, and as Department of Defense specifications (MILSPECS) replaced the Navy's, the engineering laboratory shifted its orientation closer to the mix of research and development at Carderock. Through the 1950s and 1960s, work at one laboratory supplemented work at the other. Closer coordination and planning from the managing Bureau of Ships and its successor system command concentrated the research efforts on related questions. Specialists at Carderock working with colleagues at Annapolis sensed that Annapolis was steadily moving away from its traditional testing and evaluation function. A merger became more and more logical.

Under centralized Navy command, the laboratories worked on different aspects of research questions springing from the same weapons issue. Strengthening ships to deal with airblast, studying sound and its generation on board ship, and exploring phenomena produced by high-speed jets and carriers dictated the establishment of specialized and complementary teams at both laboratories. Both facilities adopted a mix of both research and development work, coming closer together in orientation. Staff at each had contributed to the innovations arising from acoustic work, nuclear weapons and nuclear propulsion, and from the impact of the jet aircraft on the nature of the fleet.

Throughout the postwar period, researchers not only juggled demands for redesign of submarines, jet aircraft, and super carriers but also took on new experiments with new technologies through the 1950s and 1960s. Gas turbine engines, new propeller designs, and computer-assisted design all opened new fields. Researchers at the two facilities laid groundwork in each of these areas that would grow more significant in later decades.

Gas turbine development at EES during the war generated workable engines by 1949. The first turbines had a high fuel-weight to horsepower ratio, and a decade of research and design competition among Boeing, General Electric, Lycoming, Pratt and Whitney, and Solar (an engine company in Phoenix, Arizona) led to a variety of experimental applications. By 1963 twenty-six minesweepers had been equipped with Boeing-built, 220-horsepower turbines, and a 1,000-horsepower model produced by Solar powered fourteen landing craft. The high speeds of the turbines held out further possibilities for the future. By the late sixties the naval community began to investigate advanced ship concepts

Thirty-Six-Inch Variable-Pressure Water Tunnel. Researchers study a host of new propeller designs in this large water tunnel.

that would use the new, powerful gas turbines to drive hydrofoils and hovercraft.[54]

The innovative propulsion system created problems similar to those confronted by naval engineers at the beginning of the century when steam turbines began to replace reciprocating steam engines. The high torque of the plant was most efficient if the shaft revolution was directly applied rather than geared down or transmitted through a generator-electric motor system. Yet high propeller speeds produced cavitation on conventional propellers. Thus, with an eye on future applications, researchers at Carderock and Annapolis began to investigate the possibility of "supercavitating" propellers that would be designed to operate efficiently with a massive water cavity directly behind the blades.[55]

In new water tunnels and channels at the basin, researchers looked at a host of propeller design ideas that had once seemed the speculation of wild-eyed inventors. Cycloidal propellers, suspended below a vessel like eggbeaters, and tandem propellers, or two propellers mounted on the same shaft, held out possibilities for special applications. So did controllable pitch propellers that allowed a vessel to reverse motion by altering the blade angle rather than utilizing a power-wasting reverse transmission system. Theoretical work such as that by Phillip Eisenberg on the fundamental mechanics of cavitation in 1953 helped provide groundwork for studies of new propeller designs with applications in possible future ships.[56]

At the engineering station, the possibility of hybrid engine systems which would combine the high-speed virtue of the gas turbines with diesels, steam turbines, and electrical power systems attracted those who viewed one generation's science fiction as the next's technology. Magnetohydrodynamic propulsion appeared on the horizon as a possible system of the future. The use of thermoelectric materials and their application to solid state power and cooling equipment, with possible applications in refrigeration and airconditioning held promise. Fuel cells and advanced designs of nuclear power plants also competed. Technology seemed to be on the verge of a dozen breakthroughs.

Endnotes

1. Edward W. Constant, II, *The Origins of the Turbojet Revolution* (Baltimore and London: Johns Hopkins University, 1980), 230–232.
2. "Undersea Defenders: Story of Acoustic Homing Torpedoes," *General Electric Review* (Mar 1958), 30–35; copy with Karl Schoenherr, interview by David K. Allison, 15 Apr 1985, NHC, NLCCG Archives, RC 8, box 12, file 14.
3. H. S. Howard to Saunders, Ormondroyd, and Parkinson, 1 Jan 1945, WNRC, acc. 4818, S19/NP1.
4. *Centerline*, vol. 3, no. 10, 30th Anniv. Ed., 4 Nov 1969, 7 & 12; M. Strasberg and W. J. Sette, *Measurements of Propeller Noise on Three Submarines of the SS 212 Class*, DTMB Report R-205 (Apr 1944); M. Strasberg, *The Development of Cavitation Noise by Model Propellers*, DTMB Report 543 (Sep 1946).
5. Commander. J. O. Baker to V. L. Chrisler, 17 Oct 1945, WNRC, acc. 4818, box 3, A6-5-(2).
6. C. O. Kell, Memorandum, 9 Sep 1949, DTMB Records Management Office, Admin. Memos, 1949.
7. C. O. Kell, Memorandum, 12 Jun 1950, DTMB Records Management Office, Admin. Memos, 1945.
8. M. Strasberg, Memorandum, 27 Jan 1949, WNRC, acc. 11414, box 160-3, All/Noise; Joseph E. Joers and Leo F. Fehlner, *Development of a Hydrophone Towing System for Investigation of Ship Noise*, Dec 1948, DTMB Report No. C-154.
9. C. O. Kell to Chief of Bureau of Ships, Noise, Shock & Vibration, 16 Dec 1949, WNRC, acc. 11414, box 160-3, All/Noise.
10. J. O. Baker, Memorandum, 19 Aug 1949, WNRC, acc. 11414, box 160-3, All/Noise.
11. C. O. Kell to Chief of Bureau of Ships, Research, 19 Dec 1949, WNRC, acc. 11414, box 160-3, All/Noise.
12. L. Landweber to Commander, Submarine Development Group Two, U.S. Navy Submarine Base, New London, CT, 16 Mar 1950, WNRC, RG 181, acc. 12608, box 14, SS/S1-2-(5), vol. 1.
13. Mark Harrison, *Report on Some New Developments in Noise Isolation Problems*, Apr 1953, DTMB Report No. 791.
14. Robert Taggart, "Noise in Reduction Gears," *JASNE* 66 (Nov 1954): 829–847.
15. Rear Admiral Frederick R. Furth, "The Navy's Stake in Underwater Acoustics" (condensed from address to the Tenth Navy Symposium on Underwater Acoustics), Office of Naval Research, Mar 1955, *Research Reviews* (Department of the Navy, 1955), 1–5.
16. Ibid., 5.
17. Taggart, "Acoustics and Naval Engineering," *JASNE* 67 (Aug 1955): 611–629.
18. Taggart, *Derivation of Target Goals for Minesweeper Noise Reduction* 15 Dec 1953, Dept. of the Navy Bureau of Ships, Research and Development Report No. 371-N-20, WNRC, RG 181, acc. 73A-2733, box 16, 050174.
19. E. A. Wright to Director, Naval Research Laboratory, 23 Jul 1956, WNRC, RG 181, acc. 63A-2152, box 7, Propellers file.
20. E. A. Wright to Chief of Naval Research, 26 Aug 1958, WNRC, RG 181, acc. 65A-4256, box 5, 525 Towing 1958.

21. L. L. Smith to Commanding Officer and Director, DTMB, 5 Mar 1958, WNRC, RG 181, acc. 65A-4256, box 5, S11/12 Foundation Gen.

22. "Navy Is Planning Ship Conversions," *New York Times,* 16 Nov 1946.

23. Richard G. Hewlett, *A History of the United States Atomic Energy Commission,* 2 vols. (University Park: The Pennsylvania State University Press, 1962, 1969), vol. 1, *The New World, 1939–1946,* by Hewlett and Oscar E. Anderson Jr., 580–582; Lloyd J. Graybar, "1946 Atomic Diplomacy or Bureaucratic Infighting," *Journal of American History* 74 (1986).

24. Navy Department, "Miniature 'Atomic' Bomb Tests Being Conducted at David W. Taylor Model Basin," Press Releases, 4 Apr 1946, WNRC, RG 181, acc. 7681, box 1, A7-1, and 11 Apr 1946, WNRC, RG 181, acc. 7681, box 160-4, QB/Navy Industrial Association 1946.

25. E. Rassman, Memorandum, 21 Jul 1947, WNRC, RG 19, acc. 4059, box 248, NP21/A2.

26. Captain F. X. Forest to Captain E. C. Forsyth, 25 Feb 1949, WNRC, acc. 11414, box 4, 1x300/S1-2 Tests of Large & Small Models Ex *Prinz Eugen.*

27. F. X. Forest, Memorandum, 15 Mar 1949, WNRC, acc. 11414, box 4, 1X300/S1-2 Tests of Large & Small Models Ex *Prinz Eugen.*

28. R. S. Burpo to R. W. Saner, 23 Oct, 1957, WNRC, RG 181, acc. 65A- 4256, box 5, 5-11/13 Structural Air Blast; Armour Research Foundation, "Project Suggestion for Analysis of Naval Vessel Structural Components Subjected to Air Blast," 1957, 1–3, WNRC, RG 181, acc. 65A-4256, box 5, 5-11/13, Structural Air Blast.

29. R. J. Hansen to Commanding Officer, DTMB, 3 Apr 1958, WNRC, RG 181, acc. 65A-4256, box 5, 511/13 1958; A. M. Morgan to Chief, BuShips, 1 Apr 1957, WNRC, RG 181, acc. 65A-4256, box 5, 5-11/13 Structural Air Blast.

30. A. M. Morgan to Chief, BuShips, 1 Apr 1957, WNRC; and R. B. Madden to Chief, BuShips, 19 Nov 1957, WNRC, RG 181, acc. 65A- 4256, box 5, 5-11/13 Structural Air Blast.

31. C. A. Greaser to Commanding Officer and Director, DTMB, 28 May 1958, WNRC, RG 181, acc. 65A-4256, box 5, 5-11/13, 1958.

32. George Chertock, *Effects of Underwater Explosions on Elastic Structures* (reprinted from *Fourth Symposium on Naval Hydrodynamics,* ACR-92, Aug 1962), Nov 1964, DTMB Report No. 1924; William W. Murray, 16 Apr 1996, ABIF,

33. Emerson E. Fakes to Chief, BuShips, 15 Feb 1965, WNRC, RG 181, acc. 69A-5171, box 4-A52, 9111 Shock.

34. A. H. Keil to Chief, BuShips, 22 Mar 1965, WNRC, RG 181, acc. 69A- 5171, box 4-A52, 9111 Shock.

35. W. W. Murray, 16 Apr 1996, ABIF.

36. W. Tessin to Commanding Officer and Director, DTMB, 21 Apr 1965, WNRC, RG 181, acc. 69A-5171, box 4-A52, 9111 Shock.

37. E. M. Herrmann to Commanding Officer and Director, DTMB, 6 Jul 1965, WNRC, RG 181, acc. 69A-5171, box 4-A52, 9111 Shock.

38. J. T. Parady to Chief, BuShips, 30 Sep 1965, WNRC, RG 181, acc. 69A- 5171, box 4-A52, 9111 Shock.

39. Captain D. K. Ela to Chief, BuShips, 19 May 1965; and Rear Admiral N. Sonenshein to Commanding Officer and Director, DTMB, 23 Jul 1965, WNRC, RG 181, acc. 69A-5171, box 4-A52, 9111 Shock.

40. W. W. Murray to Commander, Naval Ship Engineering Center, 9 Dec 1969; Ralph A. Niemann to Commander, NSRDC, 19 Aug 1969; and H. S. Overman to Commander, NSRDC, 3 Dec 1969, WNRC, RG 181, acc. 73A-2241, box 2, 3900/AB.

41. Constant, *Origins of the Turbojet Revolution*, 240.

42. Norman Friedman, *Carrier Air Power* (Greenwich, CT: Conway Maritime Press, 1981), 59–74.

43. "Aerodynamics Laboratory Research," revised rough draft, Sep 1963, DTNSRDC RC, entry 7-1, box 4.

44. Ibid.; *Drag Effects of Various Methods of Carrying Fuselage Mounted Stores* Sep 1968, NSRDC Report No. C-2939; John F. Talbot, *Incremental Drag From Fuselage Mounted Stores* Oct 1966, DTMB Report No. C-2317, Aero Report 1120; John F. Talbot and Jonah Ottensoser, *Geometric Effects on Fuselage Mounted Store Drag*, Sep 1967, NSRDC Report No. C-2622, Aero Report 1141.

45. C. A. Peterson to Chief, Bureau of Ships, 14 Jan 1955, WNRC, RG 181, acc. 61A-2513, box 3, 070283.

46. J. W. MacDonald, Memorandum, 12 Jan 1956, WNRC, RG 181, acc. 61A-2513, box 3, 070340; R. T. Jones, *Effects of Cathodic Tank Protection on JP-5 Fuel*, 29 Feb 1956, EES Research and Development Report 070340B NS-072-504, RG 181, acc. 61A-2513, box 3, 070340; W. W. Brown to Chief, Bureau of Ships, 20 Aug 1956, WNRC, RG 181, acc. 61A-2513, box 3, 070375.

47. Friedman, *Carrier Air Power*, 60; and *U.S. Aircraft Carriers: An Illustrated Design History* (Annapolis: Naval Institute Press, 1983), 271.

48. Friedman, *Carrier Air Power*, 60; and *U.S. Aircraft Carriers*, 275.

49. E. W. Lareau to Commanding Officer and Director, DTMB, 4 Feb 1958, WNRC, RG 181, acc. 65A-4256, box 5, 5-60 Shock 1958.

50. D. K. Weitzenfeld to Commanding Officer and Director, DTMB, 27 Mar 1958, WNRC, RG 181, acc. 65A-4256, box 5, 5-60 Shock 1958.

51. "Procedure Proposed by TMB for Structural and Hydrodynamic Seaworthiness Tests on USS *Ranger*," 3 Jun 1958; and L. L. Smith to Commanding Officer and Director, DTMB, 13 Mar 1958, WNRC, RG 181, acc. 65A-4256, box 5, 5-29-12 Structural Strength.

52. A. Bodnaruk to Commanding General, Aberdeen Proving Grounds, 16 Jul 1969, WNRC, RG 181, acc. 73A-2241, box 2, 3900/Vietnam.

53. P. E. Shetenhelm, Memorandum, 25 Sep 1956, WNRC, RG 181, acc. 63A-2152, box 5, 58 Ship Trials Gen. Vol. 2.

54. G. M. Boatwright, M. Welling, and M. R. Hauschildt, "Naval Propulsion Machinery Post World War II," *Naval Engineers Journal* 75 (Dec 1963): 877–890.

55. A. J. Tachmindji, W. B. Morgan, M. L. Miller, and R. Hecker, *The Design and Performance of Supercavitating Propellers*, Feb 1957, DTMB Report No. C-807.

56. Robert J. Boswell, *A Method of Calculating the Spindle Torque of a Controllable-Pitch Propeller at Design Conditions*, Aug 1961, DTMB Report No. 1529; *Experimental Performance of a Controllable-Pitch Supercavitating Propeller*, Aug 1967, NSRDC Report No. 1636; Mary C. Dickerson, *Propulsion Characteristics Obtained With Vertical Axis Propellers for LCU(A) Represented by Model 4952*, Feb 1964, DTMB Report No. 1753-2; C. T. Davis and Richard Hecker, *Open-Water Performance of Tandem Propellers*, Jun 1973, DTNSRDC Report No. SPD-530-01; Stephen B. Denny, *A Procedure for the Design of Tandem Propellers*, Jun 1974, DTNSRDC Report No. 530-H-4; Phillip Eisenberg, *A Brief Survey of Progress on the Mechanics of Cavitation*, Jun 1953, DTMB Report No. 842.

CHAPTER 10

A Center of Excellence

THE AIR HELD A HINT OF SPRING AGAINST the lowering overcast as civilian scientists, engineers, and military officers sat in rows of folding metal chairs arrayed in front of the steps of the main office-laboratory building at Carderock on 31 March 1967. Gerald Johnson, Director of Navy Laboratories, rose to address the crowd. The day, he said, marked the "first big step toward reconstituting our Navy laboratories as a smaller number of Centers of Excellence oriented toward the major warfare categories." The event capped the merger of MEL at Annapolis with DTMB to form the first of those "Centers of Excellence," to be known as the Naval Ship Research and Development Center. The merger resulted from an intense period of organizational study, plan and counterplan, compromise and resolution that racked the Navy during the period 1961–1967. To place the merger in context, one has to look beyond the laboratories and recognize that the Navy reforms did not come in isolation.[1]

In retrospect, the merger date is a benchmark in the evolution of the laboratories, for the new organization clearly would serve to facilitate and coordinate the parallel work between the two labs that had shared BUSHIPS control since 1940. As the work at the two laboratories frequently converged in the 1960s, the projects coming on the drawing boards would require even closer coordination and planning.

The reorganization had its roots in a broad set of changes in the management of both private and governmental enterprises in the United States in the period. Deep-seated societal forces were at work to cause academic and business leaders to question existing models of the ideal organizational structure. Rising living standards, better education, organized labor, new theories of behavior, and increasingly complex technology prompted new questions about the working of bureaucracy.

From about 1910 through the 1940s, during the "classic period" of organizational theory, the rules had been simple. The theories of German sociologist Max Weber and French engineer Henri Fayol, modified by the management ideas of the American engineer Frederick Winslow Taylor, had produced a generally accepted model of the ideal bureaucratic enterprise, whether corporate, governmental, or military. In that model the familiar organizational chart was the centerpiece. Power and responsibility flowed from supervisors down to subordinates. Individuals would have a clear chain of command and would report to one superior officer, who in turn would report to yet another superior. In the ideal structure no supervisor would have more than five or six direct subordinates, representing the perfect span of control. Line and staff divisions were clear. Regulations and rules governed activities; violations led to specific punishments. The dismissal of the individual was the "ultimate" punishment in private and civil service employment, and the threat of court-martial and dishonor kept the military bureaucracy in line. The parallels and similarities among military organizations, civil service structures, and corporate enterprises were no accident, for the system of command in all three types of organizations had common roots in eighteenth- and nineteenth-century efforts to modernize and rationalize large-scale enterprise.[2]

Yet several factors during the late 1930s and through the 1940s cast doubt on the classic model of organizational structure and the assumptions about human behavior on which it was based. In the United States, collective bargaining, strengthened by legislation in the 1930s, challenged the authority of corporate decisions not only regarding hours, wages, and working conditions, but touched on the details of hiring and firing, production, work flow, and machinery speed. The behavioral sciences—psychology and sociology—suggested to management students that advancement in earning power and fear of dismissal were not sufficient tools to ensure that orders were followed. By the 1940s, rising living standards and social reforms reduced the fear of unemployment, removing at least some of the coercive power of the paycheck. Bureaucracy that ran on authority, orders, rules, and tangible rewards and punishments had grown outmoded. Other motives, such as status, regard of fellow workers, and work satisfaction might suggest that other types of structures would be appropriate.[3]

As work became more technical, complex, and professionalized, managers blurred the distinctions between line and staff. Experts low in the organizational chart would often know more about their specialized area than their superiors. The logic that decisions would be reached at higher levels and that orders would be carried out at the lower levels became less and less appropriate, especially in the more technical areas. In organizations devoted to research and development, like the model basin and the experiment station, such problems would be readily apparent, but similar issues affected industrial firms engaged in the manufacture of new and complex products. The very diversity of new products had led to the emergence of product and project managers who would do planning, advocate policy, and make executive decisions previously characteristic only of top management.[4]

By the early 1950s a ferment of ideas among management specialists indicated that a new type of model was needed. As occurred in the scientific revolutions in physics and chemistry, the "science" of management underwent a crisis in which the old theory faced multiple challenges and a search for a new, unifying general theory of organization engaged the activities of different specialists. The new model that emerged drew from several sources.

One set of ideas came from the new, specialized area of "operations research" (more grammatically called "operational research" in Great Britain). Mathematicians, scientists, and engineers assisted the military during World War II on such questions as submarine hunting, bombing patterns, and logistics. Mathematical models provided some notably successful predictions for such complex military operations as optimum size and patterns for trans-Atlantic convoys. In the postwar period the U.S. Air Force helped establish a permanent R&D contracting firm to provide operations research studies with civilian specialists who could be paid at rates competitive with private industry. RAND corporation, a contraction of R&D, flourished on Air Force contracts through the late 1940s. Its numerous reports embodied and further developed the operations research approach. In the Navy, operations research flourished during and after the war. Operations researchers began teaching their mathematical modeling methods in business schools, beginning with Case Western Reserve in 1951, and in another half-dozen universities by the late 1950s.[5]

Other management theorists held out for a humanization of bureaucracy. Some of the ideas had circulated for over a decade. Chester Barnard, the retired president of the New Jersey Bell Telephone Company, published *The Functions of the Executive* (1938). Through several editions of the book, which became a standard text, Barnard argued that authority in organizations was dependent on acceptance and cooperation rather than simple power. In the mid-1950s Peter Drucker developed the idea of "management by objective" in which goals would become explicit and work would be structured by more democratically set goals rather than simply imposed as orders down through a structure. Douglas McGregor, in *The Human Side of Enterprise* (1960), argued that persuasion could substitute for authority. He suggested that goals would be more effective when originating from below in an organization, and that management teams involving specialists from a variety of areas could better deal with the highly technical new products and processes of industry. In addition to Barnard, Drucker, and McGregor, dozens of other management specialists published articles, book-length essays, and college texts, all speculating upon the necessity of rethinking the classic organizational model of Weber, Fayol, and Taylor.[6]

By 1958 and 1959 several authors struggled toward a new "general theory" of management that would bring together the suggested reforms and creative ideas of the prior two decades. Developments in environmental biology offered a vocabulary, and management writers seized on the concept of "systems." While the word "system" had been in broad use in organizations, especially to speak of networks such as electric power grids and telephone interconnections, or school district organizations with multiple units organized under a single superintendent, the word as used in organizational theory was explicitly borrowed from biology. Some attributed their inspiration to the work of Ludwig van Bertalanffry who in 1951 had suggested that a "General Systems Theory" could provide a unifying concept for science. While the hard sciences did not respond by building on his suggestion, the concepts provided a principle and a way out of what another author had called the "management theory jungle."[7]

The word "system" took on a new definition, and the "systems approach" combined several ideas from operations research, game theory, management self-criticism and speculation, and product and project management, as well as from environmental biology. Simply put, the systems approach viewed the interaction of people and machines in the pursuit of a goal as a system, similar in its structure and its dynamics to the interaction of a natural organism and its environment. As in environmental systems, the alteration of one element would have measurable repercussions as the rest of the system adjusted.[8]

Such ideas and management concepts, current in the late 1950s and the early 1960s, did not simply represent the speculation of a few business school professors. Managers at major corporations explored their implications and put some of the new concepts to work. The ferment of innovation, however, burst upon the Department of Defense rather suddenly with the installation of the administration of President John F. Kennedy in January 1961.

The McNamara "Revolution"

When Robert S. McNamara came from Ford Motor Company to head the Department of Defense as Kennedy's appointee in 1961, he brought an energetic and personal style. It won him both admiration from a cadre of supporters and outright disdain and hostility from those who believed his reforms represented a perpetuation of the worst existing aspects of bureaucratic management. Enthusiasts claimed McNamara voiced the new theories of management and worked towards the goals of humanization, clarification, and adaption to a more technical world. Critics, including many of the scientists at the naval laboratories, regarded the new organization as an unnecessary growth in layers of bureaucracy. The ultimate verdict of history, as is so often the case, may lie between the extreme views.

Between 1961 and 1967 McNamara introduced a new set of management ideas, including new methods for planning, budgeting, and cost-benefit analysis. He sought improved control over contracts and more explicit evaluation of existing organizations in achieving their missions. The questions raised in McNamara's studies frequently uncovered serious existing problems, and the reforms he initiated were intended to address such problems.

However, his effort to centralize power in the DOD under civilian leadership and to give more decision and policymaking power to civilian specialists naturally struck many military officers as a threat to established order. In some cases the decisions and studies he initiated regarding weapons systems generated heated public debates in which the military found themselves retreating uncomfortably from contested territory—the territory of a media battle.

Several of the conflicts over weapons systems and the attempt to apply cost-benefit analyses to warfare have been studied in detail. For example, McNamara's decision to build the super carrier *John F. Kennedy* with conventional propulsion, rather than with nuclear propulsion, went forward despite naval pressure and congressional insistence on a nuclear plant. Through 1964–1965, the struggle between the Navy and the DOD over this decision spilled over to the public press and became a running controversy. In the Navy's view, McNamara's requests for studies, cost-effectiveness estimates, and operations analyses that would compare nuclear propulsion with steam propulsion consistently ignored some larger "systems" considerations. In effect, when one defined a ship and its mission equipment as a "weapons system," one conclusion would be reached. But when the weapons system was considered part of a larger system, an opposite conclusion would be reached. The Defense Department argued that to refuel a conventional propulsion carrier at sea would give it range similar to a nuclear carrier at less initial cost. The Navy responded that refueling in certain heavy seas was impossible and delays in the logistics of bringing supply tankers to rendezvous points, as part of a larger military operation or system, would favor nuclear propulsion. Systems and operations thinking, designed to provide mathematical concepts for policy decisions free of politics, could clearly be utilized in the traditional political way. When "one man's system could be another's subsystem," the appearance of cost-effectiveness-based objectivity vanished in a conflict of opinion, interest, power, and personality.[9]

The structural reorganization of research and development at the services' in-house laboratories begun by McNamara is a less popularly familiar story than the conflicts over ships and aircraft. Yet the outcome of the effort to make the laboratories more effective and to address some of the sources of discontent among civilian researchers may have had more permanent consequences than the front-page debates over particular weapons systems.

In the laboratories controlled by the military services, deep-seated and continuing problems of morale hampered creativity. During World War II, academically trained scientists had enlisted in the war effort in vast numbers. Growth similar to that at the model basin and the experiment station was reflected at every naval laboratory. Almost overnight, thousands of men and women with graduate training had entered a new world. In the university environments from which they came, the leading professors had often defined their own problems and sought grants to support their work. But in the military and in many industrial environments, scientists followed orders. The relative freedom of academia for such people had been suddenly replaced by the structures and controls of the classic bureaucracy, with its rules, procedures, paperwork, chain of command, and increasingly dated sanctions on nonconforming behavior. The change was immense; for many, it was uncomfortable.

At DTMB and EES, the experience of working for the Navy brought national issues down to a personal level. Robert Goddard, for example, had based his earlier career entirely on independent, grant-supported research. His was perhaps the most extreme case of a sudden transfer from independence to programmed task. Yet even less independent researchers, whether advanced in their careers or fresh out of college, often found day-to-day controls and the rigidity of bureaucratic decisions confining. When management theorists suggested that traditional bureaucracy stultified the creativity of professionals, or recommended that management decisions be made by technical specialists rather than distant superior officers, the new breed of civilian scientists heard echoes of their own complaints.

For the researcher, the question of exactly who made decisions regarding experimentation was no mere problem of managerial theory; it was an immediate and real matter to be resolved on a daily basis. Accomplished scientists expressed their resentment of "paper pushers," especially of those who had not risen to power from a respectable technical background. Such feelings produced a groundswell of pressure for change.

McNamara tried to impose reforms to address such discontents. The new theories of management, current in business schools and circulating among industrial managers, could apply. The "systems approach," with its advocacy of objectives and goals set on a more democratic basis, and with project management supplanting management from above, all held promise of dealing with the issue of civilian scientist morale within the military laboratories.

Management Innovation—Early Attempts Within the Navy

Even before McNamara's appointment, naval officers had made several management innovations and had slightly reformed the organization structure in attempts to maintain creative research. Through the 1950s, while management theorists searched for new concepts, piecemeal reforms in the Navy dealt with aspects of parallel problems. As new specialists at low ranks came on board, senior administrators confronted the issue of how to deal with more expertise among those with less seniority, the problem that Drucker and McGregor had found to be increasingly common in industry. The Navy generated its own independent project approaches to management, at the same time that product and project management became more widespread in private enterprise.

While Rear Admiral Hyman Rickover's program to construct the *Nautilus* and the Special Project Office for Polaris cut across traditional bureau lines, conventional research remained difficult to coordinate and consolidate. Rickover's own personal style of management, viewed by many as a revolutionary approach, reflected some of the ideas current in management theories. Yet his team, set up with few internal divisions and a great number of highly skilled individuals reporting directly to him in violation of the traditional span of control concept, depended on a personal leadership quality not easily replicated by others. Rickover prided himself on hiring brilliant young specialists, leaving them unsupervised except for his own irascible control, and plunging ahead. Rear

Admiral William Raborn's Polaris Special Project Office produced a tightly scheduled method of bringing together multiple teams working on various aspects of the work in a Program Evaluation and Review Technique (PERT). Some analysts believed that PERT could provide a model for other special innovative work and became advocates of its wider use.[10]

Other reforms addressed the cumbersome nature of the Navy's bureaucracy. The Navy bureau system itself, dating back to 1842, had been partially reformed in 1940 with the merger of Construction and Repair and Engineering into the Bureau of Ships. In 1948 the Office of Naval Material was created to coordinate innovation, development, and procurement throughout the Navy. While Special Projects Offices like those for *Nautilus* and Polaris cut across traditional bureau lines, conventional research remained difficult to coordinate and consolidate. The introduction of missiles to be launched from airplanes, for example, created overlap and wasted effort as both the Bureau of Aeronautics and the Bureau of Ordnance sought to control research and development in that area. After several years of awkward cooperation, the two bureaus were merged in 1959 into a new Bureau of Naval Weapons.[11]

Despite such patchwork reforms, problems persisted. The concept that the "material" bureaus, engaged in production, would develop products consumed by the "operations" side of the Navy seemed increasingly dated as technology and doctrinal alternatives grew more complex. Planning for military need and feedback from the fleet required constant communication across the bureaucratic lines between producers and consumers, as in the development of SUBDEVGRU-2 at New London, Connecticut. Furthermore, the discontents expressed by civilians, who found pay grades limiting and freedom of research too controlled, continued to simmer.

The McNamara Revolution—First Phase

When McNamara took office, he hoped to deal with and solve the crisis of morale among civilian scientists at the services' in-house laboratories. Professionals, he found, were quitting to take jobs in industry because of low pay, and others left out of concern with mediocrity or military control. Director of Defense Research and Engineering Harold Brown echoed his chief's views in an address at the Naval Research Laboratory late in 1961: "We must retain our talented people and we must get new blood from industry and universities," he said. "Action must be taken, and quickly."[12]

Reforming the system, Brown and McNamara believed, could reaffirm excellence and improve morale at the laboratories. As examination and study of the issues went forward, Brown's early hope for a quick solution soon proved ephemeral. Studies, reports, proposals, plans, and counterplans proliferated in a bewildering flood.

Early in the Kennedy administration the Office of the Secretary of Defense and the Office of the President launched detailed studies of naval management focusing on the organization and funding of innovative research. Shortly after taking office, McNamara and his staff developed 120 broad questions, each one of which would require a book-length report to answer. For the naval laboratories, question ninety-seven was crucial: "What must be done in order to enhance the capability of our in-house research and development laboratories?" McNamara assembled a special group to address the question, Task Force 97, to be headed by Deputy Director of Defense Research and Engineering Eugene Fubini, who later became a member of the board of Texas Instruments.[13]

Task Force 97 conducted field visits and interviews with laboratory personnel and then reported in the fall of 1961 with five basic recommendations for the services. After field visits and interviews with laboratory personnel, Fubini urged that each laboratory have a well-defined mission, adequate supplies of competent manpower, improved personnel policies to raise morale, simpler procedures for programming and budgeting, and better facilities. McNamara asked the services to provide extended tours of duty to military officers assigned to laboratories, to increase discretionary funds for the laboratories, and to raise salaries for technical personnel.[14]

President John F. Kennedy ordered a separate study headed by David Bell, director of the Bureau of the Budget, that focused on the issue of government contracting for research and development. The Bell report, similar to Fubini's Task Force 97 report, urged strengthening in-house research capacities and particularly pointed to the lack of clarity in the relationship between military officers and civilian technical staff in the service-controlled laboratories.[15]

While awaiting the outcome of the Bell investigation, Secretary of the Navy Fred Korth personally ordered, in March 1962, a third, comprehensive study of Navy management. Korth hoped to forestall any outside-imposed critiques from the other two studies. John Dillon, administrative assistant to Korth, headed the study that developed eighty-five major recommendations for changes. Dillon proposed to eliminate the Office of Naval Material and replace it with a new office that would have direct line authority over Yards and Docks, Supplies and Accounts,

Weapons, and Ships. In 1963 Korth assigned to the Chief of Naval Material new command authority over the material bureaus and, shortly thereafter, over the newly established systems commands which replaced the bureaus. This change paved the way for ending the old bureau structure by placing the chiefs under a single authority.[16]

The three reports, from the Defense Department, the Bureau of the Budget, and the Office of the Secretary of the Navy, all had some underlying similarities in urging improved management and pay scales and better career paths for civilian scientists. The three reports, in one way or another, addressed the problem identified in question ninety-seven and in Brown's NRL speech: civilian scientists' morale in the Navy laboratories.

As a step in dealing with the morale question, in November 1963 Korth issued an order mentioning the Bell, Fubini, and Dillon reports as authority. SECNAV Instruction 3900.13A spelled out the requirement that every naval laboratory would have a civilian technical director in addition to the continuing military commanding officer. The appointments of Harold Nutt at EES and Alfred Keil at DTMB as civilian technical directors met this requirement.[17]

Despite Korth's concerns with outside interference, the Navy laboratories had been strengthened. The exercise in self-study had led, in the first two years of the McNamara administration, to some steps toward recognition of professional status which had been urged by the management revisionists. Caught between pressure from McNamara's office and the groundswell of complaint from below, the Navy had adjusted.

The McNamara Revolution—Second Phase

A new phase of the "McNamara revolution" began in the summer of 1964, a phase that many in the Navy interpreted as an attempt to destroy service autonomy in the area of research. The resulting events led to supplanting the material bureaus with "systems commands" and the emergence of the "Centers of Excellence" model for laboratories that produced the consolidation of Annapolis and Carderock in 1967.

Deputy Director of Defense Research and Engineering Chalmers Sherwin, another McNamara appointee, came to his DOD office with prior experience as the general manager of Aerospace Corporation in Los Angeles and as a professor of physics. In 1954–1955 he had served as chief scientist of the Air Force. Sherwin, working with staff, conducted an extensive study of the state of in-house laboratories and began to develop recommendations in late 1964.[18]

As Sherwin formulated his thinking, it became apparent to his associates that he might recommend that all of the services' laboratories be centralized under DOD's Director of Defense Research and Engineering, Sherwin's own office. When Captain Barney Towle and Sam Rothman, both of whom worked in the office of the Chief of Navy Material, discussed with Sherwin his preliminary inclination to take the labs from under military control, they reported the news back to the Navy. Towle later recalled that his report on the Sherwin ideas caused a stir. "Suddenly," he said, "we were talking to 3- and 4-star officers from all the services. We moved up the line real fast. . . . "[19]

In November 1964 McNamara forwarded the Sherwin plan to the service chiefs for their comments. Entitled "A Plan for the Operation and Management of the Principal DOD In-house Laboratories," the proposal initiated a two-year battle, as bitter in its tone as the fight over nuclear propulsion for CVA 67, going on at the same time. The military services treated the Sherwin plan as the opening salvo in an attack on their established territory. The fear was not unfounded.[20]

While Sherwin did not ultimately suggest that the laboratories be taken away from the services, he strongly argued that the solution to civilian scientists' morale problems would come with strengthened civilian control and reduced military contact. His three basic premises were that laboratories were sensitive to the quality of their management, that only professional scientists and engineers, subject to peer review, were appropriate managers of laboratories, and that "organizational barriers" had to separate researchers from end users. Whether, in the case of the Navy, such a barrier was to be between "producers" and "consumers" or, more openly, between civilian scientific researchers and naval officers was not explicit. By either logic, however, it would be an easy step to argue that the laboratories should be entirely severed from military administration and placed directly under civilian control in the Department of Defense. At the specific level, Sherwin suggested that each service create its own director of laboratories as a civilian post, and that he should supervise large interdisciplinary laboratories ranging in size between 500 and 1,500 employees.[21]

Robert Morse, Assistant Secretary of the Navy for Research and Development, headed the effort to develop a Navy response to the Sherwin plan. Between 1964 and 1966 Morse circulated the Sherwin plan in the Navy. Most of the laboratory directors were displeased. They had just begun to implement the reforms suggested in the Task 97 report, the Dillon report, and the Bell report. Now they faced yet another threat of reorganization. Captain C. O. Holmquist of the Naval Missile Center at Point Mugu, California, responded like many of his colleagues that the Navy should have a chance to make the existing system work. "It is easy," he noted, "to imagine that all of the problems of a complex system can be solved with the magic word 'reorganization.' Experience shows that this seldom happens."[22]

Drawing on laboratory directors' responses, Morse developed a plan based on Sherwin's plan but which would ensure continued Navy control of its laboratories under the existing bureau system. Morse directed his response to the Secretary of the Navy on 4 January 1965. The central provision of his plan was the appointment of a civilian Director of Navy Laboratories, with retention of the bureau control over program and budgets for the laboratories. Morse asked Admiral Ignatius Galantin, Chief of Naval Material, to draft a "charter" for the new Director of Navy Laboratories (DNL).[23]

Surprisingly, Galantin's proposed charter came closer to the "civilianization" proposed by Sherwin than the bureau control suggested by civilian Assistant Secretary Morse. Galantin urged direct control of the laboratories by the DNL. He found the bureaus archaic. Each adhered to a different, outmoded set of procedures that he had tried to modernize. The bureaus, he said, were "incapable of continuing to exercise a sufficient authoritative management over the in-house laboratories to ensure their continued balance, vitality and stability. . . ." Galantin believed a strong Director of Navy Laboratories could reduce the power of the outmoded bureaus.[24]

The resulting compromise between Morse and Galantin was worked out under the pressure of a veiled threat from Defense that if the Navy did not get its house in order, the laboratories might be transferred entirely out of naval jurisdiction as the best way to implement the Sherwin plan. The compromise put command and administrative control under the bureaus, and personnel ceilings, facilities, and workload balance under the Director of Navy Laboratories. SECNAV Instructions issued in December 1965 set up the Office of the DNL and established the responsibilities.[25]

Galantin, as Chief of Naval Material, supported in early 1966 a further reform that abolished the material bureaus and replaced them with six functional systems commands. Galantin was to supervise the new systems commands, and he would report to the Chief of Naval Operations. This move established a system of control over both production and consumption in one structure. McNamara approved the change 7 March 1966. The laboratories, although represented by and coordinated through a civilian in the post of Director of Navy Laboratories, would be more closely directed by the Navy.[26]

Under the continued pressure from DOD to consolidate the laboratories, Galantin rearranged the fifteen former bureau laboratories under his jurisdiction. In November 1965, Director of Defense Research and Engineering John Foster asked each service to prepare a comprehensive plan for restructuring in-house laboratories. Following the thinking of the Sherwin report, Foster ordered each service to list the five to ten critical research and development areas and to determine how those areas could be reorganized into "systems laboratories." The preliminary Navy response designated six laboratories as systems development centers with each to be aligned with parts of four major problem areas: antisubmarine, amphibious, fleet defense, and strike warfare.[27]

Foster turned over the services' responses for a systems organization and a consolidation plan to a task force headed by Leonard Sheingold, vice president of Sylvania Electronic Systems. In October 1966 the "Sheingold report" suggested that the in-house laboratories should take a stronger role in defining weapons requirements, in analyzing proposals for new systems, and in the planning of future systems. Sheingold recommended the formation of "weapons centers" much along the lines of the Navy response to the Foster request. Each weapons center would provide for continuous mission-discipline interaction.[28]

The Sheingold recommendations for weapons centers included specific requirements. Each center was to be oriented toward a specific military mission. Each was to have about 1,000 professional scientists and engineers in order to achieve "critical mass." Each weapons center, which might have several geographical locations, would be a self-contained organization performing research, development, and analysis of working models. The centers would be involved in original procurement and provide support to the procurement agency on large-scale production. The Sheingold report recommended action on the formation of the Navy's first center by early 1967.[29]

Table 10-1
Reorganization Chronology

Task Force 97 Report	Fall 1961
Bell Report	30 Apr 1962
Dillon Report	15 Dec 1962
SECNAV 3900.13A	1 Nov 1963
Sherwin Plan	16 Nov 1964
Morse Plan	4 Jan 1965
Morse–Galantin Compromise/SECNAV 5430.77	20 Dec 1965
Systems Commands Established	7 Mar 1966
Sheingold Report	31 Oct 1966
Pinney Report ("Der Grosse Plan")	24 Jan 1967
DTMB and MEL merged to form NSRDC	31 Mar 1967

The Laboratory Merger

Director of Navy Laboratories Gerald Johnson translated the Sheingold recommendations into a draft plan, which was put in final shape by Rear Admiral F. L. Pinney, Deputy Chief of Naval Material. At this point, the staff of the Naval Material Command had been so bombarded with plans, proposals, and counterproposals that they developed a somewhat irreverent attitude and dubbed Pinney's draft "Der Grosse Plan."[30]

Others, too, met the new plan with a tone of weary resignation at the constant round of reorganization. Captain Deke Ela, commanding DTMB, complained to Johnson that he was "deeply perturbed," even though his own laboratory was slated to grow in size and standing. All the concern with morale, he noted, seemed to have been carelessly flouted. "I cannot conceive of any tactic more traumatic to people and programs than reorganization. Can you?" He urged, simply enough, higher salaries for the civilians.[31]

Pinney proposed to merge Carderock and Annapolis to form a Naval Ship Research and Development Center (NSRDC). In addition, he recommended five other centers: two facilities for aircraft work, two for undersea warfare, and one to concentrate on electronics. Three months after the Chief of Naval Material forwarded Pinney's plan through channels, DTMB and MEL were merged to form the first of the six centers.

The Naval Ship Research and Development Center was funded mainly by the Ship Systems Command and was at least nominally managed by the Director of Navy Laboratories and the Chief of Naval Material. However, funding from one source and command from another showed the survival of the previous compromise between Galantin and Morse. The old Bureau of Ships, surviving in the form of the Ship Systems Command, still controlled the purse strings. The Chief of Naval Material and his Director of Navy Laboratories would have a say in programs and planning.

Another underlying change coming out of the period was the shift to what became called Naval Industrial Funding. While perceived by some as simply a changed system of accounting, others found that in order to obtain funding for NSRDC, researchers had to become marketers, providing proposals, briefings, and detailed progress reports to program managers at the systems commands. In effect, the system would put the laboratories and their work groups into competition with other labs, and even occasionally with the private sector. For researchers who perceived the administrative side of their work as an interference with their mission, the constant pressure to present, justify, defend, report, and conform to program managers' expectations could have a negative effect on morale.[32]

Despite such unresolved administrative issues, NSRDC emerged as the first of the Navy's new, large, multidiscipline, civilian-directed laboratories, and it did report to a civilian Director of Navy Laboratories. Whether such changes would address the morale problems, as intended by the planners, or would only exacerbate them, as feared by Ela and the other local commanding officers, remained to be seen. Following a distinguished career in acoustics research, Alan Powell, who served as head of the Acoustics and Vibrations Laboratory became the technical director of NSRDC, a position he held for the next eighteen years. His administration of the center, both in leadership style and in management direction, coincided with the larger goals established by the reforms. As he sought to enhance the level of excellence, he also oversaw expansion.

The Panama City Laboratory

The Annapolis and Carderock laboratories merged into the Naval Ship Research and Development Center effective 31 March 1967. Through the period of the birth of the center, the Chief of Naval

Alan Powell and Harold V. Nutt. On ocasion of the merger of the Marine Engineering Laboratory (MEL) at Annapolis with DTMB, Technical Director Powell welcomes MEL Technical Director Hi Nutt aboard to serve as Deputy Technical Director of the combined facility, NSRDC.

Material sought to consolidate smaller bureau laboratories into similar, large-scale operations following recommendations by Sheingold and Pinney. Among the smaller laboratories considered for consolidation or merger into a larger center was the Mine Defense Laboratory (MDL), located in Panama City, Florida.

Compared to other naval laboratories, MDL had a relatively short history. In 1943 the Bureau of Ordnance and the Bureau of Ships had established a Mine Warfare Test Station near the mouth of the Patuxent River where it joins the Chesapeake Bay at Solomons, Maryland. The laboratory's purpose was to study mine countermeasures, including methods and equipment for sweeping, locating, and destroying mines. The work, like many of the tasks performed at both DTMB and EES, straddled the lines dividing two bureaus—Ordnance and Ships. The design of minesweeping ships and the paravanes they towed clearly fell to Bureau of Ships. Mine design and explosives belonged to Ordnance. Explosion tests at Solomons limited commercial and pleasure uses of the area, and by 1945 the Navy moved the Mine Countermeasures Station to a base outside of Panama City.[33]

Over the next two decades, the Panama City laboratory expanded. In December 1966, as its future destiny was discussed, the laboratory had 631 civilian employees and a military complement of 165. Its mission covered not only mine defense but acoustic and torpedo countermeasures and inshore warfare. It also conducted research on equipment for swimmer delivery and diver operations as well as on detection and countermeasures to use against enemy "frogman" operations. Although the systems commands had replaced the bureaus in early 1966, the proper administrative slot for the mission of the Panama City laboratory continued to be a problem. Its work fell within the scope of research conducted by both Ship Systems and Weapons Systems. Both of the former bureaus, now operating as systems commands, reported to the same Naval Material Command, which had authority to straighten out the Mine Defense Laboratory's organizational location.[34]

Even so, the search for a solution regarding the future of MDL was difficult. One of the early proposals came from E. F. Schreiter, Commander Naval Ordnance Laboratory (NOL), White Oak, in Silver Spring, Maryland. Schreiter called for incorporating NOL, the Panama City facility, and the Naval Weapons Laboratory at Dahlgren, Virginia, into a new Naval Weapons Systems Center. As the staff of the Director of Navy Laboratories discussed this concept, immediate problems emerged. How would the combined unit be administered? If the Dahlgren and Panama City facilities had reduced status and authority, how could morale be maintained at those two locations? Merger bred discontent, yet autonomy bred disunity.[35]

On 21 March 1967, the Assistant Secretary of the Navy for Research and Development established a "working group," headed by retired Admiral William A. Schoech, to study the White Oak proposal and to produce a recommendation for the Panama City laboratory. The group included Captain J.D.W. Borop, who served as commanding officer and director of the Panama City laboratory, and Gregory Hartmann, the civilian technical director of the White Oak facility, as well as staff officers from both the Weapons and Ship Systems Commands. Schoech's group, with representatives of all the parties, was to hash out a solution that would satisfy, or at least mollify, everyone.[36]

The Schoech working group found the idea of attaching Panama City laboratory to the White Oak laboratory fraught with problems. Beyond the issue of local or central control was an even more serious problem. MDL needed to work closely with the people at Carderock in such areas as acoustic silencing, ship design, ship structure, hydro-dynamics of underwater towed devices, and underwater shock protection. Since a large part of the Panama City work focused on protection against explosives, the committee concluded that its work related more closely to Ship Systems than Weapons Systems. The "straddle" that had existed in the 1940s, the working group now believed, should be resolved in the direction of ships, not ordnance. Schoech's group recommended attachment of the Florida unit to the newly formed Carderock-Annapolis NSRDC.[37]

The Schoech group filed its report in June 1967, and the Navy moved rapidly to implement it. Galantin, Chief of Naval Material, who still held line authority over both systems commands, requested that the commanding officers and directors of NSRDC and MDL work out the details of the merger, which then would be implemented by an order from his own office. Captain Borop from Panama City and Captain Manuel da Costa (Buck) Vincent, commanding officer of NSRDC, agreed on a joint memorandum spelling out details of organization and funding by the end of September 1967. The merger went into a NAV-MAT Notice, effective 1 November.[38]

Although Borop and Vincent had reached an amicable agreement, Admiral Galantin did not accept one essential element of their plan. In their proposal each of the three divisions, Carderock, Annapolis, and Panama City, would have a commanding officer or officer in charge, each of whom would report to the commander of the whole center. However, Galantin established the Carderock commanding officer with line authority over both Annapolis and Panama City on laboratory matters. While the distinction might be obscure to those outside of naval circles, the arrangement ordered by Galantin clearly did not create one center with three co-equal divisions. Rather, the structure he ordered amounted to the annexation of MEL and MDL to Carderock.[39]

Despite efforts to reform the laboratory command structure later in 1967 and through 1968, Galantin would not accept what he regarded as further "layering" of authority levels as desired by the Panama City officers and staff. Over the period of proposed revision, the struggle was watched closely by Democratic Congressman Bob Sikes from the first district of Florida. Sikes had served in Congress for two terms before World War II, then entered the Army and returned to Congress for seven more terms. He brought a clear knowledge of military bureaucracy to bear in his efforts to prevent closure of his district's Navy laboratory and to preserve its autonomy.[40]

In writing to Galantin, Sikes suggested renaming the facility. Although a name might seem a frivolous topic, Sikes captured the larger issue. He recommended "Navy Inshore and Amphibious Warfare Center." Such a name, of course, would represent a warfare area, and a center designation would justify a separate existence.[41]

The task of answering the congressman's suggestions was passed up through the naval chain of command to John Warner, Under Secretary of the Navy. With a tone not intended to endear the Navy to Congress, Warner noted, "The views which you expressed have been carefully examined, and they will receive continuing attention when actions to which they relate are under consideration in the future. I do not believe, however, that any major changes in the Navy's research and development organization are warranted at this time."[42]

The question of autonomy and role raised by Sikes would not go away, however. As the Panama City staff continued under the distant administration of Carderock, difficulties and morale problems mounted. Meanwhile, some of the focus of the Panama City laboratory on issues of coastal warfare proved valuable during the heightened level of riverine and offshore battles in Vietnam. Even as the laboratory's immediate workload increased, its status remained dubious. Although the lab had well below the so-called critical mass of 1,000 staff members suggested in the Sheingold report, the Naval Material Command finally yielded to pressure. In effect, Sikes's alternative won in January 1972, when Panama City was severed from NSRDC control and established as the Naval Coastal Systems Laboratory, with a mission to apply a wide range of science and technology to the problems of shallow-water warfare. The short and troubled marriage had led to a quick divorce.

The Materials Laboratory

Another step in the consolidation during the same period of the formation of NSRDC was similarly disruptive, although it affected a smaller group. At the New York Navy Yard in Brooklyn, a small laboratory that could trace its origins back to the 1860s faced extinction in the reorganization. At the shipyard, systematic testing of fuels had grown into a chemical laboratory by 1898 to which electrical and mechanical testing were added early in the twentieth century. By 1963 the navy yard's laboratory achieved independent status as the Naval Applied Science Laboratory (NASL). In 1966 it was transferred to the Chief of Naval Material.[43]

In 1969 Galantin ordered NASL closed and its work and personnel transferred to other facilities. Few of the civilians at the lab took offers of other federal employment since most did not care to relocate. Many either retired or took jobs in the private sector. Ninety-four staff members, however, transferred to NSRDC, mostly to Annapolis, including specialists in high-strength steel, titanium, organic chemistry, plastics, and synthetic rubber. The staff at Annapolis worked to welcome the refugees. The displaced New Yorkers soon earned the respect of their new colleagues at both Annapolis and Carderock.[44]

The Center of Excellence

Secretary McNamara had brought to the Defense Department a range of ideas from private management, including extensive mission self-study, revised planning and budgeting approaches, and the vocabulary of systems thinking. On the surface it appeared that the "McNamara revolution" had provoked the most sweeping realignment of command structure in the Navy's history. Fubini, Bell, Dillon, Sherwin, Sheingold, Morse, Galantin, and Pinney all hoped to address the issue of civilian scientists' morale in order to assure creative innovation at the laboratories operated by the Navy. The changes they instituted created a larger laboratory out of existing parts, assembled from Annapolis, Carderock, Brooklyn, and temporarily, Florida. The reforms also provided additional civilians in the chain of command. The new center had a new mission: to address problems of complete ship systems. That mission was to be achieved by existing staff, reassembled into a new organization. Despite all the administrative reorganization and the emergence of a larger center, skeptics believed that such changes had little positive impact on morale or the bureaucratic complexities of the chain of command.

With a total staff well over the so-called critical mass, now numbering more than 3,000, the center consisted of two departments at Annapolis and five at Carderock, each based on earlier staff, equipment, and scientific specializations. Annapolis hosted the Propulsion and Auxiliary Systems Department, continuing the traditional strength in mechanical engineering and electrical work. The Materials Department, enriched by the influx of people from NASL in New York, continued the earlier work of the chemical, fuels, lubricants, and metals specialists.

At Carderock, the Ship Performance Department traced its organizational heritage and roots back through Karl Schoenherr to David Taylor himself. Aviation and Surface Effects Department continued the aerodynamic work originating with aviation pioneers like Holden Richardson and Albert Zahm who had built the first wind tunnels. The Structures Department went back to the 1930s when Dwight Windenberg, one of the facility's first Ph.D.s, had conducted studies of ship strength and construction. The Computation, Mathematics and Logistics Department had become a major presence in the development and application of mathematical and computer technology to a broad range of naval problems and systems, and the department operated major state-of-the-art mainframe computer facilities. The early work in Acoustics and Vibrations from the postwar era became the fifth Carderock department as Ship Acoustics in 1963.

But essential to the implementation of a new style would be the personnel. Plans and concepts would be meaningless without strong leadership and ability to implement them. The appointment of Powell as technical director of the center in 1967 fit perfectly with the long-term goals articulated by McNamara, Brown, Fubini, and the others through the early 1960s. Powell's leadership quietly shaped the direction of the center. Bringing a reputation for accomplished research on his own part, he was never viewed as simply an administrator, but rather as a distinguished colleague and intellectual leader. Over and over through the mid-1960s, reviewers of defense laboratories like Bell and Fubini had urged that leadership be drawn from the ranks of respected scientific and technically capable civilians. In order to compete with universities in the search for new personnel, to ensure that senior staff would respect not only the authority but the intellectual rank and achievement of those appointed to lead, and to maintain and enhance an international reputation for excellence, such a choice was essential. Powell always remained aware of the heritage that had been established at Carderock. He worked to assure that the facility retain its high ranking among the world's leading towing tanks and model basins, attending conferences and maintaining liaisons with peers in the Soviet Union, Britain, Japan,

Germany, and elsewhere. His scholarly manner as well as his personal standing as an accomplished researcher more than met the objectives established by Secretary McNamara and Director of Defense Research and Engineering Harold Brown, as they sought to enhance the skill level, reputations, and creativity of the in-house laboratories.

Continuity of staff could be a strength, and heritage was a source of pride that Powell stressed over and over. However, if the naval reforms were to achieve their officially stated purposes, and if the new ship center was to become a true center of excellence, the civilian staff would be expected to depart from traditions and launch into creative, innovative work on a greater scale than ever before. Further, internal changes would be required if NSRDC was to live up to its definition of mission and to take a stronger role in the creation of new ships. Powell would work hard to pursue that enhanced mission over the next two decades.

Endnotes

1. Address by Gerald W. Johnson, Director of Navy Laboratories, at the Establishment Ceremony of the Naval Ship Research and Development Center, 31 Mar 1967, DTNSRDC RC 3-1, Gerald Johnson file, transferred to NHC, NLCCG Archives.
2. Leonard White, *Introduction to the Study of Public Administration*, 4th ed. (New York: Macmillan, 1955; earlier editions, 1926, 1939, 1948); Fremont E. Kast and James E. Rosenzweig, *Organization and Management—A Systems Approach* (New York: McGraw-Hill, 1970), 65, 71; Lydall F. Urwick, "The Manager's Span of Control" (1956), in Harold Koontz and Cyril O'Donnell, *Management: A Book of Readings*, 2d ed. (New York: McGraw-Hill, 1968), 176–179; David I. Cleland and William R. King, *Systems, Organizations, Analysis, Management: A Book of Readings* (New York: McGraw-Hill, 1969), 1–8.
3. Douglas McGregor, *The Human Side of Enterprise* (New York: McGraw- Hill, 1960).
4. Ibid.; D. I. Cleland, "Project Management," and Robert M. Fulmer, "Product Management: Panacea or Pandora's Box," in Cleland and King, *Systems*, 281–290, 26–36.
5. C. West Churchman, *Introduction to Operations Research* (New York: Wiley, 1957), 632, and *The Systems Approach and Its Enemies* (New York: Basic Books, 1979), 16; Keith R. Tidman, *The Operations Evaluation Group: A History of Naval Operations Analysis* (Annapolis: Naval Institute Press, 1984).
6. Chester I. Barnard, *The Functions of the Executive* (Cambridge: Harvard, 1938; 30th ed., 1968); Peter F. Drucker, *The Practice of Management* (New York: Harper & Row, 1954), and "Integration of People and Planning," *Harvard Business Review 33*, no. 6 (1955); McGregor, *The Human Side of Enterprise*.
7. Ludwig van Bertalanffry, "General Systems Theory: A New Approach to Unity of Science," *Human Biology* (Dec 1951): 303–361; Harold Koontz, "The Management Theory Jungle," *Journal of the Academy of Management* (Dec 1961); R. N. McKean, *Efficiency in Government Through Systems Analysis* (New York: Wiley, 1958); Max Ways, "Tomorrow's Management: A More Adventurous Life in a Free Form Corporation," and Warren G. Bennis, "The Coming Death of Bureaucracy," in Cleland and King, *Systems*, 38–41, 11–17.
8. R. E. Gibson, "A Systems Approach to Research Management," in Cleland and King, *Systems*, 63–77.
9. James M. Roherty, *Decisions of Robert S. McNamara, A Study of the Role of the Secretary of Defense* (Coral Gables, FL: University of Miami Press, 1970), 65–101.
10. Joint Committee on Atomic Energy, *Progress Report on Naval Reactor Program and Shippingport Project*, 7 Mar 1957, 26–27; *Polaris Management* (Washington: Dept. of Navy, Special Projects Office, 1961); Booz, Allen & Hamilton, Inc., *Review of Navy R&D Management, 1946–1973, Summary*, 1 Jun 1976, 10, 12; Harvey Sapolsky, *The Polaris System Development: Bureaucratic and Programmatic Success in Government* (Cambridge, MA: Harvard University Press, 1972).
11. Booz, Allen & Hamilton, *Summary*, 10, 20.

12. Harold Brown, "Research and Engineering in the Defense Laboratories," address given at the Naval Research Laboratory, 19 Oct 1961, NHC, NLCCG Archives, DTNSRDC RC 3-1, series 3, acc. 84-55, box 61.

13. The following narrative draws upon D. K. Allison, "Command History, Office of Director of Navy Laboratories/Deputy Chief of Naval Material for Laboratories For Calendar Years 1965–1982," draft of 17 Oct 1983, NHC, NLCCG Archives, DNL History file.

14. W. B. Foster, "Introduction to Panel of 8th Institute on Research Administration at the American University in Apr 1963," NHC, NLCCG Archives, DTNSRDC RC 3-1, series 4, acc. 82-18, box 14, folder "Task 97: Enhancement of DOD In-House R & D."

15. U.S. Congress, Senate, *Report to the President on Government Contracting for Research and Development*, S. Doc. 94, 87th Cong., 2d sess., 1962, Bureau of the Budget (Washington: GPO, 1962), 21–22.

16. ASN (R&D) memo to Chief, Bureau of Naval Personnel, Bureau of Medicine and Surgery, Bureau of Naval Weapons, Bureau of Ships, Bureau of Supplies and Accounts, Bureau of Yards and Docks, and Chief of Naval Research, 5 Jun 1962. More effective utilization of in-house laboratories may be found in NHC, NLCCG Archives, DTNSRDC RC 3-1, series 4, acc. 82-18, box 14, folder "Dillon-RDT&E Studies, SECNAV 3900.13A, 1962–1963."

17. Fred Korth, SECNAV Instr. 3900.13A, Nov. 1, 1963, NHC, NLCCG Archives, DTNSRDC RC 3-1, series 5, acc. 82-18, box 23.

18. "Biographical Sketch," Dr. Chalmers W. Sherwin, NHC, NLCCG Archives, DTNSRDC RC 3-1, series 4, acc. 82-18, box 15.

19. Interview with Captain Barney Towle, interview by A. B. Christman, 14 Mar 1978, 4–5, NHC, NLCCG Archives, Oral History Collection, RC 6, Interview T1-78, as quoted in Allison, "Command History."

20. "A Plan for the Operation and Management of the Principal DOD In-House Laboratories," 16 Nov 1964, NHC, NLCCG Archives, DTNSRDC RC 3-1, series 4, acc. 82-18, box 15.

21. Ibid.

22. Captain C. O. Holmquist to Rear Admiral Emerson E. Fakes, 24 Dec 1964, NHC, NLCCG Archives, DTNSRDC RC 3-1, series 4, acc. 82-18, box 14.

23. Robert W. Morse, "On the Management of Navy Laboratories," 4 Jan 1965, NHC, NLCCG Archives, DTNSRDC RC 3-1, series 3, acc. 84-55, box 6.

24. I. J. Galantin, Memorandum for the Assistant Secretary of the Navy (R&D), 28 Jun 1965, NHC, NLCCG Archives, DTNSRDC RC 3-1, series 3, acc. 84-55, box 63.

25. R. W. Morse, SECNAV Instruction 5430.77, 20 Dec 1965, NHC, NLCCG Archives, DTNSRDC RC 3-1, series 3, acc. 84-55, box 61.

26. SECNAV to ALNAV, "Reorganization of the Department of the Navy," 8 Mar 1966, NHC, NLCCG Archives, DTNSRDC RC 3-1, series 4, acc. 82-18, box 15; Booz, Allen & Hamilton, Inc., *Review of Navy R&D Management, 1946–1973*, 1 Jun 1976, 85–86.

27. John S. Foster, Jr., to Assistant Secretary of the Army (R&D), Assistant Secretary of the Navy (R&D), Assistant Secretary of the Air Force (R&D), 17 Nov 1965, NHC, NLCCG Archives, DTNSRDC RC 3-1, series 3, acc. 84-55, box 63.

28. Leonard Sheingold, "Report of the Defense Science Board Committee on In-House Laboratories," 19 Aug 1965, NHC, NLCCG Archives, DTNSRDC RC 3-1, series 3, acc. 84-55, box 61.

29. Ibid.

30. "Der Grosse Plan" materials can be found in NHC, NLCCG Archives, DTNSRDC RC 3-1, series 3, acc. 84-55, box 65.

31. Captain D. K. Ela to Dr. Gerald W. Johnson, 11 Jan 1967, NHC, NLCCG Archives, DTNSRDC RC 3-1, series 4, acc. 82-18, box 16.

32. Some of the technical people viewed Naval Industrial Funding as a major source of the more competitive approach to R&D. However, from the point of view of some long-term administrative and technical employees, NIF was seen as simply a new accounting procedure for a system of project funding which had been set up decades before. Conversations, Mary Charlotte Crook and author, 1996.

33. "Compilation of Data on Navy Research and Development Activities, Navy Mine Defense Laboratory, Panama City, Florida," 1 Dec 1966, NHC, NLCCG Archives, DTNSRDC RC 3-1, series 4, acc. 82-18, box 15.

34. J.D.W. Borop to Director of Navy Laboratories, 20 Dec 1966, WNRC, acc. 70A-5757, box A-52-1, 3900 Gen. 2.

35. E. F. Schreiter to Director of Navy Laboratories, 6 Dec 1966, DTNSRDC RC 3-1, series 4, acc. 82-18, box 15, transferred to NHC, NLCCG Archives; draft memorandum, no author indicated, but context and provenance indicate staff paper from DNL, subject: "Summary of Discussion on Union of NOL, NWL, MDL," 5 Jan 1967, NHC, NLCCG Archives, DTNSRDC RC 3-1, series 4, acc. 82-18, box 15.

36. William A. Schoech to Chief of Naval Material, 9 Jun 1967, NHC, NLCCG Archives, DTNSRDC RC 3-1, series 4, acc. 82-18, box 15.

37. Ibid.

38. M. da C. Vincent and J. D. W Borop to Chief of Naval Material, 29 Sep 1967; and A. S. Goodfellow to Commanding Officer and Director, NSRDC, 27 Oct 1967, NHC, NLCCG Archives DTNSRDC RC 3-1, series 4, acc. 82-18, box 16.

39. Goodfellow to Commanding Officer and Director, NSRDC, 27 Oct 1967.

40. Richard Boyle, "The Fleet Connection," U.S. Naval Institute *Proceedings* 108 (Sep 1980) 60–61; *Biographical Directory of the American Congress, 1774–1961* (Washington: GPO, 1961), 1600.

41. Bob Sikes to Admiral I. J. Galantin, 29 Mar 1968, NHC, NLCCG Archives, DTNSRDC RC 3-1, series 3, acc. 84-55, box 65.

42. John W. Warner to Sikes, 19 Feb 1969, NHC, NLCCG Archives, DTNSRDC RC 3-1, series 3, acc. 84-55, box 65.

43. D. K. Allison, *Organizational Evolution of Navy Laboratories, 1869–1984*, draft of 7 Mar 1985, 83. A copy in NHC, NLCCG Archives, "DNL History Study" file; a shorter treatment was published by Allison as "U.S. Navy Research and Development Since World War II," in Merritt Roe Smith, ed., *Military Enterprise and Technological Change: Perspectives on the American Experience* (Cambridge: MIT Press, 1985); see also, Rodney Carlisle, *Management of the U.S. Navy Research and Development Centers During the Cold War: A Survey Guide to Reports* (Washington: Naval Historical Center, 1996).

44. Seth Hawkins, interview by Rodney Carlisle, 17 Nov 1986.

CHAPTER 11

The Systems Approach

"**O**NE SMALL STEP FOR MAN, ONE GIANT leap for mankind," exclaimed Neil Armstrong, as he lowered himself from the ladder to the surface of the moon, 20 July 1969. The date represents a high-water mark of American technological optimism and self-confidence. Within a year, reflecting the same national mood of certainty that advances in technology depended only upon money, commitment, and will, Admiral Elmo Zumwalt Jr., Chief of Naval Operations, July 1970–June 1974, set what seemed another goal drawn from science fiction, a 100-knot Navy.

If surface ships could operate at speeds approaching 100 knots, their vulnerability to both air and submarine attack would be reduced. Speeds in the range of 100 knots would aid in antisubmarine and antiair warfare. Fast ships could control the "terms of engagement" in surface-to-surface conflict, logistics, and amphibious assault missions. Very fast merchant ships could also reinvigorate the American merchant fleet, caught in a long-range decline under competition from foreign and flag-of-convenience vessels.[1]

Many shared Zumwalt's enthusiasm for speed as a solution to the problem of the decline of the surface fleet brought on by the swift submarine and jet aircraft. Rear Admiral William H. Livingston, director of the Navy's Tactical Air Surface and Electronic Warfare Development Division, believed that high-speed ships would "restore the primacy of the surface ship over the submarine." Both Livingston and Zumwalt exaggerated in describing the potential of higher speeds, calling the concept a "Quantum jump in shipbuilding" that would rival the transition from sail to steam. The 100-knot goal, like the moon landing, provided a specific technical challenge. Advocates hoped the clearly defined objective would capture the national imagination, or at least the imagination of the Congress and the naval establishment.[2]

Such a goal represented a new departure for the Navy. The Navy would take the lead and carry through promising ideas for entirely new types of ships. In the mood of technological optimism, visionaries believed that the naval laboratories, reorganized as "Centers of Excellence," would rival NASA and bring the dream to reality.

While Navy spokesmen testified in Congress, wrote essays, and gave interviews to the media about the 100-knot Navy, the difficult tasks of actually fulfilling the dream fell to researchers and research managers, many of them at Carderock. Several prototypes already developed by the 1960s held promise of meeting the objective; all could benefit from the new focus on innovative ships. Early twentieth-century experiments with hydrofoil craft suggested one path. A hydrofoil combined elements of both ships and aircraft. At low speeds of less than 30 knots, the ship would cruise with its hull in the water. Then, with a burst of power, it would rise and "fly" on struts supporting winglike foils. At 45 to 50 knots, however, the struts and foils would be subject to cavitation. This is a phenomenon where discontinuities of the flow occur due to the rapid formation and collapse of vapor-filled cavities in the liquid. If that barrier could be overcome, the vessel, given sufficient propulsion power, could operate at speeds well above fifty knots. Early designs in the United States had failed not only because of cavitation but from stresses on the struts, insufficient propulsion power in the era before gas turbines, and limitations of control technology as well as lack of consistent long-term funding. German designs by Baron Hans von Schertel at the end of World War II provided a starting point, but those craft were still in the development stage when Germany was defeated. Working gas turbine-powered prototypes were already in the Navy's hands when Zumwalt announced his goal.[4]

Hovercraft offered other possibilities. Invented in Great Britain by Sir Christopher Cockerell, the air cushion vehicle (ACV) could fly or hover at a height of several feet over relatively flat land or water. As a variation of this concept, in 1960, at the Naval Air Development Center in Philadelphia, Allen Ford invented the solid sidewall hovercraft. It had flexible bow and stern seals and rigid air-containing sidewalls that limited the craft to overwater use. First called a captured air bubble (CAB) ACV, the Navy came to designate the solid sidewall hovercraft as a surface effect ship (SES). Both types of hovercraft would require extensive development to bring the concepts to the stage of practical application.

The Marine Corps was interested in the ACV as a heavy-duty craft that could operate over both land and water and be used to deliver troops and equipment in amphibious assault operations. It offered a means to avoid the laborious and risky off-loading of Marines and equipment from conventional landing craft in sight and artillery range of shore. Although critics doubted whether 100 knots could be achieved with either hovercraft design, both held promise if funding and support could be mustered.

A third advanced ship concept offered significant improvements in some of the capabilities of conventional ships. The idea of a large catamaran-type vessel supported on thin struts attached to submarine-like hulls below the water surface, had been conceived by a Canadian inventor, Frederick Creed, in the late 1930s. Although the British, Canadian, and American navies had rejected his idea through the war years, the development of seakeeping theory in the 1950s caused renewed interest in the concept that the U.S. Navy designated as a small waterplane area twin hull (SWATH) ship.[5] Although it did not promise high speed, it did offer a high degree of seakindliness and platform steadiness in rough seas, large deck area, improved propulsion arrangements, and other attributes superior to conventional monohulls ships.

Barriers to innovation for all such marine vehicles arose not only from particular technical problems of materials, power plant, structural strength, control, and design configuration, but from problems of management, funding, and decision making as well. Until the endorsement of the spectacular goal by Zumwalt, the Navy held to a very conservative tradition in its consideration of radically new ship designs.

Creed's lonely advocacy of a small waterplane area twin hull ship for some twenty years was a typical experience for the advocates of new departures. It was fully in the pattern of John Philip Holland's fight for the submarine in the late nineteenth century, William Mitchell's claims for aircraft in the 1920s, and Robert Goddard's advocacy of liquid-fueled rockets. Established ship designs met their missions, but it had taken decades for the Navy to define and accept each of those missions. It was one thing to be able to conceive of a faster or more steady platform, but it was an entirely different matter to develop doctrine, that is, to find a role for any new concept in modern warfare. The mere existence of a new design concept on the drawing board had never guaranteed that the ship or device would go from concept to reality through the expensive process of development, preliminary design, model testing, prototype construction, procurement, and operational deployment. The expenditure of any fraction of the finite hardware budget for an unproven idea often seemed foolhardy to those making the decisions.

But even in the technologically optimistic atmosphere of the 1960s and early 1970s when Navy policy endorsed highly innovative developments, other management problems blocked the way for bringing an untried ship or craft to production and deployment. Such new ideas, while promising, required design, development, and testing on an unprecedented scale. Furthermore, the Navy's ship research and development establishment was not well organized for such jobs. The laboratories at Carderock and Annapolis were designed around disciplines. Each laboratory with its branches and divisions had well-established functions and was organized to address specific innovations or advances in the technology base on particular components or subsystems of the total ship such as materials and the structural strength and ideal shape of the hull, the mechanism of ship control, the design of the propulsor, or the optimal size and nature of the power plant. The discipline-based organizations, while a stimulus to progress in particular technical areas, had difficulty in the integration of contributions from a range of different technical fields.

Although the Bureau of Construction and Repair and the Bureau of Engineering had merged to form the Bureau of Ships in 1940, and the laboratories at Carderock and Annapolis had been merged in 1967, the former internal units survived, usually under new names. The individual laboratories, with their roots, experience, traditions, personnel, and equipment, were really loosely coordinated separate facilities, each with its own well-defined part of the picture. They would need to work much more closely if they were to create wholly new ships. A "systems" approach of some sort would be required, one that looked at the whole ship as a system, rather than at its components.

The revolution in management theory which had swept through business schools and industry and into Robert McNamara's Department of Defense offered several different ways of organizing and coordinating such innovative work and provided a new vocabulary for thinking about systems. Top-level project and program management, similar to that used by the Navy to develop *Nautilus* and Polaris, was one alternative. For every proposed new ship design, a special project office, funded and coordinated by the Bureau of Ships, and its successor, the Naval Sea Systems Command, would oversee research, development, testing, evaluation, and eventually, production.

Project management had several advantages. A specialized and highly motivated single-purpose team could be assembled with high visibility and highly placed patronage. This would help to protect the funding and the whole project, providing the necessary political support to deal with the internecine warfare in allocating research and development resources. The excitement of being dedicated to achieving a major new design would lead to high morale, a sense of commitment, and energetically focused pursuit of project goals. In turn, the challenge and good morale would help to attract and retain talented people.

Yet the special project office concept also had its flaws. If and when a project was completed, it was expected that the team would dissolve and the staff would be reassigned or disperse. Because of its transient nature, a project organization posed dangers to individuals' career paths, dangers not inherent in functional organizations such as the established laboratories. Project office staff sometimes tried to keep their organizations alive, converting a temporary team into a permanent structure and giving it an institutional life of its own, even though the project was nearing completion. The high level of public attention could also be a drawback as well as an advantage; normal technical setbacks could receive a disproportionate degree of adverse publicity and attention. The separate, expensive project and its support office could become an easy target for cutting when political winds shifted.

A second approach, also growing out of the flurry of new administrative concepts, was matrix management. A coordinating office would work with existing functional organizations, providing a second line of authority. Specialists would stay in their departments but would also report to a team manager. This approach would take advantage of existing strengths of functional organizations and would build on the traditional structure, based on continuity and established lines of authority. Once a project was completed, members of the staff would not have to "go" anywhere but would stay in their home departments. Thus, a matrix could provide both the security of a career path associated with the traditional structure and the flexibility and team spirit of the project organization.

But there was a rub here as well. In matrix management, coordination of the effort established a second line of authority, a clear violation of a cardinal principle of classical bureaucracy—that each employee or staff member should have one, and only one, supervisor. The second line of control would often be represented on the traditional organizational chart by a dotted line, cutting across from box to box. Each dotted line signaled the potential for conflict, charges of raiding, and jealousies over daily details of assignment, power, turf, and schedule. The matrix faced constant danger of dissolution, lacking the greater stability of funding of established functional organizations and the tenuous protection that came with a highly visible special project office.

At the Naval Ship Research and Development Center, management of research and development for promising new ship designs proceeded along all three paths. They included work in traditional departments, under a project office, and in a unique matrix organization. The effort to develop innovative or "advanced ships" would produce not only working prototypes and some additions to the fleet but also would affect the way the laboratory organized its work, as the innovative management methods and efforts led to some permanent changes in the administration of the center.

Surface effect ship work developed within the Aerodynamics Department and was funded out of a project office jointly sponsored and funded by NAVSEA and the Maritime Administration (MARAD). The flow of resources and work from the late 1960s through 1979 into the department brought with it reorganization; the department, renamed the Aviation and Surface Effects Department, altered its mission to reflect study and development of the new craft, continuing in the field even after the SES Project Office closed.

Development of hydrofoil subsystem technology had been undertaken as early as the 1950s at Carderock. This effort ultimately affected laboratory organization, leading to the creation of a completely new department within the center. A matrixlike organization to develop hydrofoils was at first attached to the office of the technical director. As the structure proved innovative and capable of attracting funding, Technical Director Alan Powell endorsed its conversion into the Systems Development Office and later to the Systems Development Department (Code 11), a new functional entity. Through the 1970s this department was designated by NAVSEA as the technical agent not only for hydrofoils but also for amphibious air cushion vehicles, SWATH ships, and several other promising ship concepts. By the 1980s, the organization survived with a broader mandate, to bring a systems approach to conventional, as well as advanced, ships.

Surface Effect Ships

In two days, naval architect Allen Ford "invented" the solid sidewall air cushion concept that formed the basis of the Surface Effect Ship. In 1960, while employed by the Naval Air Development Center (NADC) at Johnsville, Pennsylvania, he had been asked to review the current literature on air cushion vehicles, then a matter of intense interest stimulated by publicity over recent British work. In July 1957, Harvey Chaplin, at DTMB, had published the first open-literature theory of ACV lift.

Ford recognized that a fundamental problem of air cushion or ground effect machines was the fact that large quantities of air escaped from under the peripheral skirts, requiring considerable power to maintain acceptable air cushion pressure and associated height above the

ground or water surface. Containing solid sidewalls and some form of
flexible end seals would, on the other hand, create additional drag and
the solid sidewalls would prevent amphibious operations from continuing from the water up on to the land and inland. Yet those limitations,
he believed, could be offset by the increased efficiency resulting from
containing most of the air in the cushion.[6]

Ford patented the solid sidewall concept for the Navy, and then, in
1965, transferred to the DTMB to work with Chaplin in the
Aerodynamics Department. Chaplin was the preliminary designer and
chief test pilot of one of the Marine Corps' early experimental air cushion vehicles, the GEM-III. At Carderock, Ford continued development
of the first manned SES test craft, the XR-1. This 10-ton research craft
was transferred with Ford from NADC to DTMB. Later modifications,
designated XR-1A through XR-1D, tested a variety of modifications to
augment stability, to improve propulsion systems, and to develop more
reliable fore and aft seals. XR-1D employed a ride-control system, using
"variable geometry fans" and cushion vent valves to regulate performance in rough water.[7]

At the same time as SES work proceeded in the Aerodynamics
Department, the Navy joined with the Commerce Department's
Maritime Administration to set up a high-level Joint Surface Effects Ship
Project Office (JSESPO). The Maritime Administration saw potential in
the SES for large, transoceanic cargo vessels that could reach high
speeds. The project manager for JSESPO, Marvin Pitkin, first worked
with Chaplin and Ford in the Aerodynamics Department offices, then
moved his burgeoning "shop" to Building 102 near the main gate at
Carderock. Ford and Chaplin welcomed the support and the local office, since Pitkin's project office reported directly to NAVMAT and to a
similarly high level in MARAD. Pitkin thus had access to top management and a source of funds at both agencies.[8]

After three years, MARAD withdrew support from JSESPO, and the
Navy downgraded the project office to the NAVSEA level. The NAVSEA-
managed project continued as PMS-304. Both Pitkin and his successor,
Carl Drenkard, continued to operate the PMS-304 project office at
Carderock rather than at NAVSEA headquarters. Most other special project managers at NAVSEA did not maintain their offices at the laboratory site but at headquarters. Both JSESPO and PMS-304 were somewhat
unique in their close physical and organizational proximity to the actual
laboratory work.

While PMS-304 channeled funds and coordinated research, the
group under Ford developed other small manned test craft, including
the XR-3, tested at Annapolis in 1973, and the XR-5, tested at a newly established SES test facility on the Patuxent River in Maryland. The XR-5,

built in the Aerodynamics Department at the center in 1974, was 47 feet long with a relatively high length-to-beam ratio. As Ford later remarked, these manned test craft helped convince Navy personnel who could not follow the logic of applying Froude scaling to miniature models. Operating in "races" with conventional outboard-driven speedboats, the SES manned craft impressed nontechnical observers with their visibly smaller wakes. In demonstrations and photographs, the wake itself served as an obvious measurement of the lower power requirements of the SES compared to conventional planing hulls making the same speed.[9]

Although Pitkin recruited several Aero Department staff to work with him on the project team, others continued on in the department, including Ford and Robert Wilson, who specialized in seal design. The highly visible project office continued to channel funds to the Aero Department's own SES group and, meanwhile, placed contracts for design and construction of two 100-ton craft. These were high-speed test craft with a low length-to-beam ratio. Designated SES 100A and SES 100B they were launched in 1971 and 1972, respectively. Aerojet-General built the "A" and Bell Aerospace-Textron built the "B"craft. Both vessels were tested and put through ship handling and maneuvering demonstrations through the mid-1970s, again serving a public relations as well as a technical function. Among the various VIPs taken out for a high-speed cruise was Secretary of the Navy J. William Middendorf. At top speed, the operators pointed out that they had achieved 100 "miles per

Surface Effect Ships.   Within the Aerodynamics Department at Carderock, work on advanced surface effect ships began as early as 1957, leading to SES 100A by Aerojet-General (foreground) and 100B by Bell-Textron in the early 1970s.

hour." They did not feel it necessary to explain to Middendorf that a "knot" is about 1.15 miles per hour. Middendorf, duly impressed, gave his blessing to continued work.[10]

Through the late 1970s the project office developed plans for a large 2,000-ton SES, dubbed the "2K SES" by those working on it. Rohr Marine Incorporated (RMI), an innovative ship design and construction firm in San Diego, became deeply involved in design studies and eagerly looked forward to serious naval procurement of a full-scale ship. Cooperating with the RMI effort, the center modified the somewhat antiquated model basin's towing carriage number three, originally built in 1940, for high-speed testing. For three years, the carriage was used to test Rohr-designed models of the 2K SES.[11]

In 1979, on the eve of funding the construction of a full-scale 2K SES, the Navy ordered a review of expenditures on all advanced ship designs. The change from the technological optimism of 1970 to the post-Vietnam, post-Watergate energy crisis and fiscal malaise of the late 1970s had its impact. No acceptable mission could be established for the 2K SES. As a result, the ship concept was "missionized" and grew to be a 3K SES. But soon after, the Navy dropped plans for it. In another year, funds for PMS-304 dried up and the Carderock project office closed. High visibility, an asset in good times, created an easy target in bad times.

Nevertheless, Ford, Chaplin, Wilson, and others in the Aero Department kept alive a variety of SES projects. The testing program at the Patuxent River Naval Air Station included continuing runs of manned prototypes. The Aerodynamics Department, now renamed the Aviation and Surface Effects Department, continued to work on perfecting high length-to-beam ratio designs that would be stable and require less power at moderate speeds. Researchers announced with some pride that they had developed the "only dynamic fan evaluation rig in the world," using it to test the stabilizing variable-vent system. Alternative designs of the side hulls required both computer modeling and tank testing.[12]

After a hiatus of high-level support and interest, the advocates of the SES eventually found a market for the concept. The Coast Guard purchased from Textron Marine Systems three 30-knot, 110-foot long, 140-ton SES patrol boats in the early 1980s for drug-traffic interdiction service in the Caribbean. In 1984 the Navy procured a "stretched" SES 200 patrol boat, lengthened from 110 to 160 feet and increased in weight to about 200 tons. It was very successful in confirming predictions of significantly lower drag and power for this high length-to-beam ratio configuration over a significant speed range. The SES 200 subsequently

SES 200. In 1984, the Navy procured a surface effect craft from Textron Marine Systems and had it lengthened to 160 feet, creating a 200-ton high length-to-beam ratio ship for research purposes.

served in NATO trials in Europe and in Navy port visits in the Caribbean as a high-speed test platform for new weapons systems. In 1984, Rohr Marine and Bell Aerospace won contracts for SES designs of even larger patrol boats and minesweeping craft, but these efforts were later canceled by NAVSEA.[13]

The lag between conception and deployment, in this case about twenty years, was not so different from the earlier timing of the submarine and the aircraft carrier. Advocates looked forward to possible applications in the multi-thousand-ton size as escort picket ships. But when it came to roles like antisubmarine and antiair warfare, Navy analysts of the 1980s frankly admitted that the question remained "whether such ships can pay their way mission-wise."[14]

The Systems Development Department

Starting as a small staff group working directly for DTMB's civilian technical director, an innovative team evolved under the leadership of

William M. Ellsworth. The mission of the group was to bring together the varied talents of the specialists at NSRDC and to develop "advanced ship" designs. By 1969, the team grew into the center's eighth technical department, the Systems Development Department. The department initially worked in very nontraditional ways. The methods and style that Ellsworth developed in the first decade gave it a highly personalized character.

By the early 1960s, hydrofoil development in the Bureau of Ships had already led to two prototype ships for the Navy: *High Point* (PCH 1), a 120-ton hydrofoil patrol craft 35.1 meters in length, which was originally scheduled to be delivered to the fleet, and *Plainview* (AGEH 1), a 320-ton ship, 64.2 meters long, at that time the world's largest hydrofoil ship. *High Point* was launched in August 1962. A year later she was ready for operations and evaluation. *Plainview*, launched in 1965, was plagued by numerous delays in construction and shipyard strikes. As a result, she was not ready for Navy testing until 1969.

The major development problems confronting the hydrofoils were not only technical, but more especially issues of funding and manage-

Hydrofoil Ships Underway.   *Plainview* (AGEH 1), foreground, at 320 metric tons the largest hydrofoil in the world when built, paced by the 120-ton *High Point* (PCH 1) in a check of the two ships combined pressure signature for minesweeping.

ment. As the two prototypes neared the sea-trial stage researchers recognized that sea-trial methods as employed by model basin staff over the past decades on conventional ships were not completely adequate to evaluate a totally new "system" with both new technology and new human aspects. If the model basin was to take the lead in the development of hydrofoils, someone would need to bring together hydrodynamicists, propulsion engineers, model testers, and experts skilled in structures, propulsion, and control systems.[18]

Under a systems approach, each weapon system has both a physical and a human side, taking into account the ways in which people deal with equipment. The human side of the hydrofoil system presented issues that did not fall within the purview of any of the existing laboratories at either DTMB or the Marine Engineering Laboratory. Decisions needed to be made as to what personnel ratings, reflecting specialized training and experience, would be required to ensure a proficient crew and officers. Since hydrofoils would "fly," with the hull lifted above the water on foils operating like aircraft wings under the surface, a pilot with flight experience might be appropriate. Repairs could dictate the need for petty officers trained in the unique propulsion and lift systems. The hydrofoil development team set out to study these human aspects as well as the purely technological aspects of the system.

The diverse problems of developing a completely new system would seem to preclude a role for the specialized laboratories at DTMB, each with its traditional disciplinary focus. Yet to pass up the opportunity would mean that hydrofoil development would go on elsewhere or, perhaps, might simply not take place at all. A new interdisciplinary method of approaching technological issues would be even more essential in this area than in some others.

In late 1965 Ellsworth proposed a special coordinating office to be run out of Carderock and worked toward obtaining Bureau of Ships' support for retaining both *High Point* and *Plainview* for further experiments and development. On 1 May 1966, BUSHIPS became the Naval Ship Systems Command. In 1966 and 1967, working closely with the NAVSHIPS manager of the Hydrofoil R&D Program, James L. Schuler, he briefed naval officers in the systems command on the program. At their request, he later briefed the Chief of Naval Material Admiral Ignatius Galantin and Assistant Secretary of the Navy for Research and Development Robert Frosch on the needs and promise of the hydrofoil program. At each step, Schuler and Ellsworth worked to develop advocates, not adversaries, carefully touching base with subordinates before dealing with their superiors.

The timing was fortunate. The usefulness of the massive reorganization of naval research during the mid-1960s could be demonstrated by such projects, serving as concrete realizations of the hopes of Galantin, Frosh, and the other planners. The implied faith in all of the reorganization had been that civilian researchers, if unleashed from the restrictions of tight military control and from the bounds of tradition, could produce greater innovations. In 1967, the very year that NSRDC was formed out of the merger of the DTMB and MEL, Schuler and Ellsworth received the go-ahead. Technical Director Powell agreed to establish a Hydrofoil Development Program Office as the technical agent of NAVSHIPS. Zumwalt's endorsement of high-speed innovation spurred on the work. Ellsworth adopted the title of technical manager for the program. Later positions in the program office included William C. O'Neill, manager of Subsystems; Dennis J. Clark, manager of Systems Integration; Fred Saxton, manager of Instrumentation Systems; and Enzo Marmentini, project engineer. O'Neill had an exceptionally strong background in a broad range of engineering disciplines, particularly in propulsion and automatic control systems. Clark, transferred from the Structures Laboratory, brought a structures background and strong bent toward systems engineering and integration. Saxton transferred from the Central Instrumentation Division and had responsibility for all trials instrumentation. Marmentini was former chief pilot of Chilean Airlines and had a background in structural design and machinery. Rather than attaching most of the other supporting personnel directly to the Development Program Office, they would retain their places in existing functional organizations, not only at Carderock and Annapolis but at other Navy laboratories as well. For example, David Washburn at the Naval Electronics Laboratory Center (NELC) in San Diego was assigned responsibility for mission subsystems. As another management innovation, the position of hydrofoil program officer, a naval officer billet, was established in the Development Program Office.

Following the concept of "buying, not hiring," the program office relied whenever possible on contracting, using subsystem managers to monitor the contracts. In addition to the manufacturers of the ships and their components, the office worked with universities and other non-profit laboratories to have work done on subsystems. More important, technical experts in the NSRDC functional departments provided extensive and vital technical support.

The program office avoided some of the pitfalls of both matrix management and project management, while retaining some of the benefits of each form. Since technical personnel in supporting activities were funded for the duration of the program, the office could lay a direct claim to their time, avoiding a dotted line, relationship. Although formally still on assignment with their home departments, they could be committed to the project without endangering their career paths or antagonizing their supervisors. Every effort was made to maintain cordial relations with their department supervisors, who could release individuals temporarily, to serve as members of the hydrofoil team. Team spirit and loyalty to the project characteristic of project management was achieved, yet individual technical personnel still would be able to return to their functional departments upon completion of their tasks.

HYSTU and Its Trials

In 1966, DTNSRDC set up special support arrangements with the Puget Sound Naval Shipyard in Bremerton, Washington. On 10 November, a Hydrofoil Special Trials Unit (HYSTU) was established as a tenant activity of the shipyard. Lieutenant Commander Karl M. Duff became the first officer in charge of HYSTU. He had recently graduated from the Navy program at MIT with a doctorate in naval architecture and marine engineering. He was supported by a small staff headed by Sumi Arima who had transferred from his position with the Supervisor of Shipbuilding, Seattle, Washington.

On 21 December, the long-awaited message from the CNO was received transferring the *High Point* to the new trials unit with the *Plainview* to be transferred upon delivery.

The "Charter and Operating Plan" for HYSTU spelled out the mission: to test *High Point* and *Plainview*, evaluate performance, identify design deficiencies, accomplish modifications, correlate trials data with model and computer predictions, and determine technical feasibility, cost, and military usefulness. The trials unit was to serve as an institutional model, to provide operational experience for similar units to follow for the testing of other advanced ship types.[19]

The HYSTU "charter" defined three lines of command and responsibility. Technical functions would be the responsibility of a uniformed naval officer serving as local officer in charge, who would report to the technical manager in the Hydrofoil Development Program Office at Carderock. Military administrative functions would also be the naval officer's responsibility, and in that respect, he would report directly to the commanding officer of NSRDC. "Military operations," the actual scheduling and logistics of the trial runs, would also be his responsibility, and in this regard, he would coordinate closely with the local Seattle operations officer, the commander of the Thirteenth Naval District.

This arrangement meant that the commanding officer of each vessel and its uniformed crew would be under the ultimate military direction of the commanding officer of the research center, rather than line officers of the Navy fleet. Even though center staff had participated in sea trials from the days of David Taylor, this was the first time that the officers and crew of a ship in its sea trials had been directly under the naval command of the center. In a naval-administrative sense, Carderock now had a "fleet" of its own, a point that the Public Information Office made with some pride.

The location at Bremerton was ideal in many respects. The Puget Sound Naval Shipyard, a massive deep-water yard capable of providing support to aircraft carriers, cooperated fully with the little project, partly because the constant flow of VIPs who came to inspect the ships and visit HYSTU led to new visibility for the yard itself. The yard provided well-equipped shops for repairs, a support barge, and other craft, as well as supplies, equipment, and quarters. Boeing Company, headquartered in nearby Seattle, and their main subcontractor, J. M. Martinac Shipbuilding, had built *High Point* and provided local contractor support. Finally, Puget Sound offered relatively sheltered waters for test runs, with easy access to the open ocean for rough water trials even though numerous floating logs presented a serious hazard, particularly those that floated vertically known as "deadheads".

The hydrofoil office found that working closely with the uniformed crew had unexpected benefits. Not only could the project develop the types of training required, but the involvement of officers and crew in the innovation process led to technical improvements that the civilians had not thought about. For example, the crew developed a method of projecting the navigation radar screen on the navigation chart so that the operator could trace the "flight" of the hydrofoil on the chart. Also, members of the PCH crew worked out a method of changing propellers under water, eliminating the need for a time-consuming dry-docking.[21]

Commanding officers of the ships recommended specific changes to improve safety and handling, some major, some minor. Lieutenant Hugh Burkons, officer in charge of *High Point*, suggested in 1969 an emergency exit hatch in *High Point*'s engine room, along with improvements in the water-distilling apparatus and upgraded and lighter bilge pumps. Literally dozens of similar modifications resulting from crew observation and engineering testing improved and altered both vessels, including instrumentation and auxiliary machinery such as lighter pumps and compressors. In the summer of 1970, *High Point* underwent a major overhaul incorporating modifications to the automatic control system, rebuilt struts, and a redesigned foilborne transmission."[22]

The rotation of naval officers for short tours of duty at first struck the civilian engineers on the team as extremely impractical. No sooner would an officer become fully familiar with the unique ship and begin to suggest modifications, he would be transferred to his next post. However, civilian managers soon recognized that there were some positive aspects to this Navy tradition. Short tours exposed more officers to hydrofoil operation, building a body of experience as well as a coterie of well-placed advocates. Furthermore, on completion of the testing program, there was no problem of finding new positions for the officers since they expected to move on. Their willingness to move contrasted with civilian engineers and scientists, whose relocation always presented difficulties as they sought to maintain ties with their homes, schools, and communities.[23]

HYSTU represented a combination of a functional organization, devoted to the test and evaluation of advanced ship designs, and a project organization that would work itself out of business on completion of the innovative process. In the long run, as the Carderock Systems Development Department began to work on other ships besides the hydrofoil, the nature of the "office" shifted and took on a more standard, functional character.

Ellsworth relinquished his position as technical manager of the hydrofoil office to David Jewell of the Ship Hydromechanics Department in order to devote full time to managing the new Systems Development Department. In April 1973, Jewell left the center to accept a teaching position. He was replaced by Robert Johnston, manager of Grumman Marine Systems and a former naval officer who had been deeply involved in the early hydrofoil program of the Office of Naval Research and the Bureau of Ships.

The improvements and evaluation on both *High Point* and *Plainview* were a significant part of the foundation of future hydrofoils delivered to the Navy. *Flagstaff* (PGH 1), a 60-ton hydrofoil gunboat built by Grumman and the water-jet propelled *Tucumcari* (PGH 2) built by Boeing both incorporated proven features.[24]

In 1974, Boeing launched *Pegasus* (PHM 1), the first of a squadron of six 235-metric-ton hydrofoil missile ships and the Navy accepted her into the fleet in 1977. The six Boeing-built patrol hydrofoil missile ships (PHMs) were equipped with a 75-mm Oto Melara rapid-fire gun and eight Harpoon missiles in launching cannisters. They operated in the eastern Pacific and off the Hawaiian Islands. They later operated out of Key West working with the Coast Guard in intercepting drug smugglers. By the end of 1984, they had accumulated a record of some 22,900 underway hours, of which over 5,000 hours were "foilborne." The mainte-

Hydrofoil Squadron. These six Boeing-built patrol hydrofoil missile ships (PHMs), resulting from advanced ship work at the center, saw action in the Pacific and in drug interdiction in the Caribbean in the 1980s.

nance record and performance specifications led Boeing to undertake marketing a smaller "jet foil" to other navies by the late 1980s, seeking purchasers in the Caribbean, the Mediterranean, and Japan. In the long run, the Hydrofoil Development Program was instrumental in bringing a new type of ship from the drawing board into the Navy fleet.[25]

Amphibious Assault Landing Craft

Between 1965 and 1968, the Navy began planning for the acquisition of a high-speed amphibious assault landing craft (AALC) under the sponsorship of NAVSHIPS R&D Program Manager Jim Schuler.

In 1968 DTNSRDC set up a technical manager for the AALC Development Program, anticipating a test and evaluation role in the new development program. For the position of technical manager, Ellsworth recruited Melvin (Mel) Brown from Bell Aerospace, a former Navy engineering duty officer and a technical professional with considerable experience in developing air cushion vehicles. The initial office staff included Bruce Benson, Marty Fink, Dick Kenefick, Jack Offutt, and Carl Brindle. Lieutenant Commander Mike Terry was assigned as the first Navy AALC project officer. The hydrofoil development pattern was repeated; success could be attributed to the firm working relationship between the development program manager in NAVSHIPS, the technical manager in the Systems Development Department, and the builders of the craft. As in the hydrofoil development, personnel from center functional departments were recruited to perform a variety of important technical tasks.

In 1971 NAVSHIPS awarded two contracts for two separate designs of AALCs. Aerojet General Corporation proceeded with one design, designated "JEFF-A," and Bell Aerosystems Corporation designed and built "JEFF-B." [27]

Following the HYSTU arrangement, in 1975 an Amphibious Assault Landing Craft Trials Unit (AALCTU) was established as a tenant activity at the Naval Coastal Systems Center in Panama City, Florida. The first

Amphibious Assault Landing Craft (AALC).   These two developmental prototype air-cushion landing craft, JEFF-A (Aerojet) and JEFF-B (Bell) soon attracted vigorous Marine Corps support.

officer in charge was Lieutenant Commander Gene Wilder who was supported by a small civilian staff headed up by Frank Hawkins. In 1977 the trials unit began an extensive series of combined trials and modifications of the JEFF craft, again integrating the crew, civilian engineers, and supporting prime contractors as a total team. Four naval officers, twenty to thirty enlisted personnel, and eight civilians from Carderock made up the local team. The charter for the AALC trials unit followed the HYSTU charter, but in briefer fashion, simply outlined a similar division of technical and military chains of command.[28]

Each of the two JEFF craft met the same specifications. They were to be capable of transporting 60 tons of payload at 50 knots in a Sea State 2, that is, a significant wave height (average of the one-third highest waves) of about 2 feet. They were designed to operate in and out of the well decks of amphibious ships such as LSDs or LPDs from over-the-horizon distances. The requirement that the AALC fit inside the well deck limited the overall dimensions to less than 100 feet in length, 50 feet in beam, and 27 feet in height when on the air cushion. The

AALC JEFF-B Enters *Spiegel Grove* (LSD 32)   With its amphibious capacity, the AALC can be launched 20 miles out from over the horizon, run into shore at high speed and deposit men and equipment inland. This two-engine JEFF-B carries a main battle tank.

Textron Marine System

LCAC. This production version of the landing craft, air cushion, built by Textron Marine Systems, transports four armored vehicles across a beach and tidal lagoon.

craft were designed to clear 8-foot surf and to fly well inland of the surf zone to unload. On land, the craft were to clear 4-foot obstacles and hold course in winds up to 25 knots.[29]

Gas turbine engines powered both JEFF-A and JEFF-B, each vessel using six AVCO Lycoming TF40s in the 3,500-horsepower range. Each craft rode on an air cushion contained by a flexible skirt around the craft. Each utilized light construction materials, including marine aluminum, fiberglass, and balsa-core sheet material. The JEFF craft, like the hydrofoils, reflected elements of design from both ships and aircraft, representing a marriage of two separate technological traditions.[30]

The cargoes carried would be Marine Corps equipment and personnel for amphibious landings. The 60-ton payload requirement would allow the Marines to deposit a fully loaded main battle tank ashore and have it move into action immediately. The long-range and surf-clearing capacity would allow an invading force to off-load at alternative landing sites, choosing the least defended and topographically favorable beach out of hundreds of miles of coast. The battle tank could debark on solid ground beyond the beach sand, where it could operate effectively. If the Marines had to engage in amphibious operations like those of World War II, they now would have an appropriate link between the deep-draft ships and the beach.

The Marines took a special supportive attitude toward the program, its progress, and the work done by development program team. Whenever Navy interest or research funding threatened to drop off, the program office could count on an energetic and aggressive Marine Corps "rescue mission," with everyone from the commandant of the Corps on down rallying to support the program. The Marines' political clout, mounted at crucial points, helped bring the air cushion landing craft program to a successful completion. By 1980 NAVSEA set up an acquisition program to buy the Bell-designed landing craft, air cushion (LCAC), using features that had been tested on the JEFF craft. In 1984 Bell, which became Textron Marine Systems, set up a manufacturing facility in New Orleans, Louisana and began to deliver the first of the operational craft to the Navy. The craft would later become a major element of Marine Corps hardware, available for use in hot spots around the world.[31]

SWATH Ships

The small waterplane area twin hull, or SWATH, ship concept can be traced to the inventive ideas of Frederick Creed, a colorful, talkative missionary and inventor. Creed had developed the teleprinter in Glasgow, Scotland, where he had resettled from Canada in the early years of the century. Although he eventually sold the teleprinter to the British Post Office system, his small fortune was dissipated in the crash of 1929 and through donations to the church. While continuing to invent devices associated with telegraphy, he developed his twin hull "seadrome" concept in the 1930s, with the idea that such vessels could serve as refueling landing pads for aircraft at intervals across the Atlantic. He then began an extensive letter-writing campaign to sell his patented ideas.

Creed persisted despite the fact that, like many independent inventors with suggestions for naval improvement, he was repeatedly put off and delayed. In 1942 the Admiralty expressed interest and issued a set of "Staff Requirements" or specifications for an aircraft carrier built along the lines of Creed's concept. He worked up a set of plans to meet the specifications, and Britain's National Physical Laboratory experimented with models built to his designs. Hydrodynamic researchers agreed the craft held promise of great steadiness in head seas. But A. V. Alexander, First Lord of the Admiralty, personally met with Creed in January 1943 and explained that his ideas could not be implemented because of steel scarcity, full construction schedules, and wartime priorities. Nevertheless, Creed's liberal distribution of plans, designs, and model results among British and American shipyards, naval architects, and government bureaus left a dispersed group of advocates by the time of his death in 1957.[32]

Serious consideration of Creed's concept became possible with the advances in theoretical work in seakeeping, or the study of ships in actual wave conditions, during the early 1950s. Conventional monohull ships in heavy seas would slam, pitch, heave, and ship water. However, seakeeping theory predicted improved performance in head seas if the hull was both longer and wider underwater than at the waterline. Theory also suggested that ships of such a design would perform best at high speeds, where the contrast with conventional hulls would be profound, particularly in the reduced impact of wave-induced motions. Yet a long, narrow monohull would roll severely in all but the calmest seas and would heel dangerously in turns. The advantages of the narrow hull in reduced wave-induced motion could be achieved in a catamaran or twin hull construction, which would be steady and have reduced roll.[33]

Research demonstrated theory in some prototype work. In 1971 Litton Ship Systems in Culver City, California, constructed a 20-foot long working model of a SWATH for the Naval Ocean Systems Center. Unlike basin testing models, this craft could be operated by an on-board operator under actual wind and wave conditions. Early test runs excited the Litton designers.

Several tests in 4-foot waves indicated that a full-sized, 9,500-ton ship of the same twin hull design would be remarkably steady at full speed in huge waves up to 60 feet. The developers could hardly believe it when the 20-foot-long craft smoothly cruised through 6-foot waves and a 25-knot wind in the southern California harbor of Marina Del Rey. Using rough scaling law estimates, a full-scale ship of the same design would be steady in a hurricane with waves cresting at 100 feet. Typhoons with lower wind and waves had sunk destroyers in the Pacific during World War II, including three during one December 1944 storm.[34]

The Litton *Trisec I* created considerable interest in the advanced ship community. The Advanced Concepts Office, a small group in the Systems Development Department that undertook early exploration and evaluation of promising new concepts, borrowed the Litton model and moved it to Carderock for carefully controlled tests in the Maneuvering and Seakeeping Basin. Tests there confirmed the broad conclusions of the Litton reports from the ocean tests, that heavy seas would induce very little pitching. However, the ship did heave, that is, rise and fall vertically like an elevator. Nevertheless, the deck stayed level and would provide, on a full-scale ship, a nearly ideal platform for helicopters or V/STOL aircraft.[35]

Seth Hawkins, first technical manager of the SWATH ship program, predicted that with a fifteen-year development program (a few years shorter than either the hydrofoil or the LCAC schedules), a full-scale operational SWATH ship could be built. Initial tests indicated that the SWATH concept would encounter less complex and expensive technical problems than the hydrofoil. But in the normal progression from model through larger scale prototypes, the intermediate stages might discourage observers and potential naval buyers, since the concept would not be displayed at its optimum size until a rather large ship was built. A full-scale, 2,000-ton ship would be likely to outperform (on scale) smaller, 20- or 200-ton versions, yet the cost of a 2,000-ton vessel would be excessive for a test prototype. Hawkins thought the best compromise was to proceed on a 190-ton work boat as a test vessel, and to keep working on the potential larger ship.[46]

Meanwhile, the SWATH Ship Program Office proceeded with mathematical modeling and planning. Used as a carrier for helicopters and V/STOLs, the SWATH ship could accommodate up to 50 percent more such aircraft than a single hull vessel of the same displacement.[37]

Other promising features not only increased steadiness but the ability to maintain high speed in rough seas. Several features of the twin hull also suggested that a sonar could operate more effectively than on monohulls, partly because the transducers could be widely separated from propellers and other noisy parts of the vessel. Studies showed that the SWATH ship should ultimately cost less per ton than either hydrofoil or air cushion vehicles, since the SWATH technical problems were less complicated. From a technical point of view, it seemed a logical option for further development.

Progress and the necessary technical steps could be predicted with some confidence. But the barrier to development of the SWATH ship was not technical. Instead, it was delayed by the careful pace of the Navy's decision- making process. The V/STOL-helicopter-carrier mission niche was already filled; the Navy at first did not see a clear military use for such a craft.

The Naval Ocean Systems Center ordered a "Semi-Submerged Platform" (SSP) as a work boat for use in connection with their Hawaiian laboratory. Built at the Coast Guard's shipyard at Curtis Bay, Maryland and launched in 1973, the 200-ton craft *Kaimalino* remained

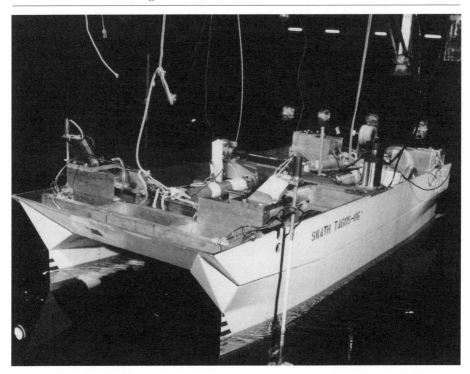

SWATH Ship Model.   The small waterplane area twin hull (SWATH) ship concept is tested at the model basin in the mid 1980s. By the 1990s, SWATH ship designs found many applications in ferry and offshore oil rig supply as well as naval vessels.

the U.S. Navy's only SWATH ship for over a decade. The ship itself incorporated a number of surplus spare parts, including used helicopter engines and chain drives. Nevertheless, in its operation in Kaneoe Bay, Hawaii by the Naval Ocean Systems Center, it served to demonstrate the practicality of the concept.[38]

Although the SWATH concept was ready for development by the mid-1970s, it would take a decade of development outside of Navy laboratories as private yachts, ferries, and merchant ships before the Navy turned once again to this design. In the early 1970s the Japanese firm of Mitsui Engineering and Shipbuilding, Ltd., began work on SWATH ship designs, using some engineering data provided openly from NSRDC. After several test designs, Mitsui built *Seagull*, a 350-ton passenger ferry, and the *Kotozaki*, a hydrographic survey ship of 240 tons. Later, a 3,500-ton ocean support ship, *Kaiyo*, was built by Japan. In the United States a private yacht of fifty tons, the *Suave Lino*, was built for Leonard Friedman at Poole Boatyard in Chula Vista, California. Rohr Marine Incorporated, the advanced shipbuilding firm located in San Diego that had worked on the SES design, constructed a 50-ton SWATH to help promote the concept in the early 1980s.[39]

In the Systems Development Department at Carderock, a dedicated group continued to work on SWATH ship concepts, despite the hiatus in Navy interest and lack of major development funding over the decade 1973–1983. Robert Lamb devoted over fifteen years of his career to the program, and commented that others, including Ray Allen and Jerry Gore, had made a similar commitment. Gore succeeded Hawkins as technical manager of the SWATH ship development program office. In 1985 one specialist calculated that Lamb and five others in advanced ship design work at Carderock together had over fifty years of SWATH ship "experience."[40]

During the period of reduced support, basic work still continued. Computer simulation studies of structural problems led to the development of a specialized SWATH ship evaluation program to find the optimum location and distribution of control surfaces on alternative designs. Other programs, using finite element analysis, could determine stress and ideal spacing of bulkheads, and the impact of severe "side loads," that is, the effect of beam seas, on various designs. As a consequence, by the mid-1980s the SWATH group claimed that they could produce SWATH structural designs with confidence and "without fear" of unexpectedly high stresses in service.

This research uncovered and quantified the benefits of the SWATH concept. It also started to define its limitations. The SWATH ship has remarkable "seakindliness" when compared to a conventional monohull surface ship. It also has much more "wetted surface" due to its twin hull configuration. This increase in wetted surface creates an unacceptable increase in frictional drag at high speeds. Attention was then focused on missions requiring relatively moderate speeds (less than thirty knots) and outstanding ride quality in heavy seas for long periods of time.[41]

Continued advocacy and the few working examples finally led to the development of a mission accepted by the Navy in 1983, an open ocean ship for towing sonar arrays. That commitment led to a rejuvenation of the concept and a procurement path calculated to bring the first SWATH ship (T-AGOS 19) into the fleet before 1990. Through the mid-1990s, SWATH ships began to find even more applications outside military circles, as in fast ferries capable of operating in rough seas.[42]

The new high-performance ship designs generated problems and research studies in other departments besides Systems Development, and Aerodynamics. Some of the new technology developments required

T-AGOS 19 SWATH Ship Under Construction.   The SWATH ship concept proved to be high in "sea-kindliness," even in extremely heavy seas.

better evaluation techniques. The Structures Department did not have the capability to evaluate large structural detail components. So the entire center bay of the structures building was committed to a versatile loading, testing, and data-gathering system that would allow the loading of ship structures in a way to accurately simulate the response to realistic at-sea conditions. The laboratory floor was used as a hold-down unit for the test set-ups; hydraulic pumping systems and loading jacks were used to provide the various loadings; and an air-conditioned room was built for controlling the tests and recording data. Rigid vinyl plastic modeling was used to study complex details as well as for modeling whole ship hulls. Drop tests generated realistic impact pressure data to validate analytic predictions and methods for design of the bottom structure of high-speed planing hulls, SES, ACVs, and hydrofoil craft. These tests consisted of dropping box structures onto calm and rough water surfaces, and using high-response pressure recording equipment to develop the data for pressure-impact design curves.[43]

Advanced Ships and Institutional Memory

Because the 100-knot goal set by Admiral Zumwalt in 1970 seemed simplistic, some of the concepts suggested to fulfill it produced little more than "cartoons" suitable for framing and posting in the halls of the Carderock offices, as was noted by George Kerr, head of Preliminary Design in NAVSEA. Nevertheless, the eventual impact of the center's work on advanced ships was of considerable significance. Although the high-visibility SES Program Office came and went, the Aerodynamics Department changed its name and its function to the Aviation and Surface Effects Department. The growth of Ford's SES group and its continuing work in testing a variety of concepts gave new vitality to the laboratory.

Even more significantly, the SES group was able to survive the demise of the program office. Operating out of departmental and center budgets, committed advocates to the principle of the SES could continue to develop working prototypes and theory. After several years, the growing interest of the Navy in fast, small craft and possibly high-speed "blue water" ships of innovative design provided new opportunities for the SES. Matrix management in the hydrofoil office, which evolved into the Systems Development Department, finally succeeded in bringing the hydrofoil, the air cushion landing craft, and eventually, the SWATH ship to the fleet. As a department, the group drew from a variety of existing units at both Carderock and Annapolis. At Annapolis, a small group that had reported to Technical Director Harold Nutt, the Advanced Ship Systems Development Group, consisting of six engineers and two support staff, had been set up in 1966 to conduct studies of amphibious ship designs and to make recommendations for candidates to be selected for further design work. After the merger of DTMB and MEL, this group was transferred to the Systems Development Department, but retained its offices at Annapolis. At Carderock, those who had participated in hydrofoil and SWATH work formed the core of the department, later supplemented by groups from Aerodynamics and from Operations Analysis work in the Applied Mathematics Laboratory.

Keeping the faith, housed in their institutional setting, the advocates and specialists could wait through the cycle of declining support. The enthusiasm of the Zumwalt era fell off in the late 1970s. But when naval interest in fast ships revived in the 1980s, the center could move rapidly to fill the new mission niches, bringing some of the background and experience in the experimental ships to bear on new problems. In the Structures Department, surface ship structural research was directed toward solutions to current design problems on more traditional dis-

Fatigue Test of Hull Structure.   In the Structures Laboratory, this large test stand subjected a ⅓-scale aluminum hull model to severe fatigue stresses. This is the largest and most complex fatigue test known to have been performed.

placement hulls. These new studies included the use of thick-skinned fiberglass hulls for minesweepers, the use of high-strength steels in helicopter landing decks located high in the hull, and the hull-deck interaction of bents in a SWATH ship. Structures Department work on surface ships also included studies in improved joining methods, the use of high strength steels, and the use of composites and aluminum.

Cross-Disciplinary Innovations in Signature Reduction

Indications that cross-disciplinary and integrative thinking were taking hold at the center showed up in the work of signature reduction and the development of low-observable ships through the 1980s. It was clear that no matter how fast a ship could skim the water, she could not outrun homing missiles. Yet, to be hit by a missile, a ship had to be detected by some means. Not only are ships visible to the eye, but they can be detected by a host of radiated "signatures" of all kinds: audible vibration, active sonar emission, heat, electromagnetic radiation including radars and radio transmission, wake in the water, and effluents such as sewage and waste. To reduce all such signatures emitted by a ship would require an effort that would cut across the traditional disciplines. Machinery would need to be silenced and its vibration reduced or dampened, and new machinery developed to handle waste. The pathways by which noise is propagated and transmitted to the air and water would need to be studied by specialists in structural mechanics. The emissions of electromagnetic radiation would require specialists in that area; the sounds of propellers and various hull forms moving through the water would require the expertise of hydrodynamicists as well as acoustics experts. The need for effective cooperative cross-disciplinary work in such areas had long been recognized at the center.

By the 1980s, the Ship Acoustics Department had played the lead role in establishing, understanding, and maturing the science of ship-generated noise from its early emphasis after World War II. For over thirty years, Carderock had brought together scientists and engineers from a broad range of technical disciplines to aggressively pursue the measurement, physical understanding, and treatment of ship-related noise. By 1980, the Ship Acoustics Department at Carderock was comprised of four broad divisions which spanned work in ship acoustics trials, sonar systems interface, ship acoustics silencing, and structural vibration and acoustics technology advancement. In addition, the Annapolis division (under the Propulsion and Auxiliary Systems Department) had broadened their efforts in machinery silencing. Some 240 Carderock personnel performed coordinated ship acoustics work in radiated and sonar self-noise trials, structure-borne and airborne noise, acoustic data processing, hydro-acoustic hull and systems vibration, and target acoustics RDT&E. Eighty Annapolis personnel were dedicated to ship machinery noise and noise isolation work. No longer would a ship be built and then "fixed" acoustically; rather, silencing considerations would be a major concern from the first design steps.[44]

As is often the case for ship design components, good hydrodynamic design does not necessarily translate to good acoustical design. Such is the case for ship propulsors. Efficient problem solving therefore required coordinated efforts between hydrodynamic and acoustics engineers. Since the mid-1970s, Maurice M. Sevik, with his strong background and interest in underwater acoustics, and William B. Morgan, with his expertise and experience leading the propulsor technology branch in the Hydromechanics Department, set the tone at the top by inspiring and promoting collaborative RDT&E efforts between personnel of both departments. During the 1980s and 1990s, this cooperative team approach was required to design quiet, efficient propulsion systems for the Navy's advanced design nuclear submarines.

Sevik envisioned a large powered submarine model operating on a quiet measurement range that would provide an improved physical understanding, through analysis and experimentation, of the overall noise mechanisms associated with dynamically interacting submarine propulsors and structures. Carderock officials proposed construction of a large-scale self-propelled horizontal-running model submarine, designated the large-scale vehicle (LSV) based on the design of the *Los Angeles* (SSN 688) class. That submarine class was chosen because of the extensive analytical, model measurement, and full-scale database that had been built up for the class. The concept was approved in 1980, but with the 1982 DOD decision to build a new class of *Seawolf* (SSN 21) nuclear submarines with advanced stealth performance, NAVSEA shifted the design of the LSV to that of the new class of submarines.

In 1984, NAVSEA awarded a contract to an industry team led by Unisys for construction of the LSV. At 88 feet long, 10 feet in diameter, and displacing 155 tons of water, the LSV became the world's largest free-running unmanned underwater vehicle. It had over 2,000 on-board sensors, on-board data recorders, guidance and navigation systems, DC motor and auxiliary machinery and propulsion and auxiliary systems batteries. The LSV, named *Kokanee*, was delivered in 1987 to the test site at Lake Pend Oreille, Idaho.[45]

Meanwhile, researchers in various departments of the center participated in the target strength reduction program. Using both full-scale models at the Idaho facility and computer-based predictive models, they helped to develop a target-strength prediction model. The prediction model proved to be a valuable design tool in assessing the potential performance of alternative hull treatments. By the mid-1980s, DTRC-developed hull treatments were installed on a number of *Sturgeon* (SSN 637) and *Los Angeles* class submarines.

Interest in controlling radar cross-section and infrared signatures of ships increased as early as 1967 after the sinking of the Israeli destroyer *Eilat* by a Soviet-built cruise missile launched from an Egyptian ship. In 1968, engineers from the Ship Materials Department conducted a demonstration on *Gyatt* (DD 712) in which several signature control measures were employed. In the mid-1970s engineers from that department developed a boundary layer induction stack suppressor system that could be used to control infrared radiation from a ship's stack. The system was installed in the *Arleigh Burke* (DDG 51) class of destroyers. At the same time, the Systems Integration Department explored total ship approaches to controlling nonacoustic signatures. Working with the

Large-Scale Vehicle (LSV).   This quarter-scale LSV is a self-powered model of the *Seawolf* (SSN 21) class. At 88 feet in length, it is the world's largest un-manned underwater vehicle.

Materials Department, they sponsored the development of the "TRACK" program at Georgia Institute of Technology, which became widely used to predict the radar cross-section of a wide variety of targets.[46]

In 1984, the mission for electromagnetic signature control was consolidated in the Central Instrumentation Department, becoming the Ship Electromagnetic Signatures Department. Engineers from both Ship Materials and Systems Integration Departments were assigned to this new department. Charles Weller worked on radar cross-sections and wake phenomena. With the development of orbital satellites that could detect ship wakes, the understanding of wakes became increasingly more important. A group including David Etherton, Peter Cervenka, and Ray Ratcliffe studied infrared phenomena on ships. In 1987, the center contracted for the acquisition of the Radar Image Modeling System to be used in measuring the radar cross-section of scaled ship models operating in the center's Maneuvering and Seakeeping Basin. In 1988, the Ship Electromagnetic Signatures Department acquired responsibility for the Santa Cruz Radar Imaging Facility.[47]

In these various ways, work on signatures more generally, and acoustic signatures in particular, had required cross-disciplinary approaches. In fact, naval acoustics work as a discipline had from its beginnings in the early post-World War II period always represented an interdisciplinary approach to problems. It brought together specialists in hydrography, oceanography, hydromechanics, physics, structures, materials, machinery, and other fields, all of whom needed to be able to think and work outside of narrow specializations. With such background, it was only natural that people concerned with silencing and with sonar detection would readily understand the need to move into further interdisciplinary and cross-departmental work.

Systems and Operational Research

Systems thinking and systems-related approaches took root in other ways at the center. As early as 1963, the DTNSRDC established an operations analysis staff, headed by John Pulos, who reported directly to Technical Director Alfred Keil. The staff of six technical specialists conducted studies related to realistic performance goals for ships and submarines, emphasizing overall ship design and operational performance effectiveness. In 1966, this small group became the military effectiveness division within a newly created ship concept research office, again, directly under the technical director. In 1968 the office was transferred to the Systems Development Office, which later became the Systems Development Department.

Meanwhile, another group developed in the Applied Mathematics Department, which also used operational theory and computer modeling of systems to quantify the relative benefits of different ship system and combat system design goals against current and projected threats. In 1966, the warfare simulation branch was formed as part of the computer-aided design division in the Applied Mathematics Department. The Warfare Simulation Branch, headed by Susan Voigt, consisted of about seven mathematicians utilizing computer models and simulations. Various computer models and simulations were acquired, developed, and used to quantify the benefits of R&D initiatives in terms of operational measures of effectiveness.[48]

Both the military effectiveness group under Pulos and the warfare simulation branch under Voigt were heavily focused on submarines and advanced ships as well as traditional surface combatants. Significant accomplishments of this group during the 1970s and early 1980s focused on conducting assessments that contributed to the introduction of significantly quieter and faster submarines with enhanced survivability and mission effectiveness. It provided a means for assessing the impact of magnetic signatures, towed arrays, torpedo evasion, acoustic counter-measures, and studies of a large number of conceptual submarine and surface designs.[49]

During the period from 1979 to 1984, the center was the technical direction agent for OPNAV 02 (Submarine Warfare) and NAVSEA 92 (Submarine) in the planning and assessment process called the Submarine Systems Engineering and Analysis (SE&A) Program. Seymour Goldstein provided on-site management and analysis program leadership interacting with these offices and with submarine program offices. The SE&A Program identified time-phased operational needs and conducted a large number of assessments leading to the definition of SSN 688 improvements and to the SSN 21.[50]

In 1984, when the Systems Development Department was reorganized into the Ship Systems Integration Department, portions of these staff groups were merged into a technical intelligence and military effectiveness office. The Director of Navy Laboratories and the Assistant Secretary of the Navy for Research, Engineering, and Systems issued guidelines. They directed the Navy's R&D Centers to "carry out programs of systems analysis comprising intelligence studies, operations research, warfare analysis, participation in fleet exercises . . . to provide an understanding of the operational support problems and opportunities facing the fleet and maritime forces."[51]

These efforts were given further external support in 1985 when DNL Gary Morton chartered a Federation of Systems Analysis Directors (FOSAD). This consisted of the heads of various center's systems analysis components. It was organized to assure that each center had a rigorous systems analysis capability to support both external sponsors and internal RDT&E programs. Furthermore, FOSAD was to facilitate and conduct integrated multicenter systems analysis trade-offs for systems or issues that crossed center charters, and to establish and utilize cost and affordability analysis as part of the systems analysis process.

When such increased emphasis on systems approaches became incorporated into naval planning and into the naval R&D establishment's approach in dealing with issues which straddled several disciplines or several R&D centers, the Carderock facility was able to bring experienced individuals and depth of background to solution of the problems. Over the next decade, as the Navy sought to apply operational research and systems thinking to larger issues of warfighting context, logistics, and signature reduction, the center was well positioned to take a leadership role in these areas.

Endnotes

1. Richard Witkin, "Missile-Armed Hydrofoil to Give U.S. Navy Light and Agile Look,"
The New York Times, 29 Nov 1971, 18; Dana Adams Schmidt, "Zumwalt Says Navy
Plans to Develop Hydrofoil and Air-Cushion Craft Faster Than Existing Vessels," *The
New York Times*, 11 Feb 1971, 13; William Beecher, "Navy Considering Plan to
Mothball 6 of 18 Carriers," *The New York Times*, 21 Oct 1970, 1, 11; "Drive For
Modern Navy—Warships That 'Fly'," *U.S. News & World Report*, 6 Dec 1971, 53–54;
Seth Hawkins, interview by Rodney Carlisle, 17 Nov 1986.
2. "Drive For Modern Navy," 53–54.
3. Ibid.; Witkin, "Missile-Armed Hydrofoil"; Schmidt, "Navy Plans to Develop
Hydrofoil"; Beecher, "Navy Plan to Mothball 6 of 18 Carriers"; John Fricker, "Air-
Cushion Vehicle Comes of Age," U.S. Naval Institute *Proceedings* 91 (Sep 1965):
139–144; M. J. Hanley, Jr., "Surface Effect Ships," U.S. Naval Institute *Proceedings* 92
(Nov 1966): 34–48; Hanley, "60-Knot Landing Force," U.S. Naval Institute *Proceedings*
93 (Mar 1967): 45–55; J. V. Jolliff and G. D. Kerr, "Designing for Change: Present
and Future," U.S. Naval Institute *Proceedings* 100 (Jul 1974): 30–38.
4. George F. Crouch to Stevens Institute of Technology, 20 Nov 1945; and T. A. Solberg
to Chief of Research and Inventions, 5 Mar 1946, WNRC, RG 181, acc. 7681, box
160-4, Misc. Inquiries 1946; James J. Stilwell and William R. Porter, "Naval Use of
Hydrofoil Craft," U.S. Naval Institute *Proceedings* 89 (Feb 1963): 60–69; Robert E.
Nystrom, "The Role of the Hydrofoil Special Trials Unit (HYSTU) in the U.S. Navy
Hydrofoil Programme," Paper presented at Second International Conference,
Hovering Craft Hydrofoils Advanced Transit Systems, RAI Exhibition and Congress
Centre, Amsterdam, 17–20 May 1976.
5. Mark Thornton, "Success, Frustration, And Now, Perhaps, Recognition," *Hovering
Craft and Hydrofoil* 18 (Aug 1979): 4–8; Nils Salvesen, "A Note on the Seakeeping
Characteristics of Small Waterplane-Area Twin-Hull Ships," AIAA SNAME-USN
Advanced Marine Vehicles Meeting, Annapolis, Maryland, 17–19 Jul 1972, AIAA
Paper No. 72-606.
6. Allen Ford, interview by Rodney Carlisle, 6 Feb 1987.
7. Ibid.; "DTNSRDC's Role in Surface Effect Ship Development," reprint from
Centerline, 4 Apr 1980 (hereafter referred to as *Centerline*, 4 Apr 1980).
8. Ford interview, 6 Feb 1987.
9. Ibid.; Edward A. Butler, ed., "The Surface Effect Ship," *JASNE* 97 (Feb 1985):
214–215; see also photographs in *Centerline*, 4 Apr 1980.
10. Ford interview, 6 Feb 1987; *Centerline*, 4 Apr 1980; Dr. Alan Powell papers, Technical
Directorate Items, Aviation & Surface Effects Department, period ending 18 Jun
1976, DTNSRDC Archives, box 1, Tech. Directorate Items 1976, file 17.
11. Ibid.
12. *Centerline*, 4 Apr 1980.
13. Butler, "The Surface Effect Ship," 210.
14. Ibid.; Cindy Howard, "From Research to Reality, 'John Wayning it' on the SES-200,"
Centerline, 9 Aug 1985, 1, 4–6.
15. William Ellsworth, interview by Rodney Carlisle, Oct 1984.

16. Ibid.
17. Nystrom, "The Role of the Hydrofoil Special Trials Unit"; Stilwell and Porter, "Naval Use of Hydrofoil Craft," 60–69. The story of these two hydrofoils is presented in William M. Ellsworth, *Twenty Foilborne Years: The U.S. Navy Hydrofoil High Point PCH-l* (DTNSRDC, 1987).
18. Ellsworth interview, 1 Oct 1984.
19. "Hydrofoil Special Trials Unit Charter and Operating Plan," WNRC, RG 181, acc. 73A-2241, box 3, 9010/Hydrofoil—Hydrofoil Design Tests.
20. Ibid.; Ellsworth interview, 1 Oct 1984.
21. Ellsworth interview, 1 Oct 1984.
22. Hugh A. Burkons to Commander, Thirteenth Naval District, and Commander, Naval Ship Research and Development Center, 24 Feb 1969, WNRC, RG 181, acc. 73A-241, box 4, 9080/High Point,; "Situation Report, Hydrofoil Development Program Office," 10 Mar 1969, 16 Jun 1969, and 1 Aug 1969, WNRC, RG 181, acc. 73A-2241, box 3, 9010/Hydrofoil—Hydrofoil Design Tests; W. M. Ellsworth to Commander, Naval Ship Systems Command, 8 Dec 1969, WNRC, RG 181, acc. 73A-2241, box 4, 9080/High Point.
23. Ellsworth interview, 1 Oct 1984.
24. William M. Ellsworth and Dennis J. Clark, "Ship Design and the Navy Laboratory," *Naval Engineers Journal* (Apr 1981): 37.
25. Boeing Marine Systems advertisement, *Naval Engineers Journal* 97 (Feb 1985): 6–7.
26. Ellsworth and Clark, "Ship Design and the Navy Laboratory," 33–46.
27. "JEFF" is not an acronym. The craft was named after Jeff Schuler, a son of Jim Schuler who was the R&D Program Manager for Advanced Ships and Craft in NAVSEA from 1961 to 1985.
28. "Amphibious Assault Landing Craft Experimental Trials Unit Charter," 16 Jun 1977, NHC, NLCCG Archives, DTNSRDC RC 7, series 6, acc. 84-12, box 6.
29. "Detachment: AALC Trials Unit," n.d., NHC, NLCCG Archives, DTNSRDC RC 7, series 6, acc. 84-12, box 6.
30. Ibid.
31. Ellsworth interview, 1 Oct 1984.
32. Thornton, "Success, Frustration, & Now, Perhaps, Recognition," 4–8.
33. Fendall Marbury, Jr., "Small Prototypes of Ships—Theory and a Practical Example," *Naval Engineers Journal* 85 (Oct 1973): 35–48; Reuven Leopold, "A New Hull Form for High-Speed, Volume-Limited, Displacement-Type Ships," Paper presented at SNAME Spring Meeting, May 1969; H. M. Jonckheere, "The Control for the Heave and Pitch of a Semi-submarine in Regular Astern Waves," Massachusetts Institute of Technology DSR Project No. 8073, Jan 1963.
34. Marbury, "Small Prototypes of Ships," 35–48; E. Stafford, *Little Ship, Big War* (New York: Morrow, 1984; paperback edition), 300.
35. Marbury, "Small Prototypes of Ships," 35–48.
36. Ibid., 49–51.
37. Seth Hawkins and Theodore Sarchin, "The Small Waterplane-Area Twin Hull (SWATH) Program—A Status Report," Paper presented at AIAA/SNAME Advanced Marine Vehicles Conference, San Diego, California, 25–27 Feb 1974, AIAA Paper No. 74-324.
38. Jerry L. Gore, ed., "SWATH Ships," *Naval Engineers Journal* 97 (Feb 1985): 84–85.
39. Ibid., 85–107.
40. Ibid., 83–84.
41. Communication, William Ellsworth to the author, 21 Aug 1987.

42. Gore, "SWATH Ships," 105; Robert Lamb, interview by Rodney Carlisle, 6 Feb 1987. For later applications, see for example, *Marine Log,* Oct 1996, cover story and advertisements.

43. Material on Structures Department derived from Peter Palermo report, ABIF.

44. Material on signature reduction derived from Brian Bowers report, 8 Oct 1996, ABIF.

45. Ibid.

46. Ibid

47. Material on operations research and FOSAD derived from Seymour Goldstein report, 18 Jun 1996, ABIF.

48. Ibid.

49. Ibid.

50. Ibid.

51. Ibid.

CHAPTER 12

Paths Taken and Not Taken

T HE ORIGINAL TASKS SET BY DAVID TAYLOR at the Navy Yard Model Basin in 1900 included several disciplines. As the laboratory grew over the years, it gradually added new fields and equipment, new talents and capabilities. The Annapolis laboratory, from its beginning, had been conceived as a laboratory with a range of experts in various engineering disciplines and the work at the two facilities always reflected a measure of diversity. By the 1970s and 1980s, that diversity had become a source of strength, even though it might be hard to summarize to outsiders in public relations literature or even to potential sponsors in NAVSEA.

In World War II the immediate and practical questions dominated: improved torpedoes, lighter diesel engines, effects of depth charges, appropriate camouflage. The pressures of war shunted long-range research and development aside, such as the gas turbine development, repeatedly postponed by priorities on metals, shop time, and personnel. In the postwar years, research expanded in hydrodynamics, wave motion, acoustics, propulsion engineering, and a growing group of materials and structural specialties.

By the 1970s the diversity had increased through the internal institutional growth and accretion of new capabilities. Other sources of the diversity were the merger of the two laboratories and the Navy's effort to consolidate its scattered facilities into larger units by bringing in groups such as the materials specialists from the Naval Applied Science Laboratory in New York. Advanced work could now be expected to come from any of about forty divisions organized within the seven major departments or laboratories. After the two facilities had merged into one center, the range of projects could be attributed partly to the rich variety of capabilities that came as a consequence of the component units' long institutional history and growth.

Researchers grumbled at the increasingly unpredictable nature of the bureaucracy that gave DTNSRDC its rudder orders. Even more frustrating, a very promising technological lead or innovation developed by the center's experts would be temporarily supported, only to be abandoned by those holding the purse strings. As a result, the leadership of the newly named David Taylor Naval Ship Research and Development Center had good reason to be concerned over adhering to their "mission," and to attempt to find resources for seeing a project through to a recognized accomplishment.

Through the 1970s and early 1980s the technical director of the center, Alan Powell, conducted meetings every two weeks with the department heads, in a group which he called the technical directorate. These discussions focused on current and possible new work, with crowded agendas regarding funding and capability. The diverse heritage and the changing needs of the Navy combined to swamp these meetings with dozens of topics. The minutes and agendas reflected a clear tension between a natural desire to be responsive to what the Navy needed done and a contrary desire to concentrate on proven areas of strength, outstanding qualifications, and the pressure to stick with a promising beginning until clear results could be demonstrated. Each meeting seemed to reflect the classic tension between technological "push" and requirements "pull." Whether or not any particular project fit the ship R&D mission, and whether it could be absorbed, if properly funded, by one or more of the Carderock or Annapolis teams became a time-consuming and difficult debate. Through the patterns of rich diversity, several themes can be identified over the decade following the war in Vietnam.[1]

Pursuing Excellence

With the acquisition of the advanced ship systems work on hydrofoils, SES, SWATH ships, and the LCAC, some special focus had emerged. Yet in aerodynamics, computer studies, and propulsion, researchers made innovations and progress on a wide variety of fronts through the 1970s that did not bear directly on the design of those particular new ships and craft.

Much of the work and progress derived from a steady application of theory and state-of-the-art equipment to agenda items inherited from the Bureau of Engineering and the Bureau of Construction and Repair, and carried forward under BUSHIPS and then under NAVSHIPS, NAVSEA, and NAVMAT. Such technology was by no means simply a matter of routine; application of contemporary equipment and knowledge to long-standing research problems could be demanding, difficult, and fascinating, and could lead to major accomplishments. But funding of applied technology was not always assured. In the 1970s, the center took pride in one growing new area of applied technology—the flourishing use of computers on a range of problems. A new tool with new capabilities was being exploited; application after application helped on long-standing processes and problems.[2]

In several areas, a defined future naval need would set the agenda. While helicopters could take off and land vertically, their top speed was severely limited to about 150 knots. By contrast, fixed-wing jet aircraft had passed through the transonic to supersonic speeds and beyond. The two developments of the helicopter and the jet had created a "presumed anomaly"—two types of aircraft, each with almost contradictory capabilities, which the Navy would like to see combined in a single craft. That had been the goal of V/STOL (vertical short take-off and landing) designs, but by the 1970s, no fully satisfactory design had emerged.[3]

Work in the Aerodynamics Department through the 1970s concentrated on a design of a helicopter that would move forward into the speed range of jet aircraft. Aero examined several promising solutions to this particular problem leading, by the 1980s, to work on a very innovative concept, the "X- wing" aircraft.

In other areas progress was driven by the fact that a particular, existing innovation could not be applied in its optimal fashion. The "front" of progress had moved forward, leaving one stubborn area behind, like an enemy salient or enclave in a battlefield, that then drew attack. Work on gas turbines, contracted out from EES in the 1940s, produced engines that moved into several application niches in the Navy. By the early 1970s they powered light auxiliary craft, hydrofoils, surface effect ships, and amphibious assault landing craft. Nevertheless, the turbine, with its high speed and torque, had not been applied to larger ships, leaving this role to the older steam turbines, diesel engines, and to nuclear power. Here was a salient that invited attack.[4]

This particular salient was attacked on several flanks, two of which led to major accomplishments at the center. The issue of transmission of power and the issue of shifting power from forward to astern motion— the "reverse gear" of an automobile or small powerboat—both engaged the center's specialists. These transmission problems paralleled those associated with the introduction of the steam turbine at the opening of the century. Like the steam turbine, the gas turbine produced such high-speed revolutions and high torque at its most efficient speeds that gearing and reduction of speed to the propeller was essential. Reduction gears, using the helical design worked out by George Melville and Joseph MacAlpine for the steam turbine, were extremely large and heavy. Increased weight of the gears worked against the turbine advantages, and the mechanical gearing system imposed limits on selection of the optimal turbine speed.

One path to a solution involved the revival of an earlier concept, that is, electrical power generation by the turbine and the use of electric motor drive. The electric drive offered several advantages, already demonstrated in practice on earlier steam turbine-electric and diesel-electric systems. Generator and motor speed could be completely independent, using electrical transmission to reduce the high revolutions of the turbine to the necessary slower revolutions of the propeller. Electric cables were far lighter than direct drive shafts. Furthermore, the cables did not have to be lined up directly between the turbine and the propeller, thus allowing for better location of equipment inside the ship. Yet there were problems that had always been associated with the electric drive approach: electric motors were themselves quite heavy, and they operated with a loss of efficiency. Methods of improving electric motor efficiency could assist in the search for a way to get the best use of a turbine. The laboratory concept of "superconductivity" offered promise. Heike Kamerlingh Onnes, a Dutch physicist, had discovered the phenomenon in 1911, winning a 1913 Nobel Prize for his work in the study of low- temperature properties of helium and metals. Onnes demonstrated that electrical resistance of certain metals almost vanished when they were cooled to near absolute zero. With the improvement in cryogenic technology in the 1960s, researchers in governmental, university, and private laboratories studied the superconductivity phenomenon, especially concentrating on applications to electronic circuitry and to electrical power transmission. Experiments with various metals and alloys led to the rapid accumulation of empirical knowledge of their properties at very low temperature.[5]

A group of physicists, including John Bardeen of the University of Illinois, developed a comprehensive theory of superconductivity for which they received a Nobel Prize in 1972. The combination of empirical studies and the new theoretical base stimulated even more studies. At the Annapolis site of DTNSRDC, a team began working on the concept of an electric motor with crucial parts cooled and working as superconductors that would be vastly more efficient than a conventional motor of the same size and weight. Such a motor, if meeting the theoretically possible efficiencies, would go far toward solving the problem of transmission of gas turbine power aboard ships of the destroyer and cruiser scale.[6]

Whether improved through superconductivity or through another approach, a turbine-generator-motor system would still present the other barrier—that is, the difficulty of changing from forward to astern motion. While an electric motor could be reversed through switching, the delay of bringing the motor itself to a full stop and reversing its shaft direction contributed to poor performance in maneuvering. While separate or auxiliary motors geared and clutched to the shaft could be used for "reverse," that alternative only increased weight. If a propeller were designed with controllable or reversible pitch, then the shaft would continue to turn in the same direction, but the shift from forward to reverse would be at the prop itself. Previous designs of controllable pitch propellers had proven the value of the concept, but for very high shaft horsepower, the approach had been rejected in favor of clutch-gear and reverse engine drives. With consideration of the best use of gas turbines, propeller designers revived the controllable pitch approach.[7]

Progress on the gas turbine had left behind the large ships; the search for solutions to the problems of transmission and reversibility in electric work and in propeller design produced, by the early 1980s, durable models of new controllable pitch propellers and compact, but large-scale, working models of highly efficient superconducting electric motors. The center could boast of major accomplishments in both attacks on the "salient" of turbine application.

In the long view, each of the three classic patterns of progress gives some keys to the diverse work of the center: applied technology bringing existing developments to bear on current or long-standing problems; presumed anomalies generating searches for a future design; and work on the stubborn gaps on the front of progress; applying either recent science, as in superconductivity, or the revival and adaptation of existing ideas, as with controllable pitch propellers. But when viewed up close at the time, progress went forward unevenly, on a wide scattering of projects. Behind that uneven pattern was the issue of financial support, which was, as always, subject to the decision-making process of the Navy. It remained centered in the systems commands and their program offices.

Vietnam Laboratory Assistance Program

In early August 1964, North Vietnamese torpedo boat maneuvers near the United States destroyers *Maddox* (DD 731) and *C. Turner Joy* (DD 951) led to an exchange of fire. In response to this "Gulf of Tonkin

Incident," on 5 August, President Johnson introduced the Tonkin Gulf Resolution to Congress. The resolution gave the President broad powers in responding to attacks on American forces and it served as the basis for the subsequent increased U.S. involvement in the Vietnam War.

In late 1966 Assistant Secretary of the Navy for Research and Development Robert Frosch asked Gerald Johnson, Director of Navy Laboratories, to increase technical support to the war effort in Vietnam as the intensity of combat increased. In response, Johnson established the Vietnam Laboratory Assistance Program (VLAP). In 1968, the Naval Ordnance Laboratory at White Oak took over coordination of the whole VLAP.

VLAP provided quick-response technical support to U.S. naval forces in combat by sending scientists and engineers to Vietnam for extended periods to observe problems of the operating forces first hand and to work quickly to solve the problems. The initial ground rules for solution to problems set a six-month time frame and a cost per solution of no more than $50,000. Most of the support was focused on Navy coastal and riverine operations and Marine Corps operations in the Northern sector.

VLAP recruited, trained, and sent sixty-one scientists and engineers as laboratory representatives to Vietnam for periods generally of four to six months. They were assigned temporary duty with the Navy R&D Unit Vietnam (NRDU-V), under the Commander Naval Forces Vietnam (COMNAVFORV). B. M. Shepard asked NSRDC Deputy Technical Director Harold Nutt to select someone from Annapolis with small craft expertise to accompany him to Vietnam. Nutt selected Jerry Gore for this assignment to solve small craft performance and suitability deficiencies plaguing the riverine forces. In the summer of 1967 Gore spent several months in Vietnam gathering data on small craft problems. Upon his return to Annapolis, he worked on a project to reduce the noise of patrol craft engines and returned to Vietnam in 1968 to test the new devices.

Barry Pifer was selected to be the coordinator of VLAP at NSRDC. He went to Vietnam in November 1967, and in March 1968 Jim Corder replaced him there. Six senior scientists, including Hi Nutt, were also sent to serve different tours as science advisors to the commander. Pifer continued to serve as NSRDC coordinator of the program until 1971. VLAP field representatives participated in combat operations to identify technical problems that impacted warfighting and reported these problems back to Navy laboratory management.

NSRDC, which during this period included the facilities at Panama City as well as at Carderock and Annapolis, completed almost 100 of the

Shock Seats, Armored Troop Carrier.   As part of some 100 projects in direct aid of U.S. forces in Vietnam, engineers at Carderock designed these special shock protection decks and seats to absorb mine detonations.

544 VLAP-sponsored projects between 1967 and 1972. Most of the NSRDC projects related to small craft, mine countermeasures, and swimmer countermeasures. For small craft, the main thrusts included acoustic quieting, shock and fragmentation protection systems, and ferro-cement as a material for boat building by the Vietnamese. While Carderock and Annapolis conducted R&D on these projects, Panama City concentrated on mine and swimmer countermeasures.

The war in Vietnam demanded of the Navy not high technology and sophistication but a return to basics in the perfection and development of long-neglected designs, such as river craft. Not since the days of

Riverine Craft, *Viper II*.   Under both the Vietnam Laboratory Assistance Program as well as direct systems command sponsorship, the center made numerous improvements to riverine craft, such as this ferro-cement boat *Viper II* that saw action in the Vietnam War.

the Civil War monitors and the China river gunboats had the Navy focused on "brown water" craft as distinct from the high seas, "blue water" ships. The challenges of riverine warfare resulted in many innovative concepts, including design and construction support for several ferro-cement coastal and riverine patrol boats, armor to defeat shaped-charge warheads, kevlar blankets to prevent fragmentation damage, collapsible decks to defeat mineblast shock, numerous systems to defeat hostile swimmers (lighting, electric barriers, detection devices, nets and drags), and mine countermeasure devices (small boat drones, and chain drags).

   The center also provided technical assistance outside of VLAP at the direct request of the systems commands. For example, problems related to general purpose bomb separation from certain aircraft led to intensive wind tunnel testing to provide solutions.

   In 1970, the success of VLAP prompted DNL Joel Lawson to set up a program to provide naval science advisors to other Navy commands. It was designated the Naval Science Assistance Program (NSAP). NSAP emphasized the advantages of improving communications with the fleet and provided a "real world" training ground for laboratory personnel.[8]

NSAP first supported the Sixth Fleet in the Mediterranean and the Commander Naval Forces Korea (COMNAVFORK). By 1975, the program expanded to thirteen Navy and Marine Corps commands. In the first five years seventy-two scientists and engineers took temporary duty with the commands supported. Thirteen scientists and engineers from the David Taylor center provided on-site support to six different operational commands between 1970 and 1983. In addition, the center worked on more than sixty NSAP projects, with about twenty-five in response to requests from the Naval Forces Korea Command. In the period from 1971 to 1975, the U.S. sought to promote Korean navy self-sufficiency, and center projects supporting Korea focused primarily on combatant craft design, manufacturing, test, and evaluation. Other navy projects related to acoustics, machinery, and materials for U.S. Navy surface and submarine operational commands.

Even as the Vietnam War wound down in the early 1970s, national concerns with energy conservation and petroleum shortages tapped some of the skills and talents of the center. Such popular concerns stimulated support for particular projects with shipboard application. Interest in energy conservation helped win advocates for the advanced electric motor work. Environmental awareness and worry over pollution happened to coincide with naval attempts to reduce the signature of ships left by oil, garbage, and sound and electromagnetic emission. Although the Navy sought undetected operation and satisfaction of a growing public worried over protecting the environment, the two objectives could coincide.[9]

On the whole, Powell and the department heads resisted the temptation to wander too far afield. Limited discretionary funds allowed preliminary pursuit of promising ideas. Furthermore, the departments were free to take on contracts from other units of the government. Despite all sorts of available funding and projects discussed at the biweekly directorate meetings, the center made it a policy to seek those that fell closest to the specialties already developed, such as taking some jobs for the Maritime Administration and the Coast Guard. Although Powell did not approve of the term "marketing," he and others within the departments worked very effectively at advancing their ideas for further research to NAVSEA and other sponsors.[10]

The X-wing—A Path Partially Pursued

Among the projects of the 1970s and early 1980s in which the center took the most pride by including in lists of "major accomplishments," were the X-wing fixed/rotor aircraft, the superconducting electric motor, the controllable pitch propeller, and new computer programs for the analysis of magnetic signatures of ships. The new propulsor design for SSN 21, installed in *Seawolf*, similarly had first been conceived in the 1970s, in a committee chaired by Maurice Sevik and then developed over a period of more than a decade, tested on *Kokanee* in Idaho. The list of "Major Accomplishments" also included many of the projects which had begun before, or that had been completed by, 1970. The list included such earlier achievements as the work on HY-80 steel, the design of deep submergence rescue vehicles (DSRVs), studies of the use of titanium for submarine structural systems, and a range of contributions in acoustics, in ship protection, and in a few areas in which the accomplishments themselves remained classified through the whole period and into the present. There were major advances in work on protection of surface ships from airblast as well as improvement of aircraft carrier magazines against missiles.[11]

Since the inception of the helicopter, aircraft designers sought ways to combine the vertical lift capability of the helicopter with the higher forward speeds possible with fixed-wing aircraft. The vertical take-off and landing (VTOL) designs of the 1960s followed two paths, both of which suffered from built-in limitations. One approach was to add wings and auxiliary propulsion to the helicopter—the so-called "compound helicopter." The other approach was to deflect the thrust of cruise engines on a fixed-wing aircraft by various designs of tilted wings or tilted engines, so that the machine could achieve lift.

While these approaches to the VTOL concept had merit, their handicaps had prevented deployment of such craft in the Navy in that era. The compound helicopter suffered from the drag of the helicopter blades and from the excess weight of added wings, dual control systems, and auxiliary engines. The deflected-thrust approach on fixed-wing aircraft required great power and fuel consumption in hover, since the area swept by the propellers was small; the direct lift of a jet engine in such a configuration had to approach rocket heat, force, and fuel consumption to achieve vertical lift. The down-wash from a jet or prop system of deflected thrust would make it impossible to fill the rescue mission of helicopters; those being "rescued" would either be fried or scrambled, or both.[12]

In both Great Britain and the United States in the late 1960s, designers sought solutions to these barriers and deficiencies to better blend the virtues of the helicopter and the airplane. In both countries one approach was the concept of a "stowed rotor." Both Sikorsky and

Lockheed proposed to the Air Force similar designs. In these plans a conventional helicopter rotor would lift the craft, then the rotor would be stopped, folded, and mechanically lowered into the fuselage, as the craft proceeded as a fixed-wing airplane. The stowed rotor would not present drag and the airplane would be able to achieve the same speeds as an equal size and weight jet or propeller-driven airplane. But this plan suffered from the problem of excessive added weight for the necessary machinery, with the consequence of reduced payload.[13]

In Great Britain in 1965, Ian Cheeseman of the University of Southampton considered a novel approach to the stowed-rotor problem for a vertical take-off and landing commercial airliner. Cheeseman planned to make use of the Coanda effect, named after Henri Coanda, a Romanian scientist who had discovered in 1911 that air forced over a curved surface will follow the contour. When applied to an airfoil, the result is increased lift. Cheeseman conducted experiments with rounded rotors, using a forced air current from inside the rotor to get the Coanda effect. The increased lift would allow for smaller and therefore lighter rotors for equivalent-sized aircraft, thus addressing the weight and payload problem on the stowed-rotor version of the compound helicopter. But the British National Gas Turbine Establishment, which sponsored Chceseman's work, had to cut back funding in 1967, and his particular approach was carried no further.[14]

Cheeseman's idea of using the Coanda effect through forced air was an early effort to utilize "circulation control" to enhance rotor efficiency. That approach soon bore fruit in a related application developed at the David Taylor Naval Ship Research and Development Center.

At the center's Aerodynamics Laboratory, Robert Williams, working with Harvey Chaplin, picked up on the Cheeseman work. Whereas Cheeseman had visualized the application of a circulation control enhanced and stowable rotor on a commercial airliner, Williams and Chaplin considered applying the idea to the Navy's need for a smaller VTOL or faster helicopter for landing and takeoff on small, destroyer-size ships. They recognized that Cheeseman's use of circulation control would allow for a smaller rotor for the same amount of lift. As they studied the problem, a new approach to increasing helicopter speed occurred to them.[15]

A technical problem in helicopter flight could be addressed through the circulation control concept. As conventionally bladed helicopters increase in speed, they normally stall at a speed in the range of 150 to 200 miles per hour. A rotor blade cuts into the air with its forward edge rounded and its trailing edge tapered to a sharp edge, providing lift. As the rotor turns, sweeping forward on the right and backward on the left in its circle, it lifts the craft. The stalling at the relatively slow flight speed of 150 miles per hour derives from the fact that at such a speed, a turning rotor on the "retreating" half of its turning circle begins to experience a change in the direction of airflow over the blade. The aircraft is simply moving forward faster than the blade is rotating rearward. In effect, the retreating blade is cutting the air backwards and is in a sense partly dead in the air (stalled) because it is not shaped to produce lift in "reversed" flow.

Circulation control could help the craft through the stalling phase by taking advantage not only of the high lift capability but also of the fact that both edges of a circulation control airfoil are rounded. Whichever edge has the blowing applied will function the same as the sharp edge of a conventional blade. Thus, it would not matter which edge of the blade faced into the wind because the blowing could simply be switched from one edge to the other as the relative airflow direction reversed locally on the rotor. Once past the stall speed, the rotor would begin to approach the efficiency of a fixed-wing aircraft.

As they worked on this approach, an entirely novel idea occurred to them. If a rotor could be aerodynamically enhanced by circulation control blowing, then it might be possible to design an aircraft without the dual lift system of both rotors and wings. With the unique properties of circulation control, it might be possible to convert rotors, by stopping them, into wings and back to rotors. Once perceived, the idea was "technically sweet" in that it made good sense. Achieving an acceptable design would, however, require surmounting many structural, control, and safety problems.[16]

When the rotor was converted to a wing, there would be no limit to the forward speed of the aircraft except that of the aerodynamics of the plane, the power of the propulsion system, and the structural strength of the wings and craft. Thus, it could readily move into the supersonic range of over 700 miles per hour. The concept could represent a true marriage in which the virtues of the helicopter and the jet were merged in the hybrid offspring.

Several factors made such an idea seem reasonable in the early 1970s, whereas it would have been immediately dismissed, or not pursued at all, in an earlier era. Advances in other areas of technology made the whole concept worth exploring when the two men conceived of the new craft. One necessary prior advance was in computer and electronic design. Rapid opening and closing of valves to change the aerodynamic characteristics on each revolution of the blade would be required. A purely electromechanical distributor system simply would

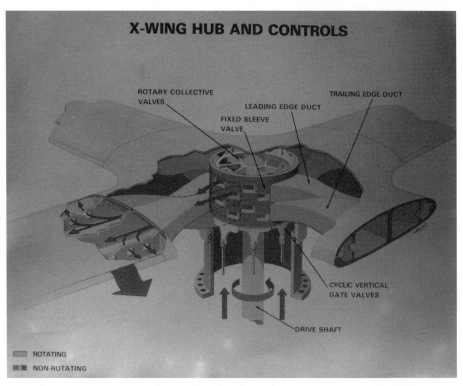

X-Wing Hub. Combining several innovative concepts, the aircraft design allowed conversion of helicopter lift blades into wings for high speed forward motion.

not keep up. Only a reliable high-speed computer could allow for such a control system.

Another necessary development was in the area of materials and structures. Only an extremely strong, lightweight material could endure the stress and remain rigid. Graphite composite materials introduced by the early 1970s made the design a conceivable possibility. Still another advance came in the design of turbine engines. By the late 1970s, General Electric produced a "convertible turbine" that could deliver power either to a shaft or as thrust, or in a mixed proportion of both shaft and thrust. Such a system would allow for a single engine set to drive the rotor, provide the pumped air for circulation control, and to be used for forward thrust.[17]

Williams and Chaplin worked on the stopped-rotor idea, using discretionary center funding in 1973 and 1974. In 1975 they developed a model rotor and tested the principles in wind tunnel experiments. In 1975-1976 they published their ideas and first used the phrase "X-wing" in the open literature to describe the whole concept. Chaplin ap-

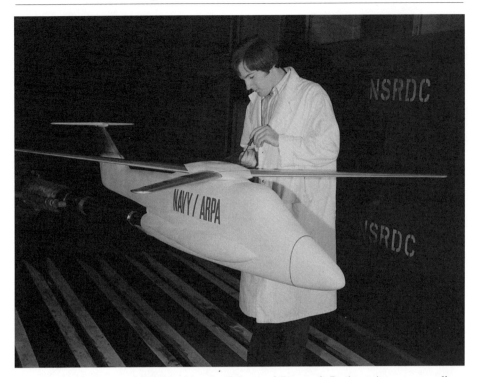

X-Wing Model.   Sponsored by the Advanced Research Projects Agency as well as by the Navy, the X-wing held out promise as an air-sea rescue vehicle. A path not taken, the Navy turned from the X-wing to the *Osprey* for V/STOL.

proached Naval Air Systems Command (NAVAIR) and the Defense Advanced Research Projects Agency (DARPA), receiving funds in 1975 to proceed with the work. While NAVAIR saw promise in the concept, DARPA's function was to fund high-risk research, and the innovative concept met their guidelines for a completely new approach to a military mission. A request for bids was issued by DARPA, and Lockheed responded with a proposal to develop a large-scale rotor to test further the concept. The Lockheed proposal was funded in October 1976.[18]

Instead of developing a small 3,200-pound demonstrator model, the program manager at DARPA decided to go directly to a contract for a 32,000-pound prototype, and to open the competition to other firms in the aircraft industry. Boeing-Vertol and Sikorsky Aircraft Company were chosen to participate. In the period 1979–1982 the two firms reviewed and assessed the status of the technology base, as DTNSRDC staff transferred what they had already learned to the two aircraft firms.[19]

Both companies helped provide independent evaluations of the work done so far. After the initial assessment of the concept, "follow-on" contracts were issued to each company to proceed with evaluation of particular designs of full-scale aircraft. Boeing-Vertol designed and fabricated a ten-foot scale model operating at full speed to confirm the capabilities of the X-wing. Sikorsky concentrated on the fabrication of the carbon-composite blades and the air valving of the circulation control system. As a consequence of these projects, DARPA identified a variety of optional designs and settled on one that would be the least expensive and that would lead to an operating model in a relatively short period. After evaluation of the DARPA-funded work, NASA joined in support of the project and helped provide funds for the development of a research craft. The RSRA/X-wing was ready for flight testing in 1987.[20]

Like the development of the hydrofoil, the SES, the LCAC, and the SWATH ship, the X-wing moved from conception to the verge of deployment along a schedule of about twenty years. However, it did not find an ultimate military customer, as the Marine Corps and industry backed other approaches to the vertical lift problem. Like many other R&D projects, the X-wing became the story of a "might have been," shelved, perhaps for a decade, perhaps forever, because alternative paths were taken.

The Promise of Superconducting Machines

The work in superconductivity through 1980s represented another promising path partially pursued. The physicists and engineers at Annapolis who worked on applying superconductivity to ship propulsion found the work exciting, innovative, and challenging. Researchers like Howard Stevens, who started at Annapolis in the early 1960s, would later remark that the work on the project made it a real pleasure to come in every day. The staff worked almost without regard to the paycheck—the demand and the excitement of the project itself, he claimed, made participation seem a privilege.[21]

By the late 1970s this enthusiastic team had built a machine that proved quite efficient. The motor, if scaled up and properly applied, would allow for efficient use of gas turbine engines on ships of destroyer and frigate classes. Propulsion systems that would incorporate such a motor would be lighter, would occupy less space, and would permit optimum operation of the prime mover, the gas turbine itself. Yet even with all this promise, the Navy did not decide to move toward the application of the system in the fleet.

That negative decision reflected the Navy's essentially conservative tradition, a conservatism that was founded on experience. "High technology," with its risk and high expense, had proven essential for particular areas such as new sensing devices, new methods of concealing a ship's location, the perfection of new weapons, and developing entirely new ships and aircraft which filled previously vacant niches, such as the LCAC.

But advanced electric drive possible with superconducting parts would only improve upon existing classes of ships, adding a margin of efficiency and reduced weight. The need for research and development expenditure was far less convincing than the higher priorities of weapons, concealment, communication, and speed. Yet the superconducting electric drive work proved that the device could be practicable. The story, like that of the X-wing, is no less a part of the history of DTNSRDC accomplishments of the 1970s than the success stories of devices introduced into the fleet.

During the rapid advances with superconductivity in the 1960s and early 1970s that grew out of work with new metals and improved cryogenic refrigeration equipment, and with the publication of the basic theory by Bardeen and others, there was a rush to find applications for superconductivity at such Atomic Energy Commission laboratories as Brookhaven, at university laboratories, and at the Bureau of Standards. The fact that one could use superconductivity to obtain a visible manifestation of a micro phenomenon at the quantum level attracted physicists all over the world.[22]

As a consequence, engineers simultaneously worked on parallel paths. At both Annapolis, Maryland, and Panama City, Florida, researchers considered how superconductivity might provide improvements in electromagnetic sensing devices used in locating submarines and surface ships. As the missions of the various laboratories became more clearly defined during the organizational revolution of the Navy in the mid-1960s, the Annapolis work on this particular application closed down. However, experience in the application of superconductivity could not be simply thrown away, so researchers turned their attention to work more clearly suited to the NSRDC mission.[23]

For the team of about twenty researchers engaged at Annapolis, the idea held several intrinsic advantages for propulsion. Since supercooled windings in a motor would have no resistance, in theory, an engineer could get four or five times as much power out of a given-size motor, without the superconducting winding. Although power would be needed to cool the parts, vacuum insulation and proper construction would mean that "a very low price would be paid" to maintain the cold state.

At the time Annapolis researchers began thinking through the concept of motor application, some parallel work went forward in Great Britain, where experimenters built a 3,000-horsepower motor incorporating superconducting parts. The innovative motor was put to work in an industrial pumping station. From an engineer's viewpoint, the device proved out the idea. Yet several elements made it less attractive as a more public demonstration. The British design used superconducting shielding around the whole motor, which increased the overall size of the unit. Furthermore, as with any innovative machine, "down time" for repairs, readjustments, and part fabrication reduced its profitability in a commercial application.

In the United States, other laboratories also worked on the possibilities of superconducting machines. The Army Corps of Engineers placed a contract with AVCO Everett Laboratories, through Fort Belvoir, to build a small generator that would demonstrate the applied principle. John Stekly, an engineer with AVCO, developed a design that embedded super-cooled windings in a copper matrix that allowed for absolute zero resistance.[24]

At Annapolis the team focused on motors as part of the drive system for ships. The use of an electric drive in ships had a long history. During World War II the shortage of gear-cutting capacity had made electric propulsion a necessary choice. Widely used on the workhorse tanker of the war, the T-2, the system had proven durable and dependable. A generator-motor "transmission" actually weighed more than an equivalent gear-train, but the electric system offered other advantages in flexibility of arrangement and reduced shaft length. The overall savings in space and weight helped offset the loss of power efficiency in generation of electricity and in the relatively low efficiency of electric motors themselves. During the war such motors were "bipolar," that is, the rotors' magnetic poles constantly alternated direction. Earlier efforts to develop an efficient "homopolar," or single, noncycling field rotor, had ceased by about 1930.[25]

In 1973, as Annapolis worked with the idea of designing a superconducting motor, the researchers made several design choices, choosing components and concepts from the growing experimental work done at Westinghouse and General Electric, and by smaller research firms, some associated with MIT. The Annapolis group revived the idea of a homopolar or "acyclic" motor, which became more attractive with the high voltage-low current expected with superconductivity. They used superconducting wire, made of the newly developed metal niobium-tin, cryogenically cooled and embedded in a copper matrix that would maintain the necessary low temperature, applying Stekly's idea developed with the AVCO experimental generator.[26]

One unreliable and bulky alternative attempted in the British work had been an attempt to provide shielding for the whole motor, using a superconducting "active shield." The Annapolis group rejected that path and chose instead heavy iron shielding to absorb the electromagnetic field produced by the motor. Shielding was needed in order to reduce the ship's detectable emitted signal, to prevent interference with electronic devices, to prevent magnetic attraction of stray tools and parts that could jump across the room, and to eliminate the exposure of personnel to the poorly understood effects of high-Gauss electromagnetic waves on the human physique.

The Annapolis designers incorporated liquid metal brushes, developed in earlier work at General Electric, which allowed for handling of the low-current and high-voltage characteristic of superconducting machines. The sodium-potassium (NaK) liquid, lodged in a tongue and groove arrangement, would be maintained at liquid temperature by completely isolating the cold niobium windings from all the warmer parts of the machine, including the brushes.

Timothy Doyle, a member of the merged Annapolis group, patented a unique arrangement of components, with a stationary magnet surrounded by a rotor, called a shaped magnetic field machine, which was utilized in all further DTNSRDC designs of superconducting motors. The Doyle design allowed for a very compact arrangement, and planners produced several notional sketches comparing the overall dimensions of the Annapolis design to equivalent-horsepower conventional electric motors.[27]

Following these design principles, the merged group produced a 400-horsepower motor that was operable by 1978. By 1980 they were able to install it in a small test craft to demonstrate the system, complete with uniquely designed 15-volt, 15,000-amp advanced switching gear.

The researchers who worked on the project, such as Howard Stevens, would later say with considerable pride, "We built a machine." The machine was unique and proved that a well-designed motor using a superconducting winding could be far more efficient, for the same weight, than a conventional electric motor. During the fuel and energy crisis of the 1970s, the idea held considerable attraction for the Navy, and the possible applications of the concept generated a spate of articles in the *Naval Engineers Journal* and other technical journals and magazines. Gas turbine engines, as great consumers of fuel, could not be operated at maximum efficiency without a variable reduction system. The Annapolis-designed motor could provide a missing link in the search for the most fuel-efficient use of gas turbines. By 1976 NAVSEA had begun to support the work, using special project office funding.[28]

NAVSEA contracted with General Electric and a smaller firm, Garrett Air Research, to build three motors using the Annapolis ideas but

Superconducting Motor. Using super-cooled niobin-tin superconducting wire, by 1978, the design group at Annapolis produced an operable 400-horsepower motor as a demonstration model. Another path not taken, the superconducting motor held promise to provide a missing link in efficient use of gas turbines in hybrid propulsion systems.

at the next order of magnitude, in the 3,000-horsepower range. Although Garrett's design did not work out because of failures in multiple "O"-rings, that company eventually concentrated on designing the necessary larger switch gear. General Electric produced two working designs. Their "drum-disc" design was completed and under test by 1986. The smaller, 400-horsepower design, together with the General Electric 3,000-horsepower design, proved that there was no problem with the superconductor or the cryogenic system—the heart of the innovation. Other problems, however, were numerous, particularly the design of the liquid metal collectors and keeping the overall motor at planned weight and size.[29]

While those engaged in the work were disappointed that the Navy did not plan to use such a motor, or even to proceed with the design of the next scale, at about 30,000 horsepower, they took solace in some other effects of their work. By causing the ship design community to focus on electric generators and motors as possible transmission systems for large-scale turbines, Annapolis researchers believed that they had stimulated other improvements in electric motor design. Through the early 1980s, plans for an experimental guided missile destroyer (DDGX) used a "conventional" electric motor, proposed by Westinghouse. Yet that motor, which did not utilize superconductivity technology, was itself considerably lighter, smaller, and more efficient than traditional electric motors, and utilized alternating current. Although the Navy rejected even that proven industrial technology as too risky and built instead a "plain" destroyer that did not reflect such progressive ideas, the discussion and work had made many marine engineers and naval architects aware that electric drive could be beneficially utilized and improved upon.[30]

In 1984, partly as a consequence of the renewed interest in ways of improving electric drive, the Navy embarked on a two-pronged approach. One path led to a request for proposals announced in December 1986 to develop a full-scale alternating current electric system for a proposed experimental missile frigate (MFX). The other path promised some funding for continued work on the homopolar advanced direct current motor, following ideas from the Annapolis work.

As an improvement in technology that would bring better size, weight, and power to the already established advantages of electric drive, superconductivity was attractive. Like earlier work on the hydrogen peroxide engine, the development required challenging searches for optimum solutions. And like those earlier workers on closed-cycle submarine engines, the builders of superconducting machines at Annapolis did not have guaranteed long-term support. The closed-cycle alternatives had been dropped with the proof of the value of nuclear power. By the late 1980s, some feared that the superconducting motor might become a similar case of a path not fully pursued.

The Annapolis researchers on superconducting machines knew that the theoretical concept could be practically applied, and they forged ahead. They understood, with a degree of resigned tolerance, that the Navy needed to put its research and development monies where they were most needed. To get from the drawing board to the fleet had never been an automatic process. The DTNSRDC leadership listed superconductivity as a major accomplishment because, whether deployed or not, the shaped magnetic field superconducting motor, like the X-wing, was a cutting-edge innovation in which the center played a crucial part.

Technology Development—A Range of Accomplishments

As in the past, the laboratories organized in the David Taylor Research Center proceeded with testing and evaluation of naval equipment, using contemporary technology and instruments to meet the growing and diverse mission. Through the 1970s, as in earlier decades, there was tremendous diversity of such work. The following descriptions can only give a partial picture of the center's "performance," in a range of technology developments in the 1970s and early 1980s.

Controllable-pitch propeller designs that allowed for changing the pitch of ship propeller blades to achieve reverse thrust and to find the most efficient "bite" for each shaft speed and torque had been conceived of and used, in a relatively primitive design, as early as the 1850s. In 1934, a hydraulic system of blade control developed by Escher-Wyss of Germany allowed for practical applications on smaller craft. Through World War II hundreds of Navy landing craft were fitted with controllable-pitch propellers that allowed for rapid reversal from beaches without stopping or clutching the engine through to the prop.[31]

Between 1940 and 1966, over 1,400 craft in the Navy, mostly in the categories of landing craft and smaller auxiliaries, used the system. However, before 1970, the highest rated shaft horsepower for a controllable-pitch propeller application had been 7,900 shaft horsepower, used on board the landing ship, tank *Newport* (LST 1179). With the development of design standards and characteristics for *Spruance* (DD 923)-class destroyers in the early 1970s, the Ships Characteristics Board (SCB) required gas turbines rated at 40,000 shp and also required that a controllable-pitch design be developed to accommodate the vastly increased power. A controllable-pitch propeller for *Barbey* (FF 1088), rated at 35,000 shp, was installed, but its structural failure during trials led to a program at DTNSRDC to investigate the difficulty.[32]

The DTNSRDC program identified the problem after study of the installations on board not only *Barbey* but also *Spruance, Oliver Hazard Perry* (FFG 7), and *Ticonderoga* (CG 47). More than 200 propellers of a controllable-pitch design on more than 100 ships were examined and then modified to increase their reliability and endurance under stress conditions, to specifications established by DTNSRDC propulsion engineers.[33]

DTNSRDC specifications and procedures, some initiated as early as 1970, were developed in the Hydromechanics, Structures, and Materials Departments. The resulting work constituted a new technology base. For example, that base included procedures for predicting hydrodynamic blade loading, developed by Robert Boswell, and structural response and strength. The base also provided guidance in the selection of materials for controllable pitch propeller designs. Furthermore, the base spelled out methods for conducting full-scale propeller stress trials, and it could be used to design and test the controllable-pitch principle with propellers rated up to 60,000 shp. The full program of testing, evalua-

Structural Test of a Full-Scale Propeller.   After studies of the failure of a controllable-pitch propeller on the *Barbey* during sea trials, center engineers modified the propeller design on over 100 naval vessels.

tion, and design of such propellers was fully in place by 1980, and the work was recognized by a presidential-level award.[34]

The funding for this work came largely out of the funds for new ship construction, with assistance from the Coast Guard. The USCG icebreaker *Polar Star* (WABG 10) was used to test the stresses encountered by controllable-pitch propellers while encountering sea ice.

Between 1975 and 1977 a team at DTNSRDC coordinated a program to test the effects of impacts of a Mark 48 torpedo against a submarine hull, to allow for actual at-sea exercises with the torpedo against U.S. submarines. Although the torpedo in such an exercise would not carry an explosive charge, the danger of impacts of a one-ton torpedo at cruise speed would be considerable. Damage to the hull, to diving planes, to hull-mounted equipment, to hull valves, and to personnel would all place the crew of a "target" submarine at risk. "Fleet readiness," on the other hand, required such exercises involving the launching of actual torpedoes at real targets, rather than at mock-ups, abandoned hulls, moored surplus submarines, or signal-emitting buoys.

DTNSRDC coordinated the effort of several laboratories, including the Naval Research Laboratory, the Naval Surface Weapons Center, the Naval Underwater Systems Center, and three different naval shipyards, as well as ship personnel who participated in tests and studies. The program developed a pneumatic launcher to set the torpedo at cruise velocity and to aim it for a specified target area on a hull moored in dry dock for the testing phase of the program. The group developed instruments to record data from both the torpedo and the target sub. They conducted a series of tests, studying such factors as hull cracking during impact. Eventually, as the data accumulated, they ran impact tests on *Drum* (SSN 677), with a submarine crew aboard, while in drydock in Puget Sound. As a result of that test series, the data collected could be used to recommend modifications to structure and to equipment mounting and location.[35]

With these modifications, submarines of the same class as *Drum*, the SSN 637 class, could be "certified" for live exercises with nonexplosive Mark 48 torpedoes. As those exercises progressed, the Navy could develop evasive tactics for the defenders as well as crew training in the use of the torpedo under conditions very close to actual warfare, without placing crews or boats at undue risk. The Mark 48 could be validated as a sophisticated, modern weapon system rather than simply existing as a partially tried part of the weapons inventory.

The range of disciplines and the wide diversity of accomplishments in the 1970s and the 1980s at DTNSRDC demonstrated a continuous and vigorous advance of naval technology. In 1970, the Office of Saline Water in the Department of the Interior had been working on several technologies to convert brackish and salt water into fresh water. One of the methods under experimentation was reverse osmosis (RO). The technique simply forces seawater through a semipermeable membrane, to produce water with less than 500 parts per million of salts, which meets modern Environmental Protection Agency standards for drinking water. In that year, the Navy became interested in shipboard applications of the RO process, particularly for the new classes of surface vessels to be driven by gas turbine engines. Unlike earlier steam-driven ships, with their high requirements for fresh water, the primary need for water on board the new ships would be for crew use. An RO system might be more reliable than older distillation methods. Furthermore, a manually operated RO system would be ideal for lifeboat use. At DTNSRDC Annapolis, the project moved from concept development through full-scale development in the early 1970s. Shipboard trials of a membrane fabricated from cellulose triacetate materials revealed that corrosion of metal piping caused membrane deterioration and premature failure. By

Recovery Engineering Inc.

Reverse Osmosis Desalinization.   At Annapolis, studies of the process for
making seawater potable moved from concept development through full-scale development in the early 1970s.

the early 1980s a new membrane, in a spiral-wrapped configuration, was developed that helped reduce requirements for special metals and treatments of piping on board ships.

By the mid-1980s, Annapolis personnel developed two prototype shipboard reverse osmosis desalination systems, installed on board *Stump* (DD 978) and *Fletcher* (DD 992). Each system had more elaborate filtration systems. On board *Fletcher,* the systems continued to operate for over three years before replacement. A lifeboat desalinization device was pursued through a competitive R&D contract, which developed pre-production prototypes. Several companies competed, including Recovery Engineering, Inc., which developed the final product. This device could produce more than thirty gallons a day, and could be stored in less than a cubic foot of space. During development of this desalinator the company began to commercialize the unit. In 1989, a couple survived in a lifeboat off South America for over fifty days, with their survival attributed to the fact that they had one of the units.[36]

Another major technological advance in the 1980s came with Materials Department work on new steel alloys. From the days of the first nuclear submarines, the Navy had adopted for hulls and structural members the high-strength steel alloys HY-80 and HY-100. The test coupons of the high-strength steels would begin to yield at 80,000 psi and at 100,000 psi, respectively. In the early 1980s, major domestic and foreign steelmakers were producing large tonnages of a new generation of high-strength, low-alloy (HSLA) steel plate with improved weldability and low-temperature toughness, particularly for the Arctic oil pipeline. Researchers at DTNRDC foresaw the advantages of developing commercial HSLA steels to meet the requirements that had already been established for HY-80 steel in naval applications.

Early in the HSLA studies, NAVSEA identified the need for weight reduction in CG 47- and DDG 51- class ships that could be obtained with HY-80 steel, but at high cost. The HSLA steels research and development program began at DTNRDC in 1981 with a goal of reducing shipbuilding costs. The first objective was the certification of HSLA-80 steel, weldable without costly preheat, which would be equivalent in performance to HY-80 steel. Type A710 steel quickly emerged as the prime candidate, which the materials researchers at DTNRDC optimized to meet the Navy requirements. The evaluation of HSLA-80 properties, welding, structural performance, and shipyard production demonstration showed that the very low carbon, copper-strengthened steel met the HY-80 requirements, and was readily weldable with no preheat, using the same welding materials and processes as used in HY-80 work. HSLA-80 was certified for use in ship construction in 1984.

Cost savings of $2,000 to $3,000 per ton of fabricated structure were estimated by using HSLA-80 in place of HY-80, when considering savings in material, labor, energy, and inspection costs. Since the commercially available alloy was used after the mid-1980s in carriers, destroyers, frigates, and smaller vessels, the Navy's investment in the HSLA-80 research and development program was paid back much more than tenfold.

Following the HSLA-80 program, materials researchers began an alloy development and qualification program in 1985 resulting in HSLA-100 as a replacement for HY-100. Unlike the earlier HSLA-80, the 100,000 psi yield strength test alloy steel was unique in being a DTNRDC alloy design, rather than a steel industry development. Researchers took the HSLA-100 program through laboratory alloy design, trial plate production, and commercial plate production for the certification program. Based on the performance of the new alloy's mechanical, physical, and fracture properties, and its weldability and structural performance, HSLA-100 was certified in 1989 for use in surface ship structures and ballistic protection, as a replacement for HY-100 steel. Approximately 12,000 tons of the new alloy was used in the construction of the nuclear-powered carrier *John C. Stennis* (CVN 74). Again, the cost savings were enormous, ranging from $500 to $3,000 per ton of fabricated structure. Similar savings were being achieved with use of the HSLA-100 in construction of the newer carriers *Harry S. Truman* (CVN 75) and *Ronald Reagan* (CVN 76.)[37]

Computer Uses—A New Generation of Tools

Throughout the center a wide variety of computer applications made the work of such groups as the Systems Development Department and the X-wing group in Aerodynamics possible. The SWATH ship database allowed testing of various designs through computer modeling of the stresses and vectors in unique, never-tried structures, and the CRUISE-4 program allowed prediction of X-wing performance even before the first physical models were constructed. Finite *difference* analysis, which in effect substitutes the computer's capacity to handle vast amounts of numbers for the methods of traditional calculus, found many applications in work with motion, flow, speed, power, and other dynamic studies characteristic of aerodynamics and hydrodynamics. Finite *element* analysis was a new computational technique that emerged as a practical tool in the 1970s, with initial applications primarily in structural analysis. The computational laboratory staff played a major role in making finite element analysis a practical tool, reducing the

High-Strength, Low-Alloy (HSLA) Steel. The island for aircraft carrier *John C. Stennis* (CVN 74) being lowered into place. The structure is one of the largest made of HSLA steel, a new low-cost, highly weldable alloy developed by the Materials Directorate of the center.

effort required in formulating the description of structures and greatly reducing the computer power and time required to solve structural analysis problems. Later finite element techniques were also applied to problems in fluid dynamics, but finite difference analysis remained the primary technique used there.[38]

Computational mechanics was a natural follow-on for the staff that had worked on the nuclear reactor program. The ultimate goal was to be able to completely and accurately simulate on a computer the performance of a real ship in realistic seas. The goal could not be immediately attained, since the complete mathematical formulation of fluid motion is not yet known, and even if it were known, would require computer power not available to date. Even so, substantial progress was made. In computational structural analysis, contributions were made in finite element analysis and in specialized computer programs that addressed individual problems. Under leadership from Betty Cuthill, plans were made to develop a general purpose finite element analysis program, when

Carderock staff learned of a similar project being undertaken by NASA. Cuthill and her team decided to participate with NASA. The resulting NASA Structural Analysis (NASTRAN) Program turned out to be a resounding success. Cuthill, James McKee, and Gordon Everstine developed the techniques and software for bandwidth reduction of the principal matrix involved in finite element methods, greatly enhancing the power of these techniques. This allowed for easier formulation of problems and reduced computer time and computer power requirements. The center was designated the Navy NASTRAN systems office, which provided training, support, and assistance to all Navy activities performing structural analysis using the NASTRAN Program.[39]

In the area of computational fluid dynamics, significant progress was made in developing computer programs based on various mathematical models of fluid flow phenomena. Hans Lugt, who joined the laboratory in 1967, became internationally recognized for his research in vorticity and autorotation. His book, *Vortex Flow in Nature and Technology* (1983), has been translated into several languages. Lugt won the Navy's Distinguished Civilian Service Award, and the Humboldt Award for Senior U.S. Scientists, the first Navy scientist to win this award.[40]

Through the 1970s specific computer applications followed the pattern that had always been part of the incremental progress of technology as equipment and tools spread from one use to another. In logistic support, ship analysis and design, the study of ship structure, and the modelling of magnetostatic signatures of ships, computers provided key assistance not available in the precomputer age. Computer software, developed at the center under the Computer Aided Ship Design and Construction (CASDAC) Program, became standard parts of the ship-designer's modern "tool kit." These tools were developed by a group under the leadership of Robert Stevens, and later, Tom Corin. They assembled a team of naval architects and engineers with experience in ship design and construction, as well as computer experts. This effort required extensive coordination with the design staff of the Navy and with the nation's shipbuilding industry, the ultimate users of the software that was developed.[41]

In the area of logistics, the power of the computer in sorting out the complexities of delivery, material inventories, and efficient schedules and routings proved valuable. In 1973 the Chief of Naval Material ordered that the Navy should study the feasibility of air-dropping high-priority spare parts to Sixth Fleet ships stationed in the Eastern Mediterranean. He requested that the system be accurate, allowing for pinpoint drops and pickups not requiring the launching of small boats or men into the sea. The system to be developed should involve the Navy as customer, the Army as "rigger" for packing and handling the parachute systems, and the Air Force as transporter of the supplies. The resulting program, developed at DTNSRDC, was the Navy Emergency Air Cargo Delivery System (NEACDS), which went into operation in 1977. As a supplemental system, the Air Deployment Delivery System (ADDS) was designed to carry smaller loads in a shorter time frame, and was ready by 1981. NEACDS was designed to resupply bulky, high-priority items, including missiles and large machinery units. ADDS was a "package delivery" service for small items less than 8 or 10 cubic feet in size. Although the program cost to develop both NEACDS and ADDS totaled less than $800,000, the outcome had widespread application and showed the ability of the Computation and Mathematics Laboratory to respond to Navy-wide concerns beyond the direct service needs of the other researchers at the center. The work in logistics led to a major new mission for the center, with responsibility for developing improved logistics systems for the Navy as a whole. Perhaps more than any other center research and development, the logistics work affected every Navy activity, and the logistics improvements that resulted continued to save the Navy vast amounts of money.[42]

Since the mid-1960s the center had been at the forefront of the effort to develop numerical techniques for the use of the computer in solving hydrodynamic and structural problems. A variety of programs and databases, regarded as "tools," came out of this work, and by 1981, the center selected thirty-seven major applications from a much larger number to illustrate the wide variety of uses. The applications ranged from structural analysis of submarine hulls, satellites, advanced ships, antennae, and aircraft, to studies of the dynamics of propulsion, torpedo impacts, propeller designs, and aircraft carrier deck motion. The development of computer vulnerability models was a decisive step in helping the Navy design tougher ships and submarines. Computers assisted in the design of the liquid metal collectors in superconducting motors, in the design of new wind tunnels, in ship transom design, and in the design of devices such as searchlights, missiles, sonar domes, radar transducers, and torpedoes. Throughout the laboratories, hundreds of engineers, spread across the various departments, made use of the computers.[43]

In their own literature the researchers referred to the programs and databases as "design tools." The term was apt. Although a stack of paper printouts or a program may be difficult to visualize as a tool, these software products served exactly the tool function in technology. One of the most widely recognized of the items in the new "tool kit" may have been the Structural Synthesis Design Program (SSDP). It was worked on from 1970 in the Structures Department and published in 1977 by NAVSEA, and distributed for use by contractors and others in the shipbuilding community. The SSDP had the capability to perform structural designs and study trade-offs for both conventional and advanced ships.[44]

The new program proved useful in a wide variety of studies. SSDP was employed in the design of guided missile destroyers, the nuclear aircraft carrier *Theodore Roosevelt* (CVN 71), the SWATH ship, the SES, and the guided missile cruiser *Vincennes* (CG 49). The Maritime Administration, the Coast Guard, the Canadian Defense Research Establishment Atlantic, and a host of civilian ship designers all made active use of it.[45]

This tool, widely used throughout the ship design community, will never have the public visibility of the SWATH ship, the hydrofoil, the air cushion vehicle or the surface effect ship. Yet from the perspective of the ship engineering and design communities, SSDP became widely regarded as a significant naval invention, coming out of DTNSRDC, and ranking with the more tangible devices, ships, instruments, and inventions in importance.[46]

Among the computer tools generated through the late 1970s, several had direct application to long-standing weapons and weapons defense problems. With the development of magnetic mines and their wide use in World War II, the Navy grew increasingly concerned with reducing a ship's "magnetostatic field." The field was generated by the steel hull itself, by machinery and steel structure, and by the various electrical direct current sources on board, such as batteries. Minesweeping and mine-hunting operations require that the minesweeper itself have a low emitted field, and ship protection of regular naval vessels also requires methods to measure, identify, and limit the ship's magnetic field.

Between 1974 and 1982 DTNSRDC developed two computer models to deal with these issues. SOURCE, developed by Darrell Nixon, allowed for planning the location of field sensors for degaussing ranges and sea trials. Again, as in SSDP, trade-offs can be studied to find the most efficient and economic geometry. A second model, using finite element analysis, designed by Myles Hurwitz, could be used to calculate the induced magnetic fields of ships. Both models were used to assist scientists and engineers in developing protection against the magnetic mine and against detection of ships by stationary magnetic "listening" buoys or stations implanted by potential enemies in strategic seabed locations.[47]

Through these years, the center led the way in the development of integrated database oriented computer systems, as distinct from individual computational programs, with application to the entire ship design and construction process, involving both government and private sector users. The computer systems had a wide variety of naval logistics functions, as well as application to engineering and scientific analysis. As noted in the prior chapter, the development and application of analytical and computational techniques, systems analysis, and warfare simulation to naval warfare issues and scenarios by center staff led to major recognition, and to the assignment of important responsibilities in submarine development. Similarly, the leadership in logistics operations and functions led to the assignment of logistics automation technology functions to the center.

CASDAC and the other programs gave Navy ship design its entry into the computerized world. However, the greater possible benefits, such as the shortening of the ship design-construction cycle, the savings of billions of dollars in the ship construction budget, and other fundamental payoffs were not achieved because the computational group could not get the Navy to spend the money to achieve an integrated design, construction, and logistic support capability. The tremendous amount of data involved in the design and construction of a warship, and the interaction among the numerous design disciplines presented major challenges to an integrated design system. While some observers thought such an idea ahead of its time, the computer specialists themselves believed that political and financial issues rather than technical feasibility were the principal impediments to implementation. Although supported by a number of flag officers, the total-system approach to shipbuilding never found a champion willing and able to take on the task of changing the way things were done. A similar approach to design and construction was adopted by NASA, but the Navy lost its opportunity to take the lead in implementing the concept of a fully integrated design approach.[48]

Through the late 1960s and early 1970s, as the acquisition and use of mainframe computers proliferated in government and elsewhere, the Navy, in response to congressional pressures, established a complex procedure for justifying and acquiring automatic data processing (ADP) equipment. By 1973, the ADP bureaucratic procedures had become oppressive, often delaying a purchase of new equipment so long that new generations of computers had come and gone before an acquisition could be completed. The laboratories were forced to compete with each other with endless justifications and reviews. After review of the problem by a special group of the Naval Research Advisory Committee (NRAC), Director of Navy Laboratories Joel Lawson created the position of special assistant for interlaboratory computing who would help establish policies and procedures that would speed up the process and make it more rational, work toward establishing a Navy Laboratory Computer Network, and lead an interlaboratory committee to promote and implement appropriate joint efforts. Gene Gleissner, head of the Computation and Mathematics Department at David Taylor, was asked to take on the new post as an additional duty, which he held until his retirement in 1986. He was replaced by Charles Schoman. Working with teams at the center, the interlaboratory group established a common program to evaluate and implement advanced computer technology. The center developed the Navy Laboratory Computer Network (NALCON) using ARPANET, which later became the INTERNET, fully twenty years before INTERNET usage became commonplace. In effect, the laboratories were using e-mail more than a full decade before the national spread of the system. The center also pioneered interorganizational standards for office automation and video-conferencing.[49]

Pollution and Energy Efficiency

Following the oil embargo of 1973–1974, a special task force called the Defense Energy Task Group assigned to the various military services the responsibility for finding ways to reduce the Defense Department's dependence on imported petroleum. NAVSEA, in charge of the Navy's portion of the program, asked DTNSRDC to develop a comprehensive plan. The result was the Shipboard Energy Research and Development Program. NAVSEA then assigned management of that program to the center in 1975.[50]

As developed, the program aimed toward a twenty percent reduction in fuel consumption by the late 1980s. The center pursued simultaneously several lines of inquiry to achieve the goal. Improved hull-cleaning methods would reduce frictional resistance of ships. The development of organotin antifouling hull coatings seemed another promising area. These coatings would prevent barnacles and other biofouling, again increasing ship performance. However, by the late 1980s, environmental concerns about the possible damage to marine life from the coatings interfered with wide application of this energy-saving method. A process to reduce the flow of bathing shower heads would reduce the energy consumed in distilling water on board ships. Other individual aspects of the program focused on improved diesel fuel, improvement of the recycling of stack gases, improved techniques of trimming propellers on the trailing or inoperative shafts on multiprop ships, increased flexibility in fuel use, and studies of the potential value of shale-derived diesel fuel. In this program, as in much of the 1970s work, computer studies helped. One program analyzed ways to optimize energy consumption, particularly in gas turbine- and diesel- powered ships.[51]

A wide variety of resulting improvements were implemented during the 1980s, gradually increasing the fuel efficiency of naval ships. The delays in acceptance of new hull coatings worked against energy savings. Nevertheless, the energy conservation effort had stimulated several accomplishments, including the low-volume shower head, which found widespread outside commercial application as well as naval uses.[52]

Popular concerns with environment not only worked against such improvements as the organotin coatings but worked to win support for other useful naval innovations. In 1971 the Chief of Naval Material assigned to DTNSRDC the lead responsibility for research, development, test, and evaluation in handling shipboard waste. A variety of oil-water separators, sewage plants, and food waste disposal systems were reviewed, new specifications set, and improved equipment purchased as a result of the effort. In particular, DTNSRDC worked on a sewage collection and incineration system on DD 963-class ships, development of 10-gallon-a-minute and 50-gallon-a-minute oil-water separators, and detoxification of the wastes generated in removing organotin antifouling paint. New food waste grinders were installed on all capital ships, and a set of operating instructions for sewage collection, holding, and transfer tanks developed. By 1975 alterations to reduce waste went into effect; by 1977 the newly designed separators, garbage, and sewage systems began to be installed.[53]

Diversity and Excellence

In the 1970s and 1980s the merged laboratories at Carderock and Annapolis practiced both theoretical science and practical engineering in a wide range of activities related to the naval ship. Despite extensive interdisciplinary work in signature reduction, and despite the systems approach that had succeeded in bringing advanced ships through the design stages, there had been some severe frustrations. Two of the projects defined by the center leadership as major accomplishments, the superconducting motor and the X-wing aircraft, had been brought to the verge of deployment, but not sold to the Navy. As in earlier decades, the choice of research focus grew out of constant juggling between available staff and equipment and current naval concerns and sources of funds. Some of the less publicly noted applied technology work, especially in the application of computer techniques to standing problems, could produce lasting and valuable results. A host of specific demands, coming out of the Defense Department and out of NAVSEA, could sometimes generate lasting contributions, For examples, the incorporation of center-developed signature-reduction concepts into the design of the next generation nuclear submarines, in the incorporation of the new steel alloys HSLA-80 and HSLA-100 into new ships, and in the development of computer design tools and technology databases.

However, by the middle of the 1980s, while there was much excellence coming out of the Center of Excellence, there was very little "centrality" to it. The very nature of the ship research and development mission, despite the language of systems analysis, was diverse and suited to further diversification. What was the central goal, mission, or ideal of the center? Various answers to such a question might emerge although many saw the diversity itself as a strength. It remained difficult to relate all of the work to a single mission statement.

One theme with which many could identify, even though their personal projects and separate disciplines took them in various distinct directions, was the advanced ship work. By the late 1970s, artists' renderings of possible future SWATH ships, air cushion landing craft, mobile ocean bases, and other notional craft derived from DTNSRDC work decorated the halls. At the same time, international developments suggested that DOD and Navy priorities in the defense area could rapidly change. The agendas, the contributions, and the very organizational identity of the center would once again be reshaped by shifting national defense policy priorities and the remaking of naval administrative structures.

Mobile Ocean Base Model.   The concept of a floating ocean base for aircraft and supplies is tested in the MASK facility.

Endnotes

1. Technical Directorate Items, 1973–1981, passim, DTNSRDC Archives, Dr. Alan Powell papers, boxes 1 and 2. The minutes reflected discussions of priorities throughout the period. Excellent examples of focus on the conflicting pressures are found in the minutes for the 8 July 1974 meeting in box 1, Technical Directorate Minutes 1974, and in memorandum, Powell to Tech. Directorate, 10 Apr 1981, box 2, T.D. Meeting Minutes 1981.

2. For development of the idea of "normal technology," see Edward W. Constant, *The Origins of the Turbojet Revolution* (Baltimore: Johns Hopkins University Press, 1980), 10–12.

3. For the concept of a "presumed anomaly," see ibid., 15–16.

4. For the development of the idea of "reverse salients," see Thomas Parke Hughes, "The Science-Technology Interaction: The Case of High Voltage Power Transmission Systems," *Technology and Culture* 17 (Oct 1976): 646–659; Hughes, Thomas Parke, *Elmer Sperry: Inventor and Engineer* (Baltimore: Johns Hopkins University Press, 1971), 64–70.

5. F. A. Freeth, "H. Kamerlingh Onnes, 1853–1926," *Annual Report of the Board of Regents of the Smithsonian Institution* (Washington: Government Printing Office, 1927), 533–535.

6. Bernard Weinraub, "6 Americans Win Nobel Prizes in Physics and Chemistry Fields," *The New York Times*, 21 Oct 1972, 1, 14; "11 Nobel Laureates Get Medals and Checks for $100,000," *The New York Times*, 11 Dec 1972.

7. F. Schanz, "The Controllable-Pitch Propeller as an Integral Part of the Ship's Propulsion System," *TSNAME* 75 (1967): 194–223; J Wind, "Principles of Mechanisms Used in Controllable-Pitch Propellers," 1st Lips Propeller Symposium, Drunen-Holland, 20–21 May 1970; Christian K. Neilsen, Jr., "A Summary of Controllable-Pitch Propeller Systems Employed by the U.S. Navy," *Naval Engineers Journal* 86 (Apr 1974): 81–90; Thomas C. Gillmer and Bruce Johnson, *Introduction to Naval Architecture* (Annapolis, MD: Naval Institute Press, 1982), 238–239.

8. "New Design Concepts in Naval Shipbuilding, Impact of Vietnam War"; and Naval History Division *Riverine Warfare, The U.S. Navy's Operations on Inland Waters* (Washington: Government Printing Office, 1968), NHC, NLCCG Archives, DTNSRDC RC 7, series 6, acc. 82-1, box 10; J. B. Chaplin, "The Air Cushion Vehicle," *Military Engineer* 61 (Jan–Feb 1969): 12–15. Lawson's role in the Vietnam Laboratory Assistance Program and the Navy Science Advisor Program is spelled out in Rodney Carlisle, *Management of the U.S. Navy Research and Development Centers During the Cold War* (Washington: Naval Historical Center, 1996), 55.

9. D. C. Hughes, Navy Pollution Control Report, 11 Mar 1975, NHC, NLCCG Archives, DTNSRDC RC 3-1, series 2, acc. 82-29, box 7; and Paul E. Pugh to Chief of Naval Material, 27 Jul 1973, NHC, NLCCG Archives, series 2, acc. 82-29, box 6; Joel S. Lawson, Jr., to Chief of Naval Material, 29 Jun 1970, NHC, NLCCG Archives, DTNSRDC RC 3-1, acc. 82-29, series 1, box 2.

10. Tech. Directorate Meeting Minutes, 22 Jan 1973, DTNSRDC Archives, Powell papers, box 1, TD Actions 1973.

11. "Major Accomplishments of the Navy Laboratories, DTNSRDC," n.d. (1981?), internal publication, DTNSRDC, typescript, DNL.
12. James C. Biggers and Arthur W. Linden, "X-Wing: A Low Disc Loading V/STOL for the Navy," *SAE Technical Paper Series* (Society of Automotive Engineers, 1985), Paper no. 851772.
13. Ibid.
14. I. C. Cheeseman and A. R. Seed, "The Application of Circulation Control by Blowing to Helicopters," *Journal of the Royal Aeronautical Society* 71 (Jul 1966).
15. Ernest Rogers, interview by Rodney Carlisle, 30 Mar 1987.
16. Ibid.
17. Ibid.
18. Ibid.
19. Ibid.; Biggers and Linden, "X-Wing," 3–4; "Sikorsky S-72X1 Rotor systems Aircraft—X-Wing," Fact Sheet, United Technologies Sikorsky Aircraft, n.d.
20. Rogers interview, 30 Mar 1987.
21. Howard Stevens, interview by Rodney Carlisle, 10 Nov 1986.
22. Charles F. Janes, "The Potential of Superconductors for Shipboard Power Applications," *Naval Engineers Journal* 79 (Oct 1967): 791.
23. Stevens interview, 10 Nov 1986.
24. Ibid.; E. G. Frankel, J. M. Reynolds, and E. H. Sibley, "Superconducting Machinery for Naval Applications," *Naval Engineers Journal* 78 (Jun 1966): 501–514; Janes, "The Potential of Superconductors," 794.
25. Stevens interview, 10 Nov 1986; Frankel, et al., "Superconducting Machinery," 502.
26. Stevens interview, 10 Nov 1986.
27. Ibid.; Janes, "The Potential of Superconductors," 795; T. J. Doyle, "The Shaped Field Drive Concept," Workshop on Naval Applications of Superconductivity, Panama City, FL, Nov 1970; Doyle and J. H. Harrison, "Navy Superconductive Machinery Program," Paper presented at SNAME Spring Meeting/STAR Symposium, New London, CT, 26–29 Apr 1978, Paper no. 20; H. O. Stevens, "Superconductive Generator Development for Ship Electric," *Transactions, IECEC* (1974); Doyle, "Superconductive Propulsion Motor Development at NSRDC," ASME Paper 75-WA/OCE-8, 1975; Stevens, Doyle, M. J. Superczynski, Harrison, and H. Messinger, "Superconducting Machines for Naval Ship Propulsion," *IEEE Transactions on Magnetics*, vol. MAG-13, no. 1, Jan 1977; Notional sketches appear in Frankel, et al., "Superconducting Machinery," 503; Janes, "The Potential of Superconductors," 796.
28. Stevens interview, 10 Nov 1986; Ralph Roberts to Chief of Naval Research, 11 Dec 1974, NHC, NLCCG Archives, DTNSRDC RC 3-1, acc. 82-18, series 5, box 30; E. F. McCann II, and C. J. Mole," Superconducting Electric Propulsion Systems for Advanced Ship Concepts," *Naval Engineers Journal* 84 (Dec 1972): 35–45.
29. Stevens interview, 10 Nov 1986.
30. Ibid.
31. Gerald M. Boatwright and John H. Strandell, "Controllable Pitch Propellers," *Naval Engineers Journal* 79 (Aug 1967): 538.
32. Ibid., 539; Technical Directorate Items, Ship Acoustics Dept., 4 Oct 1974, DTNSRDC Archives, Powell papers, box 1, file 19.
33. "Strength of Controllable Pitch Propellers," Major Accomplishments, No.16.
34. Ibid.; Technical Directorate Items, Ship Acoustics Dept., 7 Oct 1977, DTNSRDC Archives, Powell papers, box 2, file 19.
35. "MARK-48 Exercise Torpedo Impact Safety Certification of SSN 637 Class Submarine," Major Accomplishments, No. 12.

36. Annapolis files, ABIF.
37. "Development of HSLA-80 and HSLA-100 Steels," report prepared by Ernest Czryca, communication with the author from George Wacker, 29 Jan 1997.
38. Gene Gleissner report, ABIF.
39. Ibid.
40. Ibid.
41. The center's use of computer applications to solve problems of ship design was part of a much wider phenomenon at the time, in which DTRC took a leadership role. The Naval Ship Engineering Center developed several designs and tools used at DTNSRDC. See Jack Brainin, "Functional Description for the Integrated Ship Design System (ISDS)," NSRDC Report no. 4663, Apr 1975; Tom Corin to Dr. W. E. Cummins, 2 Apr 1975, WNRC, RG 181, acc. 85-125, box 3, 3900(4) CASDAC; H. Sheridan, CAPDAC Working Memorandum No. 33, 3 Jun 1976, WNRC, RG 181, RC, acc. 85-125, box 2, 3900(4) CAPDAC; Bernard W. Romberg, *CASDOS, A System for the Computer Aided Structural Detailing of Ships*, 20 Jan 1967, WNRC, RG 181, acc. 85-125, box 3, 3900(4) CASDOS. Note that all these systems—ISDS, CASDAC, CAPDAC, AND CASDOS—were developed at the Center.
42. "Emergency Logistic Support of Forces Afloat," Major Accomplishments, No. 19.
43. "Computer Techniques for Ship Analysis and Design," Major Accomplishments, No. 20.
44. "Structural Synthesis Design Program (SSDP) 'A Ship Design Tool'," Major Accomplishments, No. 14.
45. Ibid.
46. Ibid.
47. "Modeling of Magnetostatic Signatures of Ships," Major Accomplishments, No. 22.
48. Gene Gleissner, report, ABIF.
49. Ibid.
50. "Shipboard Energy Research and Development Program," Major Accomplishments, No. 28.
51. Ibid.; Paul Shatzberg, "Organotin Antifouling Paints and the U.S. Navy—A Historical Perspective," *Proceedings, Oceans-87 Conference*, Marine Technology Society, Halifax, Nova Scotia, Canada, 1987.
52. Ibid.
53. "Shipboard Pollution Abatement," Major Accomplishments, No. 25; Lawson to Chief of Naval Material, 29 Jun 1970, NHC, NLCCG Archives, DTNSRDC RC 3–1, acc. 82–29, series 1, box 2.

CHAPTER 13

Cold War Cross Currents

P RESIDENT RONALD REAGAN'S FOREIGN POLICY premises were clear: he believed in a strong defense and in a tough stand against the Soviet Union. The years of his administration, 1981–1989, are remembered as the peak of the Cold War. Yet a close examination of the 1980s reveals cross currents in policy and action that call into question that simple stereotype. On the one hand, President Reagan spoke sharply against the Soviet Union, calling it the "evil empire" in speeches and television appearances. In March, 1983 he endorsed the concept of a Strategic Defense Initiative, a high-technology missile defense system. Vast increases in defense expenditures also support the notion that the Cold War was at its height. Defense budgets climbed from $167 billion in 1981 to $303 billion by 1989. Competition with the Soviet Union for quieter, more effective, and better-performing high technology in ships and submarines continued to drive naval RDT&E.

On the other hand, several specific Reagan-era reforms stressed reduction in the size of government, sometimes touching on the defense establishment. Much of the increased defense budget went to procurement of already developed systems, while the in-house RDT&E facilities of the military services, as part of the government civil service establishment, began to face budgetary restraint, personnel ceilings, and repeated reforms designed to streamline the activities.

International events also signaled profound change. Mikhail Gorbachev won election as Soviet Communist Party secretary general in March 1985, and the Reykjavik Summit that foreshadowed later disarmament agreements met in October 1986. Negotiators from sixteen NATO nations and seven Warsaw Pact nations met in Vienna in February 1987 to begin detailed and technical discussions that later produced the

Conventional Forces in Europe Treaty limiting nonnuclear armaments in the whole area from the Atlantic to the Urals. Despite such promising signs, most American defense planners viewed Gorbachev's reforms of perestroika or restructuring and glasnost or openness, not as signs of instability in the Soviet bloc, but as moves that would potentially strengthen Soviet military and strategic capabilities. Increasing stealth capabilities of Soviet submarines served to warn American specialists that the arms race surrounding underwater silence was about to move into a new cycle of intensified quieting and improved detection.

The April 1986 air strike against Libya by U.S. forces, in Operation El Dorado Canyon, brought home to naval planners many lessons. As the first major engagement of U.S. military aircraft, weaponry, and fighting personnel since the Vietnam War, the operation tested the interaction of command, warfighters, platforms, weapons, and electronic systems, as well as interservice cooperation between Air Force and Navy. The operation brought American seamen and airmen against formidable equipment including radar-directed antiaircraft missiles, heat-seeking missiles, Styx antiship cruise missiles, and late-model Soviet and French aircraft, such as MiG-23s, Su-22s, Mirage Vs, and Mirage F-1s. One lesson of the engagement was that highly sophisticated weapons and defense systems were rapidly finding their way into the arsenals of third world countries.[1]

The mid-1980s were a period of many changes, but it was not clear exactly what those changes meant for naval research and technology. Events and trends raised questions that were difficult to answer. Would the Soviet Union emerge from its reforms as a more dangerous opponent? Would the threat from terrorist states like Libya intensify or diminish? Would America be able to maintain its competitive edge in world markets? Would the demand to reduce the size of government lead to further downsizing and reduction of the procurement establishment at the very time when resources needed to be turned to shifting military and civilian priorities?

The apparent contradiction between massive defense expansion and government shrinkage led to a series of policy changes, administrative reforms, and institutional restructurings, affecting the Navy's R&D centers in different ways. Specific reforms were spurred on by the reports of the Grace Commission and the Packard Commission, both developed in 1983. In 1985, following a general instruction by President Reagan in accord with Packard recommendations to make field activities of the government smaller, Secretary of the Navy John Lehman disestablished the Office of Naval Material. Studies by the Office of Technology Assessment and the consulting firm of Coopers & Lybrand recommended other changes with the goal of efficiency and improved responsiveness to the needs of the fleet.

During the mid-1980s, other policy initiatives generated further deep-seated changes in the goals and objectives of the defense establishment. The Goldwater-Nichols Defense Reorganization Act of 1986, requiring closer coordination and consolidation of the military services, was designed to work toward a leaner and more efficient bureaucracy. The Federal Technology Transfer Act of 1986, together with an executive order signed by President Reagan in the spring of 1987 articulated the need to increase American competitiveness in the world marketplace by encouraging the transfer of technology from the Department of Defense and Department of Energy laboratories to the private sector for commercial application.

At the David Taylor Naval Ship Research and Development Center, the response to the confusing cross currents of the era was characterized by an infusion of ideas from new administrative leaders, innovative research, and some internal restructuring.

Organizational Innovation to Deal With Ship Integration

Searching for ways to accomplish cross-disciplinary integration at the center, Technical Director Alan Powell established a program of Technology Applications Teams (TATs) in 1980. Based on programs like the White House Fellows, the plan would release a small number of individuals from current assignments to work directly for the technical director on specially designated topics for a defined period. Under the TAT program, three to eight specialists from different disciplines were to be released from their regular duties for a year to work together "to investigate innovative alternatives which fulfill the center's mission." Powell invited all GS 12–14 scientists and engineers to apply for the program, seeking self-nomination rather than selection by department heads.

Powell chose as the topic for the first TAT the development of methods of systematically evaluating the impact of emerging technologies on the total ship system for surface ships. One of the evaluation methods produced by the first team was an interactive computer program: Advanced Surface Ship Evaluation Tool (ASSET). The second TAT continued work on ASSET in 1981–1982, validating the tool, and bringing further improvements to it. One important benefit of ASSET was that it allowed planners to examine closely the interaction of subsystems within a total ship system. Frequently the best design of a subsidiary part of a ship was not necessarily the optimum design in the total ship. The difficult process of suboptimization, characteristic of many systems problems, was particularly acute as designers tried to bring together ideal propellers, hulls, armaments, machinery, electrical, and other systems. Engineers continued to refine and improve ASSET over the next decade and a half, adding subsidiary programs concerned with cost and with specialized problems in submarine design.

TATs in 1980 and 1981 focused on surface ship technology, assessing and evaluating the impact of emerging technologies. In 1982–1983 and 1983–1984, the teams incorporated examination of cost and eventual mission effectiveness of new technologies, particularly with regard to submarines. TATs 1 and 2 developed and enhanced ASSET, and TATs 3 and 4 developed technology evaluation programs, technology surveys, and three new concepts for submarines. ASSET and the other programs enabled planners to look at the impact of new technologies on the total ship, on cost, on manning requirements, and on mission capabilities.

The TAT concept itself ran into difficulties, however. As R&D budgets dwindled, heads of existing departments questioned whether the results of the program justified the temporary reassignment of five or so very valuable people from the departments. Other problems, typical of such administrative reforms when tried in other settings, plagued the TATs. "Home" departments sometimes found it difficult to provide a useful position for a returning member. After serving a year in the creative and interdisciplinary environment of the TAT, it was difficult for many to return to regular program-funded projects in their own specialties.

Budget cutbacks at the center as a whole through the 1980s resulted in reduced travel and rare promotion opportunities, making it difficult to retain many talented younger researchers. The TAT served as a "safety valve" for energetic and ambitious researchers, helping to keep some from resigning for a better position elsewhere. Even so, the center often lost staff after they returned to their departments from service on a TAT.

But the positive outcomes outweighed the problems, TAT advocates argued. The experience returned members to their departments with a centerwide perspective. Working in TAT taught the value of teamwork. Rather than decreasing available R&D monies, the TATs actually attracted new research monies through innovations such as ASSET and other products.

Despite such benefits, in the face of continued concern over restricted budget and the drain on departments losing staff, TAT was not renewed in fiscal year 1985. Among the reasons for the termination of the program was the justified complaint that many participants "migrated" from their original departments after service on a TAT. Of

twenty-one members over the four years of the program, only two continued in their same discipline, while six retired, three left Carderock,
and ten went on to continue work in systems approaches outside of their
discipline.

However, the TAT major product, ASSET, in fact did change the
way NAVSEA's design community thought in regard to conceptual ship
design. ASSET was adopted in a naval architecture course taught at MIT,
and soon a wide range of specialists, in areas from ship pollution abatement to ship silencing, began to request ASSET documentation. By the
late 1980s, ASSET became a permanent part of the toolkit of ship designers, and began to find applications beyond the U.S. Navy.[2]

Powell, who had served as technical director since 1967, retired in
December 1985. Edwin O'Neill served as acting technical director until
Richard E. Metrey assumed the post on 1 June 1986. Like Powell, Metrey
worked to address the issue of ship system integration through management innovation.

Metrey's earlier career at NAVSEA had exposed him to a series of
problems in weapons systems integration. From his experience in
weapons systems, where the coordination of electronic, mechanical,
propulsion, and command systems was essential to combat, he concluded that systems integrators had a well-established and well-recog-
nized role. However, he believed that systems integration had not gained
as much recognition in the ship design area. The final weapon system installed on a ship represented a working balance between the input from
the specialists on the subsystems. Even in weapons systems, however, the
lack of combat experience in recent years raised concerns that the technically sophisticated subsystems might not mesh properly in actual warfare. Metrey noted that on the hull, mechanical, and electrical (HM&E)
side, the Navy had never been able to establish effectively the necessary
coordination even to the level found in weapons.[3] He took steps to
strengthen the linkage between systems analysis and technology assessments by directing that existing warfare simulations be improved to represent center R&D initiatives in a warfare context. To demonstrate pay-
offs of center-developed technologies and systems in possible warfare
scenarios, he supported the establishment of a secure warfare simulation
facility: the Simulation, Planning, and Analysis Research Center
(SPARC). Over the next years the SPARC and its intellectual products
would do much to stimulate thinking about future warfare scenarios
among naval leadership.

For naval officers and crews, the systems integration issue was no
abstraction. The very survival of men and ships depended upon weapons
and ship integration. Although the United States had engaged in no

major naval war since 1945, and only a few isolated incidents like El Dorado Canyon since the end of the Vietnam War, the fleet remained at risk. Several incidents involving U.S. naval ships, such as the Iraqi attack on *Stark* (FFG 31), in May 1987, vividly demonstrated the difficulties of integration of modern systems of defense and ship command. Ideal, integrated designs that worked well in combat continued to be a crucial goal for the Navy.

At the center, the Systems Integration Department, Code 12, which had originated as Code 11, the Systems Development Department, had a natural role in ship integration. The Systems Development Department had successfully brought systems integration to high-speed small craft such as hydrofoils and air cushion AALC. In the mid-1980s, Technical Director Powell had shifted Warren Dietz, who headed Code 27 (Machinery) at Annapolis, to direct the department.

At first, Dietz attempted to broaden the responsibility of Code 12 by bringing into the department two units whose work had some ship-wide application. He brought from his department at Annapolis the ship damage control group. He also absorbed a specialist in ship survivability from the technical director's office. But the department still remained an awkward conglomeration of programs without a true, shipwide systems analysis function. The problem of moving the systems approach from a focus on advanced ships to more conventional ships remained.[4]

Dietz continued an effort begun by his predecessors, playing a support role to the Ship Design Division of NAVSEA. That office continued the function of design groups at the old Bureau of Construction and Repair and at the Bureau of Ships. To address more effectively the need to support design, Dietz established three new internal divisions of the Systems Integration Department: one for surface ships, one for submarines, and one to continue the work on advanced ships, in addition to his other collected offices. Yet such departmental reorganization did not address the fact that the other existing functional departments at the center continued to deal directly with program managers at NAVSEA to acquire their funding. Most systems coordination would have to take place at the headquarters level, while the Systems Integration Department at the center continued to coordinate only a few programs.[5]

In early 1987, another personnel shift reflected Metrey's attempt to get the Systems Integration Department to play a stronger coordinating role, by interchanging its leadership with that of NAVSEA Preliminary Design (Code 501). The head of Preliminary Design, George Kerr, transferred to direct the Systems Integration Department at the center and was replaced in NAVSEA by Deitz.

Kerr, with a cynicism born of twenty-seven years in conceptual design and administrative experience at NAVSEA, looked on the role of Code 12 very realistically. While he agreed that it should play a systems role, he also recognized that merely asserting that role would not work with the commitment to subsystems represented by the various other departments. He did not see that entrenched attachment to subsystems as anyone's fault. The specialists in propellers, machinery, hulls, and other subsystems had good reason to regard someone outside as interfering with their turf. Kerr believed that he could describe the department only in terms of its actual work. "We are what we do," he proclaimed.[6]

Kerr remembered that old-timers at NAVSEA recognized that the marriage or consolidation expected with the formation of BUSHIPS in 1939 had never really taken place, and that Ship Design at NAVSEA faced inherited and built-in problems of trying to coordinate the work of machinery and hull specialists at headquarters itself. His years of experience at NAVSEA led him to define the problem of ship integration as deeply rooted in the historic evolution of naval structure, not simply as a local problem.[7]

O'Neill, from his own experience in administering the department in 1983, saw the barriers to an integration role for Code 12 somewhat differently. He believed that ship integration, given the naval RDT&E structure, had to be a support, not a leadership and management, role. He believed that the fact that Ellsworth had built the early department around program management for advanced ships meant that the people in the department were not accustomed to a support role. A second barrier derived, in O'Neill's view, from the fact that NAVSEA was not particularly interested in seeing the center play such a role. Like Kerr, he viewed the difficulty in ship integration as a problem inherent in the Navy's organizational structure.[8]

SSN 21, a nuclear attack submarine scheduled to go into the water in mid-1990s (the *Seawolf* class), presented a major coordination challenge to Kerr and to NAVSEA in the late 1980s. Kerr estimated in 1987 that about forty percent of the center's budget derived in one way or another from SSN 21, a reflection on the very high priority placed on reaching new levels of stealth and performance that would exceed those of the Soviets. Code 12 began to serve a kind of communication and monitoring role for SSN 21, going to briefings, making presentations, entertaining visiting VIPs, representing Technical Director Metrey at a few meetings, and generally keeping up with what went on. Kerr knew, however, that such a role did not convey any power to impose systems trade-offs or to coordinate effectively, and he worried that the future submarine's final design might not turn out to be the ideal optimum.[9]

Some in the Systems Integration Department believed that it would be more logical to have their department serve as a staff office to the technical director. This concept seemed quite natural, since it began as an office under the technical director. All efforts and recommendations notwithstanding, the mission implied by the name, "The Ship Systems Integration Department," remained elusive in the mid-1980s.[10]

Although caught in a problem whose origins went back to the earliest days of steam-propelled ships, administrators at the center continued to try ideas that would bring together subsystem specialists. Powell and, later, Metrey worked on these alternatives: focusing the Technology Assessment Teams on the issue, strengthening the role of the technical director and his staff, setting up both internal and external coordination groups, and establishing a new department whose function had a broader systems basis.[11]

Following an initiative begun during Powell's administration, Metrey established an Advanced Ship Concept Demonstration Group, consisting of highly placed members from each department, to take a coordinating look at future ships. This group looked at new technology and worked towards blending it, particularly in the area of ship machinery. One focus in early 1987 had been a concept of a "podded" or modular propulsion unit that would incorporate superconducting motors and a counter-rotating propeller system that could be added to a ship almost as an outboard motor. The modular, or plug-in, nature of components would allow the Navy to more readily take advantage of future changes. Complex systems demanded replacement, rather than repair, and the modular construction would permit more rapid return to service of damaged or disabled vessels. Metrey recognized that the idea in its early stages had its critics and needed much further development. Yet in order to make progress, he believed that innovative ideas of this sort had to be explored and considered. Unlike the TAT approach, the Advanced Ship Concept Demonstration Group did not require that researchers transfer out of their departments for an extended period of time, and this approach encountered far less opposition than the TAT.[12]

NAVSEA considered another coordinating reform, the Hull, Mechanical, and Electrical (HM&E) Initiative, a proposal from the center that would establish a high-level systems office. Whether housed at the center or at NAVSEA, the proposed HM&E R&D strategy team would look at future ships, considering needs, mission, and evolving technology, and would study the economic and technical feasibility of likely innovations for periods as long as ten to twenty years into the future. Using these projections, the Navy might be able to bring integration to hull and machinery planning as it had to weapons systems.[13]

However, systems approaches were not only the province of center-wide groups. In early 1987 Metrey initiated a reconstitution of the Central Instrumentation Department (Code 29) as the Ship Electromagnetic Signatures Department (Code 14). Like the Ship Acoustics Department, this new group would focus on reducing the detectability of ships by other means including infrared signatures, radar-imaging, wake detection, and a variety of electromagnetic emissions. Similar to the Acoustics Department, its interest would cross the disciplines and involve specialists in structures, hydrodynamics, materials, and machinery. In this sense, the two functional departments concerned with reducing detectability both took a shipwide approach, rather than focusing only on specialized subsystems. As sophisticated weaponry and sensors came into the inventory of third world nations, planners recognized that reducing the detectability of submarines and surface ships took on added urgency.[14]

Although the center's research excellence derived from its specialists in a range of subsystems, those specialists had worked together for years. Responding to constant pressure to engage in cooperation and trade-off of designs, the researchers, civilian administrators, and naval officers recognized that ship integration was essential to the achievement of effective and combat-ready vessels. Deep-seated administrative and funding barriers to ship integration stood in their way, some of them local and some imposed by the Navy's system of procurement. Nevertheless, leadership at the center continued to work, both within and across departments, to address systems integration issues.

Independent Research During the Late 1980s

The policy cross currents of the 1980s created severe dilemmas for naval R&D. In the interests of economy, some forward-looking programs were being discontinued, research and travel funds cut back, and ceilings imposed on promotion. At the same time, DOD and the Navy expected continuing innovation in science and technology. One means of balancing between these conflicting goals was through support for independent research. Independent research had always been a strength of the center. From the inception of the Experimental Model Basin under David Taylor himself in 1898, private shipyards in the United States had never taken a lead role in ship research and development. Over the decades, the center, almost by default, became the lead laboratory in ship-related research.

The continued flow of innovative concepts into the fleet depended on the Navy's willingness to sponsor research that might not immediately show practical results. In the reorganization of research and pro- curement during the 1960s, a system recognizing this principle had des- ignated funding not only for programmed development but for the kinds of independent research that Ernest Eggert and others had quietly sponsored in earlier decades. Most of the Navy's budget for the center came from four RDT&E budget categories, designated by code numbers ranging from 6.1 to 6.4: Research (6.1), from the Office of Naval Research; Exploratory Development (6.2), from the Office of Naval Technology; and program funding from the systems commands for Advanced Development (6.3) and Engineering Development (6.4).

Together, 6.1, 6.2, and part of 6.3 funding supported the Technology Base or Science and Technology, which in the thinking of naval planners made fundamental contributions from which later appli- cations would be developed. However, during the 1970s and 1980s, there was a long-range decline in overall Navy expenditure in the 6.2 Exploratory Development category from about $1 billion per year to about $400 million a year (as measured in constant 1989 dollars). To an extent, this decline was partially offset in the 1980s by a rise of about $100 million in 6.1 Research funding. At the center, these Navy-wide R&D funding developments had significant local consequences, felt in a surge of independent research funded under the 6.1 guidelines.[15]

Although the center's budget in the 1980s mostly derived from the 6.3 and 6.4 categories, money managers at the systems commands controlled such funding. By contrast to the 1950s, such an arrange- ment left little latitude for independent or fundamental research. However, the relatively small center budget from both the 6.1 and 6.2 categories, running about $4 million a year during the mid-1980s, was completely discretionary. These relatively small amounts of Independent Research and Independent Exploratory Development monies could fund long-range research, which although promising, might take decades to find direct application in the fleet, in the judg- ment of local leadership. Many IR/IED projects could yield returns far out of proportion to the small amounts invested in them, and could, on occasion, begin or carry forward extremely innovative concepts that then led to follow-on developments.

David Moran, who had responsibility for such programs out of O'Neill's office, reminded the staff that the first consideration in all in- dependent research work had to be the support of identified Navy needs. But the IR/IED program, which was personally approved by the technical director, often showed an imaginative and creative style that, Moran claimed, led to "discovery of fundamental concepts and the solu- tion of technical unknowns."[16]

Moran, adopting a pattern found in academia, pointed with pride to the fact that much of the work funded under the independent parts of 6.1 and 6.2 led to publication and presentation of results at conferences and symposia, and through the period, he used peer-reviewed publications in refereed scholarly journals as a measurement of success, rather than immediate application in fleet usage. Later, numbers of patents issued would be added as another criterion or "metric" of accomplishment in such activities. Moran asserted that the center's reputation depended "entirely on the dedication of the scientists who perform the research," and for that reason, he structured his reports as a presentation of individual accomplishments, focusing on specific researchers.[17]

Moran suggested over and over in his reports that when a history of naval technology was written in future decades, the origins of weapons, machinery, and ships would be traced to such exploratory work. In fact, Technical Directors Powell and Metrey both hoped that the discretionary funds would serve as seed money, to develop ideas that had no sponsors in program offices, and that could serve as a source of future applied naval innovation.

The discretionary funds could be used to keep alive an area of science-technology innovation, even when program support dried up. A case in point came in the area of superconductivity. Despite the fact that the Advanced Electric Drive Program had developed and successfully demonstrated an engine using superconductivity, program support vanished after 1980. The team at Annapolis maintained its continuity, however, using IR/IED funding, and a series of research projects kept the program alive. In early 1987 public interest in new discoveries in superconductivity stimulated a flurry of media interest and congressional support.

Michael Superczynski, who had worked with the superconductivity group since 1971, commented that the renewed congressional support in 1987 and media concern held promise that the center would receive new program funding. The Annapolis Advanced Electric Drive Group had produced a machine, had demonstrated it on board the test vessel *Jupiter*, and had maintained the continuity of research. Superczynski felt optimistic that funding included in the armed services appropriations would flow to the center. The new developments, which suggested that superconductivity could be achieved at temperatures in the range of -203 degrees C, held great promise for machinery applications, since liquid nitrogen (at -209.86 degrees C) could yield such temperatures much more easily and less expensively than could liquid helium (at -272.2 degrees C). Much basic engineering accomplished at Annapolis with the earlier generation of superconductivity could be carried over if the new discoveries proved practical. In any case, the fact that Annapolis had established and maintained a reputation in the field led to good prospects for further work as congressional interest and support picked up once again in the 1990s.[18]

Neal Sondergaard pursued the study of liquid metal current collectors for use in high-power-density homopolar direct current machines for ship propulsion. The liquid metal collectors, whether employed in superconducting machines or more conventional homopolar direct current motors, would improve efficiency, lower weight, and increase power density to a point that would greatly reduce ship size and cost. In 1985 Sondergaard worked on current collectors that utilized niobium fibers encased in copper, with the fibers serving as a brush, holding the liquid metal as a "paint" in place against the rotor. Such an arrangement would allow for a smooth, stable electrical and mechanical contact. His particular study focused on the brushes' electrical resistance, applying theoretical models to the turbulent flow patterns of the liquid metal.[19]

Coatings and compounds that could reduce a ship's resistance in water continued to be a major concern. G. I. Loeb predicted a new generation of antifouling compounds for ship hulls. By the mid-1980s, cuprous oxide and organotin compounds had greatly reduced fouling of ship bottoms by barnacles, tubeworms, and other relatively large organisms, although such compounds had raised objections from groups and local governments concerned with environmental protection, leading to the Navy banning their use on large ships. Loeb focused on the question of exactly how microorganisms settled on metal and plastic surfaces, and investigated through electron spectroscopy the surface characteristics of the materials before and after seawater immersion. Another researcher, V. J. Castelli, looked at methods of improving speed through water by reducing friction and studied various polymer coatings for torpedoes.[20]

Some hydrodynamics projects applied contemporary computer hardware and programs to subjects of long-standing interest with possible future applications. B. H. Cheng studied the effect of nine different bulbous bows on the performance of high-speed naval ships, such as frigates, validating a design methodology for a typical naval combatant ship. J. V. Waldo Jr. and E. Battifarano developed a bubble-dynamics theory and a numerical method of applying it to study closely the effect of underwater explosions. The theory could lead to better structural design for improving ships' ability to survive weapons attacks.[21]

M. C. Mosher used numerical methods to investigate vortices in the flow from submarines and aircraft. In the case of submarines, better knowledge of vortices could help reduce the detectability of the ship, since vortex flows created detectable surface flow patterns. Mosher published his results in a German journal of flight science. Cheng modified existing computer programs to improve the study of flow fields around underwater towed bodies. Although theoretical, this study also had its practical uses. Expensive and time-consuming sea trials gathered data to measure the wake of a ship, but better knowledge of generation of flow fields would allow much of the work to be done at lower cost by computer.[22]

The wake, thermal disturbance, radar image, and infrared image of a ship would leave "signatures," all of which would make it more detectable to an enemy. Independent Research funds supported a series of investigations into wake generation and detection, detectable hydrodynamic phenomena, and radar cross-section modeling in 1985. After 1987, such work would contribute to the Ship Electromagnetic Signatures Department agenda.[23]

These projects are only a few of a much greater number funded under the discretionary funding, suggestive of the wide range of interests and disciplines engaged. Some work sponsored by Independent Research funding remained classified even in the preliminary research stages. Such projects included studies of explosive armor, some approaches to reducing the infrared signature of ships, investigation of radar-absorbing structures, and continuing improvements in acoustic stealth. Although the issues required basic research, military applications would be apparent from the inception of the work.[24]

Change of Command, Change of Name

On 15 July 1987, at his installation ceremonies as Commanding Officer DTNSRDC, Captain Clark (Corky) Graham shocked many in the audience by referring to the center as the David Taylor Research Center. Since 1975, long-term center employees chafed under a long and unwieldy name: David Taylor Naval Ship Research and Development Center. DTNSRDC added up to the longest acronym for a shore establishment in the Navy, they noted, with ironic resignation. In the audience, listeners wondered how the new commanding officer achieved the welcome name change, reflecting the center's long history, its heritage deriving from Taylor, and its research emphasis. Years later, in an interview, Graham remarked that he "just did it," and that he luckily was able to get the name change officially recognized within a few months, on 18 September 1987. The somewhat audacious and unconventional move would characterize the style of much of Graham's nearly five-year term at DTRC.[25]

In a flurry of activity, Graham spent his first weeks visiting every department, meeting not only the department heads, but men and women at the next echelons of management and many senior researchers. He immediately began to issue memos, many to all department heads, and others directed to key personnel, with suggestions, ideas, requests for information, and new initiatives. The flood of memorandums exceeded the secretarial staff's capability to produce them in typed form, and senior managers and researchers became used to receiving photocopies of handwritten memos, soon referred to as "Corkygrams," in much the same way that Admiral Elmo Zumwalt's many memorandums had become known as "Z-grams." Graham explicitly modeled several administrative ideas on those of Zumwalt.

Graham hoped to bring many new initiatives to fruition, and to work on the continuing ship integration problem. For these purposes, he worked closely with those he called "the bright number twos," including assistants to the heads of departments and accomplished researchers throughout the organization. Working with such people, and through the Strategic Planning and Assessment Center initiated by Captain Graham, he soon established communication among all of the departments, among other R&D centers, and among NAVSEA, ONR, and OPNAV sponsors. He established a "Round Table Process" that focused initially on surface combatants, bringing in individuals from each technical department at the center. Later, he established what he called "war rooms" that he hoped would serve as catalysts for strategic thinking and planning for the Navy as a whole.

In 1989, Graham and Metrey reorganized the Office of the Director, Technology, Plans and Assessment, reconstituting it as the Office of the Director of Technology, appointing Harvey Chaplin as the director, and Dennis Clark as the director of Strategic Planning. Adjusting to new developments in priorities in 1990, Graham established an "affordability" war room to respond to increasing emphasis placed on cost as a driver in the naval acquisition process. In the same year, he also established an Operation Desert Shield War Room to coordinate DTRC support and to serve as a clearinghouse for information regarding the Persian Gulf crisis. He and Metrey also established a Strategic Planning Council, which modified and used a strategic planning method employed by the U.S. Marine Corps.

Graham's leadership generated a range of reactions, from enthusiasm on the part of some who welcomed the attempt to focus on systems, planning, and the changing naval environment, to others who found his barrage of innovative ideas almost irrelevant to the established center missions. In retrospect, he admitted that his own lack of administrative follow-through, his unwillingness to go through channels, and his irreverent attitude toward many established naval traditions and interest groups had worked against achieving most of his goals. In many ways, he did not simply exercise his role as commanding officer, but attempted to go beyond that assigned duty to act as intellectual leader and provocative agent for change. Not surprisingly, such a challenge to convention and "proper" administrative structure energized some staff members while it only served to antagonize others, both within the center and higher in the chain of command.

He consciously sought to take the ideas developed at the center to wider audiences. For example, at the 4 May 1989 American Society of Naval Engineers (ASNE) meeting, he delivered the keynote address, focusing on a concept of naval force architecture developed by the center. He discussed the "D^3 + S" concept, referring to distribute, disperse, disguise, and sustain. Under this paradigm, he explained, two types of ships would be built: carriers of large objects and scout fighters. Using colored cylinders to demonstrate the ideas, with their size directly proportional to the signature magnitudes of the ships they represented, he made visual the problem of ship signature reduction. "The bottom line," he asserted, "is that we have to challenge today's concepts and start conceptualizing alternatives."[26] As he later noted, the concept of large-object carriers received lots of interest from engineers, but encountered immediate resistance from many who had built careers and developed major advances based on existing fleet architecture concepts.

Among Graham's efforts to change the corporate culture at the center was his initiation of a variety of institutional mechanisms to stimulate new ideas. He created the Innovation Center, which consisted of three pre-stocked cells or rooms furnished with desks, computers, and phones. Multi-disciplinary and multi-organizational groups would be formed and assigned to one of the Innovation Center cells. Working under a "fast-failure" guideline, the group would decide within a month whether the concept should be developed further or abandoned. If continued, the group would have up to six months to develop the innovative concept. Over the next decade, of the sixteen projects coming out of the Innovation Center, nine eventually found sponsors and funding. Graham appointed Harvey Chaplin to be an innovation advocate to assist in stimulating groups to participate in the Innovation Center and to help provide managerial support. A contest was held, with a tongue-in-cheek trophy of a giraffe, representing those most willing to "stick out their necks" with an untried technological and managerial ideas. Graham and others at Carderock took satisfaction from the fact that the Innovation Center concept spread to other activities throughout the Navy. Carderock, they claimed, built on its well-deserved reputation for developing models of ships, going on to modeling institutional or managerial structures emulated and replicated elsewhere.

Graham regarded as one of his more important achievements the endorsement he received from CNO Admiral Carlisle Trost for another idea that the round table–war room approach generated. Trost became an enthusiastic advocate of an integrated electric drive as a major new advance in naval ship propulsion. Not only did Admiral Trost order the establishment of a program office (SEA 05Z) to sponsor research and development in this technology, but he set up the program office itself at the center's Annapolis site, a departure from the usual pattern of directing such programs from NAVSEA in Crystal City, Virginia. Graham's innovative and energetic style came at a time when the Defense Department generally and the Navy in particular struggled with reshaping R&D priorities.

Continuing Innovation, Continuing Change

Despite the cross currents in the 1980s clouding the shape of future defense policy, research continued on many fronts at the center. Both Powell and Metrey sought administrative ways to address the difficult issue of fostering ship systems integration. Several departments had mandates that cut across disciplines and subsystems, such as the Computer Lab, Acoustics, Electromagnetic Signatures, and the Systems Department itself. Yet coordination among these people and with other specialists in machinery, propellers, structural mechanics, materials sciences, and hydrodynamics continued to require innovative approaches. The TATs, ASSET, the Systems Department reforms, the HM&E initiative, SPARC, the Advanced Ship Concept Demonstration Group, and other efforts all spoke to the systems problems that had haunted ship architecture for more than a century. The simultaneous demand for innovation and for budget constraint characteristic of the 1980s created increasing pressures, only partly addressed by reliance on discretionary IR/IED money. Graham focused his energy not only on issues of ship system integration, but on further means of stimulating innovation.

Meanwhile, the world continued to change beyond the fences surrounding the center. Momentous events suggested that long-held assumptions about the international balance of power were coming into question. In mid-1988 Gorbachev announced and in October 1989 ordered massive troop removals from Eastern Europe. In the fall of 1989, Hungary opened its borders, and East Germans took the opportunity to emigrate to West Germany through the open Hungarian borders. Clearly, an era was coming to an end.

Endnotes

1. Joseph T. Stanik, *Swift and Effective Retribution: The U.S. Sixth Fleet and the Confrontation with Qaddafi* (Washington: Naval Historical Center, 1997), 20–27.
2. Details of TATs (sometimes redundantly referred to as "TAT Teams") were provided through discussions on 26 Jun 1997 with Dennis Clark, a member of the first TAT. Documents in the ABIF include internal memoranda, 1978–1985, describing some of the administrative problems and positive results. See also *Centerline*, 19 Sep 1980, 26 Mar 1982, and 25 Nov 1985.
3. Richard Metrey, interview by Rodney Carlisle, 15 May 1987.
4. Warren Dietz, interview by Rodney Carlisle, 15 Dec 1986; George Wachnik, interview by Rodney Carlisle, 26 Oct 1984.
5. Dietz interview, 15 Dec 1986; "New Department Emphasizes Total Systems Integration," *Centerline*, 21 Dec 1984, 4–5.
6. George Kerr, interview by Rodney Carlisle, 12 May 1987.
7. Ibid.
8. Edwin O'Neill, interview by Rodney Carlisle, 27 May 1987.
9. Ibid.; Kerr interview, 12 May 1987.
10. William Ellsworth, interview by Rodney Carlisle, 1 Oct 1984; O'Neill interview, 27 May 1987.
11. Ellsworth interview, 1 Oct 1984; O'Neill interview, 27 May 1987.
12. Metrey interview, 15 May 1987.
13. Ibid.
14. Ibid.; O'Neill interview, 27 May 1987.
15. Trends in 6.1 and 6.2 funding are detailed in Vice Admiral P. F. McCarthy, "Navy RDT&E White Paper," 29 Mar 1989, copy in ABIF.
16. *IR/IED Annual Report, Fiscal Year 1985* (DTNSRDC publication, Jan 1986), x, xi; Michael Superczynski, interview by Rodney Carlisle, 8 Jul 1987.
17. *IR/IED Report*, FY 1985, I.
18. Ibid., 7–8, 29–30;
19. *IR/IED Report*, FY 1986, 27–28
20. *IR/IED Report*, FY 1985, 27–28, 39–40.
21. Ibid., 57–58, 51–52.
22. M. C. Mosher, "A Method For Computing Three-Dimensional Vortex Flows," *Zeitschrift fur Flugwissenschaften und Weltraumforschung (Journal of Flight Sciences and Space Research)* 9 (May/Jun 1985): 123–133.
23. *IR/IED Report, FY 1985*, 103–104, 112, 115.
24. Ibid., 99–100, 107, 109–110, 114; *IR/IED Report, FY 1986*, 47–48, 56, 67.
25. John Iler, "Center Means Progress Workshops Formed," *Centerline*, Dec, 1987; Captain Clark Graham, USN (Ret.), telephone interview by Rodney Carlisle, 28 Mar 1997. A tape of the interview is with ABIF materials. A file of Graham's memoranda in the TD's office, coupled with the interview, gave many insights to the administrative style reflected in the following paragraphs.
26. Mary Kniss, "Graham Keynote Speaker at ASNE Day 1989," *Centerline*, May 1989.

CHAPTER 14

Peace Dividends

IN DECEMBER 1989, WORLDWIDE TELEVISION audiences watched the spectacle of joyous crowds tearing chunks of concrete from the Berlin Wall that had stood as a symbol of the Cold War since 1961. Although for many the "collapse of the wall" provided a visual and memorial reference point for the end of the Cold War, many other events gave indications of changes in Soviet-American relations and within the Soviet Union itself. While international relations rapidly changed, the impact of change on the American defense establishment, on the Navy's RDT&E facilities, and on the research facilities at Carderock and Annapolis took several years to unfold, making the whole period from 1989 through the late 1990s one of multiple transitions.

By November 1989, the phrase "peace dividend" entered common parlance to describe potential defense budget cuts. Within the DOD, planners clearly understood that the congressional pressures for budget cuts had to be addressed. Rear Admiral Wayne Meyer noted that the Secretary of Defense and the Joint Chiefs of Staff were "highly responsive to political pressure," and political pressure now mounted to focus all defense planning on budget cutting.[1]

In the last months of 1991, the Soviet Union itself dissolved. With Soviet political and economic collapse, and with the elimination of Communist Party control of all but a handful of nations, the Cold War, which had been declared over by 1989, was clearly a thing of the past by 1992. By 1992–1993, the clamor for a peace dividend began to have clear and lasting institutional consequences for the defense establishment and more particularly for the Navy's RDT&E facilities.

The changes came so rapidly that old policy guidance persisted for years in the United States. By the early 1990s, many influential voices suggested policy adjustments in contradictory directions.

DOD and Naval Mission Reassessments and Restructuring

Policymakers at the Pentagon continued to emphasize goals set in earlier studies, some of which had been prepared at the height of the Cold War. For example, President George Bush directed the Secretary of Defense Richard Cheney, in February 1989, to "develop a plan to accomplish full implementation of the recommendations of the Packard Commission and to review Defense management overall."[2] The Packard Commission, had recommended a group of reforms in 1983, resulting from studies conducted over the prior two years. Thus, at the beginning of the year that would see the Berlin Wall collapse, the Secretary of Defense based his review on eight-year-old premises.

The Packard Commission goals hardly reflected any recognition of reduced Soviet threat. Even so, the commission recommended several basic management concepts that could apply quite well in a post-Cold War environment, including multiyear funding, clearer command channels, smaller staffs devoted to management, closer communications between producers and users of research and development, and lower-cost approaches using commercial products and commercial-style competition.[3] Such Packard Commission goals continued to guide Defense management reform in the late 1980s.

In his Defense Management Report delivered to the President in July 1989 (mandated under the Goldwater-Nichols Act of 1986), Secretary of Defense Cheney reviewed the implementation of Packard recommendations, indicating that there was "no basis for complacency," while noting progress. Cheney's Report recommended that the scale of defense facilities be further cut back through closure of facilities and consolidation of activities. He requested that the Service Secretaries provide specific plans reflecting how the suggested guidance on cutbacks should be implemented. In the Navy, this request led to a round of planning that in turn produced a restructuring plan that emerged in 1991.[4]

The usual delay time in publishing documents, often a year or more, contributed to the dated tone of some policy papers, especially as strategic changes out-paced the ability of scholars and planners to evaluate the situation. In the turbulent period 1989–1991, some analysts continued to assume a continuing Soviet threat as they sought to design new structures. For example, an October 1989 Department of Defense Management Report still stressed the Soviet challenge, documenting it with reference to other recently published studies.[5]

On orders from the Secretary of Navy, Director of Navy Laboratories Gerald Schiefer headed a study group to examine naval facilities and suggest possible consolidations in response to Cheney's request. This group advanced the concept of aligning several field activities with similar or related responsibilities into a single field organization and placing such organizations under a single headquarters organization to improve accountability and service.[6] This concept evolved into a restructuring plan to drastically reshape the research and development organizations at Carderock and Annapolis.[7] If the Navy produced its own plan of consolidation and closure, the best, most essential, and strongest R&D entities might be preserved, and the new structure would have a rational, not simply a political, basis. Schiefer explicitly recognized that the pressure for a peace dividend could be converted into an opportunity to achieve a long-standing management objective of consolidation.[8]

Compared with other defense policy documents issued in the period, the team's report reflected a realistic grasp of the rapid changes in the world situation and in the likely changes in domestic policy that would result. The group noted that the Secretary of Defense would restructure the Navy if the Navy did not do it for itself. The team predicted that Defense would shift to more emphasis on "low-intensity conflict," which, if less threatening to world security, seemed less predictable than the perceived threat from the Soviet bloc during the Cold War. The team also predicted withdrawal from overseas bases, fewer weapons platforms and weapons systems, as well as an uncertain threat environment.[9]

Schiefer's team reviewed potential warfare environments, the likely developments of technology, the changing acquisition system, and a more multiservice-oriented and smaller scale support organization. Using a set of sixteen questions regarding technology and function, the team produced a list of recommended closures, mergers, and interservice transitions. Based on such a well thought-out and fully justified approach, the final plan was one that politicians, special-interest groups, or special advocates found difficult to challenge.

Gerald Cann, Assistant Secretary of the Navy for Research, Development, and Acquisition, forwarded to the Under Secretary for Defense (Acquisition) a memorandum growing out of Schiefer's work. The "DOD Test and Evaluation, Research and Development Facilities Paper" (12 April 1990) outlined the Navy's evaluation of RDT&E restructuring options, considering the changes in domestic and international priorities.[10]

Cann's memorandum noted that for forty years the Navy had "placed its highest premium" on deterring and defending against possible Soviet military aggression. In the post-Cold War world, he argued, superior American technology continued to be "an essential element" in future national strength and necessary for future naval superiority.

Looking at limited intensity conflicts like Operation El Dorado Canyon in Libya, Cann noted in 1990 that crisis response missions continued to require forward-deployed and expeditionary naval forces. Those forces had to face sophisticated weaponry coming into third world arms inventories.

Cann outlined a plan for the Navy RDT&E community that would lead to four full-spectrum RDT&E centers and a fifth, "corporate laboratory": Naval Air Warfare, Naval Surface Warfare, Naval Undersea Warfare, Naval C³I, and the Naval Research Laboratory. He argued against closure of, or transfer to the private sector of, the Navy's in-house RDT&E facilities. He summarized several lines of thought for this position, most of which had appeared before in planning documents: 1) the need to be a "smart buyer," 2) the need to maintain a technological capability in areas of limited interest to the commercial sector, 3) the ability to provide a quick response in time of crisis, 4) the ability to inject the "art of the possible" into defense planning, and 5) the need to provide cradle-to-grave capability to carry technology from development through application and fleet support.[11]

The Secretary of the Navy set up the Base Structures Committee in response to the fiscal year 1991 Defense Authorization Act. In the committee's recommendations, issued in April 1991, they replicated some of the logic and approaches developed over 1989–1990 by the "tiger team studies" and elaborated by Cann. The Navy forwarded the report to the Defense Base Realignment and Closure Commission established by Congress in the fiscal year 1991 authorization.[12]

The Navy's plan for realignment of RDT&E and engineering capabilities followed the Cann and Schiefer scheme of creating four megacenters: the Naval Air Warfare Center (NAWC), the Naval Command Control and Ocean Surveillance Center (NCCOSC), the Naval Surface Warfare Center (NSWC), and the Naval Undersea Warfare Center (NUWC). The Defense Base Realignment and Closure Commission (BRAC) accepted the Navy recommendations to create four warfare centers, each to be a megacenter with several locations. The thirty-four centers, facilities, stations, and activities that were combined into the larger warfare centers are shown as follows:

Naval Surface Warfare Center
1. Naval Surface Warfare Center, Dahlgren, VA
2. David Taylor Research Center, Carderock, MD
3. Integrated Combat Systems Test Facility, San Diego, CA
4. Naval Mine Warfare Engineering Activity, Yorktown, VA
5. Naval Coastal Systems Center, Panama City, FL
6. Naval Ordnance Station, Indian Head, MD
7. Naval Ordnance Station, Louisville, KY

  8. Naval Weapons Support Center, Crane, IN
  9. Naval Ship Systems Engineering Station, Philadelphia, PA
  10. Naval Ship Weapons Systems Engineering Station, Port Hueneme, CA
  11. Fleet Combat Direction Systems Support Activity, Dam Neck, VA

Naval Air Warfare Center
  12. Naval Weapons Center, China Lake, CA
  13. Naval Air Propulsion Center, Trenton, NJ
  14. Naval Air Engineering Center, Lakehurst, NJ
  15. Naval Avionics Center, Indianapolis, IN
  16. Naval Air Development Center, Warminster, PA
  17. Pacific Missile Test Center, Point Mugu, CA
  18. Naval Weapons Evaluation Facility, Albuquerque, NM
  19. Naval Air Test Center, Patuxent River, MD
  20. Naval Ordnance Missile Test Station, White Sands, NM

Naval Underwater Warfare Center
  21. Naval Underwater Systems Center, Newport, RI
  22. Naval Sea Systems Combat Engineering Station, Norfolk, VA
  23. Naval Undersea Warfare Engineering Station, Keyport, WA
  24. Trident Command & Control Systems Maintenance Activity, Newport, RI

Naval Command, Control, and Ocean Surveillance Center
  25. Naval Ocean Systems Center, San Diego, CA
  26. Naval Electronic Systems Engineering Center, Charleston, SC
  27. Naval Electronic Systems Engineering Activity, St. Inigoes, MD
  28. Naval Electronic Systems Engineering Center, Vallejo, CA
  29. Naval Space Systems Activity, Los Angeles, CA
  30. Naval Electronic Systems Engineering Center, Washington, DC
  31. Naval Electronic Systems Engineering Center, Portsmouth, VA
  32. Naval Electronic Systems Engineering Center, San Diego, CA
  33. Fleet Command Direction Systems Support Activity, San Diego, CA
  34. Naval Electronic Engineering Activity Pacific, Pearl Harbor, HI

A Department of Defense review group headed by Charles (Pete) Adolph noted that there would be many human problems in such planned consolidation and in relocating 4,800 people, including loss of key personnel, disruption of work, and loss of continuity. The Adolph Commission recommended that the Navy attempt to minimize turbulence in as many ways as possible, and to make every effort to hold key personnel. Nevertheless, Adolph noted, the closure and realignment plan represented a coherent and logical approach to consolidation, and did reflect a sensitivity to many issues felt at the laboratory level. Employees who had hoped the long-awaited Adolph Commission report would result in a modification of restructuring plans were disappointed when the report, after warning that disruptions could affect morale, simply endorsed the plans.[13]

In this fashion, the David Taylor Research Center, including both Carderock and Annapolis, became a division of the Naval Surface Warfare Center in January 1992. Over three years of quiet behind-the-scenes planning had generated a long-range reorganization that ensured the center's survival by incorporating it into a larger institution.

Research Priorities After the Cold War

As the Cold War rapidly wound down, just how the Navy would adjust research and development priorities continued to remain unclear. Neither Cann nor Schiefer had specified the priorities which would drive post-Cold War research and development. Their planning focus had been on institutional structure, not research agenda. Several alternative paths or patterns of reactions to the rapid changes in the world appeared to lie as implicit assumptions behind different sorts of project funding which came to the center over the early 1990s. The alternate implicit driving considerations could be summarized as follows:

- Continue prior long-term research agendas and programs.
- Shift research agendas to reflect more diverse and less powerful adversaries than the former Soviet Union, often involving potential conflicts in littoral waters.
- Emphasize research agendas that reflect commercial, budgetary, environmental, social, and other priorities.
- Establish new research agendas based on estimates of future technical capabilities of potential adversaries and future R&D development.

Continuing prior and existing research and development projects (the first path in the above list) simply reflected the reality of institutional momentum. Program managers continued existing projects with funding and personnel, based on development of technologies originally initiated to meet the threats of Cold War Soviet technology. Such an approach allowed funding and established decisions as to long-range projects to continue as the "drivers."

Shifting research agendas to reflect a more diverse and less powerful set of adversaries held a certain appeal. CNO Admiral Frank B. Kelso II and the Marine Commandant, General C. E. Mundy, advocated just such a priority change in a paper published in 1992, *From the Sea*. Even prior to the release of this document, some naval planners, such as Schiefer, had begun to assume that both naval operations and naval technological development should shift their emphases away from the high-technology contest against the Soviet Union to a more diverse set of potential opponents, requiring force projection from littoral waters to the shore. Some 177 incidents involving the U.S. Navy over the period since 1945 provided realistic evidence of what the Navy's future role might be. Such an approach, based on a selective view of history, made a new strategic assessment the driver of technology agendas.[14]

Research emphasis on commercial, environmental, budgetary, and social objectives, which had flourished in 1980s, received a new boost with congressional and public expectation of a peace dividend resulting from the Cold War's end. A series of projects focused on environmental quality technology. Similar premises led to transfer of naval technology to the private sector, supporting American competitiveness in the world market. Reflecting language utilized in prior decades, such a switch to civilian priorities was termed "conversion" or "reconversion." The Clinton administration, at the highest levels, fully endorsed conversion.[15]

The concept that the expert community should carefully assess the future of naval technology, looking ahead to the possible technologies in 2010 or 2020, represented the fourth approach. The approach assumed that talented and creative technical and scientific thinkers could predict future alternative scenarios of warfighting. Using such predictions, the Navy should consider and advocate imaginative, future-based research priorities and technological developments. This approach led to the major program on integrated electric drive, and consideration of radically new ship forms during the period.

Presented thus, the alternative paths, based on different premises, might appear to be mutually exclusive. However, because of project funding and the structure of research and development decisionmaking within the Navy, R&D advanced on all four alternative paths simultaneously, with a variety of projects within each during the period through the early 1990s.

For these reasons, the usual rich variety of research and development work pursued at DTRC appeared even more diverse during the period 1988–1998. In one sense, any "critical-mass" research and development institution inherently possessed the strength of diversity. By working simultaneously on a variety of projects that reflected priorities, each based on different premises, the center was bound to be ready for whatever the future yielded. If indeed, a major new adversary with high-technology capabilities in naval warfare emerged early in the twenty-first century, early futuristic planning would help prepare the national defense. On the other hand, if the nation enjoyed several decades of international peace, punctuated by occasional low-intensity conflicts, peacekeeping missions, and other such requirements, the center would be positioned to respond. The continued emphasis on commercial and civilian priorities and on over-the-shore equipment fitted well into such a future. Being large enough and flexible enough to respond simultaneously to a wide variety of possible outcomes and, at the same time, continuing toward successful completion of major current long-term projects initiated years before meant that the center met priorities advocated by different policy groups in the defense and naval communities.

In short, the center's very diversity, springing from its complex heritage, made it well adapted to responding to the diverse cross-currents in naval technology at the end of the Cold War.

Several hundred separate R&D projects proceeded independently under different program and project fundings at the center through the years of transition from Cold War to post-Cold War. Of these hundreds, a few major projects serve to illustrate the four premises at work in the period:

1. Continuation of R&D on long-established priorities
   Construction of Large Cavitation Channel, Memphis, TN
   SSN 21—the *Seawolf* class submarines
       acoustic silencing
       propulsor design
   Large-Scale Vehicle (LSV)
       Southeast Alaska Acoustic Measurement Facility
       Replacement of *Monob* with *Hayes*
       On-going work on DDG 51—*Arleigh Burke* destroyers

2. *From the Sea* emphasis
   Advanced Amphibious Assault Vehicle (AAAV)
   Joint Logistics Over the Shore (JLOTS)
   Hovercraft, hydrofoil, and SWATH ship programs

3. Civilian/commercial/environmental emphasis
   Ship design with Advanced Surface Ship Evaluation Tool (ASSET)
   Use of HY-100 steel
   Improved structural design methods
   Computer-Aided Acquisition and Logistics Support
   Reverse osmosis desalinization
   Conversion of air conditioning from CFCs
   Environmental quality—solid waste projects

4. Future-scenario driven
   Simulation Planning and Analysis Research Center (SPARC)
   Integrated Electric Drive (IED)
   Low-Observable Ship
   Advanced Enclosed Mast/Sensor

Continuing Priorities—The Large Cavitation Channel

Among the long-term projects that dominated the middle and late 1980s, a significant addition to the experimental facilities came with the large cavitation channel (LCC), constructed in Memphis, Tennessee.

Sea Shadow.   The low radar signature shape of this experimental ship, like other innovations over the decades at the center, may once again change the shape of ships to come.

The impetus for the LCC grew out of the continuing need to do cavitation-type testing of new designs in European facilities. Begun in 1979 and dedicated in 1991, the project represented a collaboration, led by DTRC, among several industrial companies, research firms, and academic laboratories.

Many staff members at the center played a crucial role in seeing this facility through to completion. Former commanding officers from Carderock, Rear Admiral Myron Ricketts and Captain Barry Tibbits, working at NAVSEA, pushed the concept of building and installing the large cavitation facility. Richard Rothblum had been active in the design phases. Bill Middleton helped shepherd the project through managerial and financial difficulties. Commanding Officer Captain G. Richard Garritson made some 127 presentations to help focus command support for the project. Technical Director Richard Metrey worked out the legal and institutional arrangements, requiring patient and intensive negotiation regarding property transfer, jurisdiction, budgeting, and other aspects of the multiparty collaborative effort.

Advanced Enclosed Mast/Sensor (AEM/S) System. The AEM/S came out of extensive center work on signature reduction. In this installation on board *Arthur W. Radford* (DD 968), the mast is enclosed in an obelisk of nonradar reflective material and shape shown aft of the conventional mast.

Squarely in the tradition of hydrodynamic experimentation that could be traced to the earliest days at the Experimental Model Basin, it was designed to provide a tool for testing the acoustic and hydrodynamic properties of submerged or partially submerged shapes in a flow in the range of 30 to 35 knots. In its physics, the LCC resembled a wind tunnel, in which the fluid medium flowed around a fixed model, rather than the model-basin concept of a model towed through the fluid. Under construction through the late 1980s, it incorporated many new technological concepts in the design of hydrodynamic and hydroacoustic test facilities.

The LCC was built in response to the need for a U.S. facility to have a variable-pressure, closed-circuit tank large enough to conduct model tests with scaled, full-length, completely appended models. The need for model tests of the complete hull-propulsor-appendage system became more important as concerns with acoustic silencing demanded ever more sophisticated testing of final interaction of hull, propulsors, and all underwater appendages on a model of a complete ship or submarine.

Bringing a systems approach to the question of underwater flow-generated noise required that a complete ship or submarine be tested, not simply the hull shape or individual components.

As in all facility design questions, certain basic decisions had to be taken that drove the LCC's overall shape and size. In particular, decisions as to the test section size, shape, and flow velocity, drove the overall design. The section for models had to be large enough to minimize adverse viscous scaling effects and flow blockage effects. Furthermore, since engineers designed the LCC to be a hydro-acoustic test facility, low background ambient noise levels had to be achieved, and extensive acoustic instrumentation had to be accommodated. So, at the same time, the instrument had to be large and powerful, yet extremely quiet. The final dimensions represented optimization between these goals.

Concerns with the hydrodynamic performance of nonsymmetric contraction and diffuser sections led to an interesting development in which designers "modeled" the LCC itself by the construction of a 1/10-

Large Cavitation Channel (LCC).   This large variable-pressure circulating water channel constructed at Memphis, Tennessee, provides a capability for center researchers to test large-scale ship and submarine models for acoustic effects of water flow around the model.

scale wind tunnel at St. Anthony Falls Hydraulic Laboratory of the University of Minnesota. Bolt, Beranek, and Newman Inc. of Cambridge, Massachusetts built still another partial wind tunnel model of the LCC water tunnel at 1/6 scale. These wind tunnel tests measured the detailed velocity field at the impeller location for the impeller design and noise predictions, and also measured flow excitation and unsteady forces on the turning vane cascades at the channel's corners or elbows. The experiments led to recommendations for improvement in turning vane shape and for improving impeller flow velocity pattern.

In order to reduce noise generated by rotating machinery, all such equipment was mounted on double-stage vibration isolation bases, using techniques and materials evolved over decades of research at the Annapolis facility. They mounted the main 14,000-horsepower pump motor on a two-stage inertia block system, consisting of two concrete blocks measuring about 35 feet square by 9 feet thick, with a 1-inch layer of elastomeric material separating the two blocks from each other, and separating the lower block from the motor foundation. Engineers also used elastomeric drive couplings along the drive shaft leading from the motor to inside the tunnel.

This large facility represented a continuation of priorities in a number of ways. Conceived during the height of the U.S.-Soviet competition to develop the most acoustically undetectable submarines and surface ships, the LCC represented a continuation of Cold War priorities in design objectives years after the Cold War's announced end. Even more profoundly, the LCC represented a continuation of a deeply rooted combination of research objectives and equipment innovation springing from the combined skills of researchers in hydrodynamics, facilities constructors, wind tunnel designers, acoustic specialists, and materials specialists. The testing of models of ships and submarine hulls, propulsors, and appendages together required a systems orientation and the contributions of specialists from across the disciplines at both Carderock and Annapolis.

In these ways, the LCC represented not only a culmination and a continuity of a Cold War-driven naval research priority, but a bringing together and a continuation of many traditional technical and managerial strengths of DTRC.[16]

Continuing Priorities—Acoustic Stealth

In the mid-1980s the Navy initiated several important programs that developed and contributed significant advanced acoustic stealth technology to its ships and to its acoustic measurement systems. As noted by George Kerr, the *Seawolf* fast attack submarine design program accounted for upwards of forty per cent of the center's budget through the mid-1980s. Requirements for *Seawolf* called for ship signature reduction and control, with very stringent noise goals specified. With the more stringent goals, it became necessary to develop and apply new measurement technology capable of measuring the much lower submarine noise signatures expected. In effect, the requirement that submarines be even more silent drove the technology development of a whole new generation of tools.

Researchers at the Acoustic Research Detachment at Bayview used the large-scale vehicle, to test fifteen alternative SSN 21 propulsor designs to meet the acoustic goals for the propulsor. The LSV was a 1/4 scale, battery-powered, computer-controlled, autonomous 156-ton model of an SSN. Attempting to achieve the same test program at full scale would have taken five times as long to achieve. As a consequence, LSV generated immense cost savings. In the early to mid-1990s, acoustic

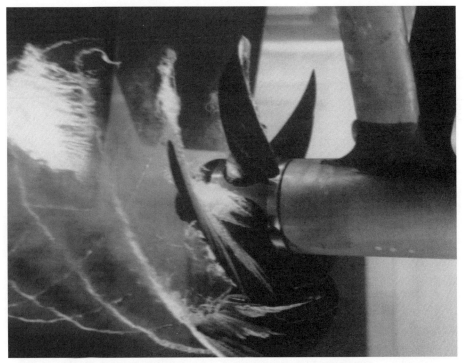

Controllable-Pitch Propeller in Large Cavitation Channel. Used for over 20 years from the 1940s, controllable-pitch propellers had been limited in the shaft horsepower (shp) they could sustain. Center work to improve their ability to take stresses up to 60,000 shp won a presidential level award.

design efforts for the Navy's new multimission attack submarine, New SSN (NSSN), involved similar work. Engineers reconfigured the LSV to support NSSN, including critical evaluations on various options related to the propulsor design. Researchers built several other new models to provide test platforms on which to evaluate performance of threat-reduction treatments, as well as to investigate several important bow design issues.[17]

In 1986, Carderock set up an Acoustic Measurement Facilities Improvement Program to develop, design, and provide systems capable of detecting and measuring the very low radiated noise signatures from the new generation of submarines. As a result of planning through this and other programs, the Ship Acoustics Department generated two new facilities. Off the East Coast, USNS *Hayes* (T-AG 195) replaced R/V *Monob* in 1991 as the fleet's submarine acoustics measurement platform. On the West Coast, the Southeast Alaska Acoustic Measurement Facility (SEAFAC) replaced the Carr Inlet Acoustic Range (CIAR) and the Santa Cruz Acoustic Range Facility (SCARF) in 1992.

With work on the *Seawolf* class, ship acoustic engineers became principal participants in the design process, working on designing and producing a quiet propulsor, special hull treatments, and acoustically improved bow features and silencing treatments. The acoustical engineers at Carderock and machinery specialists at Annapolis incorporated quieting technology they had developed over the previous two decades into the *Seawolf* design.

Hayes, converted from an oceanographic research vessel to an ultra-quiet noise measurement platform, used Exuma Sound and the Tongue of the Ocean near the Bahamas as its primary measurement sites. As a mobile platform, the ship could make acoustic measurements in littoral waters as well as in deeper sea environments. *Hayes* employed three major advanced specialized measuring systems; a special high-gain measurement array, a new high-capacity data acquisition and processing system, and a towed array measurement system.

SEAFAC, located in Behm Canal, near Ketchikan, Alaska, provided an ideal ship acoustic measurement site characterized by low ambient noise and minimal noise interference. It included the Navy's only facility capable of conducting acoustic measurements of a full-scale immobile submarine. It also could detect "transients" such as the starting of a pump, dropping of an object, or other momentary sounds that could give away the position of a submarine. The facility consisted of two measurement sites, a site to collect acoustic signatures of submerged submarines under powered and underway conditions at a variety of speeds and conditions, and a site to measure acoustic signatures of motionless

***Hayes* (T-AG 195).** In 1991, *Hayes* replaced *Monob* as the fleet's submarine acoustics measurement platform, operating in the Bahamas.

submarines with various on-board machinery under unloaded operation. At the static site, suspension barges lowered the submarine on cables and positioned it between two measurement arrays for a variety of nonpropulsive machinery operating conditions.

Engineers modified *Kamloops*, the 66-foot-long model used as an acoustic test vessel at Lake Pend Oreille since the 1960s, so that its bow came to resemble *Seawolf's* design. Starting in 1987, the model could be used to evaluate the acoustic performance of individual *Seawolf* design features. By 1990, the focus shifted to a simultaneous evaluation of the full complement of bow features in order to mitigate any related mutually interacting noise sources, to help attain the design's stringent noise goals.

The process of quieting the self-generated noise environment surrounding the sonar, in order to listen for more distant hostile acoustic sources, could be compared to peeling an onion, where the abatement of conspicuous noise exposed additional slightly less conspicuous underlying noises. Using *Kamloops* measurements, diagnostic tools, historic

Southeast Alaska Acoustic Measurement Facility. The need for silence in modern submarines demands extremely quiet waters in which to measure
noise characteristics. SEAFAC, near Ketchikan and surrounded by Tongus National
Forest, provides a unique site for acoustic testing of full-scale submarines.

full-scale and model-scale acoustical data, and thirty years of corporate
experience, acoustics engineers identified several critical constituent
contributors to *Seawolf*'s bow sonar noise environment.

As U.S. submarines became quieter and newer designs utilized
stealth technology, improved structural acoustic measurement became
necessary in order to investigate the more subdued flow of structure-
borne energy within the overall structure and the possible "hot spot"
acoustics radiation that might be detectable by hostile sensors. In 1987,
an ONR panel determined that a need existed for a large-scale model
target strength measurement capability. A team including DTRC, the
Naval Civil Engineering Laboratory, and the Ocean and Radar Systems
Division of General Electric participated in the program execution.
DTRC built the resulting facility, the Intermediate-Scale Measurement
System (ISMS), at the Bayview, Idaho site on Lake Pend Oreille.

The ISMS facility provided the capability to perform high-quality
measurements of structural acoustic responses of large-scale submarine

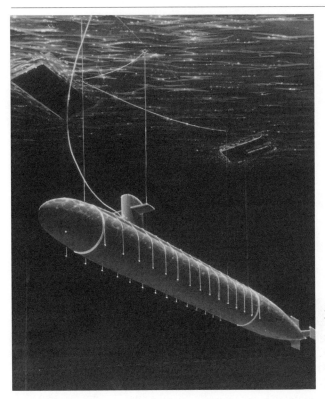

Alabama (SSBN 731).
With a submarine tethered
in Carr Inlet, engineers
can determine sources
and pathways of noise
propagation.

models in a quiet controlled environment. A large-scale test model is
controlled by an anchored handling and haul-down platform system
and remote shore winch. Most ISMS operations are controlled from the
shore through a 14-mile fiber optic command and data link to the underwater hardware. A stand-off array of thirty-six high-power acoustic
projectors transmits relevant acoustic signals to the model. Returning
acoustical energy scattered from the test model is captured by a ring of
closely spaced receiving hydrophones that encircle the model in the
same plane as the transmitting array.

All the new acoustic testing facilities developed for *Seawolf* and the
New SSN represented the greatest addition of acoustic test and measurement capability in the center's history. In the decade from the mid-
1980s through the mid-1990s, the new test-platforms, listening arrays,
large-scale models, and model-handling equipment represented the culmination of decades of ground work. Although initiated in response to
the Soviet threat in the mid-1980s, the work on acoustic detection and
acoustic stealth reached fruition over several years, providing the Navy
with the capability to meet continuing challenges from potential adversaries with advanced technology.[18]

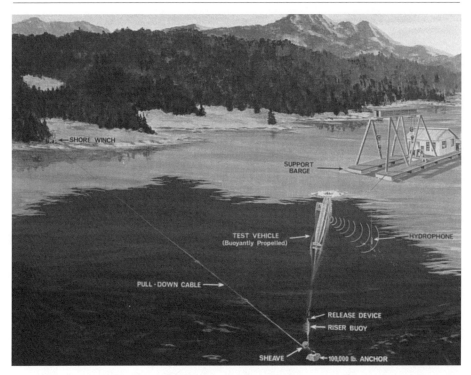

Submarine Model Testing, Lake Pend Oreille.   At the quiet and pristine lake setting, submarine model *Kamloops* surfaces from the depths by buoyancy, and flow-generated noise is recorded.

Continuing Priorities—SSN 21 and DDG 51

With the modern ships entering service in the 1980s and 1990s, the center continued many of its traditional crucial roles. Two new classes: *Seawolf* and the guided missile destroyer *Arleigh Burke* incorporated both original design development from the center and many later improvements and refinements. A few elements of center participation can serve to illustrate the continuity of this traditional mission through the years at the end of the Cold War. While the *Seawolf* design effort required stringent goals for acoustic stealth, DTRC staff participated in many other aspects of *Seawolf* development. Researchers tested some thirty alternative propulsor configurations to provide input to the final design. The center's Propulsor Manufacturing Office acted as the single point of contact for the Navy with the full-scale propulsor contractor, Oak Ridge National Laboratory, to assure on-schedule delivery.[19]

Staff at the center also engaged in SSN 21 projects regarding ship control development and studies of HY-100 steel welding and fabrica-

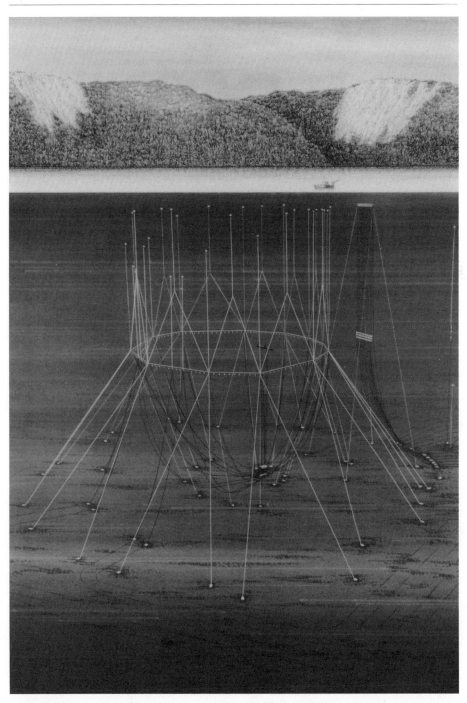

Intermediate-Scale Measurement System (ISMS). Huge underwater cable arrays at Lake Pend Oreille suspend an immobile submarine, like a fly in a spiderweb, to perform acoustic tests.

tion techniques through the late 1980s. Center control engineers developed the automatic maneuvering and control algorithms for SSN 21, providing the submarine with state-of-the-art, safe, automatic maneuvering capability in the open ocean and during under-ice operations. Center researchers evaluated alternative hull and control surface configurations and selected the final design. Electric Boat Corporation, the lead designer and builder, worked closely with the center in the implementation of automatic control system algorithms and *Seawolf* simulation design.[20]

During SSN 21 construction, inspectors discovered cracking in the HY-100 hull welds. DTRC researchers identified a form of hydrogen-induced embrittlement leading to cracking in the welds as the primary problem and worked out new welding materials and procedures with Electric Boat. Center experts played a pivotal role in developing weld wire compositions and inspection procedures to ensure crack-free welds in the future. The answers to the weld cracking issue were based on work under the HY-130 welding development program, and under studies of weldments first conducted in the Structures Department in the 1970s. The causes of the cracking problem were traced to dirty welding gas and high "carbon-equivalent" weld wire that was drawn from ingots obtained overseas.[21]

As with prior ship and submarine designs, specialists in shock protection and survivability played a crucial role in the development of the SSN 21 design. Experimental evaluations incorporating various-sized structural models and full-scale trials resulted in major design changes that reduced potential damage and increased the survivability of submarines subjected to underwater explosives, just as they had earlier for SSN 688, the *Ohio*-class fleet ballistic missile submarine, DDG 51 destroyers, and other ships.[22]

Introduced in the mid-1980s, the *Arleigh Burke* class of missile-destroyers incorporated many design elements worked out at the center. Center structural engineers had worked on improving resistance to shock for all Navy ships, and like several generations of cruisers, carriers, and submarines, DDG 51 went through a rigorous comprehensive shock-testing program involving not only modeling, but full-scale shock tests with up to 1,200 channels of data to be recorded. During the Gulf War, damage to U.S. naval vessels *Stark*, *Samuel B. Roberts* (FFG 58), and *Princeton* (CG 59) demonstrated the need to improve hull resistance to damage. Researchers developed several new armor concepts to protect vital areas aboard the ships and applied them to the DDG 51 class. The original DDG 51 design had been influenced by a Ship Vulnerability Model developed at the center in the areas of blast-hardened bulkheads, blast-resistant doors, armor concepts, redundancy evaluation and equipment separation factors.

The Office of Naval Research sponsored a project for continuing improvement on the *Arleigh Burke* class, undertaken by the center, utilizing another core capability, in this case, one that could trace its heritage to the hydrodynamic testing initiated by David Taylor himself. Researchers sought to develop a bulbous bow that reduced the resistance of a naval surface combatant and that could be integrated with an existing bow sonar dome, thereby reducing ship fuel consumption. Initial installment cost estimates for the first bulbs calculated against fuel savings resulted in a payback period of less than two years. Center personnel identified a total of seventy nine destroyers and cruisers which could benefit from the new design.[23]

For the ships coming into the fleet in the 1980s and 1990s, such as DDG 51 and SSN 21, Carderock remained a major point of origin. As it had been in the days of the EMB under Taylor and Ernest Eggert, and in the early years of the DTMB under Harold E. Saunders, the center represented the place where ship designs took form and where the fleet began.

Changing Priorities—Littoral Warfare

Throughout the Cold War, the U.S. Marine Corps retained its focus on over-the-shore capabilities and had directly participated in many low-intensity conflicts. Some of those very conflicts had formed the basis for the vision statement published by Admiral Kelso and General Mundy in their position paper, *From the Sea*. At Carderock, programs supported by the Marine Corps and reflecting the concept that the Navy's future mission would be to project forces from littoral waters over the shore continued to flourish during the 1980s and early 1990s.

The USMC program office began an exploratory program in 1983 to improve the next generation of armored amphibious vehicles. The Marine Corps hoped to develop a vehicle that could be deployed some 20 miles out to sea, travel at speeds in excess of 20 mph over water in 3-foot seas, hit the beach and then travel over land as a tracked vehicle at speeds in excess of 45 mph. Vehicles based on the concept would be potential successors to the relative low speed, 7- to 8-mph assault amphibious vehicle (AAV-A1). The existing design meant that naval amphibious ships had to drop off marines closer to shore than the ideal "over-the-horizon" position. With threats from sea mines and relatively sophisticated surface-to-surface missiles, it is hazardous to launch closer than 20 miles offshore. Thus the requirements for a high-speed

***Arleigh Burke* (DDG 51).**   Introduced in the mid 1980s, this class of missile-carrying destroyers reflected many structural and hydrodynamic improvements developed at the center.

armored vehicle clearly fit into the Marine mission and the larger naval mission of projecting force from the sea, especially in limited intensity conflicts.

Under the Marine Corps program, center engineers built three manned demonstrator vehicles between 1985 and 1993. They first constructed the High Speed Amphibian, which served purely as a hydrodynamic demonstrator, built at 0.55 scale. At Carderock, the Ship and Ocean Systems Dynamics Branch conducted trials with the second manned model, the High Water Speed Technology Demonstrator (HWSTD), in 1988–1989. The HWSTD was built at 3/4 scale primarily to demonstrate the hydrodynamic feasibility of using a planing vehicle concept. The team involved in the Demonstrator project received the Navy's 1990 award for best R&D project, which included $100,000 of 6.2 funds for discretionary use. By 1991, this project became the Advanced Assault Amphibious Vehicle (AAAV) Program. Walter Zeitfuss Jr. at DTRC served as the technical manager of the program, which developed two distinct designs produced by competing contractors, one a planing hull and the other a hybrid hydrofoil. Using the DTRC towing tanks, researchers worked with 1/8 scale hydrodynamic models of each concept in 1991 to validate drag and powering estimates, ride quality, and driver visibility.

At the same time, the center contracted for a manned, a full-scale Propulsion System Demonstrator (PSD) that underwent acceptance trials at the center's Special Trials Unit at Patuxent River, Maryland. An armored vehicle which could travel at high speed over water, if successful, could set new records. On 12 December 1991, the PSD traveled over water at speeds in excess of 32 mph; never before had a full-scale troop-carrying amphibious vehicle exceeded 20 mph in water. The PSD well exceeded the specifications of water speeds in excess of 20 knots and a land speed in excess of 40 mph. Combat loaded, the Demonstrator weighed 29 tons, and showed off not only the propulsion and hull form but a number of other advanced technologies. Engineers had designed the hull itself of a composite involving fiberglass with alumina tiles for ballistic protection, and they had included a VT-903 diesel engine for land and water modes, a T-700 gas turbine engine for the high-speed water mode, a hydraulic waterjet drive system, a retractable compressible fluid suspension system, and a global position and navigation system.[24]

A tracked vehicle requires around 25 horsepower per ton to travel on land, but to attain speeds over 20 mph in water, 70 to 80 horsepower per ton is required. To keep the total horsepower requirement as low as possible required many imaginative innovations to reduce weight and space. Innovations included electric drive components and a much lighter drive-by-wire system of steering, shifting, and acceleration controls instead of physical mechanical linkages. In such projects, DTRC built upon the earlier work by the Special Trials Unit in working with a full-scale vehicle to incorporate design changes that derived from practical experience.[25]

Through 1990 and 1991, a host of other projects reflected the same sort of strategic thinking. For example, the Joint Logistics Over the Shore (JLOTS) project, funded directly from the Office of the Secretary of Defense, provided for a $9 million dollar test that involved over 1,500 personnel from the various military services in the movement of military cargo from ship to shore. At DTRC, the Mobile Support Systems Office coordinated the technical evaluation, providing technical support, test planning documentation, and integrated support from other center departments. The center-developed air cushion landing platform, along with several center-developed

AAAV Propulsion System Demonstrator. At one-third scale, this remarkable armored assault craft developed at the center achieves high-speed planing, as the wake demonstrates.

SEABEE ship cargo handling improvements were also evaluated in the JLOTS Program.[26]

Continuing work on hydrofoil designs, work with new waterjet propulsion systems for the SES 200, support for landing craft designs, and a number of studies of methods of moving assault material and vehicles from shore waters to the beach and back to sea, all reflected the vision that future military engagements would be likely to represent a continuation of force projection from the sea to the shore. The center conducted a feasibility study of a hybrid hydrofoil multimission support vehicle in 1991, studying a 5,000-long-ton ship capable of carrying a cargo of 70 long tons and a LAMPS III helicopter. [27]

Emphasis on Conversion and Commercial Applications

Many projects that continued from earlier periods met the goals of converting defense capabilities to peacetime objectives. Center-developed computer technologies, programs, and systems held great potential for transfer to the commercial maritime community and more broadly to civilian uses. For example, the Advanced Surface Ship Evaluation Tool, or ASSET, originally developed by the Technology Applications Team in 1981–1982, led to further design synthesis computer programs. In 1990, NAVSEA Sealift design teams and others working on a variant guided missile destroyer design employed computer tools derived from ASSET. The program was exported to France through the Foreign Military Sales system and used by the French to study British/French frigate designs.[28]

Much advanced logistics work performed by the computational staff at DTRC found civilian application. The Requirements and Distribution Systems Division conducted programs in operations research and systems analysis for Navy Logistics Support programs. Areas of interest included naval distribution systems, resource analysis, material flow, transportability, distribution networks and logistics control systems, resource allocation, reliability and maintainability, and economics/econometrics. In any conversion to civilian or noncombat goals, many of these areas of interest could find ready commercial application. For example, a Cooperative Research and Development Agreement (CRADA) signed by DTRC and the Georgia Institute of Technology in 1990 focused on computer-aided warehouse design. Under this agreement, Georgia Tech got access to software developed at DTRC for use in warehouse research programs, and in turn, the Navy received the benefit of all related research at the university that resulted from work using the program. The computer-aided warehouse design system allowed the Navy to select the least-cost warehouse from alternative designs, resulting in savings estimated by the Office of Naval Research at $20 million per year.[29]

Over prior decades, the Computation, Mathematics and Logistics Department had developed a great many computer, database, and logistics programs that paved the way for the information revolution that drew media attention in the 1990s. From its earliest days in developing programming for UNIVAC in the 1960s, the center had been a leader in computer and programming circles nationally. Through the 1970s, the center demonstrated the feasibility of using tutorial, microcomputer-based systems to automate the control of logistics management operations on board Navy ships. The Navy tested a prototype system on four ships and demonstrated that ordinary sailors with no computer training could easily learn and use the system. The Navy later implemented the Data Entry Aboard Ships (DEAS) system on some 300 ships. It took sailors no more than four hours of training to be able to operate the supply inventory interactive system and to incorporate it into the work environment.[30]

Math lab personnel chose for the DEAS system, not "ruggedized," specially built computers, but off-the-shelf, commercially available computers. During sea exercises, operating directly underneath a firing 5-inch gun, sailors strapped the computer to a desk with a 1-inch rubber pad underneath. The system worked successfully. In the 1990s, the concept of Defense Department purchase and use of off-the-shelf items became quite common, and in this regard, as well, the center's math laboratory was ahead of its time.[31]

The math lab developed an onboard computer supply system for carriers in the late 1970s. A serious inventory control problem had developed on aircraft carriers. There were serious problems in keeping track of large quantities of supplies and materials stowed on board. Inventory clerks hand-recorded the information on paper, then later entered the data into the ship's main computer system, leading to multiple errors. Within a short time after departing port, a carrier could not locate 25 to 30 percent of its supplies and material. Again, using commercial microprocessors and interactive systems technology, with a menu-driven program, center personnel developed a system that was put in place by 1982.[32]

In the early 1980s, the computer staff began working on some new automation concepts emerging then in the academic world: office automation and digital computer networks. They created a prototype office automation system, Technical Office Automation and Communications System (TOFACS)—later rechristened Office Automation System (OASYS)—ultimately serving over 1,000 users at Carderock and Annapolis. Again, the center was "ahead of the curve" in developing this system. The math lab staff again showed their prescience when they built the David Taylor Network (DTNET). They envisioned a centerwide integrated data communications network that would enhance and integrate both research and management activities. From 1987 to 1989 workers installed the network connecting seventy buildings on the two campuses at Annapolis and Carderock. A high-speed telephone line connected the two sites so that the two operated as one logical communication network.[33]

In the early 1990s, the math lab became a principle technology contributor to revolutionizing the Navy's maintenance, training, system operation, and logistic support procedures through development of the Interactive Electronic Technical Manual (IETM) concept. For decades, sailors often encountered inaccurate, incomprehensible, or hard-to-use technical manuals, leading to impaired fleet readiness. The center conducted a 6.2/6.3 funded research program through the late 1970s and the 1980s, entitled the Navy Technical Information Presentation System (NTIPS). The program aimed at improving all aspects of developing and managing technical manuals, introducing the concept of replacing paper manuals with electronic ones. In the mid-1980s, researchers tested IETMs on the FA-14A Rudder Trim System at the Miramar Naval Air Station, and on a Radar Repeater at the Norfolk Naval Base. In June 1992, Carderock conducted a joint field test with the Air Force and the Marine Corps using a portably displayed IETM for the F/A-18 fire control system. The project won the 1992 Federal Leadership Award in information technology.

As the Navy moved more widely to IETMs the Carderock math lab took a lead role in further development. In the late 1990s, they worked on a cost-effective prototype system for automatically converting paper technical manuals, with both text and graphics, to the IETM system with a revisable data base. A test of this conversion system and the whole IETM system attracted much attention, not only through the Navy and DOD, but in private industry as well.[34]

A wide variety of other computer projects such as speech recognition programs, electronic signature recognition, database programs, logistics and supply management, all held promise for transfer to nonmilitary settings. All these computer developments had applications and spin-offs to the commercial sector, through publication in open literature, through presentations at conferences and expositions, as well as through the more structured Cooperative Research and Development Agreements. Researchers who did more specialized computational work in fields related to naval ship and submarine design continued to publish in professional journals and make presentations at conferences and symposiums, bringing their methods and research to the attention of wider audiences of researchers, engineers, and multidisciplinary groups.[35]

Besides such transfers of advanced design, logistics and management tools to the private sector, a number of hardware technologies under development at the center through the 1980s could also meet peacetime objectives. In 1988, the Chief of Naval Operations tasked DTRC to assume project management of a study of plastic waste management aboard ships. Over the next years, a variety of projects focused on improved methods of plastic waste disposal. In this fashion, the long-standing official Navy concern to meet international standards regarding disposal of waste at sea as well as to reduce the ship's signature through disposal of oil waste and plastics generated projects that strongly coincided with popular and governmental concerns over the

need for environmental protection. For example, in 1990, the preproduction prototype solid waste pulper developed at the center for the
purpose of pulping mixed paper waste underwent a series of tests at the
Aeronav Laboratory, College Point, New York. Technical problems discovered in the equipment led to improvements incorporated in the next
design, scheduled for shipboard evaluation the following year.[36]

Other studies looked into thermal destruction of shipboard solid
waste, environmentally acceptable antifouling hull coatings, and systems
for the recovery of chlorofluorocarbon refrigerants. Meanwhile, researchers focused on developing a non-CFC air conditioning plant, by
qualifying alternative refrigerants. Lab investigations of a hydrofluoro-
carbon demonstrated that a compound, HFC-134a, served as a satisfactory backfit alternative to the CFCs used in shipboard reciprocating
compressor air conditioning plants.

A commercially successful product from the Annapolis site, a system that produced drinking water from the ocean by reverse osmosis,
moved into production. Essential in lifeboat situations, the RO system used a highly reliable and modularized semipermeable membrane for the separation of pure water from seawater. The Navy issued a major procurement of 2,000 lifeboat reverse osmosis
desalinators in 1991.[37]

In 1992, the center's Invention Evaluation Board (IEB), made up of
specialists from various departments, together with the Associate
Counsel for Intellectual Property, routinely reviewed and evaluated invention disclosures to determine that would be the most promising for
military application and also those that had the highest potential for
commercial licensing. The IEB had been established in response to the
Federal Technology Transfer Act of 1986, which allowed for a variety of
sharing arrangements between government and the private sector, most
notably Cooperative Research and Development Agreements. The board
worked both on stimulating CRADAs and on more traditional patent-li-
censing agreements to assist in taking naval inventions to the commercial sector. They hoped that these activities in the area of commercialization, would help reposition the United States in world markets. This
emphasis showed another aspect of the center's adaptability to the pattern of conversion and commercialization.[38]

In a development that reflected an explicit conversion of a Cold
War-inspired project to commercial and post-Cold War priorities, the center obtained a defense conversion grant from the Advanced Research
Projects Agency's Technology Reinvestment Project to help apply technology from the *Seawolf*-class submarine to other uses. This project explicitly met goals set in President Clinton's "Defense Reinvestment and

Conversion Initiative." Carderock had worked with Westinghouse on a propulsion system called an Integral Motor/Propeller (IM/P). This system integrated a hermetically sealed, canned electric motor with a propeller in a shroud to form a ship propulsor, originally intended as a "take-home" motor for slow cruising in harbors and in docking situations. With no gear train and fewer parts than conventional gear-driven propulsion systems, the IM/P was lighter and more reliable. The propulsor could be applied to bow thrusters and to ships working with offshore oil platforms. At the center, the work focused on the hydrodynamic design for IM/P surface ship applications, with transfers to the commercial sector expected in the mid and late 1990s.[39]

In the mid-1990s, the Power Electronics Building Blocks (PEBB) Program held out the possibility that a programmable general purpose power controller could be developed that would be capable of performing a variety of electrical conversion functions. The program had the goal of developing effective and efficient methods of distributing and transforming electric power aboard ships, submarines, and aircraft. Carderock became involved in testing a device from Harris Semiconductor that might become a crucial component in such a PEBB. The center added a variety of center-developed and off-the-shelf equipment to come up with a complete architecture, merging critical enabling technologies. The potential for transfer from and to the civilian sector of advances in this area made it particularly attractive.[40]

The Navy of the Next Century

Through the period from 1988 through 1991, the center management organized a series of strategic planning efforts focused on the long-range future of naval technology and the possible role of DTRC in that future. In 1988 the center's department heads met for a nine-hour session, generating a list of eleven technical areas for future thrusts. These growth areas included nonacoustic and acoustic signatures and stealth, electric drive, composite materials, ship integration systems analysis, advanced concepts, automation and reduced manning, autonomous vehicles, artificial intelligence, numerical methods, ship survivability, affordability, and military effectiveness assessment capability. The Strategic Planning and Assessment Center, with its "roundtable" process and its "war rooms," generated interest in the Navy hierarchy. Using these institutions and displaying their products to visitors, Graham and Metrey hoped the ideas would become catalysts for strategic thinking and planning for the Navy as a whole.

In 1989, the futurist emphasis became even more explicit. The center established a roundtable to identify through a formal process, "long-range, quantified, time-specific goals." The center's annual Command History stated, "DTRC is creating a vision for the future Navy and the U.S. maritime industry as well." The increased visits to the center by VIPs served as means of measuring the impact of ideas from the roundtables and war rooms. In 1989, in addition to fifteen admirals (including CNO Admiral Carlisle Trost), the center hosted the Secretary of the Navy, members of the Senate Appropriations Committee, the Under Secretary of Defense for Research and Evaluation, the Federal Emergency Management Agency Director, and a variety of deputy assistant secretaries and congressional staff members. All toured the war rooms and examined displays focusing on some long-range future concepts, especially the concept of an integrated electric drive. Metrey and Graham understood very well that if DTRC's vision of the future Navy were to become part of naval planning, it would have to be promoted through exactly such channels.[41]

When Trost established an Integrated Electric Drive Program Office at the center's Annapolis site, the action represented at least a partial incorporation of the DTRC-generated future visions into the official structure of naval planning. IED held out the promise of operational and arrangement flexibility in monohull ship designs. Weight, size, and efficiency gains would be possible with the advanced machinery. DTRC participated actively in the IED Preliminary Design Review and generated and reviewed improved contract specifications for the advanced electrical machinery and the controls to be used in an IED system.

The very diversity of approaches that flourished under DOD and Navy funding at the center had many virtues. The rich variety of research and development sponsored by program managers at the systems commands and the small proportion of independent work provided many alternative solutions to the Navy's changing needs. Whether reflecting emphasis on *Continuity*, *Littoral Warfare*, *Conversion*, or *Futurism*, the center had the capability to respond.

Ultimately, the future remained unknowable, and approaches that envisioned various future scenarios, while entailing the risk that many projects would fail or not go through to completion, provided the surest path to accomplishment. Since the private sector could not provide for the specialized and high-risk research required by the Navy, the RDT&E centers had to remain active, quick to seize opportunities, and alive to imaginative possibilities.

The BRAC Years

The years from 1992 through 1997 just prior to the centennial year 1998, saw further implementation of base realignment and closure, known throughout the Navy as "BRAC." Realignment and closure took place in four separate exercises, BRAC-88, BRAC-91, BRAC-93, and BRAC-95. Through the late 1990s, another round of examination of DOD Laboratories was planned, under the heading of "Vision-21."

On 2 January 1992, the new organization "stood up," under BRAC-91. Under OPNAVNOTE 5450, DTRC was organizationally converted, as it had been a number of times in the past, becoming the Carderock Division, Naval Surface Warfare Center. The largest specific effects of the BRAC changes can be briefly summarized as follows:

1. DTRC now became a division within a larger community which incorporated Dahlgren, Virginia, Indian Head, Maryland, Port Hueneme, California, Crane, Indiana, and other naval facilities concerned with ship and ordnance-related RDT&E. Many of these institutions had their origins as shore facilities under the old bureaus, whose management had transferred and had been consolidated over the decades from the 1940s through the 1980s into the Naval Sea Systems Command. Each of the five large facilities became a division within the Naval Surface Warfare Center as part of the Naval Sea Systems Command.

2. DTRC's Annapolis site was scheduled for closure.

3. The Naval Ship Systems Engineering Station (NAVSSES) at the Philadelphia Navy Yard came under the control the Carderock Division. The new organizational unit became the Naval Surface Warfare Center Carderock Division-Ship Systems Engineering Station (NSWCCD-SSES).

4. The two DTRC departments resident at Annapolis would be transferred. After much discussion and active lobbying for other outcomes, the final decision was made by the technical director that the Materials Department at Annapolis would be transferred to Carderock and merged with the Structural Mechanics Department, and located in a new Ship Materials Technology Center. The Machinery Department would be transferred to the newly incorporated NAVSSES in Philadelphia, Pennsylvania.

5. In addition to the existing detachments in Puget Sound, Washington; in Memphis, Tennessee; and in Bayview, Idaho; the Carderock Division would take on the administration of several other remote detachments.

6. The Naval Ordnance Laboratory at White Oak, Maryland would be closed, with most of its scientific/research personnel shifted to Dahlgren, Virginia. However, some 300 personnel would be shifted to Carderock. These personnel transfers were completed by January 1997.[42]

By 1997, the Carderock Division served as headquarters for ten remote facilities:

SEAFAC Ketchikan, AL
Puget Sound Detachment—Carr Inlet Acoustic Range, WA
Acoustic Research Detachment, Bayview, ID
Large Cavitation Channel, Memphis, TN
Underwater Explosives Research Detachment, Chesapeake, VA
Combatant Craft Detachment, Norfolk, VA
Special Trials Unit Patuxent, River, Virginia
Acoustics Trials Detachment, Cape Canaveral, FL
South Florida Testing Facility, Fort Lauderdale, FL
NAVSSES, Naval Shipyard, Philadelphia, PA

New Detachments and Personnel Transfers

The former Combatant Craft Engineering Department of the Naval Sea Combat Systems Engineering Station (SEABAT) at Norfolk was also added to the Carderock Division, becoming Code 127 within the Systems Department. The newly formed detachment consisted of a Design Branch, a Test, Evaluation and Logistics Branch, and a Special Programs Branch. Of eighty-one employees located at Norfolk, none would be required to relocate.

The Naval Ship Systems Engineering Station in Philadelphia had a history that began in 1910 with the establishment of the Fuel Oil Testing Plant. George Melville is credited with providing the inspiration for founding this plant.

From a modest beginning in a single small brick building manned by twelve military and civilian personnel, it took on fuel oil tests as the Navy switched from coal to fuel oil in boilers. By effectively solving problems associated with burning fuel in Navy boilers, it became the U.S. Naval Boiler Laboratory in 1932. During the 1930s, steam turbines were added to its testing repertoire and, in 1941, its name was again changed to the U.S. Naval Boiler and Turbine Laboratory. During and after World War II, work included not only fuel oil, boilers, and steam turbines, but reduction gears, diesel engines, work on associated propulsion machinery components and systems, and hull and deck machinery.

In 1966 the laboratory was reconstituted as the Naval Ship Engineering Center, Philadelphia Division, incorporating other units into a single command, including work on submarine antennas and the Assurance Engineering Field Facility. The latter group worked on shipyard quality assurance audits, submarine safety audits, helicopter platform certification, and hardware surveys of manufacturers' plants and government facilities engaged in working on U.S. Navy ship equipment.

In October 1979, the facility was again reorganized and designated the Naval Ship Systems Engineering Station with the primary function of

Philadelphia Navy Yard. The Machinery R&D Directorate is relocated from Annapolis to the Naval Ship Systems Engineering Station (NAVSSES) in the Philadelphia Navy Yard at the confluence of the Delaware and Schuylkill Rivers.

serving as the principal activity for test and evaluation of hull, mechanical, and electrical ship systems and in providing in-service engineering support for these systems. The facility took on testing of gas turbines through the 1970s and 1980s. In 1982, NAVSSES gained added responsibility as the In-Service-Engineering Agent (ISEA) for all Navy HM&E systems and equipments. In the 1995 BRAC, the machinery R&D function of the Annapolis site was transferred to Philadelphia and plans were made to transfer personnel. [43]

Strategic Planning Effort

Long-range strategic planning at the center allowed some degree of input to the eventual reorganization. Strategic planning could go further, developing a vision to help ensure the center a secured role in the shifting future. The organization's historical roots in the earliest work at the EMB under David Taylor and the EES under Walter Worthington

Machinery Research and Development Genealogy

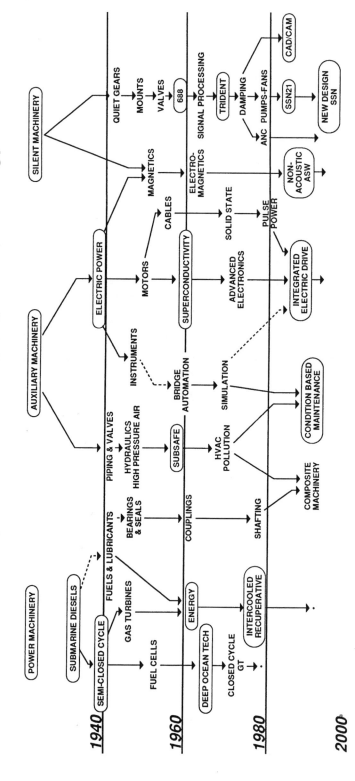

provided a basis on which to build. Both Taylor and Worthington had simultaneously worked on peacetime and war-fighting priorities, suggesting a pattern that would apply in the 1990s. Strategic planning at the
Carderock Division level took the form of exploring possible alternative
futures that might emerge from the process, and could demonstrate the
effect that those futures might have in terms of mission, effectiveness,
and specialized areas of research.

In May 1994, the Carderock Division's Strategic Planning Office,
under Dennis Clark, issued the results of a case study, *"Ready About:" A
Customer-Focused Strategy for Restructuring Key Technical Capabilities.* The
paper described the effects of potentially severe cuts in workforce faced
by the center as it moved into the post-Cold War era.[44]

The current situation, the report noted, abounded in uncertainties.
The authors identified the two opposing forces at work: diminished budgets among "customers" and the continuing requirement to deal with
potential regional conflicts. The division faced both the threat of "severe
downsizing" and "real opportunities to expand our market." The report
described a method of cutting personnel in the most cost-efficient fashion, leading to the increase in some promising technical capabilities
while shrinking others that appeared less promising.

The report came as the result of work over a seven-month period
through eight different workshops, each with about twenty participants.
Each group addressed the same task: in the face of reduced numbers of
workyears, how should the laboratory restructure its technical capabilities? In 109 key technical areas, the group sought combinations of workforce increments or reductions that would result in the most cost-effective balance of resources. For each of 109 areas, nine optional levels of
capability could be considered, resulting in an "astronomical" number
of combinations. However, the group sought to develop the overall most
cost-effective strategy, which required formal analysis and computer-
based modeling to work through the possibilities. Because more than
200 staff members participated in the process, and because the process
was formal and explicit, the staff would trust the final balances and
trade-offs as being the best that they could achieve. The end result was a
workforce allocation model that told the participants, based on their collective judgment, how restructuring should take place on a key technical
area-by-area basis. As a consequence, some areas were shown to increase,
others to decrease, and others to remain the same to achieve the ideal
balances.

The model had the virtue that it could be adjusted to varying demands from higher authority within the Navy. Thus, if asked to consider

adjustments in twenty specific core technical competencies, the model could be rerun using the collective judgments of participants. Similarly, as different budget figures were suggested, again the model could be reapplied. It could quickly generate a plan, based on the same wide-based judgment and consensus, showing how to make the most cost-effective adjustment to the proposed budget.

The model employed in *"Ready About"* soon proved its worth. At a meeting regarding Naval Surface Warfare Center planning held at Carderock, each CO-TD team from the various warfare centers was asked how they would respond to certain specific numbers of personnel to be cut. Only Carderock could come back, in very short order, with a specific plan detailing exactly how the hypothetical cuts would be implemented. In the area of strategic planning and management decision making, as in its technical areas, the center had demonstrated that it was on the cutting edge of progress.[45]

Further efforts at strategic planning continued through the late 1990s, as division leadership participated in workshops and a variety of exercises weighing alternative future scenarios and their potential effects. In January 1998, the work led to publication of a Division Strategic Plan entitled "Course and Speed." Through all the planning sessions, the division worked from a position of strength, as a large institution, with a rich heritage and with multiple abilities to respond to the needs of the fleet.[46]

The Carderock Division, Naval Surface Warfare Center that emerged from DTRC built on the heritage that incorporated the practical, industrial-based concepts that Walter Worthington and Thomas Kinkaid brought from the Bureau of Steam Engineering as well as the research emphasis that David Taylor and Ernest Eggert brought from the Bureau of Construction and Repair. In the 1990s effort to establish full-spectrum centers, with services ranging from research through developmental engineering to application engineering, the strengths of the Annapolis groups in engineering fields helped ensure the center's overall survival through the BRAC process.

Warfare Centers and Systems Commands

Originally, EES at Annapolis had been a field activity of the Bureau of Engineering and EMB had been a field activity of the Bureau of Construction and Repair. Responding to the emphasis on research, EES became the Marine Engineering Laboratory during the 1960s. More than twenty-five years after the two bureaus were united as the Bureau of

Ships, the two BUSHIPS research facilities near Washington were united into NSRDC in 1966, then into DTNSRDC. In 1987, the center became DTRC. With the conversion in the 1960s from bureaus into systems commands, some old bureau connections and traditions continued. NAVSEA supplanted NAVSHIPS, incorporating Ordnance. In the 1980s, the Navy attempted to convert the Naval Electronics Systems Command (NAVELEX) into an overall systems command, Space and Naval Warfare Systems (SPAWAR). However, with the Cold War's end, the structure was reorganized once more, abandoning the apparent division between users and suppliers, between operations and procurement systems that was essential to the bureau structure, and that had continued into the period of systems commands. The systems commands, answering to the CNO, were put in charge of operating the warfare centers. With the establishment of the Naval Research Laboratory as the Navy's "corporate laboratory," the R&D centers no longer were designated as centers for research. Rather, as warfare centers, they represented the technical suppliers to the three major branches of the operating fleet. At the very point when the Cold War ended, and a new emphasis had been placed on conversion to peace-time priorities and commercial applications, many found irony in the introduction of the term "warfare" into the title of the Navy's technical instititions.

The process of reassigning work and functions in a logical and planned fashion was given the term "mission purification." To many individuals involved, this suggested an impersonal procedure with distasteful overtones. Although "Surface Warfare" implies otherwise, the Carderock Division continued its major R&D efforts on submarines, which continued to account for a large percentage of its total effort.[47]

From a long-range perspective, much of what emerged from the downsizing and readjustment at the end of the Cold War was beneficial to the Navy and the nation. Command and control of four R&D centers was easier and more efficient than command and control of thirty-four separate activities. The warfare centers did have relatively consolidated roles, missions, and leadership functions. All of the divisions were so large that each was well above so-called critical mass; Carderock Division had over 4,500 employees. Even though transformed, the heritage, culture, and other intangible benefits of institutional identity remained preserved within the divisions, and pride in their past achievements continued to be an asset.

Such administrative and long-term advantages of consolidation and reorganization did not immediately offset the negative impact on morale that had been anticipated by Charles Adolph in his 1990 report. Reorganization brought with it uncertainty, in itself unsettling. Closure of some facilities, no matter how conducted, had the psychological effect of a repudiation or lack of recognition of prior accomplishment. At the personal level, civilian employees, unlike military personnel, usually felt uncomfortable with required long-distance relocation and the disruption it imposed on families. Management estimated that only some 15 percent or less of the machinery specialists at Annapolis would accept transfer to Philadelphia, with the rest retiring or resigning to take positions in academia or private industry.

Some of the negatives were less personal and more institutional. Adopting a new name—the Carderock Division, Naval Surface Warfare Center—meant that the international recognition and prestige that had built up around the name of David Taylor was no longer there. The formal removal of "research" from the name and mission seemed a denial of a long-established strength. The administration of personnel caps on senior civil service ranks and the reassignment by higher command of senior personnel to Carderock from other locations made it increasingly difficult to retain through promotion talented younger staff. Yet the division and its personnel had gone through many such changes before and each time they had gone on to further significant accomplishments. The institution, despite its transformations, had met challenges and had survived a turbulent century.

Enduring Excellence

As the DTRC neared its centennial, an article in the *Harvard Business Review* captured four ingredients that characterize corporations that survived a century or more in the United States. Although meant to apply to private sector corporations, the criteria presented in the article went far to explain the continued achievements of the center as an institution over a century and boded well for its future. Surviving corporations, the article pointed out, had these characteristics:

- Conservativism in financing
- Sensitivity to the world around them
- Awareness of their identity
- Tolerance of new ideas [48]

As to financial conservativism, constraints in the defense budgets imposed built-in limits. The semicompetitive system of Naval Industrial Funding required that researchers and managers secure funding for projects well in advance of a project. Further, as projects and programs wound down, managers at the center took care to reassign senior experienced personnel to new tasks of responsibility.

Sensitivity to the outside world was another characteristic that DTRC passed on to its new incarnation as the Carderock Division of NSWC. As demonstrated when the Cold War ended and the DOD/Navy establishment simultaneously pursued diverse sets of goals, the researchers and research programs at the center reflected an ability to adapt simultaneously to all the emerging trends.

Evidence of the sense of pride in identity and in heritage from the past was all around at the center. The preservation of architectural symmetry around a central greensward at Carderock during the construction of the Ship Materials Technology Center and the striking architecture of the new building itself demonstrated an aesthetic side to sense of the past. Hall displays of patents and designs by David Taylor and of many other prior accomplishments testified to the sense of the past. The equipment itself was part of the inheritance. As demanding and knowledgeable specialists, Taylor, Saunders, and their successors had required that capital-intensive construction be designed at the cutting edge of technical quality. Thus the physical facili-

Ship Materials Technology Center. In keeping with architectural themes at Carderock, this well- equipped new center building faces the greensward from the west, echoing the Moreell facade of the Main Building.

ties represented an excellent assemblage of unique and highly valuable equipment for research related to submarines and ships, ranking with the best in the world.

The tradition of combining technical knowledge, administrative acumen, and an ability to acquire first rate installations continued into the mid-1990's. George Wacker, head of the Survivability, Structures, and Materials Directorate, convinced over 83 percent of the Annapolis personnel to transfer to the new Ship Materials Technology Center at Carderock. Fittingly, Wacker received the ASNE Harold Saunders Award in 1998 for his career-long achievements in material sciences and applications.

As to tolerance for new ideas, this remained the "stock in trade" at the center. Not only in the advanced ship work that constantly focused on innovative designs of potential future ships, but in hydrodynamics, structural mechanics, materials, signatures, logistics and mathematics, the specialists at the center continued to "think out of the box" and to constantly envision the future. Researchers impressed visitors with their ability to think ahead to what technological changes would be wrought a few years or even decades into the future by contemporary developments. The sense that the projects were future-oriented remained palpable, emerging in every discussion.

One of the more notable efforts was the Smart Ship Project. Operating on the principles of the "innovation cell" earlier, this project had a very clear, yet profound objective—to identify and implement innovative technologies, policies, and procedures that offered a significant reduction in ship workload and crew size with enhanced readiness without sacrificing crew safety or mission capability. The project was initiated following a briefing given to the CNO, Admiral Jeremy M. Boorda, in October 1995 by the Naval Research Advisory Committee panel on reduced manning. The panel had concluded that the major obstacle to reducing manning levels and decreasing life cycle costs of Navy ships was Navy culture and tradition rather than a lack of technology, a point that Admiral Boorda actively advocated. Seizing the initiative, Vice Admiral George Sterner, who had become COMNAVSEA in April, and Captain James Baskerville, Commander Carderock Division, NSWC, enlisted the support of other commands in pursuing the Smart Ship Project. As a result of Baskerville's personal attention, energy, and commitment, Carderock served as host to a unique gathering of representatives from the fleet, technical activities, the Bureau of Personnel, and other organizations. The project team developed innovative methods to facilitate evaluation of numerous ideas for workload reduction from the fleet, Navy technical organizations, and the private sector. Utilizing *Yorktown* (CG 48) as a test ship, the team succeeded in developing and applying solutions which demonstrated that a significant reduction in manning levels could be achieved. Reductions came through changes in ship procedures for watchstanding, maintenance, and damage control. Many of these changes resulted from implementing distributed information systems on a new fiber-optic backbone throughout the ship. The fiber-optics enabled the employment of an integrated bridge system, common displays for damage control, and an integrated control and condition assessment system for shipboard machinery.

With the strength of a century of progress and many significant accomplishments serving the fleet behind them, the people of the Carderock Division, Naval Surface Warfare Center continued to face the future with confidence.

Endnotes

1. Admiral Wayne Meyer, interview by Joseph Marchese, 30 Apr 1990 and 9 May 1990, NHC, NLCCG Archives, RC 8, box 9, folder 13..
2. Office of the Secretary of Defense, Dick Cheney, "Defense Management: Report to the President," Jul 1989, 1. A more complete review of the development of the Navy's reorganization plan is found in Rodney Carlisle, *Navy RDT&E in an Age of Transition* (Washington: Naval Historical Center, 1997). The following section draws from that report. The policy reports cited here are on deposit at the Naval Historical Center, Operational Archives.
3. White House Science Council, "Report of the White House Science Council. Federal Laboratory Review Panel" (Packard Report), May 1983, 8–12.
4. Office of the Secretary of Defense, Dick Cheney, "Defense Management: Report to the President," Jul 1989, 1.
5. Defense Science Board, 1987 Summer Study, "Technology Base Management," Dec 1987; Office of Technology Assessment, "Holding the Edge: Maintaining the Defense Technology Base," Apr 1989, iii.
6. Staff of the DNL, "A Review of Studies Conducted from November 1989 to Apr 1990 on Restructuring the Navy RDT&E Community," 1–4 Jul 1990.
7. Schiefer spelled out his task in an interview with Joe Marchese, 1 Nov 1991, NHC, NLCCG Archives, RC 8, box 12, folder 13.
8. Ibid.
9. Ibid.
10. Gerald Cann, "DOD Test and Evaluation, Research and Development Facilities Paper," 12 Apr 1990, 4.
11. Ibid.
12. Department of the Navy Base Structure Committee, "Department of the Navy Base Realignment and Closure Recommendations, Detailed Analysis," Apr 1991, 13–15, 43–47.
13. Federal Advisory Commission, "Federal Advisory Commission on Consolidation and Conversion of Defense Research and Development Laboratories—Report to the Secretary of Defense," Sep 1991, 3, 5, 15. Conversation with Joe Sheehan, 27 May 1997.
14. Admiral Frank B. Kelso II and General C. E. Mundy, . . . *From the Sea: Preparing the Naval Service for the 21st Century*, Sep 1992. Earlier presentations of this concept, utilizing historical record of prior engagements, can be found in Adam Seigel, *The Use of Naval Forces in the Post-Cold War Era: U.S. Navy and Marine Corps Crisis Response Activity, 1946–1990* (Alexandria, VA: Center For Naval Analyses, 1991) and in Chairman, Joint Chiefs of Staff, *National Military Strategy of the United States*, Jan 1992. Such literature resulted from a regular call for a reassessment of the roles and missions of the armed services by the Secretary of Defense, a "Defense Management Review," mandated under the Goldwater-Nichols Act, passed in 1986.
15. Conversion as a model was discussed in both policy documents and in the public press during the period. See for example, Bruce B. Auster, "A Healthy Military/Industrial Complex: A Diversified Defense Industry Could Help Both the

Economy and the Pentagon," *U.S. News and World Report*, 12 Feb 1990, 42–43, 47–48. Early in the Clinton administration, documents officially endorsing conversion as doctrine appeared, as in President Bill Clinton and Vice President Al Gore, "Technology for America's Economic Growth," 22 Feb 1993. A few months later, John M. Deutsch, Under Secretary of Defense (Acquisition and Technology), testified on Defense Reinvestment and Conversion Programs before the Subcommittee on Defense, Committee on Appropriations, U.S. Senate, on 27 May 1993.

16. Robert J. Etter and Michael B. Wilson, "The Large Cavitation Channel," Paper presented at the 23rd ATTC Meeting, New Orleans, LA, 11–12 Jun 1992.

17. Brian Bowers, "Years of Silencing R&D Provide Significant Stealth Technology Contributions to the Fleet," ABIF.

18. Ibid.

19. NSWC, "Technology Developments and Applications For Today's and Tomorrow's Navy" (Bethesda, MD: NSWC, Dec 1996), C-12, hereafter, "Today's and Tomorrow's Navy."

20. Peter J. Montana, "DTRC Capabilities and Facilities—FY 1989" DTRC- 90/CT10 Sep 1990, 19–20.

21. "Today's and Tomorrow's Navy," F-12, F-13, F-14, F-15.

22. Ibid., D-11.

23. Ibid.; Dominic S. Casanelli, "Bulbous Bow Design Study on the DDG 51 Guided Missile Destroyer (Model 5422)," Summary Report CRDKNSWC/HD—0200-48, Apr 1994.

24. John Hoyt, "Propulsion System Demonstrator," Report CRDKNSWC/HD—1452-01, Jun 1994.

25. "Today's and Tomorrow's Navy," A-2, A-4.

26. Ibid., I-4.

27. DTRC Command History, 1991.

28. Seymour Goldstein, "Operations Research/Systems Analysis/Warfare Analysis, Historical Perspective at Carderock Division, NSWC," ABIF.

29. Peter S. Montana, "DTRC Capabilities and Facilities, FY 1989," DTRC- 90/CT10, p.38; "Today's and Tomorrow's Navy," I-2.

30. A. W. Camara, "CMLD Technical History Items: Computer Science and Information Systems," ABIF.

31. Ibid.

32. Ibid.

33. Ibid.

34. Ibid.; "Today's and Tomorrow's Navy," I-3; Mark Kramer, et al., "Results of a Joint Navy/Air Force Operational Test to Evaluate USAF Integrated Maintenance Information System (IMIS) Interactive Electronic Technical Manual (IETM) Technology Applied to the F/A 18 Aircraft," Naval Surface Warfare Center, Carderock Division, CARDIV-93/007, Jun 1993; Mark Kramer and Mary Zoccola, "Making IETMs Affordable," *Wavelengths*, Mar 1997.

35. Publication in open scholarly literature by Math lab personnel is extensive, as they noted in their reports for the ABIF. A few such items illustrate the point: Hans J. Lugt and S. Ohring, "The Oblique Rise of A Viscous Vortex Ring toward a Deformable Free Surface," *Meccanica* 29 (1994): 313–329, 1994; S. A. Hambric, and C. Dai, "A Prototype Artificial Intelligence Driven Marine Propulsor Design Tool," *Proceedings of the AIAA/NASA/USAF/ISSMO Symposium on Multi-disciplinary Analysis and Optimization* (Sep 1994): 334–343; J. F. Slomski, J. F. and J. J. Gorski, "Fluid Stratification at a Free Surface Induced by a Rising Vortex Pair," Paper presented at 27th AIAA Fluid Dynamics Conference, New Orleans, LA, 17–20 Jun 1996.

36. "Today's and Tomorrow's Navy," G-8.
37. Ibid., G-2, G-3, G-4, G-5.
38. Kathy Kaplan, "IEB Sets New Goals: Clark Heads Invention Evaluation Board," *Centerline*, May–Jun 1992.
39. Mary Zoccola, "Grants allow Division to Team with Industry," *Wavelengths*, Feb, 1994.
40. Conversation with Joe Boraccini, 20 Jun 1997.
41. DTRC Command History, 1988, ABIF.
42. In addition to information gained from interviews with Pete Montana, Dennis Clark, Bill Ellsworth, and Bill Middleton, these observations were documented by review of *Year in Review—95—Carderock Division* (Naval Sea Systems Command, Naval Surface Warfare Center, 1995). "BRAC" as an acronym is a bit inaccurate, representing a pronounceable version of Base Closure and Realignment Commission (BCRC). OPNAV Note 5450, Ser 09B22/1U510577 established the Naval Surface Warfare Center, transferring DTRC to CD/NSWC, and transferring NAVSSES in Philadelphia to Carderock Division control. Other actions described were accomplished in a round of realignments between 1993–1997.
43. Communication by Fax, Warren Christensen to Pete Montana, 4/30/97, ABIF.
44. Captain Dennis K. Kruse, Dennis J. Clark, and Roy M. Gulick, *"Ready About:"* A *Customer-Focused Strategy for Restructuring Key Technical* Capabilities, Carderock Division, Naval Surface Warfare Center, May 1994.
45. Conversation with Dennis J. Clark, 30 Apr 1997.
46. An extensive strategic planning exercise that considered several alternate futures was reported on in *Course and Speed: The 1995/1996 Carderock Division Strategic Planning Initiative*, Report of the Workshop conducted 23–24 Aug 1995, Hunt Valley, MD, Dec 1995.
47. Vugraph packet, "SWC, Data as of 30 September 1993." One table included details of civilian personnel shifts of 1,900 people among the various units of the NSWC to be accomplished by the end of fiscal year 1997. The table was labeled "NSWC Mission Purification."
48. Arie De Geus, "The Living Company," *Harvard Business Review* (Mar–Apr 1997).

Chronology of Significant Events

(Items in **bold** are are of particular importance to DTRC.)

1798

At the urging of President John Adams, the Congress passes an act on 30 April that established the U.S. Navy Department.

1799

The Washington Navy Yard is authorized by the first Secretary of the Navy, Benjamin Stoddert. The official date for its founding is 2 October. It is the U.S. Navy's oldest shore establishment.

1842

A reorganization of the U.S. Navy establishes separate bureaus to perform specific functions. Among them is the Bureau of Construction and Repair, a precursor of the Bureau of Ships.

The Bureau of Steam Engineering is established on 9 March.

1862

A naval battle on 9 March between the two famous Civil War ironclad ships, *Monitor* and *Virginia* (formerly the wooden hull *Merrimack*), takes place. After five hours of fighting at Hampton Roads, the battle ends in a draw although *Virginia* requires extensive repair.

1864

David Watson Taylor is born in Louisa County, Virginia, on 4 March.

1885

David W. Taylor graduates from the Naval Academy with the highest grade-point average of any graduate to date.

On 3 September, the Naval War College, located in Newport, Rhode Island, begins operations with its first class.

1886

The Naval Gun Factory is established at the Washington Navy Yard.

1890

Alfred T. Mahan publishes the first of his ten-volume history, *The Influence of Sea Power Upon History, 1660–1783.*

The USS *Maine* is launched at Brooklyn, New York.

Harold E. Saunders is born in Washington, D.C. on 29 November.

1898

The battleship *Maine* blows up in Havana harbor on 15 February with the loss of 260 officers and men.

On 25 April, the United States declares war on Spain, one day after Spain declared war on America. The war ends on 10 December after Spain sues for peace.

The Experimental Model Basin (EMB) is established at the Washington Navy Yard.

1900

On 12 October, the USS *Holland*, which was purchased from John P. Holland, becomes the first submarine commissioned in the U.S. Navy.

1901

On 4 March, David Taylor is promoted to Captain, on his 37th birthday.

Guglielmo Marconi tests radio transmissions between England and Newfoundland.

1903

On 3 March, Congress establishes the U.S. Navy Engineering Experiment Station (EES).

On 30 June, Congress appropriates $400,000 for the construction of EES at Annapolis, Maryland.

On 17 December, Orville and Wilbur Wright successfully test their gasoline-engine-powered device in Kitty Hawk, North Carolina. Lasting 12 seconds, the flight covers 120 feet.

1905

Albert Einstein proposes his Special Theory of Relativity.

1907

Lee DeForrest invents the triode vacuum tube.

1908

On 17 March, completion of EES construction allows personnel to move in.

On 15 July, EES Commanding Officer Captain Walter F. Worthington submits the first report outlining work done by the station during its first months of existence under the Bureau of Steam Engineering.

On 16 November, EES submits its first test report on steam safety valves.

The Ford Motor Company produces the first Model T auto, priced at $850.

1909

On 6 April, on his 6th attempt, Admiral Robert E. Peary reaches the North Pole.

1910

Winston Churchill is appointed First Lord of the Admiralty.

The Fuel Oil Testing Plant, inspired by Rear Admiral George W. Melville, is established in the Philadelphia Naval Shipyard.

1911

The Speed and Power of Ships, **David Taylor's book outlining guidelines for the design of hulls, is published. It becomes the basis for the Taylor Standard Series, which guides ship design for the next fifty years.**

EES finishes its two-year study of boiler corrosion with the development of the first scientific chemical water treatment and controlled test cabinet for shipboard use.

Glenn Curtiss flies the first successful seaplane.

1912

On her maiden voyage the ocean liner *Titanic* strikes an iceberg off the Coast of Newfoundland on 15 April and sinks with the loss of 1,503 lives.

On 7 December, the Navy Department places its civilian personnel under the civil service.

1913

In situ metallography techniques are developed by EES and applied to all full-size Navy machinery components.

On 1 February, the Navy opens the Postgraduate School at the Naval Academy in Annapolis, Maryland.

The Navy's first electric-drive ship, collier *Jupiter* is commissioned on 7 April.

1914

World War I begins 3–4 August. The United States becomes a belligerent on 6 April 1917; the war ends 11 November 1918.

On 1 July, the Office of Naval Aeronautics is established.

The Panama Canal is officially opened for traffic on 15 August.

The first test run in the 8-by-8-foot wind tunnel at Washington Navy Yard takes place on 8 December.

Promoted from his position as Director of EMB, on 17 December, Taylor becomes Chief of the Bureau of Construction and Repair. He is relieved by Captain William McEntee.

1915

On 25 January, the first transcontinental telephone call is made between Alexander Graham Bell in New York and Thomas A. Watson in San Francisco.

On 3 March, in Public Law 271, Congress establishes the Office of Chief of Naval Operations. It also establishes the National Advisory Committee for Aeronautics (NACA) to settle the long-standing dispute over the organization and coordination of aeronautical research.

On 25 March, the submarine *F 4* sinks off Honolulu, Hawaii, with 21 lives lost. This was the first submarine sinking in Navy history.

On 7 May, a German submarine sinks the British steamer *Lusitania* off the coast of Ireland with the loss of 1,198 lives.

On 1 June, the first Navy contract for lighter-than-air craft is awarded.

On 5 November, USS *North Carolina* (Armored Cruiser No. 12) made the first launch of an aircraft from a ship with a catapult.

On 21 November, German submarine commanders are secretly authorized to begin sinking ships in the English channel. The

Germans halt the practice after President Woodrow Wilson issues an ultimatum threatening to sever U.S relations.

Albert Einstein formulates his General Theory of Relativity.

1916

Organized by order of President Wilson to promote wartime research as well as stimulate scientific programs and information, the National Research Council is officially established on 20 September.

1917

On 1 February, Germany resumes its policy of unrestricted U-boat warfare in order to destroy the British "means and will to fight."

Sinking of U.S. ships by Germany leads to a U.S. declaration of war on 6 April.

On 23 April, USS *New Mexico* (Battleship No. 40), the first battleship to be driven by electric power, is launched.

On 26 June, the first U.S. troops arrive in Europe.

The United States adopts a convoy system to reduce Allied losses to German U-boats.

1918

On 8 January, President Wilson announces his peace program, the "Fourteen Points," to Congress.

On 7 March, the Office of the Director of Naval Aviation is established.

On 25 July, the Navy is made responsible for the development of rigid airships.

On 13 August, SECNAV authorizes the enrollment of women in the Marine Corps Reserve for clerical assignments.

On 11 November, Germany signs an armistice ending World War I hostilities.

On 1 December, helium is first used for lighter-than-air craft.

1919

On 13 March, the CNO issues a program for postwar naval airplane development.

On 31 May, the Curtiss flying boat NC-4 completes the first Atlantic crossing by air. Flying from Newfoundland to Lisbon, the seaplane makes a mid-ocean stop in the Azores.

The development of these planes had been originally suggested by Admiral Taylor during World War I.

On 28 June, the Peace Treaty ending World War I is signed at Versailles.

1920

On 20 June, The Bureau of Steam Engineering is renamed the Bureau of Engineering.

On 26 August, the 19th Amendment to the Constitution is ratified, giving women the right to vote.

On 20 August, the first regular licensed radio station begins broadcasting.

1921

On 12 July, Congress officially establishes the Navy Bureau of Aeronautics to oversee its aeronautical research and development.

On 12 November, President Warren G. Harding convenes the Washington Naval Conference to discuss naval disarmament and questions concerning the Pacific and Far East. The conference, which lasted until February 1922, results in nine treaties ratified by the Senate in 1922.

1923

Admiral Taylor retires on 16 January after 40 years of naval service.

The Naval Research Laboratory is commissioned.

1924

On 21 January, Ilyich Lenin, Chairman of the USSR Council of People's Commissars (Premier) dies; over the next three years Joseph Stalin emerges as the new Soviet leader.

1926

On 2 July, the Congress establishes the Army Air Corps.

Robert Goddard launches the first liquid-propelled rocket.

On 17 August, an exploding steam boiler at EES kills two and injures two others. The explosion is later attributed to a "progressive corrosion- fatigue crack in the back head of the steam drum."

1927

On 20–21 May, Charles A. Lindbergh makes the first solo transatlantic flight from Long Island, New York, to Paris, France, in a Ryan monohull airplane. The 3,610-mile journey takes 33 hours and 29 minutes.

On 20 June, the Geneva Conference on Naval Disarmament is held establishing limitations on the building of cruisers, destroyers, and submarines. France and Italy refuse to attend the conference, which ends on 4 August.

On 17 December, the submarine *S 4* sinks after a collision with Coast Guard destroyer *Paulding* off the coast of Provincetown, Massachusetts. Thirty-nine lives are lost.

1928

The first dirigible landing on a ship is made on 27 January when *Los Angeles* lands on *Saratoga* (CV 3).

On 17 June, Amelia Earhart is the first women to fly across the Atlantic.

1929

On 10 May, the first submarine escape lung is tested by Lieutenent C. B. Momsen and C. L. Tibbals at depths down to 206 feet.

On 29 October, sixteen million shares are traded on the New York Stock Exchange causing values to plummet. The crash intensifies the devastating economic depression that encompasses most of the western world.

On 18 December, the aircraft carrier *Lexington* (CV 2) is the first ship to furnish electrical power to a major city when Tacoma, Washington, suffers a power failure.

Captain Henry C. Dinger acquires diesel engines for the Naval Postgraduate School from the Smithsonian. Testing of power boat diesel engines is started. In 1933 additional funding allows for an expansion of the program to submarines, motor boats, and electrical auxiliaries on capital ships.

1930

From 1 January to 22 April, London hosts the International Conference on Naval Disarmament. The conference, attended by the United States, Great Britain, Japan, Italy, and France, seeks to limit construction of cruisers and achieve parity in such areas as submarine construction.

On 15 March the frigate *Constitution* is refloated at Boston, Massachusetts, after necessary repairs are made. They were financed by public subscription.

British engineer Frank Whittle patents a gas turbine engine for jet aircraft.

1931

The Welding Laboratory originally requested by Captain Dinger in December 1928 is established at EES.

Auguste Piccard makes the first manned balloon flight into the stratosphere.

Under the aegis of Admiral Taylor, the National Advisory Committee for Aeronautics constructs a 2,000-foot-long, high-speed towing tank at Langley Field, Virginia, for testing seaplane hulls and floats.

1932

Karl E. Schoenherr publishes his paper on the frictional resistance of fluids along plane surfaces. From this paper emerges the famous Schoenherr frictional resistance formula.

The Fuel Oil Testing Plant in the Philadelphia Naval Shipyard becomes a boiler development plant and is renamed the U.S. Naval Boiler Laboratory.

1933

On 30 January, Adolf Hitler is named Chancellor of Germany.

On 16 June, the Public Works Administration (PWA) is established. Some PWA funds available under the act are channeled to naval shipbuilding.

On 31 July, the frigate *Constitution* begins a tour of principal U.S. seaports.

EES sets up the Internal Combustion Engine (ICE) Laboratory for the testing of diesel engines.

The senior welding engineer at EES, Bela Ronay, develops an acronograph, "a recording instrument designed to chart arc stability when used during the process of welding."

1934

On 27 March, Congress and President Franklin D. Roosevelt approve the Vinson-Trammel Act authorizing the building of a full-treaty-strength Navy within the terms set by the Washington Naval Treaty of 1922 and the London Naval Treaty of 1930. Congress, however, fails to appropriate sufficient funds and until 1938, naval construction continues to be based almost solely on replacement needs.

The British oceanliner *Queen Mary* is launched.

1935

Scottish physicist Robert Watson-Watt patents the first practical radar system.

1936

On 6 May, Congress authorizes construction of a new model basin. The authorization includes $100,000 for acquisition of a site with total construction costs not to exceed $3,500,000.

On 26 June, the Merchant Marine Act becomes law, substituting the U.S. Maritime Commission for the U.S. Shipping Board.

The Society for Naval Architects and Marine Engineers establishes the David W. Taylor Medal in his honor. The society also presents Taylor with the first medal.

1937

On 3 May, the Association of Federal Architects awards a First Award Class A for the design of the "Naval Experimental Model Basin at Carderock, Maryland."

On 6 May, the hydrogen-filled German zeppelin *Hindenburg* burns up at its mooring in Lakehurst, New Jersey.

In May, the Navy acquires the first plot of land for the future model basin. The original plot, measuring slightly more than 107 acres, costs $61,424.

On 2 July, aviatrix Amelia Earhart disappears in the Pacific. An extensive search is unsuccessful.

On 12 August, the Navy awards the Turner Construction Company the contract for the construction of the new model basin. On 8 September, the ground is officially broken.

On 5 October, Secretary of the Navy Claude Swanson, through General Order 100, officially directs that the new establishment be known as "The David W. Taylor Model Basin."

1938

On 17 May, Congress approves the Naval Expansion Act of 1938 (an extension of the Vinson Act) allocating $1,090,656,000 for the expansion of a "two-ocean" Navy over ten years.

On 25 June, Congress, in an act entitled "Public Works, Bureau of Yards and Docks," appropriates an additional $500,000 to complete the "model testing plant."

1939

On 20 March, the Naval Research Laboratory begins an organized research program in atomic power.

On 23 May, the submarine *Squalus* (SS 192) sinks off Portsmouth, New Hampshire, in 240 feet of water. Twenty-six lives are lost but 59 crew members are rescued by diving bell in its first use in an operational environment.

On 26 June, the contractor finishes installing all services and erecting all buildings at the David Taylor Model Basin Carderock site.

On 1 September, Germany invades Poland causing Great Britain and France to declare war on Germany on 3 September.

On 5 September, the United States declares its neutrality in the European war; on 8 September, President Franklin Roosevelt declares the nation to be in a state of limited national emergency. Transatlantic passenger air service begins.

On 11 October, President Roosevelt authorizes research leading to the building of an atomic bomb.

On 4 November formal dedication ceremonies for the new model basin are held. Admiral David W. Taylor attends in a wheelchair. Transfer of personnel and equipment from EMB actually lasted until some considerable time later.

1940

On 10 May, Winston Churchill replaces Neville Chamberlain as Prime Minister of England.

On 29 May, tests of a propeller in the variable-pressure water tunnel are the first productive test runs in the DTMB tunnel.

On 11 June, Congress authorizes close to $1.5 billion for naval defense under the Naval Supply Act.

On 17 June, the CNO asks Congress for $4 billion to construct a true two-ocean Navy.

On 20 June, the Bureaus of Construction and Repair, and the Bureau of Engineering merge to form the Bureau of Ships. The Office of the Under Secretary of the Navy is also established.

On 27 June, under executive order of President Roosevelt, the National Defense Research Council (NDRC) is established with Vannevar Bush as its first chairman. Charged with correlating and supporting "scientific research on mechanisms and devices of warfare," the committee becomes a subordinate of the Office of Scientific Research and Development (OSRD) in June 1941.

On 28 July, Admiral Taylor dies at the U.S. Naval Hospital in Bethesda, Maryland.

On 27 September, Germany, Italy, and Japan sign a tripartite pact binding them to a common struggle.

In December, EES contracts with Allis Chalmers to begin design and construction of a 3,500-horspower gas turbine. Charged with the "investigation of those components which most logically might be used in a prototype shipboard plant," the station chooses J. T. Rettaliata to head the project.

Captain Harold E. Saunders is appointed the first Technical Director of DTMB and serves in that capacity through World War II. In 1946, he is appointed director.

1941

On 17 March, the 77th Congress finally makes an appropriation for a subsonic atmospheric wind tunnel to be built at DTMB. Although Congress had originally authorized funds for wind tunnels in the 1936 funding for the basin, it subsequently excluded them.

On 27 May, the British sink the German pocket battleship *Bismarck*.

On 1 November, the Coast Guard is placed under the jurisdiction of the Department of the Navy for the duration of the national emergency.

On 7 December, Japanese planes attack the U.S. Navy installation at Pearl Harbor, Hawaii. The event, "a day that will live in infamy," extends the European conflict into World War II.

On 8 December, the United States officially declares war on Japan. Three days later, Germany and Italy declare war on the United States.

On 12 December, the Air Transport Service is established.

A program of high-temperature materials research is set up at EES.

The Naval Boiler Laboratory adds steam turbines to its testing repertoire and becomes the Naval Boiler and Turbine Laboratory.

1942

On 27 January, U.S. submarine *Gudgeon* (SS 211) sinks a Japanese submarine; the only confirmed case where a U.S. submarine sinks an enemy sub while both are submerged.

On 4–8 May, the United States and Japan engage in the Battle of Coral Sea off the southern coast of New Guinea. During the battle the aircraft carrier *Lexington* (CV 2) is sunk while her counterpart *Yorktown* (CV 5) is heavily damaged. U.S. naval forces do, however, inflict heavy losses on the Japanese fleet and prevent it from landing at Port Moresby. This conflict is the first time a naval battle is fought exclusively by planes from carriers instead of by surface ships.

On 13 May, the Bureau of Navigation is renamed the Bureau of Naval Personnel.

On 3–6 June, in another extensive naval battle, the U.S. and Japanese fleets meet at Midway. Although the U.S. Navy loses *Yorktown*, the Japanese lose four of their carriers. This is a turning point of the war.

On 9 July, Robert H. Goddard arrives at EES to begin on-site testing of jet-assisted take-off (JATO) rockets. On 23 September, JATO

rockets attached to a PBY Catalina are tested on the Severn River under Goddard's direction.

After purchasing its first gas turbine from Allis Chalmers, the Navy installs the turbine at EES for testing in the recently organized Gas Turbine Lab.

On 2 December, Manhatten Project scientists under Enrico Fermi, at the University of Chicago, produce the first successful controlled fission chain reaction.

1943

On 29 January, the wind tunnel building at Carderock is completed at a cost of $282,143.

On 25 February, J. Robert Oppenheimer receives a charter authorizing establishment of a laboratory at Los Alamos, New Mexico, to design an atomic bomb.

On 15 March, the numbered fleet system is established.

On 1 April, the Naval Air Station at Patuxent River, Maryland, is established.

On 9 April, the first two subsonic wind tunnels at DTMB are completed for a total cost of $145,850.

On 30 April, construction is completed on the pentagonal test pond for underwater explosives tests on submarine models at a cost of $136,356. The instrument house cost an additional $9,968.

The Bureau of Ships and Bureau of Ordnance establish the Mine Warfare Test Station near the mouth of the Patuxent River in Maryland. In 1945, the station is moved to Panama City, Florida.

1944

On 1 January, the Aerodynamics Lab staff at EMB is officially transferred from the Washington Navy Yard to Carderock.

On 21 April, parachute tests are the first to run in subsonic wind tunnel #1.

On 19 May, James V. Forrestal, Under Secretary of the Navy since 1940, becomes Secretary of the Navy.

On 6 June (D-Day), Allied forces, led by General Dwight D. Eisenhower, begin Operation Overlord, the invasion of Normandy. Two months after D-Day, Allied forces liberate Paris. General of the Army Eisenhower becomes Supreme Commander of the Allied Expeditionary Forces.

On 5 July, the circulating water channel at DTMB is completed and filled with 600,000 gallons of water, although tests are not run in the channel until 1945.

On 17 July, the first tests are run in DTMB wind tunnel #2.

On 18 July, Secretary of the Navy James Forrestal approves the extension of the model basin by a length of 1,820 feet.

On 23–25 October, the U.S. Navy engages the Japanese fleet in Leyte Gulf. It is a major victory for the Seventh and Third Fleets and remains as one of the U.S. Navy's greatest sea battles. Seven U.S. ships and twenty-six Japanese ships were sunk.

The first tests of the Allis Chalmers engine are conducted at EES.

On 14 December, the rank of Fleet Admiral (five stars) is established.

1945

V-E Day is celebrated on 8 May with the unconditional surrender of Germany to Western Allies and Russia ending the war in Europe.

On 16 June, the Naval Air Test Center is established at Patuxent, Maryland.

On 23 June, tests of a subsurface glider are the first to be conducted in the DTMB circulating water channel, the largest such channel in the world.

On 16 July, the first U.S. atomic bomb is exploded at Alamogordo, New Mexico.

On 6 August, an atomic bomb is dropped by the United States on Hiroshima, Japan. Three days later, on 9 August, a second bomb is dropped on Nagasaki, Japan.

On 14 August, the Japanese sign a surrender which officially ends World War II on 2 September.

On 1 September, dedication ceremonies for the U.S. Navy Mine Countermeasures Station are held in Panama City, Florida.

In November, a special gas turbine project is established at EES. This project becomes part of the Mechanical Lab in September 1948.

1946

In May, DTMB receives two captured German water channels; one is 20 centimeters wide and the other is 8 by 12 centimeters.

The U.S. Navy participates in nuclear weapons tests at Bikini Atoll in the Pacific in Operation Crossroads, with an air burst on 1 July and the world's first underwater nuclear detonation on 25 July.

On 2 July, the Navy's first jet aircraft operates from a carrier.

On 1 August, the Atomic Energy Act (McMahon Act) is signed into law by President Harry S. Truman. The Atomic Energy Commission is created through the act to "direct development, use, and control of atomic energy for defense and security of the U.S. and for a variety of peaceful applications."

On 1 August, Public Law 588 of the 79th Congress establishes the Office of Naval Research.

On 1 October, the Naval Air Missile Test Center, Point Magu, California, is established.

On 31 October, the Bureau of Ships acquires the Farragut (later Bayview) Field Station on Lake Pend Oreille in Idaho for acoustic

and underwater countermeasure tests. The Secretary of the Navy officially establishes the station under the technical control and management of the David Taylor Model Basin and names it the David W. Taylor Model Basin Field Station.

Noise, shock, and vibration work in the EES Welding Lab is shifted to a newly established Wave Mechanics Lab. EES also begins work on a bearings project.

ENIAC, the first successful electronic digital computer, becomes operational.

The DTMB towing basin is extended by 1,820 feet, increasing the versatility of carriage operations.

1947

On 15 July, Captain Harold E. Saunders retires and is replaced by Rear Admiral Claude O. Kell. On 17 July, Saunders is transferred to the Bureau of Ships.

On 26 July, President Truman signs the National Security Act establishing the National Security Council as a cabinet-status agency charged with advising the President and supervising the Central Intelligence Agency. The U.S. Air Force is also established under this act as a separate branch of the military and is united with the Army and Navy as the National Military Establishment.

On 10 August, President Truman signs amendments to the National Security Act creating the Department of Defense, originally designated as the National Military Establishment, and giving subcabinet status to the secretaries of the Army, Navy, and Air Force.

On 17 September, James Forrestal, at the time serving as Secretary of the Navy, becomes the first Secretary of Defense.

On 19 October, USAF Captain Charles Yeager is the first person to achieve supersonic speed. He accomplishes the feat in an X-1 research plane built by Bell Aircraft.

At the American Towing Tank Conference, member tanks in the United States and Canada adopt the Schoenherr Friction Line as the standard for calculating frictional resistance.

Construction on DTMB's second deep-water towing basin is completed.

EES undertakes development of HY-80 steel to provide high yield strength and notch toughness.

The Office of Naval Research, Bureau of Ships, and Bureau of Aeronautics initiate a research program to develop hydrofoil craft.

On 16 December, Bell Labs introduces the transistor.

1948

On 16 June, the 80th Congress authorizes the construction of a 7-foot-by-10-foot sonic wind tunnel at Carderock. Parts of the tunnel were obtained from a 3-meter tunnel captured at Ottobrun, Germany. On 25 June, in Public Law 785, Congress appropriates money for the construction of the tunnel.

The Office of Naval Material is established.

The EES Welding Laboratory gains control of a new Electrical Branch and it is renamed the Welding and Electrical Laboratory.

1949

On 28 August, the Soviet Union detonates its first atomic bomb.

In March, the DTMB Applied Physics Laboratory is put under control of the Hydromechanics Lab.

The Naval Air Development Center is established on 1 August at Johnsville, Pennsylvania.

On 24 August, the North Atlantic Treaty Organization (NATO) is established by the United States, Canada, and ten Western European nations.

On 1 October, the Navy takes over surface transportation from the Army with formation of the Military Sea Transportation Service (MSTS), now the Military Sealift Command.

On 24 November, construction of *Albacore* (AGSS 569), the first submarine of a military type built solely for research purposes, is authorized by Congress.

The submarine *Turbot* (SS 427) is assigned to EES as a floating lab facility for acoustic testing.

The National Science Foundation is established.

1950

On 31 January, President Truman orders production of the H-bomb.

On 27 June, President Truman orders the Air Force and Navy to Korea after North Korea invades South Korea. He approves air strikes and ground forces against the North on 30 June.

On 15 September, the battleship *Missouri* bombards the coast of Korea. Naval amphibious forces carry out a historic landing at Inchon at a crucial period to help check a North Korean drive.

1951

On 11 April, President Truman dismisses General Douglas MacArthur as Commander in the Pacific for his having made unauthorized policy statements. He is replaced by General Matthew Ridgway.

On 28 September, by act of Congress, the 7-by-10-foot sonic wind tunnel is changed to a transonic wind tunnel of the same dimensions.

1952

On 6 March, the Bureau of Ships delegates the technical administration of its entire hydromechanics research program to DTMB.

On 26 April, the U.S. destroyer *Hobson* (DD 464) sinks in the mid-Atlantic after colliding with the U.S. aircraft carrier *Wasp* (CV 18).

On 28 April, the Navy announces that it will put British-designed catapults on board U.S. carriers.

On 26 May, testing of the feasibility of the aircraft carrier angled deck concept begins on board *Midway* (CVA 41).

On 26 May, after thirty-eight years of aircraft design testing, the EMB wind tunnel at the Washington Navy Yard is decommissioned.

On 14 June, the keel is laid for the first U.S. nuclear-powered submarine, *Nautilus* (SSN 571).

On 17 June, the Navy takes delivery of the world's largest nonrigid airship, *ZPN1*.

On 1 November, the U.S. detonates the first hydrogen device at Eniwetok Atoll in the Pacific.

On 9 December, the Bureau of Ships establishes an Applied Mathematics Laboratory at DTMB.

The Welding and Electrical Lab at EES is split into two separate labs.

EES finishes construction of the Wolverine Building test facilities.

The British de Havilland Comet is the first jetliner aircraft to enter commercial passenger service.

1953

The Soviet Union explodes its first hydrogen device—probably only "boosted" plutonium, not a true fusion weapon.

Jacques Piccard's bathyscape *Trieste* descends to a depth of 10,330 feet.

On 5 March, Joseph Stalin dies.

On 5 June, a 2-by-4-foot "low turbulence" wind tunnel is built as part of the Fluid Phenomena Lab at DTMB.

On 19 August, UNIVAC-A, DTMB's first electronic computer, is installed for use on a "multiplicity of Navy problems in the fields of engineering, logistics, and operations research."

On 15 September, the keel of the nuclear submarine *Seawolf* (SSN 575) is laid.

On 16 October, DTMB's Applied Mathematics Laboratory is dedicated.

On 5 December, the research submarine *Albacore* is commissioned at the Portsmouth Naval Shipyard, Kittery, Maine.

1954

On 21 January, Mrs. Dwight D. Eisenhower christens the nuclear submarine *Nautilus* at Groton, Connecticut. It is the first time a First Lady is given that honor for a submarine.

An electrical equipment building and cooling tower is built for the Carderock continuous-flow transonic wind tunnel.

1955

On 11 February, the Experimental Model Basin at the Washington Navy Yard is officially decommissioned.

On 29 April, the Navy Mine Countermeasures Station in Panama City, Florida, is renamed the Navy Mine Defense Laboratory.

Construction of the DTMB continuous-flow transonic wind tunnel is completed.

Low-cycle fatigue is identified and evaluated at EES, which leads to the use of low-cycle fatigue materials for submarine design and construction.

EES-reengineered atmospheric control systems are used in nuclear submarines, significantly increasing time on station submerged.

1956

In March, the continuous-flow transonic wind tunnel at Carderock becomes operational for subsonic testing. Transonic testing did not begin until February 1958.

On 26 April, the Naval Air Engineering Facility replaces the Naval Aircraft Factory in Philadelphia, Pennsylvania.

On 1 August, a groundbreaking ceremony for the Maneuvering and Seakeeping Basin (MASK) is held at DTMB.

1957

On 10 January, the Navy commissions the Naval Air Mine Defense Unit at Panama City, Florida.

On 20 May, Harold V. Nutt becomes the first Technical Director of EES.

On 4 October, the USSR launches the first artificial satellite, Sputnik I.

Air cushion vehicle (ACV) research begins at DTMB.

A second building for the Applied Math Lab is built at DTMB.

An EES modernization program begins, including a $1.2 million renovation of the fifty-year-old mechanical engineering test building.

1958

On 1 January, Explorer I, the first U.S. artificial satellite, is launched by a Jupiter rocket. A Navy satellite, Vanguard I, the size of a grapefruit and weighing 3.25 pounds, is put into orbit three months later on 17 March.

On 1 May, the new 12-foot pressure tank begins operation at DTMB.

On 3 August, the nuclear submarine *Nautilus* reaches the North Pole under the polar icecap.

On 27 August, the development of the super-cavitating propeller, by Marshall Tulin of DTMB, is announced. The design is compared "in magnitude to the development of jet propulsion for aircraft."

In September, DTMB greatly expands its mission statement to include "fundamental and applied research in the fields of hydromechanics, aerodynamics, structural mechanics, mathematics, acoustics, and related fields of science."

On 1 October, the National Advisory Committee on Aeronautics is disestablished and the National Aeronautics and Space Administration (NASA) is created in its place.

On 6 October, the submarine *Seawolf* completes a record sixty-day submerged voyage.

EES consolidates its seven labs into four technical departments under the management and control of civilian Technical Director Harold (Hi) Nutt. The four departments are Chemistry, Mechanical Engineering, Applied Physics, and Metallurgy.

The National Defense Education Act passes authorizing federal funds for research projects at U.S. universities.

DTMB begins a study of HY-80 steel to "establish a method for characterizing dynamic, metallurgical, and static weld properties."

The United States launches the first intercontinental ballistic missile (ICBM).

1959

On 4 February, the keel of the world's first nuclear aircraft carrier *Enterprise* (CVAN 65) is laid at Newport News, Virginia.

On 9 March, a Bureau of Ships Instruction officially expands the mission of EES from "testing and determination of the suitability of certain steam machinery for use in naval vehicles" to the "conduct of applied research, development, investigations, evaluations, and tests in the fields of physics, chemistry, metallurgy, and electricity."

Rear Admiral Ralph K. James relieves Rear Admiral Albert Mumma as Chief of the Bureau of Ships.

On 9 June, the first nuclear fleet ballistic missile submarine, *George Washington* (SSBN 598), is launched at Groton, Connecticut.

On 18 August, Public Law 86-174 disestablishes the Bureaus of Aeronautics and Ordnance. The Bureau of Naval Weapons is

created in their place, taking over administration of the DTMB Aerodynamics Lab.

On 27 August, a Polaris missile on board *Observation Island* (AG 154) is fired for the first time from a ship at sea.

On 1 November, the Weapons Effects Branch of the Underwater Research Division at Norfolk Naval Shipyard is put under control of the DTMB Structural Mechanics Lab. DTMB also establishes a new Department of Applied Science headed by Danos H. Kallas.

EES originates a program to conduct machinery vibration tests on the first of each class of nuclear submarines.

On 10 November, the 447.5-foot submarine *Triton* (SSRN 586) with two nuclear reactors, is launched.

Sir Christopher Cockerell tests the first air cushion vehicle.

The Boeing 707 enters commercial airline service.

1960

On 10 May, Captain Edward L. Beach, USN, commander of the submarine *Triton*, completes a circumnavigation of the globe underwater in this 109 million dollar nuclear submarine.

In July, a launch of the Polaris missile is made successfully from *George Washington*.

American physicist Theodore H. Maiman demonstrates the first successful laser.

Jacques Piccard and Don Walsh descend in the ocean to a depth of 35,000 feet in the bathyscape *Trieste*.

On 1 December, the High Speed Phenomena Division of the Hydrodynamics Lab at DTMB takes control of the hydrodynamic research facilities at Langley Research Center, Langley Field, Virginia.

The hypersonic wind tunnel at DTMB becomes operational. Used in the development and design of high-speed missiles, it also assists in the selection of materials for their construction.

1961

In January, DTMB's mobile noise barge (*Monob*) is put into operation in the Atlantic, Tongue of the Ocean, becoming the primary engineering and noise measurement facility for Atlantic Fleet submarines.

On 21 January, newly inaugurated President John F. Kennedy names Robert S. McNamara as Secretary of Defense.

On 12 April, Yuri Gagarin, of the Soviet Union, becomes the first man to venture beyond the Earth's atmosphere into space.

On 16 May, the Livermore Atomic Research Computer (LARC) is dedicated in the Model Basin's Applied Math Lab.

On 20 June, named in honor of Captain Harold Saunders, the Maneuvering and Seakeeping Basin, a simulated ocean covering 5 acres and a rotating arm basin 260 feet in diameter, is dedicated at the David Taylor Model Basin.

On 1 July, the Underwater Explosions Research Department (UERD), formerly a division of the Norfolk Naval Shipyard, becomes a detachment of DTRC. The underwater explosions barge (UEB 1) is acquired and assigned to the Structural Mechanics Laboratory. Alfred Keil, head of UERB, reports as head of the Structural Mechanics Laboratory at Carderock.

In October, President Kennedy sends his military advisor, General Maxwell Taylor, to South Vietnam to evaluate the country's economic and military condition. Based on his report of the impact of continuing infiltration by the Viet Cong, American aid is stepped up. During the next two years more than 16,000 military advisors are sent to South Vietnam and more than 400 million dollars is spent in military aid alone.

EES dedicates the Ralph James Magnetic Field Laboratory. Partially completed and opened in 1960, the lab becomes fully operational in 1961 with the addition of the high-speed magnetic field measuring system.

Captain Harold E. Saunders dies on 11 November just 18 days before his seventy-first birthday.

On 25 November, the nuclear-powered carrier *Enterprise* joins the fleet in Newport News, Virginia.

1962

DTMB's 36-inch variable-pressure water tunnel is put into operation.

On 20 February, Colonel John H. Glenn Jr. becomes the first American astronaut to orbit the earth, piloting *Friendship* 7 through three orbits.

On 11 May, Operation Swordfish tests the destroyer delivery of an underwater nuclear weapon. This is one of the last tests before activation of the treaty with the Soviet Union banning nuclear testing.

On 15 July, French explorers in the bathyscape *Archimedes* descend to a depth of 30,365 feet in the Pacific's Japan Trench.

1963

On 1 March, Alfred Keil, head of the Structural Mechanics Laboratory, is appointed the first civilian technical director of DTMB.

On 10 April, the nuclear submarine *Thresher* (SSN 593)sinks after a test dive off the New England coast. All hands are lost.

In April, the Instrumentation Division in the Industrial Department, the Technical Information Division in the Administrative Department, the Operations Research Staff, the Programming Office, and the Long-Range Planning Office are moved to the DTMB technical director's staff.

On 29 April, Rear Admiral William A. Brockett relieves Rear Admiral Ralph K. James as Chief of the Bureau of Ships.

On 1 July, Karl E. Schoenherr, head of the Hydromechanics Laboratory, retires and is replaced by William E. Cummins.

On 1 July, the Engineering Experiment Station (EES) changes its name to the Marine Engineering Laboratory (MEL).

On 10 October, William W. Murray is appointed acting head of the Structural Mechanics Laboratory.

In November, the Acoustics Branch in the Hydromechanics Laboratory, the Vibrations Branch of the Structural Mechanics Laboratory, and the Underwater Acoustics staff under the technical director, are merged to create the Acoustics and Vibrations Laboratory (AVL) in order to "assure that surface ships, submarines, underwater weapons, and underwater detection and evasion devices for the U.S. Navy shall have acoustic and vibration characteristics which will permit the accomplishment of their intended missions."

On 22 November, President John F. Kennedy is fatally wounded as he rides in a motorcade in Dallas, Texas.

On 2 December, the Office of Naval Material is redesignated the Naval Material Support Establishment (NMSE).

The first study of HY-130 steels is initiated by MEL, joined by the Navy Applied Science Laboratory (NASL) in Brooklyn, New York.

Nickel- and cobalt-based superalloys for use in marine gas turbines operating in a corrosive saltwater environment are developed by MEL working in conjunction with manufacturers.

1964

On 1 March, William Murray is officially appointed head of the Structural Mechanics Laboratory.

In June, the SEABED summer study is convened at the Naval Postgraduate School in Monterey, California. John Craven, chief scientist in the Polaris program office, is the chairman and Alfred Keil, technical director of DTMB, is chairman of the Undersea Technology Panel.

On 2 and 4 August, night attacks by South Vietnam patrol boats are said to have been made on two U.S. ships in the Gulf of Tonkin. As a result, President Johnson requests the Congress to give him authority to use whatever force is necessary to protect U.S. and allied forces from attack. The Congress gives him that authority in the Gulf of Tonkin Resolution passed on 7 August and a massive buildup of U.S. military forces in Vietnam begins soon thereafter.

On 1 August, Captain Patrick Leehey, head of the DTMB Acoustics and Vibrations Laboratory, leaves the Navy to accept a faculty position in MIT's Department of Naval Architecture and Marine Engineering.

The submersible *Alvin*, measuring 20 feet in diameter, is launched by the Woods Hole Oceanographic Institution.

The Civil Rights Act is passed by the U.S. Congress.

1965

On 6 April, Intelsat I, the first commercial communications satellite, is launched.

On 29 June, a groundbreaking ceremony for the new Structural Mechanics Laboratory building is held at Carderock.

On 1 October, Gene Gleissner becomes head of the Applied Mathematics Laboratory replacing Harry Polachek.

On 20 December, SECNAV issues Instruction 5430.77 setting up the position of Director of Navy Laboratories (DNL) in the Office of Naval Material. The position is filled by Gerald Johnson.

1966

On 31 January, Rear Admiral Edward J. Fahy relieves Rear Admiral William A. Brockett as Chief of the Bureau of Ships.

SECNAV ALNAV of 8 March directs a major reorganization of the Navy. This provides for establishment of naval systems commands.

Bureau of Ships letter of 28 March requests DTMB to assume responsibilities as technical agent for the Navy's Hydrofoil Development Program.

On 1 April, the Navy's R&D labs are put under the Director of Navy Laboratories in the Naval Material Support Establishment (NMSE).

On 19 April, DTMB establishes the Systems Development Office, Code 0H01, under Technical Director Alfred Keil. The Hydrofoil Development Program Office, Code 0H50, is also established.

On 1 May, the Bureau of Ships becomes the Naval Ship Systems Command (NAVSHIPS) and the Naval Material Support Establishment (NMSE) becomes the Naval Material Command (NAVMAT).

On 30 June, Alfred Keil retires as Technical Director of DTMB and accepts a position as head of the Department of Naval Architecture and Marine Engineering at MIT.

In July, Robert A. Frosch becomes Assistant Secretary of the Navy for Research and Development.

On 12 October, Alan Powell, head of the Acoustics Laboratory, replaces Alfred Keil as Technical Director of NSRDC.

On 10 November, the DTMB Hydrofoil Special Trials Unit (HYSTU) is established as a tenant activity of the Puget Sound Naval Shipyard (PSNS) in Bremerton, Washington. Lieutenant Commander Karl M. Duff is given additional duty as officer in charge.

On 21 December, the CNO transfers *High Point* (PCH 1) to HYSTU with *Plainview* (AGEH 1) to be transferred when delivered.

1967

On 31 March, the David Taylor Model Basin and the Marine Engineering Laboratory in Annapolis merge to form the Naval Ship Research and Development Center (NSRDC) with headquarters at Carderock, Maryland. MEL Technical Director Harold V. Nutt becomes Deputy Technical Director of NSRDC.

The first large-scale model submarine test vehicle, *Kamloops*, is delivered to the center's Acoustic Research Detachment (ARD) at Lake Pend Orielle, initiating ARD's increasingly important role in submarine silencing.

On 1 August, the center awards a contract for construction of an anechoic test facility.

On 1 November, the Navy Mine Defense Laboratory in Panama City, Florida becomes the third component of NSRDC.

The NSRDC Structural Mechanics Laboratory Building, containing high-pressure test tanks for deep-submergence studies, is completed.

At Annapolis, the Degaussing Control System Test Facility, is completed.

1968

On 19 January, construction of the Instrument Calibration Facility is completed at Annapolis.

In March, Lieutenant Commander Karl Duff is given PCS orders as officer in charge of the NSRDC Hydrofoil Special Trials Unit.

On 21 March, *Plainview* operated by the contractor, Lockheed Ship, makes its first foilborne flight lasting eleven and one-half minutes.

On 31 May, Vietnam peace talks begin in Paris, France.

On 7 November, an OPNAV Notice officially announces the name change of the Annapolis Division, NSRDC, to the NSRDC Laboratory, Annapolis, Maryland. The Navy Mine Defense Lab is renamed the NSRDC Laboratory, Panama City, Florida. Also, the title of Commanding Officer and Director of NSRDC is changed to Commander.

NAVSHIPS designates NSRDC the Principal Technical Development Laboratory for air cushion vehicles. An amphibious assault landing craft (AALC) program is established in the Systems Development Office to aid in the technical support and direction of the AALC advanced development.

Reorganization of the Annapolis Division to become the NSRDC Laboratory, Annapolis, Maryland, results in the formation of three laboratories: Electrical, Machinery, and Materials.

Without casualties, the research submarine *Alvin* accidentally sinks off the coast of Cape Cod. It is subsequently recovered.

1969

Several functions and 94 members of the staff of the Naval Applied Science Laboratory in Brooklyn are transferred to the Annapolis Laboratory. Following this, on 27 March, the Annapolis Lab modifies the names of its technical labs. The Electrical Lab becomes the Department of Electrical Engineering, the Machinery Lab the Department of Machinery Technology, and the Materials Lab the Department of Materials Technology.

On 7 April, the center's LARC computer is decommissioned.

On 29 April, the title of Chief is replaced by the title of Commander. For example, Chief NAVSHIPS becomes Commander NAVSHIPS.

On 20 July, Neil Armstrong sets foot on the moon.

On 31 July, Rear Admiral Nathan Sonnenshein relieves Rear Admiral Edward Fahy as Commander NAVSHIPS.

1970

On 2 March, the *Plainview*, at 320 tons the world's largest hydrofoil ship, is accepted by the U.S. Navy.

On 2 July, the building housing the Carderock anechoic test facility (ATF) is dedicated with a ribbon-cutting ceremony. It is later renamed the Anechoic Flow Facility (AFF).

Development of the titanium-100 alloy is completed by NSRDC and it is used as the material for construction of the pressure spheres of the deep-ocean submersibles *Alvin* (1972/12,000-foot depth), and *Sea Cliff* (1984/20,000-foot depth).

1971

On 18 April, the Systems Development Department (SDD), Code 11, is established headed by William M. Ellsworth.

On 19 April, David D. Jewell is appointed technical manager of the Hydrofoil Development Program Office, Code 115.

The SES 100A is launched by the builder, Aerojet General.

1972

On 24 January, the NSRDC Laboratory in Panama City, Florida, is officially separated from NSRDC and on 1 February is renamed the Naval Coastal Systems Laboratory.

On 30 March, North Vietnam launches its biggest attack in four years across the demilitarized zone.

On 3 April, John H. Chafee resigns as the Secretary of the Navy.

On 15 April, the U.S. resumes bombing of Hanoi and Haiphong after a four year lull.

In April, the NATO Patrol Hydrofoil Missile Ship (PHM) Project Office is established in NAVSHIPS under Captain James Wilkins, USN.

On 8 May, President Nixon announces the mining of Vietnam ports.

On 1 August, Vice Admiral (Sel) Robert C. Gooding relieves Rear Admiral Nathan Sonnenshein as Commander Naval Ship Systems Command.

On 11 August, the last combat troops leave Vietnam.

The SES 100B is launched by Bell Aerospace.

In November a memorandum of understanding (MOU) is signed by the United States and the Federal Republic of Germany for the design and development of two lead PHMs.

On 18 December, full-scale bombing of Vietnam is resumed after Paris peace talks reach an impass.

1973

On 27 January the United States ends the military draft.

On 9 April, Robert Johnston, formerly manager of Grumman Marine Systems, becomes head of the Hydrofoil Development Program Office, Code 115.

The Navy's Rubber Laboratory and RDT&E Paint Group are transferred from Mare Island Shipyard to DTNSRDC Annapolis.

On 31 December, Harold (Hi) Nutt retires from federal service.

1974

On 29 June, Admiral James Holloway becomes CNO.

On 1 July, the Naval Ship Systems Command merges with the Naval Ordnance Command to form the Naval Sea Systems Command.

Facing impeachment over the Watergate affair, on 8 August, President Richard Nixon resigns. He is replaced by Vice President Gerald Ford the same day.

On 9 November, *Pegasus* (PHM 1) is launched on Lake Washington at the Boeing plant in Renton, Washington.

An investigation of controllable-pitch propeller blade attachment loading, design, and material selection is undertaken by NSRDC after failure of the CP propeller on *Barbey* (FF 1088). Application of the results leads to trouble-free operation of the gas turbine-powered DD 963, FFG 7, CG 47, and DDG 51 classes.

1975

On 25 February, *Pegasus* makes its first foilborne flight.

In April, after ten years of war and the loss of 58,000 Americans, the United States, along with some of their South Vietnamese supporters, withdraw from Vietnam. North and South Vietnam become united under communist rule.

On 9 July, OPNAV Notice 5450 announces the renaming of the Naval Ship Research and Development Center to the David Taylor Naval Ship Research and Development Center in honor of the founder and first director of the original Experimental Model Basin.

1976

In January, the DTNSRDC Amphibious Assault Landing Craft Experimental Trials Unit is established as a tenant activity of the Naval Coastal Systems Laboratory in Panama City, Florida.

1977

On 26 May, R&D responsibility for the PHM 1 is assigned to the center's HYSTU. The ship is commissioned in July.

On 7 September, President Jimmy Carter signs a treaty with Panama, agreeing to turn over the Panama Canal and the surrounding zone to Panama by the year 2000. The treaty is ratified by the U.S. Senate in 1978.

Installation of first-generation environmental quality control systems, developed by DTRC, begins on board Navy ships.

In December, the CNM Group on functional realignment issues its draft report, which comes to be known as the Gavazzi Study.

1978

The towing tank at Langley Field, Virginia, is placed in standby status.

In June, fleet-wide underwater hull cleaning of ships begins and produces a significant reduction in fuel consumption.

The air cushion assault landing craft program test craft JEFF-B is delivered to the Navy by Bell Aerospace on 28 July.

The hydrofoil R&D ship *Plainview* is inactivated on 22 September.

1979

In May, *Plainview* is sold to a private party for $127,000. Its original cost was $21 million.

Full-scale development of the landing craft air cushion (LCAC) begins in December after successful operation of the JEFF-A and JEFF-B test craft. The LCAC program is launched with the award of a contract to Bell Aerospace for six preproduction craft.

DTRC introduces thermal-sprayed aluminum coatings for corrosion protection and machinery repair/restoration in the fleet.

1980

In January, a refurbished high-speed towing carriage is put into operation at DTNSRDC. The facility is designed to test models of high-speed craft.

On 1 August, NAVMATINST 5450.27D is issued. It states that DTNSRDC's mission is: "To be the principal Navy RDT&E Center for naval vehicles and logistics, and for providing RDT&E support to the Maritime Administration and the maritime industry."

1981

The Navy announces the intent to reactivate four *Iowa*-class battleships.

DTNSRDC develops a sensor-based adaptive control for arc-welding. This ultimately leads to development of the fully integrated Programmable Automated Welding System (PAWS).

1982

In January, Frank Kendall retires as head of the center's Central Instrumentation Department.

In February, periodic cleaning of submarine propellers is instituted to provide increased speed and reduced noise.

Admiral James O. Watkins is nominated to relieve Admiral Thomas B. Hayward as CNO.

The computer-based Advanced Surface Ship Evaluation Tool (ASSET) is developed by the center's Costing and Design Systems Office of the Systems Development Department (Code 11).

1983

On 1 January, William Ellsworth retires as head of the Systems Development Department.

On 19 June, Sally Ride on board orbiter *Challenger* becomes the first woman to fly in space.

On 25 October, U.S. Marines and Army Rangers, as part of a seven-nation Task Force, invade Grenada to prevent it from becoming a Cuban-style dictatorship.

Toshiba and Konigsberg VaaPenFabrikk illegally sell to the Soviets fine-tolerance milling machines crucial to the precise fabrication of propellers.

First use of fracture mechanics fitness-for-service analysis of *Saratoga* (CV 60) boiler failure results in a cost saving of one million dollars and minimal operational impact.

1984

In January, as a result of DTNSRDC's evaluation of high-strength low-alloy (HSLA) steels, an 80-ksi yield-strength steel to replace is introduced in surface ship construction.

In January, NAVSEA disestablishes the Surface Effect Ship Test Facility (SESTF) at the Naval Air Station, Patuxent River, Maryland and authorizes the SES Support Office to continue to maintain and operate the SES 200 test craft.

On 28 May, the 30-year-old submarine *Nautilus*, which had been decommissioned on 3 March 1980, goes to sea for the last time under tow from Mare Island Naval Shipyard to the Naval Submarine Base at New London, Connecticut. She is scheduled to go on permanent public display in the spring of 1986. Commissioned on 30 September 1954, she went to sea the first time on 17 January 1955, signaling back the historic message "underway on nuclear power."

The mission requirement for ship electromagnetic signature control is consolidated in the Central Instrumentation Department, which then becomes the Ship Electromagnetic Signatures Department.

The center changes the name of the Systems Development Department to the Ship Systems Integration Department "to capitalize on the synergistic gains available from the combination of new technologies."

DTNSRDC installs the first developmental-scale metal spray forming facility in the United States for nonreactive metals such as iron- and nickel-based alloys.

The Navy successfully demonstrates organometallic polymer antifouling bottom paints in the fleet with eight years of service free

of fouling. The development is transitioned to the commercial maritime industry.

On 11 November, DTNSRDC Detachment, Puget Sound, is created by merger of the Hydrofoil Special Trials Unit and the Ship Silencing Division, under Charles P. Henson.

1985

In March, Mikhail Gorbachev is elected Soviet Communist Party Secretary General.

On 6 May, the Naval Material Command is abolished. The Director of Navy Laboratories and the CNM Centers and Laboratories are placed under the Chief of Naval Research.

In July, the U.S. Army and the center's Surface Effect Ship Support Office (SESSO), Code 1232, begin a three-year test program at Patuxent, Maryland, on the Army's lighter amphibious air cushion vehicle (LACV 30).

On 27 December, Alan Powell retires after serving for almost two decades as the center's technical director. Edwin O'Neill is appointed acting technical director.

1986

On 24 February, DTNSRDC and seven other Navy R&D Laboratories are reassigned from the Office of Naval Research to the Space and Naval Warfare Systems Command (SPAWAR).

In March, George Wacker replaces J. Robert Belt as head of the Ship Materials Department, Code 28.

On 6 May, DTNSRDC celebrates its 50th anniversary since authorization by the Congress on 6 May 1936.

On 1 June, Richard E. Metrey takes over as technical director of DTNSRDC.

On 3 June, Robert C. Allen, head of the Propulsion and Machinery Department, Code 27, since 1984, retires. Larry Argiro becomes acting department head.

The center's Applied Mathematics Laboratory, Code 18, buys a Cray supercomputer and installs it in an extension of Carderock Building 17.

In October, Warren Dietz, head of the Ship Systems Integration Department, Code 12, and George Kerr, head of the NAVSEA Concept Design Division, SEA 501, exchange Senior Executive Service positions.

In December, SES 200 is loaded on a merchant ship and delivered to Portsmouth, England where it begins an extended demonstration tour of Europe.

1987

In February, major breakthroughs in high-temperature superconductive materials are reported in the United States.

On 1 May, the Ship Electromagnetic Signatures Department is established under Gerald G. Switzer, replacing the Central Instrumentation Department, Code 29. Its divisions include Observables Technology; Measurement Technology; and Control, Instrumentation, and Mechanical Systems.

On 31 August, ground is broken for the large cavitation channel (LCC) on President's Island in Memphis, Tennessee.

In September, History Associates, Inc., delivers a draft of a history of the Navy's David Taylor Research Center and its antecedents titled *Where the Fleet Begins* written by Rodney Carlisle.

On 18 September, the name of the center is officially changed to the David Taylor Research Center. This was the result of a special initiative of the center's new commander, Captain Clark C. (Corky) Graham.

On 18 September, Dennis Clark and David Moran are appointed to new positions as assistant technical directors. These positions were established as an experiment in personnel development.

In October, a memorandum of understanding is signed by NAVSEA Codes 017 and 50C, and DTRC, giving the center access to ship cost data and cost models.

In October, Jerry L. Reed becomes the new Director of Navy Laboratories under SPAWAR.

Responsibility for the operation of the Santa Cruz, California, Radar Imaging Facility (SCRIF) is transferred to DTRC.

1988

In January, construction begins on the large cavitation channel in Memphis, Tennessee.

In November, the center begins tests to evaluate a new submarine propulsor design which offers greatly improved acoustic performance. A 1/4-scale, self-propelled model of the SSN 21-class submarine is used as a test bed. Named the *Kokanee*, the model is the world's largest autonomously controlled submarine model and is operated by the center at the Acoustic Research Detachment on Lake Pend Orielle.

On 9 December, DTRC closes the Hydrofoil Trials Branch, PSNS (formerly HYSTU) after more than twenty-two years of providing technical support to the Navy's Hydrofoil Development Program.

1989

In March, the DTRC Innovation Center is established at Carderock. Facilities for the Innovation Center are completed in May, providing an environment for multidisciplinary teams to conceptualize innovative new systems.

In March, HSLA-100 steel is certified for use in surface combatant structures by the Naval Sea Systems Command. It is first used in the aircraft carriers CVN 74 and CVN 75.

USNS *Hayes* (T-AGOR 16) arrives at Tacoma Boat on 20 May to begin refurbishment as a replacement for *Monob* to conduct acoustics trials.

On 13 July, Secretary of Defense Richard Cheney delivers to the President a Defense Management Report (DMR) recommending further cuts in the scale of Defense facilities by cooperative programming, extensive cooperative use of facilities, closure of facilities, and consolidation of activities within and among the services.

On 1 September, OPTEVFOR reports favorably on the evaluation of the DTRC reverse-osmosis desalinator for lifeboats and recommends approval for fleet introduction.

DTRC adopts a new logo in September.

On 1 December, the Center Business Directorate, Code 30, is formed. It includes the Comptroller, Civilian Personnel, Supply, Technical and Administrative Services, and the Computer and Information Services Department. At the same time, the Aviation Department is disestablished and most of its functions are transferred to the Ship Systems Integration Department, Code 12, which is renamed the Systems Department.

On 20 December, U.S. troops invade Panama in an attempt to capture General Manuel Noriega.

The concept of the Simulation, Planning, and Analysis Research Center (SPARC), advanced in 1986 by Technical Director Richard Metrey, becomes operational in Building 191.

The position of director of the David Taylor Institute is established and David Moran is appointed to this position.

Aluminum anodes are first installed on submarines, resulting in a savings in weight of 4 tons and a cost saving of about $600,000 per boat.

In December, worldwide television audiences watch as joyous crowds tear chunks out of the Berlin Wall that had stood as a symbol of the Cold War since 1961.

1990

Congress passes the Defense Base Closure and Realignment Act of 1990, PL 101-510, which sets up a Defense Base Realignment and Closure Commission (BRAC).

In June, the DTRC-developed high solids coating of submarine ballast tanks for preservation is implemented. It extends tank maintenance schedules from two or three years to four to six years.

In July, the 7-foot-by-10-foot continuous-flow transonic wind tunnel suffers a catastrophic blade failure with extensive damage to the power section shell and power train.

Also in July, a modern state-of-the-art welding and non-destructive testing laboratory is completed and starts operation at the DTRC facility in Annapolis, Maryland.

In September, a DTRC Strategic Planning Council (SPC), chaired by Dennis Clark, is established to develop a draft center Strategic Plan.

On 1 October, parts of the Computation, Mathematics, and Logistics Department, Code 18, merge with the Systems Department, Code 12.

In October, a new Fracture Mechanics Laboratory is constructed at DTRC Annapolis with the latest in computer-interactive servo-hydraulic test systems for evaluation of naval alloys and material processes.

On 5 November, the Navy forwards its report to the BRAC, recommending that programs previously executed at the Annapolis facility of DTRC be reassigned to the Carderock, Maryland, site.

1991

The Persian Gulf War begins on 16 January and ends on 6 April with a six-week ground assault known as the Desert Storm Operation.

On 12 April, SECNAV approves a plan to consolidate RDT&E, Engineering, and Fleet Support facilities into a "corporate community." The plan calls for the merger of DTRC and the Naval Ship Systems Engineering Station (NAVSSES), in Philadelphia, Pennsylvania, and the move of materials facilities and personnel from Annapolis to Carderock.

On 21 April, the DTRC large cavitation channel is dedicated in Memphis, Tennessee. It is the world's largest and quietest high-speed variable-pressure water channel. Acceptance tests are completed in May and initial operation begins in June

On 1 July, the Defense Base Realignment and Closure Commission, BRAC, sends its report to the President.

On 4 July, *Arleigh Burke* (DDG 51) is commissioned at Norfolk, Virginia. It becomes the most advanced class of destroyers at sea.

On 10 July, President George Bush approves and sends to the Congress the recommendations of the 1991 BRAC without change.

In November, the center's newly constructed Southeast Alaska Acoustic Measurement Facility (SEAFAC) is dedicated. It is the most technologically sophisticated acoustic test range in the country. It replaces CIAR and SCARF as the fleet's Pacific-based ship-related acoustic measurement facilities.

On 20 December, the Under Secretary of the Navy authorizes implementation of the 1991 Base Realignment and Closure Act.

USNS *Hayes* (T-AG 195), the center's newest and largest, ultra-quiet, and capable noise measurement vessel, replaces R/V *Monob* as the fleet's "underway" submarine acoustical measurement platform.

In December, the USSR is formally dissolved. On 25 December, Gorbachev resigns his position as Secretary General of the Soviet Communist Party.

After over a decade of R&D, a unique concept for a quiet propulsor for SSN 21 application that the center recommended to NAVSEA, is now successfully powering this new submarine.

Metal spray-forming technology development at the center transitions to the Manufacturing Technology Program with the availability of Inconel-625 piping for *Seawolf* (SSN 21)-class submarines.

1992

On 2 January, the Navy forms four warfare centers; the Naval Air Warfare Center (NAWC), the Naval Surface Warfare Center (NSWC), the Naval Undersea Warfare Center (NUWC), and the Naval Command Control and Ocean Surveillance Center (NC-

COSC), along with the Naval Research Laboratory (NRL), from thirty-six RDT&E, Engineering, and Fleet Support Activities. Included are fifteen SPAWAR, six NAVAIR, thirteen NAVSEA, and two CNR activities. Rear Admiral George R. Meinig becomes the first commander of NSWC and reports to the commander of NAVSEA. DTRC becomes the Carderock Division of NSWC with Headquarters in Bethesda, Maryland. The Center Commander becomes Division Commander and the Technical Director becomes Division Director.

On 2 January, the Combat Craft Engineering Department, Code 60, based in Norfolk, Virginia, becomes a detachment, Code 1270, of the Carderock Division Systems Intergation Department.

On 12 April, SECNAV issues a RDT&E, Engineering, and Fleet Support consolidation plan.

In July, Rear Admiral Edward S. McGinley II relieves Rear Admiral George R. Menig as Commander NSWC.

In August, the Mobile Support Systems Office, under Ted Vaughters, is moved from Annapolis to Carderock.

In December, Harvey Chaplin, former head of the Aviation and Surface Effects Department, replaces George Kerr as head of the Systems Integration Department, Code 12. The Communications and Information Systems Division, Code 122; the Requirements and Distribution Systems Division, Code 129; and the Mobile Support Systems Office, Code 1235, are transferred from the Systems Integration Department to the new Logistics and Machinery Systems/Programs Directorate, Code 10. The remainder of the Systems Integration Department is reformed as the Ship Systems and Programs Directorate, Code 20.

On 12 December, the Carderock Division of NSWC is reorganized into eight directorates: Logistics and Machinery Systems/Programs, Code 10; Ship Systems and Programs, Code 20; Business, Code 30; Hydromechanics, Code 50; Survivability, Structures and Materials, Code 60; Signatures, Code 70; Machinery Research and Development, Code 80; and Machinery In-Service Engineering, Code 90.

The first real-time weld process monitor and controller based on acoustic emissions of the welding process is transitioned from a laboratory model to a full-scale unit. The unit uses a neural network and self-checking algorithms for welding process control.

1993

In January, forty-three NAVSEA 03 employees are reassigned to the Carderock Division to expand the division's role in Navy ship design.

On 3 March, Rear Admiral McGinley signs a memorandum of agreement between the U.S. Army Aviation and Troop command (ATCOM) and NSWC, defining R&D and engineering support for Army watercraft to be provided by the Carderock Division, following disestablishment of ATCOM's Belvoir Research, Development, and Engineering Center.

On 1 April, CDNSWC Code 35 ceases operation of the Cray supercomputer and the Control Data CDC-860 mass storage system.

On 23 June, the submarine *Turbot* is scrapped and removed from the Carderock Division Annapolis site. It was originally launched uncompleted in April 1945 and was transferred to EES on 27 October 1950 for use as a platform for testing submarine auxiliary machinery.

Light-off of the intercooled recuperated (ICR) gas turbine occurs on 15 July at the Royal Navy's Admiralty Test House in Pyestock, England. It had been under development by the Marine Division of Westinghouse since 1991 as part of the Advanced Development Machinery Program (ADMP) managed by Cyril Krolick, Code 808, in Annapolis. It will be tested in the CVN 76 and is expected to result in a thirty percent savings in fuel.

30 July, at the Amphibious Base, Little Creek, Virginia, the Navy decommissions the entire squadron of six patrol hydrofoil missile ships (PHMs). This is the first time in history that the Navy has decommissioned an entire class of ships at one time.

In August, the Southeast Alaska Acoustic Measurement Facility (SEAFAC) static site installation is completed. It provides the Signatures Directorate with the capability to conduct acoustic measurements on a suspended submarine.

On 9 October, the USNS *Hayes* is dedicated in Cape Canaveral, Florida, to serve as a Carderock Division ship for underwater acoustics trials.

The NAVSEA Weapons and Combat Systems Directorate (SEA06) is abolished on 10 October. Most of the responsibilities and resources are realigned within the Surface Ship Directorate (SEA91).

1994

On 14 April, Rear Admiral (Sel) David P. Sargent Jr. relieves Rear Admiral Edward S. McGinley II as Commander NSWC.

On 24 April, Vice Admiral George R. Sterner relieves Vice Admiral Kenneth C. Malley as Commander NAVSEA.

In May, tests of a model of a mobile ocean basing system (MOBS) are run in the MASK facility.

On 23 June, the air cushion vehicle landing platform (ACVLAP) technology demonstration with a maritime prepositioning RO/RO ship is successfully completed. A total of thirty-seven landings are made with an amphibious landing craft air cushion (LCAC).

On 6 June, ground is broken for the new world-class Ship Materials Technology Center at Carderock, Maryland.

On 8 July, Dahlgren's Fort Lauderdale Detachment is transferred to the Carderock Division to become the South Florida testing facility operated by the Signatures Directorate. The facility is to support the fleet in its role in littoral warfare.

In October, the Survivability, Structures and Materials Directorate (Code 60) is reorganized to provide more clarity and emphasis on work areas. The following departments were formed: Metals (61), In-Service Engineering (62), Environmental Quality (63), Non-Metallic Materials (64), Structures and Composites (65), Underwater Explosions Research (67), Protection and Weapons Effects (68), and Weapons Materials (69).

1995

On 3 March, Harvey Chaplin retires as head of the Carderock Division Ship Systems and Programs Directorate, Code 20. He is replaced by Robert Keane from NAVSEA.

On 15 March, the Advanced Amphibious Assault Vehicle (AAAV) Program enters the Demonstration/Validation Phase of development.

The Undex Test Facility (UTF) at Aberdeen Proving Grounds is calibrated and becomes fully operational in July. This unique shock test facility, known as Superpond, is 1,100 feet long, 800 feet wide, and 800 feet deep. It enables the Navy to test submerged submarine models and full-scale platforms such as the MHC-51.

On 7 July, the 12-ton, 37-knot hydrofoil small-waterplane-area ship (HYSWAS) demonstrator is rolled out at the builder Maritime Physics Corporation's facility in Laurel, Maryland. The craft named *Quest* was launched on 31 July at Carderock Division's Annapolis facility.

A Carderock Division retreat is held 23–24 August to help set the course for the Division to enter the twenty-first century.

On 15 September, the Intermediate-Scale Measurement System (ISMS) begins operations at the Acoustic Research Detachment, Lake Pend Orielle, Idaho. It provides a means to better understand the underlying physics of the target strength of submarines.

On 11 October, management of the National Shipbuilding Research Program (NSRP) is transferred from NSWCCD, Code 20, to NAVSEA.

The BRAC approves the Navy's plan to consolidate the Machinery R&D personnel and facilities at Annapolis with the Machinery ISE facilities and personnel at NAVSSES Philadelphia, and close the Annapolis site.

1996

On 26 January, the U.S. Senate approves the Strategic Arms Reduction Treaty (START II) more than three years after Presidents George Bush and Boris Yeltsin had signed it. It requires reduction of long-range nuclear weapons to one-third of 1990 levels.

On 13 March, Carderock Division NSWC is the first DOD organization to receive a International Standards Organization (ISO) 9001 Certificate of Compliance from ABS Quality Evaluation, Inc. The ISO 9001 Quality System is universally recognized as the model for quality assurance in design, development, production, installation, and servicing.

In the spring, *Monob*, *Deer Island*, and several other Navy ships are transferred to the Mexican government.

On 16 May, Admiral Jeremy M. Boorda, the first sailor to rise from the lowest enlisted ranks to become Chief of Naval Operations, takes his own life. He is replaced by Admiral J. L. Johnson.

Construction of the Ship Materials Technology Center at Carderock is completed in May and the building is dedicated in June.

The Carderock Division is selected as a Beta test site for the Navy Laboratory Center/Coordinating Group's (NLCCG) Navy Distributed Virtual Library (NDVL) initiative. Tests are scheduled for July–December. The NDVL is planned to be a World Wide Web library system.

On 18 July, Rear Admiral Kathleen K. Paige relieves Rear Admiral David P. Sargent Jr. as Commander NSWC.

1997

In January, 300 personnel engaged in ship materials and weapons technology programs are transferred from Annapolis and White Oak to the Carderock site.

On 24 January, William S. Cohen is sworn in as Secretary of Defense.

On 17 May, a traditional "Mast Stepping" is held on board the *Spruance-* class multimission destroyer *Arthur W. Radford* (DD 968) at the Norfolk Naval Shipyard. The U.S. Navy's first advanced hybrid composite structure, known as the Advanced Enclosed Mast/Sensor (AEM/S), is installed. The DTRC Code 6501 project manager is Jeffrey L. Benson.

On 18 June, *Seneca* (ATF 91), a multipurpose ship test facility for the Power Systems Department, is towed from the Annapolis site to Portsmouth, Virginia, where a salvage contract is to be awarded.

On 18 June, the Carderock site hosts a grand opening ceremony for the new Ship Materials Technology Center (SMTC). It is attended by many distinguished guests.

On 20 June, William A. Middleton retires as head of the Carderock Division's Business Directorate, Code 30. Comptroller Todd Parker is temporarily double-hatted as acting head.

On 25 June, Jacques Cousteau dies at the age of eighty-seven. For forty legendary years he traveled the oceans of the world in his research vessel *Calypso*.

In July, the world's fastest, quietest, and most heavily armed nuclear-powered attack submarine, *Seawolf* (SSN 21), is commissioned at Electric Boat shipyard in Groton, Connecticut.

At sunset on 31 July, the flag is lowered for the final time at the NSWC White Oak site, formerly occupied by the Naval Ordance Laboratory. In October, it is to become a federal research center and will house the Federal Drug Administration.

On 28 August, a contract is awarded to Bedwell, Inc., for construction of test facilities, labs, and office space to house the Machinery Research and Development Directorate (Code 80) in preparation for the move from Annapolis to Philadelphia.

On 7 September, *Louisiana* (SSBN 743), the last Trident submarine, is commissioned.

On 1 October, the Machinery In-Service Engineering Directorate (Code 90), headed by Gregg D. Hagedorn, is reorganized formalizing a merger of Codes 10 and 90 which took place last year. The new directorate comprises seven departments; Programs and Platforms (Code 91), Steam and Auxiliary Systems (Code 92), Machinery and Electrical Systems (Code 93), Integrated Logistics and Assessment Systems Support (Code 94), Instrumentation, Communications and Control Technologies (Code 95), Submarine Sail Systems (Code 96), and Hull and Deck Machinery (Code 97).

21 October, the *Constitution*, nicknamed "Old Ironsides" because of her oak hull's resistance to battle damage, is 200 years old. Her forty-four-month restoration and rehabilitation was completed in 1996 and she set sail again in July. She is the Navy's oldest commissioned warship.

On 24 October, Navy Secretary John Dalton announces the Navy's decision not to build the maritime fire-support demonstrator (MFSD), formerly called the arsenal ship.

On 3 November, Steve D. Roush, former head of technical operations in NSWC, becomes the head of the Carderock Division Business Directorate.

Experiments on airplane wake vortex dynamics, sponsored by Boeing, are conducted in the model basin deep-water towing tank.

1998

In January, a Carderock Division Strategic Plan that sets forth the Division's course and speed for the future, is completed and published.

On 30 January, a ceremony is held at Carderock, Maryland, during which the American Society of Mechanical Engineers designates the David Taylor Model Basin as a National Mechanical Engineering Landmark.

Historical Documents

DOCUMENT 1

After a congressional introduction as H.R. 7542, the bill establishing the original model basin became part of an 1897 naval appropriations bill signed into law on 10 June 1896.

AN ACT

Be it enacted by the Senate and House of Representatives of the United States of America in Congress assembled, that the following sums be, and they are hereby, appropriated, to be paid out of any money in the Treasury not otherwise appropriated, for the naval service of the Government for the year ending thirty June eighteen hundred and ninety-seven, and for other purposes.

For making plans, examining and preparing the ground and other preliminary work toward the construction of a model tank, with all buildings and appliances, to be built upon the grounds of the navy yard at Washington, District of Columbia, under the Bureau of Construction and Repair of the Navy Department which shall conduct therein the work of investigating and determining the most suitable and desirable shapes and forms to be adopted for United States naval vessels, seven thousand five hundred dollars: Provided, That upon the authorization of the Secretary of the Navy experiments may be made at this establishment for private shipbuilders, who shall defray the cost of material and of labor per diem employees of such experiments: And provided further, That the results of such experiments shall be regarded as confidential and shall not be divulged without the consent of the shipbuilder for whom they be made.

Approved June 10, 1896

DOCUMENT 2

Congress incorporated 5.2471, a bill establishing the Engineering Experiment Station, into a 1904 naval appropriations bill approved as law on 3 March 1903.

AN ACT

Be it enacted by the Senate and House of Representatives of America in Congress assembled, That the following sums be and they are hereby, appropriated, to be paid out of any money in the Treasury not otherwise appropriated, for the naval service of the Government for the year ending June thirtieth, nineteen hundred and four, and for other purposes.

Bureau of Steam Engineering

BUILDING ON LAND OWNED BY THE GOVERNMENT, ANNAPOLIS, MARYLAND: Bureau of Steam Engineering: For a building to be used as an experiment station and testing laboratory in the department of marine engineering and naval construction (the cost not to exceed two hundred and fifty thousand dollars). For the complete equipment of this building with all the necessary appliances and apparatus as an experiment station and testing laboratory, one hundred and fifty thousand dollars.

Approved 3 March 1903

DOCUMENT 3

Following the suggestion in the memorandum from Jerry Land to Admiral Brown, USN, the Secretary of the Navy named the facility the David Taylor Model Basin on 5 October 1937.

NAVY DEPARTMENT
Bureau of Construction and Repair
Washington, D.C.

Personal

17 March 1936

MEMORANDUM
For: Admiral Brown, USN
       Aide to the President.

1. The Model Basin Authorization Bill passed the House 16 March 1936.

2. The money for this "Experimental Model Basin" is in the Naval Appropriation Bill, which will be reported to the House this week. Information available indicates that the Senate will take up the House Authorization Bill in the very near future and favorable action is expected both in the Committee and in the Senate itself.

3. My particular personal and professional gratitude is hereby given to the President for his interest and action in this matter.

4. It seems to me that it would be most fitting if this new "Experimental Model Basin" could be named in honor of Rear Admiral D.W. Taylor, (CC), USN, who was the wartime Chief Constructor and served under the President when the latter was Assistant Secretary of the Navy.

5. Admiral Taylor is and has been in the Naval Hospital for a number of years with his left side paralyzed but his mind entirely unaffected and as keen as ever. It is unnecessary for me to add that Admiral Taylor is the most outstanding naval architect this country ever produced and some of us feel that he is the most outstanding naval architect the world has ever produced.

(signed) Jerry Land

DOCUMENT 4

On 16 March 1936, the House of Representatives passed H.R. 10135 providing for the establishment of a new model basin. It subsequently passed the Senate and was signed into law on 6 May 1936.

AN ACT

Be it enacted by the Senate and House of Representatives of the United States of America in Congress assembled, that the Secretary of the Navy is hereby authorized to acquire a site at a cost not to exceed $100,000 in the vicinity of Washington, District of Columbia, and to construct thereon a model basin establishment, with buildings and appliances, in which the Bureau of Construction and Repair of the Navy Department shall conduct the work of investigating and determining the most suitable and desirable shapes and forms to be adopted for United States vessels, including aircraft and the investigation of other problems of ship design, at a cost not to exceed $3,500,000: Navy experiments may be made at this establishment for private parties, who shall defray the cost thereof under such regulations as the Secretary of the Navy may from time to time prescribe: Provide further, That the results of such private experiments shall be regarded as confidential and shall not be divulged without the consent of such private parties, except that the right is reserved to the Secretary of the Navy to use data so obtained for governmental purposes, subject to the patent laws of the United States.

Approved 6 May 1936

DOCUMENT 5

DEPARTMENT OF THE NAVY
Office of the Secretary
Washington, D.C. 20350

SECNAVNOTE 5450
OP-09B3
Ser 21
MAR 20 1967

SECNAV NOTICE 5450

From: Secretary of the Navy
To: Distribution List

Subj: David W. Taylor Model Basin, Carderock, Maryland—Navy Marine
Engineering Laboratory, Annapolis, Maryland—David W. Taylor Model
Basin, Field Station, Bayview, Idaho; modification of

1. *Purpose.* To modify the activity titles, missions and titles of official in
command of the subject shore (field) activities.

2. *Modification.* Effective 31 March 1967 the following shore (field) activities assigned to the Chief of Naval Operations for command and support are modified:

From:	*To:*
Official Title and Mail Address	*Official Title and Mail Address*
Commanding Officer and Director David W. Taylor Model Basin Development Carderock, Maryland (MAIL ADDRESS) Washington, D.C. 20007 *3865-333* (Short Title: DTMB (SNDL L45A)	Commanding Officer and Director Naval Ship Research and Center Washington, D.C. 20007
Commanding Officer and Directo Navy Marine Engineering Laboratory Annapolis, Maryland 21042 *3865-100* (Short Title: MEL	Officer in Charge Annapolis Division Naval Ship Research and Development Center Annapolis, Maryland 21402

Director	Officer in Charge
David W. Taylor Model Basin	Naval Ship Research and
Field Station	Development Center
Bayview, Idaho 83803	Test Facility
3865-250	Bayview, Idaho 83803
(Short Title: DTMB)	

3. *Mission*

    a. *NAVAL SHIP RESEARCH AND DEVELOPMENT CENTER, WASH-INGTON, D.C.*
    To conduct an RDT&E program in Naval Architecture, Marine Engineering, Ship concepts, and related fields of science and engineering.

    b. *ANNAPOLIS DIVISION, NAVAL SHIP RESEARCH AND DEVELOP-MENT CENTER.*
    To support the mission of the Naval Ship and Development Center by carrying out assigned ships research and development tasks in scientific and engineering fields.

    c. *NAVAL SHIP RESEARCH AND DEVELOPMENT CENTER TEST FACILITY, BAYVIEW, IDAHO.*
    To support the mission of the Naval Ship Research and Development Center by maintaining a deep water testing facility (where deep depths, stable temperature gradients, and clarity is a controlling factor) for the utilization of other research activities, and to provide support services for their utilization.

4. *Implementation.* The Chief of Naval Operations will promulgate implementing instructions including such delegation of command, support, and area coordination responsibilities as he deems appropriate.

5. *Cancellation.* This Notice may be retained for reference purposes or canceled when no longer needed.

                      (Signed)
                      Graeme C. Bannerman
                      Assistant Secretary of the Navy
                      (Installation and Logistics)

DOCUMENT 6

DEPARTMENT OF THE NAVY
OFFICE OF THE CHIEF OF NAVAL OPERATIONS
WASHINGTON, D.C. 20350-2000

OPNAVNOTE 5450
Ser 09B22/1U510577
23 DEC 1991

OPNAV NOTICE 5450

From: Chief of Naval Operations

Subj: ESTABLISHMENT OF NAVAL SURFACE AND UNDERSEA WARFARE CENTERS, MODIFICATION OF TITLE AND DISESTABLISHMENT OF SHORE ACTIVITIES AND DETACHMENTS.

Ref: (a) OPNAVINST 5450.169D
    (b) SECNAV memo dtd 12 Apr 91
    (c) OPNAVINST 5450.171C
    (d) SNDL, Part 2

1. *Purpose.* To implement, in accordance with reference (a), Secretary of the Navy (SECNAV) decisions, as contained in reference (b). These decisions called for the establishment of Warfare Centers; the establishment, disestablishment or realignment of specicic shore establishments and detachments; and the assignment or revision of missions for the Naval Surface Warfare Center and the Undersea Warfare Center and their components.

2. *Background.* SECNAV announced his approval of a plan to consolidate Navy research, development, test and evaluation, engineering, and fleet support activities via reference (b). The recommendations of the 1991 Base Closure and Realignment Commission (BCRC) were approved on 01 October 1991. The Naval Command Control and Ocean Surveillance Center plan was included in the BCRC recommendations. The plan called for the transfer of various activaties between the Systems Commands, establishment of a Surface Warfare Center and an Undersea Warfare Center under COMNAVSEA, and the subsequent realignment of a number of existing NAVSEA and former SPAWAR shore activities and detachments. The objectives of these actions are to preserve core mission capabilities while accomodating reduced navy budgets and achieving substantial savings.

3. *Organization Changes.* The following changes to the shore establishment are effective immediately:

    a. *Established*—the following shore activities are established:

        (1) Commander
             Naval Surface Warfare Center
             Washington, DC 20362-5101

        (2) Commander
             Naval Undersea Warfare Center
             Washington, DC 20362-5101

    b. *Title Modification*—The titles of the following shore activities and detachments are modified:

NAVAL SURFACE WARFARE CENTER

From	*To*
Commander David Taylor Research Center Bethesda, MD 20084-5000	Commander Carderock Division Naval Surface Warfare Center Bethesda, MD 20084-5000
Officer in Charge David Taylor Research Center Detachment Acoustic Research P.O. Box 129 Bayview, ID 83803-0129	Officer in Charge Naval Surface Warfare Center Carderock Division Detachment Bayview P.O. Box 129 Bayview, ID 83803-0129
Officer in Charge Annapolis Laboratory David Taylor Research Center Detachment Annapolis, MD 21402-1198	Officer in Charge Naval Surface Warfare Center Carderock Division Detachment Annapolis, MD 21402-1198
Director David Taylor Research Center Detachment Puget Sound Naval Shipyard Bremerton, WA 98314-5215 Bremerton, WA 98314-5215	Director Naval Surface Warfare Center Carderock Division Detachment Bremerton Puget Sound Naval Shipyard Bremerton, WA 98314-5215

Commanding Officer
Naval Ship Systems Engineering
Station
Naval Base
Philadelphia, PA 19112-5083
Naval Base

Commanding Officer
Naval Ship Systems Engineering
Station
Carderock Division
Naval Surface Warfare Center

Philadelphia, PA 19112-5083

c. *Disestablish*—the following shore activities and detachments are disestablished:

> Officer in Charge
> Carderock Laboratory
> David Taylor Research Detachment
> Bethesda, MD 20084-5000

4. *Mission Statements.* Missions for the new and modified shore activities are as follows:

a. Naval Surface Warfare Center

(1) *Naval Surface Warfare Center, Washington, DC.*
Operate the Navy's full spectrum research, development, test and evaluation, engineering, and fleet support center for ship hull, mechanical and elictrical systems, surface ship combat systems, coastal warfare systems, and other offensive and defensive systems associated with surface warfare.

* * *

(4) *Carderock Division, Naval Surface Warfare Center, Bethesda, MD.*
Provide research, development, test and evaluation, fleet support, and in-service engineering for surface and undersea vehicle hull, mechanical and elictrical systems, and propulsors; provide logistics R&D; provide support to the Maritime Administration and the maritime industry. Execute other responsibilities as assigned by the Commander, Naval Surface Warfare Center.

(5) *Naval Ship Systems Engineering Station, Carderock Division, Naval Surface Warfare Center Philadelphia, PA.*
Support the mission of the Carderock Division of the Naval Surface Warfare Center by providing engineering and technical management of ship systems, equipment, and material, test and evaluation of ship systcms (HME), and in-service engineering support for those systems and equipments. Execute other responsibilities as assigned by the Commander, Carderock Division, Naval Surface Warfare Center.

* * *

Command and Support. Commander, Naval Sea Systems Command (COMNAVSEASYSCOM) will exercise the following command and support structure for the Naval Surface Warfare Center and the Naval Undersea Warfare Center:

Eschelon   Command and Support

Naval Surface Warfare Center. . . .

3   Commander, Naval Surface Warfare Center, Washington, DC

4   Commander, Carderock Division, Naval Surface Warfare Center, Bethesda, MD

        Officer in Charge, Carderock Division, Naval Surface Warfare Center Detachment, Bayview, ID

        Officer in Charge, Carderock Division, Naval Surface Warfare Center Detachment, Annapolis, MD

        Director, Carderock Division, Naval Surface Warfare Center Detachment, Bremerton, WA

5   Commanding Officer, Naval Ship Systems Engineering Station, Carderock Division, Naval Surface Warfare Center, Philadelphia, PA

6. *Action.*

a. COMNAVSEASYSCOM will take appropriate action, consistent with reference (c), to issue a mission, functions and tasks directive for the Naval Surface Warfare Center and the Naval Undersea Warfare Center within 90 days from the date of this directive. CNO (OP-09B22) will be included in the distribution.

b. CNO (OP-09B22) will revise reference (d).

7. *Cancellation Contingency.* This notice may be retained for reference purposes. The organization action will remain effective until changed by CNO (OP-09B).

                    (signed)
                    R. M. Walsh
                    Rear Admiral, U.S. Navy
                    Assistant Vice Chief of Naval Operations

DOCUMENT 7

DEPARTMENT OF THE NAVY
NAVAL SEA SYSTEMS COMMAND
WASHINGTON, D.C. 20362-5101

5400
OPR NSWC
Ser NSWC/29
2 Jan 92

From: Commander, Naval Surface Warfare Center

Subj: STAND-UP OF NAVAL SURFACE WARFARE DIVISIONS

Ref (a) UNSECNAV memo of 20 Dec 91 (Notal)
(b) OPNAVNOTICE 5450 Ser 09B22/1U510577 of 23 Dec 91
(c) Naval Surface Warfare Center Charter of 2 Jan 92

1. *Purpose:* To authorize stand-up of the Naval Surface Warfare Center's divisions.

2. *Background:* By reference (a), the Under Secretary of the Navy authorized the stand-up of the Naval Warfare Centers. Reference (b) established the Naval Surface Warfare Center within the Naval Sea Systems Command. Reference (c) was signed by Commander, Naval Sea Systems Command on 2 January 1992.

3. *Action:* Effective this date, division commanders of the Naval Surface Warfare Center are authorized to stand-up their respective divisions.

(signed)
G. R. MEINIG, JR.
Rear Admiral, U.S. Navy
Naval Surface Warfare Center

Distribution:
Commander, NAVSURFWARCEN, Carderock Division Bethesda MD
Commander, NAVSURFWARCEN, Crane Division Crane IN
Commander, NAVSURFWARCEN, Dahlgren Division Dahlgren VA
Commander, NAVSURFWARCEN, Indian Head Division Indian Head MD
Commander, NAVSURFWARCEN, Port Hueneme Division Port
   Hueneme CA

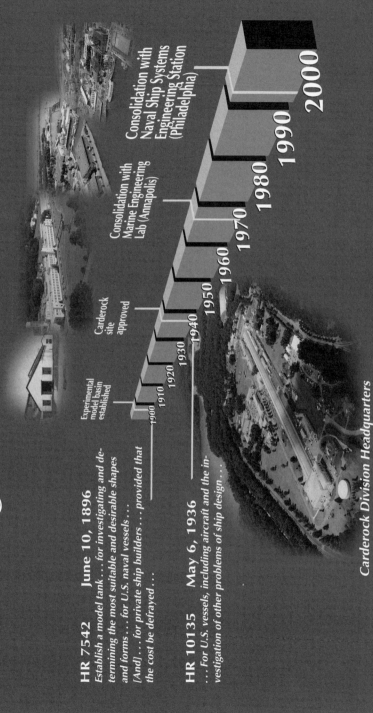

Organizational Timeline

HR 7542   June 10, 1896
*Establish a model tank . . . for investigating and de-
termining the most suitable and desirable shapes
and forms . . . for U.S. naval vessels . . .
[And] . . . for private ship builders . . . provided that
the cost be defrayed . . .*

HR 10135   May 6, 1936
*. . . For U.S. vessels, including aircraft and the in-
vestigation of other problems of ship design . . .*

Experimental
model basin
established

Carderock
site
approved

Consolidation with
Marine Engineering
Lab (Annapolis)

Consolidation with
Naval Ship Systems
Engineering Station
(Philadelphia)

1900 1910 1920 1930 1940 1950 1960 1970 1980 1990 2000

Carderock Division Headquarters

Command Structure

THESE CHARTS ILLUSTRATE CHANGES in the command structure over the laboratories throughout their hundred-year history. The charts do not include sections of the naval organization outside the direct chain of command. They were prepared by Charles Schoman, former Director of Plans and Programs and later head of the Computation, Mathematics, and Logistics Department.

Experimental Model Basin (EMB)
1896 – 1967 (see note)

1896 – 1940	1940 – 1947	1947 – 1963	1963 – 1967
		SECRETARY OF DEFENSE	
Secretary of the Navy	Secretary of the Navy	Secretary of the Navy **E**	Secretary of the Navy **A E F**
Assistant Secretary of the Navy	Assistant Secretary of the Navy	Under Secretary of the Navy	Chief of Naval Material
Bureau of Construction and Repair	Bureau of Ships	Bureau of Ships	Bureau of Ships
Experimental Model Basin (EMB)*	David Taylor Model Basin (DTMB)	David Taylor Model Basin (DTMB)	David Taylor Model Basin (DTMB)

*1937 David W. Taylor Model Basin (DTMB) Established

**1967 David W. Taylor Model Basin (DTMB) and Marine Engineering Laboratory (MEL) Merged to Form Naval Ship Research and Development Center (NSRDC)

Staff, Secretary of Navy

A Ass't Secretary Navy (Research & Development)

B Ass't Secretary Navy (Research, Engineering & Systems)

C Ass't Secretary Navy (Research, Development & Acquistion)

D Director of Navy Laboratories (DNL)

E Chief of Naval Operations

F Under Secretary of Navy

Staff, Chief of Naval Material

M Deputy Chief of Navy Material
Deputy Chief of Navy Material (Development)
Deputy Chief of Navy Material (Laboratories)

P Director of Laboratory Programs (DLP)

Note: Dates are approximate. Data from Naval Archives primarily from Department of Navy Management Guide(s) NAVSO P-2457

Engineering Experimental Station (EES)
1903 – 1967 (see note)

1903 – 1920	1920 – 1940	1940 – 1947	1947 – 1961	1961 – 1967
			SECRETARY OF DEFENSE	
Secretary of the Navy	Secretary of the Navy	Secretary of the Navy	Secretary of the Navy	Secretary of the Navy
Assistant Secretary of the Navy	Assistant Secretary of the Navy	Assistant Secretary of the Navy	Under Secretary of the Navy	Under Secretary of the Navy
Bureau of Steam Engineering	Bureau of Engineering	Bureau of Ships	Bureau of Ships	Bureau of Ships
Engineering Experimental Station (EES)	Engineering Experimental Station (EES)	Engineering Experimental Station (EES)	Engineering Experimental Station (EES)	Marine Engineering Lab (MEL)

**1967 David W. Taylor Model Basin (DTMB) and Marine Engineering Laboratory (MEL) Merged to Form Naval Ship Research and Development Center (NSRDC)

Note: Dates are approximate. Data from Naval Archives primarily from Department of Navy Management Guide(s) NAVSO P-2457

Consolidated Organizations
1967 – 1998 (see note)

1967 – 1969	1969 – 1983	1983 – 1985	1985 – 1991	1991 – 1998
SECRETARY OF DEFENSE				
Secretary of the Navy	Secretary of the Navy	Secretary of the Navy	Secretary of the Navy	Secretary of the Navy
Under Secretary of the Navy ⒶⒹ	Under Secretary of the Navy ⒶⒹ	Under Secretary of the Navy ⒷⒹ	Under Secretary of the Navy ⒷⒹ	Under Secretary of the Navy Ⓒ
Chief of Naval Operations	Chief of Naval Operations	Chief of Naval Operations	Chief of Naval Operations	Chief of Naval Operations
Chief of Naval Material Ⓟ	Vice Chief of Naval Operations	Vice Chief of Naval Operations	Vice Chief of Naval Operations	Vice Chief of Naval Operations
Naval Ships System Command	Chief of Naval Material	Chief of Naval Material	Space and Naval Warfare Systems Command (SPAWAR)	Naval Sea Systems Command (NAVSEA)
Naval Ship Research and Development Center (NSRDC)**	Vice Chief of Naval Material ⒹⓂⓅ	Vice Chief of Naval Material	David Taylor Research Center (DTRC)	Naval Surface Warfare Center (NSWC)
**1967 David W. Taylor Model Basin (DTMB) and Marine Engineering Laboratory (MEL) Merged to Form Naval Ship Research and Development Center (NSRDC)	Naval Ship Research and Development Center (NSRDC)	Deputy Chief of Naval Material (Laboratories)	**5/85 – 12/86** **Note:** Upon Abolishment of Chief of Naval Material (Naval Material Command) Navy R&D Laboratories/ Centers and Director of Navy Laboratories placed under Chief of Naval Research	NSWC Carderock Division (formerly DTRC)
		David Taylor Naval Ship Research and Development Center (DTNSRDC)		

Note: Dates are approximate. Data from Naval Archives primarily from Department of Navy Management Guide(s) NAVSO P-2457

Commanding Officers and Technical Directors

Commanding Officers

EXPERIMENTAL MODEL BASIN

**RADM
David W. Taylor
USN
1899 – 1914**

**CAPT
William McEntee
USN
1915 – 1920**

**CAPT
Ernest F. Eggert
USN
1920 – 1924**

**CAPT
William McEntee
USN
1924 – 1927**

**CAPT
Everett L. Gayhart
USN
1927 – 1928**

**CAPT
Ernest F. Eggert
USN
1928 – 1938**

**CAPT
Lewis O. McBride
USN
1938 – 1940**

DAVID TAYLOR MODEL BASIN

**CAPT
William G. DuBose
USN
1939 – 1940**

**CAPT
Lewis O. McBride
USN
1940 – 1942**

**CAPT
Herbert S. Howard
USN
1942 – 1946**

**CAPT
Harold E. Saunders
USN
1946 – 1947**

**RADM
Claude O. Kell
USN
1947 – 1950**

**RADM
George A. Holdern
USN
1950 – 1951**

DAVID TAYLOR MODEL BASIN (continued)

RADM
Albert G. Mumma
USN
1951 – 1954

RADM
William H. Leahy
USN
1954 – 1956

RADM
E. Alvey Wright
USN
1956 – 1960

CAPT
Jack A. Obermeyer
USN
1960 – 1963

CAPT
John M. Ballinger
USN
1963 – 1964

CAPT
Dennett K. Ela
USN
1964 – 1967

CAPT
Manual da C. Vincent
USN
1967 – 1967

ENGINEERING EXPERIMENT STATION

CAPT
Walter F. Worthington
USN
1904 – 1910

RADM
Thomas W. Kinkaid
USN
1910 – 1920

CAPT
John Halligan, Jr.
USN
1920 – 1923

CAPT
Paul B. Dunigan
USN
1923 – 1926

CAPT
Henry C. Dinger
USN
1926– 1930

CAPT
Halford R. Greenlee
USN
1930 – 1933

RADM
Ormond L. Cox
USN
1933 – 1939

RADM
Alert T. Church
USN
1939 – 1944

RADM
Claude A. Jones
USN
1944 – 1946

ENGINEERING EXPERIMENT STATION (continued)

RADM
David H. Clark
USN
1946 – 1947

RADM
Wilson D. Leggett, Jr.
USN
1947 – 1951

CAPT
Fred W. Walton
USN
1951 – 1954

CAPT
C. A. Peterson
USN
1954 – 1956

CAPT
William W. Brown
USN
1956 – 1957

CAPT
R. L. Mohan
USN
1958 – 1961

CAPT
Francis H. Huron
USN
1961 – 1963

MARINE ENGINEERING LABORATORY

CAPT
Francis H. Huron
USN
1963 – 1964

CAPT
William Tessin
USN
1964 – 1965

CAPT
Fred A. Hooper
USN
1965 – 1967

NAVAL SHIP RESEARCH AND DEVELOPMENT CENTER

CAPT
Manuel da C. Vincent
USN
1967 – 1970

CAPT
Randolph W. King, Jr.
USN
1970 – 1972

CAPT
Perry W. Nelson
USN
1972 – 1975

DAVID TAYLOR NAVAL SHIP RESEARCH AND DEVELOPMENT CENTER

CAPT
Perry W. Nelson
USN
1975 – 1975

CAPT
Michael C. Davis
USN
1975 – 1977

CAPT
Myron V. Ricketts
USN
1977 – 1981

CAPT
Barrick F. Tibbitts
USN
1981 – 1984

CAPT
G. Richard Garritson
USN
1984 – 1987

CAPT
Clark C. Graham
USN
1987 – 1987

DAVID TAYLOR RESEARCH CENTER

CAPT
Clark C. Graham
USN
1987 – 1991

CAPT
Dennis K. Kruse
USN
1991 – 1991

NAVAL SURFACE WARFARE CENTER—CARDEROCK DIVISION

CAPT
Dennis K. Kruse
USN
1992 – 1994

CAPT
James E. Baskerville
USN
1994 – 1997

CAPT
John H. Preisel, Jr.
1997 –

Technical Directors

EXPERIMENTAL MODEL BASIN   1899–1940

CAPT
Harold E. Saunders
1938 – 1940

DAVID TAYLOR MODEL BASIN   1940–1967

CAPT
Harold E. Saunders
1940 – 1947

Dr. Alfred H. Keil
1963 – 1966

Dr. Alan Powell
1966 – 1967

ENGINEERING EXPERIMENT STATION   1907–1963

Harold V. Nutt
1957 – 1963

MARINE ENGINEERING LABORATORY   1963–1967

Harold V. Nutt
1956 – 1967*

* During the reorganization that accompanied the merger of the David Taylor Model Basin and the Marine Engineering Laboratory, Nutt's position as Technical Director of MEL was reclassified to Deputy Technical Director. Dr. Powell became the Technical Director of the entire Center.

NAVAL SHIP RESEARCH AND DEVELOPMENT CENTER 1967–1974

Dr. Alan Powell
1967 – 1974

DAVID TAYLOR NAVAL SHIP RESEARCH AND DEVELOPMENT CENTER 1974–1987

Dr. Alan Powell
1974 – 1985

Edwin B. O'Neill
(Acting)
1985 – 1986

Richard E. Metrey
1986 – 1987

DAVID TAYLOR RESEARCH CENTER 1987–1992

Richard E. Metrey
1987 – 1992

NAVAL SURFACE WARFARE CENTER—CARDEROCK DIVISION 1992–

Richard E. Metrey
1992 –

Sites and Major Facilities

IN JANUARY 1992, THE NAVAL SHIP Systems Engineering Station, Philadelphia, Pennsylvania, and the Combatant Craft Department of the Naval Sea Combat Systems Engineering Station, Norfolk, Virginia, were merged with the David Taylor Research Center to form the Carderock Division, Naval Surface Warfare Center. This appendix describes the Sites and Major Facilities of the Carderock Division in July 1997. It was prepared by Peter Montana from information provided by Beverly Booker, Brian Bowers, James Burns, Donald Collins, Douglas Garbini, Robert Hardy, Donald Martin, Richard Messalle, Joseph Sheehan, and Larry Wellman.

Property Owned by the Navy and Managed by the Carderock Division, Naval Surface Warfare Center

Location	Land (Acres)	No. of Buildings	Building Size 10³ FT²	Land Purchase Price[1] ($K)	Building Current Value[2] ($M)
Ketchikan, Alaska		5	24.7		10.3
Fort Lauderdale, Florida	9	3	7.0	5.3	0.4
Bayview, Idaho	22	23	62.9	27.5	9.4
Kootenai, Idaho		3	3.0		1.1
Annapolis, Maryland	44	75	576.8	144.4	190.2
Arnold, Maryland	47	18	34.5	67.6	5.0
Carderock, Maryland	186.2	71	1535.4	106.0	486.5
Philadelphia, Pennsylvania	224	45	1168.6	654.8	281.0
Memphis, Tennessee	88	11	492.0	9.2	135.9
Fox Island, Washington	2	2	6.4	22.0	5.1
Totals	**622.2**	**256**	**3911.3**	**1036.8**	**1124.9**

[1] Land purchase price is shown in then-year dollars.
[2] Building value is the cost of replacing the building in 1996 dollars.

Property Leased by the Navy and Managed by the Carderock Division, Naval Surface Warfare Center

Location	Land (Acres)	No. of Buildings	Build. Area 10^2 Ft^2	Lease Cost $K /year
Ketchikan, Alaska	15.0[1]			
Port Canaveral, Florida	1.5	2	17.0	86.9
Panama City, Florida[2]		1	5.0	20.4
Bayview, Idaho	9.0[1]			
Kootenai, Idaho	2.0[1]			
Patuxent River, Maryland[3]	2.5	3	41.0	100.0
Chesapeake, Virginia[4,5]	9.3	1	18.5	314.0
Norfolk, Virginia	1.0	1	22.0	490.0
Bremerton, Washington[6]		2	18.9	
Totals	**40.3**	**10**	**122.4**	**1011.3**

[1] Land use is provided through a special use permit from the U.S. Forest Service.

[2] The building is located on the Coastal Systems Station, Dahlgren Division, Naval Surface Warfare Center.

[3] Property is located on the Naval Air Test Station, Patuxent River. The lease cost is a funds transfer between Navy activities.

[4] The land is located on the Portsmouth Naval Ship Yard. The lease cost is a funds transfer between Navy Activities.

[5] The leased building is commercial property located in the city of Chesapeake.

[6] Use of the buildings is provided at no cost by the Puget Sound Naval Ship Yard.

Major Facilities at the Carderock, Maryland Site

The Carderock site serves as the headquarters for the Carderock Division and is the Navy's principal source for surface and undersea vehicle hull and propulsor research, development, test and evaluation (RDT&E) in the areas of hydrodynamics and hydroacoustics, structures and materials, hull and propulsor signatures, and vehicle design. Facilities located at Carderock include:

Acoustic Data Analysis Center (ADAC)

This is Carderock's principal ship signature reduction and acoustic analysis center. It provides acoustic signal and data processing services for a wide variety of research and measurement missions such as full-scale trial analysis, modeling and noise measurements, and sonar performance evaluation. It utilizes specialized data processing equipment for the reduction and analysis of submarine and surface ship radiated noise and sonar self-noise data collected during full-scale, at sea evaluations. The systems process steady state and transient acoustic signatures data using conventional and advanced algorithms.

Sites and Major Facilities

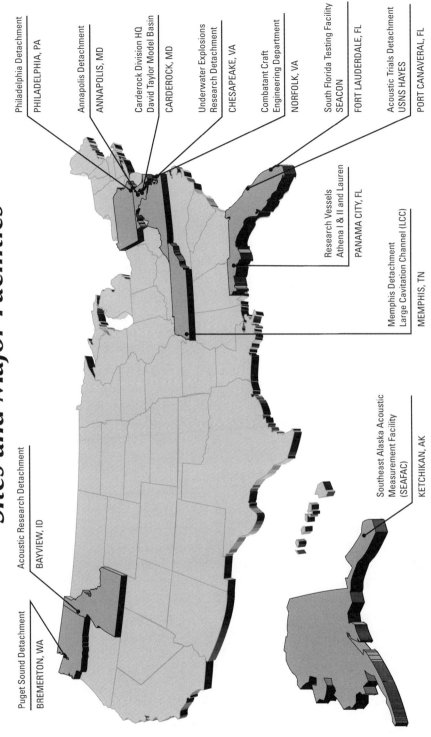

Philadelphia Detachment
PHILADELPHIA, PA

Annapolis Detachment
ANNAPOLIS, MD

Carderock Division HQ
David Taylor Model Basin
CARDEROCK, MD

Underwater Explosions
Research Detachment
CHESAPEAKE, VA

Combatant Craft
Engineering Department
NORFOLK, VA

South Florida Testing Facility
SEACON
FORT LAUDERDALE, FL

Acoustic Trials Detachment
USNS HAYES
PORT CANAVERAL, FL

Research Vessels
Athena I & II and Lauren
PANAMA CITY, FL

Memphis Detachment
Large Cavitation Channel (LCC)
MEMPHIS, TN

Acoustic Research Detachment
BAYVIEW, ID

Puget Sound Detachment
BREMERTON, WA

Southeast Alaska Acoustic
Measurement Facility
(SEAFAC)
KETCHIKAN, AK

Anechoic Flow Facility (AFF)

This is the first large facility of its kind in the world. It consists of a special wind tunnel for model testing of flow-generated noise components related to features of Navy ships. The facility combines the properties of an anechoic (echo-free) chamber and a low-noise, low-turbulence closed-circuit wind tunnel. The large test sections (8 feet square closed and 23.5 feet square open), with low turbulence and low acoustic interference make this a unique facility. It has supported a broad range of fundamental experimental studies on flow-induced noise over smooth and rough surfaces, appendages and cavities, and partial or full model hull forms. Initially built to support model propeller evaluations, tests in the facility have led to design improvements in the external features of ship hulls, propulsors, and many other naval applications. In particular, the wake distribution of models of naval structures such as submarines, torpedoes, and propulsors have been extensively studied.

Circulating Water Channel

The Circulating Water Channel is a 670,000-gallon recirculating, variable- speed channel with a free-surface test section open to the atmosphere. The test section is rectangular, 18.3 meters (60 feet) long and 6.7 meters (22 feet) wide. The maximum water depth is 2.7 meters (9 feet) with a maximum water velocity of 5.1 meters per second (10 knots). The rate of the flow of water is regulated by adjusting the pitch of two propeller pumps that are connected to a 1,250-horsepower motor. Flow around underwater bodies may be observed by using nylon tufts, dye, or other flow visualization techniques. It can be viewed from ten large windows at different elevations on either side of the test section, and nine windows in the bottom. A moveable bridge spans the test section for ease and versatility in mounting models. The bridge is capable of taking towing loads at any one of numerous points up to 35,584 N (8,000 lbs). An overhead traveling bridge crane is also available for handling large and heavy models. Filters keep the water photographically clear.

This facility is used for high accuracy flow visualization experiments on ship model hulls up to 30 feet in length, rudders, fairings, struts, bilge keels, other appendages, stack gas flow studies over ship superstructures at various headings, wakes from air flow around aircraft carrier bridges, and tests of cable-towed bodies. It has been used regularly in recent years by other government agencies and industry in conjunction with development testing programs. One such program was on commercial fishing trawl nets. According to Massachusetts Institute of

Technology, the innovative trawl design work performed in this DTRC test facility was of significant benefit to the U.S. fishing industry.

Computer-Aided Acquisition and Logistics Support (CALS) Facility

The CALS facility contains the computer-aided design (CAD) components, prototype automated data processing (ADP) equipment, production environment equipment, communications equipment, and other test node devices necessary for the development, testing and validation of CALS technology for naval systems. Efforts focus on the development and test of CAD & computer-aided manufacturing (CAM) systems, technical manual automation, and communications and ADP integration and interoperability.

Deep Submergence Pressure Tank Facility

The deep submergence pressure tank facility contains pressure tanks which are designed to provide the Navy and the maritime industry the capability to test structures, components and systems in an environment that simulates as near as possible the ocean depths. The tanks range in size from 15 inches in diameter and 3.5 feet in length to 13 feet in diameter and 40 feet in length. Each tank has the highest operating pressure for its diameter of any quick-opening test tank in the United States. The 10-foot-diameter spherical tank is the only NAVSEA explosive-rated tank in the U.S. and may be used to study shock effects on submarine structures at depth.

Pressure Tank Capabilities

Year Operational	Diameter (Feet)	Length (Feet)	Maximum Pressure psi
1961	6	21	6,000
1964	4	20	15,000
1966	10	Sphere	10,000
1972	5	9	17,000
1976	13	40	3,000

The tanks are installed vertically with separate pumping systems and are served by an overhead crane having 35-ton lift capacity. Primarily intended for structural model tests of submarines and submersibles, the tanks have multiple ports for bringing sensor wires and cables out of the tank for monitoring the test article's response. Over

1,000 response channels may be recorded for a typical test to evaluate structural performance of a large model under hydrostatic load. Every class of U.S. submarine constructed over the past 40 years has had pressure hull confirmation models tested in this facility prior to proceeding to full-scale construction. The pressure tanks, piping systems and pumping systems can use either oil, fresh water, or salt water as the pressurizing medium. The temperature of the pressurizing medium may be lowered to near zero degrees Celsius. The capability exists to cycle the pressure in the tanks for fatigue evaluation of the test item. Some of the tanks use a method called soft cycling where the tank pressure is held constant and the test article's internal pressure is cycled. The 5-foot-diameter-yoke tank may be hard cycled, i.e., the tank can be subjected to the same fatigue cycles as the test article. In addition to certifying Navy submarine structures, the tanks have been used to certify the deep submersible pressure hulls for *Alvin* and *Sea Cliff,* France's *Nautile,* and Japan's *Shinkai 6500.*

Explosives Test Pond

The explosives test pond was designed for use in conducting underwater explosive (UNDEX) shock testing of ship and submarine models and components. The pond was constructed in 1943, and tests were conducted on models in preparation for the then-secret Normandy invasion during World War II. It is the only explosives-rated pond in the U.S. with the capability of providing high-speed underwater photography of UNDEX model response. The water is continuously filtered to provide clarity necessary for viewing underwater tests through portholes in a caisson on one side of the pond. The pond contains over 3,000,000 gallons of water.

Its shape is pentagonal and measures 135 feet along the top of each side. During test operations, the water depth is maintained at 26 feet. Explosive weights of up to three pounds may be used in the pond. Magazines for storage of explosives are located in an adjacent area. Personnel with the necessary expertise are available to safely and efficiently conduct UNDEX experiments in this controlled and environmentally safe location.

Experiments are conducted to support development of analytical procedures such as finite element analysis to predict underwater explosion behavior of ship and submarine structures. Recording systems available for data collection include analog and digital straingage recording equipment as well as transient data recorders for recording high-speed phenomena such as underwater shock waves and subsequent bubble pulsations. Approximately fifty tests per year are conducted in the test pond which has been safely and efficiently operated since its construction.

Infrared Measurement System

The infrared measurement system can be employed at Carderock, at a shore site, or from a helicopter for signature reduction experiments on full-scale ships and scale-models. Studies include evaluation of signature characteristics of ships, special craft, wakes, and other investigations such as material characterization and environmental effects. The system consists of a variety of infrared and visual sensors, ancillary mounting equipment, environmental measurement systems, and associated calibration equipment. The primary sensors include imaging radiometers, spectral radiometers, visual imaging systems, and low-light and night-vision systems.

Maneuvering and Seakeeping Basin (MASK)

The seakeeping basin of MASK is rectangular concrete fresh water tank with pneumatic wavemakers on two adjacent sides which is used to study the effect of wave conditions on ships, submarines, and ocean platforms. It is 240 feet wide, 360 feet long, and 20 feet deep. One section, 50 feet wide and 322 feet long, is 35 feet deep. This section is used to conduct free-running tests of submerged models. Both restrained and free-running ship models of up to 30 feet in length may be tested. A 376-foot-long steel bridge spans the length of the basin and supports a 15-knot, 16.5-ton aluminum towing carriage. The bridge can be rotated at angles up to 45 degrees and the towing carriage can traverse one half the width of the basin. The facility's unique pneumatic wavemakers can simulate both regular and confused seas as strong as gale force conditions. Experiments on conventional craft, high-performance craft and ocean systems (i.e. platforms) are conducted in waves at all headings including regular singular waves, crested waves, programmed long-crested irregular waves, and programmed short-crested waves. Wave absorbers consisting of a "beach" of 2-inch concrete bars nearly 36 feet long are installed along the wall opposite a total of 21 wavemakers. Models can be towed at any angle to the waves by the towing carriage. In this way, model motions, accelerations, control surface deflections and strains may be measured. The basin's "instant ocean" is the only one of its kind in the world.

A rotating arm facility is also housed in the MASK. It is circular basin of reinforced concrete 260 feet in diameter and 21 feet deep. There is a rotating arm carriage structure that pivots on a bearing located on an island in the center of the tank and is supported on a track around the outer circumference. Steady-state speeds of up to 30 knots can be reached in half a revolution at a radius of 120 feet. Top speeds of up to 50 knots at the same radius can be reached in a little more than one complete rotation. Measurements are made of the forces on models that are induced and maintained in a turn. Rotary coefficients required in the equations of motion are obtained from model tests conducted in this facility. Design data can be acquired relating to directional stability; strut side force problems; and maneuverability and control of submarines, torpedoes, surface ships, air-cushion vehicles, and hydrofoil craft. The facility can accommodate submarines up to 20 feet in length and surface ship models up to 30 feet in length.

Radar Imaging Measurement System (RIMS)

RIMS is a mobile radar-imaging system used for measuring the signatures of ships and craft in the S, X, and Ku bands. It provides high-fidelity imagery at horizontal and vertical polarizations, making possible the identification of returns from individual reflectors. Its output is therefore useful for diagnostics as well as for operational applications. RIMS can provide quick-response radar measurements at virtually any location convenient to the fleet, including Atlantic, Pacific, and Gulf Coast sites, Puerto Rico, and St. Croix. For research purposes, RIMS provides useful data on scale models, which are used in Carderock's maneuvering and seakeeping facility where an ocean environment can be simulated. The system is housed in a shielded, 28-foot custom van, which features the radar electronics, computers for signal processing, telemetry and communications equipment, and a marine search radar for rapid all-weather localization of the test vessel.

Ship Materials Technology Center

The new Carderock Ship Materials Technology Center (SMTC) is a world-class facility having a pivotal role in advancing the use of advanced materials and processes in the Navy fleet of the 21st century. The SMTC encompasses capabilities for developing advanced materials, engineering mechanics, chemical formulation, testing and characterization of metallic and non-metallic materials, and the prototype production and testing of materials and ship systems and components. The laboratory functional capabilities include:

Advanced Ceramics Laboratory—a comprehensive ceramics synthesis, processing, and characterization laboratory. Ceramics processing capabilities include traditional powder preparation and shape-forming equipment, as well as isopressing, injection molding, hot pressing, and slip casting. Advanced techniques include hot-isostatic pressing and a chemical vapor deposition. Heat treatment and oxidation equipment includes 1,700 degrees C air furnaces and graphite or carbon-element 3,000 degrees C inert-atmosphere/vacuum furnaces. Analytical capabilities include: an x-ray diffractometer for phase analysis, mechanical testing equipment (Instron high temperature mechanical testing system, macro-hardness tester, acoustic fatigue), optical microscopy, thermal analysis (1,600 degrees C dilatometer, 1,600 degree TGA), mass spectrometry, particle size and distribution analyzers, surface area and density measurement, and metallographic sectioning and polishing equipment.

Biotechnology Laboratories—provide expertise and facilities for studies in environmental microbiology, molecular biology, biosensors, and materials-microbe interactions. It includes equipment and capabilities in microscopy (transmitted and reflected light, epifluorescence, autoscan, photomicroscopy), protein/enzyme purification and characterization, protein patterning, genetic analysis, gas and liquid chromatography, image analysis, microbial characterization and identification, biodegradation/biodeterioration analysis, and microbiological monitoring.

Dosimetry Laboratories—dedicated to all aspects of the Navy's personnel dosimetry program. A gamma radiation range provides calibration and quality assurance to ensure the accuracy and integrity of the system. Gamma, beta, and x-ray radiation as well as mono-energetic neutrons produced from a 3MeV tandem positive ion accelerator are available for dosimeter calibration. Complementary laboratories are used to investigate the fundamental optical properties of materials for potential use in dosimetry as well as development, testing, and evaluation of prototype dosimetry badges and their accompanying electronics.

Electrochemical/Battery Laboratories—include chemistry labs for the study of basic materials and processes in electrochemical cells; a controlled atmosphere dry room for work with moisture sensitive materials; a thermal analysis laboratory; and special facilities for the evaluation of batteries under normal and abusive conditions such as discharge, charge, short circuit, high and low temperature, etc.

Environmental Protection Laboratories—used for investigation of processes, operations, and systems designed to abate shipboard-generated liquid, solid, and gaseous discharges; allowing the development and evaluation of pilot-plant size discharge processing, full-scale waste treatment, solid and plastics waste disposal, and thermal destruction hardware and systems; and for hazardous materials reduction and pollution prevention.

Fatigue and Fracture Laboratories—an extensive facility for characterization of low-temperature fracture, dynamic fracture, low-cycle and high-cycle fatigue and fatigue crack growth properties. It consists of five major areas of equipment and instrumentation: computer-interactive servo-hydraulic fracture and fatigue test systems; high load, variable-stiffness computer-interactive fracture test systems; dynamic fracture servo-hydraulic test systems; dynamic fracture impact towers; and thick weldment low-cycle fatigue test systems.

Fire-tolerant Materials Laboratories—have the capability to assess shipboard fire safety performance with small-scale tests for candidate shipboard materials for such properties as flame spread, smoke generation, heat release, and products of combustion; includes NIST and Factory Mutual calorimeters and analytic equipment.

Magnetic Materials Laboratory—has a variety of instruments to measure magnetic properties. The vibrating sample magnetometer can measure magnetization from cryogenic temperatures to above room temperature. Other experiments can measure magnetostriction and magnetization as a function of magnetic field with forces as high as 100,000 pounds applied. These measurement capabilities support the magnetic materials group's efforts to develop new magnetic materials for Navy applications.

Marine Coatings Laboratories—an extensive facility consisting of a paint formulation and application lab, a paint test and evaluation lab, and a biosurface analytical lab; capable of formulating and manufacturing paints, coatings and adhesives, and analyzing and evaluating these materials for input into design guidance, specifications, and manuals.

Marine Corrosion Control and Evaluation Laboratories—consist of the aqueous corrosion and electrochemical lab; environmentally assisted cracking lab; marine corrosion analysis lab; low-velocity burner rig lab; and a small-scale high-temperature lab. They provide the capability of testing materials in a simulated gas turbine environment, conducting corrosion research, metallurgy failure analysis, and electrochemical testing of Navy seaborne materials.

Marine Organic Composites Laboratories—dedicated to all aspects of composites from basic research into the components of their manufacture, their physical and mechanical properties, and prototype construction and evaluation; this includes a large prototype production and test area, filament winder (control system capability with 6 degrees of free-

dom to wind complex parts), autoclave (capable of processing parts up
to 3 feet by 6 feet at temperatures up to 950 degrees F and pressures of
200 psi), and polymer synthesis labs.

Materials Characterization and Analysis Laboratory—consists of advanced instrumental analysis techniques including metallography and
optical microscopy, scanning electron microscopy, dynamic mechanical
thermal analysis, energy dispersive x-ray analysis, electron micro-probe
analysis, scanning-auger analysis, transmission electron microscopy, and
x-ray diffraction.

Nondestructive Evaluation (NDE) Laboratories—used to conduct NDE
of Navy materials with the following capabilities: radiography lab (400-
kV x-ray machine) and dark room; ultrasonics and electromagnetics lab;
laser optics lab; and penetrant testing and magnetic particle test lab.

Signature Materials Laboratories—provides the prototype production
capability for experimental shipsets of target-strength-reduction materials; measurement of both reflected and radiated signatures in the
acoustic, infrared, ultraviolet, visible, and microwave regions; the materials evaluation capability includes large acoustic pulse tubes capable of
submarine depth simulation, a unique bidirectional infrared spectral
emittance measurement system and a laser coordinate-axis ultra-precision dimensional metrology machine.

Spray-metal Forming Laboratory—Carderock Division NSWC is the
only government activity with the Osprey process capability; it has a 200-
pound melt capacity, a deposition rate of ferrous and nonferrous metal
alloys on the order of 100 to 400 lbs. per minute, sensors to provide real-time information on critical properties for intelligent processing, and
manipulators for multi-axial motion to make nonsymmetric components
and geometries.

Welding Process and Consumable Development Laboratories—a complete
welding capability consisting of the arc-welding laboratory (welding
process development; weld simulation; weldability evaluation; and welding sensors and robotics); and the welding consumable development
laboratory (electrode production and wire fabrication prototype; flux
evaluation; and moisture evaluation).

Ship Motion Simulator Facility

This facility consists of electronic analog computers to solve ship
and submarine differential equations of motion; a submarine diving-station to simulate the control room and pitching motion of the submarine; and numerous kinds of auxiliary equipment such as instrument displays, automatic plotting boards, and strip-chart recorders. The facility

can simulate the motion of a ship under action of forces on its hull, appendages, and control surfaces. By use of this facility a wealth of data can be obtained in a fraction of the time it would take using other means such as model or full-scale testing. It has been used to solve a variety of complex problems in stability and control of motions in 6 degrees of freedom of submarines, surface ships, hydrofoil craft, torpedoes, and missiles. Design variations which normally would have required trajectory studies for satisfactory evaluation were simulated allowing corrective actions to be taken early in the design process there avoiding major changes to design specifications and hardware.

Strategic Planning and Assessment Center (SPARC)

The SPARC consists of a warfare simulation facility, four war rooms and associated office spaces. The purpose of the center is to evaluate current and future ship and battle-force-related technologies and tactics for both U.S. and potential adversaries to assess predicted pay-offs in realistic operational scenarios.

Structures Evaluation Laboratory

This laboratory provides the facilities and expertise needed for testing large heavy structures like full-size ship components and sections. It is capable of developing loads necessary to test a 1/3-scale model of a destroyer to failure. The facility includes a strong floor measuring 40 feet by 100 feet constructed of heavily-reinforced concrete 7 feet thick with tie-downs located on 5-foot centers, each rated at 250,000 pounds. Loads are applied to the test structure through hydraulic rams. Computer-controlled instrumentation is available to monitor loads and the response of test articles. For typical large-scale tests several hundred channels of data are recorded simultaneously.

Also part of this facility are various universal static load machines with up to 600,000 pounds load capacity, and various fatigue load machines which cycle models at loads up to one million pounds of either constant or programmed amplitude loading.

Subsonic Wind Tunnel

This wind tunnel is one of two wind tunnels brought to Carderock from the Experimental Model Basin in the Washington Navy Yard. These tunnels were once the Navy's primary resource for aircraft aerodynamic testing. The remaining tunnel has a 8-by-10-by-14-foot test section and is capable of speeds from 20 to 150 knots (Mach 0.1–0.3) at atmospheric pressure. The tunnel is used to produce certain types of low-speed aerodynamic data that are unique to Navy missions. These studies include ship wake surveys, submarine flow studies, and stack-gas flow studies as well as conventional aerodynamic testing of aircraft and weapons at low speed.

Towing Tanks

One of DTRC's original structures houses three towing basins. A deep-water basin, 2,775 feet in length, 51 feet wide and 22 feet deep, permits tests of models up to 32 feet long, 5 feet wide and weighing up to 5 tons. Its pneumatic wavemaker can generate regular waves up to 2 feet high with a wave length of 40 feet. A shallow-water basin, 303 feet long, 51 feet wide, and 10 feet deep, joins the deep-water basin and doubles back in a J-shaped curve at one end to form a turning basin. The turning basin is used for tests of ship models in maneuvering and turning up to 180 degrees. A high-speed basin, 2,968 feet long, 21 feet wide, and 10 feet deep for one third of its length and 16 feet deep for its remaining length, completes the structure. It is used for model tests of high-speed planing hulls, hydrofoils, air cushion craft, surface effect ships, and submarines at speeds up to 60 knots.

3-Inch Pipe Flow Facility

This quiet-flow facility is used to conduct boundary layer flow and noise experiments. The results are applied directly to ship hull and coating designs to ensure future ships and submarines retain their acoustic advantage.

12-Inch Variable-Pressure Water Tunnel

This water tunnel is used primarily to determine cavitation inception characteristics and pressure distributions on fairings, ship appendages, submerged bodies, fins, and hydrofoils. It is inexpensive to operate and can be used for a variety of basic hydrodynamic research projects including acoustic measurements of cavitation noise, boundary layer flow studies, bubble research, flow visualization techniques, and dissolved gas effects. It can also be used to determine the cavitation characteristics of small propeller models. The tunnel is a vertical-plane, closed-loop recirculating water circuit with a variable-pressure test section. The working section is a rectangular open jet with a circular entrance nozzle throat diameter of 12 inches. Maximum working section velocity is 6.1 m/s (12 knots). Minimum working section absolute pressure is 10 kPa (1.5 psia). The minimum working section cavitation number, sigma = 0.4 (at 1.5 psia and 12 knots).

24-Inch Variable-Pressure Water Tunnel

This intermediate-size water tunnel is used primarily to determine the cavitation characteristics of propellers and to conduct six-component unsteady propeller force measurements in simulated wakes. This cost effective (single operator) facility also is used to determine cavitation inception characteristics and pressure distributions on fairings, ship appendages, submerged bodies, fins, and hydrofoils. The tunnel is a vertical-plane, closed-loop recirculating water circuit with a variable-pressure test section. The working section is an open jet with a circular entrance nozzle throat diameter of 24 inches. Maximum working section velocity is 17 m/sec (33 knots). The entrance and exit nozzles can be removed and a cylindrical liner installed to convert to a closed-jet test section. Dynamometers for measuring steady and unsteady propeller forces are located on both the upstream and downstream shafts. Minimum working section absolute pressure equals 14 kPa (2 psia), maximum working section absolute pressure equals 241 kPa (35 psia). Minimum working section cavitation number, sigma = 0.08 (at 2 psia and 33 knots).

36-Inch Variable-Pressure Water Tunnel

This facility was constructed when increased propeller sizes and speeds proved that the 12- and 24-inch water tunnels, erected in 1929 and 1941 respectively, were inadequate for evaluating full-scale propeller operations. In addition to testing full-scale propellers operating at high speeds, the 36-inch tunnel can also predict and simulate propeller cavitation patterns. Two chambers allow for these tests. The closed section accommodates models up to 18 inches in diameter while the open section can test 27-inch models of various shapes, including sonar domes and torpedoes, Water is circulated through the vertical, closed-duct circuit at speeds up to 50 knots and pressures up to 60 pounds per square inch by a 3,500-horsepower electric pump. Elbows with diffusers or vanes to reduce turbulence, located at the corners of the closed-loop tunnel, turn the flow. A 78-foot deep "resorber" chamber, placed in an excavation blasted out of solid bedrock, also serves to eliminate turbulence. At the test chamber, located in the upper portion, two 1,750-horsepower motor-dynamometers, capable of achieving speeds up to 10,000 revolutions per minute, turn two rotating shafts driving the propeller model. At the same time, these motor-dynamometers measure the propeller's thrust and torque. By controlling both water and propeller speed through the motors, a wide range of thrust and torque variables can be tested. Vacuum pumps lower the air pressure on the model, thus simulating the combined effect of the atmosphere and water pressure on the propeller and permitting the investigation of full-scale cavitation patterns on the models.

140-Foot Towing Basin

This towing basin is currently being used primarily to develop particle velocimetry technology and flow visualization using laser light sheets for complicated flow regions. The facility has been extensively upgraded for this laser work and also is used for seakeeping evaluations in head seas, resistance tests on bare hull models, canal lock studies, and ship passing experiments in restricted channels. It is a 52,000-gallon rectangular basin 1.5 meters (5 feet) deep, 42.7 meters (140 feet) long, and 3 meters (10 feet) wide. It has a pneumatic wavemaker at one end and a wave absorbing beach at the other. The wavemaker can create regular waves from 0.6 to 4 meters (2 to 13 feet) in length with corresponding maximum heights of 25 to 191 millimeters (1 to 7.5 inches). The towing carriage has a maximum speed of 3.2 meters per second (6.1 knots) and operates over the basin from a suspended track system. Model-size range is 1.5 to 3 meters (5 to 10 feet) in length. The carriage is equipped with special mounting fixtures and instrumentation for conducting flow visualization experiments with laser light sheets.

Major Facilities at the Annapolis, Maryland Site

The Annapolis Detachment is the Navy's principal source for shipboard machinery systems research and development (R&D), and concept integration for ships and submarines in the areas of propulsion, auxiliary and electrical machinery including machinery acoustic and electromagnetic signatures. The main site is located across the Severn River from the U.S. Naval Academy; a satellite site is located in Arnold, Maryland. The Annapolis detachment will be closed as a result of the base closure and realignment decision of 1995. Major facilities and personnel will be relocated to the Philadelphia and Carderock sites. Facilities located at Annapolis include:

Advanced Electric Propulsion Machinery Development Facility

This unique facility contains advanced current collectors ranging from small-scale, high-speed to large full-scale facilities to develop technology necessary to handle the extremely high density currents in superconducting machines. It also includes a 3,000-horsepower model superconducting electric drive train, including control and data-acquisition system, turbine, generator, switch gear, motor, load device, and cryogenic system. The purpose of this facility is to conduct technology development programs critical to implementation of conventional and superconducting electric propulsion systems for ships. Technologies include advanced current collectors, cryogenic refrigeration systems, liquid cooling, superconducting materials and magnets, high-current switchgear, fabrication technology, electromagnetic structures and high-power electronics. Activities include research, design, fabrication, experimental development, analysis, and testing.

Advanced Shipboard Machinery Development Facility

This facility is comprised of a computer-controlled submarine shaft seal test fixture, a submarine propulsion thrust bearing test site, a ventilation fan test site, a new submarine steering and diving test facility, and an air conditioning test facility. Virtually any submarine or surface ship auxiliary machinery system can be tested at full performance levels including submarine main shaft seals and thrust bearings. This unique facility is used to conduct research of new machinery concepts, confirm heat transfer and fluid mechanic computer models, and to qualify fullscale shipboard machinery including: air conditioning systems; hydraulics systems; compressed air systems; ventilation systems; seawater systems; desalination systems; and submarine shaftline systems. Most of these research sites are equipped with monitoring and control instrumentation that enable unattended operation.

Deep Ocean Pressure Simulation Facility

The main pressure tank in this facility is unique in the world by virtue of its size and capabilities. It can simulate the ocean pressure, temperature and salinity to depths of 27,000 feet (pressure of 12,000 pounds per square inch) and can accommodate submersibles (or equipment) up to 20 feet in diameter and 27 feet in length. It can simulate diving and surfacing from 4,000 pounds per square inch at a rate of once a minute. Its purpose is to provide the Navy, other government agencies, universities, industry, and foreign governments with unique pressure testing capabilities. The work performed in the facility is mainly in support of R&D for naval applications.

In addition to the physical capabilities of this pressure tank, the facility is certified for testing of manned vehicles while under operational load and in their normal horizontal plane of operation. Other pressure tanks within the facility complex are listed in the accompanying table.

Pressure Tank Capabilities

Feature	Tank A	Tank B	Tank J	Tank H	Tank V
Diameter	10 ft	4 ft	30 in	30 in	18 in
Length	27 ft	12 ft	8 ft 6 in	8 ft	5 ft 3 in
Maximum Static Pressure	12,000 psi	12,000 psi	10,000 psi	7,000 psi	10,000 psi
Pressurizing Fluid	Sea or Fresh Water		Fresh Water		Oil
Tank Axial Centerline	Horizontal				Vertical
Pressure Cycling	Yes	Yes	Yes	No	No

Electric Power Technology Laboratory

This unique facility contains seven sources of electrical power to simulate and test for various ship system conditions for solving fleet problems with new equipment. Power sources include ship-service motor generator sets, a turbine simulator, an uninterruptible power supply, station power, and multiple solid state power converters. The laboratory supports the development of advanced shipboard machinery control and electric power distribution and conversion technology. Among the diverse uses of the laboratory are; development of advanced power generation and distribution components and system performance assessment in the 500-kw to 1-mw range in a machinery systems facility; computer simulation of large machinery systems and development of control algorithms; development of advanced sensors and instrumentation; development of advanced power conversion topologies and advanced semiconductor device application up to several hundred kilowatts; development of submarine power-conditioning equipment for improved power quality and reduced submarine radiated noise; development of innovative electrical distribution component designs for reduced noise; and development of modeling techniques to predict and minimize motor noise and to predict and optimize full-scale propulsion motor size and weight.

Environmental Non-CFC Facility

This facility is a large complex composed of many test facilities integrated and interconnected by a variety of shared water systems, electrical power distribution systems, and data acquisition and analysis systems. The complex was developed to meet U.S. and international laws banning the use of chlorofluorocarbon compounds (e.g. Freon) in cooling systems aboard Navy ships and submarines. The facility, which encompasses 30,000 square feet of floor space, has three major components—centrifugal compressor test facility, naval air-conditioning plant water test facility, and refrigeration plant development facility. The complex is used to develop replacement compressor-refrigerant combinations for installation in existing cooling plants on board ships and to develop cooling plants for ships and submarines of the future.

Machinery Acoustic Silencing Laboratory

This is the only facility within the Department of Defense used to provide direct support in the development of quiet naval machinery and noise isolation devices. It has been extensively used to develop quiet machinery technology and prototype hardware in support of *Seawolf-* and *Ohio*-class submarines, surface ships, and other quiet machinery development programs. This laboratory, by its design, provides a unique capability to measure low-level airborne and structure-borne noise. Hardware which has been developed and evaluated has contributed significantly to achievement of the low-detectability edge enjoyed by U.S. submarines.

The laboratory has several unique facilities including anechoic chambers with vibration-isolated floors used in conducting research and development of quiet fans, ventilation system components, quiet pumps, fluid flow devices, isolation materials, resilient mounts, and other noise isolation devices for submarines and naval surface ships. The development of active noise cancellation technology and the acoustical development of machinery foundations and other ship structures, including damping treatments for these structures and for piping systems are supported by the laboratory.

Ralph K. James Magnetic Fields Laboratory

This facility is unique within the U.S. in that it can simulate the magnetic environment anywhere in the northern hemisphere and, with its three layers of magnetometers at different levels below the main floor, it can measure and map the magnetic fields of shipboard equipment at their full rated loads. The specific purpose of the facility is to provide the Navy with a magnetically clean and controlled environment for the accurate measurement of magnetostatic field signatures beneath full-size electrical machinery designed for use on board mine counter-measure (MCM) ships.

The test building is constructed entirely of nonmagnetic materials and is located remote from vehicular traffic and other sources of magnetic noise. It is set into the side of a hill and contains four floors. The top floor is the main test floor that is capable of supporting shipboard machinery weighing up to 40 tons. The lower three floors contain magnetic field measurement sensors. The geometrical arrangement between test item and sensors simulates the passage of a ship over mine sensors.

Submarine Fluid Dynamics Facility

This facility was originally designed and constructed for the study of the ballast and blow process in submarines. It has been upgraded to accomplish its primary task which is to conduct research and development concerned with the design and performance of quiet fluid system components for shipboard applications. In this role, the facility has the capability for acoustic and operational evaluation of components requiring high pressures and/or high rates of flow of air or water. It is also used extensively to test, evaluate, and qualify fluid system components designed and manufactured by private industry and proposed for shipboard use.

Major Facilities at the Philadelphia Site

As a result of the base closure and realignment decision (BCRD) of 1991, the Naval Ship Systems Engineering Station (NAVSSES) was merged with the David Taylor Research Center in January 1992 to form the Carderock Division of the Naval Surface Warfare Center. NAVSSES, located at the Philadelphia Naval Business Center (the former property of the Naval Station Philadelphia and Philadelphia Naval Shipyard), is the Navy's only comprehensive source for full-scale test and evaluation and in-service engineering of ship and submarine propulsion, electrical, and auxiliary machinery systems.

NAVSSES was originally founded by Rear Admiral George Melville as the Fuel Oil Testing Plant, which opened in 1910. Through the years, it has grown in size, scope, funding, and responsibility. The name has been changed numerous times. In 1932 the site became the U.S. Naval Boiler Laboratory; in 1941 the U.S. Naval Boiler and Turbine Laboratory, in 1966 the Naval Ship Engineering Center Philadelphia Division; and in 1979 the Naval Ship Systems Engineering Station. Facilities located at Philadelphia include the following:

Advanced Propulsion and Auxiliary Machinery Facility

This facility is being constructed as a replacement for a facility to be closed at the Annapolis Site as a result of the BCRD of 1995. It will support R&D functions and include full-scale submarine propulsion shaft and thrust bearing, composite propulsion shaft, line shaft bearing, shaft seal, and gas turbine rotary engine, and piston-engine test capabilities. The full-scale propulsion shaft, thrust bearing, and shaft seal test sites are unique within the free world.

Air Conditioning and Refrigeration Test Facility

This facility supports surface and undersea vehicle auxiliary systems and components test and evaluation; acquisition and in-service engineering; and environmental, logistics, and materials-processing RDT&E for surface and submarine ships classes. Materials and components investigated include alternative CFC's, air conditioning and refrigeration, ventilation, oxygen generation, and air purification systems for surface ships and submarines. Since ships are designed as integrated systems, system testing is critical to determination of the effectiveness of modifications of shipboard systems. These facilities do not exist anywhere else in this country. Their use for evaluation of proposed submarine life support, air conditioning, refrigeration, and ventilation systems enhances the Navy's capability to be a smart buyer of these ship systems.

Boiler Components Test Facility

This facility supports surface machinery propulsion auxiliary machinery system and component RDT&E and in-service engineering for numerous ship classes. It was originally constructed as a 1,200 psig cruiser boiler room that was used to train the Navy's boiler technicians. It has remained operational to conduct testing on associated boiler components and was used most recently to provide part of the steam required for *Seawolf* (SSN 21) main propulsion testing. It was also used extensively by the alternative fuels program to test boiler performance using "synthetic" shale fuels oils. Typical components testing performed includes combustion optimizers for fuel efficiency, gas- analysis systems for environmental compliance, smoke indicator systems, burner systems, control systems, fuel oil control valves, strainers, fuel oil pumps, boiler water-level indicating systems and newly designed boiler refractory. The only other alternative to use of the facility is shipboard testing. It plays a prominent role in providing the technical expertise to enable the Navy to be a smart buyer of these components.

Cargo and Weapons Systems Facility

This facility consists of a contiguously located suite of full-scale and component test facilities. The site was constructed in 1986 to address and solve the technical problems encountered from the diverse population of cargo and weapons systems in the fleet (e.g., over 600 different types of elevators, with 21 different capacities, of 250 different designs, and made by 64 different manufacturers). It includes a full-scale 6-story cargo and weapons elevator on a land-based engineering site; a vertical package conveyor test site; temperature- and humidity-controlled machinery; electrical control, and power unit rooms; and a modular layout to provide for shipboard configuration and other testing that is cost-prohibitive at sea.

Compressed Air System Facility

This is a one-of-a-kind test facility capable of conducting full-scale system and component testing. Systems testing includes high-pressure air, low-pressure vital and non-vital air, electronics dry air, submarine ballast-blow air, and electronic cooling water. Component testing includes high- and low-pressure air compressors, reducing valves, dehydrators, moisture monitors, air control panels for radar wave guides, chill water system refrigerant controllers, chilled water heat exchangers for demineralizer systems, duplex strainers, flow switches, and temperature-regulating valves. Environmental controls allow for operation over a wide range of temperature and humidity in order to duplicate actual shipboard conditions. A temperature-controlled, closed-loop salt water cooling system supports facility operation to simulate world-wide ocean conditions.

Data Collection and Calibration Facility

This facility consists of the test operations analysis and control center and a calibration laboratory. The control center consists of independent, computer-controlled data acquisition and analysis systems which permit the monitoring and interpretation of data from tests located throughout NAVSSES. Test sites are connected via a multiconductor fiber optic network. Data are displayed and analyzed (on line and off line) then stored to allow for future trending analysis. The center is capable of active control of remote facilities and tests, and facilitates the rapid modification of test and hardware configurations to meet customer needs.

The calibration lab provides the fleet with efficient, affordable machinery health monitoring, cost-effective predictive maintenance and maximum system readiness and operation, and qualified enlisted personnel through on-site training. The standards used in this facility are traceable to the National Institute of Standards and Technology.

Diesel Engine Development Facility

This facility supports testing of main propulsion and auxiliary diesel engines. The propulsion support facility includes a full-scale propulsion system that duplicates the port engine room of the LSD 41- and LSD 49-class amphibious ships. This system includes two 92-ton, 8,500-horsepower diesel engines, main reduction gear, control system, and associated auxiliary support equipment. The facility also includes the capability for tests of small propulsion and auxiliary diesel engines used on other class ships (e.g. minesweepers and minehunters) and diesel support systems (e.g. submarine snorkels). Part of this facility also duplicates the complete ship-service diesel generator set for FFG 7-class ships.

Electrical Systems R&D Facility

This facility is being constructed as a replacement for a facility to be closed at the Annapolis site as a result of BRAC 1995. It will be capable of evaluating the unique aspects of maritime electrical machinery performance with respect to advanced system prototyping, development of fabrication technology, emulation of ship interfaces and state-of-the-art computer simulation, data acquisition, and data analysis. The facility's primary purpose is to support the development of new technology, active ship construction programs, and future ship designs while providing supplemental capability to service active fleet assets. It will include both large integrated machinery system prototypes test stands, and high technology research laboratories. Major capabilities will include a multi-megawatt electric drive, including 200,000 ampere power supply and full-scale current collector test facility; cryogenics systems; superconducting magnetic system design; and a fabrication capability. Laboratory areas include power generation and distribution, electroacoustics, solid state power, machinery sensors, machinery and electrical systems simulation, 400 Hz and dc power distribution, aircraft and avionics support power systems, and zonal electrical systems.

Environmental Systems Facility

This facility provides the capability to provide the fleet with effective shipboard pollution abatement systems and operators trained in environmentally sound maintenance processes. It contains fully operational oil-water separators, injection systems, oily-waste conditioners, variable-speed separator pumps, oil content monitors and all associated support system tanks, piping, valves, and controls. The solid waste section has both working garbage grinders and classified document destructors as well as incinerator feed chute mock-ups used in the testing of automated feed systems. The lab includes air/gas emission test equipment and a complete EPA Method 5 sampling train to conduct incinerator and prime-mover emissions testing. An isolated lab enclosure for testing hazardous waste treatment-analysis methods is also available and is used for PCB field-test-kit analysis and hazardous materials waste-processing equipment such as the HM/W spill response kit. The facility has an analytical lab that is used to conduct oil-in-water analysis, biochemical oxygen demand, solids analysis, coliform concentrations, total hydrocarbons analysis, and other tests that are used to characterize waste constituents. Some of the equipment includes a high-resolution photo-capable microscope, particle counters, infrared analyzers, incubators, computers, and air/gas analyzers. The facility is also outfitted with a portable GC/MS for both lab and field analysis of effluent waste streams for PCBs, dioxins and metals. The water-jet test and wastewater recycling facilities are used to test alternative water-jet systems, components, applications, and water reuse and recycling methods.

Fiber Optic Facility

This facility provides test and evaluation, research and development, design, integration, installation and maintenance engineering, fleet engineering support, acquisition and lifetime support, and fleet training for fiber optic cable plant topology, fiber optic networks, and fiber optic sensor systems for shipboard and land-based military installations. This laboratory was developed as a facility for both integrated systems evaluation and component testing for fiber optic equipment and applications. This results in maximized efficiency for components and systems integration testing, reduced operating costs, and improved system-wide impact assessments from fiber optic system or component upgrades. This laboratory is used to investigate a wide range of fiber optic shipboard and land-based equipment which includes cable plant topology components, network communications hardware components, local area network (LAN) architectures, system applications software, sensors, and the associated control units. System-level testing prior to shipboard deployment is critical to ensure the success of fielded fiber optic systems.

It is the only DOD-certified fiber optic qualified products list (QPL) testing laboratory for verifying component performance to functional military requirements.

Gas Turbine Development Facility

This facility consists of several major components including the DDG 51 land-based engineering site (LBES) and the integrated propulsion system (IPS). The DDG 51 LBES consists of two General Electric LM-2500 marine gas turbines, three ship-service gas turbine generators (SSGTG), and associated auxiliary equipment configured as engine room #2 of the *Arleigh Burke* (DDG 51) destroyer class. This site became operational in 1989 and is used in a variety of component and system-oriented tests that include integration testing of propulsion machinery (reduction gears, lube oil systems, air systems, and water systems) as well as machinery control, and data acquisition and information systems. The facility is also used for operational testing of the advanced turbine systems program and has the capability for integration testing of advanced electromechanical systems (e.g. hybrid fuel cell/gas turbine technology, advanced electrical distribution networks, and integrated propulsion systems).

Machinery Acoustic Silencing Laboratory

This facility is being constructed as a replacement for a facility to be closed at the Annapolis site as a result of the BCRD of 1995. It will be the only facility capable of developing and assessing the quietness of full-scale naval machinery under system operating conditions. The laboratory will provide anechoic spaces with seismic floors and low-level background noise and will have test equipment for evaluating fan noise, quiet pumps, resilient machinery mounts, and for performing structural acoustics R&D.

The laboratory will contain two major test cells—a anechoic acoustic chamber and a quiet evaluation facility—with over 7,500 square feet of test area, an anechoic platform, and extensive support space. Test cells will have very thick concrete walls and massive seismic floors that will be physically isolated from the rest of the building and set on their own foundations.

This laboratory will be used to develop and improve silencing technology and machinery components for surface ships and submarines, including the SSN 21 new attack submarine, DDG 51, and future combatants. In addition, it will support fleet acoustic operational requirements, habitability, environmental compliance, and quiet machinery developments for other services and commercial applications.

Materials and Processing Facility

This facility provides for rapid direct fleet support, test and evaluation, qualification of candidate seaborne materials, and failure analysis of a wide variety of materials and processes related to hull, mechanical and electrical systems. Capabilities for investigations include paints and coatings for ship's super-structure, interior and underwater hull nondestructive testing, failure analysis, materials evaluations of mechanical and electrical machinery, corrosion control, steam plant analysis, lube, fuel, and aqueous fluid systems contamination control, particulate monitoring of fluid and air systems, thermal spray paint coatings, and prototype shipboard monitoring equipment.

Power Generation T&E Facility

This facility provides the dual capability of testing a CG 47-class ship- service gas turbine generator (SSGTG) set, and 60 Hz, 400 Hz and direct current electrical distribution systems and components for the entire fleet. As the only CG 47 SSGTG test site, it provides for incorporation, testing, and evaluation of engineering improvements set forth in engineering change proposals prior to implementation in the fleet. Engineering improvements are focused on reducing maintenance and operating costs, improving reliability, and eliminating safety issues. Full-load testing of a generator set is accomplished by connection to resistive and inductive load banks. The naval shipboard power distribution facility provides the capability to test all shipboard 60 Hz, 400 Hz, and direct current electric power distribution equipment utilizing shipboard-type electric power (60 Hz and 400 Hz) or local utility power and a shipboard power inverter.

Small Gas Turbine Test Facility

This facility provides a broad range of equipments that support small to medium gas turbines up to 10,000 horsepower and gas turbine marine aerosol/separator intake systems. It is designed to accommodate rapid response testing for emergent fleet problems as well as to test and validate design modifications (e.g. exhaust diffusers, foreign object damage screen, exhaust gas turbine limiter, carbon and ceramic seals, electronic sequencing unit, flexible fuel manifolds, air movement control, air conditioning, particulate monitoring).

Steam Propulsion Test Facility

This facility supports surface and undersea vehicle propulsion and auxiliary system test and evaluation, acquisition, in-service engineering, logistics, and materials/processing RDT&E for numerous ship classes. It was developed as an integrated, cost-effective alternative to shipboard testing. Systems evaluated include surface ship and submarine main propulsion auxiliary equipment, generator sets, and main boilers. Use of this facility results in reduced costs by lowering the manpower required and evaluations are improved by enhanced data acquisition and reduction techniques. It is capable of supplying one million pounds per hour of superheated or saturated steam to major turbine or component test sites. It also has the capability to supply feedwater at 1,500 pounds per square inch, cooling water of 180,000 gallons per minute flow and 500,000 horsepower heat rejection. The facility has supported SSN 21, the LHD boiler superheater, SSN and CVN main feed and steam valves, and performance tests for pumps and heat exchangers.

Survivability Engineering Facility

This facility supports environmental testing and hardening of shipboard components and systems used throughout the surface and subsurface fleet. It consists of a wide array of environmental and stress test equipment and vibration testing equipment capable of producing linear and logarithmic swept-sine and random waveforms. In addition, it possesses the capability to test components and systems weighing up to 10,000 pounds and as large as 64 square feet. Shock tests are routinely performed in accordance with MIL-S-901D on components and systems weighing up to 300 pounds. Components tested include main propulsion equipment, generator sets, controllers, electronics, and fiber optic system controllers.

Undersea Sail and Deployed Systems Facility

This facility supports the technical capability for in-service engineering, full-scale test and evaluation, research and design support, acquisition and life-cycle engineering for undersea vehicle sail and deployed system hull, mechanical and electrical equipment.

It is unique, combining in-service technical expertise with the only existing complex of sail and deployed system test facilities to ensure their safe and reliable operation. Undersea vehicle radar, antennas, and periscope components are tested and evaluated to assess performance and technical risk prior to fleet introduction.

Facilities at Other Sites

In addition to the facilities available at Carderock, Annapolis, and Philadelphia, the Carderock Division has RDT&E facilities at various sites located in other sites across the United States. These are described below.

Alaska

Southeast Alaska Acoustic Measurement Facility (SEAFAC)

SEAFAC, located in Behm Canal, near Ketchikan, Alaska, provides an ideal ship acoustic measurement site characterized by low ambient noise and minimal noise interference. Replacing the Carr Inlet Acoustic Range (CIAR) and the Santa Cruz Acoustic Range Facility (SCARF) in 1992, SEAFAC is the Navy's only acoustic signature facility in the Pacific area capable of performing submarine passive radiated noise measurements and diagnostics over the full frequency range specified by the Navy. SEAFAC is also capable of supporting submarine target strength measurements. It consists of a site to collect acoustic signatures of submerged submarines underway, and a unique site to measure acoustic signatures of motionless (static) submerged submarines with various onboard machinery secured or under unloaded operation. Acoustic signatures can be collected for a variety of speeds and operating conditions as the submarine transits back and forth between the dual bottom-mounted acoustic arrays. At the static site, suspension barges lower the submarine on cables and position it between measurement arrays to evaluate acoustic signatures of individual machinery components.

Florida

Athena *Research Ship System*

The *Athena* research ships have been configured to provide the speeds, onboard laboratories, instrumentation, and handling equipment necessary to support sea-based tests. They include full-scale validation of model theory for propeller wake surveys and propeller stress studies; towed acoustic arrays, mine classification and neutralization systems; communication systems; and development of means to solve fleet operational problems. The *Athena* ships are based in Panama City, and include three converted *Asheville*-class patrol gunboats. Two have been converted to support general hydrodynamic and acoustic testing, and one supports electromagnetic signatures testing. These ships are 165 feet in length with a beam of 23.5 feet, a design displacement of 245 tons, and have 13,000 shaft horsepower. They have a top speed greater than 35 knots, and a towing loads of 15,000 to 20,000 lbs at 25 to 30 knots.

South Florida Test Facility (SFTF)

SFTF is the only ship, submarine, and mine-effectiveness test range with simultaneous air, surface, and subsurface tracking capability. It is located just South of Port Everglades in Fort Lauderdale. It became a part of the Carderock Division in 1994. The site location on the continental shelf provides a near-shore range that covers water depths from the surf zone to 1,500 feet. There are three permanent measurement ranges each with electromagnetic and acoustic arrays in 30, 60, and 600 feet of water respectively. There are also several simulated minefields with strategically placed sensors. High-precision air, surface, and subsurface tracking systems provide continuous vehicle locations throughout the measurement areas.

Hayes *(T-AG 195)*

Hayes, converted from an oceanographic research vessel to an ultra-quiet noise measurement vessel began operation in 1991 as the fleet's submarine acoustical measurement platform on the East Coast. Utilizing advanced measurement systems developed under the Acoustic Measurement Facilities Improvement Program (AMFIP), *Hayes* provides the platform and system capability of measuring radiated noise signatures of the Navy's quietest submarines. It conducts deep-water measurements at a variety of locations off the Florida coast and the Bahamas. Special measurement arrays, a new high capacity data acquisition and processing system (MAX), and a towed array measurement system (ATAMS) provide enhanced measurement capability of various noise deficiencies including sources that may be transient in nature. The ship is based in Port Canaveral.

Idaho

Acoustic Research Detachment (ARD)

ARD conducts ship stealth-related research and evaluations at various static and dynamic sites at secluded Lake Pend Oreille in northern Idaho near the town of Bayview with a remote site near the town of Kootenai. The 42-mile long, 1,150-foot-deep lake provides stable temperatures, clear water, and low background noise making it a unique environment for ship-related acoustical measurements. Historically, the detachment has conducted research and development in a variety of areas including advanced propulsors, structural acoustics, radiated noise and target strength, submarine sonar dome development, SSN bow design and acoustic performance evaluation, advanced special sonar design performance, sonar countermeasures, and transducer and hydrophone calibration. Many one-of-a-kind facilities such as data acquisition and processing systems support the diverse studies performed at ARD. Buoyantly propelled large-scale models such as *Kamloops* and *Dolly Varden,* a self-propelled large-scale submarine model (LSV), and the intermediate-scale measurement system (ISMS) are the principal facilities in operation at ARD. The 7.4-foot-diameter, 66-foot-long *Kamloops* has performed since the late 1960s as a unique unmanned buoyantly propelled test platform for submarine flow-noise experiments using a specially devised haul-down and release system. Originally a model of an SSN 637-class design, during the 1970s and early 1980s, *Kamloops* has been used for a variety of flow-noise studies of submarine bow domes, advanced sonar concepts, quieting device applications, and hull-related features and appendages as well as for static target strength measurements. In 1986, *Kamloops* was reconfigured to the *Seawolf* design and has supported flow-noise investigations of SSN 21 design features into the early 1990s.

Dolly Varden, a model of the SSN 688-class submarine, was acquired in 1978 and performed flow-noise investigations relevant to design features of that class until it was used in the mid- and late 1980s in support of the SSN 21 program. In 1995, the original *Dolly Varden* bow was modified to replicate the acoustically relevant features of the New SSN design and is supporting that program.

The LSV, named *Kokanee,* is a 1/4-scale, self-propelled model of the SSN 21-class submarine, delivered to the ARD test site in 1987. It is used for evaluations of the radiated noise characteristics of propulsors and hull appendages; hydrodynamic maneuvering and powering characteristics of advanced propulsor designs; hull vibration and acoustic radiation; and non-acoustic wake-detection. Capable of preprogrammed powered operations at full-scale speeds and depths, the LSV is autonomously maneuvered through a dedicated measurement range approximately 2.5 miles long, where bottom-mounted hydrophone arrays collect radiated noise data that are transmitted to the mission barge. At 88 feet in length, 10 feet in diameter, and displacing 155 tons, it is the world's largest free-running unmanned underwater vehicle (UUV). Results of LSV evaluations have been key to the design of advanced propulsors for SSN 21 and New SSN applications.

The intermediate-scale measurement system is the most advanced target strength and structural acoustic research facility in existence. It provides the capability to perform precise high-quality measurements of target strength and structural acoustic responses of large-scale submarine models and modeled onboard ship-related features in a quiet controlled environment. The standard test configuration is a large-scale static model whose submerged position and orientation at the test site is controlled by an anchored handling and haul-down platform system and remote shore winch. A stand-off array of high-powered acoustic projectors transmit acoustic signals to the model. Returning acoustical energy scattered from the test model is collected by a ring of hydrophones that encircle the model at an appropriate distance in the same plane as the transmit array. The model can be positioned in azimuth, roll, and pitch. In another standard mode of operation, the hydrophones are used to measure noise radiated from the test model resulting from powered onboard structural excitation shakers placed in specific patterns. A 14-mile fiber optic command, control, and data link between the site and the

ISMS control center provides manual or programmed model positioning, and transmission of data to the shore-based computers and processing equipment.

Maryland

Special Trials Unit

This unit, located at the Patuxent River Naval Air Station, is under the management of the Division's Combatant Craft Department. It was established in 1971 to support the Surface Effects Ship Program. It currently supports a wide variety of vehicle research, development, test, and evaluation projects. The site facilities, which are located on a protected harbor, include pier space, a synchrolift drydock and transfer system, high-bay boat house space, offices, shops capable of limited construction, and variety of other support instrumentation and equipment.

Tennessee

Memphis Detachment

This detachment, located on a 94-acre site on President's Island, near Memphis, became part of DTRC on 1 August 1988. It includes a 500,000 square foot industrial facility with a 10-story clear space and 35,000 square feet of office space. The detachment was developed as the operating site for the large cavitation channel (LCC). This is the largest water tunnel of its kind in the world. It is capable of testing all types of ship and submarine propellers and propeller-hull interactions with model scales sufficiently large to match the largest towing and turning basins in the world. The tunnel test section has a cross-section area of 100 square feet (10 feet by 10 feet) and can accept models up to 40 feet in length. Test pressure range is 0.5 to 60 psia and flow control speeds in the test section are up to 30 knots. This is the only large water tunnel specifically designed for hydroacoustic testing. The dynamic range of pressure and hydroacoustic performance-parameter combinations exceeds all other water tunnel systems. The physical control parameters and size provide for full compatibility with the large towing tanks located at the Carderock Division's Bethesda, Maryland site.

Virginia

Combatant Craft Department

This department, now under the Division's Ship Systems and Programs Directorate, has performed full life-cycle and full-spectrum support for combatant craft and boats from its facilities located in the Norfolk area since 1967. The facilities are located near the largest and most varied inventory of DOD and non-DOD boats and craft in the United States. Their assigned mission is to perform total craft systems engineering and technology integration including: research and development, test and evaluation, design, acquisition (smart buyer), construction technical support, integrated logistics support, program management, life-cycle management, technology advancement and transfer, in-service engineering, and fleet support for combatant craft, boats, patrol coastal class ships, other water craft, and associated systems.

Underwater Explosions Research Detachment

UERD became operational in 1942 and has been organizationally a part of DTRC since 1961. Formerly located in the Norfolk Naval Shipyard, it is currently is located in Chesapeake. It is the principal activity for shock analysis and testing of large-scale models and Navy ships and submarines. Personnel have an average of 15 years experience and possess skills and unique corporate knowledge which supports Navy requirements for ship survivability design concepts, ship shock trials, and live fire assessments. UERD is a full-service testing activity providing integrated pretest analytical studies, test planning and direction, post trial analyses, and interpretation of experimental results with state-of-the-art capabilities of advanced data acquisition and data processing systems.

Washington

Carr Inlet Acoustic Range (CIAR)

CIAR, located on Fox Island, Washington, provides underway and static sites for acoustic signature measurements of surface ships and submarines. In addition to its data acquisition and analysis systems, CIAR has a bottom-mounted tracking system for submarine maneuvering and positioning. As larger and faster submarines entered the fleet, CIAR gradually became too confining an area to perform high-speed maneuvers during noise trials, and work is gradually transitioning to SEAFAC.

Puget Sound Detachment

This detachment, located in the Puget Sound Naval Shipyard, Bremerton, provides management and logistic support for West Coast full-scale ship and submarine acoustic trials. It is responsible for the operation of the Southeast Alaska Acoustic Measurement Facility (SEAFAC) near Ketchikan, Alaska, and the Carr Inlet Acoustic Range.

Awards

The David Taylor Award

ESTABLISHED IN 1960, THIS HONORARY AWARD is presented annually by the Commanding Officer to employees for superior technical achievements. The Society of Naval Architects and Marine Engineers established a separate David Taylor Medal in 1936. Unlike the David Taylor Award, eligibility for the SNAME Medal is not limited to Carderock employees, although the Commanding Officer may nominate an employee.

Year	Name
1960	Pao C. Pien
1960	Feodor Theilheimer
1961	Murray Strasberg
1962	N. H. Schauer
1963	Lt. Commander M.C. Davis
1964	Martin A. Krenzke
1965	Harvey R. Chaplin
1966	Lt. Commander Henry Cox
1967	William M. Ellsworth
1968	Fred Schloss
1969	Robert M. Stevens
1970	Paul S. Granville
1971	William E. Cummins
1972	Allen G. Ford
1973	William B. Morgan
1974	Hans J. Lugt

Year	Name
1975	Robert M. Williams
1976	Elizabeth H. Cuthill
1977	Robert D. Rockwell
1978	Robert Englar
1979	Thomas T. Huang
1980	Nathan Bales
1981	Gideon Maidanik
1982	Terry E. Brockett
1983	Darrell R. Garrison
1984	William K. Blake
1985	G. Robert Lamb
1986	Marcel L. Salive
1987	David Feit
1988	Gerald E. Brunkhart
1989	Robert J. Boswell
1990	Milton O. Crutchfield
1991	Robert R. Jones
1992	Melvyn L. Rumerman
1993	Alfred L. Disenbacher
1994	Stuart D. Jessup
1995	Yuan-Ning Liu
1996	No award
1997	Jonathan L. Gershfeld

The George Melville Award

Presented annually by the Commanding Officer to employees of the Annapolis facility, this honorary award recognizes "distinguished scientific and engineering accomplishment."

Year	Name
1960	Larry J. Argiro
1961	William W. Anderson
1962	Matt V. Smith
1963	Ronald A. Darby
1964	N. Robert Gross
1965	Ralph Snapp
1966	Yung-Fa Wang
1967	Richard Schoeller Jr.
1968	C. Joseph Rubis
1969	John W. Henry

Year	Name
1970	Guy L. Johnson
1971	Richard A. Milroy
1972	John R. Ward
1973	Harold H. Singerman
1974	Timothy J. Doyle
1975	Lawrence C. Davidson
1976	Ernest J. Czyryca
1977	Edwin M. Petrisko
1978	Jean A. Montemarano
1979	John J. Eynck
1980	Michael J. Superczynski
1981	John P. Gudas
1982	Joseph L. Cavallaro
1983	Harold O. Stevens
1984	Wayne L. Adamson
1985	Thomas W. Montemarano
1986	James E. Smith
1987	Paul Schatzberg
1988	Bruce R. Hood
1989	Thomas E. Calvert
1990	Craig S. Alig
1991	Joseph W. Dickey
1992	Michael G. Vassilaros
1993	Chester R. Petry
1994	Roger M. Crane
1995	David H. Clayton
1996	No award
1997	Herman B. Urbach
	William Flickinger

Navy Distinguished Civilian Service Award

Awarded by the Secretary of the Navy, this honorary award recognizes accomplishments by Navy employees. The center may nominate employees it feels merit the award, although achievements may also be recognized by the Secretary without a formal nomination. The following are EES, DTMB, and center employees who have received this award.

Year	Name
1945	James Franko
1946	George W. Cook

Year	Name
1946	Vivian L. Chrisler
1946	Leon Wedding
1946	Karl E. Schoenherr
1954	Fred Schloss
1960	Harry Polachek
1961	Norman Jasper
1962	Alfred H. Keil
1963	William W. Murray
1971	Donald Ross
1975	William E. Cummins
1980	William M. Ellsworth
1982	Hans J. Lugt
1983	Larry J. Argiro
1994	Martin A. Krenzke
1994	Richard Schoeller Jr.

Department of Defense Distinguished Civilian Service Award

Awarded by the Secretary of Defense, this honorary award recognizes the achievements of a select few employees in the Department of Defense.

Year	Name
1961	Dr. Harry Polachek
1961	Dr. Norman Jasper
1975	Dr. William W. Murray

Significant Accomplishments

SIR ISAAC NEWTON IS SAID TO HAVE OBSERVED, "If I have seen farther it is by standing on the shoulders of giants." Similarly, technical achievements are usually built on and composed of many contributions large and small, past and recent, and from sources within and without. The significant technical accomplishments of the David Taylor Research Center and later the Carderock Division, Naval Surface Warfare Center, set forth here are the result of such contributions.

This appendix was prepared by Brian Bowers and is based on information published in December 1996 by the Office of the Director of Technology (Code 011), in a report entitled "Technology Developments & Applications for Today's and Tomorrow's Navy." The purpose of that report was to document the particularly noteworthy developments achieved by the center during the 50 years since the end of World War II. Specific criteria used to select from a long list of accomplishments are set forth in that report. Technical accomplishments that entered the fleet must have changed the way warfare is conducted; reduced cost, increased operational effectiveness, or improved maintenance of ships, craft, and submarines; corrected significant system or subsystem failures; or brought the U.S. Navy into compliance with new national or international laws. Otherwise, accomplishments must have significantly changed the state-of-the-art in a technical field of importance to achievement of the mission of the center.

SURFACE SHIPS AND CRAFT

AMPHIBIOUS ASSAULT LANDING CRAFT (AALC)
(Early 1970s onward)—Developed and demonstrated prototype air cushion vehicles featuring a 100-ton lift and 40-knot amphibious assault capability. Other participation

included NAVSEA, Naval Personnel Research & Development Center, Naval Coastal Systems Center, Aerojet General, Bell Aerospace, Bell-Avon, Lycoming, Hughes, Band-Lavis Associates, Bell-Textron and Lockheed. **IMPACT:** Most successful experimental prototypes and technologies were transitioned to the landing craft air cushion (LCAC) acquisition program. As of mid-1996, 91 LCACs were under contract and 77 had been delivered providing a revolutionary new capability for the U.S. Marine Corps.

SMALL WATERPLANE AREA TWIN HULL (SWATH) SHIP

(Late 1960s onward)—Developed the technology base and design methods for the SWATH ship concept that provides greatly improved seakeeping and seaway performance, particularly in small and medium size ships. Other participation included Naval Command Control and Ocean Surveillance Center, NAVSEA, American Bureau of Shipping, and McDermott Shipbuilding. **IMPACT:** The inherently superior SWATH ship concept is clearly demonstrated in T-AGOS 19-class ocean surveillance ships which are able to carry out their vital mission while operating in the winter in Sea State 7, conditions that severely limit or preclude operation of the monohull counterparts of T-AGOS ships. The SWATH ship concept has been adopted worldwide for a growing number of commercial applications. By the mid-1990s, about forty naval and commercial SWATH ships had been built worldwide.

HIGH-WATER SPEED TECHNOLOGY DEMONSTRATOR (HWSTD)

(Late 1980s onward)—Developed and demonstrated a concept for tracked amphibious landing vehicles with 25-plus-knot capability. Other participation included ONR, U.S. Marine Corps., AAI Inc., MTU, and Bird-Johnson. **IMPACT:** HWSTD technology permits operations in realistic environments from offshore to over-the-beach positions, without sacrificing desired overland capabilities. This results in greatly increased tactical flexibility and greatly reduced vulnerability of ships, troops, and equipment. HWSTD will become the advanced amphibious assault vehicle (AAAV) as it moves into its demonstration/validation (pre-production) phase. It is scheduled for initial operational capability (IOC) by the year 2008.

OPEN-OCEAN HYDROFOIL

(1960s onward)—Developed, demonstrated, and implemented technology permitting realization of an open ocean hydrofoil capability. Other participation included NAVSEA, Boeing, Lockheed, Aerojet, General Electric, and smaller companies and academic institutions. **IMPACT:** The first squadron of six patrol hydrofoil missile (PHM) hydrofoil ships provided a 40-plus-knot, all-weather capability for the Navy—a capability not achievable by standard monohulls more than twenty times their size. These ships clearly demonstrated the potential for hydrofoils of up to about 750 tons and opened up the application of the technology to commercial vessels, most notably high-speed ferries used in the U.S., Europe, and Asia.

SHIP SIGNATURE MEASUREMENT & SILENCING

LARGE-SCALE VEHICLE (LSV)

(Mid-1980s onward)—Developed concepts for a quarter-scale, self-propelled, autonomous model of *Seawolf* (SSN 21), along with its system support facility. It was designed, built, and operated for the purpose of ensuring the achievement of full-scale noise goals for the *Seawolf* class and later New SSN-class submarines. Other participation included NAVSEA, Naval Coastal Systems Center, UNISYS, Southwest Research Inc., Vitro, Applied Measurement Systems Corp., and Newport News Shipbuilding. **IMPACT:** Investment in the LSV test facility was a major risk reduction effort by the Navy to develop sufficient design data to ensure that *Seawolf* and future SSNs would meet more stringent goals for noise reduction. Attempting to achieve the same test program using full-scale submarines is estimated to have taken five times longer with an immense cost differential.

SIGNATURE MEASUREMENT TECHNIQUES & FACILITIES
(Mid-1940s onward)—Developed radiated noise and target strength measurement techniques and facilities for conducting signature measurements on surface ships and submarines. Other participation included ONR, NAVSEA, ARL/University of Texas, and other support contractors. **IMPACT:** The ability to acquire radiated noise signature information led to the identification of specific noise sources. Forty years of research and engineering development generated successive reductions in noise levels of sources, incrementally reducing signature levels of navy ships and submarines. This aggressive approach led to submarines with significant tactical advantages over their potential adversaries, and surface ASW ships that are highly effective in performing their missions.

QUIET BEARING TECHNOLOGY
Developed materials and design technology to permit manufacture of extremely quiet machinery bearings for ship and submarine machinery. Bearing design and material selection, lubricity additives, and surface finish requirements all impacted this quieting effort. Other participation included ONR, NAVSEA, and bearing and machinery equipment manufacturers. **IMPACT:** Waterborne noise signatures at slow shaft speeds were reduced significantly, thus contributing to the overall stealth of Navy ASW forces.

QUIETING TREATMENTS FOR SONAR DOMES
(1978 onward)—Conceived, designed, developed, and implemented quieting treatments for submarine bow sonar domes. Other participation included NAVSEA, Navy shipyards, HITCO Inc., and Goodyear. **IMPACT:** The quieting treatments developed for submarine sonar domes resulted in major improvements in high-speed sonar self-noise, thus permitting greatly increased tactical speeds for U.S. submarines. These improvements have been implemented on all classes of U.S. submarines including *Seawolf* and the New SSN submarines.

COMPOSITE SONAR BOW DOME
(Early 1980s onward)—Developed composite bow domes for submarine sonars. Other participation included NAVSEA, and Hitco Inc. **IMPACT:** The development and fleet deployment of glass-reinforced-plastic (GRP) sonar domes by Carderock in the early 1970s led to material and structural refinements. Significant RDT&E efforts by the center resulted in the introduction of composite bow domes in the mid-1980s that exhibited major acoustical improvements, reduced production costs, high impact resistance, ease of removal, and lower life cycle maintenance costs for operational submarines. It was so successful that the domes are now incorporated in all classes of U.S. submarines including *Seawolf* and New SSN.

REMOTELY SENSED SURFACE SHIP WAKE SIGNATURES
(Mid-1980s onward)—Developed ocean surveillance technology to understand and exploit methods for the remote detection and tracking of ships. Other participation

included ONR, NRL, MIT, Erim Inc., APL/Johns Hopkins, Arete Inc., TRW, and Lockheed. **IMPACT:** The first space experiment on measuring ship wakes documented the vast potential for all-weather remote-sensing and tracking of ships from space. A technology program successfully documented the causal phenomenology and provided an adequate technical foundation for the eventual use of this powerful ocean surveillance tool.

SHIP SILENCING BY AIR EMISSION SYSTEMS

(1950s onward)—Developed an air emission quieting system to significantly reduce surface ship radiated noise. Other participation included NAVSEA, ONR, and several industry and academia efforts. **IMPACT:** The innovative underwater noise masking system developed by Carderock called PRAIRIE and MASKER, resulted in enormous reductions in radiated noise. This greatly increased ASW effectiveness for all ships using these systems. These highly effective systems were applied to virtually all frigates, destroyers, and mine warfare ships after the late 1950s and early 1960s (well over 175 ships) and, to this day, provide the backbone of the surface ship quieting effort in the U.S. Navy.

SPECIAL HULL TREATMENTS & INSTALLATION PROCEDURES (Late 1960s onward)—Developed, demonstrated, and implemented submarine target strength reduction materials and a novel cast-in-place approach for installing them in the fleet. Other participation included NAVSEA, PMO 450, Tracor, Seaward Inc., Electric Boat Corp., and Newport News Shipbuilding. **IMPACT:** Carderock-developed special hull treatment materials are molded in place to eliminate many of the added costs and maintenance difficulties inherent in the use of conventional tiles. This molding process saves at least $6M per installation. The technology is used extensively—through SHIPALTS—on older SSN 637 and 688 submarines, and was incorporated in the SSN 21 class. It is also planned for the New SSN.

SSN 688 CLASS PROPELLER CAVITATION SUPPRESSION

(Late 1970s through mid-1980s)—Developed special bolt-on propeller blade tips that significantly increased cavitation inception speeds on operating submarines. Other participation included NAVSEA, Philadelphia Naval Shipyard, and several manufacturing companies. **IMPACT:** The high technology, low cost, specially designed bolt-on propeller blade tip greatly increased the tactical operating speed of the SSN 688-class submarine, without degrading the overall acoustic signature. The effective and inexpensive propeller blade tip was backfitted to forty two SSN 688-class submarines. By reducing instances of propeller changes and repairs, annual cost savings is estimated to be about $3.6M.

SUBMARINE COMMUNICATIONS BUOY HYDRODYNAMIC FIXES Developed and demonstrated alternate designs to improve performance of submarine communications buoys and their towing systems. Other participation included NAVSEA, ONR, NRL, Naval Undersea Systems Center, and Spears Associates Inc. **IMPACT:** The communications buoy design changes and towing system improvements permit more covert operation, higher towing speed , and longer life of buoy systems for a series of new classes of SSNs, and SSBNs.

SUBMARINE SILENCING

(Late 1940s onward)—Developed hull, mechanical and electrical quieting technologies for submarine silencing, and supported transitioning of these technologies to the U.S.

submarine fleet. Other participation included ONR, NAVSEA, NUWC, Portsmouth and Mare Island Naval Shipyards, and many industry and academia participants. **IMPACT:** Over forty years of successive silencing developments have kept U.S. submarines the quietest in the world. They have never been surpassed by another nation's submarines in underwater acoustic performance, thus sustaining our undersea warfare advantage for both our attack and ballistic missile submarines.

SURFACE SHIP ADVANCED QUIETING SYSTEM
(Mid-1980s onward)—Developed and conducted full-scale testing of an advanced quieting system for reducing the radiated noise of surface ships. Other participation included ONT and Pearl Harbor Naval Shipyard. **IMPACT:** The center developed and demonstrated an advanced surface ship quieting concept which reduced by an order of magnitude the detectable radiated noise, first on an ex-patrol craft and then on the FF 1077. The ex-patrol craft still deploys this concept; however, with the reduction in Navy ASW priorities, the advanced quieting system technology remains on-the-shelf in case of future Navy need.

SURFACE SHIP "TOWED SONAR" FIXES
(1960s to early 1990s)—Developed modifications to the tow line and towed bodies of the Navy's surface ship variable-depth (towed) sonars that eliminated towing instabilities. Other participation included NAVSEA, ONR, NUWC, and Edo Corp. **IMPACT:** The AN/SQS 10 and the follow-on AN/SQS 13 variable-depth towed sonars were a primary surface ship ASW system. Early on they were plagued with towing instability, self noise, and equipment reliability problems. The center developed modifications that alleviated most of these problems, thereby permitting these sonars to be more effective throughout their useful lives until they were replaced by towed line array systems.

LOW FREQUENCY VERTICAL LINE ARRAY (LFA) SYSTEM
(Early 1990s onward)—Developed LFA sonar array system fixes to eliminate hydrodynamic instabilities during development. The LFA system is a massive towed array consisting of up to 30 large transducer bodies that are towed from a single towing cable at low speeds. Other participation included the Space and Naval Warfare Command, NCOSC (formerly NOSC), Naval Civil Engineering Laboratory, APL/Johns Hopkins, SAIC, General Electric, Hydroacoustics, Inc. and Weston Corp. **IMPACT:** The hydrodynamic fixes developed by Carderock permitted operation within design specifications of this important ASW array system during critical sea tests, and eliminated a critical fault in the original design that impaired effective acoustic operation. The prototype design led to further development (and a name change) of the newer LTS system installed on T-AGOS 19-class ships.

OHIO CLASS SILENCING PROGRAM
(1986 onward)—Developed numerous quieting design modifications to *Ohio*-class hull and machinery systems. Other participation included NAVSEA, NRL, the submarine bases at Bangor, Washington, and Kings Bay, Georgia, and Electric Boat Corp. **IMPACT:** The SSBN 726 *Ohio*-class submarines are the most quiet in the world; in fact, they are an order-of-magnitude quieter than the previous nuclear submarine class. DTRC was a major contributor to that success with more than a dozen modifications made since 1986 that have reduced or eliminated machinery, hull, propeller, and other sources of noise from the ships' signatures. These accomplishments ensure that *Ohio*-class submarines are the most effective and least vulnerable of our strategic platforms.

HULL/PROPULSORS

NEW METHOD FOR SHIP WAVE CALCULATION

(Late 1960s onward)—Developed a revolutionary computational method for calculating the Kelvin wave system and its associated drag for a given ship form and speed. Other participation included ONR. **IMPACT:** The new computational method, called the Dawson Method after its developer, radically changed and improved the ability of hydrodynamicists to accurately and rapidly perform Kelvin wave system calculations for a ship. The method has emerged from peer-review as a revolutionary step in the ability to compute wave drag and Kelvin wave system characteristics. Recent extensions of the Dawson Method to the seakeeping problem are producing similar improvements to the calculation of ship motions and radiated wave fields for forward moving ships in waves.

ADVANCED POLYMER DRAG REDUCTION & QUIETING

(Early 1960s onward)—Developed new drag reducing polymers and injection distribution systems for increased submerged speed of submarines. Other participation included NRL, NCOSC, ONR, and ARL/Penn State. **IMPACT:** The new advanced polymers and injection system is projected to increase submarine submerged speed by 20%. Quieter operations at tactical speeds are also expected from its use. These developments were nearly complete when ASW priorities were revamped in the early 1990s curtailing a scheduled full-scale demonstration aboard an SSN 688-class submarine. The technology has now been documented and is available if ASW priorities change again.

DDG 51 HYDRODYNAMIC DESIGN

(Early 1980s onward)—Developed hydrodynamic hull-form technology to achieve improvements in seakeeping, powering, and acoustic performance of DDG 51-class ships. Other participation included NAVSEA, ONR, and Hydronautics Inc. **IMPACT:** The DDG 51 class has superior seakeeping, powering, propeller quieting, and acoustic performance due to the innovative efforts by Carderock in the area of hull form R&D. The hydrodynamic characteristics were thoroughly evaluated during the design and construction process, and have been extensively tested in sea trials and in the normal operations of the first ships of this new class of destroyers. This accomplishment is of major significance and is a direct result of years of investment in efficient hull form technology R&D and the ability to measurably influence the design of a monohull combatant in early design stages.

CONTROLLABLE-PITCH PROPELLER DESIGNS

(Mid-1970s)—Conducted timely and comprehensive model and full-scale experiments and analyses that identified the cause of premature failure of controllable reversible pitch (CRP) propeller blades on Navy ships. Other participation included ONR and NAVSEA. **IMPACT:** The prototype propeller blade failure on *Barbey* would have caused a massive setback in fleet readiness, but it was avoided by timely and thorough analysis and redesign of serious structural inadequacies in these propeller systems. At the time of the failure in the mid-1970s, the design was scheduled to be installed on all *Spruance-* class destroyers, the entire *Perry*-class of frigates, and later, *Ticonderoga* and *Burke* classes: over 100 gas-turbine-powered ships. The potential negative budget impact was in the order of tens of billions of dollars.

HIGH-PERFORMANCE PROPELLER FOR 170-FOOT PCs

Developed and tested a more efficient propeller design to achieve improved acoustic and propulsive performance. Other participation included NAVSEA, Bird-Johnson Inc., and Bollinger Shipyards. **IMPACT:** The Carderock-designed, high-performance propeller for the Navy's high-speed, 170-foot PC-class ship is more efficient than its predecessor. It is also quieter, thus relieving a serious noise problem in the crew's quarters. Reductions in cavitation erosion also results in lower maintenance costs.

HIGH-SPEED SUBMARINE HULL FORM DEVELOPMENT

(Late 1940s onward)—Pioneered development of a new set of submarine hull forms that enabled high submerged-speed operation at speeds far in excess of those obtainable with more traditional World War II submarines and their predecessors. Other participation included NAVSEA and ONR. **IMPACT:** The development of Series 58 hull forms in the late 1940s and early 1950s proved to be a revolutionary development. *Albacore,* the first submarine prototype of this design, reached submerged speeds well in excess of 30 knots. When combined with the parallel development of nuclear power, then being tested in *Nautilus,* true submarines with high-speed capabilities became a realistic alternative to the submersible surface ships in use at that time. *Skipjack* (SSN 585) was the first of a new class of this design. These revolutionary developments rewrote the book on submarine warfare and was emulated worldwide by friend and foe alike.

HIGHLY SKEWED PROPELLER DEVELOPMENT

(Late 1950s)—Developed a highly skewed propeller design that greatly reduced levels of fluid-borne vibration excitation on ships and submarines. Other participation included MARAD, NAVSEA, National Steel Shipyard, Ferguson Propellers Inc., and numerous small R&D firms and academic institutions. **IMPACT:** The highly skewed propeller, first introduced in the early 1970s, made possible previously unachievable low levels of fluid-borne vibration excitation and noise on naval and merchant ships. The technology brought about significant reductions in structural, machinery, and shafting vibrations with the concomitant major effects on reduced detection, maintenance costs and greatly increased habitability. The first naval application in the U.S. came with the FFG 7-class ships in the mid-1970s. Highly skewed propellers are now widely applied to thousands of naval and merchant ships of all types worldwide.

REDUCED ENERGY CONSUMPTION FOR NAVAL SHIPS

Developed and implemented numerous significant innovations in the fleet to reduce energy consumption and operating costs. Other participation included ONR, NAVSEA, and numerous industry contractors and manufacturers. **IMPACT:** The energy conservation innovations have resulted in savings of tens-of-millions of dollars each year in reduced fuel consumption by U.S. Navy ships. Most of these innovations, once implemented, continue to save the Navy both in the form of lower fuel expenditures and in other ways, such as maintenance, for the life of the ships involved.

RUDDER ROLL STABILIZATION (RRS) FOR SHIPS

(Mid-1970s onward)—Developed effective, low-cost ship roll stabilization by modifications to ships' own rudder (steering) systems. Other participation included USCG, ONR, NAVSEA, Jered/Brown Brothers, Advanced Peripherals Inc., and Sperry Marine. **IMPACT:** Reductions of 20% to 50% in the roll motions of destroyer and frigate size ships operating in a Sea State 5 can now be achieved utilizing RRS with minor modifications to existing steering equipment while using the same rudders. This effective, inexpensive, is being installed on the ships of the DDG 51 class. The use of RRS results in substantial increases in all-weather operability, particularly while launching and recovering helicopters, and in many other important operations such as the loading of weapon systems. Commercial applications are also expected.

SSBN HOVERING SYSTEM DEVELOPMENT

(Early 1960s onward)—Developed basic technology that defined the magnitude, as a function of time, of wave forces acting on a submarines operating near the surface. Other participation included NAVSEA and ONR. **IMPACT:** The center effort provided the basis for eliminating the highly undesirable broaching effect of waves acting on a submarine when operating near the surface at slow speeds. The unexpected broaching effect on the earliest SSBNs might have seriously influenced the success of the Navy's strategic missile defense system.

SSN 21 PROPULSOR DESIGN & MANUFACTURE

(Mid-1980s onward)—Developed and demonstrated concepts that met stringent noise and performance goals and performed manufacturing oversight for the *Seawolf* (SSN 21) propulsor. Other participation included NAVSEA, Oak Ridge National Laboratory, Martin-Marietta, and APL/Penn State. **IMPACT:** The delivery of the SSN 21 propulsor system to Electric Boat one month ahead of schedule was primarily the result of the efforts of the center. From the outset, the propulsor design was driven by very stringent noise goals. These goals led to a plan to analyze and experiment with an extended series of concepts. Each concept was experimentally evaluated, many at various scales, until a final configuration could be selected. Specifications were then developed and a special manufacturing arrangement was made with ORNL. Carderock acted as the Navy single-point-of-contact to assure on-schedule completion of the propulsor. The timely delivery of the SSN 21 propulsor avoided a chain reaction of other expensive construction delays.

SSN 21 SHIP CONTROL DEVELOPMENT

(Mid-1980s onward)—Developed and evaluated state-of-the-art automatic maneuvering and control algorithms for SSN 21. Other participation included NAVSEA, Naval Training System Center, and Electric Boat. **IMPACT:** The control system algorithms provide the SSN 21 class with state-of-the-art, safe, automatic maneuvering capability in the open ocean and during under-ice operations. This was arrived at after an extensive period of development where hull form and control system design trade-offs were evaluated analytically and experimentally in terms of safety and operability. The resulting control system was used by the lead design and construction shipyard and will be used in *Seawolf*-class training for operators.

SUBMARINE TOWING TECHNOLOGY

(Mid-1970s onward)—Developed technology to permit stable and safe towing of submarines in the open ocean. Other participation included NAVSEA and ONR. **IMPACT:** The experimental and analytical towing technology that was developed prevents unstable and frequently dangerous yawing or kiting excursions when a submarine is being towed on the surface in the open ocean. This permits submarines of different classes and configurations to be safely and expeditiously towed over substantial distances whether they are being moved between storage sites, to shipyard facilities, or being salvaged at sea.

SUB-SAFE DEVELOPMENTS

(Early 1960s onward)—Developed stability and control, structures and materials, and flooding technologies to increase the operational safety of submarines. Other participation included NAVSEA, Mare Island and Portsmouth Naval Shipyards, Electric Boat Division and Newport News Shipbuilding, and Branson Instruments. **IMPACT:** The *Thresher* disaster in the early 1960s fostered the SUB-SAFE program. The loss of *Scorpion* a few years later re-emphasized the need for the program. The center developed and tested various means to ensure stability and control for all submarines. Safe operating envelopes were clearly defined. Structural and material changes were made in areas where increased margins of safety were judged to be desirable, such as seawater piping systems and other hull structural details. These developments resulted in an unprecedented record of submarine safety for the fleet in the ensuing period of more than thirty years.

SURFACE SHIP HULL FORM CHARACTERIZATION
(1906 onward)—Pioneered and developed the experimental and analytical bases for ship hull form designs called the Taylor Standard Series, that have been applied for nearly 100 years to naval combatants, auxiliaries, and merchant ships. Other participation included Maritime Administration, ONR, NAVSEA, and Society of Naval Architects and Marine Engineers. **IMPACT:** One of the primary outgrowths of the establishment of the Experimental Model Basin manifested itself in the creation of several ship model series. The data were widely disseminated and became the basis for thousands of ship designs worldwide for nearly 100 years. The series helped the designer assure optimal performance for a given set of payload/cargo capacity, and operating characteristics. The original Taylor Standard Series covers 221 models and is still in use today as a benchmark for modern designs. Other series of particular note are: Series 60, developed in the late 1950s and early 1960s, covering the range of new, moderately high speed container ships and tankers as well as numerous naval auxiliary designs. Series 62, 64, and 65 cover a wide range of high-speed boat hull forms ranging from the PG 84 gunboat to Navy hydrofoil ships. They are used worldwide for military, commercial, and pleasure craft designs.

STRUCTURES AND MATERIALS

22-MEGAWATT GENERATOR ROTOR DESIGN REVIEW
Conducted independent design review that identified serious safety deficiencies associated with a preproduction design of a 22-megawatt generator for the Navy integrated propulsion system (electric drive) program. Other participation included NAVSEA and Kaman Electric. **IMPACT:** The center design review of a proposed 22-megawatt generator, an integral part of the Navy integrated propulsion system program, found serious design flaws that could well have resulted in catastrophic failure under the specified operating conditions. The results were reported to the sponsor and a redesign of the entire generator was carried out in order to meet safety concerns.

VERTICAL LAUNCH SYSTEM SUPPORT STRUCTURE REDESIGN
(Late 1980s onward)—Developed structural design modifications that eliminated structural failures related to vertical launch system (VLS) installation in the original design of *Ticonderoga*-class guided missile cruisers, CG 52 through 73. Other participation included NAVSEA, NRL/Bay St. Louis, Wright Patterson A.F. Base, Bath Iron Works, Casde Corp., George Washington University, and Vector Corp. **IMPACT:** Serious structural failures that limited the operational capabilities of the CG 52 and follow-on ships fitted with the VLS were eliminated as a result of an intensive program of analyses, model experiments,

and full-scale trials. Modifications recommended by the center assured the full scope of *Ticonderoga*-class operations to be conducted during a hull structure fatigue-life for a period in excess of twenty years.

COATINGS FOR CORROSION CONTROL

Developed and tested new corrosion control coatings for shipboard use. Other participation included NAVSEA, ONR, NRL, the major naval shipyards, Sherwin Williams Paint Company, Devoe Marine, and Lehigh University. **IMPACT:** New coatings for corrosion control reduce maintenance costs for Navy ships and submarines by tens-of-millions of dollars each year by reducing maintenance work and by eliminating or greatly delaying the need for expensive drydockings. The reductions in maintenance also enable the ships to have more time for training and operational availability.

HIGH-STRENGTH STEELS FOR NAVAL SHIP CONSTRUCTION

Developed and supported certification of high-yield strength, high-toughness steels for structural applications in naval ships. Other participation included NRL, the naval shipyards, Newport News Shipbuilding, Electric Boat Corp., United States Steel Division of USX, Lukens Steel Co., Lincoln Electric Co., Hobart Bros. Corp., and L-TEC/Alloy Rods Division of ESAB Corp. **IMPACT:** Development and certification of high yield strength steels such as HY-100 and HY-130, and of compatible welding systems, has resulted in significant increases in submarine operating depth, survivability, and stealth in the SSN 21 class. Successful development of HY steel systems made possible a reduction in costs and weight for pressure-hull and non-pressure-hull structures. This has also led to ship protection systems and structural weight reduction in the construction of the CVN 71-class carriers.

HIGH-STRENGTH LOW-ALLOY STEEL

Developed and supported certification of weldable high-strength low-alloy (HSLA) 80 and 100 steels for reduced costs of ship construction. Other participation included NIST, Mare Island Naval Shipyard, NAVSEA, ONR, Amax Corp., Phoenix Steel Corp., Lukens Steel Co., Colorado School of Mines, Ingalls Shipbuilding, and Bath Iron Works. **IMPACT:** Major increases in shipbuilding productivity and reductions in cost were made possible by the development and certification of HSLA-80 and -100 steels for ship and submarine construction. This major development reduced the cost of plate acquisition and permitted large increases in welding productivity by eliminating the costly process of weld preheating. By the early 1990s, substitution of HSLA-80 steel had already saved the Navy $84M in the construction of the CG 47 class, DDG 51 class, CVN 71 class, and LHD 1 class. As its use increases, the savings are anticipated to grow to $50M per year. HSLA-100 is being used for flight deck, island, and ballistic protection structures on the CVN 75-class carriers, with savings on the order of $50M per ship. In 1995 HSLA-100 was certified for submarine non-pressure-hull structures, and is expected to be utilized in the New SSN.

IMPROVED SUBMARINE STRUCTURAL DESIGNS

(1940s onward)—Pioneered, developed and validated procedures enabling more efficient and cost-effective design and construction of submarine structures. Other participation included ONR; NAVSEA; the fleet; Portsmouth, Norfolk, and Mare Island Naval Shipyards; NASA; Lockheed; Electric Boat Corp.; Newport News Shipbuilding; Excelco Corp.; Southwest Research Institute; and Stanford University. **IMPACT:** Forty years of sustained investment in submarine structural technology development has led to large weight savings, major cost savings, and increased survivability, without sacrificing either the safety or the structural integrity of each new submarines class. A few of the improved designs contributing to the continued excellence of the U.S. submarine safety record are: basic design procedures for HY-100 and HY-130 steel structures, reactor, and engine room hull design methods; end-closure design methods; structural response to underwater explosions; and recent results that support under-matched frame weld techniques for cost reduction in SSN 21-class submarines.

LOW YIELD-STRENGTH WELDS
(Late 1960s onward)—Developed and implemented a cost-effective technique for utilizing weld metal with a strength less than the plate metal. Other participation included ONR, NAVSEA, Mare Island Naval Shipyard, Electric Boat Corp., Newport News Shipbuilding, and The Center for Excellence in Metal Working Technology. **IMPACT:** The concept of utilizing welds with a material strength less than that of the plate metal was developed as a safe and cost-effective way to deal with submarine construction that uses high-strength steels such as HY-100 and HY-130. Important advantages of under-matched welds are the wide range of flexibility available to the welder when utilizing HY-80 weld materials, and the avoidance of costly time consuming postweld treatments that are necessary when using higher strength materials. The concept was initially employed on some SSN 21 tee joints. Utilization of under-matching welds on NSSN will be much more extensive, pending completion of an exhaustive development and testing program.

PROGRAMMABLE AUTOMATED WELD SYSTEM (PAWS)
(Mid-1980s onward)—Developed automated welding technologies for reduced ship construction costs. Other participation included OPNAV, ONR, NAVSEA, NIST, Idaho National Laboratories, McDermott Shipbuilding, Adept Technologies, Babcock and Wilcox, Carnegie Mellon University, and Newport News Shipbuilding. **IMPACT:** Implementation of the PAWS in U.S. shipyards in 1997 will represent a major milestone in the application of advanced technology for reduced construction costs and improved quality of shipyard welding processes for both naval and commercial ship construction. PAWS cost savings will accrue for years to come and it also will make a major contribution to make our commercial shipyards competitive worldwide.

RESOLUTION OF SSN 21 HY-100 WELD CRACKING
(1990–1991)—Participated in a Navy team that responded to the discovery during construction of weld cracking in the hull of SSN 21. Other participation included PMS 350, NAVSEA, Electric Boat Corp., Newport News Shipbuilding, and materials experts from industry and academia. **IMPACT:** New welding materials and procedures that preclude the development of weld cracking due to this form of hydrogen-induced cracking were expediently developed, and construction of *Seawolf* resumed with minimum disruption to its schedule.

SPRAY METAL FORMING DEVELOPMENTS
(Late 1980s onward)—Optimized spray metal (nonreactive) forming technology for manufacturing (high purity) affordable, near-net shaped metallic products for Navy and industry usage. Other participation included NAVSEA, ONR, MTS Systems. **IMPACT:** Navy intended usage of spray metal forming technology includes special submarine piping applications, and precision shaft sleeves and seals. For industry, metal matrix com-

posites, super-plastic-forming tooling dies, automotive tooling dies, and super-alloy piping are examples of special products that have been produced.

TITANIUM FOR SHIPS AND SUBMERSIBLES

(1960s onward)—Developed the titanium alloy, metal processing, welding, and fabrication technologies leading to the construction of titanium alloy pressure hulls for two deep submergence vehicles (DSVs). Also developed the technology for the application of titanium to pumps, piping systems, condensers, and heat exchangers in numerous ships and submarines. Other participation included NRL, naval shipyards, RMI Corp., Timet Corp., Excelco Development Corp., and CBI Corp. **IMPACT:** A significant R&D effort in the area of titanium, to re-fitting hulls for DSVs *Alvin* and *Sea Cliff* in the 1960s and 1970s. The operating depth of *Alvin* doubled and that of *Sea Cliff* more than tripled. In addition, the development program in the 1980s made possible the use of lighter weight, corrosion immune (and safer) machinery system components for SSN 21 and selected surface combatants.

MACHINERY COMPONENTS

LSD 41 AUXILIARY BOILER CONTROL SYSTEM

(Early 1990s onward)—Developed and implemented a replacement auxiliary boiler control system that greatly improved operations and safety. Other participation included NAVSEA, SUPSHIP organizations, and a number of contractors working for shipyards. **IMPACT:** LSD 41-class amphibious ships were experiencing a chronic series of problems with their auxiliary boiler control systems. The center developed a replacement system that greatly reduces previously experienced difficulties, and provides a safer and more effective operation of this important ship subsystem for the LSD 41 and other ships of the class.

SARATOGA (CV 60) BOILER FAILURE

(1983)—Conducted analysis of voyage-interrupting boiler failures on newly overhauled *Saratoga* and developed repair methods. Other participation included NAVSEA, Charleston and Philadelphia Naval Shipyards, and University of Tennessee. **IMPACT:** Immediately after completing an extended shipyard overhaul in 1983, and on its way to operational development, *Saratoga* suffered a severe loss of steam through the superheater section of the main boilers. Ship operations were curtailed and the ship put into Mayport, Florida. Due to timely expert on-site inspections and repairs, and subsequent analyses by the center, *Saratoga* made a rapid return to service, and an estimated $1.5M additional cost for extensive boiler repairs was avoided.

INTEGRATED POWER SYSTEMS (IPS)

Developed technology, ship design concepts, and impact analyses utilizing integrated electric drive, propulsion-derived ship service systems, advanced machinery control systems, and efficient propulsion gas turbines. Other participation included NAVSEA, ONR, Naval Postgraduate School, General Electric, Lockheed-Martin, Cegelec Inc., Newport News Shipbuilding, Kaman Electromagnetics, CAE-LINK, Propulsion Dynamics, Gibbs & Cox, and Westinghouse. **IMPACT:** Integrated power system technology can provide large improvements in ship payload, range, operating costs, affordability, and signature reduction by enabling new ship design arrangements. An early use of IPS technology was its application in the installation of an AC Zonal Electric system on a

DDG 51 Flight II ship. This application alone will save between $1M and $2M. Other examples of IPS technology are the ICR engine that is scheduled for large-scale land-based testing in 1998, the Standard Monitoring and Control System (SMCS) presently in the testing stage, and a large-scale, fully integrated motor generator for propulsion and ship service power currently being developed under NAVSEA contract.

REVERSE OSMOSIS DESALINATION SYSTEMS
(Mid-1970s onward)—Developed Reverse Osmosis (RO) desalination systems for Navy ships. Other participation included ONR, NAVSEA, Navy Bureau of Medicine, LaQue Center for Corrosion Technology Inc., Westinghouse, Village Marine Technology, Recovery Engineering, Inc., Electric Boat Corp., Separation Systems Technology Inc., Argo Scientific, Chemistry Department UNC/Wilmington, Industrial Maintenance Corp., and Oxford Laboratories Inc. **IMPACT:** Developed an improved alternative technology to meet the unique freshwater requirements of the Navy shipboard environment. RO systems significantly reduce the weight, volume, cost, and manpower requirements of desalinating seawater when compared to distillation systems. Single pass RO plants were successfully developed and used for potable water needs aboard Navy ships, including destroyers, hydrofoils, landing craft carriers, and life rafts. Multiple-pass plants are now being placed on Navy ships for meeting more stringent water requirements for boiler makeup, electronic cooling, and gas turbine washdown needs.

SUPERCONDUCTING ELECTRIC MACHINERY
(Late 1960s onward)—Developed and demonstrated technology for superconducting electric machinery and technology through 3000-horsepower sizes. Other participation included ONR; NAVSEA; NRL; NSWC/White Oak; NIST; Creare Corp.; A.D. Little; Air Products Inc.; Universities of Virginia, Illinois, and Texas; Westinghouse Science and Technology Center; Intrascience Corp.; General Electric; AiResearch Manufacturing Co.; and Westinghouse. **IMPACT:** In addition to the scientific achievement, the successful development and verification of superconducting electric machinery through 10-, 400-, and 3000-horsepower sizes provides the foundation for its future use on ships. The primary advantages derived from superconducting electric power are large reductions in machinery spaces, greatly increased design and arrangement flexibility, greater range or increased payload. Increased savings are possible because smaller ships could be used to carry out required tasks.

CVN 65 MAIN FEEDWATER PIPING REPAIR DEFERRAL
Sophisticated fracture analysis techniques applied to a main feedwater piping cracking problem on *Enterprise* (CVAN 65) allowed deferral of untimely and expensive repairs. Other participation included ONR, NRC, NAVSEA, Westinghouse, and Battelle. **IMPACT:** Prior to its last deployment preceding a scheduled overhaul, cracking was discovered in the main feedwater piping system on the CVAN 65. Immediate repair would have delayed ship deployment and cost $1.2M. The welds were non-destructively inspected and flaw sizes measured. Ductile fracture mechanics analyses were used to determine that the flaws would not lead to catastrophic failure prior to scheduled overhaul. Based on this analyses, CVAN 65 was able to maintain its schedule and complete deployment.

PROTECTION, WEAPONS EFFECTS, & DAMAGE CONTROL

SURFACE SHIP PROTECTION
(1960s onward)—Conducted analyses and experiments which resulted in the development of technologies to increase the protection of ships and their vital systems when

under attack. Other participation included ONR, NAVSEA, Aberdeen Proving Grounds, Atlantic Fleet Weapons Training Facility/Roosevelt Roads, PR, Naval Air Warfare Center/ Patuxent River, Hi-Test Inc., DTI Inc., T. Carrol Associates, and PMC Inc. **IMPACT:** The damage that occurred to *Stark, Samuel B. Roberts,* and *Princeton* during the Gulf War clearly demonstrated the need to improve the resistance of ship hulls to weapons damage. The application of technology developed from three decades of experience with model and full-scale size experiments, in addition to comprehensive computer-based analyses, resulted in ship design changes to reduce potential damage. It also brought about the installation of armor concepts to protect vital areas of ships from damage by weapons. These were applied most recently to the DDG 51 Flight II and LPD 17-class ships.

AIRCRAFT CARRIER MAGAZINE PROTECTION SYSTEM
Developed an aircraft carrier magazine protection system after years of research, scale-model testing, and design. Other participation included NAVSEA, ONR, Aberdeen Proving Grounds, Holloman A.F. Base, NSWC/White Oak and Chesapeake, Newport News Shipbuilding. **IMPACT:** *Theodore Roosevelt* (CVN 71), is the first of the class to have installed the center-developed carrier magazine protection system. The system represents an improvement of major significance in terms of protection to the large magazine areas on a carrier, and manifests the culmination of years of analytical and experimental R&D. All other ships of this class have this system.

VULNERABILITY MODELING & ANALYSIS METHODS
(1960s onward)—Developed computer models for assessing the damage to ships and submarines from a wide range of weapons. Other participation included DOD Joint Coordinating Group for Munitions Effectiveness. **IMPACT:** The ship vulnerability model (SVM) and the submarine vulnerability model (SUBVEM) are used continually within the Navy for evaluation of ship and submarine design options and weapons effectiveness evaluations. SVM has influenced ship designs such as DDG 51, LPD 17, CVN 76, and others in the areas of blast-hardened bulkheads, blast-resistant doors, armor concepts, redundancy evaluations, and equipment separation factors. SVM has been used in the development of new warhead designs for Tomahawk and Penguin missiles. SUBVEM has been used in support of development of the Mk 46 and Mk 50 lightweight torpedoes and the Mk 48 ADCAP heavyweight torpedo. SUBVEM was also a major player in support of the congressionally mandated Livefire program.

SHOCK RESISTANCE OF SURFACE SHIPS & SUBMARINES (Early 1940s onward)—
Developed, applied, and verified technology that enables ships and submarines to resist shock levels encountered under wartime conditions. Other participation included NAVSEA, ONR, Aberdeen Proving Grounds, EPA, NSWC/Indian Head, NUWC/Newport, NRL, Electric Boat Corp., Wiedlinger Associates, Lockheed/Palo Alto, NKF, Northwestern University, University of Colorado, Boston University, Georgia Tech., Hi-Test Inc., and DTI Inc. **IMPACT:** Shock resistance of Navy ships is part of the design process from the outset of an acquisition program. The success of the application of these design methods is validated by extensive and comprehensive shock testing of mission-critical components, and shock trials for each new class of ships. *Whidbey Island* (LSD 41), *Mobile Bay* (CG 53), *Theodore Roosevelt* (CVN 71), *Jacksonville* (SSN 699), and *John Paul Jones* (DDG 53) have undergone successful full-scale shock trials. Comprehensive analyses of the Navy UNDEX shock database have supported development of advanced shock testing methods and criteria, development of advanced shock

hardening requirements for new ship acquisition programs, and verification and validation of advanced computational techniques for LFT&E program applications.

MHC 51-CLASS MINESWEEPERS SHOCK RESISTANCE
Conducted a massive computational effort to rapidly assess the shock resistance of the MHC 51 prior to construction. Other participation included NAVSEA, Casde Corp., Designers and Planners, JJMA Inc., and Weidlinger Associates. **IMPACT:** Because the shock resistance calculations were carried out in a timely manner, the Navy, in negotiations with the prospective shipbuilder, advised that significant design changes were required before construction could begin. The design changes were necessary to enable this new class of glass-reinforced-plastic minesweepers to meet the shock levels prescribed in the Navy top-level requirements, thereby avoiding the potential of expensive refits.

SUBMARINE PROTECTION
(Mid-1960s onward)—Increased the survivability of submarines through analytical and experimental programs to increase the shock hardness of submarine structures and systems. Other participation included ONR, Defense Nuclear Agency, NAVSEA, Aberdeen Proving Grounds, NSWC/Indian Head, Lawrence Livermore National Laboratory, Sandia and Los Alamos National Laboratories, DTI, Hi-Test, Electric Boat Corp., Wiedlinger Associates, Lockheed/Palo Alto, NKF, Northwestern University, University of Colorado, Boston University, and Georgia Tech. **IMPACT:** Experimental evaluations incorporating various size structural models and full-scale trials, in addition to comprehensive computer based analyses, resulted in major submarine design changes that reduce potential damage and increase the survivability when subjected to underwater explosions. Many of the recommendations resulting from this work are incorporated in the-submarine designs of the *Los Angeles, Ohio,* and *Seawolf* classes. They are also being adopted in the New SSN design.

EXERCISE TORPEDO IMPACT SAFETY ON SUBMARINES
Developed and conducted an analytical and full-scale experimental project with full-scale inert torpedoes operating at full speed to determine impact loading and responses on various areas of an SSN 688 submarine structure. Other participation included NAVSEA, the Fleet, Naval Weapons Station/Keyport, NUSC/Newport, NSWC/White Oak, NKF Engineering, and M&T Inc. **IMPACT:** The exercise torpedo impact safety program proved that operational submarines can participate in full-scale exercises with inert torpedoes, provided certain constraints are observed, thus facilitating important war-like at-sea training. The project also saved the Navy at least $130M by clearly demonstrating that planned modifications to the submarines were not required.

ANTISHIP AND ANTISUBMARINE WEAPON EFFECTIVENESS
Developed a capability to perform weapon effectiveness evaluations and applied them to operational and developmental weapons against threat targets. Other participation included NSWC Indian Head, NUWC Newport, NSWCDD Panama City, the U.S. Army Aberdeen, T. Carroll Associates, Hi-Test Inc., and DTI Inc. **IMPACT:** These studies influenced the design, construction, and deployment of many major weapon systems employed by the Navy today. Weapon effectiveness assessments resulted in modification of warhead designs to enhance damage effectiveness and influence development of guidance systems that allow optimum weapon placement for maximum damage. Data from antiship weapon effectiveness assessments were used to set acquisition and tactical air mission requirements, and were incorporated in basic warfare guides. Warhead effective-

ness assessments made by the SUBVEM supported Live Fire analytical efforts and played a major role in the development and approval of both the heavyweight Mk 48 ADCAP and lightweight Mk 50 torpedoes allowing them to go into production.

NUCLEAR WEAPONS EFFECTS DESIGN CRITERIA

(Mid-1940s through early 1960s)—Developed ship and submarine design and operational criteria for use in nuclear warfare. Other participation included ONR, NAVSEA, Long Beach Naval Shipyard, and EG&G. **IMPACT:** From the mid-1940s through the early 1960s, a number of full-scale nuclear burst tests were conducted in the Pacific. They successfully established a range of vulnerability and protection criteria for Navy ships and submarines in the postwar era. They also permitted development of operational procedures for naval nuclear warfare, including operational safe delivery ranges.

SAILOR HAT AIRBLAST EXPERIMENT

(Mid-1960s)—Enabled the verification of air-burst blast effects on surface ships through a series of tests, using massive amounts of conventional explosives. Other participation included ONR, NAVSEA, Defense Nuclear Agency, Long Beach Naval Shipyard. **IMPACT:** The Sailor Hat experiments conducted in the mid-1960s provided the solution to a surface ship protection design gap regarding verification of existing design methods for airblast effects of nuclear explosions. Five hundred tons of TNT were detonated on Kahoolawe island with the fully instrumented and specially configured Navy reserve cruiser *Atlanta* moored nearby. Other operational and support ships were stationed significantly further away to collect supporting data. Developed criteria are still in use some thirty years later for surface ship designs.

INTEGRATED SURVIVABILITY MANAGEMENT SYSTEM

Developed, tested, and implemented a new system for collecting, recording, displaying, and transmitting information between damage control central, repair lockers, the bridge, and CIC on board ships—a segment of the overall system that is called the integrated survivability management system (ISMS). Other participation included ONR, NAVSEA, PMS400, Johnson Space Flight Center, NSWC/Indian Head and Louisville, Hughes Data Systems, PDI Inc., and other software development contractors. **IMPACT:** The new system was developed to accelerate the shipboard damage control process, minimize the spread of damage, ensure the safety of the ship and personnel, maximize the remaining mission capability, and provide important damage control training. It accomplishes this by merging traditional safety and survivability efforts with improved survivable communications, computer readout support throughout the ship, and computer-aided damage control prediction.

FIRE PROTECTIVE INSULATION

Developed new shipboard fire zone bulkhead insulation designs to improve fire containment on board Navy ships. Other participation included NRL, BB&N, Southwest Research Institute, Omega Laboratories, and Hughes Associates. **IMPACT:** The development of fire zone bulkhead insulation increases the ability of a ship to resist fire spread across principal watertight boundaries by a factor of two to ten. This provides time for firefighters to contain, attack, and extinguish major shipboard fires before they can spread. The center has been a partner with industry and other government organizations to enhance shipboard safety against fires on naval and commercial vessels.

FIRE RESISTANT ELECTRICAL CABLES

(1970s onward)—Conducted fire tests and developed performance characteristics and specifications for fire resistant shipboard electrical cables used in current Navy ships. Other participation included NAVSEA, NRL, Raychem Corp., Brand-Rex Cable Company, Monroe Cable Company, American Cable Company, and Delta Supernaunt Cable Company. **IMPACT:** Fire resistant electrical cables reduce the spread of fire and smoke. They also result in the near elimination of noxious and corrosive elements in the smoke caused by burning electrical cables.

COMPOSITES FLAMMABILITY AND MIL STANDARD-2031

Developed fire and toxicity test methods and qualification procedure for composite material systems used in hull, machinery, and structural applications inside Navy submarines. Other participation included NAVSEA, NRL, ONR, and Hughes Associates. **IMPACT:** The development of MIL-STD-2031 and the fire requirements and methods contained therein provided the impetus for screening and qualification of commercially available composite materials for both submarines and surface ships. It has resulted in an extensive Navy database on the fire properties of available composite systems and fire barrier technology. This has resulted in the timely transition of the design requirement for the use of composites for surface ship topside structures, e.g., *Arthur W. Radford* (DD 968) advanced enclosed mast/sensor system.

FINE-WATER-MIST FIRE PROTECTION

(Late 1970s onward)—Developed and demonstrated technology for using fixed system, fine-water-mist fire protection in ship compartments as an alternative to halon-based systems. Other participation included ONR, NAVSEA, NRL, and NKF Engineering. **IMPACT:** Fine-water-mist systems, developed in the late 1970s and early 1980s are effective because of the tremendous heat absorbing surface area of the mist particles, the mist tends to precipitate heavy smoke particles rapidly, and they use relatively small amounts of water when compared to conventional fire hose systems. When tested, using the latest in nozzle design, the concept proved successful; within seconds fires could be extinguished, and within a few minutes a compartment could be cooled enough to prevent a reflash of the fire. With the current need for an alternative to Halon firefighting systems, which are in the process of replacement, the fine-water-mist system is getting worldwide attention.

ENVIRONMENTAL QUALITY

CFC ALTERNATIVE FOR NAVY MACHINERY

(Late 1980s onward)—Conducted extensive land-based and at-sea tests of large air conditioning and refrigeration plants to establish HCR-134a as the candidate non-ozone depleting compound for Navy machinery. Other participation included NAVSEA, NRL, NIST, EPA, Navy Environmental Health Organization, Carrier Corp., York International, Castrol, and Dupont. **IMPACT:** International agreements banning the production of ozone-depleting substances such as CFCs (chlorofluorocarbons) by the year 2000, necessitated Navy compliance for many shipboard and land-based kinds of machinery. As a result of a center development, test, and evaluation program, a new non-ozone-depleting compound called HFC-134a was selected. It has been successfully tested in the laboratory and in full-scale machinery at sea on board Navy ships. Necessary equipment and lubricant modifications have been made and work continues in applying this basic technology to types of existing CFC machinery until all ships and land-based facilities are brought into compliance with the international law.

ELECTROLYTIC DISINFECTANT GENERATOR (EDG)

Developed a shipboard potable water electrolytic disinfectant generator (EDG). Other participation included NAVSEA, Norfolk Naval Shipyard, Eltech Research Corp., and Eltech International Corp. **IMPACT:** Electrolytic disinfectant generators improve potable water disinfection effectiveness, reduce cost, eliminate use of a hazardous waste source, and improve safety aboard ship. Laboratory evaluations of the generator demonstrated readiness for shipboard evaluation on CVN 71 in 1996. Plans call for the installation of EDG units in all aircraft carriers and in new surface ships starting with CVN 76 and LPD 17.

INNOVATIVE USES OF PROCESSED PLASTIC WASTE

Completed utilization of processed plastic waste as a core material for manufacturing composite marine pilings. Other participation included Strategic Environmental Research and Development Program, Norfolk Naval Station, Seaward International, Recycling Research and Technology, Plastics Forming Enterprises, Cumberland Engineering Division, East Coast Recycling Inc., and Lehigh University. **IMPACT:** Plastic disks that are a product of the Navy plastic waste processor program were turned into a functional product with economic benefit. Long-life composite marine pilings were produced using an estimated four million pounds of disk material per year and other recycled plastics from ships of the fleet. These pilings are safer for the environment when compared to commonly used treated wood pilings. Estimated yearly cost avoidance amounts to over $0.8M.

OILY WASTE ULTRA-FILTRATION SYSTEM

(1980s onward)—Developed ultra-filtration technology to reduce oil-water separator discharge levels to meet more stringent oily-waste compliance levels. Other participation included NAVSEA, NAVFAC, Naval Weapon Station/Earle, *L. Y. Spear* (AS 36), *Carney* (DDG 64), NRL, Advanced Marine Enterprises Inc., Westinghouse Machinery Technology Division, Mantech Corp., Separation Systems Inc., and Geo Centers Inc. **IMPACT:** Navy facilities located in port areas can now meet stringent oil-waste-discharge standards as a result of the development of a practical, effective, and highly efficient membrane technology when used in conjunction with appropriate oil-water separators. The prototype ultra-filtration system successfully meets local pollution standards by concentrating the amount of wastewater to 1/100 of its original volume, while realizing a cost savings of nearly $1M per year.

SHIPBOARD OIL-WATER SEPARATORS

(Late 1970s onward)—Developed technology and equipment for a range of shipboard oil/water separators. Other participation included NAVSEA, Norfolk Naval Shipyard, G.E., Johns Hopkins University, J. J. McMullen, and M. Rosenblatt & Sons. **IMPACT:** The MARPOL 1990 international agreement to reduce pollution at sea provides strict levels of oil allowances for discharge into waters in port and at sea. The OPB-3F 1 gallon-per-minute (gpm), the OPB-10NP 10 gpm, and the 100-gpm high-capacity oil-water separators developed by the center provide a range of equipment for use in ships from small craft to large carriers. These separators enable ships to comply with MARPOL 1990. The 10-gpm units are in use fleet-wide. The 100-gpm high-capacity unit is in use on board *Eisenhower* (CVN 69), and is expected to be installed in other carriers.

SHIPBOARD PLASTIC WASTE PROCESSOR TECHNOLOGY

(Late 1980s onward)—Developed technology, prototypes and equipment for the fleet to deal with the large amounts of plastic waste accumulated on board ship that by law cannot be discharged. Other participation included NAVSEA, Navy Bureau of Medicine, naval shipyards, Navy Environmental Health Center, Westinghouse Machinery Technology Division, Northrop/Grumman, and Universal Technologies Inc. **IMPACT:** The new plastic waste processor technology reduces the volume of plastic wastes by a factor of thirty to one, and produces a 20-inch disk that is 1.5 inches thick. The disk is easily stored, unloaded, and disposed of in port, or it can be recycled. This achievement will bring the Navy into compliance with the Marine Plastic Pollution Research and Control Act of Fiscal Year 1995 and will vastly reduce the handling/storage problem for ships at sea.

SOLID WASTE PULPERS

(Late 1980s onward)—Developed large and small solid waste pulpers for shipboard use during the late 1980s which process 70% of all solid waste generated on board ships. Other participation included NAVSEA, Norfolk Naval Shipyard, Westinghouse Machinery Technology Division, and Somat Corp. **IMPACT:** Solid waste pulpers allow for rapid and sanitary disposal of paper, food, and classified documents, producing a wet slurry that can legally be discharged when ships are more than three nautical miles off shore. The discharge does not interfere with flight operations because it does not create a foreign object damage hazard. These pulpers now perform successfully on CVN 71, CVN 73, LHD 1, and FFG 48.

OPERATION, MAINTENANCE, & REPAIR

BOILER FEEDWATER TREATMENT

Developed and supported fleet implementation of a new method for chemically treating boiler feedwater. Other participation included NAVSEA. **IMPACT:** The chelant (chemical) water treatment method results in greatly reduced amounts of deposits inside boilers and also results in the elimination of the requirement to inspect and clean boilers every 1,800 steaming hours. Aggregate savings in maintenance and repair on the 122 ships affected by this accomplishment are estimated to be more than $30M annually.

FUEL FLASHPOINT MEASURING DEVICE

Developed and implemented a safer, more efficient, and automated shipboard fuel flashpoint measuring device for the fleet. Other participation included NRL, and Petrolab Corporation. **IMPACT:** The need for open flames and the use of mercury thermometers as parts of the original fuel flashpoint test was eliminated, making the device much less hazardous than its predecessor. The measuring device provides accurate measurements equivalent to those of the ASTM Standard methods. It is safe, simple to operate, requires minimal training, and is a valuable asset now that Navy acceptance is complete. British, Australian, and Canadian Navy evaluations of the development are underway.

FUEL TANK SOUNDING KIT

Developed and supported implementation of an efficient and effective fuel tank sounding kit that is compatible with Navy shipboard requirements. Other participation included NAVSEA and KA-CE Associates. **IMPACT:** The development of an efficient, effective, and inexpensive fuel tank sounding kit eliminated many problems that plagued fleet personnel as they carried out a routine procedure on Navy ships. Sounding tube and test procedure incompatibilities, leakage problems, and the use of hazardous material to carry out the test were some of the problems that were eliminated by the new tank sounding kit. The kit is about one-fifth the cost of the old equipment. It is used in hundreds of Navy ships and is also available for commercial use.

IMPROVED CLEANING OF SHIPBOARD DISTILLERS
Developed an online method of cleaning shipboard distillers using a citric acid mixture. Other participation included NAVSEA. **IMPACT:** The new cleaning method for shipboard distillers results in significantly reduced maintenance, less down-time, and greatly increased crew morale due to virtual elimination of water rationing on board ship. Fleet implementation was accomplished and the transition to the private sector is underway.

IMPROVED GAS TURBINE ENGINE COATINGS
Developed advanced metal coatings that improve the performance of high-pressure-stage gas turbine engine blades. Other participation included NAVSEA, NRL, Naval Ship System Engineering Station/Philadelphia, General Electric, Detroit Diesel-Allison, and Prattt & Whitney. **IMPACT:** The development of advanced metal (chromium-aluminum-yttrium) coatings for the high-pressure stage of Navy marine gas turbine engines resulted in significant improvements in the efficiency, life, and reliability. Achieved a factor of four improvement in mean time between overhaul (MTBO) and $35,000 per engine savings in direct acquisition costs.

INTEGRATED CAPABILITY ASSESSMENT SYSTEM (ICAS)
Developed a shipboard, computer-based machinery data acquisition, diagnostic, and condition-analysis system. Other participation included NAVSEA, the fleet, Idax Corp., Lifecycle Engineering Inc., Engineering Visions Inc., Information Technology Solutions Inc., and Xenotechnics Inc. **IMPACT:** ICAS greatly reduces the manhours necessary to operate and maintain many parts of a ship's machinery system. Examples of ICAS payoffs are reduced depot-level maintenance costs of $0.5M per ship availability for LHD 1-class ships, 20% fuel savings during normal operation of CG 47-class ships, time reductions of 70% to 80% in complex boiler tests for conventional aircraft carriers, and 25% reduction in preventative maintenance actions for an AE-class ship. The success of ICAS is indicated by the fact that it is already installed and operational in twenty-three ships representing nine classes, from aircraft carriers to mine warfare ships. Ten more ships received the system in 1996 and 160 ships will have ICAS by the year 2000.

LASER OPTIC TUBING INSPECTION SYSTEM (LOTIS)
(1980s onward)—Developed and supported implementation of a laser-optic tubing inspection system primarily for ship boilers and condensers. Other participation included NAVSEA, Atlantic and Pacific Fleets, Watervliet Arsenal, and Quest Integrated Inc. **IMPACT:** LOTIS greatly improves the ability of operating personnel to non-destructively, efficiently, and accurately inspect the internal condition of equipment such as boiler and condenser tubes in order to detect deteriorated or damaged areas that might present a safety problem. Since its introduction in the mid-1980s, LOTIS has also been identified as a candidate for other uses such as inspecting the material condition of the interior of gun barrels and diverse types of piping systems.

SHIPBOARD LUBRICANT & FUEL OIL MONITORING

Developed new equipment that permits safe and accurate shipboard monitoring of diesel lubricants. Other participation included NAVSEA, Microsensor Systems Inc., and Cambridge Applied Systems Inc. **IMPACT:** This new equipment permits accurate and safe determination of marine lubricant characteristics without having to send samples to a laboratory, and it can be used by all crew members. By addressing a number of routinely encountered shipboard engineering problems, these developments provide for more effective and less expensive operation of ships' equipment. In addition, it provides quick readouts that can be accepted with confidence in assessing lubricant characteristics. Commercial as well as military use of these devices has been achieved.

SUBMARINE SHAFT SEAL CORROSION CONTROL

Developed corrosion control and materials for the reduction of corrosion problems on submarine shaft seal systems. Other participation included NAVSEA, Naval shipyards, the TRIDENT Refit Facility/Bangor, NRL, and LaQue Center for Corrosion Technology. **IMPACT:** Over the last thirty years, shaft seal corrosion and repair problems have consistently led to expensive and premature shaft replacement in every class of submarine. A focused center program identified causal factors, developed a range of techniques to mitigate shaft corrosion problems, and tested them in the fleet thus increasing fleet availability.

LOGISTIC SYSTEMS

COMPUTER-AIDED WAREHOUSE DESIGN

Developed a computer-aided warehouse design (CAWD) system. Other participation included ONR, Naval Supply Systems Command, Air Force, Army, Marine Corps, GSA, and Georgia Institute of Technology. **IMPACT:** The CAWD system was developed to help the Navy determine methods for selecting the least-cost warehouse design from alternatives in terms of construction cost, and operations and maintenance costs on a life cycle cost basis. This system also satisfies specific storage requirements. It has been successfully used by the Navy and is being used by GSA, Air Force, Defense Logistics Agency, and Marine Corps. The Office of the Chief of Naval Research and NAVSUP estimate that it saves up to $20M per year in costs to construct, operate, and maintain Navy warehouses.

IETM AUTOMATED CONVERSION SYSTEM (ACS)

Developed the technology to permit automated conversion of key interactive electronic technical manuals (IETM) into a standard database format while reducing or eliminating the need for labor-intensive human interaction. Other participation included ONR, Naval Air Systems Command, NADEP/North Island, NSWC/Port Hueneme, Lockheed-Martin, and Mantech Services Corp. **IMPACT:** The automated conversion system (ACS) developed by the center allows the Navy and other services to cost-effectively convert paper documents and other legacy technical manuals to the IETM revisable database format. ACS is projected to reduce the cost of conversion by more than 60 percent, thereby making the implementation of IETM feasible and the maintenance of the technical information affordable. Utilization of ACS is currently underway with the Aegis weapon system, the F/A-18 by NAVAIR, and the F-16 by the Air Force. Commercial utilization and adoption by foreign governments is under negotiation.

JOINT LOGISTICS OVER THE SHORE (JLOTS)
(Mid-1960s onward)—Developed capabilities over thirty years to permit commercial cargo ships carrying military cargoes to be unloaded from offshore locations in time of war. Other participation included Naval Facilities Engineering Command, ONR, NAVSEA, Naval Facilities Engineering Service Center, MAR Inc., Advanced Marine Enterprises, and Band-Lavis Associates. **IMPACT:** JLOTS emerged during the Vietnam War when merchant ship design changed so radically that DOD was forced to develop means to permit these new configurations to be unloaded from offshore locations in time of war. The ensuing twenty to thirty years have seen a series of pragmatic and innovative designs of subsystems that permit large commercial ships to be specially handled during wartime conditions. Military cargo can now be unloaded at offshore and near-shore locations. Frequent joint-service exercises, which include chartered merchant ships with the JLOTS subsystems, have verified many times the success of the JLOTS capability. Without important JLOTS developments, DOD would have been forced to develop and acquire an expensive system utilizing its own ships to serve the armed forces in wartime.

UNDERWAY REPLENISHMENT (UNREP)
(Mid-1980s onward)—Developed and demonstrated technology and hardware to transfer and stow or load dry cargo, weapons and ammunition, and fuel under high sea-state conditions. Other participation included ONR, NAVSEA, NSWCCD Coastal Systems Station, EG&G, and Washington Analytical Services. **IMPACT:** Center developments of UNREP technology and hardware significantly increases the ability of fleet assets to perform critical on-board functions safely under higher sea-state conditions than capabilities allowed in the past. Further refinements will result in an increase in UNREP capability up to the goal of at least a fully developed Sea State 5 which can be compared to the present limitations of Sea State 3 for some UNREP evolutions. These developments result in cost savings due to the use of fewer pieces of equipment and reduction of shipboard maintenance.

MISCELLANEOUS

CIRCULATION CONTROL AERODYNAMICS
(1969-Present)—Developed and demonstrated concepts that permit circulation control to be used for numerous lift-enhancement-related applications for aircraft and marine vehicles. Other participation included NAVAIR, ONR, DARPA, NASA, Lockheed, Kaman Inc., Boeing, Sikorsky and Grumman. **IMPACT:** Circulation control is now possible for simpler, more affordable, and more effective short-take-off and vertical-take-off and landing aircraft. It also has great potential for a number of other high- payoff ship and submarine applications. This technology, some of which has been demonstrated at full-scale, remains a potent resource for future application to numerous aircraft situations, particularly in the short-take-off and vertical-take-off areas.

ENHANCED TRIDENT II MISSILE MOTOR QUALITY CONTROL
Developed techniques for assuring detection of critical flaws in missile motors, casings, and hardware. Other participation included NIST, Lockheed-Martin, Thiokol, Alliant Techsystems, UT-Chemical Systems Division, Kaiser Corp., and Brunswick Corp. **IMPACT:** Provides a dependable means for detecting critical flaws in missile motors, casings, and

hardware, greatly enhances safety, and provides improved reliability to ensure a missile will function effectively.

LITHIUM BATTERIES FOR FLEET NEEDS
Developed and implemented safe lithium batteries for the fleet. Other participation included ONR, NAVSEA, NSWC/Crane, Naval Ordnance Center, and primary battery manufacturers. **IMPACT:** Lithium batteries provide two to three times the energy content per unit volume and two to ten times the energy content per unit weight compared to traditional batteries such as silver-zinc or alkaline. They are also reliable, inexpensive, low maintenance, and environmentally friendly. The Navy has successfully adopted lithium batteries for use in mines, missiles, communications devices, countermeasure devices, decoys, air and underwater vehicles, emergency beacons, and sensor arrays.

SUPERCONDUCTING WIRE FOR MINESWEEPING MAGNETS
(1970s onward)—Developed a new type of compatible wire material using aluminum stabilized niobium/titanium (NbTi) for use with superconducting minesweeping magnet systems. Other participation included NAVSEA, PMO407, Naval Coastal System Station, Supercon Inc., and R&R Engineering. **IMPACT:** This development produces a much lighter wire, one that is more amenable to conductive cooling, and is more resistant to shock and vibration than commercially available wires. The result is a more effective superconducting minesweeping system than was previously in use. Since its success—in prototype form—was demonstrated, the new superconducting wire has moved to full-scale development and has become commercially available.

TRIDENT OPERATOR GUIDANCE SYSTEM (EMOGS)
Developed and implemented a system to provide transit guidance through the entrance channel to the Kings Bay Trident submarine base in Georgia. Other participation included Strategic Systems Program Office, NAVSEA, Naval Facilities Engineering Command, Seatex of Norway, ORI Inc., Woods Hole Oceanographic Institution, University of Virginia, and Offshore Technology Inc. **IMPACT:** The EMOGS system significantly reduces the risk of grounding for submarines transiting the entrance channel as a result of sea-state-induced motions, tidal-level variations, and channel sedimentation. It is an inexpensive alternative to channel dredging and follow-on maintenance.

APPENDIX **H**

Interviews

Interviews by Rodney P. Carlisle and History Associates staff:

William M. Ellsworth, 1 October 1984
John R. Belt, 22 October 1984
Owen K. Ritter, 26 October 1984
Z. George Wachnik, 26 October 1984
William W. Murray, 29 October 1984
Harvey R. Chaplin, 2 November 1984
Robert C. Allen, 5 November 1984
William B. Morgan, 1 March 1985
Gene H. Gleissner, 5 April 1985
Alan Powell, 19 December 1985
William F. Brownell Jr., 27 April 1986
Robert Chomo, 7 July 1986
Harvey H. Singerman, 7 July 1986
Larry J. Argiro, 10 November 1986
Howard O. Stevens Jr., 10 November 1986
Seth Hawkins, 17 November 1986
Warren C. Dietz, 15 December 1986
Allen G. Ford, 6 February 1987
G. Robert Lamb, 6 February 1987
Ernest O. Rogers, 30 March 1987
Edward Wenk Jr., 17 April 1987
G. Richard Garritson, 8 May 1987
George D. Kerr, 12 May 1987
Richard E. Metrey, 15 May 1987
Edwin B. O'Neill, 27 May 1987
Michael J. Superczynski, 8 July 1987
Richard E. Metrey, 14 October 1990
Clark C. Graham, 28 March 1997

Richard E. Metrey, 25 April 1997
Peter S. Montana, 1 May 1997
William A. Middleton, 16 May 1997

Other Interviews:

Harold V. Nutt, by David K. Allison, 22 October 1982
Louis Landweber, by Seth Hawkins, 28 October 1983
Alfred H. Keil, by David K. Allison, 2 November 1984
Karl Schoenherr, by David K. Allison, 15 April 1985
Louis Landweber, by David K. Allison, 20 January 1986
Wayne Meyer, by Joseph Marchese, 30 April 1990
Gerald Schiefer, by Joseph Marchese, 1 November 1991

Note: This list of formal interviews does not include the numerous informal conversations, telephone discussions, and meetings with the Editorial Advisory Board that provided enrichment, explanations, and pertinent data. Documentation of the above interviews is in the Operational Archives of the Naval Historical Center, Washington Navy Yard, Washington, D.C.

Bibliographical Notes

T HE BEST SOURCES FOR ANY INSTITUTIONAL history are usually found
in the internal management files of the organization itself. In the
case of the Carderock Division, Naval Surface Warfare Center, the
institution has survived through internal reorganizations and several
major restructurings of the naval bureau system and naval research management. Consequently, the preservation of files relating to the David
Taylor Model Basin and the Engineering Experiment Station is inconsistent. Despite the scattering of documents among repositories, a number
of rich primary sources were located. Readers should note, however, that
many of the files used in the initial writing of this work have since been
transferred to other depositories, as described below.

For the earliest period, David Taylor's bound correspondence, held
at the Technical Information Center (TIC), Carderock, Maryland,
proved useful. Other files covering the first years are now preserved at
the Operational Archives of the Naval Historical Center in Washington,
D.C. Early records of the Bureau of Steam Engineering and the Bureau
of Construction and Repair are located in Record Group 19 at the
National Archives and Records Administration, Washington, D.C.

For the interwar period, Bureau of Engineering and Bureau of
Construction and Repair records were quite rich. The collection that
was located at the National Archives' Suitland, Maryland facility, cited in
this work as the Washington National Records Center (WNRC), Record
Group 19 (Bureau of Ships), and filed under the Navy Filing Manual
numbering system, has been transferred to the National Archives in
downtown Washington.

The personal papers of Emory Land, Chief of the Bureau of
Construction and Repair in the period leading up to the site selection
and construction at Carderock, are housed in the Manuscript Division of
the Library of Congress. These documents reveal Land's personal commitment and political style.

Bureau of Ships documents for the 1940–1949 period, also found at
WNRC Suitland, enriched the story of wartime and postwar work at both
the Engineering Experiment Station and the David Taylor Model Basin.
Useful collections in the Records of Naval Shore Establishments (RG
181) in several accessions are also arranged under Navy Filing Manual

numbers. These records were moved to the new National Archives facility in College Park, Maryland, in the mid-1990s.

The collection gathered in the old historical office of the David Taylor Research Center is relatively significant for the 1950s and 1960s. The mid-1960s naval reorganization, with the complex sequence of studies, reports, and plans dealing with Secretary of Defense Robert McNamara's effort to address civilian management of military research, is well documented in the historical files of the now defunct Director of Navy Laboratories. David K. Allison's analyses of these documents and his preliminary draft reports on laboratory reorganization, filed with the documents, serve as a road map through the politics of Navy research management. All of these files have been transferred to the Operational Archives of the Naval Historical Center.

Some four cubic feet of office records from Alan Powell's term as technical director of David Taylor Research Center provide insight into the internal management in the 1970s and 1980s, and are now at the Naval Historical Center.

A particularly valuable source of technical information is the Technical Information Center's collection of reports documenting research, tests, and facilities construction. Although these reports are not widely available in libraries, archival copies, including test reports from EES, are available at TIC Carderock. They are cited as primary documents in the endnotes and do not appear in the bibliography of secondary sources. Articles and conference papers describing center research, however, were published in periodicals such as *Naval Engineers Journal* and the U.S. Naval Institute *Proceedings* and are included in the bibliography.

As listed in Appendix H, interviews by the author provide another sort of primary documentation. For coverage of the last fifty years, oral histories, originally collected for the Director of Navy Laboratories and since transferred to the Naval Historical Center, were also quite helpful. These were supplemented with formal taped interviews, as well as with informal telephone discussions and personal queries. Together, the interviews, conversations, and oral histories round out the picture on both technical matters and management and policy questions. In every case, use of these materials is explicitly listed in the endnotes. When an interviewee expresses his point of view or provides specific information, an attribution often appears in the text proper without recourse to endnotes.

Finally, the members of the Editorial Advisory Board, established in 1996, offered input and advice on the innovations of recent decades. Their considerable discussions on many of the technical programs summarized in the text are filed in the Advisory Board Information File (ABIF) at the Technical Information Center and cited in the endnotes.

Since this book was researched and written for the open literature, classified materials were not used or discussed. This approach avoided time-consuming declassification reviews of the manuscript and procedural difficulties in handling research materials and draft manuscripts. While it is possible to draw classified conclusions from unclassified sources, the focus of this work did not lead to such analysis. As a consequence of this open approach, certain areas of classified technical research at Carderock and Annapolis, although briefly summarized in the text, could not be treated at length or in detail proportionate to their naval significance.

Secondary Sources

The literature on naval ship types is extensive, with detailed and well-illustrated design histories of aircraft carriers, submarines, battleships, and destroyers in particular. Solidly researched monographs and journal articles that include the history of science and technology and histories of particular technologies, such as turbines, aircraft, radar, diesels, and computers, provided an important level of detail as did the many technical articles and conference papers reporting on laboratory research. Internal naval organizational histories, texts and histories of management theory, political analyses of naval strategy and planning, and memoirs and biographies brought in the necessary perspectives for a more complete treatment. For the convenience of the reader, the secondary works used in the preparation of this book are presented in a single list, as titles are sufficiently explicit to identify the subject.

Bibliography

Albion, Robert Greenhalgh. *Makers of Naval Policy, 1798–1947.* Edited by Rowena Reed. Annapolis: Naval Institute Press, 1980.

Albion, Robert Greenhalgh, and Robert Howe Connery. *Forrestal and the Navy.* New York: Columbia University Press, 1962.

Alden, John D. *The American Steel Navy: A Photographic History of the U.S. Navy from the Introduction of the Steel Hull in 1883 to the Cruise of the Great White Fleet, 1907–1909.* Annapolis: Naval Institute Press, 1972.

_____. *The Fleet Submarine in the U.S. Navy: A Design and Construction History.* Annapolis: Naval Institute Press, 1979.

Aldrich, William S. "Engineering Research in the Navy." *Transactions of the Society of Naval Architects and Marine Engineers* 3 (1895).

Allard, Dean C. "Naval Rearmament. 1930–1941: An American Perspective," *Revue internationale d'historie militarie* 73 (1991).

Allison, David K. *New Eye for the Navy: The Origins of Radar at the Naval Research Laboratory.* Washington: Naval Research Laboratory, 1981.

_____."U.S. Navy Research and Development Since World War II." In Merritt Roe Smith, ed., *Military Enterprise and Technological Change: Perspectives on the American Experience.* Cambridge: MIT Press, 1985.

Anderson, Commander William R., with Clay Blair Jr. *Nautilus 90 North.* Cleveland, OH and New York: The World Publishing Co., 1959.

Auyh, Richard. *Death of the Battleship.* New York: Macmillan, 1963.

Baer, George W. *One Hundred Years of Sea Power: The U.S. Navy 1890–1990.* Stanford, CA: Stanford University Press, 1994.

Bagnasco, Ermino. *Submarines of World War Two.* Annapolis: Naval Institute Press, 1977.

Baker, William. *Engine Powered Vessel: From Paddle Wheeler to Nuclear Ship.* New York: Grossett & Dunlap, 1965.

Baldwin, Hanson W. *The New Navy.* New York: E. P. Dutton & Co., 1964.

_____. *What the Citizen Should Know About the Navy.* New York: Norton, 1941.

Ballantine, Duncan. *U.S. Naval Logistics in the Second World War.* Princeton, NJ: Princeton University Press, 1947.

Barnaby, Kenneth C. *Basic Naval Architecture.* London, New York, and Toronto: Hutchinson's Scientific & Technical Publications, 1949.

_____. *The Institution of Naval Architects, 1860–1960.* London: Royal Institution of Naval Architects, 1960.

Barnard, Chester I. *The Functions of the Executive.* 1938. 30th ed. Cambridge: Harvard University Press, 1968.

Basler, R. E. "The Origins of Engineering Duty Only." *Journal of the American Society of Naval Engineers* 65 (November 1953).

Baxter, James Phinney III. *Scientists Against Time.* Boston: Little, Brown, 1946.

_____. *The Introduction of the Ironclad Warship.* Hamden, CT: Archon Books, 1968.

Bernstein, Jeremy. *The Analytical Engine: Computer Past, Present and Future.* New York: Morrow, 1981.

Bieg, F. C. "On the Necessity and Value of Scientific Research in Naval Engineering Matters as Related to the U.S. Navy and the Necessity of an Engineer Training for the Younger Members of the Engineer Corps of the U.S. Navy." *Journal of the American Society of Naval Engineers* 7 (August 1895).

Biggers, James, and Arthur W. Linden. "X-Wing: A Low DiscLoading V/STOL for the Navy." Paper no. 851772. Society of Automotive Engineers, 1985.

Biographical Directory of the American Congress, 1774–1961. Washington: Government Printing Office, 1961.

Boatwright, Gerald M., and John H. Strandell. "Controllable Pitch Propellers." *Naval Engineers Journal* 79 (August 1967).

Boatwright, G. M., M. Welling, and M. R. Hauschildt. "Naval Propulsion Machinery Post World War II." *Naval Engineers Journal* 75 (December 1963).

Booz, Allen & Hamilton, Inc. *Review of Navy R&D Management, 1946–1973.* 1 June 1976.

Borklund, C. W. *Men of the Pentagon: From Forrestal to McNamara.* New York: F. A. Praeger, 1966.

Bowen, Harold G. *Ships, Machinery & Mossbacks: An Autobiography of a Naval Engineer.* Princeton, NJ: Princeton University Press, 1954.

Bowen, H. G., and Leo Loeb. "The Engineering Experiment Station; Some Results." *Journal of the American Society of Naval Engineers* 26 (1914).

Bowers, Peter M. *Forgotten Fighters and Experimental Aircraft.* New York: Arco Publishing Co., 1971.

Boyle, Richard. "The Fleet Connection." U.S. Naval Institute *Proceedings* 108 (September 1980).

Bradford, James C. (ed.) *Admirals of the New Steel Navy: Makers of the American Naval Tradition, 1880–1930.* Annapolis: Naval Institute Press, 1990.

Brayton, Harris. *The Age of the Battleship, 1890–1922.* New York: Franklin Watts, 1965.

Breemer, Jan S. *U.S. Naval Developments.* Annapolis: Nautical & Aviation Publishing Co., 1983.

Breyer, Siegfried. *Battleships and Battle Cruisers, 1905–1970.* Translated by Alfred Kurt. London: Macdonald & Jones, 1973.

Brodie, Bernard. *Sea Power in the Machine Age.* Princeton, NJ: Princeton University Press, 1941.

_____. *A Guide to Naval Strategy.* Princeton, NJ: Princeton University Press, 1944.

Brown, David. *Aircraft Carriers.* New York: Arco Publishing Co., 1977.

Buell, Augustus C. *The Memoirs of Charles H. Cramp.* Philadelphia and London: Lippincott, 1906.

_____. *Master of Sea Power: A Biography of Fleet Admiral Ernest J. King.* Boston: Little, Brown, 1980.

Bureau of Engineering. *History of the Bureau of Engineering Navy Department During the World War.* Washington: Government Printing Office, 1922.

Burns, R. W. "Impact of Technology on the Defeat of the U-Boat: September 1939-May 1943," IEEE *Proceedings A: Science, Measurement and Technology* 141 (September1994).

Bush, Vannevar. *Science: The Endless Frontier. A Report to the President.* Washington: Government Printing Office, 1945.

_____. *Modern Science Against Time.* Boston: Little, Brown, 1946.

_____. *Modern Arms and Free Men.* New York: Simon and Schuster, 1949.

Butler, Edward A., ed. "The Surface Effect Ship." *Naval Engineers Journal* 97 (February 1985).

Calhoun, C. Raymond. *Typhoon, The Other Enemy: The Third Fleet and the Pacific Storm of December 1944.* Annapolis: Naval Institute Press, 1981.

Calvert, Monte A. *The Mechanical Engineer in America, 1830–1910: Professional Cultures in Conflict.* Baltimore: The Johns Hopkins Press, 1967.

Canan, James W. *The Superwarriors: The Fantastic World of Pentagon Superweapons.* New York: Weybright and Talley, 1975.

Carlisle, Rodney P. *Sovereignty for Sale: The Origins and Evolution of the Panamanian and Liberian Flags of Convenience.* Annapolis: Naval Institute Press, 1981.

_____. *Powder and Propellants: Energetic Materials at Indian Head, Maryland, 1890–1990.* Washington: Government Printing Office, 1991.

_____. *Management of the U.S. Navy Research and Development Centers During the Cold War: A Survey Guide to Reports.* Washington: Naval Historical Center, 1996.

Cathcart, William Ledyard. "George Wallace Melville." *Journal of the American Society of Naval Engineers* 24 (1912).

Chaplin, J. B. "The Air Cushion Vehicle." *Military Engineer* 61 (January-February 1969).

Cheeseman, I. C., and A. R. Seed. "The Application of Circulation Control by Blowing to Helicopters." *Journal of the Royal Aeronautical Society* 71 (July 1966).

Christman, Albert B. *Sailors, Scientists, and Rockets: Origins of the Navy Rocket Program and of the Naval Ordnance Test Station, Inyokern.* Vol.1. Washington: Naval History Division, 1971.

Churchman, C. West. *Introduction to Operations Research.* New York: J. Wiley & Sons, 1957.

_____. *The Systems Approach and Its Enemies.* New York: Basic Books, 1979.

Clark, J. A., and A. J. Tucker. "Optical Measurements of Structural Intensity Destributions." *The Proceedings of the Second International Congress on Acoustic Intensity.* Senlis, France, 23–26 September 1985.

_____. "Power Flow and Traveling Waves in Structures." *JASA* Paper 28. Paper presented at the 110th Meeting of the Acoustical Society of America, Nashville, TN, November 1985.

Cleland, David, and William R. King. *Systems, Organizations, Analysis, Management: A Book of Readings.* New York: McGraw-Hill, 1969.

Coletta, Paolo E. *Admiral Bradley A. Fiske and the American Navy.* Lawrence, KS: Regents Press, 1979.

_____. *The United States Navy and Defense Unification, 1947–1953.* Newark: University of Delaware Press, 1981.

Collins, J. Lawton. *War in Peacetime: The History and Lessons of Korea.* Boston: Houghton Mifflin, 1969.

Connery, Robert Howe. *The Navy and the Industrial Mobilization in World War II.* Princeton, NJ: Princeton University Press, 1951.

Constant, Edward. *The Origins of the Turbojet Revolution.* Baltimore: Johns Hopkins University Press, 1980.

Cooling, B. Franklin. "The Formative Years of the Naval Industrial Complex: Their Meaning for Studies of Institutions Today." *Naval War College Review* 27 (March–April 1975).

Cooney, David M. *A Chronology of the U.S. Navy, 1775–1965.* New York: F. Watts, 1965.

Corbett, Julian S. *Some Principles of Maritime Strategy.* Annapolis: Naval Institute Press, 1972.

Creswell, John. *Sea Warfare, 1939–1945.* Revised edition. Berkeley: University of California Press, 1967.

Curtis, A. V., and L. F. Hewing. "Some Results of Tests of Model Propellers." *Transactions of the Society of Naval Architects and Marine Engineers* 13 (1905).

Cuthill, Elizabeth H. "Digital Computers in Nuclear Reactor Design." *Advances in Computers.* New York: Academic Press, 1964.

_____. "FLAME, A Three-Dimensional Burn-up Code for LARC." *Codes for Reactor Computations.* Vienna: International Atomic Energy Agency, 1961.

Daniels, Josephus. *The Wilson Era: Years at War and After, 1917–1923.* Westport, CT: Greenwood Press, 1946, 1974.

Davis, George T. *A Navy Second to None: The Development of Modern American Naval Policy.* New York: Harcourt, 1940.

Davis, H.F.D. "Building Major Combatant Ships in World War II." U.S. Naval Institute *Proceedings* 73 (May 1947).

Davis, Vincent. *Postwar Defense Policy and the U.S. Navy, 1943–1946.* Chapel Hill: University of North Carolina Press, 1966.

_____. *The Admirals Lobby.* Chapel Hill: University of North Carolina Press, 1967.

_____. *The Politics of Innovation: Patterns in Navy Cases.* Denver, CO: University of Denver, Social Science Foundation & Graduate School of International Studies, 1967.

De Gues, Arie. "The Living Company." *Harvard Business Review* (March–April 1997).

Deputy Chief of Naval Operations (Air). *U.S. Naval Aviation, 1910–1970.* Washington: DCNO Air, 1970.

Deitchman, Seymour J. *New Technology and Military Power: General Purpose Military Forces for the 1980s and Beyond.* Boulder, CO: Westview Press, 1979.

Douhet, General Giulio. *The Command of the Air.* 1942. Reprint. Washington: Office of Air Force History, 1983.

Doyle, T. J., and J. H. Harrison. "Navy Superconductive Machinery Program." Paper presented at SNAME Spring Meeting/STAR Symposium, New London, CT, 26–29 April 1978.

Drake, Frederick C. *The Empire of the Seas: A Biography of Rear Admiral Robert Wilson Shufeldt, USN.* Honolulu: University of Hawaii Press, 1984.

Drucker, Peter F. "Integration of People and Planning." *Harvard Business Review* 33 (1933).

_____. *The Practice of Management.* New York: Harper & Row, 1954.

Dupree, A. Hunter. *Science in the Federal Government.* 1957. Reprint. Baltimore: Johns Hopkins University Press, 1986.

Durand, William F. *The Resistance and Propulsion of Ships.* 2d edition. New York: J. Wiley & Sons, 1909.

Eiffel, Gustave. *La Resistance de l'air et l'aviation: experiences effectuees au laboratoire du Champs-de-Mars.* Paris: H. Dunot et E. Pinat, 1911.

Ellsworth, William M. *Twenty Foilborne Years: The U.S. Navy Hydrofoil High Point (PCH–1).* Washington: DTNSRDC, 1987.

Ellsworth, William M., and Dennis J. Clark. "Ship Design and the Navy Laboratory." *Naval Engineers Journal* (April 1981).

Emmet, William LeRoy. *The Autobiography of an Engineer.* ASME, 1940.

Englar, Robert J. "STOL—The Potential of the Circulation Control Wing Concept." *Naval Engineers Journal 91* (April 1979).

Enthoven, Alain C. *How Much is Enough? Shaping the Defense Program, 1961–69.* New York: Harper & Row, 1971.

Erickson, John. *The Military-Technical Revolution: Its Impact on Strategy and Foreign Policy.* New York: Published for the Institute for the Study of the USSR by F. A. Praeger, 1966.

Fagle, C. Ernest. *The War and the Shipping Industry.* London, Eng.: Oxford University Press, 1927.

Fassett, Frederick Gardiner. *The Shipbuilding Business in the U.S.A.* New York: SNAME, 1948.

Featherstone, Frank. "A.E.D.O.: A History and Heritage." U.S. Naval Institute *Proceedings* (February 1968).

Feld, B. T., et. al. *Impact of New Technologies on the Arms Race.* Cambridge: MIT Press, 1971.

Fiske, Rear Admiral Bradley A. *From Midshipman to Rear Admiral.* New York: Century, 1919.

Fordyce, T. K. "Officer-Civilian Relationships in Semi-Military Technical Organizations." *Journal of the American Society of Naval Engineers* 65 (February 1953).

Forrestal, James. *The Navy: A Study in Administration.* Chicago: Public Administration Office, 1946.

Fox, J. Ronald. *Arming America: How the U.S. Buys Weapons.* Cambridge: Harvard Business School, 1974.

Frankel, E. G., J. M. Reynolds, and E. H. Sibley. "Superconducting Machinery for Naval Applications." *Naval Engineers Journal* 78 (June 1966).

Freeth, F. A. "H. Kamerlingh Onnes, 1853–1926." *Annual Report of the Board of Regents of the Smithsonian Institution.* Washington: Government Printing Office, 1927.

Fricker, John. "Air-Cushion Vehicle Comes of Age." U.S. Naval Institute *Proceedings* (September 1965).

Friedman, Norman. *Carrier Air Power.* Greenwich, CT: Conway Maritime Press, 1981.

_____. *U.S. Aircraft Carriers: An Illustrated Design History.* Annapolis: Naval Institute Press, 1983.

_____. *U.S. Submarines Since 1945: An Illustrated Design History.* Annapolis: Naval Institute Press, 1994.

_____. *The US Maritime Strategy.* London: Janes, 1988.

_____. *US Naval Weapons: Every Gun, Missile, Mine, and Torpedo Used by the US Navy from 1883 to the Present Day.* Annapolis: Naval Institute Press, 1982.

Frothingham, Thomas Goddard. *The Naval History of the World War: The United States in the War, 1917–1918.* Cambridge: Harvard University Press, 1924–1926.

Froude, William. *The Papers of William Froude, 1810–1879.* Memoirs and an evaluation of William Froude's work by Sir Wescott Abell. London: Royal Institution of Naval Architects, 1955.

Fuller, J.F.C. *Armament and History: A Study of the Influence of Armament on History from the Dawn of Classical Warfare to the Second World War.* New York: C. Scribner's Sons, 1945.

Furer, Rear Admiral Julius Augustus. *Administration of the Navy Department in World War II.* Washington: Government Printing Office, 1959.

_____. "Naval Research and Development in World War II." *Journal of the American Society of Naval Engineers* 62 (February 1950).

Galambos, Louis. "Technology, Political Economy and Professionalization: Central Themes of the Organizational Synthesis." *Business History Review* 57 (Winter 1983).

Garzke, William H. *Battleships: United States Battleships, 1935–1992.* Annapolis: Naval Institute Press, 1995.

George, James L. *The U.S. Navy in the 1990s: Alternatives for Action.* Annapolis: Naval Institute Press, 1992.

Gilfillan, S. C. *Inventing the Ship*. Chicago: Follett, 1935.

Gillmer, Thomas C., and Johnson, Bruce. *Introduction to Naval Architecture*. Annapolis: Naval Institute Press, 1982.

Goddard, Esther C., and G. Edward Pendray, eds. *Papers of Robert H. Goddard*. Vol. 3, *1938–1945*. New York: McGraw-Hill, 1970.

Goodier, J. Norman, and Nicholas J. Hoff. "Structural Mechanics." *Proceedings of the First Symposium on Naval Structural Mechanics (1958)*. New York: Pergamon, 1960.

Gore, Jerry L., ed. "SWATH Ships." *Naval Engineers Journal* 97 (February 1985).

Graybar, Lloyd J. "1946 Atomic Diplomacy or Bureaucratic Infighting." *Journal of American History* 74 (1986).

Hacker, Barton C. "Military Institutions, Weapons and Social Change: Toward a New History of Military Technology," *Technology and Culture* 35 (October 1994).

Hagan, Kenneth J. *American Gunboat Diplomacy and the Old Navy, 1877–1889*. Contributions in Military History No. 4. Westport, CT: Greenwood Press, 1973.

———. *This People's Navy: The Making of American Sea Power*. New York: Free Press, 1992.

Halpern, Paul G. *A Naval History of World War I*. Annapolis: Naval Institute Press, 1994.

Hanley, M. J., Jr. "Surface Effect Ships." U.S. Naval Institute *Proceedings* 92 (November 1965).

———. "60-Knot Landing Force." U.S. Naval Institute *Proceedings* 93 (March 1967).

Hart, Robert A. *The Great White Fleet: Its Voyage Around the World, 1907–1909*. Boston: Little Brown, 1965.

Hartman, Gregory F. *Weapons That Wait: Mine Warfare in the U.S. Navy*. Annapolis: Naval Institute Press, 1979.

Hewlett, Richard G., and Oscar E. Anderson Jr. *A History of the United States Atomic Energy Commission*. Vol. 1, *The New World, 1939–1946*. University Park: Pennsylvania State University Press, 1962.

Hewlett, Richard G., and Francis Duncan. *A History of the United States Atomic Energy Commission*. Vol.2, *Atomic Shield, 1947–1952*. University Park: Pennsylvania State University Press, 1969.

Hewlett, Richard G., and Francis Duncan, *Nuclear Navy, 1946–1962*. Chicago and London: University of Chicago Press, 1974.

Historical Section, Bureau of Ships. "An Administrative History of the Bureau of Ships During World War II." Manuscript. Navy Department Library.

Hitch, Charles J. *Decision-Making for Defense*. Berkeley: University of California Press, 1965.

Hodges, Peter, and Norman Friedman. *Destroyer Weapons of World War II*. Annapolis: Naval Institute Press, 1979.

Hoegh, Carl. *The Cylinder Wear in Diesel Engines*. New York: Chemical Publishing Co., 1945.

Holley, I. B. *Ideas and Weapons*. 1953. Reprint. Hamden, CT: Archon Books, 1971.

Hooper, Edwin B. *United States Naval Power in a Changing World*. New York: Praeger, 1988.

Hooper, Edwin Bickford., Dean C. Allard, and Oscar P. Fitzgerald. *The U.S. Navy and the Vietnam Conflict*. Vol.1, *The Setting of the Stage to 1959*. Washington: Naval History Division, 1976.

Hounshell, David A. *From the American System to Mass Production, 1800–1932: The Development of Manufacturing Technology in the United States*. Baltimore: Johns Hopkins Press, 1984.

_____. "Ford Eagle Boats and Mass Production during World War II." In Merritt Roe Smith, ed., *Military Enterprise and Technological Chance: Perspectives on the American Experience*. Cambridge: MIT Press, 1985.

Hovgaard, William. "Biographical Memoirs of David Watson Taylor, 1864–1940." *Biographical Memoirs of the National Academy of Sciences*, Vol. 22. Washington: National Academy of Sciences, 1941.

_____. *Modern History of Warships*. 1920. Revised edition. Annapolis: Naval Institute Press, 1971.

Howarth, Stephen. *To Shining Sea: A History of the United States Navy, 1775–1989*. New York: Random House, 1991.

Hughes, G., ed. *Fifth Conference of Ship Tank Superintendents: Papers and Discussions*. 14–17 September 1948. London: His Majesty's Stationery Office, 1949.

Hughes, Thomas Parke. *Elmer Sperry: Inventor and Engineer.* Baltimore: Johns Hopkins University Press, 1971.

_____. "The Science-Technology Interaction: The Case of High Voltage Power Transmission Systems." *Technology and Culture* 17 (October 1976).

Hunsaker, Jerome C. *Aeroplane Design.* Annapolis: U.S. Naval Institute, 1914.

_____. *Aeronautics at Mid-Century.* New Haven, CT: Yale University Press, 1952.

_____. "Forty Years of Aeronautical Research." *Annual Report of the Board of Regents of the Smithsonian Institution, 1955.* Washington: Government Printing Office, 1956.

Janes, Charles F. "The Potential of Superconductors for Shipboard Power Applications." *Naval Engineers Journal* 79 (October 1967).

Joint Committee on Atomic Energy. *Progress Report on Naval Reactor Program and Shippingport Project.* 7 March 1957.

Jolliff, J. V., and George D. Kerr. "Designing for Change: Present and Future." U.S. Naval Institute *Proceedings* 91 (July 1974).

Karsten, Peter. *The Naval Aristocracy: The Golden Age of Annapolis and the Emergence of Modern American Navalism.* New York: The Free Press, 1972.

Kast, Fremont E., and James E. Rosenzweig. *Organization and Management—A Systems Approach.* New York: McGraw-Hill, 1970.

Kaufmann, William W. *The McNamara Strategy.* 1st edition. New York: Harper & Row, 1964.

Keller, Emil E., and Francis Hodgkinson. "The Steam Turbine in the United States; I—Developments by the Westinghouse Machine Company." *Mechanical Engineering* (November 1936).

Kelso, Frank B., II, and Mundy, C. E. . . . *From the Sea: Preparing the Naval Service for the 21st Century.* Washington: Department of the Navy, U.S. Marine Corps, 1992.

Kevles, Daniel J. *The Physicists: The History of a Scientific Community in Modern America.* New York: Alfred A. Knopf, 1978.

Keyes, Roger John Brownlow. *Amphibious Warfare and Combined Operations.* Cambridge, Eng.: The University Press, 1943.

King, Ernest J. "The U.S. Naval Engineering Experiment Station, Annapolis, Md." *Journal of the American Society of Naval Engineers* 25 (August 1913).

King, Randolph. *Naval Engineering and American Seapower*. Baltimore: Nautical & Aviation Publishing Co. of America, 1989.

Knox, Dudley. *A History of the United States Navy*. New York: Putnam, 1948.

Koontz, Harold. "The Management Theory Jungle." *Journal of the Academy of Management* (December 1961).

Kuhn, Thomas. *The Structure of Scientific Revolutions*. 2d edition. Chicago: University of Chicago Press, 1970.

Kuzmak, Arnold. *Naval Force Levels and Modernization*. Washington: Brookings Institute, 1971.

Land, Emory S. *Winning the War with Ships: Land, Sea and Air—Mostly Land*. New York: R. M. McBride, 1958.

Landweber, Louis. "Skin Friction: A Contribution to the Discussion of Subject 2." *The Sixth International Conference of Ship Tank Superintendents: Discussions, Conclusions and Comments*. September 1951. Washington: 1951.

Lasby, Clarence G. *Project Paperclip: German Scientists and the Cold War*. New York: Atheneum, 1971.

Lasky, Marvin. "A Historical Review of Undersea Warfare Planning and Organization, 1945-1960, with Emphasis on the Role of the Office of Naval Research." *Journal of Underwater Acoustics* 26 (1970).

Layton, Edwin T., Jr. *The Revolt of the Engineers: Social Responsibility and the American Engineering Profession*. Baltimore: Johns Hopkins University Press, 1986.

Leggett, Wilson D. "The U.S. Engineering Experiment Station." U.S. Naval Institute *Proceedings* 77 (May 1951).

Leopold, Reuven. "A New Hull Form for High-Speed Volume-Limited Displacement-Type Ships." Paper presented at Society of Naval Architects and Marine Engineers Spring Meeting, May 1969.

Leslie, Stuart. *Boss Kettering*. New York: Columbia University Press, 1983.

Long, John D. *The New American Navy*. 2 volumes. New York: Arno Press, 1979.

Love, Robert W., Jr. *The Chiefs of Naval Operations*. Annapolis: Naval Institute Press, 1980.

_____. *History of the U.S. Navy.* Harrisburg, PA: Stackpole Books, 1992.

Madaler, R. B. "The Bureau of Ships and Its E.D. Officers." *Journal of the American Society of Naval Engineers* 67 (February 1954).

Magdenburger, E. C. "Diesel Engine in the United States Navy." *Journal of the American Society of Naval Engineers* 61 (1949).

Marbury, Fendall, Jr. "Small Prototypes of Ships—Theory and a Practical Example." *Naval Engineers Journal* 85 (October 1973).

Marolda, Edward J., and Pryce, G. Wesley. *A Select Bibliography of the United States Navy and the Southeast Asian Conflict, 1950–1975.* Washington: Naval Historical Center, 1982.

Martin, L. W. *The Sea in Modern Strategy.* London: Institute for Strategic Studies, 1967.

McCann, E. F., II, and C. J. Mole. "Superconducting Electric Propulsion Systems for Advanced Ship Concepts." *Naval Engineers Journal* 84 (December 1972).

McEntee, William. "Some Applications of the Principles of Naval Architecture to Aeronautics." *Transactions of the Society of Naval Architects and Marine Engineers* 19 (1911).

_____. "Variation of Frictional Resistance of Ships with Condition of Wetted Surface" *Transactions of the Society of Naval Architects and Marine Engineers* (1915).

_____. Notes from the Model Basin." *Transactions of the Society of Naval Architects and Marine Engineers* (1916).

_____. "Cargo Ship Lines of Simple Form." *Transactions of the Society of Naval Architects and Marine Engineers* (1917).

_____. "Variations of Shaft Horsepower, Propeller Revolution, and Propulsion Coefficient with Longitudinal Position of Parallel Middle Body in a Single Screw Cargo Ship." *Transactions of the Society of Naval Architects and Marine Engineers* (1918).

_____. "The Propulsive Efficiency of Single Screw Cargo Ships." *Transactions of the Society of Naval Architects and Marine Engineers* (1919).

McGregor, Douglas. *The Human Side of Enterprise.* New York: McGraw-Hill, 1960.

McKean, R. N. *Efficiency in Government Through Systems Analysis.* New York: J. Wiley & Sons, 1958.

McNamara, Robert *The Essence of Security: Reflections in Office.* New York: Harper & Row, 1968.

Mitchell, Donald W. *History of the Modern American Navy, from 1883 through Pearl Harbor.* New York: Alfred A. Knopf, 1946.

Morison, Elting. *Admiral Sims and the Modern American Navy.* Boston: Houghton Mifflin, 1942.

_____. *The War of Ideas: The United States Navy 1870–1890.* Colorado Springs: United States Air Force Academy, 1969.

_____. *From Know-how to Nowhere: The Development of American Technology.* New York: Basic Books, 1974.

Morris, R. K. *John P. Holland, 1841–1914: Inventor of the Modern Submarine.* Annapolis: Naval Institute Press, 1960.

Morrow, John H., Jr. *The Great War in the Air: Military Aviation from 1909 to 1921.* Washington: Smithsonian Institution Press, 1993

Mosher, M. C. "A Method For Computing Three-Dimensional Vortex Flows." *Zeitschrift fur Flugwissenschaftes und Weltraumforschung* (*Journal of Flight Sciences and Space Research*) 9 (May/June 1985).

Mostert, Noel. *Supership.* New York: Alfred A. Knopf, 1974.

Muir, Malcolm. *Black Shoes and Blue Water: Surface Warfare in the U.S. Navy, 1945–1975.* Washington: Naval Historical Center, 1996.

Murdock, Clark A. *Defense Policy Formation: A Comparative Analysis of the McNamara Era.* Albany: State University of New York, 1974.

Naval History Division. *Riverine Warfare: The U.S. Navy's Operations in Inland Waters.* Washington: Government Printing Office, 1968.

_____. *The Submarine in the United States Navy.* 3d edition. Washington: Government Printing Office, 1969.

Neilsen, Christian K., Jr. "A Summary of Controllable Pitch Propeller Systems Employed by the U.S. Navy." *Naval Engineers Journal* 86 (April 1974).

Nichols, John F. "The Development of Marine Engineering." *SNAME: Historical Transactions 1893–1943.* New York: SNAME, 1945.

Nitze, Paul, Leonard Sullivan Jr., and the Atlantic Council's Working Group on Securing the Seas. *Securing the Seas: Soviet Naval Challenge and Western Alliance Option.* Boulder, CO: Westview Press, 1979.

"Notes from the Engineering Station." *Bulletin of Engineering Information.* 1 July 1929.

Nystrom, Robert E. "The Role of the Hydrofoil Special Trials Unit (HYSTU) in the U.S. Navy Hydrofoil Programme." Paper presented at Second International Conference, Hovering Craft Hydrofoils Advanced Transit Systems, RAI Exhibition and Congress Centre, Amsterdam, Netherlands, 17–20 May 1976.

O'Connell, Robert. *Sacred Vessels: The Cult of the Battleship and the Rise of the U.S. Navy.* New York: Oxford University Press, 1993.

Office of Naval Intelligence. *The United States Navy as an Industrial Asset— What the Navy Has Done for Commerce and Industry.* Washington: ONI, 1922.

O'Neill, J. G. "Endurance Test of Force Feed Oils." *Journal of the American Society of Naval Engineers* 33 (1921).

————. "Examination of Oils from the Atlantic Fleet Before and After Use." *Journal of the American Society of Naval Engineers* 29 (1917).

Palmer, Michael A. *Origins of the Maritime Strategy: American Naval Strategy in the First Postwar Decade.* Washington: Naval Historical Center, 1988.

Paullin, Charles Oscar. *Paullin's History of Naval Administration, 1775–1911.* 1912. Reprint. Annapolis: Naval Institute Press, 1968.

Peck, Taylor. *Round-Shot to Rockets: A History of the Washington Navy Yard and U.S. Naval Gun Factory.* Annapolis: U.S. Naval Institute, 1949.

Polmar, Norman. *The Ships and Aircraft of the United States Fleet.* 12th edition. Annapolis: Naval Institute Press, 1981.

————. *The American Submarine.* Annapolis: Nautical & Aviation Publishing Co. of America, 1983.

Possony, Stefan T., and J. E. Pournelle. *The Strategy of Technology: Winning the Decisive War.* Cambridge: Dunellen, 1970.

Potter, E. B. *Sea Power: A Naval History.* 2d edition. Annapolis: Naval Institute Press, 1981.

Puleston, William Dilworth. *Mahan: The Life and Work of Captain Alfred Thayer Mahan, USN.* New Haven, CT: Yale University Press, 1939.

Rand Corporation. *The Rand Corporation: Its Origin, Evolution, and Plans for the Future.* February 1971.

Reilly, John C., Jr., and Robert L. Scheina. *American Battleships, 1886–1923: Predreadnought Design and Construction.* Annapolis: Naval Institute Press, 1980.

Reynolds, Clark G. *Famous American Admirals.* New York: Van Nostrand Reinhold, 1978.

Richardson, Alex. *The Evolution of the Parsons Steam Turbine Engineering.* London: 1911.

Roherty, James M. *Decisions of Robert S. McNamara: A Study of the Role of the Secretary of Defense.* Coral Gables, FL: University of Miami Press, 1970.

Roland, Alex. *Model Research: The National Advisory Committee for Aeronautics, 1915–1958.* Washington: Scientific and Technical Information Branch, National Aeronautics and Space Administration, 1955.

Rosinski, Herbert. *The Development of Naval Thought.* Edited by Mitchell Simpson. Newport, RI: Naval War College, 1977.

Roskill, Stephen. *Naval Policy Between the Wars.* 2 volumes. Vol. 1, *The Period of Anglo-American Antagonism, 1919–1929;* and Vol. 2, *The Period of Reluctant Rearmament, 1930–1939.* London: Collins, 1968, 1976.

Rossell, Henry Eastin, ed. *Principles of Naval Architecture.* New York: SNAME, 1939.

Ruge, Friedrich. *The Soviets As Naval Opponents, 1941–1945.* Annapolis: Naval Institute Press, 1979.

Salvesen, Nils. "A Note on the Seakeeping Characteristics of Small-Waterplane-Area-Twin-Hull Ships." AIAA Paper no.72–606 given at AIAA/SNAME/USN Advanced Marine Vehicles Meeting, Annapolis, MD, 17–19 July 1972.

Sandler, Stanley. *The Emergence of the Modern Capital Ship.* Newark: University of Delaware, 1979.

Sapolsky, Harvey M. "Academic Science and the Military: The Years Since the Second World War." *The Sciences in the American Context: New Perspectives.* Edited by Nathan Reingold. Washington: Smithsonian Press, 1979.

_____. *The Polaris System Development: Bureaucratic and Programmatic Success in Government.* Cambridge: Harvard University Press, 1972.

Saunders, H. E. "The David W. Taylor Model Basin." *Transactions of the Society of Naval Architects and Marine Engineers 46,* Part 1, 1938. New York: SNAME, 1939.

_____. "The David W. Taylor Model Basin." *Transactions of the Society of Naval Architects and Marine Engineers 48,* Part 2, 1938. New York: SNAME, 1939.

_____. ed. *Sixth International Conference of Ship Tank Superintendents: International Committee Reports, Introductory Remarks, Discussions, and Conclusions.* 10–15 September 1951, New York: SNAME, 1953.

Schanz, F. "The Controllable Pitch Propeller as an Integral Part of the Ship's Propulsion System." *Transactions of the Society of Naval Architects and Marine Engineers* 75 (1967).

Schurman, D. M. *The Education of a Navy: The Development of British Naval Strategic Thought, 1867–1914.* Malabar, FL: Robert E. Kreiger, 1984.

Seager, Robert II. *Alfred Thayer Mahan: The Man and His Letters.* Annapolis: Naval Institute Press, 1977.

_____. "Ten Years Before Mahan: The Unofficial Case for the New Navy, 1880–1890." *Mississippi Valley Historical Review* 40 (December 1953).

Sexton, Donald J. "Forging the Sword: Congress and the American Naval Renaissance, 1880–1890." Ph.D. dissertation, University of Tennessee, 1976.

Shatzberg, Paul. "Organotin Antifouling Paints and the U.S. Navy—A Historical Perspective." Paper presented at Oceans 87 Conference, Halifax, Nova Scotia, August 1987.

Singer, Charles, E. J. Holmyard, A. R. Hall, and Trevor I. Williams. *A History of Technology.* Vol. 5, *The Late Nineteen Century, c.1850 of c.1900.* Oxford, Eng.: Clarendon Press, 1958.

Smith, Edgar C. *A Short History of Naval and Marine Engineering.* Cambridge, Eng.: The University Press, 1938.

Smith, Merritt Roe. *Harpers Ferry Armory and the New Technology: The Challenge of Change.* Ithaca, NY: Cornell University Press, 1977.

_____. ed. *Military Enterprise and Technological Change: Perspectives on the American Experience.* Cambridge: MIT Press, 1985.

Sokol, A. E. *Seapower in the Nuclear Age.* Washington: Public Affairs Press, 1961.

Sokolsky, Joel J. *Seapower in the Nuclear Age: The United States Navy and NATO, 1949–80.* London: Routledge, 1991.

Special Projects Office. *Polaris Management: Fleet Ballistic Management Program.* Washington: Government Printing Office, 1961.

Spector, Ronald. *Professors of War: The Naval War College and the Development of the Naval Profession.* Newport, RI: Naval War College Press, 1977.

Sperry, Elmer. "The Gyroscope for Marine Purposes." *Transactions of the Society of Naval Architects and Marine Engineers* 18 (1910).

Sprout, Harold and Margaret. *Toward a New Order of Sea Power: American Naval Policy and the World Scene, 1918–1922.* Princeton, NJ: Princeton University Press, 1940, 1943.

St. Denis, Manley, and Willard J. Pierson. "On the Motions of Ships in Confused Seas." *Transactions of the Society of Naval Architects and Marine Engineers* 61 (1963).

Stafford, Edward Peary. *Little Ship, Big War.* Paperback edition. New York: Morrow, 1984.

_____. *The Far and the Deep.* New York: Putnam, 1967.

Stanik, Joseph T. *"Swift and Effective Retribution": The U.S. Sixth Fleet and the Confrontation with Qaddafi.* Washington: Naval Historical Center, 1997.

Stewart, Irvin. *Organizing Scientific Research for War: The Administrative History of the Office of Scientific Research and Development.* Boston: Little, Brown, 1948.

Stilwell, James, and William R. Porter. "Naval Use of Hydrofoil Craft." U.S. Naval Institute *Proceedings* 89 (1963).

Swanborough, F. Gordon, and P. M. Bowers. *United States Navy Aircraft Since 1911.* London: Putnam, 1968.

Taggart, Robert. "Noise in Reduction Gears." *Journal of the American Society of Naval Engineers* 66 (November 1954).

_____."Acoustics and Naval Engineering." *Journal of the American Society of Naval Engineers* 67 (August 1955).

_____. *Marine Propulsion: Principles & Evolution.* Houston, TX: Gulf Publication Co., 1969.

Tai, T. C. "An Integral Prediction Method for Three-Dimensional Flow Separation." AIAA Paper no. 84-0014. Paper presented at the American Institute of Aeronautics and Astronautics (AIAA), 22d Aerospace Sciences Meeting, Reno, NV, January 1984.

Taylor, David W. *Resistance of Ships and Screw Propulsion.* New York: Macmillian, 1907.

_____. *Speed & Power of Ships.* 1910. Reprint. Washington: U.S. Shipping Board, 1933.

_____. "The United States Experimental Model Basin." *Transactions of the Society of Naval Architects and Marine Engineers* 8 (1900).

_____. "A Dynamometer and Revolution Counter for Fan Testing." *American Machinist* (June 1903).

_____. "On Ships' Forms Derived by Formulae." *Transactions of the Society of Naval Architects and Marine Engineers* 11 (1903).

_____. "Some Recent Experiments at the Model Basin." *Transactions of the Society of Naval Architects and Marine Engineers* 12 (1904).

_____. "Model Basin Gleanings." *Transactions of the Society of Naval Architects and Marine Engineers* 14 (1906).

_____. "An Experimental Investigation of Stream Lines Around Ships' Models." *Transactions of the Society of Naval Architects and Marine Engineers* 15 (1907).

_____. "Some Model Experiments on Suction of Vessels." *Transactions of the Society of Naval Architects and Marine Engineers* 17 (1909).

_____. "The Effect of Parallel Middle Body Upon Resistance." *Transactions of the Society of Naval Architects and Marine Engineers* 17 (1909).

_____. "Some Model Basin Investigations of the Influence of Form of Ships Upon the Resistance." *Transactions of the Society of Naval Architects and Marine Engineers* (19 November 1911).

Thornton, Mark. "Success, Frustration, and Now, Perhaps, Recognition." *Hovering Craft and Hydrofoil* 18 (August 1979).

Tidman, Keith R. *The Operations Evaluation Group: A History of Naval Operations Analysis.* Annapolis: Naval Institute Press, 1984.

Todd, F. H. "Hydrodynamics Research Programme of the Bureau of Ships, U.S. Navy." *Transactions of the Institute of Naval Architects* 46 (1954).

Todorich, Charles. *The Spirited Years: A History of the Antebellum Naval Academy.* Annapolis: Naval Institute Press, 1984.

Tollmein, Walter. *Ludwig Prandtl Collected Treatises on Applied Mechanics, Hydro- and Aerodynamics.* Washington: NASA, 1988.

Turnbull, Archibald Douglas, and Clifford Lee Lord. *History of United States Naval Aviation.* New Haven, CT: Yale University Press, 1949.

_____. "Undersea Defenders: Story of Acoustic Homing Torpedoes." *General Electric Review* (March 1958).

Urick, Robert. *Principles of Underwater Sound.* 3d edition. New York: McGraw-Hill, 1983.

Urwick, Lydall F. "The Manager's Span of Control." *Management: A Book of Readings, by Harold Koontz and Cyril O'Donnell.* 2d edition. New York: McGraw-Hill, 1969.

U.S. Department of the Navy. *Annual Report of the Secretary of the Navy.* Various years.

Van Bertalanffry, Ludwig. "General System Theory: A New Approach to Unity of Science." *Human Biology* (December 1951).

Van Borselen, Jan Willem. *Human Bias in R&D Policy Machinery.* Rijswijk: GBS Tekstverking, B.V., 1976.

Van Wyen, Adrian O. *Naval Aviation in World War I.* Washington: Chief of Naval Operations, 1969.

Weir, Gary. *Forged in War: The Naval Industrial Complex and American Submarine Construction, 1940–1961.* Washington: Naval Historical Center, 1993.

Weisgall, Jonathan M. *Operation Crossroads: The Atomic Tests at Bikini Atoll.* Annapolis: Naval Institute Press, 1994.

Wenk, Edward, Jr. *Making Waves: Engineering, Politics, and the Social Managemenat of Technology.* Urbana: University of Illinois Press, 1995.

West, Michael. "Laying the Legislative Foundation: The House Naval Affairs Committee and the Construction of the Treaty Navy, 1926–1934." Ph.D. dissertation, Ohio State University, 1980.

Westervelt, George Conrad, et al. *The Triumph of the NCs.* Garden City, NY: Doubleday and Page, 1920.

White, Leonard. *Introduction to the Study of Public Administration.* 4th edition. New York: Macmillan, 1955.

White, Leonard, John Gaus, and Marshall Dimick. *The Frontiers of Public Administration.* New York: Russell of Russell, 1936. Reissued 1967.

Who Was Who in America. Vol. 1, *1897–1942.* Chicago: Marquis, 1943.

Williams, D.S.D. *The Modern Diesel.* London: Newnes Butterworths, 1972.

Wing, J. "Principles of Mechanisms Used in Controllable Pitch Propellers." 1st Lips Propeller Symposium, Drunen-Holland, 20–21 May 1970.

Wise, George. "Science and Technology." OSIRIS. 2d series, vol. 1. Philadelphia: University of Pennsylvania, 1985.

Wolfe, Thomas W. *Soviet Strategy at the Crossroads.* Cambridge: Harvard University Press, 1964.

Woodhouse, Henry. *Textbook of Naval Aeronautics.* Introduction by Bradley Fiske. New York: Century, 1917.

Worthington, Walter F. "Government Testing and Inspection for the Naval Service." *Journal of the American Society of Naval Engineers* 24 (1912).

Wright, E. A. "Naval Mathematics at the David Taylor Model Basin." *Journal of the American Society of Naval Engineers* 29 (May 1957).

_____. "The Bureau of Ships: A Study in Organization." *Journal of the American Society of Naval Engineers* 71 (February & March 1959).

Yeh, H.Y.H. "Series 64, Resistance Experiments on High-Speed Displacement Forms." *Maritime Technology* 2 (July 1953).

Zumwalt, Elmo, Jr. *On Watch: A Memoir.* New York: Quadrangle Press, 1976.

Index

Prepared by Richard and Anne Bassler

Bureau of Engineering *See also* Bureau of
   Ships
   and agenda items inherited from, 366
   and Bowen, 163
   and EES tradition, 166
   effect of performance control on, 93
   and increases in performance monitor-
      ing, 93
   and merger with Construction and
      Repair, 153, 164
   and merger into Bureau of Ships, 332,
      477
   and merger with Construction and
      Repair, 164
   opening of, in 1908, 4
   renaming of, 151, 471
Bureau of Naval Construction, 152
Bureau of Naval Personnel, 478
Bureau of Naval Weapons, 312
Bureau of Navigation, 37
Bureau of Ordnance, 312
Bureau of Ships
   Applied Science Division of, 280
   and design groups, 408
   equipment and knowledge at, 366–367
   formation of, 409, 477
   inspection requirements, relaxation of,
      170
   laboratories, crush of war work on, 170
   and low potential for research work, 196
   new, 277
   and notice of noise problem, 260
   policy, 173
   and request for work, 200
   research program, 198
   as Ship Systems Command, 318
Bureau of Ships Fundamental
   Hydromechanics Research, 232
Bureau of Standards, 74, 380
Bureau of Steam Engineering
   Chief of, 37
   establishment of, 465
   and New Navy movement, 14
   renaming of, 151, 471
   and requirement for work facility, 34
   and standard strength tests, 62
   and tests on asbestos sheet packing, 68
   and Yarrow system, 55
Bureau of Yards and Docks, 29, 143
Burkons, Hugh, 343

Bush, George, 422, 507, 511
BUSHIPS *See* Bureau of Ships
Bush, Vannevar
   and case for heavy funding, 163–165
   as chairman of NDRC, 477
   and commitment to research, 196
   and meeting with Army and Navy officers,
      196
   and previously secret research, 195
BUWEPS *See* Bureau of Naval Weapons

C
C. Turner Joy (DD 951), 369
CAB *See* air bubble, captured
Cabin John, Maryland, 139
Cal Tech *See* California Institute of
   Technology
California Institute of Technology, 175
Call, Wilkinson, Senator, Florida, 27
Calypso, 513
Canadian Defense Research Establishment
   Atlantic, 394
canal vessels, 132, 143
Cann, Gerald, 423–424, 426
capability assessment system, computer-
   ized, 596
Cape Horn cruise and *Ranger* (CV 4), 297
capital ships, emergence of modern, 12
Capps, Washington L., 152
Captive Flight/Launch Aerodynamics of
   Aircraft Stores, 292
carbon dioxide generated by submarine
   crew, 257
Carderock
   and Annapolis, merged laboratories at,
      397
   continuous-flow transonic wind tunnel
      at, 486
   research facilities at, 421
   reshaping of R&D organizations at, 423
Carderock-Annapolis NSRDC, 321
Carderock Division, NSWC and major
   R&D effort, 457
Carderock, Maryland, 4, 144
career anxiety of naval officers, 15
career discrimination, engineers and, 18
North Carolina (Armored Cruiser No. 12),
   469
carriages propelled by hydraulic gear, 140

ISBN 0-16-049442-7

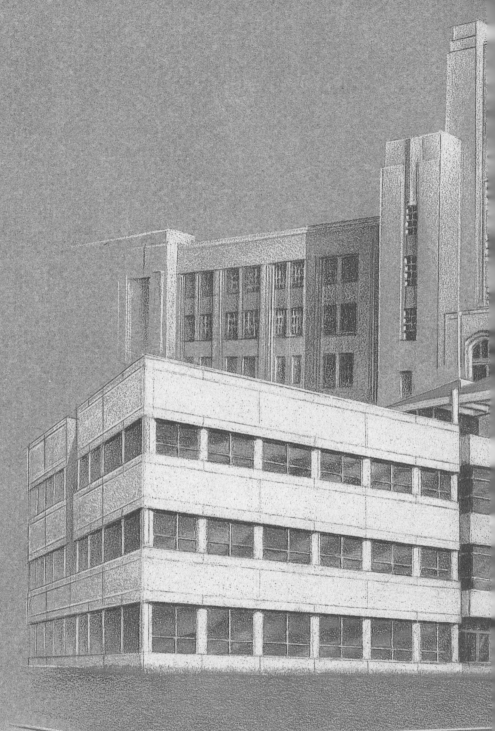